SOCIAL INFORMATICS: AN INFORMATION SOCIETY FOR ALL?

In Remembrance of Rob Kling

Proceedings of the Seventh International Conference on Human Choice and Computers (HCC7), IFIP TC 9, Maribor, Slovenia, September 21-23, 2006

Edited by

Jacques Berleur
University of Namur
Belgium

Markku I. Nurminen
University of Turku
Finland

John Impagliazzo
Hofstra University
United States

 Springer

IFIP – The International Federation for Information Processing

IFIP was founded in 1960 under the auspices of UNESCO, following the First World Computer Congress held in Paris the previous year. An umbrella organization for societies working in information processing, IFIP's aim is two-fold: to support information processing within its member countries and to encourage technology transfer to developing nations. As its mission statement clearly states,

> *IFIP's mission is to be the leading, truly international, apolitical organization which encourages and assists in the development, exploitation and application of information technology for the benefit of all people.*

IFIP is a non-profitmaking organization, run almost solely by 2500 volunteers. It operates through a number of technical committees, which organize events and publications. IFIP's events range from an international congress to local seminars, but the most important are:

• The IFIP World Computer Congress, held every second year;
• Open conferences;
• Working conferences.

The flagship event is the IFIP World Computer Congress, at which both invited and contributed papers are presented. Contributed papers are rigorously refereed and the rejection rate is high.

As with the Congress, participation in the open conferences is open to all and papers may be invited or submitted. Again, submitted papers are stringently refereed.

The working conferences are structured differently. They are usually run by a working group and attendance is small and by invitation only. Their purpose is to create an atmosphere conducive to innovation and development. Refereeing is less rigorous and papers are subjected to extensive group discussion.

Publications arising from IFIP events vary. The papers presented at the IFIP World Computer Congress and at open conferences are published as conference proceedings, while the results of the working conferences are often published as collections of selected and edited papers.

Any national society whose primary activity is in information may apply to become a full member of IFIP, although full membership is restricted to one society per country. Full members are entitled to vote at the annual General Assembly, National societies preferring a less committed involvement may apply for associate or corresponding membership. Associate members enjoy the same benefits as full members, but without voting rights. Corresponding members are not represented in IFIP bodies. Affiliated membership is open to non-national societies, and individual and honorary membership schemes are also offered.

SOCIAL INFORMATICS: AN
INFORMATION SOCIETY FOR ALL?

b 29234978

Library of Congress Control Number: 2006931006

Social Informatics: An Information Society for All?

Edited by J. Berleur, M. Nurminen, and J. Impagliazzo

p. cm. (IFIP International Federation for Information Processing, a Springer Series in Computer Science)

ISSN: 1571-5736 / 1861-2288 (Internet)
ISBN: 10: 0-387-37875-8
ISBN: 13: 9780-387-37875-8
eISBN: 10: 0-387-37876-6
Printed on acid-free paper

9 8 7 6 5 4 3 2 1
springer.com

HM
851
.I345
2006

Contents

PART 2: SOCIAL INFORMATICS: UBIQUITY? AN INFORMATION SOCIETY FOR ALL?

"As ICT are everywhere, social informatics should be everywhere."

Ethics and Culture

Politics and Law

Economic, Organizational and Technical Issues

Methods and Concepts

Cross-cutting Issues

PART 3: FAIR GLOBALIZATION

Preface

Markku I. Nurminen, Jacques Berleur, and John Impagliazzo
University of Turku (Finland), mnurmi@utu.fi
University of Namur (Belgium), jberleur@info.fundp.ac.be
Hofstra University (USA), john.impagliazzo@hofstra.edu

Human Choice and Computers (HCC) is the flagship conference of IFIP-Technical Committee 9 (TC9), dedicated to the study of the relationships between 'Computers and Society'. These proceedings cover the seventh of such conferences. We give as an annex to this Preface the sequence of the six first conferences as well as the references of their proceedings.

*

*   *

On 15 May 2003, Rob Kling, Professor of Information Systems and Information Science and Director of the Center for Social Informatics (CSI) at Indiana University, Bloomington, passed away. He was 58 years old. The day of his death, Indiana University's Dean Blaise Cronin at the School of Library and Information Science (SLIS) said, "Rob Kling's accomplishments are legion, and well documented. He was quite simply the brightest bloke with whom I have had the pleasure of working. Infectiously curious, playfully serious, razor sharp, generous of spirit, and wonderfully open-minded." We share that appreciation, as so many of his friends.

Rob was a founding father of IFIP-TC9. For several years since the inception, he was also chair of the so-called 'American core' of IFIP-Working Group 9.2 on Social Accountability.

What is this rather new field of research that, after discussion with colleagues and friends, Rob decided to call 'Social Informatics'? [RKCSI, 1996]

"Social Informatics (SI) refers to the body of research and study that examines social aspects of computerization - including the roles of information technology in social and organizational change and the ways that the social organization of information technologies are influenced by social forces and social practices. SI includes studies and other analyses that are labelled as social impacts of computing, social analysis of computing, studies of computer-mediate

Please use the following format when citing this chapter:

Nurminen, M. I., Berleur, J., Impagliazzo, J., 2006, in IFIP International Federation for Information Processing, Volume 223, Social Informatics: An Information Society for All? In Remembrance of Rob Kling, eds. Berleur, J., Numinen, M. I., Impàgliazzo, J., (Boston: Springer), pp. 1–16.

communication (CMC), information policy, 'computers and society,' organizational informatics, interpretive informatics, and so on. SI sets agendas for all the technical work in two ways: 1) more superficially, by drawing attention to functionalities that people value, thus setting priorities for design and implementation; and 2) more fundamentally, by articulating those analytical categories that have been found useful in describing social reality, and that which therefore should also define technical work in/for that reality as well." [Kling, 2001a]

We decided to dedicate HCC7 to Rob Kling's personality and his work. He is the founding father of the 'Social Informatics' school of thought.

*
* *

'An Information Society for All?': this is the question of the second part of the title of HCC7.

Geneva 2003 (December 10-12) – Tunis 2005 (November 16-18): the two phases of the UN World Summit on the Information Society (WSIS) that mobilized international authorities, governments, civil society, business people, computer scientists... [WSIS, 2003-2005], [Civil Society, 2003-2005].

The main issue at stake, as stated in a UN Resolution [UN, 2001], was the linkage between the development of Information and Communication Technology (ICT) and the UN *Declaration of the Millennium* goals. Among these goals were the eradication of extreme poverty (1.1 billion people, World Bank estimate) and hunger and the achievement of universal primary education, the target date being 2015. [UN, 2000] In other words, and more largely: how can we build up, whatever we may call it, an Information Society, a Knowledge Society, a Digital Society *for all*?

Wasn't this a way of meeting Rob's deep insight and intuition and updating one of his ideas that we can find in another definition he gave of Social Informatics? Rob wrote: "A more formal definition (of Social Informatics) is the interdisciplinary study of the design, uses and consequences of information technologies that takes into account their interaction with institutional and cultural contexts." [Kling, 1999, Kling, 2001b] We may expand this definition in many ways, among which would be the inclusion of the critical evaluation of the benefits and beneficiaries of ICT, including those left out in the process.

Using the vocabulary of UNESCO or of the European Union, we choose to give as second part of the title for our HCC7 Conference: 'An Information Society for All?' [UNESCO, 2002], [eEurope, 2002], which was a way to take into account the UN way of thinking: "Knowledge and technology must be put at the service of development for all", as the text of the UN 2001 Resolution indicates. We believe, *if ICT are everywhere, so should Social Informatics be everywhere.*

*
* *

Social Informatics is a construction open to many different interpretations; it is nearly impossible to find the orthodox formulation to it. We asked the contributors (represented in Part 1 of the Call for Papers) to expose their understanding of Social Informatics. We also wanted to explore various applications of Social Informatics thinking (Part 2). This turned out to be the more attractive of the two parts.

Nevertheless, keep in mind that we cannot separate sharply these two parts because each contribution in the more practical application field necessarily must articulate an interpretation of the nature of Social Informatics to be qualified as being an application of it. Such an interpretation can be found in all papers, if not explicitly, at least implicitly. On the other hand, all definitions of Social Informatics are likely to be based on an intuitive understanding of the motivation of the framework, often even expressed as the desire of certain types of applications or their impacts on social affairs. This means that the two parts are overlapping to a great extent.

Observing the contributions in the two parts, what kind of picture do we get about Social Informatics and its applications?

Before we can find answers, we had better to first formulate the questions. What are the particular issues addressed in Social Informatics? What makes Social Informatics different from other disciplines or approaches? What gives Social Informatics its special profile?

One question concerns the technical characteristics of informatics, namely, how technical is Social Informatics when compared to other approaches on informatics? The clear answer of Social Informatics is that informatics is more than technical. We cannot explain or understand many consequences of information technology by means of a reference to technology alone; we must also take into account various social aspects. Nevertheless, we cannot ignore technology totally, for without it, there would be no mechanism that would create those consequences of interest we wish to study.

It is probably fruitless to debate the 'egg and hen' and which was first. The interplay between the technical and the social aspects depends upon the characteristics of both parts of the interaction. We will get more out of this confrontation when we recall other slogans frequently associated with Social Informatics. One states, 'People first!' while another proclaims, 'Information society for all'. Eureka: we need the involvement of people in informatics for it to be Social Informatics.

Fortunately, Social Informatics is not alone when demanding greater attention to human beings in the context of computing. Many current approaches to information technology also view human subjects as inseparable parts of their theoretical and conceptual frameworks. Participative design and situated action are good examples, as is the interest for tacit knowledge and communities of practice. What is important is that we do not treat people only as objects of study; indeed, we should emphasize their role as active actors. For example, we should not interpret the slogan 'Information Society for All' so that some experts should design all the features of society and then deliver the outcome to *all* of the members of the society. This is not enough. *All* people are supposed to participate in this shaping of information society.

We objectify people when we treat them as objects of study, work, or change. It is no wonder that many people feel themselves as cogs of a machine while those who have the power or the knowledge manipulate them. Indeed, participative design has been one member in the Social Informatics family that has helped in the struggle against this danger of objectification.

Let us call this kind of denial of people as subjects 'subjectless-ness' as opposed to 'subject-ness'. However, this denial is not the only form of objectification. We can divide people into parts. Some parts that we usually envision as inherent parts of human beings are their objects and thus separated from the people themselves. This is what happens when values or motivation, knowledge or understanding are taken as objects of manipulation. When objectified, these characteristics become just another means of production. From afar, we regard human work as an object, and we bracket or ignore the genuine activity in which the actor can engage. Social Informatics has the mission to keep these people as individuals and collectives visible and significant. People first!

Another issue that Social Informatics has emphasized from its very first formulations is the concern regarding the consequences of information technology. Since many of the changes are unintended and undesired, we cannot regard the implementation as a deterministic process with discrete entities. The web of computing describes much better the situation. Notwithstanding, Social Informatics cannot stay as a 'besserwisser' (know-it-all) observatory witnessing the mistakes and breakdowns that people do with ICT. Some alternatives are good and others are bad. The choice is an ethical question. It broadens the scope of the 'ethics of computing'. While particular ethical issues still exist, Social Informatics is likely to view all aspects of the use, development, and implementation as moral questions of good versus evil, whereby people's interests should come first.

The reader now faces nearly forty contributions that display different views on Social Informatics. We could have sorted and classified these contributions in many ways. For example, there was no clear line between the two parts on what informatics is and its ubiquitous applications. The two themes on 'subject-ness' and moral issues embedded in all ICT develop from this material more than in many earlier contexts of Social Informatics. This is how we further bring the real message of 'Human Choice and Computers'. It is up to the reader to find all the themes and their counterpoint in the material of this conference. In what follows, we provide 'snapshots' of each contribution.

1 Social Informatics, What is It?

Alice Robbin, Roberta Lamb, John Leslie King, and Jacques Berleur have written a remembrance of Rob Kling as an introduction that will be found after this Preface. As it already provides one answer to the question of the identity of Social

Informatics, it nicely opens the concept remembrance itself. The authors regard remembrance as reflection, legacy, and vision. In the spirit of Vannevar Bush's visionary thinking – *As We May Think* (1945) –, they have named their chapter *As We May Remember*.

Alice Robbin and Ron Day discuss Social Informatics and the work of Rob Kling in terms of theoretical, methodological, and critical underpinnings of Kling's work. Even if he had no time to present a synthesis of all of these areas, Kling's contributions in all of them transcend many borders typical for traditional settings of research and practice. One of Kling's conceptual frameworks was Socio-Technical Interaction Networks (STIN). This is the specific object of Eric T. Meyer's paper. He gives a good overview about STIN and its application, strengths and weaknesses. STIN is not the only theoretical framework that we can successfully apply to Social Informatics. Steve Sawyer and Michael Tyworth apply another framework called the 'Social Actor Approach', first introduced by Roberta Lamb and Rob Kling on through STIN. Because of their empirical work, they discovered that these two approaches lead to different insights. Because both approaches can be both true and useful, Social Informatics is not a singular theory, but rather an analytic perspective and a set of principles.

Teaching Social Informatics

The dilemma of teaching Social Informatics is that in most of the imaginable contexts it is bound to happen to the audience who already is familiar with informatics as a technically oriented discipline. The message in such a situation often takes the form of explaining that the traditional presentation of informatics is not the truth or at least not the whole truth. It is rather exceptional for a student to start his studies at the very beginning with the conceptualizations of Social Informatics!

Lilla Juhász and László Z. Karvalics report their experiences of teaching Social Informatics at their university in Budapest. Social Informatics offers to engineering students a significant set of minor studies. They structure and justify the subject very carefully, first by interpreting information as an exclusively human phenomenon. Further discussions deal with the IT-'information and knowledge' industry, the axioms of ICT, a history and prehistory of IT, and the profession world of the information complex. This is an interesting and ambitious enterprise.

Another university with particular teaching of Social Informatics is the University of Ljubljana. Vasja Vehovar takes us to an exciting sightseeing through the history and geography of information systems research. He identifies many conceptualizations that complement each other. The concern is rather similar than in the recent debate on the IS Core: the desire of a core for Social Informatics is clear.

Social Informatics as a discipline has also been the main concern of Per Flensburg and Arianit Kurti. They are not, however, satisfied with the analysis of Social Informatics as an academic discipline; they want instead to step out to the practical problems and crises of the world. They discuss many central themes frequently found in the critical analyses of current globalization and they attribute some fresh views toward the potential role of information technology affecting origins and solutions. To some extent, the broad legitimacy justifies the unorthodox format of the contribution.

2 'Social Informatics': Ubiquity? An Information Society for All?

In our understanding, we should not understand Social Informatics in such a way that a part of informatics is social whereas the rest of the discipline is not social. The need for Social Informatics comes from the ignorance of the social dimension of information technology that is too common still today. To the contrary, we argue that all use and development of IT are socially determined. Moreover, as ICT is everywhere, Social Informatics should also be everywhere. In today's terminology, Social Informatics should be ubiquitous. Otherwise, it would not make sense to talk about an 'Information Society for All'.

We have clustered the contributions in various classes: Ethics and Culture, Politics and Law, Information Society and ICT Policies, Economic, Organizational and Technical Issues, Methods and Concepts, and finally a couple of papers on Crosscutting Issues.

2.1 Ethics and Culture

Social Informatics is replete with ethical concerns and it has an inherently cultural dimension. In many ways, ethics and culture also complement each other; that is, one of them is meaningful only as far as it can refer to the other.

Göran Collste is concerned about the ethical principles in various applications of e-medicine. We should be aware that we do not accidentally throw away old traditional aspects characteristic of the relationship between doctor and patient. Also new situations of care will emerge in the Internet era that requires formulation of new ethical principles. Trust on information and services mediated electronically are good examples of this type of ethical concern.

The technical progress of the ICT and the relatively high degree of anonymity in Internet operations offer important new opportunities for the freedom of speech and equality. Unfortunately, it is also a free jungle for many types of criminals. Child pornography is one criminal area that has grown towards more intensive market place for this type of criminals. Marie Eneman presents an IS research agenda that aims at a better understanding of this phenomenon. Know your enemies in order to beat them!

Quite often information systems come to the desks of their users who have no other choice than to accept the artifact as given. This is because users, for all practicality, lack the ability to tailor the system or to find alternative pieces of software to accomplish the tasks they are to do. To a certain extent, the users are controlled rather than becoming controlling. Yu-Wei Lin and Enrico Zini suggest the use of free/libre open source software (FLOSS) as one way to reduce this degree of control. They report experiences of implementing FLOSS in an Italian high school. Ubiquitous and pervasive computing also raises the concern of control to the surface. If the user cannot escape pervasive applications or if he is not aware of all active ubiquitous applications, we cannot expect him or her to be in control of the applications.

Giuseppina Pellegrino analyses the increasingly mediated character of everyday life, various types of technological artifacts are mediating our activities particularly in mobile working situations. Yet another ethical concern is the transparency of economic activity that takes place in firms. The companies do have justified business secrets, but on the other hand, they are under pressure to reveal information on their activities to convince the authorities and other interested parties about their fair and acceptable principles.

Information and communication technology allows many different opportunities to make the activities transparent. Antonino Vaccaro and Peter Madsen introduce a model called the five-force model to analyze and make sense of the pressures towards greater transparency.

2.2 Politics and Law

Societies create laws as shared and explicit expressions for rules of ethical character. They tell in more operative terms, what is right, and what is wrong. Politics should not be a reason to violate laws, even if they give greater freedom for individuals to promote their shared values. Issues in this class vary from intellectual property rights to the freedom of expression.

We may regard many databases as shared resources for all users who have access to them. Tom Dedeurwaerdere reports about the work on databases with microbiological information. He studies their production and use as public good and common pool resource. Quality forms a crucial basis for the usefulness of such a shared resource. One needs a complicated network of incentives, property rights, licenses, and contracts for the governance of the collaborative database. The databases are not the only resources shared for general benefit and creativity. Software is perhaps an even more important resource in this respect, because we view it as an intellectual property of its author(s). Paul B. De Laat offers an outline of 'open source software' and he offers various means for protecting and sharing these resources.

We can limit freedom of expression in cyberspace by various forms of restrictions on publishing expressions or on access to undesired pages. Mathias Klang presents a good overview on such censoring techniques and their backgrounds.

Information society does not come by itself; we need to welcome it by various measures performed by the society. Vasileios Laopodis presents the strategy of the European Union to introduce Research and Development Programmes. The purpose of these projects is to use ICTs and their pervasive role in economy and society for greater economic growth, sustainable development, and social cohesion.

One part of information society is to organize a part of services electronically, with good examples of e-commerce, e-government, or e-health. Many companies develop their *Customer Relationship Management* (CRM) system utilizing the power of ICT. Francoise Massit-Folléa and Cécile Méadel introduce a parallel concept useful in electronic administration *Citizen Relationship Management* and continue by using it in order to turn the concept of administration to a more market oriented direction with its supply and demand.

The ethical concern of Social Informatics also has its long-term dimension. We should not compromise the ability of future generations to meet their needs. This general formulation of sustainability is the point of departure for Christian Fuchs in his exploration of the different facets of sustainability in the information society. He is not satisfied with the ecological sustainability alone; he is asking for technological, economic, political, and cultural sustainability.

2. 3 Information Society and ICT Policies

One may view an information society as a possible portrait of Social Informatics. Governments often show their interest and responsibility by formulating strategies and policies for promoting the development of ICT and information societies. Supporting the creation of infrastructure governments often also promote the development of various new electronic methods for government and other services.

Electronic services are an important feature in an information society because it creates the possibility to change significantly the structures of production and the delivery of services. Such changes are not deterministic and we can choose its different directions of development. Elisabeth Davenport and Keith Horton have analyzed e-government and they have been able to identify two frames. They call one the 'technology action frame' that prefers the use of processes, which is likely to lead to a dehumanized concept of a *managed citizen*. They base the other frame on notions of interaction, solidarity, and shared practice that is close to the Kling's frame of 'web of computing'.

We can agree that the Internet and the web is the engine of an information society. Who invented them? This is a wrong question in Social Informatics perspective. The Internet is not a discrete entity and its invention and governance follow much more complicated rules. William H. Dutton has applied the concept ecology of games to illustrate innovatively the indeterminist character of such processes that have multiple actors.

An Information Society for All? is the second part of the title of this conference. The IS researchers should keep in mind this slogan as well, as Tanja Urbancic, Olga Stepankova, and Nada Lavrac require. Whenever a conflict exists between people and other values, people should be in the first place. The authors make their argument more convincing by a few illustrating examples.

The scientific community does not often leave too much room for human subjects or 'subject-ness'. The desire for objectivity could easily lead to a misunderstood one-sided objectification. However, several theoretical approaches exist that address the subjective character of human beings. Katarina Lindblad-Gidlund has taken social constructionism as derived from Berger & Luckmann as such a theory. They use it as a bridge between two notions of usability: empirical usability and usability as ideology.

We would expect ICTs to promote democracy in the information society. We can make information available with the purpose of improving transparency thereby controlling and making sense of social phenomena. Simon Delakorda has taken his target in the core of democratic processes–political parties. He has reviewed the parties' web sites and found out that most of their designs were for one-way communication. Such designs foster the desire for power and control rather than a genuine social movement.

The second part of the title of this conference is *An Information Society for All?* Bruno Oudet, Jean-Pierre Pinet, Corinne Chevrot, and Gwenaël Navarette have taken this challenge seriously by bringing technology to very poor people in their project called *Internet in the Street*. They report their experiences about the problems and barriers of reaching this audience and of giving them the opportunity to use the Internet.

The digital divide is one of the concerns in information societies. It is perhaps even more critical at the global level. Access to computers is essentially more difficult if the supply of devices is scarce; however, we must also guarantee the infrastructure and availability of adequate software. Pia Krakowski analyses the use of Free Open Source Software (FOSS) in developing countries. She discovers that the issue is not only in the cost of FOSS, but also in the freedom and flexibility it gives in circumstances that did not have a high priority in the designer's mind.

2.4 Economic, Organizational, and Technical Issues

People believe that information is a more important factor of production than capital or labor. Capitalism has shifted to 'informational capitalism' in the conceptual framework derived by Castells. Rudi Schmiede assumes Castells' notion as the point of departure and takes us 'sightseeing' through the information society. He is especially concerned about human subjects and consequently about anthropocentric development of technology.

Responsibility and accountability become easily fuzzy when we introduce ICT. The danger is greater when the systems are wide and integrated. Enterprise architectures are useful for creating overview and keeping track of accountability. In their paper, Gian Marco Campagnolo and Gianni Jacucci discuss this issue on design for accountability, making use of the 'actor-network theory'. Context of an IS is an important concept for Social Informatics, because the social aspects of information technology are likely to reside in the context. One issue about contexts is whether there are any recurrent factors in contexts even if they seem to be different from one case to another. Tuija Tiihonen, Anja Mursu and Mikko Korpela have made an attempt to identify such factors in terms of scopes, categories and levels. The authors' work in developing countries drives this attempt.

2.5   Methods and concepts

Concepts are part of the definition of the research and methods are more or less consequences of it. The contributions in this category therefore help also the building the notion of Social Informatics. It is natural that the discussion on the interpretations of Social Informatics continues here as it does thorough the entire conference. Gunilla Bradley desires to bring ICT, people, and society to a fruitful interaction. Equipped with three roles as a professional, private person and citizen, people could become empowered when these things and roles become more integrated.

The ICT has an enabling role in this convergence process. The identity of Social Informatics is not a narrowly defined entity. Even in this conference, it has received many slightly different interpretations. Pertti Järvinen draws the profile of Social Informatics by comparing it to the mainstream information systems research. He uses two stereotypic ideal types introduced by Kling and Lamb called the 'standard tool model' and the 'socio-technical model.' [Kling, 2000] He continues his discussion by emphasizing the role of human beings in information systems and in Social Informatics at least to some extent.

The 'subject-ness' is, indeed, a thoroughgoing theme in this conference. One weakness of Social Informatics is in its generality; operationalizing empirical research does not always receive very strong support. The way of research design may be long. Markku I. Nurminen suggests that we could operationalize Social Informatics more greatly and he gives an example of this by starting to define a sub-discipline that he calls *Work Informatics*.

Social Informatics also needs foundational support with deeper philosophical thinking. Rocío Riueda Ortiz, Henrik Herlau, and Leif Bloch Rasmussen do this by starting with Churchman and Singer, continuing with Kant and Habermas, and ending up to Derrida and Feyerabend. They profile nicely the particular characteristics of Social Informatics during this journey through different philosophers. The modern ICT offers the possibility to access enormous amounts of data in databases connected to the Internet or to other networks. Social Informatics has taken a critical stance on this issue as long as people regard this opportunity as merely a technical feature.

Data without adequate interpretation is worthless – if not dangerous. Klaus Fuchs-Kittowski introduces the concept of an information centre – a centre of thought that would play an important role in this challenge of collective sense making. The suggestion gives an interesting view to many problems of knowledge management and organizational learning.

Access to ICT and the Internet are important features of an information society because lack of access is likely to increase the digital divide. Access has been the object of many studies, even at this conference, that aim at finding ways to promote the access for all. Olle Nilsson has taken the complementary approach: instead of analyzing the driving forces of access, he has decided to identify and classify barriers of access leading to a *User Centred Access Model*.

2.6   Cross-Cutting Issues

The diffusion and use of information technology is dependent on the beliefs that potential users have about this technology. Pille Pruulmann-Vengerfeldt has collected two longitudinal surveys with Estonian people. By classifying the respondents into users and non-users, she has been able to make some distinctions that indicate barriers to ICT use. Perhaps we may transcend these barriers to some degree by distributing corrective information.

Social Informatics as a key area for understanding socio-technical change is the focus of the paper by Edouard J. Simon, Monique Janneck, and Dorina Gumm. In the spirit of Social Informatics, the innovative change is also an ethical challenge by definition. The key of Social Informatics in this approach turns out to be multidisciplinary. We operationalize this by the concept of *Mikropolis*, which means the collective of researchers with a perspective from different disciplines. However, through their joint research activity, *Mikropolis* develops into a conceptual framework that we can regard as a tentative embryo for the theory of Social Informatics.

3   'Fair Globalization'

The third part of these proceedings is very short and does not fit very well with the style of the others. However, we decided to keep it for two reasons.
- People will use this text for a youth forum, which is a side event to HCC7 conference. Obviously, as this book will be published before the event, we are not able to expose its results!
- It is a text that shows how the agencies of the United Nations, namely the International Labor Organization (ILO), have adopted the goals of the *Millennium Declaration* for their own sphere of competence, and influence [UN, 2000], [ILO, 2004].

This text provides a kind of blueprint showing how an *Information Society for All* should be. In a way, it provides an agenda for such action.

4   As a Matter of Stage

In a posthumous book, Rob Kling et al. refer to three orientations of Social Informatics: normative, analytical, and critical [Kling et al., 2005]. Quoting Kling,

"The critical orientation refers to examining ICTs from perspectives that do not automatically and uncritically accept the goals and beliefs of the groups that commission, design, or implement specific ICTs. (…) It encourages information professionals and researchers to examine ICTs from multiple perspectives (such as those of the various people who use them in different contexts, as well as those of the people who pay for, design, implement, or maintain them) and to examine possible failure modes and service losses, as well as ideal or routine ICT operations."

We hope that the different contributions have brought forth a first patchwork of answers to this methodological preoccupation. It is surely of utmost importance for today when most people are fascinated by the wonders of the technology. Yet, they forget that we must develop these technologies for the people – for *all* people.

Let us return to the questions that we posed earlier. What are the particular issues addressed in Social Informatics? What makes Social Informatics different from other disciplines or approaches? What gives Social Informatics its special profile?

As a result of our reading, it seems more fruitful to ask which research questions or areas do *not* belong to Social Informatics. This is because Social Informatics can analyze critically practically any research project in terms of its people dimension, that is, Where are the people? What roles do they play? How does ICT affect them? It is not enough for Social Informatics to take into account some social factors when the social actors remain objects of manipulation. Social Informatics is in favor of 'subject-ness' and against 'subjectless-ness'.

We can interpret this so that research and development in the ICT field, the area of informatics, is too important for technical experts to do alone. We need social expertise on the side of the technical one. Nevertheless, we must continue our critical orientation to cover the work of these socially oriented experts. For example, if an organization had established an internal board for ethical issues, it would not mean that the employees should perform their jobs without any attention to its ethical aspects. Quality systems do not create quality. People must infuse quality in their own work and they must have a desire to see that quality is a genuine happening. It is not possible to outsource and ethical social issues, even if they open 'controversies' as Rob observed them [Kling, 1991, 1996].

References

[Civil Society, 2003-2005] Civil Society Declaration to the World Summit on the Information Society WSIS, Civil Society Plenary *Shaping Information Societies for Human Needs,* Geneva, 8 December 2003, (Version with corrections 12 December 2003); Civil society statement on the World Summit on the Information Society, *Much more could have been achieved,* 18 December 2005 (Revision 1 – 23 December 2005). Nearly all the documents of the Civil Society related to the WSIS are available on the CONGO website at http://www.ngocongo.org/index.php?what=resources&id=278 (May 3, 2006)

[eEurope, 2002], eEurope 2005: An information society for all - An Action Plan to be presented in view of the Sevilla European Council, 21/22 June 2002, COM(2002)263/F of

28 May 2002. <http://ec.europa.eu/comm/secretariat_general/regdoc/liste.cfm?CL=en>

[ILO, 2004], World Commission on the Social Dimension of Globalization, February 2004, Report: 'A Fair Globalization: Creating opportunities for all', ILO, Geneva, Switzerland.

[Kling, 1991, 1996] Kling, R., & Dunlop, C. (Eds.). (1991), *Computerization and controversy: Value conflicts and social choices*, .San Diego: Academic Press. Kling, Rob (Ed.). (1996). *Computerization and controversy* (2nd ed.). San Diego, CA: Academic Press

[Kling, 1999,], Rob Kling, What Is Social Informatics and Why Does It Matter? In *D-Lib Magazine*, January 1999, volume 5, Number 1, ISSN 1082-9873, <http://www.dlib.org/dlib/january99/kling/01kling.html>

[Kling, 2000], Rob Kling and Roberta Lamb, IT and Organizational Change in Digital Economies: A Socio-Technical Approach. In: *Understanding the Digital Economy - Data, Tools and Research*. Brian Kahin and Erik Brynjolfsson (eds). The MIT Press.

[Kling, 2001a], Rob Kling, What is Social Informatics?, <http://www.slis.indiana.edu/SI/concepts.html>, or <http://rkcsi.indiana.edu/index.php/about-social-informatics>, and <http://rkcsi.indiana.edu/index.php/history-of-the-term>

[Kling, 2001b], Rob Kling, Social Informatics, in: *Encyclopedia of LIS*, Kluwer Publishing, July 5, 2001, <http://www.slis.indiana.edu/SI/si2001.html>

[Information Society], *The Information Society, An International Journal*, <http://www.indiana.edu/~tisj/index.html> [Rob Kling was Editor-in-Chief from 1981 to 2003]

[Kling et al., 2005], Rob Kling, Howard Rosenbaum, and Steve Sawyer, *Understanding and Communicating Social Informatics: A Framework for Studying and Teaching the Human Contexts of Information and Communications Technologies*. Medford, New Jersey: Information Today, Inc.

[RKCSI, 1996], Rob King Centre for Social Informatics, *History of the term*, <http://rkcsi.indiana.edu/article.php/about-social-informatics/35>

[UN, 2000], United Nations, *The Millennium Declaration*. 8 September 2000 <http://www.un.org/millennium/>

[UN, 2001], United Nations, Resolution adopted by the General Assembly, 56/183: World Summit on the Information Society, 90th Plenary Meeting, 21 December 2001.

[UNESCO, 2002], UNESCO, Information for All Programme (IFAP), An intergovernmental Programme of UNESCO, http://www.unesco.org/webworld/ifap

[WSIS, 2003-2005], World Summit on the Information Society, *Declaration of Principles, Building the Information Society: a global challenge in the new Millennium*, WSIS-03/GENEVA/DOC/4-E, 12 December 2003; *Plan of Action*, Document WSIS-03/GENEVA/DOC/5-E, 12 December 2003); *Tunis Agenda for the Information Society*, WSIS-05/TUNIS/DOC/6(Rev.1)-E, 18 November 2005; *Tunis Commitment*, WSIS-05/TUNIS/DOC/7-E, 18 November 2005. All those documents are available on the ITU website: http://www.itu.int/wsis.

Annex

The *Human Choice and Computers* Conferences

The First World Conference on *Human Choice and Computers* was held in 1974 (April 1-5), in Vienna. The initiative came from Heinz Zemanek, President of IFIP (1971-1974) and at the time also President of IBM Austria. Fred Margulies, Secretary of the International Federation of Automatic Control (IFAC), who was mainly leading the reflection of unions on the computerization in the work place, assisted him.

The success of HCC1 was such that IFIP-TC9 has always considered it as a founding event, if not its birthplace. This is not the place to provide a history of TC9, as Heinz Zemanek and Jacques Berleur have already documented that narration. Furthermore, the recognition of TC9 as a technical committee within IFIP was a challenge and the leaders at that time had to overcome the opposition from the Russian Academy of Science. For convenience, the Academy preferred to consider 'computer science' as a neutral area. We can still find anachronously such information in the IFIP Statutes that state, "IFIP does not take any account of the political, social or economic aspects of its Member organizations because IFIP is totally dedicated to the transfer of scientific and technical information and experience" (art. 1).

TC9 came to birth in 1976, two years after HCC1. Its creation was fortunate: having a technical committee reflecting on the issues raised by the nascent Information Technology was a blessing.

Kelly Gotlieb (CDN) was the first TC9 Chair. With Fred Margulies, he organized *HCC2*, which took place in Baden (Austria) in 1979 (June 4-8). This was the first attempt to clarify the field of 'Computers and Society'. In the HCC2 Proceedings, Abbe Mowshowitz attempted to list the main social issues in computing.

The third world conference *HCC3* was held in Stockholm, 2-5 September 1985. 'Comparative Worldwide National Computer Policies' was its main theme. HCC3 tried to go further in the way the different nations were approaching the policies of ICT in different domains such as in working life, public policies, and culture. Hal Sackman was the TC9 Chair.

HCC4 took place 6-12 June 1990 in Dublin. TC9 prepared HCC4 with Klaus Brunnstein as its chair and with Riccardo Petrella leading the European FAST Programme. The concept of 'technology assessment' applied to the field of information technology was surely the first attempt to federate the main reflection on social aspects of science in the field of ICT.

The fifth world conference on HCC—*HCC5*—was held in Geneva (25-28 August 1998) with the help of Silvio Munari and the 'Hautes Etudes Commerciales' (HEC) of the University of Lausanne. It was the first time that TC9 faced the role of

ICT in the issue of globalization. Pertti Järvinen was the TC9 Chair.

HCC6 was in Montreal as a track of the 17th IFIP World Computer Congress. The main theme concentrated on one of the scopes of TC9. Its Aims and Scope state 'Issues of Choice and Quality of Life in the Information Society'. Klaus Brunnstein and Jacques Berleur (TC9 Chair) were at the root of that worldwide initiative. They also organized the IFIP-WG9.2 Namur Award Ceremony in honor of Deborah Hurley, Director of the Harvard Information Infrastructure Project.

HCC Conferences Proceedings

1. Human Choice and Computers, Enid Mumford & Hal Sackman, Eds., Proceedings of the Conference on Human Choice and Computers, Vienna (Austria), April 1-5, 1974, Elsevier, North-Holland, Amsterdam, 1975, ISBN 0-7204-2826-2

2. Human Choice and Computers – 2, Abbe Mowshowitz, Ed., Proceedings of the Second IFIP-TC9 Human Choice and Computers Conference (HCC-2), Baden (Austria), 4-8 June, 1979, Elsevier, North-Holland, Amsterdam, 1980, ISBN 0-444-85456-8

3. Comparative Worldwide National Computer Policies, Harold Sackman editor, Proceedings of the 3rd IFIP-TC9 Conference on Human Choice and Computers, Stockholm (HCC-3), Sweden, 2-5 September 1985, Elsevier, North-Holland, 1986, 486 pages, ISBN 0-444-70056-0

4. Information Technology Assessment: Human Choice and Computers, 4, Jacques Berleur & John Drumm, Eds., Proceedings of the Fourth IFIP-TC9 International Conference on Human Choice and Computers (HCC-4), Dublin, July 8-12, 1990, Elsevier, North-Holland, Amsterdam, 1991, 394 pages, ISBN 0-444-88759-8

5. Computers and Networks in the Age of Globalization, Leif Bloch Rasmussen, Colin Beardon and Silvio Munari, Eds., Proceedings of the 5th IFIP-HCC (Human Choice and Computers) International Conference, HCC-5, Kluwer Academic Publishers, 2000, ISBN 0-7923-7253-0

6. Human Choice and Computers, Issues of Choice and Quality of Life in the Information Society, Klaus Brunnstein & Jacques Berleur, Eds., Proceedings of the IFIP-TC9 HCC-6 Conference, 17th World Computer Congress, Montreal, August 2002, Kluwer Academic Publ., 2002, ISBN 1-4020-7185-X

Acknowledgments

On behalf of IFIP and TC9, the editors of these proceedings would like to thank:

- our partners: the Slovene Association Informatika, the University in Maribor, the Municipality of Maribor, the Institute of Information Science (IZUM), Arctur Nova Gorica, Agenda Open systems, and Vercer;
- Franci Pivec, from IZUM, and the members of the Organizational Committee who made so many efforts during the preparation of HCC7;
- the authors, as well as our invited speakers Roberta Lamb and John Leslie King, and
- the members of the International Programme Committee, who drafted the first Call for papers, made the review of the submitted papers, and decided for the Conference programme.

May this conference, dedicated to Rob Kling, bear its fruit in research and in action.

As We May Remember

Alice Robbin, Roberta Lamb, John Leslie King and Jacques Berleur
Rob Kling Centre for Social Informatics, Indiana University,
arobbin@indiana.edu
University of California Irvine, rlamb@uci.edu
University of Michigan, jlking@si.umich.edu
University of Namur (Belgium), jberleur@info.fundp.ac.be

Introduction

By now, many retrospectives have been offered on Rob Kling. Some have focused on personal and professional reflections about what motivated his intellectual pursuit and shaped his socio-technical perspective. Others have looked carefully at the whole 'package' of Rob's work as a legacy of scholarly publications and a community of connected researchers who care about informatics and social worlds. His own characterization of his lifelong project was as an institution builder devoted to illuminating analytically understandings of the complex relationships between the design and use of advanced information and communication technologies (ICTs) and the character of social life in settings where people use them.

Many remembrances note that Rob was an idealist. His achievements, impressive and laudable as they were, have not yet produced a discipline as inclusive and socially realistic, nor an ICT-infused world that is as socially equitable, as Rob would have wished for. Our purpose in this short paper is to remember Rob as we knew him – warts and all – in our personal and professional lives. We have drawn together a series of historical links to events and influences that we know about to explain his approach, motivations, personal style and intellectual biases.

Please use the following format when citing this chapter:

Robbin, A., Larab, R., King, J. L., Berleur, J., 2006, in IFIP International Federation for Information Processing, Volume 223, Social Informatics: An Information Society for All? In Remembrance of Rob Kling, eds. Berleur, J., Numinen, M. I., Impagliazzo, J., (Boston: Springer), pp. 17–21.

Remembrance as Reflection

Our first memories are a reflection of Rob over time. At the time Rob began his career in the early 1970s, discussions of the relationships between computers and society were largely speculative and prescriptive. There were relatively few computer systems and computer networks to serve as a basis for empirically anchored and analytically-oriented research, which he believed was required because social improvements do not always accompany substantial technological advances. Rob also believed that fundamental changes in science education were needed so that IT professionals would be trained to identify and evaluate the social consequences of ICT-based systems. Throughout his life he articulated a responsibility-centered role for information professionals that flowed from his convictions about the ethical self.

He was acutely mindful that technology was complicit in many aspects of human suffering, and he could not abide the dismissive or disinterested attitude of many technologists toward the growing body of empirical evidence that technology often had unintended negative consequences. He embraced a critical perspective that placed these contradictions at the heart of the technological conundrum. In executing his critical worldview, he opened the eyes of many people to the complexities of problems that seemed relatively simple on the surface. At the same time, however, many of Rob's zealous predictions about computerization failed.

Our reflections about the future of Social Informatics have begun to consider how he might have avoided some of the traps of a critical empirical approach. We remember heated arguments with Rob about socio-technical futures that stretched visions of computing to their logical (i.e. absurd) limits. But, perhaps due to inherent biases of critical and positivist perspectives, those limits were often simple linear extensions of the current context, rather than exponential or recursively accumulative imaginings of ICT-infused social worlds.

Remembrance as Legacy

We are cautiously mindful of the shortcomings that grew out of Rob's idealism, yet we are at the same time enormously admiring and appreciative of his overall legacy. Over the course of his life, Rob contributed insights from his wide-ranging empirical research and policy studies on computing, in more than a hundred articles and several books that were published in journals of diverse disciplines. He critically examined computing in the workplace. He wrote about the interactions between the public and organizations dependent on computer-based systems. He explored people's self conceptions in dealing with machines and about the computing world as a social institution. He was particularly attentive to the relationship between computing and public policy and, beginning with his first papers, addressed policy issues on privacy, the ethical dilemmas of computing, legal issues, and the social accountability of the IT professional. In one form or another his writings always addressed the normative implications of computerization, the roles and responsibilities of the public and private sectors and professions, and public policy design and its consequences for social life, work life, and the citizen.

Through European colleagues in the early 1980s, he was introduced to the term 'social informatics' to describe this research area, and he adopted the term as a workable label to facilitate the integration of a heterogeneous body of research and to help communicate key theories and findings. By 1996, he had developed what he called a 'serviceable definition' of the discipline of Social Informatics, which he wrote 'refers to the interdisciplinary study of the design, uses and consequences of information and communication technologies that takes into account their interaction with institutional and cultural contexts." He intended that Social Informatics would be a genuine socio-technical systems perspective that included analytical, critical and normative approaches, multiple methodologies, innovations in research design, and true interdisciplinarity. His corpus of work introduced North American scholars to seven important social informatics ideas:

1. The context of ICT use directly affects their meanings and roles; the design of ICTs is linked to social and organizational dynamics.
2. ICTs are not value neutral; their use creates winners and losers.
3. ICT use leads to multiple, unexpected, and often paradoxical or time-dependent, effects (e.g. the 'paperless office' has actually generated more paper; and during the 1980s and early 1990s, the introduction of technology into the workplace did not appear to increase productivity).
4. ICT use has moral and ethical aspects, and these have social consequences.
5. ICTs are configurable 'packages'; they are actually collections of distinct components whose social use of similar components may lead to different technical networks in each social system.
6. ICTs follow trajectories that often favor the status quo. 7
7. ICTs co-evolve during design, development, and use, that is, before and after implementation.

Rob's institutional contribution was to educational program design that incorporated a study of society and technology, whose concepts he thought had been undervalued and unappreciated in science education. During the 1990s, concerned that various disciplines were not preparing their students to address the interdependencies of the social, the technical, and the ethical, he turned his attention to developing a program of critical inquiry for a Social Informatics education that would prepare IT professionals to respond appropriately and ethically in their future careers. This led to two editions of a reader designed for undergraduates, *Computerization and Controversy*, that was published along with an instructional manual for teachers (2nd edition). His goal was to provide the conceptual foundation for a critical appreciation of the benefits and limitations provided by ICTs. He believed that IT professionals needed to understand that ICT is a socio-technical process and that social and organizational forces affected the functionality embedded in ICTs; that techniques needed to be developed to help identify and evaluate the social consequences of ICT-based systems. He also believed that information professionals needed to carefully consider elements of power and influence, resources available to and employed by various interests, and the consequences of their personal decisions and of public policies. And IT professionals needed to apply what he called 'person-centered standards' for the design of computerized information systems that promoted a sense of personal competence and authority.

At the time of his death in May 2003, Rob had written the outline of a new book, provisionally entitled *Computerization Within Societies: A Social Informatics Perspective*. It was intended as a new conceptual synthesis of key ideas from social informatics research that would be translated into insightful ways of viewing the development, use and consequences of IT applications in workplaces, organizations, and institutional arenas. He wanted to explicitly articulate concepts and bring them alive with vivid illustrations, so that readers could "take them away" and apply them in their own life-worlds and their own research. The book would have a distinctive theoretical approach, one that treated ICTs as socio-technical networks, viewed the configuration of ICTs as situated in organizations or other social settings, and was also influenced by the relevant 'technological frames' that circulate through intersecting social worlds. Parts of the theoretical approach would come from neo-institutional political sociology. However, his goal was to encourage readers to understand how socio-technical configurations play a role in influencing the range of common social behavior. The first chapters on discourses about ICTs and social change and the socio-technical character of ICTs were more conceptually oriented. Subsequent chapters would examine ICT applications, including computerization in workplaces and organizations, and transorganizational ICTs, such as dot-coms, scholarly communication and distance education. The book design concluded with a discussion of information societies in critical perspective.

Remembrance as Vision

Rob Kling's last book remains unfinished as a literary work, but its outline succinctly expresses his vision for the social informatics research community. Many of us who worked with Rob believe that his greatest gift was making us think differently – whether it was about something new, thinking in a new way, or adding back in some messy consideration that had been excluded intentionally. Through decades of intense, interpersonal, scholarly interaction, he played a unique, essential, and lasting role in the creation of a domain of research called Social Informatics. He contributed to a critical perspective on the nature, role, and dynamics of computerization. He was committed to empirical evidence and theoretical analysis. He challenged the assumptions about computerization -- his work a powerful indictment against the sloppy conjecture and hyperbolic statements about outcomes from computerization. He offered a convincing alternative interpretation of society and technology. Like Vannevar Bush's vision of the 'memex' device, Rob's vision of social informatics was based on in-depth, on-the-ground knowledge about what is, what is possible, but also what is likely – without knowing exactly how and when that vision might be realized. Maybe he overcompensated in his predictions for the tendencies toward technological determinism by other scholars of computing; but in so doing he developed a set of research skills in himself, his students and his colleagues for empirical inclusion, expansive consideration, concern for those left out, analytical synthesis, rapid characterization, and concrete conceptual anchorings of scholarly work. Above all, he perpetuated an idea that, through this kind of scholarship, we can develop an informatics know-how that curbs our enthusiasm about the technologies we love just enough to really implement better social worlds. To paraphrase Bush, Kling's social informatics disciplinary 'device' would be capable of

> ...*making more accessible our bewildering store of knowledge about ICTs in social contexts; it would help us establish a new relationship between thinking professionals, the sum of our knowledge, and the implications of our actions.*

This conference honors Rob Kling's legacy and his vision. It is a testament to his commitment and to the relevance of his ideas about the value of Social Informatics.

PART 1 – SOCIAL INFORMATICS:

AN INFORMATION SOCIETY FOR ALL?

On Rob Kling: The Theoretical, the Methodological, and the Critical

Alice Robbin and Ron Day
School of Library and Information Science Indiana University, USA
arobbin@indiana.edu, http://ella.slis.indiana.edu/~arobbin/
roday@indiana.edu , http://ella.slis.indiana.edu/~roday/

Abstract. We explore Rob Kling's conceptual scaffolding for Social Informatics: his integration of theory, method and evidence and philosophical underpinnings and moral basis of his commitment to a critical stance towards computers and social life. He extended his focus on organizational practices and a lifelong meditation on democracy, value conflicts and social choices to the discourses of computerization and social transformation and to the education of the information professional. He came to his project through careful observation of organizational life and a critical reading of research conducted by other scholars and the rhetoric about ICTs, As Kling conceptualized it, the project of Social Informatics was to intervene in the social construction of the meaning, value, use and even design of technologies as shaped by discourse and education.

Keywords: Rob Kling, Social Informatics, intellectual trajectory, theory, social critique

1 Introduction

Rob Kling is lovingly remembered by colleagues and friends around the world.[1] He is described with a host of adjectives that include: engaged, lively, enthusiastic, energetic, charismatic, intellectually curious and playful, open to ideas and criticism, socially aware, and politically committed. Kling was not the first to assign the name 'Social Informatics' to what has evolved to become a legitimate domain of study.[2] He was, however, its central figure, promoter and proselytizer, a 'scholar on a mission.' He was a major scholar and contributor to the conceptual scaffolding of Social Informatics through sustained inquiry and a very public record of his work. His scholarly contributions have been cited in a wide array of fields.[3]

His observations of the empirical world led to research questions that crossed disciplinary boundaries and invigorated disciplines, transformed our thinking, and

Please use the following format when citing this chapter:

Robbin, A., Day, R., 2006, in IFIP International Federation for Information Processing, Volume 223, Social Informatics: An Information Society for All? In Remembrance of Rob Kling, eds. Berleur, J., Numinen, M. I., Impagliazzo, J., (Boston: Springer), pp. 25–36.

helped us develop a working vocabulary about technology and social life. His extensive, worldwide social network of colleagues and students and enduring relationships with trusted assessors were responsible for creating a community of scholars committed to Social Informatics [Cronin & Shaw, 2006]. It is for all these reasons that this international conference recognizes him as a tireless institution builder.

We explore Kling's conceptual scaffolding: how he integrated theory, method and evidence and the philosophical underpinnings and moral basis of his commitment to a critical stance towards computers and social life.[4] Our analysis relies on a close reading of his most highly cited works and other papers that extended his study of organizational practices and his lifelong meditation on value conflicts and social choices to the discourses of computerization and social transformation and to the education of the information professional. We note that Kling used 'technology' to refer to computers and information technology, which 'morphed' at the end of his career into 'information and communication technologies' (ICTs); thus, we use the terms interchangeably throughout our discussion.

The ideas that guided him, his sensibilities about the problem space, and his theoretical position were clearly articulated at the beginning of his career and continued well into the 1990s and early 21st century. He attended to macro- and micro-levels of analysis and core sociological concepts of context, social situation, embeddedness, identity, role, and authority (power). He considered the influence of history on thought and action and the dynamics, contingencies, fluidity, and uncertainty of the outcomes of social relations. He understood that the relationship between technology and social life was problematic and a complex, contingent process. This relationship was mediated by history, context, structure and agency, culture and meaning systems, symbolic and material interests and resources, and political and social processes. His approach subsumed the analytical approaches of 'social shaping of technology' and 'social construction of technology' under the more general arena of study that he called 'Social Informatics'.

Kling's intensive exploration into scholarly work on organizational life and information systems was fruitfully married with his training as a computer scientist. He had an intimate knowledge of the logic of computer systems and the social world of computer scientists and management information systems professionals. His training also contributed to conceptualizing problems in terms of causal structures (as in the relationship between social forces and the effects of computerization). His awareness of the language systems employed by practitioners contributed to his later writings on the use of metaphors as constitutive of the language of public policy and social action.

He translated questions about 'how we know the world' into questions of research design. He critiqued quantitative and qualitative methods used to study information systems design and called for improved methodological rigor in the study of computerization in organizations [see Kling, 1987, 1991a, 1992b].

Humanistic and moral concerns contributed to his investigations of the problematics of the social and the technical. The notion of 'the critical' emerged very early in his work as the analysis of the disjunctions between popular and professional claims about the social values and uses of ICTs and their empirical reality. The 'critical' was given prominence in the 1990s with his writings on professional education which argued that 'critical' analysis was the foundation of Social Informatics [Kling 2003].

2 Theory, Method, and Evidence

Kling came to his project of Social Informatics through two sources: a critical reading of research on computerization conducted by other scholars and his own careful observations about how computers were introduced into organizations. His thinking was also influenced by what he deemed inflationary rhetoric about the social use and meaning of ICTs and their actual performance. The research conducted by other investigators provided Kling with ammunition for his own argument: that actual outcomes of computerized information systems implementation differed significantly from what their theories argued. In addition, his own empirical research sensitized him to the underlying premises of the theoretical approaches of other scholars and to the speculative rhetoric that he later criticized.

The central premises of his life-long critique of the consequences of computerization for organizational and social life may be summarized in the following way: He believed that rational actor theory (public choice, economic rationality, systems rationalist) dominated the study of organizational practices, computer technology, politics and public policy. The control, efficiency, and productivity features of management dominated the study of technology-in-organizations. These approaches constituted a highly prescriptive or normative form of theorizing that exuded a certainty about the consequences, outcomes, and benefits of computerization. These approaches to modeling technology adoption suggested that technology shaped organizational practices in a deterministic and unidirectional causal direction.

Kling concluded that the theoretical claims made by these dominant approaches were not supported with adequate empirical evidence and were "based on a highly simplified conception of computing and social life" [Kling & Scacchi 1982, p. 2]. He contended that their claims to universality were unfounded and their analytical explanatory power was limited and, thus, inadequate for the task of understanding the dynamics of the social context of computing [Kling 1976, 1978c, 1980a; Kling & Scacchi 1980]. Contingency and complexity were, instead, key to understanding the adoption and use of computer technology in organizations. Kling [1974] was also convinced that politics were part of social life and computerization; technology had consequences for the polity and for the individual.

However, it is important to emphasize that Kling never rejected outright the dominant models and theoretical perspectives; he criticized them because they inadequately explained socially complex technologies. His evaluation of the limitations of their conceptions of computing and social life was motivated by a desire to find good explanation for the empirical evidence he had accumulated through his own research investigations. When these theoretical approaches offered explanatory power, he used them, incorporating multiple social and political theories and methods from a variety of scholarly literatures to inform his own investigations.

He extracted concepts and a working vocabulary from theories he came in contact with to construct a better explanation of computerization in organizations and social life. His strategy linked theory and evidence through methodologies that depended on close observation to understand the social world of the organizational actor. He applied various forms of interpretive epistemology and associated methodologies to study organizational practices. Political theory was employed to find explanations for the social order that he observed inside organizations and the polis. Values, power, ideology, domination, legitimacy, authority, and influence relations and their consequences for both the bureaucracy and the policy process were at the heart of Kling's analysis of organizational and political life.

Symbolic interactionism, for its attention to micro-processes of the social order and its associated concepts, metaphors and methods, was the 'orienting strategy' [Berger, Willer, & Zelditch, 2005] that exerted the greatest influence on Kling's thinking about the relationship between social and technical systems. Its theoretical lens offered a way to understand the social structure of the computing world in interactional context and as a web of relationships. It also provided a language for decoding the consequences and impacts of computerization on organizational practices and the polity and the symbol and meaning systems that shaped interpretative action. Organizational life was a negotiated social order of both conflict and cooperation, structurally complex, contingent, ambiguous, ritualistic, and symbolic. The individual was a reflexive social actor with 'interests' who acted strategically. This approach, particularly with its emphasis on emergent and dynamic properties of the social order, also helped Kling recognize the historical aspects of the dynamic processes of computerization in organizations [see Kling & Iacono, 1989]. The ideas of Blumer, Goffman, Becker, and Berger and Luckmann infuse his writings [see Kling, 1980a; Kling & Gerson, 1977, 1978; Kling & Scacchi, 1982; Iacono & Kling, 2001/1998; Kling & Iacono, 1988, 1995; Kling & Courtright, 2004; Lamb & Kling, 2003].

Symbolic interactionism's approach provided Kling with three evocative metaphors as a way to examine the social context of computerization: technology as a 'package' (as in 'a socio-technical package') of a 'complex array of commitments,' a 'production lattice,' and 'web models' (as in a 'web of computing'). Through the next decades until his death these metaphors remained central to his analysis [see Kling, 1980a; Kling & Scacchi, 1979, 1980, 1982; Kling & Dutton, 1982; Kling & Iacono, 1989; Kling & McKim, 2000]. The web of computing and package metaphors evolved towards the end of his career into the "characterization of ICTs as 'socio-technical interaction networks' (STINs – not tools or objects that could be analyzed separately from their users, but which 'co-constituted each other' and required that 'both technologies and users be analyzed integrally'" [Robbin, Courtright, & Davis, 2004, p. 415, citing Kling, 2000a, 2000b].

Kling's affinity for the symbolic interactionist conception of social life also led him to move easily from theorizing about organizational practices as dynamic and emergent processes to a theoretical approach whose central premise was the organization as an organic and open system and institutions as symbol systems

[Kling, 1992a; Kling & Jewett, 1994; Kling & Iacono, 1988, 1995; Covi & Kling, 1996; Iacono & Kling, 2001/1998]. And the institution as symbol system, coupled with the concepts of structure and agency, led Kling naturally to work by sociologists of what would later be conceptualized as the 'new institutionalism' [Kling & Jewett, 1994; Lamb & Kling, 2003; Lamb, King, & Kling, 2003].

Symbolic interactionism also provided Kling with the theoretical grounding and a sociological explanation for his two other long-standing preoccupations regarding the dynamics of macro-level processes and consequences of computerization for collective action: the political discourse about computerization at the societal level and political life as manifested in public policy and politics. The public discourse of social movements, to which symbolic interactionists had devoted decades of study, reinforced his interest in the competing narratives and discursive repertoires about computerization. Kling reframed their research in collective behavior, specifically the study of the interactional processes of groups as social movements, ideology, conflict, and the social construction of public problems, as 'computerization movements.'

The adoption of the theoretical lenses of conflict, ideology and frame construction gave Kling the necessary theoretical tools to make explicit the linkages between micro- and macro-level processes as they related to technology adoption; and to clarify the utopian and dystopian stances that advocated for and against computerization. Computerization implied change, change implied conflict, and conflict was endemic to social transformation [Kling & Scacchi, 1979]. Power and ideology, which Kling conceptualized as a 'computing world view,' were linked, and computing developments were identified as a political process where key actors built support and quieted opposition [Kling & Iacono, 1984]. His quasi-linguistic studies on the genres of 'computerization' applied concepts from the theories of ideology and frame construction to the analysis of the rhetoric of computerization and the rhetorical devices employed by the various interests which he labeled 'utopian and dystopian stories' [Kling, 1994, 1996; Iacono & Kling, 2001; Kling & Iacono, 1988].

3   The Critical

Symbolic interactionists' interests originated from an action-oriented sociology committed to creating a more just and equal society and from their theoretical interest in the social aspects of the political processes of protest, resistance, mobilization and action. Philosophically, their commitments resonated with Kling's own philosophical tendencies, humanistic impulses, and public policy interests [Kling, 1973, 1974, 1978a, 1978b, 1978d, 1978e, 1980b, 1986, 1990, 1991b; Kling & Star, 1998; Iacono & Kling, 1987; Teich, Frankel, Kling, & Lee, 1999]. His theoretical and political sensibilities and empirical investigations aligned in the early 1970s with an emerging culture of concern by computer professionals with social values and uses of computers. Their critique made visible the contradictions between popular and professional claims about the social values and uses of ICTs and their empirical reality. Their critique also exposed what Kling [1992a, p. 351] called the 'radical dimension' to "working in this terrain [of practical computerization efforts]": The analyst who questioned the "arguments and structures that legitimated social domination, who raised the critical questions in these practical domains sometimes [came] in conflict with powerful organized interests."

Over the next decades Kling would write extensively on the consequences of public policies on computerization for democracy, consequences that raised questions of social choices and whose choices always engaged value conflicts. His wide-ranging policy critique included a continuing concern about the loss of personal privacy and the development of mass surveillance systems. He analyzed the consequences of electronic funds transfer systems. He had a long-standing interest in the quality of school preparation for the digital age, including issues of enfranchisement and the digital divide. He wrote on the quality of work life in an information society and the effects of restructuring labor markets for information work and growing social stratification. His participation in a variety of national public policy assessments undertaken by professional associations and the National Academy of Sciences led him to considerations about the design of a national computing and information infrastructure, the role of the scholar in policy design and evaluation, intellectual property, censorship, information production and distribution, the nature of public decision making, and scholarly communication. His association with library and information science yielded provocative thinking about the role of the library in society. His sensitivity to language contributed to his writings on the abuses of anonymous communication on the Internet. In all these matters his critique was both humanistic and moral.

Based on his empirical investigations into organizational life and his analyses of popular and professional claims about the social values and uses of ICTs, Kling concluded that computer professionals were inclined to believe the most utopian (or equally dystopian) narratives about the social values and uses of computers. Not only were these claims 'uncritical' statements and narratives divorced from 'empirical' reality, he contended, but 'many of [their] visions delete[d] people and social order in important ways.' To what extent, he asked, could "computer-based technologies play key roles in restructuring major social relationships – interpersonal, intergroup, and institutional" [Kling, 1991b, p. 344]?

As Kling conceptualized it, the project of Social Informatics was to intervene in the social construction of the meaning, value, use and even design of technologies as shaped by discourse and education [Kling, 1994, 2003]. The purpose of Social Informatics was not to continue the prescriptive and speculative practices of the computer industry, professional education, and 'social life' in regard to their evaluations of ICTs and social life and professional activity. The purpose was to *intervene* in the practice of theory of ICTs by means of critical examination and discourse.

Intervention required changing professional education and professional norms [Kling, 2003]. To accomplish these goals, professional computer-related education needed to be improved by infusing Social Informatics in professional programs of study, so that students would not just be trained. Computer (information) professionals needed to understand how people were affected by various computer systems. They needed to be engaged in the development of policy models to "ensure computing arrangements which [would] better serve the public" [Kling, 1980b, p.

166]; and the design of human-centered systems [Kling, 1973, 1978b; Kling & Star, 1998]. Computer (information) professionals needed more than a technical education directed to problem solving and that "identified mathematics as the only legitimate kind of theoretical orientation" [Kling, 2003, p. 408]. Students required a critical education that intervened in the narrative and institutional constructions of reality and that included critically reflective conceptual, historical, and interpretive analyses in computer science and research.

A critical orientation would reflectively question the value and meaning of discourse and other activities in an interventionist manner. Students would learn how to analyze ICTs from perspectives that did not automatically and uncritically accept the goals and beliefs of groups that had commissioned, designed, or implemented specific IT applications. Research approaches and methods would go beyond the quantitative and mathematical to embrace those used in the qualitative, conceptual, social sciences and, particularly, the humanities. They would learn appropriate methods of conceptualizing, reflecting on, and analyzing the possibilities and limits of computer technologies in institutional and other social settings.

4   Concluding Remarks

The area of research that defines all of Kling's work is the relation of information and communication technologies with social life and with professional education, in particular, the professional education of computer scientists and, later for Kling, 'information professionals.'

He argued for an analytical and empirical approach to the study of society and computerization. He connected empirical evidence to an eclectic variety of modern social and political theory to address the problematics of information and computer technologies (ICTs) in organizations and the polity. This emphasis placed on 'empirical' methods and 'problem-driven' analyses in social informatics dominates its legacy today.

Kling also employed interpretive methods of analysis that were argumentative and based in conceptual analysis, textual analysis and sometimes historical analysis. Emergence and contingency were foundational principles for him, and called for a multi-method strategy for understanding these processes.

He adopted a critical stance towards ICTs that is not traditionally associated with the empiricist approach. Indeed, his notions of method and the 'empirical' in Social Informatics may be more broadly than generally realized as belonging to Social Informatics. The implications of developing a cultural, 'critical' analysis (per historical and conceptual methods) are explored, *pace* Kling [2003] in the areas of professional education and social life.

We can view his critiques as interventions designed to destroy false illusions embedded in prescriptive education, research, and the ideologies of ICT use in social life. His critiques challenged what we are doing and why. He advocated for professional social responsibility, and his later paper on professional education implicitly argued that 'critical analysis' is the foundation for Social Informatics.

In one form or another his writings focused on various elements of the normative implications of computerization, the roles and responsibilities of the public and private sectors and professions, and public policy design and its consequences for social life, work life, and the citizen. He articulated a responsibility-centered role for information professionals, which flowed from his convictions about the ethical self. He contended that technology was not (politically) neutral and went far beyond the technical: it had consequences for the polity, society, organizational life and individuals, and it was implicated in social change and transformation. "These issues," he wrote,

concern the ways and means that computer technology can help foster a mature and humane society. They involve judgments of social value as well as technical comparisons. As a beginning we must understand how computer technology can be used to enhance (or diminish) the humaneness of the people who are affected by various computer systems [1973, p. 387].

Thus, information professionals needed to carefully consider elements of power and influence, resources available to and employed by various interests, and the consequences of their personal decisions and of public policies. And they needed to apply what Kling [1974] called 'person-centered standards' for the design of computerized information systems that promoted "a sense of personal competence and authority" (p. 6).

If we are to read Kling's work seriously—what he always challenged us to do, that is, in non-hagiographic fashion, we must confront the inherent epistemological tensions of causal assumptions and interpretive analysis in his corpus of work. By suggesting that the causal relation of 'society' and computers/IT/ICTs constituted the central issue for Social Informatics, he risked reifying the notion of the social as a causal agent and did the same for a category of technological objects ('computers,' 'IT,' 'ICTs'). His work, we argue, demonstrates the impossibility of directly correlating technological materials to cultural expressions and social uses, and the difficulty of constructing direct, efficient, causal relations between 'technology' and 'society.'

All the same, we recognize that he passed away before developing a robust and coherent theoretical framework to explain the relations that he studied. We must also acknowledge what his corpus of work did *not* examine as a central concern of Social Informatics: information (and communication) as a culturally and historically specific form of knowledge. We need to recognize, as well, that the cornerstone of Social Informatics, *the critical*, remains undeveloped. Indeed, Kling recognized these gaps in the conceptual frameworks that had grounded Social Informatics in the previous decades. Shortly before he died he wrote an outline for a book directed at scholars and students who were interested in technology and social change. His commitments to history, conceptual analysis, interpretive analysis, and the critical are to be found in this book prospectus.

Although this book was, alas, never completed, Kling's oeuvre provides us with the intellectual scaffolding for Social Informatics. He urges us to be theoretically informed, empirically grounded, and historically oriented. We need to develop good theory and good evidence if we are to achieve a more complete understanding of the relation of technology and social life. Social Informatics can and should engage other approaches and disciplines. We can recognize that future investigations in Social Informatics will benefit in their greater historical engagements, their richer conceptual analyses, and their less ambiguous commitments to strictly interpretative and conceptual analyses. We can examine techniques and technologies in their production of 'information.' And we are encouraged to follow some of the paths suggested by critical cultural research. This is his legacy.

References

Berger, J., D. Wille, and M. Zelditch, Theory Programs and Theoretical Problems, *Sociological Theory*, **23**(2), 127-155 (2005).

Covi, L. and R. Kling, Organizational Dimensions of Effective Digital Library Use: Closed Rational and Open Natural Systems Models, *Journal of the American Society for Information Science*, **47**(9), 672-689 (1996).

Cronin, B., in: Designing Virtual Communities, edited by S. A. Barab, R. Kling, and J. H. Gray (Cambridge University Press, Cambridge, England, 2004), pp. xxi-xxv.

Cronin, B. and D. Shaw, Peers and Spheres of Influence: Situating Rob Kling. Forthcoming *Information Technology & People* (2006).

Day, R. Theory, Practice, Social Informatics, presented at the annual meeting of the American Society for Information Science and Technology, Charlotte, North Carolina, October 28-November 2, 2005.

Day, R. Kling and "the Critical": Implications for Professional Education and Social Life (unpublished) (2005b).

Dutton, W. Forward, in: R. Kling, H. Rosenbaum, and S. Sawyer, *Understanding and communicating social informatics: A Framework for Studying and Teaching the Human Contexts of Information and Communication Technologies* (Medford, NJ: Information Today, Inc., Medford, NJ, 2005).

Haigh, T. Rob Kling, *Annals of the History of Computing*, **25**(3), 92-94 (2003).

Iacono, S. and R. Kling, in: Technology and the Transformation of White Collar Work, edited by R. Kraut (Hillsdale, NJ: Lawrence Erlbaum Publishers, Hillsdale, New Jersey, 1987), pp. 53-75.

Iacono, S. and R. Kling, in: Information Technology and Organizational Transformation: History, Rhetoric, and Practice, edited by J. Yates and J. Van Maanen (Sage Publications, Thousand Oaks, California, 2001), pp. 93-136.

Kling, R. Towards a Person-centered Computer Technology, *Proceedings of the Annual Conference of the ACM*, 387-391 (1973).

Kling, R. Computers and Social Power, *Computers and Society* **5**(3), 6-11 (1974).

Kling, R. EFTS: Social and Technical Issues. What are EFTS?, *Computers & Society* **7**(3), 3-10 (1976).

Kling, R. Automated Welfare Client-tracking and Service Integration: The Political-economy of Computing, *Communications of the ACM* **21**(6), 484-493 (1978a).

Kling, R. Six Models for the Social Accountability of Computing, *Information Privacy* **1**(2), 62-70 (1978b).

Kling, R. Value Conflicts and Social Choice in Electronic Funds Transfer System Developments, *Communications of the ACM* **21**(8), 642-656 (1978c).

Kling, R. Information Systems in Policy Making: Computer Technology and Organizational Arrangements, *Telecommunications Policy* 2(1), 3-12 (1978d).

Kling, R. Value Conflicts and Social Choice in Electronic Funds Transfer Systems Developments, *Communications of the ACM* 21(8), 642-657 (1978e).

Kling, R. Social Analyses of Computing: Theoretical Perspectives in Recent Empirical Research, *Computing Surveys* 12(1), 61-110 (1980a).

Kling, R. Models for the Social Accountability of Computing, *Telecommunications Policy* 4(3), 166-182 (1980b).

Kling, R. The Struggle for Democracy in an Information Society, *The Information Society* 4(1/2), 1-7 (1986).

Kling, R. in: *Critical Issues in Information Systems* edited by R. Boland and R. Hirschheim (John Wiley, New York, 1987), pp. 307-362.

Kling, R. More Information, Better Jobs? Occupational Stratification and Labor Market Segmentation in the United States' Information Labor Force, *The Information Society* 7(2), 77-107 (1990).

Kling, R., in: The Information Systems Research Challenge: Survey Research Methods, edited by K.L. Kraemer (Harvard Business School, Boston, Massachusetts, 1991a), pp. 337-350.

Kling, R. Computerization and Social Transformations, *Science, Technology and Human Values* 16(3), 342-367 (1991b).

Kling, R. Audiences, narratives and human values in social studies of science. *Science, Technology and Human Values* 17(3), 349-365 (1992a).

Kling, R. When Gunfire Shatters Bone: Reducing Sociotechnical Systems to Social Relationships, *Science, Technology and Human Values*, 17(3), 381-385 (1992b).

Kling, R. Designing Effective Computing Systems in a Web of Social and Technical Relations, *Human-Computer Interaction* 9(1), 86-90 (1994).

Kling, R. Computers and Controversy: Value Conflicts and Social Choices (2nd ed.) (Academic Press, New York, 1996).

Kling, R. Learning about Information Technologies and Social Change: The Contribution of Social Informatics, *The Information Society* 16(3), 217-232 (2000a).

Kling, R. Social Informatics: A New Perspective on Social Research about Information and Communication Technologies, *Prometheus* 18(3), 245–264 (2000b).

Kling, R. Critical Professional Education and Information and Communications Technologies and Social Life, *Information Technology & People* 16(4), 394-418 (2003).

Kling, R. and C. Courtright, Group Behavior and Learning in Electronic Forums: A Sociotechnical Approach, *The Information Society* 19(3), 221-235 (2003).

Kling, R. and W.H. Dutton, in: *Computers and Politics: High Technology in American Local Governments*, edited by J.N. Danziger, W.H. Dutton, R. Kling, and K.L. Kraemer (New York: Columbia University Press, 1982), pp. 22-50.

Kling, R. and E. Gerson, The Social Dynamics of Technical Innovation in the Computing World, *Symbolic Interaction* 1(1), 132-146 (1977).

Kling, R. and E. Gerson, Patterns of Segmentation and Intersection in the Computing World, *Symbolic Interaction* 1(2), 24-43 (1978).

Kling, R. and S. Iacono, The Control of Information Systems Development After Implementation, *Communications of the ACM* 27(12), 1218-1226 (1984).

Kling, R. and S. Iacono, The Mobilization of Support for Computerization: The Role of Computerization Movements *Social Problems*, 35(3), 226-243 (1988).

Kling, R. and S. Iacono, The Institutional Character of Computerized Information Systems, *Office: Technology and People* **5**(1), 7-28 (1989).

Kling, R. and S. Iacono, in: *Ecologies of Knowledge*, edited by S.L. Star (SUNY Press, New York, 1995), pp. 119-153.

Kling, R. and T. Jewett, The Social Design of Work Life with Computers and Networks: An Open Natural Systems Perspective, *Advances in Computers* **39**, 239-293 (1994).

Kling, R. and G. McKim, Not Just a Matter of Time: Field Differences and the Shaping of Electronic Media in Supporting Scientific Communication, *Journal of the American Society for Information Science* **51**(14), 1306-1320 (2000).

Kling, R., and W. Scacchi, Recurrent Dilemmas of Routine Computer Use in Complex Organizations, *Proceedings of the National Computer Conference* **48** (AFIPS Press, Montage, New Jersey, 1979), pp. 107-115.

Kling, R. and W. Scacchi, Computing as Social Action: The Social Dynamics of Computing in Complex Organizations, *Advances in Computers* **19**, 249-327 (1980).

Kling, R. and W. Scacchi, The Web of Computing: Computer Technology as Social Organization, *Advances in Computers* **21**, 1-90 (1982).

Kling, R. and S.L. Star, Human Centered Systems in the Perspective of Organizational and Social Informatics, *Computers and Society* **28**(1), 22-29 (1998).

Lamb, R. and R. Kling, Reconceptualizing Users as Social Actors in Information Systems Research, *MIS Quarterly* **27**(2), 197-235 (2003).

Lamb, R., J.L. King, and R. Kling, Informational Environments: Organizational Contexts of Online Information Use, *Journal of the American Society for Information Science and Technology* **54**(2), 97-114 (2003).

Robbin, A. Rob Kling in Search of One Good Theory, Forthcoming *Information Technology & People* (2006).

Robbin, R., C. Courtright, and L. Davis, in: Annual Review of Information Science and Technology, edited by B. Cronin (Information Today, Medford, New Jersey, 2004), 411-462.

Robbin, R., N. Hara, and R. Day, Social Informatics Education in I-Schools, presented at the I-conference 2005, Pennsylvania State University, University Park, Pennsylvania, September 28-30, 2005.

Teich, A., M.S. Frankel, R. Kling, and Y-C. Lee, Anonymous Communication Policies for the Internet: Results and Recommendations of the AAAS conference, *The Information Society* **15**(2), 79-90 (1999).

---

[1] See "Dr. Rob Kling Remembered" at the Indiana University School of Library and Information Science web page [Retrieved March 9, 2006, from http://rkcsi.indiana.edu/article.php/about-rob-kling/28]. A memorial service was held for him in October 2003 [Retrieved March 9, 2006, from http://vw.indiana.edu/talks04/kling.php]. For some of the remembrances see also: Haigh [2003]; volume 19, number 3 (2003) and volume 20, number 2 (2004) of *The Information Society*; Cronin [2004]; volume 19, number 1 of *Information Technology and People* (2005); volume 12 of *Communications of the Association of Information Systems* (2003); and the National Science Foundation-supported "Social Informatics Workshop" held at CRITO, University of California at Irvine, March 11-12, 2005 [Retrieved March 9, 2006, from http://www.crito.uci.edu/si/].

2   To this we owe our thanks to the Norwegian sociologist Stein Bråten whom Rob visited in Oslo in the early 1980s. Personal communication from Ingar Roggen, October 17, 1995. See also Dutton's [2005] remarks about discussions he had with Kling in the early 1980s.

3   Although there are known problems with ISI's "Web of Science" coverage, a search conducted in mid-December 2005, of Kling's cited works reveals just how extensive his influence was. He was cited by authors who reside in 35 countries. The subject categories include, in addition to the majority of articles classified as "library science and information science," 9 different or related subfields of computer science; 20 fields or subfields in the social sciences; ethics; 3 subfields of business/management; 5 subfields of engineering; 4 fields or subfields of health; philosophy and history of science, and law.

4   This paper draws on ideas first developed in Day [2005a, 2005b], Robbin [2006], and Robbin, Hara, & Day [2005].

Socio-Technical Interaction Networks: A Discussion of the Strengths, Weaknesses and Future of Kling's STIN Model

Eric T. Meyer

Rob Kling Center for Social Informatics, Indiana University, USA
etmeyer@indiana.edu, http://mypage.iu.edu/~etmeyer

Abstract. The Socio-Technical Interaction Network (STIN) strategy for social informatics research was published late in Rob Kling's life, and as a result, he did not have time to pursue its continued development. This paper aims to summarize existing work on STINs, identify key themes, strengths, weaknesses and limitations, and to suggest trajectories for the future of STIN research. The STIN strategy for research on socio-technical systems offers the potential for useful insights into the highly intertwined nature of social factors and technological systems, however a number of areas of the strategy remain underdeveloped and offer the potential for future refinement and modification.

Keywords: Social informatics, Socio-Technical Interaction Networks, STIN, Rob Kling

1   Introduction

Kling, McKim, & King's [2003] article on electronic scholarly communication forums is Kling's attempt to detail the assumptions and use of what he called the Socio-Technical Interaction Network (STIN) methodology. This STIN strategy is an elaboration of Kling's earlier web models [Kling, 1992; Kling & Scacchi, 1982] designed to give social informatics and other researchers a tool for understanding socio-technical systems in a way that privileged neither the social nor the technical. Unfortunately, Kling's untimely death in 2003 left the STIN strategy without its prime evangelist. Other researchers, however, are taking up the STIN strategy in an attempt to more fully test and develop the concept.

This paper is organized in the following manner. First is a discussion of Socio-Technical Interaction Networks (STINs) and their salient features. Next is a discussion of some of the studies that have used STINs in a variety of settings. Third, the methods used in STIN research are discussed. Next is a discussion of the

Please use the following format when citing this chapter:

Meyer, E. T., 2006, in IFIP International Federation for Information Processing, Volume 223, Social Informatics: An Information Society for All? In Remembrance of Rob Kling, eds. Berleur, J., Numinen, M. I., Impagliazzo, J., (Boston: Springer), pp. 37–48.

weaknesses and limitations of STINs. Finally, the paper concludes with some thoughts for the future of STIN research.

2 Theory

2.1 Similarities and Differences between Bijker, Latour and Kling

Kling's STIN approach [2003] is "an emerging conceptual framework for identifying, organizing, and comparatively analyzing patterns of social interaction, system development, and the configuration of components that constitute an information system" [Scacchi, 2005:2]. The STIN model is a more fully developed version of what Kling earlier [Kling, 1992; Kling & Scacchi, 1982] referred to as web models:

Web models conceive of a computer system as an ensemble of equipment, applications and techniques with identifiable information processing capabilities...as an alternative to 'engineering models,' which focused on the equipment and its information processing capabilities as the focus of analysis, and formal organizational arrangements as the basis of social action. [Kling, 1991]

The STIN approach draws both on the Social Construction of Technology (SCOT) approach associated with Bijker, Pinch and others, and on Actor-Network Theory (ANT), which is associated with Latour, Law, Callon and others. While these approaches are related, they are not identical. All are approaches which help to understand the role of social behavior in the of creation and use of technological artifacts, and all reject technological determinism as being too simplistic [Bijker, 2001:15523]. SCOT is particularly interested in the social construction process, wherein relevant social groups establish technological frames which help to understand the interpretive flexibility of artifacts and help to move toward a state of closure or stabilization [Bijker, 1995, 2001; Callon, 1987; Pinch & Bijker, 1987]. ANT can be viewed as a subset of SCOT, when SCOT is broadly defined [Bijker, 2001]. ANT adds a number of elements to other SCOT research, including the idea that non-human actants can have agency [Hanseth, Aanestad, & Berg, 2004; Latour, 1988], and that the closure discussed in SCOT results in black-boxing artifacts after a process of translation and enrollment [Callon, 1986]. The processes by which translation and enrollment occur are particularly important they help to explain some of the 'how' and 'why' questions raised by SCOT as various social groups come into contact and, potentially, conflict as they construct technology. As we will see below, the STIN approach differs from ANT in being much more conservative in attributing agency to non-human actants, is more prescriptive than SCOT or ANT, and focuses on patterns of routine use more frequently than patterns of adoption and innovation. The STIN approach is consistent with SCOT and ANT, however, in the sense that the identification of relevant social groups, understanding interpretive flexibility, and examining processes of translation and enrollment are crucial to developing a STIN model.

2.2   Socio-Technical Interaction Networks (STINs)

The STIN approach emphasizes that "ICTs do not exist in social or technological isolation" [Lamb, Sawyer, & Kling, 2000]. According to Kling:

Several fundamental assumptions underlie the application of the STIN methodology, and drive the methods used to construct STINs. These assumptions include [1] the social and the technological are not meaningfully separable..., [2] Theories of social behavior...should influence technical design choices..., [3] system participants are embedded in multiple, overlapping, and non-technologically mediated social relationships, and therefore may have multiple, often conflicting, commitments..., [and 4] sustainability and routine operations are critical. [Kling et al., 2003:56-57]

The first assumption, that the social and technological are not meaningfully separable, should be familiar to those familiar with the theoretical approaches of SCOT [Bijker, 1995; Pinch & Bijker, 1987] and ANT [Latour, 1987; Latour & Woolgar, 1979; Law, 1999], particularly ANT's concept of actants that can be human or non-human participants in a socio-technical system. The STIN approach extends SCOT and ANT, however, by problematizing information technologies and making the "association between STS [Socio-technical systems] concepts and IS research [which] is often not explicitly articulated as such in contemporary literature" [Lamb et al., 2000:1]. One of the major differences between Latour's and Kling's approached is that "Latour theorizes about how new technologies come to be; Kling and Scacchi theorize about how new technologies come to be used" [Orlikowski & Iacono, 2001:126]. The STIN approach is also less committed to ANT's concept of 'radical indeterminacy' [Hanseth et al., 2004; Latour, 1988] and is "much more conservative in attributing action to nonhuman agents" [Kling et al., 2003:66].

Kling argues that this integrated concept of socio-technical systems is more useful than the more common use of the term socio-technical to argue merely that technologies have consequences for social and organizational behavior. This highly intertwined nature of the social and the technical is central to the STIN approach.

The second and fourth assumptions reflect a normative element of the STIN approach. Arguing that theories of social behavior should influence technical design choices and that it is critical to consider the sustainability of socio-technical systems both reflect Kling's background in computer science and concern for social issues. This differs from SCOT, which does not generally concern itself with such prescriptive concerns, and also differs from ANT, which is much more theoretically oriented, to the extent that even ANT's methodological prescriptions are primarily methods of analysis and not methods of collection [Bowden, 1995]. While Kling did not reference the Technology Assessment (TA, or *Technikfolgenabschätzung*) literature, his interest in improving future technological systems based on outcomes of STIN research is consistent with TA's emphasis on influencing policy and communicating the results of socio-technical studies with a wider audience [Mohr, 1999].

Kling's third assumption regarding the multiplicity of social relationships and commitments for system participants is the key to understanding the contribution STIN makes to research into change in socio-technical systems. This ecological element of the STIN approach looks beyond the socio-technical system under study and also examines how other portions of an actor's social world are connected to their use and understanding of technology. Thus, when analyzing the physics pre-print online server arXiv.org, a STIN model includes not just authors, readers and file servers, but also institutional linkages, funding models, the non-technical social responsibilities of authors, the nature and size of research collaborations, and the socio-political behavior of arXiv's founders [Kling et al., 2003; Meyer & Kling, 2002].

Another concept that Kling was also involved in developing ties in with the STIN framework, the social actor concept as an alternative to the concept of technology users: "A social actor is an organizational entity whose interactions are simultaneously enabled and constrained by the socio-technical affiliations and environments of the firm, its members, and its industry. In short, social actors are not primarily users of ICTs" [Lamb & Kling, 2003:218]. The social actor concept allows for analysis of less computer-intensive professionals who nevertheless routinely use information and communication technologies (ICTs) which shape what they do, how they perceive themselves and others, and how they interact with others. They are influenced by their affiliations, environments, interactions and identities as they shape and are shaped by ICT use [Lamb & Kling, 2003].

2.3   STIN Studies

Despite its relatively recent introduction, the STIN approach has been used to study a growing number of IT topics, including scholarly communication forums [Kling et al., 2003], democratization of scholarly publishing [Meyer & Kling, 2002], web information systems [Eschenfelder & Chase, 2002], online communities [Barab, Schatz, & Scheckler, 2004], digital libraries [Joung & Rosenbaum, 2004], and free/open source software developers [Scacchi, 2005]. A common element of these studies is that all not only deal with complex social systems, but that the STIN approach is used to explain the complexity rather than reduce it to overly simplistic terms. This is one way that the STIN approach shares a common view with both SCOT and ANT; all three approaches reject simplistic, positivistic explanations for complex social systems all too common among more mainstream sociological approaches [Star, 1988]. One way this complexity is addressed in the STIN approach is that many of the studies include STIN diagrams, graphical representations of the relationships between various elements within the STIN, including technologies, human actors, institutions, relationships, roles, and other relevant elements.

Kling et al. [2003], in their main article laying out what they call the STIN 'methodology', examined electronic scholar communication forums (e-SCFs) including arXiv.org, Flybase, ISWORLD, and CONVEX. Among the conclusions offered in the article are that technological developments themselves will not overcome issues embedded in the social contexts into which the technologies are introduced. Fast connections and good interfaces, they argue, would not have caused medical researchers to support PubMed Central, since the primary reasons for their non-support were based on long-standing institutional arrangements and the vested interests of gatekeepers and various interest groups[1]. They also found that for the e-SCFs, understanding the business models of the supporting organizations was necessary for understanding the STIN, and that understanding the social relationships embedded in the STIN helped to understand how the technological innovations of electronic publishing are used and sustained.

Scacchi [2005] uses STINs to understand Free and Open Source Software Development (F/OSSD). Scacchi argues that STINs have formed most clearly in four areas: joining and contributing to F/OSSD, building communities of practice, coordinating projects, and co-evolving systems for F/OSS. These STINs are not independent of one another, but interdependent and overlapping. Scacchi argues that using STINs to understand F/OSSD is particularly appropriate since the F/OSS developers are only loosely connected through a fragile web of alliances and communities, and thus the social connections within the STIN are often as important as the technological innovations of the software in explaining how well the web of relations for any given F/OSS project holds together over time.

In Scacchi's article, STINs are treated as entities that independently arise in the world, and that researchers are then able to uncover using the STIN 'conceptual framework' (in his terms). This is a somewhat different approach that Kling et al. [2003] took in which the analysts constructed STIN models that were somewhat simplified views of reality. This underscores one of the confusing aspects of STINs: are STINs entities that occur in the world, or are they models that reflect patterns of organization in the world?

Eschenfelder & Chase [2002] use the STIN 'framework' as a *post hoc* 'heuristic tool' (again, their terms) to understand web information systems at four large U.S. manufacturing companies. A key finding in this study was that some nominally peripheral actors, such as order fillers and professional peer groups, were key players in the success and use of the web IS. The various players identified in the research participated in the social construction of web IS by lobbying for configurations most suited to their needs, with the interests of some groups inevitably being privileged over those of other groups.

Barab et al. [2004] use STINs to understand the Inquiry Learning Forum (ILF), a web-based forum for math and science teachers. One important aspect of this article to note is that it combines STIN explanations with a theoretical perspective (activity theory) drawn from the authors' main field of education, an approach they argue synergistically "provides a richer view of the design activity and community functioning than either can offer in isolation" [p. 27]. This points to one aspect of STIN research, and social informatics in general, that is worth noting. Social informatics is both by circumstance and design a transdisciplinary approach [Lamb & Sawyer, 2005] that offers researchers perspectives that can be applied to studying technology in a variety of settings, particularly when the more traditional fields studying various groups have not adequately problematized technology in their domain. So, in the case of education where technology may be viewed as a simple phenomenon, social informatics and STIN offers a way to bring the technical more into consideration in an educational socio-technical system.

Meyer & Kling [2002] use STINs to examine arXiv.org, the electronic pre-print archive for physics and math research papers and to examine the claims of the Standard Model (as evidenced by numerous claims by arXiv's founders) that the resource served as a democratizing influence in scientific research. Using analysis of the authors posting articles to arXiv.org over time, Meyer & Kling find that the resource is not functioning as a leveling resource, at least with regards to authorship, and use a STIN model to explain how other social factors limit who publishes articles to arXiv.org.

Joung & Rosenbaum [2004] argue that it is possible to distinguish between successful and unsuccessful STINs in their discussion of whether the Library of

Congress' American Memory Project was widely used. Although they don't fully engage the question of what it means for a technical system to be successful, this raises a point for those interested in STINs: are they to be judged as successes or failures, and by what criteria? It is important, of course, not to exclude failed STINs, or even technology-implementation attempts that failed to develop any sort of sustainable network, from our analysis. Failures can be telling, often more so than uncomplicated successes [Brown & Capdevila, 1999; Markus & Keil, 1994; Suchman, 1996].

3   Methods

3.1   STIN Methods

Kling et. al. [2003] identify a list of heuristics for researching STINs that is meant to be illustrative rather than enumerative. These steps constitute a method for modeling a STIN. The eight steps are:
1. Identify a relevant population of system interactors
2. Identify core interactor groups
3. Identify incentives
4. Identify excluded actors and undesired interactions
5. Identify existing communication forums
6. Identify resource flows
7. Identify system architectural choice points
8. Map architectural choice points to socio-technical characteristics [Kling et al., 2003:57]

Some of these steps share elements with SCOT and ANT, but with important differences. For instance, Kling is careful to point out that while identifying the relevant interactors is similar to ANT's following the actor, in STIN research the analyst also attempts to understand the ecology of the interactors <u>before</u> undertaking the field work to identify likely interactors and, in step 2, likely groups of interactors. Step 3 involves understanding incentives (and thus, potential motivations) for interactors.

Step 4 is an important but often overlooked step in other types of socio-technical research – identifying actors who are left out of the socio-technical system and interactions that are undesirable to interactors. In most network diagrams, these actors and interactions would exist only in the white space between nodes and connections, but may play a key role in influencing the system's outcomes. Step 5 involves examining communication systems, which ties back into the communication regime framework discussed at the beginning of this paper. Step 6 can be thought of, according to Kling, as 'following the money.'

The last two steps are what allows STIN researchers to analyze social change in socio-technical systems. By examining choice points where alternatives are available to interactors within the STIN, the analyst can map those choice points onto the socio-technical characteristics of the STIN identified in the earlier steps of the research.

In reality, STIN research tends to also create a 'Standard Model', which is then subsequently disassembled. Kling et al. [2003] discuss in great detail the Standard

Model of e-SCFs, which includes beliefs in easy and ubiquitous access, low costs of production, and fast publication leading inevitably to widespread adoption of e-SCFs by scholars who will come to see the value of these technological systems and alter their behavior accordingly. Joung & Rosenbaum [2004], argue that the Standard Model of the American Memory Project focuses on the technology needed to digitize historical materials and create search interfaces, and "assumes that if digital libraries adopt these processes, they will have been constructed successfully, independent of the types of libraries and fields to be serviced by them" [p. 30]. Eschenfelder & Chase [2002] identify a range of studies that contribute to the Standard Model of web IS research[2], which views post-implementation processes as essentially an "orderly logical process unaffected by social phenomena", studies that "overlook the wide array of social influences continually shaping web IS" [p. 2].

This raises a point: if there is no Standard Model, no widely accepted understanding of technology held by those within the system and those operating within disciplinary boundaries, does the STIN approach work? Does using STINs require something to demolish? More importantly, is it engaging in the construction of straw men? I would argue that this is not the case. Instead, the creation of a Standard Model is both part of the critical perspective inherent in social informatics research [Lamb & Sawyer, 2005] and part of the storytelling that makes the arguments more accessible to the transdisciplinary audience for STINs.

Storytelling was one of the tools Kling used in his research, in his public speeches, and in his teaching. Many is the time that he would listen to several people debating a topic and then cut in with "Look, it is a simple story..." and then proceed to tell a compellingly simple story that also incorporated elements of complexity in the data that made his story seem more plausible than the 'common-sense' explanation that was dominating the public discourse on a topic[3]. This storytelling approach is inherent in how he chose to explain STIN research. First, set up a story about what 'everyone believes,' present data that draws these beliefs into question, and then tell a better story that incorporates social realities with technological features to better incorporate the available data.

4   Discussion

4.1   STIN Weaknesses and Limitations

One of the weaknesses of STIN that must be acknowledged is that to date it has mainly been adopted by close colleagues and former students of Rob Kling. If the STIN strategy is to have any longevity either in information science or in other fields that use the transdisciplinary approach of social informatics, it must be cited, used, modified and extended. Actor-Network Theory, for instance, has achieved widespread use beyond its initial audience in science and technology studies. Even ANT, however, did not achieve instant success. The earliest complete explanation of ANT is probably 'Science in Action' [Latour, 1987]. While this work has been cited over 2000 times by the end of 2005 according to the Social Science Citation Index, in the first two years after its publication it had been cited on a comparatively modest 38 times. Kling's main STIN paper [Kling et al., 2003] has been cited in 10 published articles by the end of 2005, and in a number of other unpublished manuscripts and conference papers, some of which have been discussed in this paper. One test will be to see whether this number increases in the coming years.

Robbin [2005] has argued that Kling's publication record in general did not "create, (re)construct, or extend theory, or create new methodologies for understanding the empirical world of computers in organizations" [p. 23]. Instead, Robbin argues, Kling took a practical approach to appropriating theory and method as necessary to explain computerization in organizations and to build a corpus of empirically-based research that "made the unobvious, the taken-for-granted, and the ignored explicit, problematic, and visible" [p. 24].

As might be obvious from the discussion of selected STIN studies above, there is some lack of clarity regarding the language of STINs. STINs are described as a methodology [Kling et al., 2003], a type of entity [Barab et al., 2004; Scacchi, 2005], a framework [Barab et al., 2004; Eschenfelder & Chase, 2002; Scacchi, 2005], and a *post hoc* heuristic tool [Eschenfelder & Chase, 2002].

I would like to suggest that a better term to describe STIN research is to refer to the 'STIN strategy'. It is fairly clear that STIN does not reach the level of theory, nor is it a proper methodology. What I would like to suggest is that STIN is really an analytic strategy. No particular methods are tied to STIN research; in fact, STIN research, like most of social informatics, is wide-ranging in the selection of specific methods that can be used to gather the data necessary to construct STIN explanations at the analytic level.

I suggest the term STIN strategy is appropriate in the sense that a strategy is a goal-oriented plan of action. The goal in this case is to find more complete explanations and thorough understandings of the relationship between the social and the technical in socio-technical systems. Strategies are ways of going about things. STIN diagrams can help visualize relationships and important network nodes, but they are not a method in and of themselves. The STIN strategy leads to choosing particular methods, to favoring certain kinds of understandings about the world, but maintains the overall social informatics open-mindedness towards a variety of methods, and a preference for multiple method approaches to research questions. The STIN strategy is really an analytic perspective based on a strategic way of seeing the world. It is a strategy of approach, research problem selection and analysis, not a strategy of method.

At meetings of social informatics researchers, it has been remarked that in some sense we study the hyphen in socio-technical systems, the area where the connections between social organizations (as studied by sociologists and political scientists) and the technological artifacts (as studied by computer scientists and engineers) lie. Kling argues that "the STIN model shares the views of many socio-technical theories: that technology-in-use and a social world are not separate entities—they co-constitute each other. That is, it is fundamental to STIN modeling that society and technology are seen as 'highly' (but not completely) intertwined" [Kling et al., 2003:54].

One of the main concerns that has been expressed to me by several people in personal communications about the STIN strategy is whether a system that embodies both people and technology can be demonstrated not to be a STIN. In other words, is the notion that a system can be analyzed using the STIN strategy amenable to the null hypothesis that system X is not a STIN for reasons Y and Z. If this is not the case, then everything involved with technology becomes a STIN, and thus weakens the argument that STINs actually shed light on particular sorts of behaviors and institutional arrangements. This is not, in my mind, a resolved issue, and is an area where I hope that future research will strengthen the STIN strategy.

Some of the weaknesses of STIN, while not published, have been discussed informally among social informatics researchers. For instance, the STIN strategy's inherently organizational bias limits its ability to deal with the broader non-organizational social implications of technology. Another limitation that STIN shares with social informatics research in general stems from its use of a variety of methods: "combining the need for extensive data collection with the complex conceptualizing of socio-technical phenomena means it is a difficult methodological toolkit for many scholars" [Sawyer, 2005:12]. This also points to another STIN limitation: the ability to successfully identify and analyze STINs is heavily dependent on the skill of the investigator at eliciting information from respondents and gaining access to individuals and organizations.

4.2   Future of STIN studies

A primary test of using STINs as a research and analytic strategy is whether scholars begin to adopt, test, modify, and extend the strategy in their studies. While some of Kling's close colleagues and former students are pursuing the STIN strategy, there has not yet been much adoption beyond this. It is hoped that this paper as well as research that the author is currently pursuing to refine and extend the STIN strategy for his dissertation on the use of digital photography will contribute to the further development of the STIN strategy.

The next step for the STIN strategy is to rigorously test it against empirical data. There are key questions researchers doing this should ask. First, is the STIN strategy falsifiable? Can it be shown that there are boundaries beyond which the STIN strategy fails to be useful? What types of problems exist within those boundaries? In other words, what is the appropriate STIN problem space? Second, for the problems that exist within the STIN problem space, is the STIN approach the most fruitful way to understand the problem at hand? What does the STIN approach offer that other, more widely adopted approaches cannot offer? What kinds of problems within the problem space are most amenable to STIN research?

A third challenge is a practical one necessary if more researchers are to be enrolled into using the STIN strategy: to more clearly articulate the methods and tools one would use to undertake a study using the STIN strategy. While it is not desirable to have a simplistic approach that involves plugging data into a rigid framework, at the current time the STIN strategy is probably too nebulous to attract the interest of new researchers and graduate students who may understandably be drawn to more concrete approaches. Part of this challenge is more clearly defining the terminology related to the STIN strategy. For instance, as mentioned above there is confusion over whether STINs are entities that occur in the world, or are models that reflect patterns of organization in the world. In other words, does one *uncover* a STIN that exists independently of the analyst, or is a STIN a model *constructed* by an analyst to better understand the world?

Sawyer & Tapia [2005] argue that while theory building is desirable in the extension of a new field like social informatics, a "more modest approach is to focus on developing, demonstrating and exporting analytic approaches...to bring theory and evidence together" [p. 13] and cite the STIN model as an example. The STIN strategy allows for a nuanced examination of socio-technical systems by integrating the social and the technical, and provides a useful addition to SCOT's focus on case studies of mutual shaping and ANT's methods of following the actants, opening blackboxes, and examining inscriptions. STIN's inclusion of the social roles of interactors beyond their roles specific to the socio-technical system under analysis, the ability to track social actors whose roles are not primarily technical, an attention to excluded actors and undesirable interactions, and a focus on the importance of social change in socio-technical networks all make STIN a worthwhile addition to the social studies of technology and social informatics literature. Together, these approaches offer a set of analytic concepts and tools for studying technology in society.

Acknowledgements

Earlier versions of this paper have benefited from useful comments from Howard Rosenbaum, Noriko Hara, Barry Bull, Alice Robbin, and attendees at various public talks given by the author on this topic, as well as from anonymous reviewers. The author is also deeply indebted to Rob Kling, an unparalleled mentor, teacher, and inspiration.

References

Barab, S., Schatz, S., & Scheckler, R. (2004). Using Activity Theory to Conceptualize Online Community and Using Online Community to Conceptualize Activity Theory. *Mind, Culture, and Activity, 11*(1), 25-47.

Bijker, W. E. (1995). *Of Bicycles, Bakelites, and Bulbs: Toward a Theory of Sociotechnical Change*. Cambridge, MA: The MIT Press.

Bijker, W. E. (2001). Social Construction of Technology. In N. J. Smelser & P. B. Baltes (Eds.), *International Encyclopedia of the Social & Behavioral Sciences* (Vol. 23, pp. 15522-15527). Oxford: Elsevier Science Ltd.

Bowden, G. (1995). Coming of Age in STS: Some methodological musings. In S. Jasanoff, G. E. Markle, J. C. Petersen & T. Pinch (Eds.), *Handbook of Science and Technology Studies* (pp. 64-79). Thousand Oaks, CA: Sage.

Brown, S. D., & Capdevila, R. (1999). *Perpetuum Mobile:* substance, force and the sociology of translation. In J. Law & J. Hassard (Eds.), *Actor Network Theory and after* (pp. 26-50). Malden, MA: Blackwell Publishers.

Callon, M. (1986). Some Elements of a Sociology of Translation: Domestication of the Scallops and Fishermen of St Brieuc Bay. In J. Law (Ed.), *Power, Action and Belief: A New Sociology of Knowledge?* . London: Routledge.

Callon, M. (1987). Society in the Making: The Study of Technology as a Tool for Social Analysis. In W. E. Bijker, T. P. Hughes & T. Pinch (Eds.), *The Social Construction of Technological Systems* (pp. 83-103). Cambridge, MA: The MIT Press.

Eschenfelder, K. R., & Chase, L. C. (2002). *Socio-Technical Networks of Large, Post-Implementation Web Information Systems: Tracing Effects and Influences*. Paper presented at the 35th Hawaii International Conference on System Sciences, Big Island, Hawaii.

Hanseth, O., Aanestad, M., & Berg, M. (2004). Actor-network theory and information systems. What's so special? *Information Technology and People, 17*(2), 116-123.

Joung, K. H., & Rosenbaum, H. (2004, November 13-18). *Digital libraries as socio-technical interaction networks: A study of the American Memory Project.* Paper presented at the ASIST 2004 Annual Meeting; 'Managing and Enhancing Information: Cultures and Conflicts' (ASIST AM 04), Providence, Rhode Island.

Kling, R. (1991). Computerization and Social Transformations. *Science, Technology, and Human Values, 16*(3), 342-367.

Kling, R. (1992). Behind the Terminal: The Critical Role of Computing Infrastructure in Effective Information Systems' Development and Use. In W. Cotterman & J. Senn (Eds.), *Challenges and Strategies for Research in Systems Development* (pp. 153-201). London: John Wiley.

Kling, R., McKim, G., & King, A. (2003). A Bit More to IT: Scholarly Communication Forums as Socio-Technical Interaction Networks. *Journal of the American Society for Information Science and Technology, 54*(1), 46-67.

Kling, R., & Scacchi, W. (1982). The Web of Computing: Computer Technology as Social Organization. *Advances in Computers, 21*, 1-90.

Kling, R., Spector, L., & Fortuna, J. (2004). The Real Stakes of Virtual Publishing: The Transformation of E-Biomed Into PubMed Central. *Journal of the American Society of Information Science & Technology, 55*(2), 127-148.

Lamb, R., & Kling, R. (2003). Reconceptualizing Users and Social Actors in Information Systems Research. *MIS Quarterly, 27*(2), 197-235.

Lamb, R., & Sawyer, S. (2005). On extending social informatics from a rich legacy of networks and conceptual resources. *Information Technology & People, 18*(1), 9-20.

Lamb, R., Sawyer, S., & Kling, R. (2000). A Social Informatics Perspective on Socio-Technical Networks. In H. M. Chung (Ed.), *Proceedings of the Americas Conference on Information Systems.* Long Beach, CA.

Latour, B. (1987). *Science in Action: How to follow scientists and engineers through society.* Cambridge, MA: Harvard University Press.

Latour, B. (1988). Mixing Humans and Nonhumans Together: The Sociology of a Door-Closer. *Social Problems, 35*(3), 298-310.

Latour, B., & Woolgar, S. (1979). *Laboratory Life: The Social Construction of Scientific Facts.* Beverly Hills: Sage.

Law, J. (1999). After ANT: complexity, naming and topology. In J. Law & J. Hassard (Eds.), *Actor Network Theory and after* (pp. 1-14). Malden, MA: Blackwell.

Markus, M. L., & Keil, M. (1994). If we build it, they will come: Designing information systems that people want to use. *Sloan Management Review, 35*(4), 11-25.

Meyer, E. T., & Kling, R. (2002). *Leveling the playing field, or expanding the bleachers? Socio-Technical Interaction Networks and arXiv.org (Center for Social Informatics Working Paper Series WP-02-10).* Retrieved April 2, 2002, from http://www.slis.indiana.edu/CSI/WP/WP02-10B.html

Mohr, H. (1999). Technology Assessment in Theory and Practice. *Techné: Research in Philosophy & Technology, 4*(4), 22-25.

Orlikowski, W. J., & Iacono, C. S. (2001). Research commentary: Desperately seeking the 'IT' in IT research - A call to theorizing the IT artifact. *Information Systems Research, 12*(2), 121-134.

Pinch, T. J., & Bijker, W. E. (1987). The Social Construction of Facts and Artifacts: Or How the Sociology of Science and the Sociology of Technology Might Benefit Each Other. In W. E. Bijker, T. P. Hughes & T. Pinch (Eds.), *The Social Construction of Technological Systems* (pp. 17-50). Cambridge, MA: The MIT Press.

Robbin, A. (2005, March 11-12). *Rob Kling In Search of One Good Theory: The Origins of Computerization Movements.* Paper presented at the workshop 'Extending the Contributions of Professor Rob Kling to the Analysis of Computerization Movements', Irvine, CA.

Sawyer, S. (2005). Social Informatics: Overview, Principles and Opportunities. *Bulletin of the American Society for Information Science and Technology, 31*(5), 9-12.

Sawyer, S., & Tapia, A. (2005, March 11-12). *From Findings to Theories: Institutionalizing Social Informatics.* Paper presented at the workshop 'Extending the Contributions of Professor Rob Kling to the Analysis of Computerization Movements', Irvine, CA.

Scacchi, W. (2005). Socio-Technical Interaction Networks in Free/Open Source Software Development Processes. In S. T. Acuña & N. Juristo (Eds.), *Software Process Modeling* (pp. 1-27). New York: Springer Science+Business Media Inc.

Star, S. L. (1988). Introduction: The Sociology of Science and Technology. *Social Problems, 35*(3), 197-205.

Suchman, L. (1996). Supporting Articulation Work. In R. Kling (Ed.), *Computerization and Controversy: Value Conflicts and Social Choices, 2nd. Ed.* San Diego, CA: Academic Press.

Notes

[1]   This case is more thoroughly described in Kling, Spector, & Fortuna [2004].

[2]   However, the authors don't actually use the term 'Standard Model' in their paper.

[3]   An example that springs to mind came during the early days of collapse of Enron. The public explanation for Enron was that a bunch of greedy people let their greed overcome their common sense: the "bad apple" version of events. Rob felt that this was too simple and pat. Instead, he offered an alternate story that incorporated an understanding of the system of accounting rules, technological features within the corporate and government oversight system, and policy choices to understand how Enron came to fail. This broader point of view is now easy to find in discussions of Enron, but Rob was quite early in thinking in a systematic way about this issue. [Kling, R., personal communication, ca. 2001].

Social Informatics: Principles, Theory, and Practice

Steve Sawyer, Michael Tyworth
College of Information Sciences & Technology
The Pennsylvania State University, USA,
sawyer@ist.psu.edu, mtyworth@ist.psu.edu

Abstract. Through this paper we make two contributions to social informatics: the interdisciplinary study of the design, development, uses and consequences of information and communication technologies that takes into account their interaction with institutional and cultural contexts. Our first contribution is to make a connection from social informatics to general principles of socio-technical theories. We do this to both connect social informatics scholarship more directly to the large and growing literature(s) that engage socio-technical theorizing and to advance these principles more directly through social informatics. Our second contribution to social informatics is to engage two contemporary theoretical approaches that draw on social informatics principles: socio-technical interaction networks and principles of social actors and apply them to current practice. We do so to demonstrate that these analytic approaches are the needed tools to help scholars and reflective professionals in practice engage social informatics analyses. By doing this we highlight the potential of social informatics while honouring Rob Kling's legacy in helping to establish this transdiscipline.

Keywords: social informatics, socio-technical principles, social actors, socio-technical interaction networks, integrated criminal justice information systems

1 Introduction

In this paper we advance the work of Rob Kling and in doing so continue the empirical, theoretical, and critical engagement of social informatics. By social informatics we mean "…the interdisciplinary study of the design uses and consequences of information technologies that takes into account their interaction with institutional and cultural contexts [Kling, 1999]." Through this paper we make two contributions to the ongoing efforts to engage social informatics principles, concepts and analyses. First, we make a direct connection between social informatics

Please use the following format when citing this chapter:

Sawyer, S., Tyworth, M., 2006, in IFIP International Federation for Information Processing, Volume 223, Social Informatics: An Information Society for All? In Remembrance of Rob Kling, eds. Berleur, J., Numinen, M. I., Impagliazzo, J., (Boston: Springer), pp. 49–62.

and general principles of socio-technical theories. We do this to both connect social informatics scholarship more directly to the large and growing literature(s) that engage socio-technical theorizing and to advance these principles more directly through social informatics.

Our second contribution is to identify nascent theories that draw on social informatics principles. We do so because these theories present an opportunity for scholars and reflective professionals in practice engage social informatics analyses (e.g., Lamb and Sawyer, 2005). Pursuing this second contribution we contrast two emerging theories – socio-technical interaction networks (STIN) and social actor approaches – that reflect these socio-technical principles and build on social informatics[i]. The STIN approach provides a system-level framework for analyzing socio-technical networks / systems that views the social and the technological as fundamentally inseparable components of the system [Kling, McKim, & King, 2003]. The social actor approach models users as social beings, embedded within an enabling and constraining social context but with individual agency to shape that context [Lamb & Kling, 2003]. Both the STIN and social actor approaches represent current theorizing activities within social informatics. In our study of integrated criminal justice systems (ICJS), we have found that these theoretical frameworks inform our understanding of design, deployment, and use of ICJS. More importantly, STIN and social actor theories point us to relevant issues in the design of technologically and socially complex interorganizational ICT.

This paper continues with a discussion of socio-technical principles. Building on this foundation we then tie the principles to both STIN models and social actor theory, followed by an application of those theories to the study of ICT in practice. We conclude by discussing future directions for social informatics research.

2   Socio-technical Principles

Social Informatics is grounded in the principles that guide socio-technical theory. We build here on Bijker's [1995] argument that socio-technical theories reflect four principles: (1) the *seamless web*, (2) the *change and continuity*, (3) the *symmetry*, and (4) *action and structure*. In doing this we note that in engaging these principles we are not engaging a particular theory: we are arguing that social informatics reflects principles seen as common to theories of socio-technical change and action.

The *seamless web principle* states that any socio-technical theory should not *a priori* privilege the technological or material explanation ahead of the social or vice versa. In the parlance of academic disciplines, neither the computer science nor the sociology views should be privileged. In social informatics, we focus on the web of computing, treating the material artefacts and social practices as bound up together in situated and mutually-constituted activity.

The *principle of change and continuity* states that socio-technical theories must account for both change and stability and not one to the exclusion of the other. Socio-technical phenomena are at once both continuous and evolving, retaining an inherent structure while adapting over time[ii]. In social informatics, the temporal and historical trajectories of both human activity and technological development are intertwined and continuously evolving.

The *principle of symmetry* states that the successful working of technology must be viewed as a process rather than an end-state (this relates directly to the principle of change and continuity). Focusing on the workings of technology as a process rather than an end-state, avoids the trap of technologically deterministic analyses that are too often found in other perspectives. In social informatics, this principle also steers us towards engaging situated empirical studies as part of the research.

The *principle of action and structure* states that socio-technical theories should address both the agency of the social actor and the structural constraints. In this view, people have agency in shaping, changing, and enacting their social context and uses of ICT. But, they are also constrained by social institutions (Scott, 2001). In social informatics this steers scholars to focus on both the structural and agentic activities of both people and ICT.

The simply-stated (but difficult to engage conceptually or empirically) premise underlying these four socio-technical principles is that neither technology nor social context are isolated, isolatable, or unchanging. Instead the social contexts and technological artefacts are perpetually interacting and shaping each other.

2.1 Socio-technical Principles and Social Informatics

Some might see social informatics as a subset of socio-technical scholarship: one focused on particular forms of technology that directly engage information processing and communications technologies (ICT). This suggests that these ICT have particular characteristics that distinguish them from other forms of technology[iii]. That is, there must be particular characteristics that distinguish a computer and its applications from, say, a nuclear reactor, microscopes, or electrical power grids.

We argue that ICTs configurational nature is one distinguishing characteristic from other forms of technology. By configurational we mean that that in their design and use, ICT are interpretively flexible, multiply adaptive in use, and always evolving [Fleck, 1994; Quintas, 1994; Suchman, 1987, 2003]. Some may argue that these differential characteristics are but a matter of degree. We defer to other venues that discussion, and here claim that social informatics is premised on the study of ICT as a specific and volatile type of socio-technical ensemble.

The practice of social informatics is trans-disciplinary – spanning such diverse fields as computer science, sociology, communications, education, information systems, information science, and others. Social informatics is neither a theory nor a method: it is a perspective in the same way as are human-computer interaction and family studies. In action, social informatics is an approach to understanding, theorizing and engaging ICT that reflects five specific principles on social analysis of computing [Lamb and Sawyer, 2005]:

1. In social informatics ICT are seen as a socio-technical system: a web-like arrangement of the technological artefacts, people, and the social norms, practices, and rules. As a result, for the social informaticist the technological artefact and the social context are inseparable for the purposes of study and

analysis [Kling, McKim, & King, 2003]. It is this principle that most directly links to socio-technical principles.

2. Social-informatics is problem-oriented. This means that social informatics research focuses on the 'real-world' design, development, and use of ICT. The purpose of which is to inform the discourse on ICT to help individuals, organizations, and societies make better use of ICT. There is no correlate for this in the socio-technical principles.

3. The design, development and use of ICT are contextualised and socially-situated. The social and historical contexts pervade every element of ICT from conceptualisation to design to implementation and use.

4. People are social actors [Lamb & Kling, 2003]. People have individual motivations, interests, practices, values that influence how and why they use ICT. Though constrained and enabled by the social institutions in which they are embedded, people have individual agency that both shapes those institutions and influences their adoption and use of ICT.

5. The social informatics researcher adopts a critical orientation and prioritizes an empirical view of ICT. By 'critical orientation' we don not mean to convey synonymy with *critical theory* ands its orientation towards emancipation and Marxist theory [Orlikowski & Baroudi, 1991]. Here, critical denotes an orientation that challenges the accepted wisdom and taken-for-granted assumptions regarding ICT. It is through this challenging of assumptions that the social informaticists avoid simplistic technological determinism and gain deeper insight into the complexity of ICT's design, development, deployment and ongoing uses.

Using these principles, social informatics researchers have over time consistently revealed in their empirical studies a number of consistent findings (See for example: Kling, Rosenbaum, & Sawyer, 2005b). These common findings include:

1. The paradoxical effects of ICTs take up and uses,

2. That ICTs uses shape action and thoughts that benefit some over others,

3. That the design and implementation of ICTs have moral and ethical consequences, and

4. That the phenomenon of interest will vary with level of analysis

Given that these are so commonly found in empirical studies of computing's design, development, adoption and use, we argue that these are worthy to report, but do not constitute new insight. Indeed, the progress of social informatics must be based both on the constant presentation of these common findings and, more importantly, the additional detailing that reflects how these common findings are suppressed or magnified through particular actions, events or arrangements, the temporal sequencing of engagements, and the contextual differences (and measures) between better and worse computerization efforts. To do this, we and others have argued for analytic approaches that are grounded in social informatics principles [Horton, Davenport, & Wood-Harper, 2005; Lamb & Sawyer, 2005; Sawyer & Crowston, 2004; Wood-Harper & Wood, 2005].

2.2 Socio-technical principles in theory

For social informatics to continue expanding on its potential as an alternative and insightful approach to studying ICT, scholars in this area must capitalize on the empirical work done to date, and move into the realm of theorizing more specifically on the nature and roles of ICT. This does not mean we think the social informatics researcher should abandon the commitment to empirical work. Rather, we believe that development and refining of social informatics theories is tied to improved analytic approaches that will, in turn, better guide the empirical activities of social informatics research. And, in turn, this work will illuminate issues with the design, development, take up and uses of ICT that other approaches neglect or misrepresent. Improved analytical methods will be useful to practicing professionals, will be more useful in formal education of IT professionals, and will serve as a counterpoint to the unsupportable but comforting direct effects analytic approaches to understanding ICT [Kling, Rosenbaum, & Sawyer, 2005b].

As noted earlier, there are number of viable and approaches to engaging social informatics analyses. For example, one approach is to continue incorporating and extending concepts and approaches from other domains [Orlikowski & Barley, 2001]. Continuing to 'borrow' theories from other disciplines and apply them to ICT provides social informatics with an opportunity to continue demonstrating the value of social theories in the study of ICT.

A second approach is the development of 'native' social informatics theories, ones that arise from within the social informatics community. Social informatics scholars can produce and then demonstrate the utility of social informatics theory, and then 'export' those theories to other fields social informatics establishes itself as a reference discipline to others [Baskerville & Myers, 2002] [iv]. By becoming a reference discipline, social informatics not only communicates its results to other researchers but also develops a more distinct identity. We see greater intellectual value in the development and refining of theories native to social informatics.

Theoretical development in social informatics has value beyond communicating the results of social informatics research to other scholars and establishing identity. The development of social informatics theory presents the opportunity for social informatics researchers to benefit people who use ICT through contributing to better designed ICT that accounts for the social and the technical.

2.3 Socio-technical Interaction Networks

Conceptually, a socio-technical network is a view of a system as a network of people and technologies which are inseparable when trying to examine and understand the system [Kling, McKim, & King, 2003]. Socio-technical interaction network models (STINs) present a method for understanding the interactions between individual socio-technical networks (nodes) that comprise the socio-technical interaction networks [Kling, McKim, & King, 2003]. This is accomplished through the mapping of relationships between people, people and technology, and technologies [Kling, McKim, & King, 2003].

Four assumptions that echo both the socio-technical principles and social informatics bases serve as the foundation for STIN [Kling, McKim, & King, 2003]:
- the social and technical are not meaningfully separable,
- social theories should influence design,
- system participants (people) are embedded in multiple social relationships,
- sustainability and routine are critical elements of design.

These assumptions are what separate STIN from those theories that focus on either the social or the technological to the exclusion of the other.

2.4   Users as Social Actors

Roberta Lamb and Rob Kling [Lamb & Kling, 2003] published their theory of users as social actors as way of conceptualizing users of ICTs to get beyond the simple abstract models that populate much of the human-computer literature. Their conceptualization of the user is more socially-rich and situated. According to concept of a social actor, people are not simply users of ICT, but are socially-complex individuals who are engaging uses of ICT as members of one or more organizations that make use of ICTs to engage in mediated social interactions. Social actors are both enabled and constrained in their uses of ICTs by the social milieus in which they exist. The constraints of their social environment means that social actors are often limited in what they can do. However, social actors also have active agency in shaping these milieus. The degree to which structure and action are allowed are dependent in part on situated contexts and elements such as the task, roles, timing, nature of interdependencies, particular ICTs being used, and goals.

Lamb & Kling [2003] identify four dimensions of the social actor: *affiliations*, *environments*, *interactions*, and *identities*. *Affiliations* are the social ties the social actor maintains – for example professional networks – and occur both within and across organizational boundaries. *Environments* represent the normative, regulatory, and cognitive institutions that both enable and constrain social actors use of ICTs. *Interactions* are the information, modes of communication, and resources employed by social actors as they socially engage with other members of the organization or other organizations. *Identities* comprise both the identity articulated by the social actor as well as the identity of the social actor articulated by the organization. These four dimensions are not entirely discrete; rather there is some overlap between dimensions. In fact it is the way in which the theoretical dimensions of the social actor overlap that gives it much of its power.

3   Empirical Work

As an empirical base to support our comparison of these two theories, we draw on our ongoing work in the development and uses of ICJS. We see ICJS as one area that presents a significant opportunity for social informaticists to both develop theory and contribute to practice. E-Government, or digital governance, is both an emerging area of scholarship and a fast evolving phenomenon in society. This is particularly true for issues of law enforcement and national defense where there is increasing pressure to computerize or modernize existing ICT given the recent attention to international terrorism [National Commission on Terrorist Attacks upon the United States, 2004]. And, for the United States at least, it may be that there is no other area where the consequences of adhering to the deterministic view of ICT are as potentially catastrophic. Simply, and in spite of these risks and evidence against such a view, the deterministic model continues to be advocated.

For example, in his article on improving intelligence analyzing systems Strickland [Strickland, 2004] focused exclusively on technological change as the solution to the problems of information sharing among agencies. For example, he identifies data disintegration, problems in analytical methodology, and technological obsolescence as the primary areas of concern. Yet, as Richard Shelby [Shelby, 2002] noted in his addendum to the Senate Select Committee investigating pre- and post-9/11 intelligence:

> The CIA's chronic failure, before September 11, to share with other agencies the names of known Al-Qa'ida terrorists who it knew to be in the country allowed at least two such terrorists the opportunity to live, move, and prepare for the attacks   without hindrance from the very federal officials whose job it is to find them. Sadly, the CIA seems to have concluded that the maintenance of its information monopoly was more important that stopping terrorists from entering or operating   within the United States.

Though Senator Shelby's language is polemic, the message is clear: without significant changes to organizational norms of action, simply implementing new technological systems or updating existing ones will in many instances fail to achieve policy goals. It is exactly this type of problem for which social informatics is particularly applicable.

An e-Government policy area directly related to the issue of intelligence sharing is the problem of integrating information systems among law enforcement and criminal justice agencies. Prior to, but especially after 9/11, there has been a significant movement within government to integrate ICT across law enforcement and criminal justice agency boundaries in order to facilitate cross-agency communication and information sharing [See for example: General Accountability Office, 2003].

Criminal justice information systems have historically been developed in an ad hoc manner, tailored to the needs of the particular agency, and with minimal support resources (either fiscal or expertise) [Dunworth, 2000, 2005; Sawyer, Tapia, Pesheck, & Davenport, 2004]. As a result federal and state governments have begun the process of trying to develop and implement integrated criminal justice systems that allow agencies to share information across organizational boundaries. Examples of such systems are Pennsylvania's Justice Network (JNET), the Washington D.C. metro area's Capital Wireless Integration Network (CapWIN), and the San Diego region's Automated Regional Justice Information System (ARJIS) among others.

We find ICJSs to be ideal opportunities to conduct social informatics research for three reasons. First, law enforcement is a socially complex domain comprised of and embedded in multiple social institutions [Sawyer, Tapia, Pesheck, & Davenport, 2004]. Such institutions include organizational practice and culture, societal norms and values, and regulatory requirements. Second, law enforcement agencies have long been adopters of ICT to the point where ICT are now so ubiquitous that they are viewed as integral to policing [Hoey, 1998]. This remains true in spite of a decidedly mixed record of success [Baird & Barksdale, 2003; Bureau of Justice Assistance, 2002]. Third, the historical practice of ad hoc and siloed systems development suggests that law enforcement is an area where new systems development approaches are needed.

3.1   Automated Regional Justice Information System (ARJIS)

Currently we are completing a case study of the ARJIS system in San Diego, California. The Automated Regional Justice Information System (ARJIS) of San Diego, California is one of the pre-eminent criminal justice information systems initiatives in the United States. Initially a mainframe records management system accessible by multiple jurisdictions in the San Diego area, ARJIS has evolved over the past 20 years both organizationally and technologically. Organizationally ARJIS has become its own organization embedded in the county government structure. Technologically ARJIS is in the process of developing wireless communications systems, global query application, and public safety cable television channel.

We used five forms of data collection. Three focus on gathering primary data: interviews (face-to-face, by phone, and via email, depending on the point of the interaction), ride-alongs with – and other direct observation of – users. We also gathered secondary documents such as reports, memos and locally-relevant material (we, of course, have done and continue to do extensive web and library research to support the field work) as well as data about device uses, data transmission, and ARJIS usage via unobtrusive means (such browser logs, server logs, and telecom activity logs).

Data from the sources are transcribed into digital format or collected at source in digital format. Data from the usage logs came in digital format. This supports our analysis across different data sets and data collection approaches. To do this analysis we are using traditional qualitative/case study data analysis approaches [See: Miles & Huberman, 1984]. In particular, we draw on three techniques: (1) interim analysis of the data to guide data collection and interpretation in the future, (2) explanatory event matrices, and (3) content analysis of the interview/focus group transcripts and field notes. When the study is complete we expect to have more than fifteen interviews (of from one-to-two hours duration, each), notes and details from six officer ride-alongs, and over 650 pages of documents.

3.2   Socio-technical principles and Social Informatics theory reflected in practice

Preliminary analysis of our case study data indicates the ARJIS system is very much a socio-technical network as theorized by Kling *et al.* [2003]. ARJIS is both a governmental agency and a technological infrastructure, and both are highly intertwined. To understand the design and evolution of the ARJIS system, one must understand the design and evolution of the organization, and vice versa. We find support here for the seamless web principle (that both the technical and the social have equal standing). This is reflected in the STIN principle of the inseparability of the technical and social and the social actors principle of use in context.

Socio-technical Principle	STIN	Social Actor	ARJIS
Seamless Web	Social and technical not meaningfully separable	Use is socially contextual and role specific	Embedded in governmental and technological infrastructures. Contextual setting of use greatly shapes user behavior.
Change and Continuity	Sustainability and routine are critical elements of system design	Design in use	ARJIS is tied to existing technological systems, government agencies which both constrain and enable system and agency design.
Symmetry	System participants are embedded in multiple social relationships	Relationships are dynamic, multilevel, multivalent, and multi-network	ARJIS designers and managers engage multiple relationships both vertically and horizontally.
Action and Structure	The ways in which STIN evolve is through both structural adherence and agentic actions.	People's actions are guided by existing structures, but they retain some amount of agency	ARJIS management and designers are subject to historical institutional pressures. ARJIS leaders act as brokers among and between individual agencies. They seek to find commonality across individual normative systems.

Table 1 - Social Informatics Principles, Theories, and Practice – ARJIS

The technological system has been developed in conjunction with the establishment of ARJIS as an independent Joint Powers Agency. As such, individual design decisions are fundamentally linked to the manner in which the ARJIS organization has been established and embedded in the existing government structure. Similarly, we found that use of the system was very specific to the context the social actor was engaged in because context had great influence on the actions available to the actor. This dual nature of ARJIS reflects the socio-technical principle of a seamless web.

The principle of change and continuity stipulates that both system stability and evolution must be accounted for. STIN theory reflects this as sustainability and routine as key to system design. Social actor theory refers this to 'design in use,' or the phenomenon of actors in effect changing the ICT through use in unanticipated ways. ARJIS current design plan consists of maintaining the legacy system while developing a parallel system to incorporate new applications and technology is an example of the principle of change and continuity. Similarly the emergent nature of the parallel system allows for on-the-go design decisions as long as they are consistent with the overall development plan. We observed design in use in the use of the wireless handheld system. In experimenting with the handhelds, agents discovered they could take photographs and record sound with the devices and incorporated those uses into their investigatory practices. The critical point here is that the design of ARJIS is not static, either in development or after deployment; but continues to be adjusted both in development and use.

The principle of symmetry views the successful working of ICT as a process not an end-state. This reflects the ongoing evolutionary nature of ICT. STIN theory articulates this principle as participants embedded in multiple social relationships that shape their participation in the network and result in a constantly evolving network. Social actors present the user in a similar manner: as embedded in dynamic, multilevel, multivalent and multi-network relationships. ARJIS managers have relations with policymakers, users, developers, and vendors, among many others. These relationships have had and continue to have a direct impact on the how they approach the development of ARJIS. For example, the costly failed attempt to comprehensively upgrade the original ARJIS system through a private vendor continues a decade ago continues to drive ARJIS' focus on incremental but focused initiatives that can demonstrate a return on investment.

The principle of action and structure reflects the role of structure and individual agency in shaping design and use. Social actor theory articulates this principle as the environments the actor is embedded in, the affiliations of the actor and organization, and the interactions available to the actor. The organization of ARJIS is embedded in the larger institutions of local, regional, state, and federal governance as well as cultural, technological, and economic institutions. Norms in those institutions directly shape ARJIS management and design decisions. ARJIS also has agency and exercises this agency through guiding the ARJIS agenda and acting as a broker between individual agencies, policymakers, etc. ARJIS management and designers network nationally, helping to shape national integration initiatives such as data standards. Similarly, ARJIS mandates the regional data standards and ensures compliance by requiring it for participation.

In our observations of users we also found that institutional and technological structure played a large role in their use of the ARJIS system. For example, we found that officers from one agency rarely used the ARJIS system as part of their normal routines. They felt the functionality of the ARJIS system was not consistent with their objectives as patrol officers; the organizational culture was not oriented towards extensive use of ARJIS by patrol officers, and technological limitations such as access problems made using ARJIS prohibitive in comparison to competing systems.

In contrast, agents in the federal agency we observed used ARJIS extensively viewing the system as a better resource than other agency resources such as dispatch which often had long response delays and was resource limited.

4 Discussion

Drawing from the ongoing work in ARJIS, as briefly outlined in the previous section, in comparing STIN and social actor approaches we make note that these models have different foci and lead to different insights. Both the STIN and social actor approaches reflect the principles of socio-technical theories and engage social informatics principles. Yet, in the STIN, the attention is directed towards the ways in which the technological elements are embedded into the large socio-historical context. This ensemble approach steers attention to the shape of the network in which the particular technological elements are embedded. In contrast, the social actor approach focuses attention towards the ways in which people negotiate among the structural and agentic forces, with the ICT serving as elements of both. The social actor model engages the processes of action more directly, while the STIN engages the structure of the socio-technical network of arrangements.

The differential foci of these two approaches lead to different insights. STIN analyses highlight the structural engagement of the technological artefacts with the socio-historical environment. And, in the context of ARJIS, illuminate the ways in which the RJIS functionality is both shaped and embedded in the larger and smaller scale institutional trajectories. Conversely, the social actor approach points our attention to the actions of the ARJIS leadership, the officers using the systems, and the political pressures both face in negotiating development and use of these technologies.

What does this say about social informatics? First, in contrasting STIN with the social actor perspective we note that these differing approaches to engaging the principles of socio-technical theorizing support the contention that social informatics is not a singular theory, but rather an analytic perspective and set of principles. The social informatics lens is neither monocular, nor rigidly focused on one set of activities and issues. The STIN and social actor approaches help to illustrate the intellectual opportunity to develop analytic models that reflect socio-technical principles as they apply to ICT.

We further note that the treatment of ICT demands additional attention. Both the STIN and social actor model engage ICT but struggle with how best to represent the particular technological features, functions and behaviors that these systems allow, support, and defer. The configurational and interpretive nature of ICT suggests that practice-based approaches (See for example: Orlikowski, 1992; Orlikowski, Yates, Okamura, & Fujimoto, 1995) are likely to be fruitful vehicles to developing this added conceptual and empirical depth to social informatics depictions of the design, development and uses of computing.

References

Baird, Z., & Barksdale, J. (2003). Creating a Trusted Network for Homeland Security: Second Report of the Markle Foundation Task Force. *Task Force on National Security in the Information Age* Retrieved January 1, 2005, from http://www.markle.org/downloadable_assets/nstf_report2_full_report.pdf

Baskerville, R., & Myers, M. (2002). Information systems as a reference discipline. *MIS Quarterly, 26*(1), 1-23.

Bijker, W. E. (1995). *Of Bicycles, Bakelites, and Bulbs : Toward a Theory of Sociotechnical Change.* Cambridge, MA: MIT Press.

Bureau of Justice Assistance. (2002). *Mission Possible: Strong Governance Structures for the Integration of Justice Information Systems.* Retrieved November 3, 2004. from http://www.ncjrs.org/pdffiles1/bja/192278.pdf.

Dunworth, T. (2000). Criminal Justice and the IT Revolution. *Policies, Processes, and Decisions of the Criminal Justice System, 3,* 371-426.

Dunworth, T. (2005). Information Technology and the Criminal Justice System: A Historical Review. In A. Pattavina (Ed.), *Information Technology and the Criminal Justice System* (pp. 1-28). Thousand Oaks, CA: Sage Publications, Inc.

Fleck, J. (1994). Learning by trying: the implementation of configurational technology. *Research Policy, 23*(6), 637-652.

General Accountability Office. (2003). *Information Technology: FBI Needs an Enterprise Architecture to Guide Its Modernization Activities.* Retrieved. from http://www.gao.gov/new.items/d03959.pdf.

Hoey, A. (1998). Techno-Cops: Information Technology and Law Enforcement. *International Journal of Law and Information Technology, 6*(1), 69-90.

Horton, K., Davenport, E., & Wood-Harper, T. (2005). Exploring sociotechnical interaction with Rob Kling: Five 'big' ideas. *Information Technology & People, 18*(1), 50-65.

Kitcher, P. (1982). Believing what we cannot prove. In P. Kitcher (Ed.), *Abusing Science: The case against creationism* (pp. 30-54). Cambridge, Mass.: MIT Press.

Kling, R. (1999). What is Social Informatics and Why Does it Matter? *D-Lib Magazine* Retrieved September 1, 2004, from http://www.dlib.org/dlib/january99/kling/01kling.html

Kling, R., McKim, G., & King, A. (2003). A Bit More to IT: Scholarly Communication Forums as Socio-Technical Interaction Networks. *Journal of the American Society for Information Science and Technology, 54*(1), 47-67.

Kling, R., Rosenbaum, H., & Sawyer, S. (2005a). Teaching Key Ideas of Social Informatics. In *Understanding and Communicating Social Informatics: A Framework for Studying and Teaching the Human Contexts of Information and Communications Technologies* (pp. 83-103). Medford, N.J.: Information Today Inc.

Kling, R., Rosenbaum, H., & Sawyer, S. (2005b). *Understanding and Communicating Social Informatics: A Framework for Studying and Teaching the Human Contexts of Information and Communications Technologies.* Medford, New Jersey: Information Today, Inc.

Lamb, R., & Kling, R. (2003). Reconceptualizing users as social actors in information systems research. *MIS Quarterly, 27*(2), 197-235.

Lamb, R., & Sawyer, S. (2005). On extending social informatics from a rich legacy of networks and conceptual resources. *Information Technology & People, 18*(1), 9-19.

Miles, M., & Huberman, A. (1984). *Qualitative data analysis : a sourcebook of new methods.* Newbury Park: Sage Publications.

National Commission on Terrorist Attacks upon the United States. (2004). *The 9/11 Commission report: final report of the National Commission on Terrorist Attacks upon the United States : official government edition.* Washington, D.C.: U.S. Government Printing Office.

Orlikowski, W. (1992). The Duality of Technology: Rethinking the Concept of Technology in Organizations, *Organization Science, 3*(4), 380-398.

Orlikowski, W., & Barley, S. (2001). Technology and institutions: What can research on information technology and research on organizations learn from each other? *MIS Quarterly, 25*(2), 145-164.

Orlikowski, W. J., & Baroudi, J. J. (1991). Studying Information Technology in Organizations: Research Approaches and Assumptions, *Information Systems Research, 2*(1), 1-19.

Orlikowski, W. J., Yates, J., Okamura, K., & Fujimoto, M. (1995). Shaping electronic communication: The metastructuring of technology in the context of use. *Organization Science, 6*(4), 401-423.

Quintas, P. (1994). Programmed Innovation? Trajectories of Change in Software Development. *Information Technology & People, 7,* 25-47.

Sawyer, S., & Crowston, K. (2004). Information Systems in Organizations and Society: Speculating on the Next 25 Years of Research. In B. Kaplan, D. Truex, D. Wastell, A. Wood-Harper & J. DeGross (Eds.), *Information systems research: relevant theory and informed practice,* (pp. 35-52) Boston: Kluwer Academic Publishers.

Sawyer, S., Tapia, A., Pesheck, L., & Davenport, J. (2004). Mobility and the First Responder. *Communications of the ACM, 47*(3), 62-66.

Scott, W. R. (2001). *Institutions and organizations* (2nd). Thousand Oaks, CA: Sage Publications.

Shelby, R. (2002). *September 11 and the Imperative of Reform in the U.S. Intelligence Community: Additional Views of Senator Richard C. Shelby Vice Chairman, Senate Select Committee on Intelligence.* Retrieved November 1, 2004. from http://www.fas.org/irp/congress/2002_rpt/shelby.pdf.

Strickland, L. (2004). Analytic Myopia, Data Disintegration and Homeland Insecurity. *Bulletin of the American Society for Information Science and Technology, 30*(6), 7-21.

Suchman, L. (1987). *Plans and situated actions : the problem of human-machine communication.* Cambridge: Cambridge University Press.

Suchman, L. (2003). Figuring Service in Discourses of ICT: The Case of Software Agents. In E. Wynn, E. Whitley, M. Myers & J. DeGross (Eds.), *Global and organizational discourse about information technology,* (pp. 33-45). Boston: Kluwer Academic Publishers.

Winner, L. (1986). Do Artifacts Have Politics? In *The Whale and the Reactor : A Search for Limits in an Age of High Technology* (pp. 19-39). Chicago: University of Chicago Press.

Wood-Harper, T., & Wood, B. (2005). Multiview as social informatics in action: past, present and future. *Information Technology & People, 18*(1), 21-26.

Ziman, J. M. (1968). What is Science? In J. M. Ziman (Ed.), *Public Knowledge: An Essay Concerning the Social Dimension of Science* (pp. 5-27). London: Cambridge University Press.

Endnotes

---

[i]   We further note that these two models reflect a convenience sampling of available approaches to theorizing in social informatics. The intent here is not to review this large and growing collection, rather to highlight the intellectual insight and analytic opportunities that contemporary social informatics scholarship provides.

[ii]   To continue with the evolution analogy, the penguin evolved over time to become a flightless bird covered in thick feathers to insulate it from extreme cold and the ability to swim underwater with great dexterity. Even with these adaptations, the penguin retains the fundamental structure of a bird in that it has wings, a beak, lays eggs, etc. Similarly the socio-technical system, for example the personal computer, retains fundamental components such as the processor, RAM, and monitor, while evolving in its design, configuration, and use (for example as a game platform or a word processor).

[iii]   It may also be that the difference reflects more academic field differences than phenomenological. As philosophers of science and technology note, these field differences, while socially constructed, serve as boundaries in the practice of science (Kitcher, 1982; Winner, 1986; Ziman, 1968).

[iv]   We realize that in practice one discipline does not truly export a theory to another, rather the latter imports from the former. We use the term export to denote the net effect of the adoption of a theory from one discipline by another.

Teaching Social Informatics

Teaching Social Informatics for Engineering Students

László Z. Karvalics, Lilla Juhász
Dept. of Information and Knowledge Management,
Budapest University of Technology and Economics, Hungary
zkl@itm.bme.hu, juhasz.lilla@ittk.hu, http://www.itm.bme.hu/

Abstract. Courses on Social Informatics at the Budapest University of Technology and Economics have been offered since 1992. After 25 semesters, with more than 1200 students (mainly electrical engineering majors) who have taken the courses, our views on the subject, together with a comprehensive report on teaching experiences are now presented in a two volume handbook. We would like to share our notions on Social Informatics as a subject in its own right through an in-depth analysis of our curriculum philosophy and teaching methods.

Keywords: Social informatics, curriculum development, information as a cultural value. Ethics and IT, Budapest University of Technology and Economics

1 Introduction

On a professional meeting held in Budapest in December 2005 a young informatician having made a brilliant business career, recognizing one of the authors of this study, said to the audience: *"And here sits my dear ex-teacher who prevented me from becoming a narrow-minded engineer, whose course titled 'Introduction into Social Informatics' rose my interest in continuously watching and interrogating the over-technology aspects."*

The researcher and lecturer aim which led us to introduce our Social Informatics courses at the Technical University of Budapest in 1991 is better expressed by this quotation than by anything else. From the very beginning we set out from the opinion that in today's social theory it is 'information society studies' that gives the most comprehensive reflection of the challenges of this era, however, the *technical intellectuals* (primarily the informaticians) need to be able to *connect the well-known informatics aspects and background knowledge to the relevant over-technology*

Please use the following format when citing this chapter:

Karvalics, L. Z., Juhász, L., 2006, in IFIP International Federation for Information Processing, Volume 223, Social Informatics: An Information Society for All? In Remembrance of Rob Kling, eds. Berleur, J., Numinen, M. I., Impagliazzo, J., (Boston: Springer), pp. 65–72.

social aspects (Z. Karvalics – Székely, 1995, Z. Karvalics, 1998). In other words: the disadvantages emerging from the one-sided technical approach of informatician / engineer training must satisfactorily be counter-balanced. Consequently, the focus point of our attention has been permanently directed at *scientific reflection to the current practical challenges*.

This approach is slightly different from the mainstream standpoints (Kling, 1999, Sawyer – Rosenbaum, 2000, Ljubljana, 1985, Kling, 2001). The topics, subjects, our domains linking computer culture and the society are the same – we absolutely agree in what Social Informatics as a discipline is. The essential difference lies in *what and how is represented in the university curriculum from this discipline, in the pedagogical targets we follow* (Z. Karvalics, 2004).

So the basic target of our Social Informatics curriculum is to transmit, to impart a special approach in the possession of which the technical intellectuals (having the necessary technological knowledge) are open to the problems of the social sub-systems, they have knowledge of its operation, they are able to evaluate empirical data and to make in-depth investigations of the main phases of information flow. We strive to give our students organized knowledge so that they will not be compelled to rely on resources dispersed here and there while getting to know the problems of social informatics.

The 'minimum' we have to perform is as follows:
- 'Building the non-shannonian conceptual net' related to information (introduction of the cultural, cognitive and economic-social concept network of information),
- Channeling the Perception,
- Building a new identity environment for the engineers,
- Mapping the topic.

2.   The Education Modules of Social Informatics

2.1   Problem Description

In an informatics context we always speak of *hybrid systems*: a kind of system of human and signal processing machine(s). In this sense, the Internet is not 'a network of computers connected through communications lines' but a giant hybrid of people, content and complex informatics systems. Consequently, the performance and the possible system errors do not refer to the 'Computer' but to the human constructing, operating and maintaining it. Artificial intelligence does not 'conquer the human being' but helps him to achieve an operation performance exceeding his biological possibilities. On the other hand, we take *information as a cultural value*: in our opinion, information is nothing else but a special interaction through which a human being is able to establish and keep contacts with his environment. The six modules of our curriculum try to organize the course in line with this opinion.

2.2   The Phenomenon of Information

We take the interpretation domain of 'information' exclusively as a part of the world of human phenomena, a kind of 'atom' of the ability of getting to know. Starting from the opinion that *all information is (inter)action but not every (inter)action is information,* we exclude the analogue moments of the material and living systems (genetic 'information', information as a 'physical' entity equal in value to scope, time and energy) from the discussion universe. The Shannon-Weaver transmission model is insufficient for the recognition of social interactions: the basic notions of the information universe are to be deduced from somewhere else. We found the source of our categories in cognitive psychology and the history of culture.

Table 1. Information and information technology

Meanings and fundamental concepts – theoretical introduction
Elementary information, information sets and supersets
Channels of elementary information
Information and action
Basic model of information flow
Informational activity forms and modes of objectivation
Information tools, information instruments, information technology

2.3   Information and Knowledge Industry

In the background of today's information technology industry and the developments we find the accelerating restructuring of the economic sectors, the transformation of reality almost impossible to be followed. Thus the second module surveys the questions of information and knowledge economy. In parallel with the sudden advance of the Internet and the *'network economy'* the examination of *'e-economy'* and *'new economy'* has become to the foreground, and on the other hand, the categories of *knowledge economy* and *knowledge-based economy* have started to replace the use of information economy. Meanwhile, however, it is inevitable to give a summarizing and historical picture on the big blocks of computer industry, telecommunication and the media (content industry), in the terms of convergence.

Table 2. IT- Information- and Knowledge industry

World economy, international trade, business and information
Origins and Basics of Information and Knowledge Economy
Information Economy and Information Policy
Education
Research, Development and Innovation
The IT sector: clusters, dynamics, convergence
Internet-business, E-commerce

2.4   The 5 axioms of social informatics

The third module presents the 5 axioms of social informatics through case studies and examples:

The human component is present in the hybrid systems triply: as 'producer' of the computer side, as 'user' or operator being in interaction with the computer, and as the one concerned by the results (outputs). The examination of the human factor is the deepest substance of the discipline. The most important Axiom of social informatics is: *People first*.

Table 3. How to think of ICT? The Five Axiom

Standpoint (Axiom)	Modality	General category
World concept	Approach	*Moral/ Ethics*
Culture	Embeddedness	
PEOPLE		*Substance*
FIRST		
Community	Size	*Evolution*
Environment	System	

The hardware and software development of the hybrids is typically a collective performance. The human side of hybrid systems generally means 'a human connected into a network'. Each of the communication actions makes a community scope. Although the digital universe has problem sections that can be surveyed exclusively on an individual level, the examination of the characteristic contexts always need grouped or collective frameworks. (Axiom 2) The personal and community dimension of IT-universe is embraced by the 'culture' as the entity in the widest sense. (Axiom 3)

The persons and their communities possible to be described with certain cultural factors ask for the help of information technology in a certain environmental scope. Informal social environment, formal institutional environment, media environment and natural environment can be considered *environmental elements*. (Axiom 4). Finally, Axiom 5 is the entity that all the spectators and analysts approaching the IT-world must cross unperceived. Namely, the student, researcher, reporter, politician, or user interprets and analyzes the facts known properly or not by adjusting them to the models according to which they actually see the world. How do they look at the eternal questions of Life, Society or the World? What kind of samples do they mobilize in case they meet a problem?

The category of ethics becomes an essential category in the meeting-point of world concept and culture like this – it is not by chance that the first prototypes of social informatics taking up the form of university courses were the 'Ethics and IT' courses at the universities of the Francophone world at the beginning of the seventies.

The *modalities* together constructing the general category of 'evolution' are size and the dynamics determining it in the case of community, and system view in the case of the environment. The more complexly we approach the macro-level questions of IT, the more our view is based on the evolutional approach (Z. Karvalics, 2004).

2.5 History as context

The traditional fields of informatics must be given a new meaning embedded in a social scientific context. The aim is to *adjust the history of technology into a socio-historical framework*, to get to know the applier culture, to investigate the processes going on in the deep layers of society and to survey the common factors forming the relationship between technology and society from the pre-historical phase up to this day.

Table 4. Pre-history of IT

World economy, international trade, business and information
Social History of Computing
Conceptual and Social History of 'Network'
Social History of Internet
Social History of Data Storage and Processing
History of IT Industry
History of information sciences
History of IT-politics, IT-strategies

2.6 Professions and Knowledges

In the fifth module we examine the profession world of the information complex. As a result of the spread of the information technology tools and their becoming decisive factors on a social scale, as well, the knowledges necessary to execute information operations are moving more and more from the technical to the social or social scientific domain. This change, which has not yet been satisfactorily analyzed, also results in the re-thinking of the engineer knowledge worlds which we see possible to be presented in the activity matrix of social informatics. The matrix consists of the horizontal categories of researcher, engineer, technologist, broker and manager knowledges, their pre-history and trends and the vertical categories of HW, SW, system, information and knowledge. Filling up the abstract categories of the role players and knowledge types being present at the various points of IT, media, science and economy with real professions, brings about the recognition and understanding of several enlightening inter-connections.

Table 5. Building an identity environment. Who are they ?

RESEARCHER	ENGINEER	TECHNO-LOGIST	BROKER	MANAGER	
Knowledge researcher	Knowledge engineer	Knowledge technologist	Knowledge broker	Knowledge manager	KNOWLEDGE
Information researcher	Information engineer	Information technologist	Information broker	Information manager	INFORMATION
System researcher	System engineer	System technologist	System broker	System manager	SYSTEM
SW/HW researcher	SW/HW engineer	SW/HW technologist	SW/HW broker	SW/HW manager	SOFTWARE/ HARDWARE

2.7. Problem Axes, Problem Maps

Social theory has long been striving to define the sub-systems together making (constituting) Society as a whole. Since the great system builder, Talcott Parsons, several rival paradigms have tried to give the best systematization. Of the many possible models, the one standing nearest to us is that arranging the most important system categories of the life and survey of society into four-element groups (quads) – exactly into four.

Table 6. The four quads

	'Name'	Elements
1. quad	Basic Elements	Economy
		Politics
		Society
		Law
2. quad	Forms of mind and knowledge	Science
		Art
		Religion
		Everyday Mind
3. quad	Everyday life	The world of labour
		Transport and environment
		Health (care)
		Leisure time
4. quad	Basic Elements	Economy
		Politics
		Society
		Law

Let us imagine that the 4 quads form 16 problem axes each of them running into the ICT (Information and Communication Technologies) centre. The problems that can appear at all in a socio-informatics context are arranged on theses axes.

And how does the axis become a problem map? The first step is the arrangement of all the possible issues evolving when the certain sub-system and the IT-universe meet. Depending on the 'saturation' of the axis, we can find 5-25 typical questions or problem fields which can be illustrated as meeting-points or 'nodes' on the axis. For example, economy is especially rich – it is not by chance that economy informatics is an independent knowledge world –, while the number of the elements of the node of religion and ICT is not very high (although very interesting).

We can speak of two types of nodes. Specific nodes indicate a problem being characteristic of only the certain sub-system, horizontal nodes are issues possible to study uniformly concerning each axis. These are, for example:

- the informatization process of an institution belonging to the certain sub-system
- the historic aspect: where does informatization process start from (with the involvement of the pre-digital information environment)
- the actual philosophical problems of the certain sub-system generated by the ICT

And since Reality does not care for socio-theoretical systematizations, some of the problems are not possible to be ordered to only one axis or to one of the nodes, but may refer to several nodes of several axes. Let us take, for example, the problem of 'intellectual property on the Internet': it is part of the Media sub-system as 'content', but the content itself is Art or Science. Regulation is a task of the Law sub-system, however, it is strongly influenced by Politics – while deep economic interrelations appear in the background. Consequently, the *issues of social informatics are the various combinations of nodes in many cases.* (Z. Karvalics, 2004)

3   Conclusion

We are aware of the fact that the very same topics can be discussed in various pedagogical – didactical forms. Our education package has been developed for engineer students, with practical aims; still we believe that it will also contribute to the tracing of the disciplinary borderlines of social informatics. Of these aspects we highlight the *historical dimension* and the *identity and professional environment* which we consider as our own innovative contribution to the subject.

References

Kling, Rob (1999): What is Social Informatics and Why Does it Matter? *D-Lib Magazine,* January 1999 Volume 5 Number 1. http://www.slis.indiana.edu/SI/si2001.html

Kling, Rob (2001): Social Informatics. *Encyclopedia of LIS,* Kluwer

Ljubljana (1985): Social Informatics Web-site http://social-informatics.org/

Sawyer, Steve – Rosenbaum, Howard (2000): Social Informatics in the Information Sciences: Current Activities and Emerging Directions Informing Science - *Special Isssue on Information Science Research,* Vol. 3. No. 2 (2000) pp. 89-95.

Z. Karvalics, László (1998): Information Society and Social Informatics: Extended topology of the research fields/ In: *Research for Information Society.* Proceedings, Vol.II. Warsaw, 1998 October 15-17.

Z. Karvalics, László (2004): Designing a Discipline: Social Informatics Revisited. In: Jose V. Carrasquero et al. (eds): *Informatics and Society,* PISTA Proceedings Vol. I. IIS, 2004 pp. 317-321.

Z. Karvalics, László – Székely, Iván (1995): Informatics and informaticians: Changing concepts and a realized example of teaching and understanding informatics beyond computer technology In: *Key players in the introduction of information technology: Their social responsibilities and professional training* (Proceedings, Namur, July 5-7 1995) 237-244.o.

Social Informatics: An Emerging Discipline?

Vasja Vehovar

Faculty of Social Sciences, University of Ljubljana, Slovenia
vasja@ris.org, http://vasja.ris.org

Abstract. The concept of Social Informatics emerged along with the growing role of information and communication technologies ('ICT') in the 1970s and was articulated in Rob Kling's work in the 1980s and 1990s. In recent years, the notion of Social Informatics has been rapidly expanding in various contexts. Following an overview of related activities on the University of Ljubljana website (http://social-informatics.org) we can identify three broad contexts of Social informatics. The first area is the interaction of ICT with humans at the personal, organizational and society levels. The second direction involves ICT applications in the public/social sphere, encompassing modelling, simulations and information systems through to various e-applications and information architecture. The third segment relates to ICT as a tool in social science research ranging from ICT-supported statistical analysis, computer-assisted data collection to virtual collaboration and cyber-infrastructure. Within this scope we encounter numerous research activities (i.e. journals, events, associations, research institutes, projects...) related to Social Informatics, including a growing number of university study programmes. However, the dynamics, dispersion, fragmentation and lack of common framework, as well as the increasing number of competitive concepts (e.g. e-social science) could prevent Social Informatics effectively establishing itself as a discipline with all the necessary formal attributes and well-defined boarders.

Keywords: information society, cyber-infrastructure, e-social sciences, Internet research, university programmes.

1   Introduction

There is a complex relationship between information communication technology ('ICT') and the corresponding social context. We could even say that modern societies and ICT have become intertwined – we cannot understand one without

Please use the following format when citing this chapter:

Vehovar, V., 2006, in IFIP International Federation for Information Processing, Volume 223, Social Informatics: An Information Society for All? In Remembrance of Rob Kling, eds. Berleur, J., Numinen, M. I., Impagliazzo, J., (Boston: Springer), pp. 73–85.

understanding the other. One specific approach to address this interaction is the concept of Social Informatics ('SI'). Various definitions of SI exist; however, SI is typically understood as a multidisciplinary study of the social aspects of ICT. In its broadest sense, SI covers an extremely wide range of areas, from the usability of computer hardware to information privacy, from information sociology to specific web applications. In addition, the notion of SI considerably overlaps with the concepts of informatics (particularly community informatics) and the notion of information society. Various competitive concepts also exist which integrate the technical aspects of modern ICTs with social, economic, legal and ethical dimensions such as the e-social sciences and cyber-infrastructure.

In the following sections, we first describe the development of SI and then, in the third section, we discuss definitions and contexts of SI. In the fourth section we overview SI activities by making an online overview of the Social Informatics website (http://social-informatics.org). Finally, in the fifth section we investigate the prospects of SI becoming a scientific discipline.

2   The Development of Social Informatics

Informatics or information science is basically the study of information. It is primarily concerned with the structure, creation, management, storage, retrieval, dissemination and transfer of information [Wikipedia, 2006]. However, very often the label *informatics* is used with a narrower meaning, i.e. to describe applied information sciences *per se*. In any case, the term itself is relatively new. It was only in 1962 that the French *informatique*, *informatics* (English), *informatik* (German) and *informatica* (Italian, Spanish) was coined by Dreyfus to refer to the application of computers to store and process information [Fourman, 2002]. Informatics in its broader sense includes the study of applications of information in organizations, its perception among users and the corresponding interaction between users, organizations and information systems. Frequently, but not always, informatics is also perceived as a specific branch of the computer sciences. However, informatics is more problem-oriented whereas computer science is technology-oriented. There are also some regional specifics; in the US, for example, the term computer science dominates while in Europe we encounter the labels 'information science' and 'informatics' much more often.

Since the 1970s, the term *informatics* has been increasingly adopted to describe the application of information technology to various fields such as law informatics, medical informatics, organizational informatics, library informatics etc. [He, 2003]. However, if we use strict criteria to identify a scientific discipline (i.e. international associations, study programmes, occupational profiles, large conferences, professional journals, ethical codes etc.), then medical informatics was perhaps the first to fully establish itself as a new informatics-generated discipline. The other areas have either not been successful or are still in earlier development stages.

Within this context Social Informatics (SI) has also emerged as another potential discipline related to informatics. Historically, the first activities appeared in the early 1970s when computerization started to be observed in a broader social context. In the late 1970s, a critical and explicit SI discourse was advanced by computer scientists in the US, including: Kling (1980), Mowshowitz (1976) and Weizenbaum (1976) [Kling, 2003]. At the very beginning, SI sought to discredit the technological determinism that was dominating the field of computer applications. SI researchers addressed social aspects in computer science with simple issues like 'What kinds of impact does computerization have on personal privacy?' and 'What is the ability of voters to get more complete information through online sources?' [Kling, 1999].

In the US the term SI is closely linked to the University of Indiana where the concept of Social Informatics [CSI, 2005a] was formally introduced. According to [Jackewitz, Janneck, Krause, Pape and Strauss, 2003] the English term 'Social Informatics' was finalized by Kling in 1997. The term 'emerged from a series of lively conversations in February and March 1996 among scholars with an interest in advancing critical scholarship about the social aspects of computerization, including Phil Agre, Jacques Berleur, Brenda Dervin, Andrew Dillon, Rob Kling, Mark Poster, Karen Ruhleder, Ben Shneiderman, Leigh Star and Barry Wellman' [CSI, 2005b]. Before that, different labels like 'social analysis of computing', 'social impacts of computing' or 'behavioural information systems research' had been used.

Perhaps the oldest formal use of the term SI can be identified in the programme of Social Informatics at the Faculty of Social Sciences of the University of Ljubljana in Slovenia. The undergraduate four-year study programme within the Department of Sociology started in 1985 and was at the very outset labelled a programme of Social Informatics (in Slovenian 'Dru_boslovna informatika'). Besides courses from social sciences (i.e. sociology as well as political, communication and organizational sciences) half of the courses were from 'technical' disciplines: Mathematics, Statistics, Informatics, Computer Science, and Survey Methodology. A strong emphasis on social science methodology was one of the key specifics of this programme. As a consequence, the corresponding perception of SI was also strongly related to the role of ICT as a social-science research tool [Social-informatics.org, 2006]. After 20 years, as part of EU Bologna reform redesigns in 2005 this became an independent study programme at the first (undergraduate) level. In addition, the programme now articulates much more strongly another dimension of SI – the role of ICT in contemporary societies. At the same time, the master's programme (i.e. the second level) of SI was also established with three modules: Information Society, Applied SI, and Social Science Methodology.

We encounter another early introduction of SI in Norway where the Ministry of Education established SI as a discipline at the University of Oslo [Norwegian Parliament, 1984-5] in the mid-1980s. SI was originally called socio-informatics and defined by Stein Bråten in Dialogens vilkår i datasamfunnet as a "scientific domain between psychology, sociology and informatics" in 1982 [Roggen, 1998].

We should also mention SI developments in the former Soviet Union, where the importance of the relationship between ICT and society was recognized early on. As a consequence, the first scientific paper – as recorded in the ISI Web of Science database – explicitly related to SI comes from the former USSR Academy of Science: 'On the shaping of Social Informatics' [Ursul, 1989].

With the expansion of the Internet in the mid-1990s we can observe entirely new momentum in the development of the SI concept; the multiple directions taken and corresponding activities are discussed in the next section.

3   Social Informatics: Definitions and Practices

According to Rob Kling, Social Informatics (SI) is defined as the 'interdisciplinary study of the design, uses and consequences of information technologies that takes into account their interaction with institutional and cultural contexts' [Kling, 1999]. SI refers to the body of research that examines the social aspects of computerization, including the roles of information technology in social and organizational changes, the uses of information technologies in social contexts and the ways that the social organization of information technologies is influenced by social forces and social practices [Kling, Crawford, Rosenbaum, Sawyer and Weisband, 2000].

A similar concept of SI originating in the organizational aspects of ICT was elaborated by [Dahlbom, 1996] and in the June/July 2005 issue of the American Society for Information Science and Technology Bulletin with guest editor W. David Penniman from the University of Buffalo [Penniman, 2005].

Another approach of this type defines SI as 'a body of rigorous empirical research that focuses on the relationships among people, ICTs, and the social structures of their development and use' [Lamb and Sawyer, 2005].

A somewhat more informatics-oriented definition [Ohta, Ishida and Okada, 2001] describes SI as 'an interdisciplinary study to explore the function of information within a social system and to design a system for exchanging information within a society. Focusing on information, SI researchers observe various aspects of human behaviour and social systems, and examine various information networks in the society, including an economic information system, a management information system, a political information system, an administrative information system, a life information system, and so on.' According to this approach, SI consists of three main theories: a social system theory, an information system theory and a theory of the semantics of social information.

Also close to the above definition is the understanding of SI as a 'complex interdisciplinary approach, which consolidates/integrates the knowledge from mathematics and physics, computer sciences, management and humanity sciences. SI considers the problems of receiving, transformation, investigation, and modelling and explores the informational flows in large social systems and their models' [Makarenko, 1998].

In addition to the above definitions, the notion of SI appears in various other contexts which can be observed on the SI website [Social-informatics.org, 2006], which systematically collects evidence of research and educational practices relating to the concept of SI. The SI-related areas recorded on this website are presented in Fig. 1. They are roughly structured in three directions: (1) ICT's interaction with society; (2) ICT applications in the social sciences; and (3) ICT as a tool in social research. While the first branch (ICT and society) – particularly (1b) and (1c), which are circled in Fig. 1 – closely overlap with Rob Kling's initial definition, this is somewhat less clear with the other areas. In part, the second branch (ICT applications) – particularly (2a) and (2c) – seems to be closer to the understanding revealed in [Ohta, Ishida and Okada, 2001] and [Makarenko, 1998]. On the other side, the third branch (ICT as a research tool) is closer to the understanding of SI at the University of Ljubljana described above.

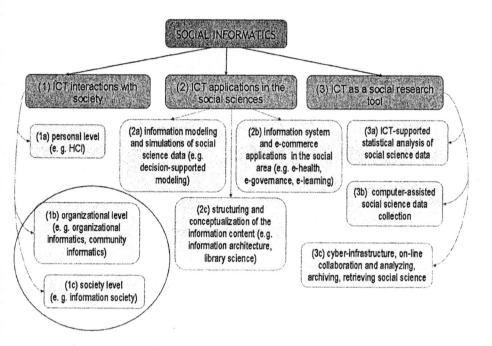

Fig. 1. The broad areas covered by Social Informatics

Let us briefly comment on the three areas and nine sub-areas shown in Fig. 1.

In relation to 1) Interaction between ICT and humans

The social aspects of computerization can be further observed at three levels:

1. *interaction with ICT at the personal level* relates to the individual's experience with ICT (e.g. HCI – human computer interaction, cognitive aspects, physiological issues etc.);
2. *interaction of ICT at the organizational (micro) level* relates to the socio-organizational aspects of implementing ICT applications. In part, it also overlaps with ICT managerial aspects;
3. *interaction of ICT and society at the macro level* relates to general changes in society due to ICT, i.e. societal change and issues related to the information society; national, regional and global aspects are incorporated here.

According to the definition of SI found on the University of Indiana's Social Informatics homepage [CSI, 2005a], SI predominantly relates to (1b) and (1c). Within this context, the notion of Community Informatics may be understood as a subfield (1b) of SI [Bieber, Gurstein, Civille, White, Silver and Kolko, 2002]. More specifically, Community Informatics ('CI') can be defined as 'the study and the practice of enabling communities with ICTs' [JCI homepage, 2006]. CI thus relates to building up communities, developing information, and providing access to technology [Stoecker, 2004]. However, SI includes broader social aspects and less problem-solving attributes, making the differences between SI and CI similar to those between biology and medicine [Bieber, Gurstein, Civille, White, Silver and Kolko, 2002].

We should also add here that while, in principle, SI covers the area of human-computer interaction (1a) this has already become a large and independent scientific field, which can hardly be squeezed under the SI umbrella even though it fits into the majority of SI definitions.

In relation to 2) Applications of ICT in social sciences

These applications can be further structured in three directions:

1. *computer modelling of social science data*, including computer simulations in the area of the social sciences, together with decision-making models, intelligence and knowledge discovery applications;
2. *information systems and e-business applications in the social sciences*, including applications in the public sector, social services etc. In particular, this relates to the corresponding e-business models of e-government, e-health, e-learning etc.;
3. *structuring and conceptualization of the information content*, i.e. the information architecture for web sites and other ICT applications in areas related to the social sciences.

With respect to this second branch, a parallel with other substantial applications of informatics can be drawn. Similarly as, for example, how medical informatics actually relates to ICT applications in medicine, SI should relate to ICT applications in the social sciences; this includes visualization, modelling, organizing and analyzing social science data, as well as developing corresponding ICT applications and solutions. According to this analogy, ICT modelling tools for social science data (2a) and the corresponding ICT applications (2b) would represent the **core meaning of SI**, and not the ICT interaction with society (1b and 1c). We should also add here that the number of substantial areas in the social sciences is extremely broad, ranging from communication, political and library sciences to sociology, public administration, social welfare studies, social science methodology and military studies. Perhaps the most typical example of these specifics is the German notion of '*Sozialinformatik*' as the application of informatics to the social care system [Sozialinformatik, 2006].

The third sub-segment (2c) relates to structuring of the content on the web and it is rapidly articulating itself as a new independent discipline and a new profession of information architecture [Morrogh, 2003]. Although it initially emerged from the library sciences, it is now expanding across various social and communication sciences, as well as across informatics. The information architecture in fact provides a prototype case of a SI subfield, nested deeply within the definition of SI, (i.e. the interaction of ICT and the social sciences), but having been developed entirely outside of the notion of SI.

In relation to 3) The use of ICT as a tool for studying social phenomena

This direction covers a wide range of areas from data mining to computer-assisted data collection. Of course, this partly overlaps with various other scientific disciplines, but also with some other areas of SI, particularly (2 in Fig. 1). We can break this segment up into three sub-areas:

1. *computer (intensive) methods for the statistical analysis of social science data*, which includes various statistical packages and specific tools: analysis of large social networks, bootstrapping, Gibbs sampler, data mining, data fusion etc.;

2. *computer-assisted data collection* in quantitative (i.e. survey data collection) and in qualitative empirical social research (e.g. virtual ethnography, online focus groups). In particular, web survey methodology stands here one of the most popular ICT applications in social science empirical research [WebSM, 2006];

3. *ICT tools for manipulating, organizing, analyzing and presenting* social science data, including platforms for co-operation and virtual collaboration in the social sciences. This also relates to all infrastructure applications that simplify the search for and access to data archives and bibliographies, online analytical tools (e.g. tabulation), as well as the new forms of scientific collaboration supported by modern ICT (e.g. grid technologies).

The majority of ICT tools in (3a) are closely related to statistical computing and social science methodology so they overlap with survey methodology, marketing research, social science methodology, applied statistics and official statistics. Similarly, computer-assisted data collection (3b) has successfully positioned itself as an independent subfield in the area of social and marketing research. ICT has also changed the infrastructure, communications and the process of scientific work, i.e. the ways in which we organize data, human potential and computer resources (3c). We have already mentioned the notions of cyber-infrastructure and the e-social sciences, which here provide two examples of alternative/competitive concepts. In part, of course, these also overlap with (2a) and (3a).

To further illustrate the above three-category (nine-sub-category) structure, we checked the ISI Web of Science portal for scientific papers related to the keyword search 'Social Informatics'. In January 2006 only 33 bibliographic units were found in response to this specific search request [Web of Science, 2006]. Most papers were at the 'ICT interaction with society at the macro (society) level' (1c), 'modelling and simulation of social science data' (2a) and in 'information systems and e-commerce in the social area' (2b). The weakest component was the notion of SI as a research tool and platform (3a-c).

4   Establishing a Discipline: Formal Activities

Let us now briefly overview activities related to SI where, in the last few years, we can observe a true explosion of appearances of the term Social Informatics.

- Thematic Journal: The *Social Informatics Magazine* (*Revista de Informatica Sociala*) published by the Social Computer Science Laboratory at the West University of Timisoara has since June 2004 appeared twice a year and it contains scientific papers in Romanian, English and French languages [Social Informatics Magazine, 2006].
- Special issues of established journals: Special issues of the *American Society for Information Science and Technology Bulletin* [Bulletin, 2005] and *Information Technology & People* [IT & People, 2005] were devoted to SI in 2005.

- Social Informatics Fair: *The Social Informatics Fair* in Kyoto was held in September 2005 with the aim to become a regular event [Fair, 2005].
- Social Informatics Associations: The Japan Association for Social Informatics [JASI, 2006] and the Japan Society for Socio-information Studies [JSIS, 2006] are already formally arranged as professional organizations.
- Blogs: Various blogs related to SI are appearing: the *Subject Tracer™ Information Blog* by Marcus P. Zillman, which monitors Social Informatics resources [Zillman, 2006], while the *Social Informatics* [SI blog, 2005a], the *Blog on Steve Sawyer's publication* [SI blog, 2005b] and *CiteULike* are devoted to academic papers and discussion [CiteULike, 2006].

In addition, at the beginning of 2006 we can find various research units/institutes that explicitly include SI in their names:
- Social Informatics Research Laboratory, University of Electro-Communications, Tokyo, Japan [SI research laboratory, 2005];
- Social Informatics Research Unit (SIRU), University of York, UK [SIRU York, 2006];
- Social Informatics Research Unit (SIRU), University of Brighton, [SIRU Brighton, 2004];
- The Social Informatics Research Group, Napier University, UK [SI research group, 2006];
- The Social Informatics Cluster, University of Edinburgh, UK [SI cluster, 2006];
- Institute for Social Informatics, Copenhagen, Denmark [ISI, 2005]; and
- Center for Social Informatics, Indiana University, [CSI, 2005a].

Similarly, we can currently (early 2006) find at least 12 university programmes of SI in seven countries:
- *United States:* University of Indiana, USA [Indiana University, 2006], University of Toledo University, [Toledo University, 2005], Bradley University in Illinois, [Bradley University, 2006];
- *Japan:* Kyoto University, [Kyoto University, 2005], Chuo University, [Chuo University, 2001];
- *Ukraine:* Kiev National Taras Shevchenko University, [Taras Shevchenko University, 2000], Kharkov National University of Radio Electronics, [Kharov University, 2005], National Technical University of Ukraine, [National Technical University, 2005];
- *Germany:* Berufsakademie Stuttgart, [Sozialinformatik, 2006];
- *Taiwan:* Yuan Ze University, [Yuan Ze University, 2005];
- *Romania:* West University of Timisoara, [Grosseck, 2004]; and
- *Slovenia:* University of Ljubljana, [Social-informatics.org, 2006].

Of course, the above lists may not be exhaustive particularly because units with slightly different names were not included, e.g. 'Socio-Informatics' in South Africa [University of Stellenbosch, 2006], in Japan [Keio University, 2002] and in Germany [The International Institute for Socio-Informatics, 2006]. Of course, all other activities and institutions from overlapping areas - without an explicit mention of the term 'Social Informatics' - were also excluded. The full lists covering all related areas and those of indirect relevance are shown on the SI website [Social-informatics.org, 2006].

If we structure the above activities into the categories in Fig. 1 we could say that, roughly speaking, in the US they typically follow the initial Rob Kling understanding (1b and 1c, Fig. 1). In part, this is also true for institutions and activities in Japan; however, very often in Japan they overlap with the understanding of SI as ICT applications in the social sphere (2a-2c, Fig. 1). This is also true for a large part of SI-related organizations and activities in Europe. With respect to the third variation, i.e. ICT as a tool and infrastructure (3a-3c, Fig. 1), we can find it articulated at the University of Ljubljana [Social-informatics.org, 2006].

5   Conclusions

Information and communication technologies (ICT) form an essential aspect of modern societies. Within this context, Social Informatics (SI) represents a specific approach to addressing the relationship of ICT and contemporary society.

SI is a relatively new concept, which started to emerge in the 1970s in close connection to the computer sciences. With the rise of the Internet in the 1990s the notion of SI rapidly expanded. How SI is understood varies across countries, scientific fields, and areas of application and terminological backgrounds. Nevertheless, the main stream of understanding follows the initial concept of Rob Kling who defined SI in a broad context where the design, use, configuration and consequences of ICT are studied in their interaction with society. However, no explicit separation of SI has been drawn yet from neighbouring areas of informatics or from ICT applications in the social sciences.

We can observe a considerable expansion of formal SI activities in recent years with respect to publications, events, research units and study programmes. At the same time, the number of contexts where SI appears is also rapidly broadening. Unfortunately this expansion is often fragmented, separated and isolated, with little or no cohesive power. Obviously, with the growth of SI-related activities we miss a stronger definition and more formal bonds, which could constitute a profession and scientific discipline: international associations, regular conferences, explicit journals, codes and standards etc. A danger thus exists that SI will continue to remain on the periphery because it lacks a clear operational definition and more coordinated formal activities.

We have structured the notion of SI in three segments and nine sub-segments. The overall range in which SI can appear is thus very broad, spanning from the interaction of ICT with society, ICT applications in the social sciences to the understanding of ICT as a tool in the social science research. Of course, due to rapid ICT-generated changes the quest to more precisely define areas covered by SI is becoming increasingly complicated.

To summarize, despite the expansion and ever greater articulation of SI there is a danger that SI will not established itself as a discipline because some areas are continuously moving under the umbrella of other fields (e.g. computer-assisted survey data collection to social science methodology). On the other hand, some areas have already become independent outside of SI (e.g. human-computer interaction or business informatics), while others are on their way to becoming independent (e.g. e-social sciences, information architecture). Even within the very core segment of SI, the community informatics is perhaps better-organized discipline with much more clear profile than SI. Similar is true for the area of information society.

On one hand, SI seems to be gaining momentum and a critical mass of activities, which could support attempts to fully formalize it as a discipline. However, on the other hand, we face an even sharper increase in its fragmentation, which might render such an undertaking very difficult, particularly because of the abundance of competing concepts addressing the relationship of ICT and modern societies.

References

[Bieber, Gurstein, Civille, White, Silver and Kolko, 2002], M. Bieber, M. Gurstein, R. Civille, N. White, D. Silver and B. Kolko, Trends and Issues in the Emerging Field of Community Informatics, A White Paper Exploring Research – final draft, 2002 (March 10, 2006); www.is.njit.edu/vci/vci-white-paper.doc.

[Bradley University, 2006], Minor in Social Informatics, Bradley University, 2006 (March 10, 2006); http://www.bradley.edu/las/soc/soc/si.html.

[Bulletin, 2005], W. D. Penniman, S. Sawyer, A. Halavais, E. Davenport and K. R. Eschenfelder, Special issue devoted to the Social Informatics, *American Society for Information Science and Technology Bulletin*, June/July 2005, Volume 31, Number 5 (February 1, 2006); http://www.asis.org/Bulletin/Jun-05/index.html.

[Chuo University, 2001], Overview of Chuo University and Social Informatics, School of Social Informatics, Chuo University, 2001 (March 10, 2006); http://www.saitolab.com/english/overchuo.html.

[CiteULike, 2006], Tag social-informatics, 2006 (March 10, 2006); http://www.citeulike.org/tag/social-informatics.

[CSI, 2005a], About Social Informatics, Rob Kling Center for Social Informatics, 2005 (February 1, 2006); http://rkcsi.indiana.edu/index.php/about-social-informatics.

[CSI, 2005b], History of the Term, Rob Kling Center for Social Informatics, 2005 (February 1, 2006); http://rkcsi.indiana.edu/index.php/history-of-the-term.

[Dahlbom, 1996], B. Dahlbom, The New Informatics, *Scandinavian Journal of Information Systems*, 1996, 8(2), pp. 29-48 (February 1, 2006); http://www.e-sjis.org/journal/volumes/volume08/articles/no2/02_dahlbom_p29-48.pdf.

[Fair, 2005], Social Informatics Fair 2005, Kyoto, Japan, 2005 (March 10, 2006); http://www.lab7.kuis.kyoto-u.ac.jp/sifair2005/.

[Fourman, 2002], M. Fourman, Division of Informatics, in *Encyclopedia of Information and Library Science*, second edition, edited by J. Feather and P. Sturges (Routledge, London, 2002), (February 1, 2006); http://www.inf.ed.ac.uk/publications/online/0139.pdf.

[Grosseck, 2004], G. Grosseck, Repere Indentitare privind Informatica Sociala, *Revista de Informatica Sociala*, June 2004, Number 1, pp. 30-38 (March 27, 2006); http://www.ris.uvt.ro/RIS%20nr%201.pdf.

[He, 2003], S. He, Informatics: a brief survey, *The Electronic Library*, April 2003, Volume 21, Number 2, pp. 117-122 (February 1, 2006); http://www.emeraldinsight.com/Insight/viewContentItem.do?contentType=Article&contentId=861993.

[Indiana University, 2006], Social Informatics, School of Library and Information Science, Indiana University, 2006 (March 10, 2006); http://www.indiana.edu/~bulletin/iub/grad/2004-2005/si.html.

[ISI, 2005], Institute for Social Informatics, Denmark, 2005 (March 10, 2006); http://isi.secureid.org/.

[IT & People, 2005], R. Lamb, S. Sawyer, R. Mansell, T. Wood-Harper, B. Wood, K. Horton, E. Davenport and J. P. Allen, Special issue: Rob Kling Festschrift, *Information*

Technology & People, 2005, Volume 18, Number 1 (February 1, 2006); http://www.itandpeople.org/mainpage181.htm.

[Jackewitz, Janneck, Krause, Pape and Strauss, 2003], I. Jackewitz, M. Janneck, D. Krause, B. Pape and M. Strauss, Teaching Social Informatics as a Knowledge Project, in: *Informatics and the Digital Society*, Kluwer Academic Publishers, 2003, pp. 261-268, (February 1, 2006); http://www.wisspro.de/publications/jackewitz_etal_teaching_2003.pdf.

[JASI, 2006], Japan Association for Social Informatics, 2006 (March 25, 2006); http://wwwsoc.nii.ac.jp/jasi/.

[JCI homepage, 2006], About Community Informatics, *The Journal of Community Informatics, 2006* (March 10, 2006); http://ci-journal.net/index.php.

[JSIS, 2006], Japan Society for Socio-information Studies, 2006 (March 25, 2006); http://www.soc.nii.ac.jp/jsis/.

[Keio University, 2002], Socio-Informatics: Undergraduate Program Guide, Keio University Shonan Fujisawa Campus, 2002 (March 10, 2006); http://www.sfc.keio.ac.jp/english/undergrad/si.html.

[Kharov University, 2005], Department of Social Informatics, Faculty of Applied Mathematics and Management, Kharkov National University of Radio Electronics, 2005 (March 10, 2006); http://si.kture.kharkov.ua/index_eng.html.

[Kling, 1999], R. Kling, What Is Social Informatics and Why Does It Matter?, *D-Lib Magazine*, January 1999, Volume 5, Number 1, ISSN 1082-9873 (February 1, 2006); http://www.dlib.org/dlib/january99/kling/01kling.html

[Kling, 2003], R. Kling, Critical professional education about information and communications technologies and social life, *Information Technology & People*, December 2003, Volume 16, Number 4, pp. 394-418 (February 1, 2006); http://www.emeraldinsight.com/10.1108/09593840310509635.

[Kling, Crawford, Rosenbaum, Sawyer and Weisband, 2000], R. Kling, H. Crawford, H. Rosenbaum, S. Sawyer and S. Weisband, Learning from Social Informatics: Information and Communication Technologies in *Human Contexts*, National Science Foundation, Center for Social Informatics, 2000 (February 1, 2006); http://rkcsi.indiana.edu/archive/SI/Arts/SI_report_Aug_14.pdf.

[Kyoto University, 2005], Social Informatics Model, Graduate School of Informatics, Kyoto University, 2005 (March 10, 2006); http://www.soc.i.kyoto-u.ac.jp/sim_e.html.

[Lamb and Sawyer, 2005], R. Lamb and S. Sawyer, On extending social informatics from a rich legacy of networks and conceptual resources, *Information Technology & People*, March 2005, Volume 18, Number 1, pp. 9-20 (February 1, 2006); http://www.emeraldinsight.com/Insight/viewContentItem.do?contentType=Article&contentId=1464566.

[Makarenko, 1998], A. Makarenko, Social Informatics – New educational speciality in the applied mathematics and computer science curriculum, Report of the Ukrainian branch of euroscience working group for technology transfer, 1998 (March 9, 2006); http://www.kiev.technology-transfer.net/socialinfo.doc.

[Morrogh, 2003], E. Morrogh, *Information Architecture: An Emerging 21st Century Profession* (Prentice Hall, Upper Saddle River, 2003).

[National Technical University, 2005], The List of Specialities, National Technical University of Ukraine, 2005 (March 10, 2006); http://ntu-kpi.kiev.ua/en/admissions/specialities.html.

[Norwegian Parliament, 1984-5], Report to the Norwegian Parliament, no. 66, 1984-5, p. 171 in: G. Grosseck, Repere Indentitare privind Informatica Sociala, *Revista de Informatica Sociala*, June 2004, Number 1, pp. 30-38 (March 27, 2006); http://www.ris.uvt.ro/RIS%20nr%201.pdf.

[Ohta, Ishida and Okada, 2001], T. Ohta, K. Ishida and I. Okada, Social Informatics, Social Informatics Research Laboratory, University of Electro-Communications, Tokyo, 2001 (February 1, 2006); http://www.ohta.is.uec.ac.jp/SI/intro.htm.

[Penniman, 2005], W. D. Penniman, Social Informatics, *Bulletin of the American Society for Information Science and Technology*, June/July 2005, Volume 31, Number 5 (February 1, 2006); http://www.asis.org/Bulletin/Jun-05/penniman.html.

[Roggen, 1998], I. Roggen, 1998, Specialization Course in Web Sociology and Social Informatics (February 1, 2006); http://folk.uio.no/iroggen/WEBsociologyINFOeng.html.

[SI blog, 2005a], Social Informatics: What is Social Informatics, IAwiki, 2005 (March 10, 2006); http://www.iawiki.net/SocialInformatics.

[SI blog, 2005b], Informatics vs. Information Science debate, CemCom, 2005 (March 10, 2006); http://cemcom.infosci.cornell.edu/blog/?p=48.

[SI cluster, 2006], Social Informatics Cluster, University of Edinburgh, United Kingdom, 2006 (March 10, 2006); http://corealisation.inf.ed.ac.uk/.

[SI research group, 2006], Social Informatics Research Unit, Faculty of Engineering and Computing Napier University, United Kingdom, 2006 (March 10, 2006); http://www.soc.napier.ac.uk/researchgroup/researchgroupid/256826/op/displayonegroup.

[SI research laboratory, 2005], Social Informatics Research Laboratory, Graduate School of Information Systems, The University of Electro-Communications, Tokyo, Japan, 2005 (March 10, 2006); http://www.ohta.is.uec.ac.jp/SI/.

[SIRU Brighton, 2004], Social Informatics Research Unit, University of Brighton, 2004 (March 10, 2006); http://www.cmis.brighton.ac.uk/Research/siru/home.htm.

[SIRU York, 2006], Social Informatics Research Unit, Department of Sociology, The University of York, United Kingdom, 2006 (March 10, 2006); http://www.york.ac.uk/depts/soci/siru.html.

[Social Informatics Magazine, 2006], *Social Informatics Magazine* or *Revista de Informatica Sociala*, West University of Timisoara, Romania, 2006 (March 1, 2006); http://www.ris.uvt.ro/Engleza/SIM.htm.

[Social-informatics.org, 2006], Social Informatics homepage, University of Ljubljana, Slovenia (February 1, 2006); http://www.social-informatics.org/index.php?fl=0&p1=181&p2=5&p3=197&id=197.

[Sozialinformatik, 2006], Sozialinformatik, Berufsakademie Stuttgart, 2006 (March 1, 2006); http://www.ba-stuttgart.de/2407.0.html?&no_cache=1&sword_list%5b%5d=Sozialinformatik.

[Stoecker, 2004], R. Stoecker, Is Community Informatics Good for Communities? Questions Confronting an Emerging Field, 2004 (March 10, 2006); http://comm-org.wisc.edu/drafts/communityinformatics.htm.

[Taras Shevchenko University, 2000], The educational plan for bachelors in 'Social informatics', Faculty of cybernetics, Kiev National Taras Shevchenko University, 2000 (March 10, 2006); http://www.unicyb.kiev.ua/Site_Eng/bakalavr/bachel_si.html.

[The International Institute for Socio-Informatics, 2006], IISI - The International Institute for Socio-Informatics, 2006 (March 10, 2006); http://www.iisi.de/70.0.html?&L=3.

[Toledo University, 2005], Social Informatics, Department of Sociology and Anthropology, University of Toledo, 2005 (March 10, 2006); http://sasweb.utoledo.edu/siwhat.htm.

[University of Stellenbosch, 2006], Socio-informatics, Department of Information Science, University of Stellenbosch, 2006 (March 10, 2006); http://academic.sun.ac.za/socio-informatics/.

[Ursul, 1989], A. Ursul, On the Shaping of Social Informatics, *International Forum on Information and Documentation*, Volume 14, Number 4, pp. 10-18, 1989.

[Web of Science, 2006], Search by keyword 'Social Informatics, ISI Web of Science portal, 2006 (January 20, 2006); http://sub3.isiknowledge.com/error/Error?Domain=isiknowledge.com&Error=IPError&Src=IP&PathInfo=%2Fportal.cgi&RouterURL=http%3A%2F%2Fisiknowledge.com&IP=194.249.57.26.

[WebSM, 2006], Web Surveys Methodology, 2006 (March 10, 2006); http://www.websm.org/.

[Wikipedia, 2006], Informatics, Wikipedia: Free Encyclopedia, 2006 (February 1, 2006); http://en.wikipedia.org/wiki/Informatics.

[Yuan Ze University, 2005], Introduction – Programs of Study, Yuan Ze University, 2005 (March 10, 2006); http://www.studyintaiwan.org/schools/YZU.htm.
[Zillamn, 2006], M. P. Zillman, M.S. and A.M.H.A., Social Informatics Subject Tracer™ Information Blog, 2006 (March 10, 2006); http://www.socialinformatics.net/.

Social Informatics in the Future?

Per Flensburg, Arianit Kurti
School of Mathematics and Systems engineering, Växjö University,
Sweden, per.flensburg@vxu.se, http://w3.msi.vxu.se/~per/
arianit.kurti@vxu.se

Abstract: When Internet in the middle of the 1990s made its breakthrough a revolution occurred compared to the industrial revolution. Suddenly the cost for information transport was reduced to almost zero and genuinely new opportunities arose. Work, that can be performed by unskilled workers, are outsourced and the focus is on the business process. This requires a genuine new way of doing business; we see a need for trust, loyalty, and sharing of values. Education of users at the workplace will be a major concern and a common language and a mutual and deep understanding of the concepts and social contexts used is a prerequisite. A 3D apple model for context is described. For defining the social context, a user centred approach must be used. We need genuinely new informatics paradigms adapted to the network economy. This requires a massive re-education of all workers, both white and blue collar. To sum it all up: Reliable and sustainable production, availability of reliable information, trust, and flexibility are the means for us to survive in this new economy.

Keywords: network society, outsourcing, supply chain, Habermas

1 Introduction

This paper is not a traditional scientific paper. It is a story presenting our view on the topic of social informatics. As such, it does not follow the traditional scientific form; instead, we have chosen the form of the Catholic mass. That also tells a story and the structure has proven to be sustainable for about 2000 years, which is far beyond the current scientific structure.

We think we have to explain why and how we have decided to use this crazy idea. The first part, Introitus, gives a background and historical reason why social informatics is important. This is seen from a Scandinavian and mainly Swedish perspective. After that comes the Kyrie that describes all the miseries we have seen (well, almost all!). It really indicates that something has to be done. The Gloria part,

Please use the following format when citing this chapter:

Flensburg, P., Kurti, A., 2006, in IFIP International Federation for Information Processing, Volume 223, Social Informatics: An Information Society for All? In Remembrance of Rob Kling, eds. Berleur, J., Numinen, M. I., Impagliazzo, J., (Boston: Springer), pp. 87–96.

praise the new economy and introduces social informatics as the salvation. The next section, the Credo, describes our beliefs of where we want to go. We strive for this ideal word. Next part is Sanctus; what we have to do in order to achieve what we believe. Finally, we talk about Benedictus, the salvation and the implementation of what we have to do in order to achieve what we believe.

We have chosen this form because the difference between science and religion is not that big, in the end it all boils down to faith [1]. Some has faith in religion and some has faith in Science, still it is faith in both cases. Hence, we chose a structure suitable for faith. That is the reason we have ended up with the mass, despite the fact that none of the authors is religious or a strong believer. Now, let the organ sound and the community enter!

2   Introitus

When Internet in the middle of the 1990s made its breakthrough a revolution occurred which in our mind is compared to the industrial revolution. Suddenly the cost for information transport was reduced to almost zero and genuinely new opportunities arose. To understand that, we have to examine the current situation that concerns the economy, industry, and the environment. The information system is only a part of these bigger systems.

Previously there was a focus on rationalisation and making things as cheap, automatic, and efficient as possible. Partly we saw other trends, seeing the computer system as a tool to help people in their work [2]. Sometimes there is awareness about the consequences of the technique, when introduced in society and in companies. Already in 1972, Kristo Ivanov pointed to the fact that the quality of the information can be judge by humans only [3]. At the beginning of the 1970s the ideas of the socio-technique was further developed and put into the trade union conflict oriented framework [4-8]. Internationally, these ideas were supported by a few 'crying voices in the desert' [7, 9-13]. In the Manchester, Kolloqvium [14] the specific nature of information systems research was recognised as being non-positivistic and research methods suitable for researching social systems from non-positivistic approaches was approved. The situation of today is however, a misery and here our mass begins.

3   Kyrie

The global systems

Today, Western industry faces the challenge from low paid countries. Work that can be performed by unskilled workers is outsourced. This applies also for programming and systems construction, which are mostly outsourced to India. The Indian programmers are very qualified and can fully compete with our programmers.

In the customer-oriented business of today, much emphasis is placed on low prices, but despite that, the products must have a high quality. With refined production methods and efficient logistic flows, this is possible. We have to keep in mind that about 95% of the time used for production is used for information processing [15] mostly done by human beings. Here is a big potential to cut costs, but at the expense of human work! Less, but more qualified work are left over. Consequently, unemployment will increase as well as the economic gaps. The question is of course: Can we avoid this? If so, how? Let us move on to the next part of the mass.

4   Gloria

The usual picture in media today is the picture of the wealthy and healthy young jet set and everybody is sophistically encouraged to join that group of people. The status of the companies is measured in the stock rate leading to a very shortsighted economy, the quarterly economy. So far, this has been a success and unconsciously everybody seems to believe in the infinite growth of the economy. The new Internet economy, with e-business, e-commerce, and other e-phenomena, seems to support this idea since there is no loyalty at the net; leaving a company is as easy as clicking link.

However, some researchers and journalists like [16, 17] see another perspective: The competition is hard and it is mainly based on price. It costs much get new customers; a better strategy is keeping the customers you already have. Establishing common values and relationships with the present customers is considered much more important than finding new ones. The advertisements make people suspicious but messages from people they know could make them try a new vendor. We call this the new economy and it is much more based on sustainability than on the old ones. We think this is much more praiseworthy than the capitalistic version. However, the technical development might seemingly point at a different direction. Taking into account the quotation from Rob Kling on the HCC7 homepage, we realise that we are facing a new social reality and this must create a new vision of the technology.

5   Credo

Economy and industry as a whole

Since IT is dependent on many things, we start in macro scale. We believe there is a growing tendency to outsource, not only IT but as much other functions as possible. For the manufacturing industry, we see a system of suppliers in several tiers. The automotive industry is a good example. Instead of yesterday's gigantic car factories, we see today a set of suppliers design and deliver a specific module of the car according to certain specifications. What counts is the ability to deliver, both in time and in the desired quality. This is a step towards the network economy described in [18-20].

The focus is on the business process, not on the single company. This strategy requires a genuine new way of doing business, we see a need for trust, loyalty and sharing of value [16, 21, 22] instead of the usual increase of benefit.

In Sweden, we see a good economical growth, but we see a decrease in the number of employees due to efficient production. We think this is a worldwide trend, which will have severe effects on the labour market, in addition to creating political instability and conflicts between countries. An example is the upcoming budget negotiation in the EU where the new members expect huge contributions whereas the old members (such as France and Great Britain) are not willing to give up their privileges.

We also believe the current economical focus on short time benefits must be replaced with more sustainable reasoning. Within the manufacturing industry we se a growing focus on sustainability and this must sooner or later, unfortunately probably later, put the focus on more long-term issues.

Implications for information systems

We have already indicated that about 95% of the time used in industry is for information processing. We have talked to industrial workers about this situation such as [15], but we have to admit, we have no hard scientific evidence. However, further rationalisation is more likely to be due to better information processing than better production. It is true that certain areas of production such as maintenance require more attention, which will help decrease production costs. However, it is our firm believe that information processing, that is, providing the right information to the right person at the right time at the right place in the right format with the right content and to the right cost [23] is the key to survival of the western industry!

The industry of today must be extremely flexible and able to produce small series with high quality and short lead-time. The business process is almost tailor-made for every transaction and covers many organisations. Having information systems based upon the MIS model with its roots in the 1960s is no longer possible. Neither is it possible to develop new systems in the way prescribed in systems development models, such as for instance RUP [24-26]. Changes occurs very fast leading to very diverse and varying information requirement. The new service oriented architecture [27-29] is one model for doing this that draws considerable attendance. However, in our mind the ontological aspects are not covered sufficiently [30]. One issue we point at is that information requirements and information needs are not always possible to foresee and the only way to be sure to get it right is letting the users do it themselves [31]. Hence, education of users at the workplace will be a major concern as well as development of suitable and comprehensible tools. In both cases a common language and a mutual and deep understanding of the concepts used is a prerequisite.

The meaning of a certain concept and the knowledge thus achieved is based upon the context at hand. The context definitions so far have been related mainly to environmental and task/activity attribute [32-34]; but that is not enough. Context should be related also to personal and cultural attributes as well. We regarded those three contextual attributes as almost independent, the *context apple model* (Figure 1).

As an example, we will briefly describe a research project of introducing the mobile contextual service in the library settings. Ten library workers participated in this project. The idea was to 'translate' the social context into the content of the mobile service. We realised that it would not be possible to translate the social context into the content of a new service without using participatory approach, since it is not possible to identify personal/cultural attributes without direct user involvement. The other two attributes can to some extend be identified (using sensor technology, cameras, work descriptions etc.) without direct user involvement. In our library settings, the environmental attributes were known since the location and its attributes were not changing while our efforts were mainly focused in identifying the activity/task and personal/cultural context. Based on a survey we were able to identify that most of the time library workers were dealing with visitors, they provided information about the content of the book. This information was confirmed during individual structured interviews as well. This was core information about their activity/task.

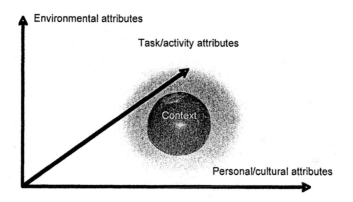

Figure 1 Three attributes of the context, *the context apple model*.

Based on this and the personal/cultural context (users mobility perception and use), we were able to shape the content of new service. The new service was audio book reviews provided through mobile wireless channels. In our evaluation survey, seven subjects answered that the service would be useful but they would need more time to explore it. One subject answered that yes, it is completely useful and this service should be introduced already next year. Another subject answered that maybe the service might be useful, but it will be difficult to find time and resources to produce the content. The important thing to mention is that none of the subjects answered that the service cannot be useful at all for them even if they had that answer as a possible choice. The explanation was that the users understood the service and identified it as a proposal from them.

Based on this experience we realised that for defining the social context a user centred approach must be used. This is mainly because social context is both complex and unique in the same time, since it contains personal/cultural attributes. These are genuinely human attributes and can be identified only with direct user involvement. The service that has content that correspond to the user social context has higher usability and acceptance. This is mainly due to service that is more related and familiar to user social context and due to the user perception of new service and their contribution as well. This was proven correct with the users in our trail project since they have very well accepted the new service.

Therefore, the role of social informatics can be in grasping and mapping the user social context to service content. This process is bidirectional way of learning. We learn from users to understand their social context and users learn from us regarding the service that has content based on their social context.

New informatics domain

Today, we no longer perform in-house systems development as performed in the 1970s and the 1980s. The reason is simple. It costs too much (Figure 2).

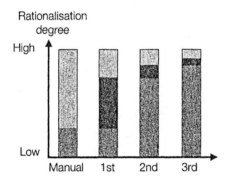

Figure 2 Increase of rationalisation potential for different systems generations [35]

When the first generation of computer-based information systems came into use, the rationalisation potential was very high since the starting point followed manual routines. The tasks that were rationalised were also rather easy because 80% of the transactions required 20% of effort. However, when the next generation became involved, the situation was very different. Now the starting point was a high degree of rationalisation so the possible benefit was considerably less. Furthermore, the tasks were trickier and thus the systems development cost was higher. Seen from an economic point of view, it is easy to understand why systems from the 1980s still are working.

Today, standard systems are used, but they are configured to suite the specific company. The configuration is often cumbersome, tricky, difficult to do, and it takes a long time. SAP/R3 is a well-known application for the complexity of the configuration. However, the drawback occurs when a new release of the standard system becomes available; then the configuration must be done again. The result is the same: IT systems become great hinders for change and they conserve the current work praxis.

The solution to this problem is dividing the BIG systems in smaller, easier to use, understand, and maintain. The needed exchange of information in the network society is done with help of Web Services and the whole system is build in a service oriented architecture (SOA), [29]. This architecture is useable for local and even individual systems, provided the users are well enough educated.

However, the network society requires totally new applications and a new way of seeing things [36]. The IT community does not yet identify this in general, but when it is the case, it will be a dramatic change for all IT-processing.

Education

We have already indicated the need for workplace related education, but we think there will much more need for education in many aspects and in many jobs. After all, the education of our workers is the primary competition weapon! However, we also need education to cope with our complex everyday and to maintain the job carrier. Hence, we will see use of IT, in all forms, for education of people; we will see a society full of applications such as communities, games, chats, and virtual reality. Since we see a growing specialisation of companies, this will also be the case for the business systems. Today we talk about e-health, e-care, e-government, and e-learning. Tomorrow, there will be many more and many specialised areas; unfortunately, there is no education for them.

Finally, we believe that this entire phenomenon and many other yet unknown circumstances will lead to an increased discussion of IT and its use and its impact on society. The area of IT in society will become an actual consideration!

6   Sanctus

Industry

Our chance to survive in the current western culture is to lower the production cost, increase the quality, and shorten the delivery time with increased reliability. Besides the production must be more environmental friendly. This seemingly impossible equation is possible due to more efficient and reliable production processes, especially the information processing part. Thus, we can do a flexible production in short series, provided the machinery does not break down. Good maintenance is also a part of the total quality and many will overlook it.

Economy

We need genuinely new informatics paradigms adapted to the network economy. This requires a massive re-education of all workers, both white and blue collar in order to be able to take advantage of the IT-technologies advantages. It requires also a de-learning with subsequent re-learning of the IT-experts in order to make them think more according to business needs and less according to technical possibilities. One economical advantage, which the manufacturing industry already is aware of, is the fact that sustainable production pays off, not only in reduced environmental load but also in tax reduction and selling advantages. The new economy is based upon reliability and trust, manifested in the relation management [16]. They also say that the most valuable asset of the company is its knowledge. An interesting thing is that sharing of knowledge increase it, thus the company should be as open as possible. For conventional economic thinking, this is ridiculous; nevertheless, in the light of trust and reliability, it does make perfect sense.

Critical resources

To sum it all up: Reliable and sustainable production, availability of reliable information, trust, and flexibility are the means for us to survive in this new economy. How shall we implement it?

7   Benedictus

We suggest three different activities that are under implementation in our network. In order to improve industrial production, we must create a research centre dealing with sustainable production and information availability and reliability. Issues addressed by the institute include:
- Decrease information processing time in a supply chain
- Develop IT-systems for total quality maintenance
- Develop sustainable economy models for the network society
- Identify areas where the region industry can compete
- Develop a holistic and sustainable model of production in a local region

The centre is supposed to operate at regional basis and in cooperation with the industries in that region. The specific region we have in mind is southern part of Sweden. This network provides us with companies[1] willing to join research activities. This is necessary in order to achieve research foundlings from EU or government. With a set of well-known and trusted collaboration partners the base for writing research applications is achieved.

Since companies require very broad competence due to the diversity of their problems, the centre must have access to very broad competence. We can secure this by the second activity: Establishment of a nationwide competence network for research and research education. Here we establish common learning activities with shared teachers and partly shared students. Thus, the researchers know what is going on in the different universities and can draw upon that competence when needed. We also have a greater body of researchers and smart students who can do specific parts of the work. This is supposed to be carried out on mutual base; there is no extra payment and no extra administration.

Now we have companies and we have competence; only the projects are lacking. The process to reformulate company problems is to engage in researchable questions within available competence; we do this in the project formulation phase. We carry this out in another 'centre for project management and innovations', which in fact is

---

1 'Companies' includes both private and public organisations.

organised as a course in project formulation and development. During the course the participants (which can be students or researchers) formulates projects and tries to get them founded. In some cases, it will succeed. There is an example from Copenhagen business school, which resulted in nine million DKK!

In doing all three activities, we do hope for beneficiation through many interesting and challenging research projects!

8   Exodus

As well as an introitus, we have an exodus – a departure when the community leaves the church. Here it will be close to a combined conclusion and summary. We have drawn a scenario where the future for the western industry is not so very bright, but we have indicated some areas and some ways of doing things where the there might be a brighter future. As far as we can see, taking the use situation into account, focus on the content and the specific, customise instead of standardise is the key success factors. In other words, replace traditional informatics with social informatics!

References

1. Churchman, C., W, *Design of inquiring systems*. 1971, New York: Basic Books.
2. Nurminen, M.I., *People or computers: three ways of looking at information systems*. 1988, Lund, Bromley: Studentlitteratur, Chartwell-Bratt. 202.
3. Ivanov, K., *Quality-control of information: on the concept of accuracy of information in data-banks and in management information systems*. 1972, Stockholm, [Ca 250] bl. (var. pag.).
4. Bergo, O.T., K. Nygaard, and V. bedriftsklubb, *En €vurdering av styrings- og informasjonssystemeet KVPOL*. Forskningsrapport fra Norsk Jern- og Metallarbeiderforbunds forskningsprosjekt Nr. 4. 1974, Oslo: Tiden Norsk Forlag. 121 s.
5. Kyng, M. and L. Mathiassen, *Computers and design in context*. 1997, Cambridge: MIT Press. xvii, 418 p.
6. Ehn, P., *Work-oriented design of computer artifacts*. 1988, Umeå,. 492 (Ca 250 bl.);.
7. Tricker, R.I. and R. Boland, *Management information and control systems*. 2nd ed ed. 1982, Chichester: Wiley. xi, 346 s.
8. Kyng, M., G. Bjerknes, and P. Ehn, *Computers and democracy: A Scandinavian challenge*. 1987, Aldershot: Avebury. 434.
9. Kling, R., *The Organizational Context of User-Centered Software Designs*. MIS Quarterly, 1977. **Vol. 1**(Dec77 Issue 4): p. p41, 12p.
10. Greenbaum, J.M., *In the name of efficiency : management theory and shopfloor practice in data-processing work*. 1979, Philadelphia: Temple Univ. Press. xi, 210.
11. Kling, R., *Computerization and controversy*. 2. ed. 1996, San Diego: Academic Press.
12. Mumford, E., *Values, technology and work*. Sijthoff & Noordhoff series on information systems 3. 1981, The Hague: Nijhoff. x, 318 s.
13. Mumford, E. and D. Henshall, *Designing participatively*. Repr. ed. 1983, [Manchester]: Manchester Business School. x,191 s.
14. Mumford, E., *Research methods in information systems*. 1985, Amsterdam: North-Holland. xii, 320 s.
15. Kallin, S., *Meeting with the information logistics group*. 2000: Ljungby.

16. Keen, P.G.W., *Relationships – The Electronic Commerce Imperative*, in *Information Technology and the Future Enterprise,*, d.G. Dickson G W, Editor. 2001, Prentice-Hall Inc.

17. Kelly, K., *New Rules for the New Economy – 10 ways the network economy is changing everything.* 1998, London: Fourth Estate Limited.

18. Castells, M., *The Information Age. Economy, Society and Culture, Volume I: The Rise of the Network Society.* 1996, Oxford.

19. Castells, M., *The Information Age. Economy, Society and Culture, Volume II: The Power of Identity.* 1997, Oxford.

20. Castells, M., *The Information Age. Economy, Society and Culture, Volume III: End of Millennium.* 1998, Oxford.

21. Habermas, J., *The Theory of Communicative Action. Vol I: Reason and Rationalization of Society.* 1984, London.

22. Habermas, J., *The Theory of Communicative Action. Vol II: The Critique of Functionalist Reason.* 1988, London.

23. Karlsson, C., P. Flensburg, and S.F. H©\0153rte, *Knowledge spillovers and knowledge management. edited by Charlie Karlsson, Per Flensburg, Sven-©\FFFDke H©\0153rte.* 2004, Cheltenham: Edward Elgar. x, 510 p. ; ill.

24. Bergström, S. and L. Råberg, *Adopting the rational unified process : success with the RUP.* Object technology series. 2004, Boston, Mass.; London: Addison-Wesley. xxiii, 245 p.

25. Pollice, G., *Software development for small teams: a RUP-centric approach.* Addison-Wesley object technology series. 2004, Boston, Mass.; London: Addison-Wesley; 2003. xxiii, 272 p.

26. Kroll, P. and P. Kruchten, *The rational unified process made easy : a practitioner's guide to the RUP.* Addison-Wesley object technology series. 2003, Boston, Mass. ; London: Addison-Wesley. xxxv, 416 p.

27. Krafzig, D., K. Banke, and D. Slama, *Enterprise SOA : service-oriented architecture best practices.* 2005, Indianapolis, IN: Prentice Hall Professional Technical Reference. xxvi, 382 p.

28. Newcomer, E. and G. Lomow, *Understanding SOA with Web services.* Independent technology guides. 2005, Upper Saddle River, NJ ; London: Addison-Wesley. xxxii, 444 p.

29. MacKenzie C M, et al. *Reference Model for Service Oriented Architectures Working Draft 10, 15 November 2005.* 2005 [cited 2005 Dec 5].

30. Flensburg, P. and M. Milrad. *On the Scandinavian Approach in the Network Economy – Some Reflections on the Importance of Content and Context.* in *26th Information Systems Research Seminar in Scandinavia.* 2003. Haikko Manor, Finland, August 9-12 2003.

31. Flensburg, P., *Personlig databehandling – Introduktion, konsekvenser, möjligheter (PhD thesis).* Lund Studies in Information and Computer Sciences, no 5. 1986, Lund: Studentlitteratur.

32. Park H and Lee J. *A framework of context-awareness for ubiquitous computing middlewares.* 2005: IEEE.

33. Zhang D, Chin C, and Gurusamy M. *Supporting Context-Aware Mobile Service Adaptation with Scalable Context Discovery Platform.* . 2005.

34. Raverdy P and Issarny V. *Context-Aware Service Discovery in Heterogeneous Networks* . 2005: IEEE.

35. Flensburg, P. and S. Friis, *Mänskligare datasystem – Utveckling, användning och principer (in Swedish).* 1999, Lund: Studentlitteratur.

36. Flensburg, P. Using information systems for collaboration in a network society. in IRIS 25. 2002. Bautahøj, Denmark.

PART 2 – SOCIAL INFORMATICS: UBIQUITY? AN INFORMATION SOCIETY FOR ALL?

Ethics and Culture

The Ethics of e-Medicine

Göran Collste

Centre for Applied Ethics, Linköping University, Sweden,

gorco@cte.org.liu.se,

http://www.liu.se/cte/organisation/Goran_Collste.PDF

Abstract. 'E-medicine', i.e. the possibilities for patients to have access to medical information and medical consultation at Internet raises new ethical issues. In this paper e-medicine is discussed in terms of how it will affect the patient-doctor-relation, patient autonomy and the moral and professional responsibility of doctors.

Keywords: e-Medicine, ethics, Internet, patient-doctor relation, autonomy, responsibility.

1 Introduction

Since many years information and communication technology is used in health care. However, lately one can notice an accelerated interest for different kinds of ICT-applications. Internet is more and more used for providing medical information, medical consultation and drug prescriptions. Medical information can be accessed from an increasing number of medical information sites, patients can consult doctors on line, patients can get access to their medical record through Internet and drugs can be bought on line. Hence, health care is going through a transformation due to different applications of e-medicine. ICT can in different ways enhance the practice of health care. However, it is necessary to examine the application in the light of the ethical values of health care. As Pellegrino and Thomasma argue "Medicine is at all levels a moral enterprise where 'moral enterprise' means action involving values" [Pellegrino and Thomasma, 1981, p.112]. The new technologies must be instrumental in achieving the goals and values of health care and they must fit into health care practices.

When a patient uses Internet as a source of information about a disease, medicines or ways of treatment, it is an example of, what has been called, 'do-it-yourself healthcare.' Consultation via the Internet is a way for those with sufficient economic resources to obtain a second opinion, yes, even a second doctor. There are

Please use the following format when citing this chapter:

Collste, G., 2006, in IFIP International Federation for Information Processing, Volume 223, Social Informatics: An Information Society for All? In Remembrance of Rob Kling, eds. Berleur, J., Numinen, M. I., Impagliazzo, J., (Boston: Springer), pp. 101–109.

many possible reasons for this demand: the patient may have lost confidence in her ordinary doctor, she has heard of some specialist in the particular disease she is suffering from, she finds herself in a desperate situation, etc. E-medicine is also a potential asset for health care in poor countries with limited health care resources.

The number of health sites on Internet is increasing. There are between 15,000 and 100,000 health-related sites in Great Britain and they have been visited by approximately 30 million people. [Parker and Gray, 2001]. A Swedish survey showed that of those who accessed Internet, about 20% had been looking for health-related information. [Garpenby and Husberg, 2000]

According to Swedish law, a patient has a right to access his or her medical record. However, in practice it is rare for patients to request to read their records spontaneously. [Ross and Lin, 2003, Sundberg, 2003, Bruzelius, 2004] A system for patient Internet accesses to his or her medical record is presently tried out in Swedish health care. Through a so-called 'patient portal' a patient can have direct access to his or her own medical record. This implies for example that the patient will have access to information about laboratory results before meeting a doctor. The technique used is similar to the technique for Internet banking. I.e. the patient will get a personal certificate with a pin code that secure that no one else will have access to the portal. The patient portal is so far tried out in a trial involving 100 voluntary patients, but will eventually be part of ordinary health care.

2   The Relationship between Doctor and Patient

The possibility to consult a doctor on line will have implications for the patient-doctor relationship. The clinical encounter has for many years been an issue for discussions in medical ethics. The relation between doctor and patient is embedded by values of commitment, trust, privacy, confidentiality and responsibility. One can distinguish between different kinds of relationship like, for example, caring and contractual. In connection to the new possibility of consultation on Internet one can ask what kind of relation will be established between patient and doctor on line. A new doctor-patient relationship is being established, i.e. between the Internet doctor and the patient, and this will also most likely affect the relation between the patient and the general practitioner.

The patient is in a vulnerable situation when his or her health is threatened and the clinical encounter is a means to recovery with the doctor as a mediator. [Pellegrino and Thomasma, 1981] With this bare description of the relationship between doctor and patient as a starting-point, I will outline the clinical interaction in different models, each focusing on specific aspects of the encounter. Which of the models resembles the relationship between the Internet doctor and the patient?

According to the engineering-model, the patient is an object for treatment, in relevant aspects similar to a broken car taken to the garage for repair. In the engineering-model of a clinical encounter, the doctor collects information in order to make a diagnosis and a decision on therapy. The information needed is, for instance, data on temperature, blood pressure etc. This model fits Tristran Engelhardt's description of "Medical care from passing strangers." [Engelhardt, 1986]

Secondly, the clinical interaction may also, in accordance with Pellegrino and Thomasma, be modelled as a 'healing relationship' [Pellegrino and Thomasma, 1981]. Then, it is seen as an encounter between two persons, the doctor and the patient, which serves the purpose to achieve a mutual understanding, or, in the words of Martin Buber, an 'I/Thou relationship' [Buber, 1923]. This model pays attention to the fact that in many cases a disease is not only a threat to the health of the patient but also to her existential balance.

Thirdly, the relationship can also be modelled as one of trust or fidelity. [Ramsey, 1970]. Trust is based on two pillars, competence and sympathy. The patient can trust the doctor knowing that he/she is competent and knowing that he/she cares. The latter pillar highlights the moral aspects of the clinical encounter. The doctor cares about the patient and is obliged to do his/her best.

These models stress different aspects of the relationship between doctor and patient. They rather complete than exclude one another. The engineering model with its emphasis on scientific and technical relevance is essential for good treatment but the hermeneutic approach of the 'healing relationship' is needed to allow the doctor to make the right decision and to involve the patient in the treatment. In real life the doctor-patient relationship will more or less resemble any of these models.

How will medical care and the relation between doctor and patient be affected by Internet consultation? With which model does it correspond? There are now two parallel patient doctor relationships established, on the one hand between the patient and the GP and on the other hand between the patient and the Internet doctor. Firstly, one can assume that Internet consultation tends to resemble the engineering-model rather than a healing relationship. Consultation is made at a distance and based on raw data, at least as long as the technical possibilities for a web-based dialogue between doctor and patient are limited. However, this may change as a consequence of the development of interactive media communication. Still, one may doubt whether this kind of mediated form of communication, ever will be a valid substitute for a person-to-person dialogue. Similarly, one can argue that the trust model requires a personal encounter. If, however, trust is based on competence rather than care, it is possible that even Internet consultation could be of this kind. This, of course, presupposes that the Internet doctor is highly competent.

3   e-Medicine and Patient Autonomy

The principle of autonomy has become increasingly important in modern health care. The principle implies that anyone who is affected by a decision should be able to influence it and if a decision only concerns one individual, he/she should decide for him/herself. When applied to health care, the principle implies that the patient should be empowered to play a more active role in his/her own care. One-way to do this is that the patient has the opportunity to give informed consent to the decisions that concern her own treatment.

The principle of autonomy, or, the derived principle of informed consent, depends on some conditions. One is that there are alternatives available in the decision-making situation, another that the patient is competent and a third that the patient has access to relevant information.

Only in situations where patients have a choice is it meaningful to speak of patient autonomy. Further, in order to be able to make an autonomous decision the patient must be competent. Competence implies an ability to understand and process information and to form a decision on the basis of the information. The information provided must be reliable and relevant.

What implications will access to medical consultation and information via Internet have for patient autonomy? One could argue that Internet would provide the patient with more information and, thus, enhance his/her autonomy. Access to an Internet doctor gives the patient a choice of a second opinion and access to medical information via Internet gives him/her access to new sources of information. However, in reality it is not as simple as that. When the patient contacts a doctor via Internet, how can she judge the quality of the doctor? Is it a competent doctor or just a quack?

A similar problem is connected to medical information via Internet. One can, at present, find a lot of websites for any disease. Presumably, these websites are normally trustworthy and contain reliable information. But this is not always the case. A study by American gastroenterologists found that one in ten of the health-related sites in the field offered unproven treatments. [Barkham, 2000] Pharmaceutical companies are responsible for some medical sites. Although they are presumably of a high standard, they are biased for commercial reasons. Thus, the patient will have problems distinguishing between reliable and less reliable sites. As a consequence, a patient looking for information about his/her disease and possible ways of treatment runs the risk of being misinformed. [Silberg, et al, 1997] Besides, all the problems connected to the transfer of information from health care provider to patient in ordinary health care will be present in e-medicine in more aggravated forms: Is the information provided in an understandable language? Is it adjusted to the ability of the patient to process the information? Does the patient really understand the prescription?

Beauchamp and Childress distinguish between three standards of disclosure of information: professional standard, the reasonable person standard and the subjective standard [Beauchamp and Childress, 2001]. Medical websites that disclose information for professionals provide new sources of information for doctors, but are of limited value for the ordinary patient. The sites for ordinary patients are usually written in a way that is understandable to a 'normal' reader. These sites can provide the patient with valuable information, helpful for anyone who wants to know more about a disease. Finally, the subjective standard takes the informational needs of the specific patient into consideration. This standard requires an interactive site, which provides the patient with opportunities to question the information presented. Thus, it seems that medical information via Internet can be a valuable source for patients wanting to learn more about their disease, provided that there are means to discern which sources are reliable. In this way, Internet will facilitate the fulfilment of the principle of patient autonomy in health care.

4   Will the Patient Portal Enhance Patient Autonomy?

Patient electronic access to the medical record might also facilitate patient autonomy in health care. However, more information does not necessarily make patients better informed. For a patient to be able to handle information and use it in a constructive way, information provided must be comprehended and relevant. For sure, through access to the medical record the patient will have access to much information but – one may ask - has he/she tools to handle it? If not, the information will not help in empowering the patient, but instead leave the patient confused and insecure. Some studies of non-electronic patient access to medical records confirm that patients commonly have difficulties in understanding parts of their records [Ross and Lin, 2003].

There is so far little empirical evidence of how electronic patient access to the medical records will influence autonomy. However, the evidence from other forms of patient access is predominantly positive. The majority of patients in several studies reported that reading their records educated them about their medical condition. Further, these studies do not confirm that the access generated anxiety or concern among the patients. Especially seems the access of obstetric patients to their records have had a positive effect on their sense of autonomy and self-efficacy [Ross and Lin 2003]. But, in contrast to the patient portal this access was mediated by a care –giver, who could explain the content and answer questions.

As a consequence of the introduction of patient portals, the notes in the medical record should rather be of a 'reasonable person standard', i.e. understandable for an 'average' patient, than of a 'professional practice standard', i.e. understandable for doctors only [Beauchamp and Childress, 2001]. However, this may also imply that the doctors write their notes with this restriction in mind and that some important information that requires to be written in a professional and technical language will be left out.

Then, is it a good idea to give the patient full access to his/her medical record? The record might contain information about the patient that is necessary for the doctor to record, but that can be harmful for the patient to read. For example, a doctor may have to record that a patient is untalented and therefore will not be expected to take his or her medicine as prescribed, or that battering may have caused some wounds on a child's body etc. The fact that the doctor has to record even unfavourable facts about patients in their best interest can be seen as a kind of weak paternalism. Thus, in cases like these what is in the best interests of the patient may come into conflict with the patient's right to have a full access to his or her own medical record.

Thus, there are two problems with giving the patient direct access to his/her medical record. It may lead to a less precise way of expressing relevant medical information and it may contain for the patient harmful information. A possible solution to these problems is that the information given to the patient is filtered. However, this would be very costly and also very difficult to implement. It would also lay a too heavy burden on the 'filterer' who is to decide what information that could pass through and according to what standard of language.

5   Consultation via Internet and the Principle of Responsibility

How will medical consultation via Internet influence responsibility in health care? Before discussing this question I will outline a bare meaning of the concept of responsibility.

We say that some person P is responsible for the outcome O of an action A, when P has intentionally done A in order to achieve O. P who is responsible must be prepared to answer questions like: Why did you do A? Why did you want O? As a result of being responsible, if O is a bad outcome, this is a reason to blame or punish P and, vice versa, if the outcome is good this is a reason to praise P. [Lucas, 1995]

However, in order to hold a person responsible, there are some conditions that have to be fulfilled. If the outcome, due to some factors that P reasonably could not foresee, is different from what P intended, say O1 instead of O, P is not responsible for O1. However, if P acts without bothering to get the necessary information, P is responsible for O1, if O1 could have been foreseen, had P bothered to inform him/herself sufficiently? Neither is it reasonable to say that P is responsible for O, if O is caused by an action that P was forced to do.

The concept 'responsibility' is used both in moral and legal senses. The main differences are the criteria for evaluating the outcome and the sanctions following a blameworthy action. In law, a sovereign legislator formally decides the criteria for evaluation and sanctions. In morality, on the other hand, the social ethos provides the criteria for evaluation and sanctions.

There is also a third usage of responsibility, referring to professional practice. Professional responsibility is a kind of responsibility that combines traits of legal and of moral responsibility. The criteria for evaluation are basically moral, outlined in professional ethical codes. However, professional responsibility is similar to legal responsibility when the professional association has decided on some sanction, e.g. expulsion from the profession, for those who do not comply with the professional moral duties.

Let us now apply the concept of responsibility to medical practice. P, the doctor, recommends A, for instance medication or surgery, in order to achieve O, i.e. the restoration of a patient's health. The doctor is responsible for medical treatment. This means that the doctor with the best intentions, and to the best of knowledge, makes a decision on treatment and prescription of medicine. If something goes wrong, the doctor will be questioned; 'Why did you recommend A?'

From the point of view of both moral and legal responsibility there are problems connected to therapy at distance via Internet. Firstly, the patient information provided might be insufficient. This is obviously the fact if the diagnosis is based solely on the patient's own story. If the Internet doctor also has access to the patient's records, there is a better basis for diagnosis and therapy. However, the doctor is still lacking the information otherwise received through a personal encounter face to face with a patient, as well as information obtained through a physical examination of the patient's body. Secondly, while lacking a personal encounter, the Internet doctor is less confident than a regular GP that the patient will follow the recommendations. The possibility of misunderstanding increases the risk that the patient will take the wrong drug or the wrong dosage. Taken together, these factors increase the risk of maltreatment. But it is a risk that the Internet doctor ought to be conscious about and, thus, he/she is morally responsible for the possible maltreatment.

When we ask about the Internet doctor's legal responsibility in the case of maltreatment we are entering precarious ground. Assuming that the Internet doctor is licensed as a doctor, principles for advisory services should be applied. However, one has to establish in what country the consultation is taking place. Is it in the country of the patient, of the doctor or somewhere between, in cyberspace perhaps? The answer is also decisive for the question: which law that should be applied? Thus, if, say, it can be decided that the consultant is an American citizen, a summons has to be issued against him/her in an American court. Further, if maltreatment leads to injury and the patient needs money for medical treatment, in what country, if any, will the insurance be paid? Possibly, even the operator of the server can be legally responsible in cases of medical service provided by non-professional consultants.

Is it possible to apply codes of professional responsibility in the case of maltreatment? If the Internet doctor is a member of the World Medical Association, he/she will be subject to the professional code of the association. This would imply that the professional criteria for evaluation and the sanctions for non-compliance would be applied, irrespective of the nationality of the doctor. This is an example of the advantage of an international professional association when dealing with a global technological system.

6   What is the Difference?

The possibility to consult doctors on Internet is of recent date. But, does the Internet doctor represent anything new? Have not people always consulted other doctors than their regular ones, for instance a friend or a radio doctor? And what is the difference between using Internet as a source of information and other media like medical handbooks and encyclopaedias?

There are similarities as well as differences between consulting a friend who is a doctor and an Internet doctor. One similarity is that the patient consults a second doctor and, as a consequence, this doctor becomes involved. A difference is that one important reason to seek help from a friend, i.e. the emotional component of trust, is lacking in the case of the Internet doctor. And this difference is important. You can count on the friend caring.

There are also similarities between a radio doctor and a doctor's question and answers column in a magazine on the one hand and the Internet doctor on the other. In all cases a sick or worried person gets advice concerning his/her particular worries. And this advice is given without the component of a personal emotional involvement. One difference, however, is that while the Internet doctor engages in a particular consultation, the radio or magazine doctor usually does not establish a personal doctor to patient interaction. Instead, he/she answers the particular questions in a general way so that anyone interested can take advantage of the recommendation.

There are some obvious similarities between Internet as a source of medical information and medical handbooks. Both will provide the reader with information about diseases. An advantage with an Internet site is that it can continuously be updated. A possible difference is, as we have noticed, that it is more difficult to control the reliability of the Internet site, i.e. to distinguish a reliable source from a bluff.

7   A Code of Conduct

So far, there seems to be a lack of trust among the public in e-medicine. A Swedish survey showed that in a scale from 1 to 7, where 1 represents 'no trust' and 7 represents 'great trust', the GP rates 6, medical handbooks 4 and the Internet 2,5. [Garpenberg and Husberg, 2000]

Organisations involved in e-medicine have, in order to counteract the lack of trust among the public, formulated a code of conduct. The code contains eight principles referring to trust, reliability and transparency. The first principle states:

"Any medical or health advice provided and hosted on this site will be given only by medically trained and qualified professionals unless a clear statement is made that a piece of advice offered is from a non-medically qualified individual or organisation."

The fourth principle states:

"Where appropriate, information contained on this site will be supported by clear references to source data..." Other principles refer to confidentiality, fairness and transparency concerning both authorship and sponsorship. [Health on the Net]

8   Conclusion

The continued evolution of e-medicine is a probable prospect for the future. This development has some obvious advantages. It will provide an increased access to doctor's consultation and it will make medical information more accessible. E-medicine will in different ways change the conditions for health care and the relationship between doctor and patient. As argued in this paper, there is a need to reconsider the implementation of principles of medical ethics in the light of this development. To meet this new situation, health care authorities should, in line with the maxim 'to guide rather than to guard', inform their patients about the reliable information sites. Through peer reviews, licensing or other ways of authorisation, it should be possible to identify those sites that are reliable. A digital signature can then mark these. Some kind of authorisation is also needed in order to distinguish professional Internet doctors and medical information sites from non-professional ones. The Code of Conduct established by the Health on the Net Foundation is a step in this direction.

The patient portal seems to be problematic from an ethical point of view. Even though it will provide patients with updated information about their health status, it may lead to impairment of the medical record and it may even be harmful for the patient. Hence, the patient portal is questionable both with reference to the principle of beneficence and the principle of non-malfeasance.

References

Barkham P. Is the net healthy for doctors? *The Guardian Online* 2000 Jun 8: 2.

Beauchamp, T. and Childress, J. *Principles of Biomedical Ethics*, (Oxford, Oxford University Press, 2001).

Bruzelius, M, Sammanfattning och slutsatser. Patientportalen. SKILL Studentkompetens AB, (unpublished) Linköping 2004.

Buber, M., *Ich und Du*, (Leipzig, Insel, 1923).

Engelhardt, T, *The Foundations of Bioethics*, (New York: Oxford University Press, 1986).

Garpenby, P & Hisberg, M, 2000, Hälsoinformation idag och imorgon, CMT Rapport 2000:3, Linköpings universitet, Linköping (unpublished)

Health on the Net Foundation Code of Conduct, [http://www.hon.ch/HONcode/Conduct.html] 2006-03-09

Lucas, J R, *Responsibility*, (Oxford: Clarendon Press, 1995)

Parker, M & Muir Gray, J A, What is the role of clinical ethics support in the era of e-medicine?, *Journal of Medical Ethics*, 2001; 27, suppl I:i, pp 33-35

Pellegrino, E.D., Thomasma, D.C. *A Philosophical Basis of Medical Practice*, (New York, Oxford University Press, 1981), p.112

Ramsey, P, *The Patient as Person. Explorations in Medical Ethics*, (New Haven: Yale University Press, 1970).

Ross, S.E. and Lin, C-T., The Effects of Promoting Patient Access to Medical Records: A Review. *Journal of the American Medical Informatics Association*, Vol 10, Nr 2, 2003.

Silberg, W M, Lundberg, G D, Musacchio, R A, , Assessing, Controlling, and Assuring the Quality of Medical Information on the Internet, *Journal of American Medical Association*, 277:1244-1245, 1997

Sundberg, A, Nulägesbeskrivning av attityder till patientportalen 2003, Landstinget i Östergötland, (unpublished), 2003.

Digital Child Pornography: Reflections on the Need for a Critical IS Research Agenda

Marie Eneman
Informatics, University of Göteborg, Sweden.
eneman@informatik.gu.se

Abstract. The purpose of this paper is to argue for the need for systematic empirical information systems research within the field of digital child pornography. This research area is today primarily driven by non-technical disciplines. This paper argues that without the IS perspective an adequate understanding of the role of ICT, its use and effects for child pornography cannot be obtained. The IS perspective is an important complement to the existing body of research attempting to understand the area of digital child pornography. The paper is based on the argument that the research area of digital child pornography is well suited to the application of critical information systems research.

Keywords: digital child pornography, IS perspective, critical information systems research

1   Introduction

The introduction of information and communication technologies (ICT) in everyday usage has greatly increased the problem of child pornography [1, 2]. Child pornography is an emotive topic, where public discourses tend to be dominated by subjective opinions and moral positions rather than rationale debates based on empirical findings [3].

Research disciplines such as law [4, 5, 6, 7] and psychology [8, 9, 10] have been early to explore the connection between ICT and child pornography. In comparison, the information systems (IS) discipline has been slow to recognise the key role it has to play in the study of child pornography [1]. The purpose of this paper is to argue for the need for systematic empirically based IS research within the field of digital child pornography. The focus of IS research is ICT, its use and effects [11, 12] while the focus of other disciplines is to respond to their own questions. Therefore, the

Please use the following format when citing this chapter:

Eneman, M., 2006, in IFIP International Federation for Information Processing, Volume 223, Social Informatics: An Information Society for All? In Remembrance of Rob Kling, eds. Berleur, J., Numinen, M. I., Impagliazzo, J., (Boston: Springer), pp. 111–121.

results of a legal study on child pornography and ICT will provide valuable insights into the legal situation but will not provide an adequate understanding of the technology effects involved since the non-technical disciplines lack a technical focus and competence. This paper will show that the study of the use of ICT outside the traditional scope of organisations is an important field of endeavour and lies within the field of expertise of the IS discipline. Furthermore this paper argues that digital child pornography is a suitable area in which to apply critical information systems research (CISR).

This paper begins with an overview of CISR. This will be followed by a section, which places child pornography in a wider context, and thereafter follows a section on the effects of ICT on child pornography. This is followed by a section where CISR is applied to the research area. In conclusion the author reviews this paper's contribution to the CISR and digital child pornography research fields.

2   Critical Information Systems Research

Within IS research the discussion on the widespread dissemination of ICT in society has mainly focused upon the benefits involved in ICT usage [13, 14]. This simplified approach tends to omit the fact that the technology is not one-sided and that the dissemination of any technology brings with it both pros and cons [15]. This paper will give examples of how well established uses of ICT are being used for harmful purposes, such as digital child pornography. This follows Wajcman's [13] argument that despite efforts to inscribe users and uses in technology design we cannot predict the future uses of the technology.

CISR can be seen as a reaction to the mainstream IS research which tends to assume that technological innovation is 'inherently desirable' and beneficial to all [16]. In the field of IS, the call to engage in critical research has been explicitly voiced by a growing numbers of researchers [14, 17, 18, 19, 20, 21, 22, 23, 24, 25 26, 27]. The adoption of CISR can also be understood as a rejection of the understanding of technology development within society as being based on solely economic terms [14, 27].

CISR encompasses a wide range of different research subjects, objectives, methods and philosophical starting points. However, these disparate applications of CISR all share a common denominator in their critical perspective [14, 28]. One example of a research agenda within CISR is Social informatics (SI). SI is the study of the social aspects of computers, telecommunications and related technologies [29, 30, 31, 32]. One of the key issues with SI is that it takes the study of ICT beyond organisational boundaries and therefore is able to ensure that IS plays an active part in the study of social phenomena connected with technology, such as digital child pornography [29].

Engaging in CISR entails the study of the research object with the aid of concepts relevant to critical theory, for example domination, power and control, emancipation empowerment etc [28]. In addition to using the relevant concepts the research object should be placed in a wider historical, political, social and economic context [33]. According to Alvesson and Deetz [33] three central elements should be included when conducting critical research, (insight, critique and transformative re-definition).

Insight is the process where the research area is investigated and interpreted. This process includes: how the data should be collected, the collection process, and the interpretation. Insight is achieved by questioning and challenging established assumptions and definitions and by interpreting the non-obvious aspects of the studied phenomenon. The following process (critique) involves the critical analysis of the insights obtained in the previous stage and relates this analysis to wider social and historical processes. The last process (transformative re-definition) is the natural complement to insight and critique. It is, however, the most difficult part of the three elements. The goal is to develop critical knowledge, practical understanding and to offer alternatives to the established dominant assumptions and definitions. The purpose of this developed knowledge is to enable change and through this to contribute to a process of emancipation.

Therefore critical IS researchers are not primarily concerned with the efficiency of technology, but with questioning and challenging established assumptions and definitions regarding the technology, its use and effects in society [14]. The purpose with this approach is to move beyond established assumptions, which dominate the public discourses [34]. Kling et al [34] argue that the public discourses on technology are often both one-sided and simplified 'disconnected discussions'. This disconnected discussion is well represented by the debate of digital child pornography presented by the media. It is often one-sided, inadequate and often lacking in empirical basis [35, 36].

These types of public disconnected discourses create a hinder if the goal is to establish positive social change in relation to ICT use. One way in which such discourses act as hindrances is that they create oversimplified conceptual models [34] of the role of ICT in society. In order to go beyond vague generalisations it is important to be more specific and define what is meant with the term ICT [37]. Orlikowski and Iacono [12] argue that the focus should be on the IT artefact and Walsham [27] argues that the area of use should be presented. Despite the common terminological misuse, ICT is not one homogenous technology. It consists of several different technologies, which have different characteristics, and there are also variations in how different technologies are interpreted and used [11].

One of the difficulties with engaging in critical IS research is that the guidelines for how to conduct critical IS research are scarce and sketchy. Critical IS researchers have focused on defining what it means to be critical, but largely ignored to explicitly define how criticality can be achieved in IS research [16]. McGrath [16] argues that CISR has not yet reached a position where theory and practice of critical research inform each other. CISR, as a field, would benefit if its researchers become more explicit in their approach, especially when carrying out empirical studies.

This paper is part of a larger ongoing research project regarding digital child pornography, where empirical studies are conducted in line with the CISR agenda. One of the difficulties with researching the area of digital child pornography relates to methodology. This is due to the fact that many actions surrounding the phenomenon constitute criminal offences and are, at the same time, considered highly unacceptable in society. Examples of empirical material used within this project are: Swedish court findings concerning child pornography during the period of 1993-2003, Swedish criminal investigation records and in-depth interviews with convicted offenders. The importance of using empirically based data in studying social consequences of ICT has been pointed out by Kling [30].

3   Contextualising Child Pornography

The central idea in critical research is that all social phenomena are historically created and conditioned [38, 39, 40]. Therefore the research object, digital child pornography, will here be placed in a wider historical, political, social and economic context of the research field [41, 42].

Child pornography is not a new phenomenon. Historically, the dissemination and consumption of child pornography was achieved through costly magazines, photographs and videos and therefore child pornography was limited by economic, physical and logistical boundaries [43]. Child pornography has been produced in different forms, using whatever technological media was available at the time [8]. Similar patterns can be seen in the technical developments within the pornography industry. Technological developments and pornography are deeply interconnected with pornography driving technological advancements and new technologies affecting pornography content [44, 45]. The economic context of digital child pornography has not been adequately studied but there is evidence of a growing commercialisation in this area [46].

The term digital child pornography refers to child pornography where ICT has been used as a medium in some form. While legal definitions of child pornography can differ greatly between jurisdictions, it is possible to discern a generally accepted definition of the term. One such generally accepted definition is: representations where a child is engaged, or appears to be engaged, in some kind of sexual act or situation [10]. The content can vary from posing pictures [8] to physical sexual abuse of children [47].

There is some debate as to the adequacy of the term child pornography. Some researchers [47, 48, 8] argue that the term child pornography is unfortunate and misleading as it reduces the gravity of what the material portrays and invites comparisons with adult pornography. Gillespie [48] argues for the use of the terms 'indecent' or 'abusive' images since these terms better describe the material. Notwithstanding this terminological debate, research [1, 8, 49] shows that there is an obvious connection between pornography and child pornography. This connection constitutes an important argument that these phenomena should not be studied as isolated research areas. Child pornography should be placed in the wider pornography context [1, 43]. However, there are obvious and important differences between the two due to the clear asymmetrical power relationship [1, 50] between the adult and the child.

When discussing pornography and/or child pornography one should be aware of the longer ongoing debate concerning pornography versus issues as freedom of expression and censorship [51, 52]. An example of this debate can be found in the Swedish debate, which took place in the beginning of 1990s and concerned the criminalization of the possession of child pornography. This debate was dominated on the rights of the child versus the limitations on constitutional rights of freedom of expression. The possession of child pornography was criminalized in 1999 in Sweden. The current Swedish legal position criminalises the production, distribution and possession of child pornography (Swedish legislation has proven to be inadequate in parts [e.g. 48, 2]).

4 Digital Child Pornography

Child pornography has changed radically since the mid-1990s [46]. The underlying reasons for this change can be explained partly by the effects of the dissemination of ICT and partly by the effects of changes in child pornography laws [2]. This section will illustrate how ICT is being used for child pornography. Following activities will be used as examples: production, distribution, consumption, networking and grooming.

First ICT simplifies the production of child pornography and enables it to be conducted at low cost [8]. By using digital technology, images and films can easily and quickly be produced and stored. The development of ICT has enabled non-technically skilled users to record, store and manipulate images in a way which was previously only available to people with the requisite technical skills and costly equipment [43]. Therefore, today even non-technically skilled users can record their abuse of children and thereafter easily distribute the material through ICT. Secondly ICT offers software tools, which can easily be used to produce so-called morphed images, also called pseudo-photographs. Morphing images entails the use of digital graphics software, to combine two images into one, or to distort pictures [4]. This means that non-pornographic images of real children can be made to appear as child pornography, and child pornographic images of 'virtual' children can be generated [53].

Similarly ICT have affected the volume of material which it is now possible to distribute and consume across networks [1]. The technology offers features to manage large amounts of data easily, rapidly, at low cost and is readily available without a high level of technical knowledge [43].

Computer networks also allow paedophiles to create online communities [54]. The communities function as places where paedophiles share and trade information and material. These communities allow them to meet other paedophiles. Together in the community they can legitimise their interests and establish important contacts. The importance of the legitimising effect can be explained by the fact that it is important for paedophiles to feel that their sexual interests for children are accepted by people around them, and that they feel they obtain social status and support within these environments [8, 55].

Further, ICT have created new ways and conditions for people to establish contacts and to interact with other people [56], including children. A development, which has come in the wake of online communication, is the problem of grooming [7]. Grooming refers to the activity when an adult initiates and establish contacts with a child online with the intention of preparing the child for later physical meeting [57] or with the intention to communicate with the child online to attain sexual gratification (with no intention of arranging physical meetings) [58]. ICT offers features for users to portray themselves to better fit their purpose [59] and, of course, they can retain their anonymity by using pseudonyms. The ability to contact children through ICT also increases the number of children available compared to real life, where geographical limitations and social exposure decrease this availability [7]. Another aspect that facilitates paedophiles in contacting, communicating and interacting with children through ICT is the lack of parental knowledge. Parents often do not know what their children are actually doing when spending time online [60].

5   Digital Child Pornography and CISR

The approach taken in this work follows the eloquent motivation posited by Walsham [61]: "To simplify, a critical stance is focused on what is wrong with the world rather than what is right. It tends to focus on issues such as asymmetries of power, alienation, disadvantaged groups or structural inequity." The role of the critical researcher within this study is to, through research, lay the foundations for a more open, well founded societal debate on digital child pornography. This is best achieved by providing alternatives to the dominant understanding within society. [33]. In this section the paper will discuss the three elements of critical research (insight, critique, transformative re-definition) [33] in relation to digital child pornography.

Insight

This stage concerns itself with the collection and interpretation of data. The goal is to bring about a questioning of established assumptions of digital child pornography. In the previous section certain digital child pornography activities were highlighted with the intention to show how technology is being used.

The identified activities exemplified above (production, distribution, consumption, networking and grooming) have emerged from the empirical data [8, 2]. By studying these activities, through the interpretation of the empirical data, the following insights have been reached. They are based upon a technological focus i.e. the empirical data is studied to increase our understanding of the use of technology (which activities and which ICT has been used). By employing this focus the researcher avoids the practices of black-boxing technology [37] or viewing technology as a neutral, autonomous tool [62].

Among the insights identified in this paper are: child pornography is a serious social problem, which has been made worse with the advent of digital technology. Despite the important role of technology within this area the IS discipline has been slow to recognise this as an important research area. Research within this area has been driven by non-technical disciplines (e.g. law, psychology). The public discourse on this topic is seldom based in adequate empirical research. One of the difficulties within this field is the access to empirical data since the acts are criminalised in most western countries and often viewed as socially unacceptable.

Critique

The next stage is the critique of the insights by placing them in a wider context [41]. Prior to this it is important to reflect upon the empirical sources, which are the basis of the insights [14]. When studying digital child pornography one of the sources of material is to be found in court findings and criminal investigation records. It is important to be critically aware of the consequences of the choices of using this material [33]. This material is produced in a specific context and for a specific purpose. The consequences of this are that the role of technology is not the focus of the material, which means that the researcher must attempt to understand what is not obvious in the material [33]. To counteract the bias of the material interviews with convicted paedophiles can be carried out. Even in this case the researcher must be aware that the topic of the interview is a sensitive subject. Despite these limitations in the empirical data the material provides a rich source of information about the use of technology in the child pornography context.

Alvesson and Skoldberg [63] argue that there is a natural tendency to interpret existing social reality from a taken-for-granted perspective and that this approach must be counteracted. One approach to developing a dialectic understanding of technology is by problematizing the effects of ICT [41]. The use of ICT as a medium for child pornography should not simply be seen as an additional channel of communication: the harnessing of digital technologies in relation to child pornography has changed the traditional problem, creating a new, more serious, situation [44]. This paper adopts the perspective that ICT is not a neutral tool [62] and that it poses qualitative changes to child pornography [2].

This paper has shown that allowing the non-technical research disciplines to drive this field is an inadequate approach in developing a well-rounded understanding of digital child pornography. This is because other disciplines have their own research agendas, just as the IS discipline has it own. The important difference here is that within the IS discipline the technology, its use and effects [12] are in focus, which is not the case for non-technical disciplines.

Digital child pornography is a phenomenon influenced by different rationales (e.g. technological, power, emotion) [40, 50] and these rationalities are constructed and shaped within wider contexts. The emotional rationale [50] is well represented in the public discourse on digital child pornography as it is particularly emotional and tends to rely more on morality and subjective opinion than empirical findings. In addition to the public discourses being inadequate as a base for further development and social change they may also act as an obstacle to the development of a more well-founded discussion [3].

Transformative Re-definition

The goal of the transformative re-definition is to build upon insight and critique to provide alternative understanding of the research area [33]. The goal is to develop knowledge with an aim to enable change and emancipation [28]. To enable change within this area a well founded understanding of the technology involved is essential. Without such an understanding it is not possible to present credible alternatives to those presented by other research areas or accepted in the one-sided media discourse. By providing a realistic understanding of the effects of technology the social change can be enacted through law, policy or social practice. A brief example can be seen in the discussion on the application of filtering technology to prevent child pornography. While these technologies have received popular acceptance in the media they are based on a lack of understanding of the diversity of ICT used for digital child pornography [55].

6   Conclusion

This paper has argued for the need for systematic empirically based IS research within the field of digital child pornography. This is important since it acts as an important complement to existing non-technical research within the area. The significant role played by ICT in child pornography demands the contribution of IS research to understand the complexity of child pornography. It is not adequate that non-technical disciplines such as law and psychology attempt to lead research within this area since these disciplines are not primarily concerned with the technological orientation.

Despite the fact that the presented area is onerous to study, systematic research must be carried out. This paper has shown that digital child pornography can benefit from being the subject of CISR since this perspective attempts to also study the negative effects of ICT in society by looking at aspects such as e.g. structural inequalities and disadvantaged groups. It is important to take the step from speculative theories and uninformed public discourses to well-founded empirical research. To be able to conduct critical research with the ultimate goal of social change, the IS discipline must be prepared to take social responsibility and participate in a larger social discourse beyond organizational boundaries.

References

1. A. Adam, *Gender Ethics and Information Technology* (Palgrave Macmillan, New York, 2005).
2. M. Eneman, The New Face of Child Pornography, in: *Human Rights in the Digital Age*, edited by M. Klang and A. Murray (Cavendish Publishing, London, 2005).
3. R. Kling, H. Rosenbaum, and S. Sawyer, *Understanding and Communicating Social Informatics: A Framework for Studying and Teaching the Human Contexts of Information and Communication Technologies*, (Information Today, Inc, New Jersey, 2005).
4. A. Gillespie, Child Pornography: Balancing Substantive and Evidential Law to Safeguard Children Effectively from Abuse, *The International Journal of Evidence & Proof*, 9, 1-21, (2005).
5. K. Williams, Child Pornography Law: Does it protect children? *Journal of Social Welfare and Family Law*, 26(3), 245-261, (2004).
6. Y. Akdeniz, Controlling illegal and harmful content on the Internet, in: *Crime and the Internet*, edited by D. Wall (Routledge, London, 2001).

7. S. Ost, Getting to Grips with Sexual Grooming? *Journal of Social Welfare and Family Law*, **26**(2), 147-159, (2004).

8. M. Taylor and E. Quayle, *Child Pornography: An Internet Crime*, (Brunner-Routledge, Hove, 2003).

9. G. Holland, Identifying Victims of Child Abuse Images: An Analysis of Successful Identifications, in: *Viewing Child Pornography on the Internet*, edited by E. Quayle and M. Taylor (Russell House Publishing, 2005).

10. J. Wolak, D. Finkelhor and K. Mitchell, The Varieties of Child Pornography Production, in: *Viewing Child Pornography on the Internet*, edited by E. Quayle and M. Taylor (Russell House Publishing, 2005).

11. G. Walsham, *Making a World of Difference: IT in a Global Context* (John Wiley & Sons Ltd., Chichester, 2004).

12. W. Orlikowski and C. Iacono, Research Commentary: Desperately Seeking the 'IT' in IT Research – A Call to Theorizing the IT Artifact, *Information Systems Research*. **12**(2) 121-134 (2001).

13. J. Wajcman, *Feminism confronts technology* (Polity Press, Cambridge, 1991).

14. D. Howcroft and E. Trauth (eds), *Handbook of Critical Information Systems Research* (Edward Elgar, Cheltenham, 2005).

15. J. Thompson, *The Media and Modernity – A Social Theory of the Media* (Polity Press, Cambridge, 1995).

16. K. McGrath, Doing critical research in information systems: a case of theory and practice not informing each other, Information Systems Journal **15**, 85-101 (2005).

17. K. Lyytinen and H. Klein, The critical theory of Jürgen Habermas as a basis for a theory of information systems, in: *Research Methods in Information Systems*, edited by E. Mumford, R. Hirschheim, G. Fitzgerald and A. Wood-Harper (North-Holland Publishing, Amsterdam 1985).

18. R. Hirschheim and H. Klein, Four paradigms of information systems development, *Communications of the ACM*, **32**(10), 199-216 (1989).

19. R. Hirschheim and H. Klein, Realizing emancipatory principles in information systems research: the case for ETHICS, *MIS Quarterly*, **18**(1), 83-109 (1994).

20. S. Jonsson, Action Research, in: *Information Systems Research: Contemporary Approaches and Emergent Traditions*, edited by H. Niessen, H. Klein and R. Hirschheim (North-Holland Publishing, Amsterdam, 1991).

21. O. Ngwenyama, The critical social theory approach to information systems: problems and challenges, in: *Information Systems Research: Contemporary Approaches and Emergent Traditions*, edited by H. Niessen, H. Klein and R. Hirschheim (North-Holland Publishing, Amsterdam, 1991).

22. K. Lyytinen, Information systems and critical theory, in: Critical Management Studies, edited by M. Alvesson and H. Willmott (Sage, London, 1992).

23. M. Myers and L. Young, Hidden Agendas, Power and Managerial Assumptions in Information Systems Development: An Ethnographic Study, *Information Technology and People*, **10**(3), 224-240, (1997).

24. F. Wilson, The truth is out there: the search for emancipatory principles in information systems design, *Information Technology and People*, **10**(3), 187-204 (1997).

25. K. Saravanamuthu, K. and T. Wood-Harper, Developing Emancipatory Information Systems in: (Re-)Defining Critical Research in Information Systems - An International Workshop, edited by A. Adam, D. Howcroft, H. Richardson and B. Robinson, (The University of Salford, 2001).

26. B. Doolin and A. Lowe, To reveal is to critique: actor network theory and critical information systems research, *Journal of Information Technology*, **17**, 69-78 (2002).

27. G. Walsham, Learning about being critical, *Information Systems Journal*, **15**, 111-117 (2005).
28. D. Cecez-Kecmanovic, Basic assumptions of the critical research perspectives in information systems, in: *Handbook of Critical Information Systems Research*, edited by D. Howcroft and E. Trauth (Edward Elgar, Cheltenham, 2005).
29. R. Kling, What is Social Informatics and Why Does it Matter?, *D-Lib Magazine*, **5**(1) (1999).
30. R. Kling, Social Informatics, in: *The Encyclopaedia of LIS*, (Kluwer Publishing, Amsterdam, 2001).
31. R. Lamb and S. Sawyer, On extending social informatics from a rich legacy of networks and conceptual resources, *Information Technology and People*, **18**(1), 9-20 (2005).
32. S. Sawyer and H. Rosenbaum, Social Informatics in the Information Sciences: Current Activities and Emerging Directions, *Informing Science*, **3**(2), 89-95 (2000).
33. M. Alvesson and S. Deetz, *Doing Critical Management Research*, (Sage, London 2000).
34. R. Kling, H. Rosenbaum, and S. Sawyer, *Understanding and Communicating Social Informatics: A Framework for Studying and Teaching the Human Contexts of Information and Communication Technologies*, (Information Today, Inc, New Jersey, 2005).
35. S. Cohen, *Folk Devils and Moral Panics* (Routledge, London, 2002).
36. P. Jenkins, *Moral Panic: Changing Concepts of the Child Molester in Modern America* (Yale University Press, New Haven, 1998).
37. E. Monteiro and O. Hanseth, Social shaping of information infrastructure: on being specific about the technology, in: *Information technology and changes in organisational work*, edited by W. Orlikowski, G. Walsham, M. Jones and J. DeGross (Chapman & Hall, London, 1995).
38. M. Horkheimer and T. Adorno, *Dialectic of Enlightenment*, (Herder, New York, 1972).
39. M. Horkheimer, Traditional and critical theory, in: *Critical Theory: Max Horkheimer*, (Seabury, New York, 1972).
40. E. Klecun, Competing rationalities: a critical study of telehealth in the UK, in: *Handbook of Critical Information Systems Research*, edited by D. Howcroft and E. Trauth (Edward Elgar, Cheltenham, 2005).
41. H. Richardson, Consuming passions in the 'global knowledge economy', in: *Handbook of Critical Information Systems Research*, edited by D. Howcroft and E. Trauth (Edward Elgar, Cheltenham, 2005).
42. B. Doolin, Information technology as disciplinary technology: being critical in interpretive research on information systems, *Journal of Information Technology*, **13**, 301-311 (1998).
43. D. Hughes, The Use of New Communications and Information Technologies for Sexual Exploitation of Women and Children, *Hastings Women's Law Journal*, **13**(1) (2002).
44. B. Chatterjee, Last of the rainmacs? Thinking about pornography in cyberspace, in: *Crime and the Internet*, edited by D. Wall (Routledge London, 2001).
45. F. Lane, *Obscene Profits: the Entrepreneurs of Pornography in the Cyber Age* (Routledge, New York, 2001).
46. H. McCulloch, Interpol and Crimes against Children, in: *Viewing Child Pornography on the Internet*, edited by E. Quayle and M. Taylor (Russell House Publishing, 2005).
47. S. Edwards, Prosecuting 'child pornography', *Journal of Social Welfare and Family Law*, **22**(1), 1-21 (2000).
48. A. Gillespie, The Sexual Offences Act 2003: Tinkering with 'child pornography', *Critical Law Review*, 361-368 (2004).
49. L. Nilsson, Sexuell exploatering av barn – vad döljer sig bakom sexualbrottsstatistiken? (Brottsförebyggande rådet, Sweden, 2003).

50. C. Avgerou and K. McGrath, Rationalities and Emotions in IS Innovation, in: *Handbook of Critical Information Systems Research*, edited by D. Howcroft and E. Trauth (Edward Elgar, Cheltenham, 2005).
51. C. MacKinnon and A. Dworkin, *In Harm's Way: The Pornography Civil Rights Hearings*, (Harvard University Press, Cambridge Massachusetts, 1997).
52. S. Easton, *The Problem of Pornography: Regulation and the Right to Free Speech*, (Routledge, London, 1994).
53. L. Edwards, Pornography and the Internet, in: *Law & the Internet: A Framework for Electronic Commerce*, edited by L. Edwards and C. Waelde (Hart Publishing, Oxford, 2002).
54. H. Rheingold, *The Virtual Community: Homesteading on the Electronic Frontier*, (MIT Press, Cambridge Massachusetts, 2000).
55. M. Eneman, A Critical Study of ISPs Filtering of Child Pornography in *Proceedings of 14th European Conference on Information Systems*, Gothenburg, June 12-14, (2006).
56. M. Smith and P. Kollock, (eds) *Communities in Cyberspace*, (Routledge, London, 1999).
57. T. Krone, Combating Online Child Pornography in Australia, in: *Viewing Child Pornography on the Internet*, edited by E. Quayle and M. Taylor (Russell House Publishing, 2005).
58. K. Durkin, Misuse of the Internet by Paedophiles: Implications for Law Enforcement Probation Practice, *Federal Probation*, **14**, (1997).
59. N. Baym, Interpersonal Life Online, in: *The Handbook of New Media*, edited by L. Lievrouw and S. Livingstone (Sage, London, 2002).
60. S. Livingstone, Children's use of the Internet: reflections on the emerging research agenda, *New Media & Society*, **5**(2), 147-166 (2003).
61. G. Walsham, Critical engagement: why, what and how?, in: *Handbook of Critical Information Systems Research*, edited by D. Howcroft and E. Trauth (Edward Elgar, Cheltenham, 2005).
62. A. Feenberg, *Transforming Technology: A Critical Theory Revisited* (OUP, Oxford, 2002).
63. M. Alvesson and K. Skoldberg, *Reflexive Methodology* (Sage, London, 1999).

An Empirical Study on Implementing Free/Libre Open Source Software (FLOSS) in Schools

Yuwei Lin and Enrico Zini
National Centre for E-Social Science, University of Manchester, UK
yuwei@ylin.org, http://www.ylin.org
Debian GNU/Linux
enrico@enricozini.org, http://www.enricozini.org

Abstract. This empirical paper shows how free/libre open source software (FLOSS) contributes to mutual and collaborative learning in an educational environment. However, unlike proprietary software, FLOSS allows extensive customisation of software and supports the needs of local users better. In this paper, we observes how implementing FLOSS in an Italian high school challenges the conventional relationship between end users themselves (e.g. teachers and students) and that between users and developers. The findings will shed some light on the social aspects of FLOSS-based computerization -- including the roles of FLOSS in social and organizational change in educational environments and the ways that the social organization of FLOSS are influenced by social forces and social practices.

Keywords: free/libre open source software (FLOSS); FLOSS implementation in schools; collaborative learning; mutual learning; OpenOffice.org; blog

1   Introduction

Many recent studies have pointed out that the relationships between lay and expert, users and developers, knowledge consumers and producers can be greatly challenged in a computer-supported knowledge-based society (e.g. Millen and Muller 2001; Hine 2001, 2002). In such a complicated knowledge system, mutual learning is a prominent phenomenon observed in various sectors. Educational sector is one of them that has been experiencing digital transformation.

In this paper, we observe such digital transformation in schools fostered by the implementation of free/libre open source software (FLOSS). We argue that FLOSS, unlike many other educational institutes that use proprietary software such as WebCT to facilitate the teaching and learning in schools (e.g. Pearson & Koppi

Please use the following format when citing this chapter:

Lin, Y., Zini, E., 2006, in IFIP International Federation for Information Processing, Volume 223, Social Informatics: An Information Society for All? In Remembrance of Rob Kling, eds. Berleur, J., Numinen, M. I., Impagliazzo, J., (Boston: Springer), pp. 123–132.

2002), has greater potentials of stimulating cross-boundary learning, and of shaping the technologies into the desires of users.

Istituto Statale di Istruzione Superiore J.M.Keynes (hereafter 'the Keynes High School'), located in the outskirt of the city Bologna in north Italy, initiated the implementation of FLOSS-based ICT to facilitate e-learning. Given the transparency of the technologies itself with openly available source code (Perens 1999; DiBona et al. 1999), the schools not only reduce management costs of existing IT systems (e.g. licensing fees of proprietary software, the cost for periodical update to fix vulnerability, and the fare for improvement of capability), but also allow them to customize the software to their specific reality. Working closely with the technicians and the system designer, the teachers and students at Keynes also contribute to the construction of the system and the software they consume.

These experiences are valuable for the development of effective environments for learning, and more importantly, they shed light on how FLOSS can be implemented in schools, and benefit both the users and developers. These examples also denotes a celebrated chapter about how social actors can participate in the technological development and configure the technologies to meet their demands (Fleck 1993, 1994). While earlier work on e-learning and computer supported cooperative work (CSCW) has attempted to use ICTs as effective medium for interactive teaching and learning, few of them have discussed the possibility of including learners and teachers in the design process of the learning technologies. Thus, this paper will be one of the most novel papers about how to design learning technologies with the participation of users in the design process.

2   Research Methods

We employ a qualitative methodology for this study in order to understand the social-technical dynamics in the implementation process. The research methods employed include ethnographic observation, informal face-to-face interview, and document analysis. One of the authors, Enrico Zini, was a student at the Keynes high school and is now both the designer of the system and a teacher of communication courses. As a student, a teacher, researcher and supporter of the system, he has had the opportunity to see the use of new technologies in education from a variety of perspectives. Being involved in the development process makes it easier for the researcher to observe and investigate the learner/user perspectives on e-learning, rather than just follow the promising functions envisaged by the system builders/providers. Apart from his participatory observation, we also collect other second-hand documents (e.g. students' and teachers' on-line discussions and off-line presentations) and informal conversations and interview with the students, teachers and technicians. These multiple sources of data provide rich information for an in-depth case study (Yin 2002).

3   The Keynes High School and their Information System

3.1   The Keynes High School

The Keynes High School is an aggregation of different former high schools located in the same area. It offers a range of didactic paths: a scientific lyceum, a technical business high school, a geometer technical high school and a tourism-oriented professional high school. It is also responsible for High School education inside the penitentiary of Bologna.

The school has 6 computer labs with 140 computers and 4 servers (based on the GNU Linux operating system) supported by 5 technical staff to serve 607 students, 96 teachers. Currently, the 4 Linux servers provide services such as routing the laboratories to the Internet, firewall with possibility of isolating different computer rooms in case the teacher does not need to use the Internet, LDAP centralized user management, file sharing including shared space and personal space and desktop accessible from every computer, DHCP services, local Debian mirror for faster upgrading of Linux machines, web server with school portal, school wiki and personal web space for teachers and students, webmail, mail server with virus scanning and spam filtering, mailing list services, IMAP server, print server, HTTP proxy cache to speed up the lessons where 20 to 30 computers connect to the same website at the same time. Some facilities, such as the webmail or internal communications, are also available remotely from home.

3.2   The Introduction of Free/Libre Open Source Software (FLOSS)

The computer laboratory has been established since 1985 to support computer lessons in the technical business courses, and the initial equipment of Olivetti M20 has been slowly upgraded and expanded.

FLOSS first came into the school in summer 1998, when the technicians decided to try and install Linux on a testing computer. At the beginning of 1999, a Linux server was deployed to share the dialup Internet connection and provide shared disk space over the network. The server has kept continuously evolving since then, partly due to the needs of the school (such as working as a print server) and partly due to the interest of the technicians to learn and experiment with new technology (such as installing a web server and CMS, or a VPN between the two campuses).

In 1999 the school faced an expense plan of about 35000000 lire (ca. 18075 euros) to buy proper Microsoft Office licenses for a new laboratory plus some of the existing seats[1]. Since the school staff had already experience with FLOSS, facing that big cost, the school decided to try other office replacements. At that time, Sun had just acquired Star Division and released Star Office 5.1 under a free software license, and so the school installed Sun's Star Office (which later on became OpenOffice.org), instead of Microsoft Office, in one new laboratory.

Such a switch encountered a strong resistance from many teachers, who feared of having to be reeducated to acquire new skills. The students, instead, had little problems with the change. The switch experiment ended up in a trade-off, where only about 13000000 lire (ca. 6710 euros) were spent on Microsoft Office licenses. The rest of the budget was used to buy new hardware.

3.3   The Growth with Free Software

After the installation of Star Office, new FLOSS-related services were deployed in the servers and the school staffs started to have more contacts with the developers' community. With the increasing awareness about free software, the school started to learn how to utilize the FLOSS-based infrastructure they built – not only passively use the system but more positively participate in the design and development process. The concept of inclusion in participatory design is gradually grounded in Keynes high school. They started to have students moderate mailing lists where mutual help was provided. The mailing lists were also open for the public so that prospect students could subscribe to the mailing lists and ask about the future school environment. Through the communication on the mailing lists, not only could prospect students start making progress in the social network they were going to be a part of, but also could the moderators – the senior high school students - have more advanced computer experience of moderating and facilitating an on-line community.

Moreover, the students were also issued a CD with the free software used at school (e.g. OpenOffice.org, Mozilla Composer, Free Pascal) to install in their home computers. In so doing, the students experiment different operating systems and software. Therefore, as Daniela, the teacher in charge of the computer lab at the Keynes high school says[2],

> In using free software, our students realize that working with computers does not mean working with a single software. [...] They understand that it is possible to switch easily from one software to another [to complete a task]. When sitting in front of computers, they don't search for 'Word', but they look at what software is installed and what can be useful to them.

Apart from starting implementing open source technologies, open contents, which share the same philosophy with the free/libre open source software movement, were also employed in the daily teaching and learning. The teachers and students started to use information on Wikipedia[3] for extensive teaching/learning materials. Meanwhile, some of them also contributed to translating webpages on Wikipedia or adding new contents to the on-line encyclopedia shared openly by Internet users around the world. The implemented ICT fosters a greater learning environment for both students and teachers at the Keynes high school with more interactive activities locally and globally, and more importantly, with the FLOSS-based system, the school members are empowered to influence and contribute to the technological design and knowledge production potently. Their participation in the design and knowledge-making process changes not only the power relationship between users and developers but also that between students and teachers. In the following, we will present a couple of examples how their uses of FLOSS-based technologies transform local experiences, understandings and social formations. We will focus on particular digital practices – developing the OpenOffice.org Italian thesaurus and creating a school weblog - and analyze representations of these technologies in discourses.

4 The Open 'Office.org' Italian Thesaurus

Hitherto, we have described the current computer-supported learning environment at the Keynes high school and the motivation for them to switch to a FLOSS-based infrastructure. Additionally, open contents are also employed in the daily teaching and learning. Both open technologies and contents on the one hand enable the teachers and students to take more active part in the technological design process and on the other hand also shape their learning behaviors and activities. Technological design and pedagogy thus indeed have the potential to co-evolve in the new medium (Bruckman 2003). The following case on OpenOffice.org is illuminated.

OpenOffice.org is open source office software suite for processing text documents, spreadsheets, presentations and drawings. The language customization of this software usually is developed and maintained by a local community of volunteers, though sometimes funded by Sun Microsystems Inc. The Progetto Linguistico Italiano Openoffice.org (PLIO), the Italian OpenOffice.org project, develops, maintains and distributes the localized Italian version of OpenOffice.org. And the source code is freely available for interested people to download, modify, study and redistribute.

In year 2004, students of the class III H were asked by their Italian teacher, Daniela Volta, who was also responsible for the computer infrastructure at the Keynes high school, to write up synonyms as a reflection of their linguistic and lexical skills. Because the Open Office they were using did not have an Italian thesaurus, the teacher thought it would be a good idea to collect students' work on synonyms and submit it to the Italian Open Office development team PLIO as an enhancement.

However, bringing students into the development of free software requires some basic training. To prepare the students to work on a Free Software project, the second author was invited to give a background lesson about the concepts and mundane practices of free software. The lesson also included a short history of OpenOffice.org as a background on the free software project the students were about to get involved with. Later on, through the coordination of Mrs. Daniela Volta, the work on the list of synonyms, began with the synonyms letters A & B drawn up by the class III H at the Keynes high school, is continued by the students at different high school and others from the wider FLOSS community.

The creation and development of Italian Open Office thesaurus shows active cross-boundary learning and developing activities based on social networking and mutual support. Because of the teacher's link with other high schools, she can call more people to participate in this project. Students, crossing the school boundary, contribute their learning results to one of the biggest free software project in the world that can be used by many others coming from different social worlds (Strauss 1987). Drawing on heterogeneous knowledge from diverse actors, the thesaurus for the Italian Open Office resembles a boundary object (Star 1989) that has been and will be constantly shaped by people who share the software. The construction of the technological artifact (i.e. the Italian Open Office thesaurus) thus embeds and embodies students' learning experiences and results. Technological innovation is no longer just within the strong expert-led industrial-supported research environment; learning is no longer just within schools. Instead, this case shows how innovation is fostered by a 'community' (Lave and Wenger 1991) including diverse actors traveling across multiple boundaries.

Moreover, as written in the Debian package documentation 'openoffice.org-thesaurus-it', the students reflected what they've learned "This experience shows that in the school it is possible to achieve an active and experimental approach to the computer technologies, with the aid of competences concerning different subjects, in this specific case the Italian language." Such interactive, community-based and cross-boundary learning thus proves to be more effective than other one-way passive Internet-based learning with websites providing course resources (text, graphics, maybe audio, video). However, it also entails that such a learning community based on FLOSS technologies is more dynamic and it requires further studies in order to understand why some tools are chosen over others, and how are they implemented in a context determined by the teachers, the subject matters, and the social, cultural and political environment of the institution.

4   Blog: A Collaborative Instrument

The blog is another facility that fosters a collaborative learning environment at the Keynes high school. Moreover, it also shows how students build both the learning community and their collective identity based on the shared learning experiences.

Students come from various backgrounds and therefore have various learning styles. Their knowledge is heterogeneous, dynamic and situated (Lave and Wenger 1991; Gomez et al. 2003). It would be effective if their different knowing and learning experiences can be shared through the rapidly developed information technologies, part.

One of the objectives of the new media education at Keynes is to help students to step back and ask critical questions about what they're seeing- rather than just absorbing media messages passively and unconsciously. To develop Internet literacy in schools, the Keynes high school initiated a new module on communication technologies covering issues such as how to provide and present information on the Internet. Trying to be neither passive information receivers nor disinterested knowledge consumers, the students were invited to play a more active role in the Internet-based society. On the class, examples such as Internet news websites Slashdot.org or Indymedia.org were presented to the students. Moreover, as a practical ground for experiencing independent information providers, a FLOSS-based weblog infrastructure using technologies such as pyblosxom[4], apache[5], planet[6], weblog-add[7] was set up in early 2005.

This weblog system can also aggregate all individual blogs of students and staffs automatically and turn them into a community blog (e.g. a class blog collecting all teachers and students' blogs from the class II H; a school blog collecting all blogs of staffs and students). In so doing, information collected from different sources and contexts can be rearranged and presented for different purposes and shared amongst wider interested audiences. Compared with other Internet technologies, this blog system contains the following advantages:

1. With a simplified interface, the blog is comparatively easier to use than web pages or wiki pages because the weblog only allows posts in plain text, and then the content will be automatically edited, display and archived. In this

regard, the school did not just blindly accept any 'cool' new technologies. A careful evaluation of the educational needs in a specific situation has been made before applying technologies (Fox 1998; Huysman and de Wit 2002). The technologies thus were less likely to discourage participation of teachers and students (Dougiamas 1999; Dougiamas and Taylor 2003; Shirky 2004).

2. Unlike on-line forums, no topic needs to be pre-given on a blog for discussion. Thus, users are offered great freedom (except for the rule that the blog is not used to insult people) to express themselves in whatever content, and whatever style they want.

3. Unlike a mailing list, a weblog is universally accessible by any user on the Internet. The information can be disseminated further and network more actors (both information providers, mediums and receivers).

It is worth noting that this concept of linking different blogs together is a common practice amongst free software developers to create an aggregation of the blogs of all the developers working on the same project (e.g. Planet Debian[8] for Debian GNU/Linux; Planet Ubuntu[9] for Ubuntu GNU/Linux). This technology implemented in the school thus was technically trivial, yet socially very effective. The creation of *Planet Keynes*[10] with the blogs of everyone in the Keynes high school fosters a greater learning community where mutual learning takes place not only between students themselves but also between students, teachers and technicians.

For example, when learning about a Greek epic poem, one student had been posting the lyrics of a popular song that was inspired by this ancient Greek poem onto the class webblog. Shared with everyone on-line, the teacher indicated in her follow-up message that this lyric would be discussed at the next lesson for drawing parallels between ancient narrative artwork and modern pop music. In this case, the teacher learned from the students about the current teen culture. In sharing the lyrics, it shortened the gap between the teacher and the students. Being applied in the teaching on the class, the spontaneous information shared on-line had become useful material to reflect something taught in the textbook. This instance illustrates how ICTs are used to integrate the physical off-line life and the digital on-line life, and more importantly, motivate the students to reflect and share what they've learnt with not only each other but also the rest of the world. In other words, such a community-based blog system not only enhances peer-support but also hinders the hierarchy in a traditionally educational environment where teachers own the power to deliver knowledge and students passively receive the information given. Moreover, it also helps provide information on-line and bridges learners around the world. Although not yet prominently observed, the technicians could also learn from the activities of their users and design better devices and services for them. A learning community with active exchanges between diverse actors thus is built and so is their collective identity based on the shared learning experiences.

Another implication found in the implementation of webblog technology is related to the feature of free software. The system designer, Enrico Zini, had been paying extra attention on minimizing the divergence of the customized software from the upstream project for easier maintenance and better integration. He also created new features to automatically install (and mass-install) the pyblosxom weblog in any user's webspace. The bugs found and fixed in the customization and implementation process together with the new features added were reported back to the original developers. Since this is the first of such a FLOSS-based webblog system implemented in a school, documentation[11] was also produced to share this experience of customizing and implementing FLOSS-based webblogs at schools. This proves that the implementation of a FLOSS-based webblog system at the Keynes high school is indeed a socio-technical innovation.

5 Conclusion and Future Research

Hitherto, we have introduced the cost-saving and effective FLOSS-based technologies implemented in the Keynes high school. This system not only fosters a local learning community integrating the physical school and on-line learning environment, but also bridges the local knowledge-sharing and learning with the global Internet society. We have presented two eminent examples showing how FLOSS-based technologies improves the current e-learning technological development in encompassing both students and teachers in the development process. The first example is the usage of OpenOffice.org, the open source office software developed by volunteers, at the Keynes high school. Apart from being the software users, the students are also developers contributing their lists of Italian synonyms to the construction of the Italian thesaurus. In this process, the students not only learned Italian synonyms, but also actively participated in the free software development and made contact with the outside world. Their learning across the boundary between users and developers brings socio-technical dynamics into both the free software development and school education. Another example on using FLOSS-based webblog technologies also shows how on-line knowledge-sharing subverts the traditional power relationship between teachers and students and empowers all actors to learn from each other. Software bugs found and new features developed in the customization and implementation process were also reported back to the original free software developers. To sum up, the Keynes high school benefits from the FLOSS development for having cost-saving and customizable e-learning and knowledge-sharing software, and the FLOSS development benefits from the Keynes high school for having users feedback and contributions. Compared with similar proprietary software, the FLOSS technologies can be tailored to suit the users' specific requirements and therefore empower users to play a more participatory role in the design process.

In this paper, we have examined the highly dynamic and socially complex processes of collaborative learning at the Keynes high school bolstered by the FLOSS-based technologies. We have also investigated the changed role of teachers and students in such a community-oriented educational settings from an integrated socio-technical perspective, taking socio-cultural processes as well as technical infrastructures into account. However, we have also observed some phenomenon that requires further studies. For example, we found that not every student had dedicated the same amount of time to blogging, and that the teacher played an important role of adopting FLOSS-based technologies and motivating students' learning activities on-line. To get a better understanding of such a FLOSS-based learning community, consistent investigation is needed in order to understand how the experience earned with a long period of blogging can be leveraged, how shared interests can be built and enhanced amongst all participants, and how to motivate students to continue blogging. Additionally, in the future, we are also expecting to study whether implementing FLOSS and using non-proprietary data formats indeed helps teaching pupils about exactly how computers operate, making them learn about the formats and the tools by letting them experiment with them (Marson, 2004). Finally, we would like to strengthen that such an implementation process should never be considered as smooth and straightforward as there were some socio-political factors (particularly human factors) involved in the implementation process (such as the disfavoring of some math and science teachers at the school in the beginning). These socio-political factors should always be taken into account when planning such implementation.

Acknowledgements

Special thanks to the students, teachers and technicians at the Keynes high school for sharing their experiences of being involved in the construction of the FLOSS-based IT system.

References

A. Bruckman, Co-evolution of technological design and pedagogy in an online learning community. In *Designing Virtual Communities in the Service of Learning* edited by Sasha Barab, Rob Kling, and James Gray. Cambridge University Press (2003).

C. DiBona, S. Ockman, and M. Stone, (Eds.) *Open Sources: Voices from the Open Source Revolution* (O'Reilly UK, 1999).

M. Dougiamas, Developing tools to foster online educational dialogue. In K. Martin, N. Stanley and N. Davison (Eds), *Teaching in the Disciplines/ Learning in Context*, 119-123. Proceedings of the 8th Annual Teaching Learning Forum, The University of Western Australia, February 1999. Perth: UWA. http://lsn.curtin.edu.au/tlf/tlf1999/dougiamas.html (1999).

M. Dougiamas, and P. C. Taylor, Moodle: Using Learning Communities to Create an Open Source Course Management System. Proceedings of the EDMEDIA 2003 Conference, Honolulu, Hawaii (2003).

J. Fleck, Configurations: crystallizing contingency, *International Journal of Human Factors in Manufacturing*, 3(1), 15-36 (1993).

J. Fleck, Learning by trying: the implementation of configurational technology', *Research Policy*, 23, 637 -652 (1994).

R. Fox, What are the shortcomings inherent in the non-problematic perception of new technologies? In Black, B. and Stanley, N. (Eds), *Teaching and Learning in Changing Times*, 96-101. Proceedings of the 7th Annual Teaching Learning Forum, The University of Western Australia, February 1998. Perth: UWA (1998).

M-L Gomez, I. Bouty, and C. Drucker-Godard, Developing knowing in practice: behind the scenes of haute cuisine. In *Knowing in organizations: A practice-based approach* edited by Davide Nicolini, Silvia Gherardi and Dvora Yanow (London: M. E. Sharpe, Inc., 2003).

C. Hine, Ideas of audience in World Wide Web design: the meaning of a mouse click. *Information, Communication and Society* 4(2): 182-198 (2001).

C. Hine, Cyberscience: and social boundaries: the implications of laboratory talk on the Internet. *Sociological Research Online*. 7(2) http://www.socresonline.org.uk/7/2/hine.html (2002).

M. H. Huysman, and D. de Wit, *Knowledge sharing in practice* (Dordrecht: Kluwer Academic Publishers, 2002).

J. Lave, and E. Wenger, E. *Situated learning: Legitimate peripheral participation* (New York: Cambridge University Press, 1991).

D. R. Millen and M. J. Muller, Computer-Supported Communities of Practice, paper presented at the 2nd *ECSCW Workshop on Community Knowledge,* 16-20 September 2001, Bonn, Germany (2001).

E. J. Pearson and A. J. Koppi, A WebCT Course on Making Accessible Online Courses, WebCT Asia-Pacific Conference, Melbourne, Australia, March 2002 (2002).

B. Perens, The open source definition. In Open Sources: Voices from the Open Source Revolution, *Chris DiBona, Sam Ockman, and Mark Stone (Eds).* (O'Reilly UK, 1999).

C. Shirky, Situated software, firstly published March 30, 2004 on the 'Networks, Economics, and Culture' mailing list. Available online at http://www.shirky.com/writings/situated_software.html (2004).

S. L. Star, The structure of ill-structured solutions: boundary objects and heterogeneous distributed problem solving. In Gasser, L. & Huhns, M. (eds.) *Distributed artificial intelligence,* vol. 2 (London: Pitman, 1989), pp. 37-54.

A. Strauss, *Qualitative Analysis for Social Scientists* (Cambridge University Press, 1987).

R. K. Yin, *Case Study Research, Design and Methods,* 3rd ed. (Newbury Park: Sage Publications, 2002).

---

[1]   At the same time, the expense plan to buy hardware for a completely new laboratory was a little more than 30000000 lire (ca. 15500euros)

[2]   This paragraph is translated from her presentation at the seminar 'Software Libero - Un'opportunità per la pubblica amministrazione e il sistema economico regionale', June 16, 2003, Emilia Romagna Regional Administration.

[3]   http://wikipedia.org

[4]   http://pyblosxom.sourceforge.net/

[5]   http://www.apache.org/

[6]   http://planetplanet.org/

[7]   http://pyblosxom.sourceforge.net/blog/registry/input/weblog-add

[8]   http://planet.debian.org

[9]   http://planet.ubuntu.com

[10]   http://keynes.scuole.bo.it/planet

[11]   The documentation is available at the Keynes wiki page http://keynes.scuole.bo.it/phpwiki.

Ubiquity and Pervasivity: On the Technological Mediation of (Mobile) Everyday Life

Giuseppina Pellegrino
University of Calabria, Department of Sociology and Political Science
Italy, gpellegrinous@yahoo.com, g.pellegrino@unical.it

Abstract. This paper aims to contribute to the debate about relationships between technology *and* society, or technology *in* society, starting from the categories of ubiquity and pervasivity. The analysis will try to understand ubiquitous/pervasive computing as a new frontier in contemporary movements of computerization [cf. Iacono and Kling, 2001], framing it in the interrelationships between different interests expressed in public discourse. Convergence in hi-tech industry and technological artefacts emerging from organizational and socio-cultural arrangements put forward the categories of ubiquity and pervasivity as key-words in design, functionality and perception of technological artefacts. The concept of ubiquity focuses on both the mobility and the pervasivity/embeddedness of technological artefacts that support the emergence of mobile Internetworking in a mobile society. Mobility and a set of affiliated concepts (e.g. miniaturization, portability, integration) constitute the main discursive frame in mobile and ubiquitous computing. Different layers of public discourse emerge as pertinent to this technology: a technology-driven and a social software perspective, both featured in the media discourse. All of them frame, eventually, inclusionary and exclusionary patterns of sociotechnical action, emerging from different politics of signification.

Keywords: ubiquity, mobility, discursive frames, mobile and ubiquitous computing, computerization movements

1   Introduction

This paper draws from the analysis of emerging concepts like mobility and mobile society, ubiquitous and mobile computing, pervasive nomadic information environments, to understand how they constitute a relevant dimension to frame, imagine and represent change and transformation in contemporary everyday life. In

Please use the following format when citing this chapter:

Pellegrino, G., 2006, in IFIP International Federation for Information Processing, Volume 223, Social Informatics: An Information Society for All? In Remembrance of Rob Kling, eds. Berleur, J., Numinen, M. I., Impagliazzo, J., (Boston: Springer), pp. 133–144.

this sense, mobile and ubiquitous computing is an open laboratory where links between the designers' work, new sociotechnical arrays, social imagery concerning technology in everyday life are experienced, enacted and drawn. Ubiquity and pervasivity are the main keywords that inform the designers' work, their practices for systems development and the very (social) 'nature' of technology in contemporary society.

Therefore, the aim is to portray, accordingly with Iacono and Kling's analysis of computerization movements [2001], some of the macro-social and cultural forces involved in the emergence of ubiquitous and mobile computing as the next wave in computerization development and specific sub-culture in computerization movements. In fact, the metaphor of ubiquity provides a key-access to discursive and organizational practices of inclusion/exclusion linked with the emergence of a mobile Internetworking, a mobile society, and the everyday life 'on the move'.

The arguments presented in this contribution also aim to draw a starting theoretical framework to enquire intersections at crossroads of mobility, technologies, everyday life and different social groups using mobile devices in their work and non-work everyday life.

Mediatized everyday life

The everyday life of individuals and organizations is increasingly mediated by various types of technological artefacts aimed to share information and allow communication at a distance. These artefacts are more and more embedded in the texture of everyday life, in at least two senses.

First and foremost, this embeddedness passes through a process of 'naturalization' of artefacts, which renders them invisible and transparent to the user's attention and sight. This process, named as 'domestication' [Silverstone, 1994] constitutes the very essence of contemporary everyday life: what we progressively take for granted, among other things, is the routine to cope with always new technological artefacts.

Silverstone provided various examples of domestication of television as both an object and a medium, but any new technology, at its beginning, requires to be domesticated, appropriated by users, through various strategies. Everyday life as more and more mediatized, that means mediated and shaped by Information and Communication Technologies. coincides, among other things, with the routinization of multiple sociotechnical innovations.

Secondly, there is an even more materialistic aspect in the process of embedding technology and rendering it invisible: literally, technology 'disappears', o 'hides itself', in our pocket, hand, body and environment. This is what is called 'ubiquitous' computing, that means the encounter between mobile and pervasive computing, which associates computing with a high degree of both mobility and embeddedness in the fabric of everyday life [Lyytinen and Yoo, 2002a]. Nomadic information environments are said to move towards "ubiquitous computing, in which computers will be embedded in our natural movements and interactions with our environments - both physical and social. Ubiquitous computing will help organize and mediate social interactions wherever and whenever these situations might occur" [Lyytinen and Yoo, 2002b: 63]. In fact, increased physical and virtual mobility is fostered and enhanced by mobile and ubiquitous computing environments, which blur boundaries between work and non-work settings and contribute to make everyday life of individuals and organizations more and more mediatized. These technologies are taken for granted more easily than others, as they tend quite literally to disappear in our pockets or hands. Invisibility [Weiser, 1994] is the metaphor used to describe this type of technologies: again such a metaphor fits in the concept of everyday life and shared meaning based on taking for granted what is defined as 'reality' from a phenomenological approach and constructivist viewpoint [Berger and Luckmann, 1967]. Furthermore, invisibility and miniaturization contribute to make sociotechnical relationships more complicated, fragile and complex as technologies are pervasively embodied in sociotechnical environments. Awareness of technology use and its participation to daily action and interaction are partly masked and weakened by this embodiment. New (dis)continuities in space and time, and in (mobile) everyday life emerge.

As a consequence, technology is not simply (and not anymore) 'out there': even before being domesticated by social groups who appropriate it into their own culture, technology is invisible, or less visible than it was before. Far from being a trivial aspect of the question, the increased invisibility of technological artefacts, their miniaturization and portability re-frame in a relevant way social use and perception of technology in everyday life. New configurations emerge along the sociotechnical continuum of the conception, development and use of technological systems and the social construction of them. Adhering to the stream of a clear anti-deterministic approach to technology, the analysis of the social and imaginary genealogy of these sociotechnical configurations becomes crucial. Such a hot issue – of not seeing technology as separated from its constitutive 'sociality' or 'socialness' – can be faced with tools and concepts provided by Social Informatics as devoted to examine social aspects of computerization.

"Social Informatics studies aim to ensure that technical research agendas and system designs are relevant to people's lives. The key word is relevance, ensuring that technical work is socially-driven rather than technology-driven" [http://rkcsi.indiana.edu/article.php/about-social-informatics/35]. Social-ness does not constitute a separate requirement or dimension in/of computerization, instead shaping it since the very beginning.

2   Discursive frames around ubiquity: a set of 'affiliated concepts'

The main reference in this paper is constituted by Iacono and Kling's analysis of computerization movements [2001] as providing a clear theoretical framework to understand mobile systems development and the emergence of mobile technological devices These phenomena are framed here in the context of the mobility and mobilities paradigm [Urry, 2003] but also as current manifestation (a kind of subculture) of computerization movements. By referring to the model of public discourse and discursive frames as alternative conceptualization of the

Internetworking, it will be possible to understand how macro social discursive frames are enacted to make sense of an increasing number of technological artefacts (e.g. wifi architectures, smart mobile phones, PDAs, I-pods and so on).

Iacono and Kling [2001] provided us with an in depth analysis of the Internetworking and distant forms of work as sociotechnical arrays emerging from the joint action of computerization movements, rather than from mere economic or technical factors. They put together the emergence of a new technological architecture (Internetworking) and the societal issues framed in layered discursive practices, which constituted the outcome and inspiration of computerization movements' action.

"(...) Participants in computerization movements build up frames in their public discourses that indicate favourable links between Internetworking and a new preferred social order. These frames help to legitimate relatively high levels of investment for many potential adopters and package expectations about how they should envision a future based on Internetworking" [Iacono and Kling, 2001: 97].

Iacono and Kling identified three components to explain at a theoretical level how macro-social and cultural components become part of the process of societal mobilization that makes the Internetworking (or any other technology, e.g. the mobile) work and develop. The three components are *technological action frames*, *public discourse* and *organizational practices*. "These three elements (...) are related (...) Technological action frames shape and structure public discourse whereas public discourse shapes and structures organizational practices (...) But these relationships are nondeterministic (...) Relationships among the three elements also can be recursive. People may enrich their discourses and even modify their frames as they struggle to discuss the actual complexity of their practices. As a consequence, practices can generate new discourses, and new discourses can build up new technological frames" [Iacono and Kling, 2001: 100-101].

Universal access, death of distance, obliteration of time and space, totalizing rhetoric of progress and belief in a new (better) social order: around these *topoi*, the computerization movements built up their idea of Internetworking. It is noticeable that all of these concepts evoke and are evoked again in the idea of ubiquity and pervasivity associated with the rise of mobile Internetworking and ubiquitous computing. What wifi architectures and mobile computing devices add to this rhetoric is the belief in an almost totally invisible, transparent and embedded computing network: the disappearance of any materiality of Internetworking and hardware architectures, to the extent of their total 'softening'. Here ubiquity suggests the capacity and ability to indefinitely navigate into invisible spaces that annihilate time, space and (potentially), any other difference.

Around ubiquity, a set of 'affiliated concepts' are built up to reinforce the development and adoption of mobile (ubiquitous) technologies: miniaturization, pervasivity, wearability, portability and, of course, mobility. All of them contribute to draw a complex picture of the new technology: they are the 'bricks of meaning', which constitute the technological action frame for ubiquitous computing, and they also pervade the different types and sources of public discourse about ubiquitous technologies. In fact, "technological action frames circulate in public discourses and act as a form of currency whose structure and meaning remain relatively constant across a variety of discursive practices" [Iacono and Kling, 2001: 110-111].

Iacono and Kling identified four layers of public discourse: government discourse, scientific discipline discourse, mass-media discourse, professional and institutional discourse [2001]. Combinations and hybridations among these layers can be traced: for example, mass-media discourse is the most pervasive as it feeds and amplifies the other layers of public discourse.

Also, to some extent we could observe overlaps between professional and scientific discourses, especially with reference to the design and development of mobile and ubiquitous computing systems (see par. 4.1).

Mass-media and professional discourse will be shortly analyzed with reference to ubiquitous technology in this paper. Of the concepts constituting the technological frame for this technology, mobility will be analyzed in particular, as key-carrier of meaning. In fact, all the other affiliated concepts and frames can be understood and highlighted as a continuous re-call to mobility and ubiquity, both enabled and enhanced by mobile technological artefacts.

3 Mobilizing support for mobility and ubiquity

Contemporary Western societies can be depicted, among other things, as affected by what Urry [2003] calls 'compulsion to mobility'. Such a compulsion comprises representations of travel (of both people and cultures) as well as the idea of a contemporary citizen 'on the move'.

For the aim of this paper it is crucial to link the trend towards an increased mobility ['hypermobility,' cf. Urry, 2002] to the trend towards an increased 'mediatization' [hypermediatization, cf. Pellegrino, 2004] of organizational and social life, at both macro and micro context level. The intersection between hypermobility and hypermediatization – what I call 'mediatized mobility' – is of particular interest as discursive frame to understand current transformations in the paradigm of Internetworking.

"(...) People in prosperous industrialised societies are both increasingly on the move and communicating more to reach and connect with absent others. Thus developments in transport and communication technologies not merely service or connect people but reconfigure social networks by disconnecting and reconnecting them in complex ways. Thus as easy availability of cars, trains, planes and communication technologies spread social networks beyond cities, regions and nations, so they reconnect them by helping to afford intermittent visits, meetings and communication at-a-distance. People can travel, relocate and migrate and yet still be connected with friends and family members 'back home' and elsewhere. So increasingly, people that are near emotionally may be geographically very far away; yet they are only a journey, email or a phone call away" [Larsen et al., 2005: 10].

Intermittent and at-a-distance communications are part of both ubiquity and pervasivity: they are not simply based on the overcoming/obliteration of distances in time and space as in the rise of Internetworking [Iacono and Kling, 2001] but on their restructuration, based on mixed forms of co-presence, travel and mobilities.

"Indeed all forms of social life involve striking combinations of proximity and distance, combinations that necessitate examination of the intersecting forms of physical, object, imaginative and virtual mobility that contingently and complexly link people in patterns of obligation, desire and commitment, increasingly over geographical distances of great length" [Urry, 2002: 1].

The idea of a mobile society and of interconnected, different 'mobilities' on which this society is structured [Urry, 2002; Larsen et al., 2005] can be identified as the main framework that feeds and reinforces the technological frame for ubiquitous technologies. In this respect, emphasis on miniaturization and portability is strongly associated with a perceived increase of travel. Travelling in the information age means new and different things: there is a corporeal travel, which does not either end or exhaust the possibilities of mobility. Mobilities of objects and information do accompany and transform corporeal travel. The combination of instrumental means of communication and humans brings about, while replacing "the spatiality of 'co-present sociality', new modes of objectified stranger-ness" [Urry, 2002: 7]. The idea of ubiquity resides in this shift from a co-presence based on physical proximity to being 'anywhere anytime' through a combination of distance and proximity increasingly enabled and supported by mobile devices.

Dispersed symptoms and traces of a societal mobilization towards mobility are in the air and start to widespread; similarly to the death of distance and the rhetoric of a new social order based on Internetworking, the mobile Internet has its founding framework into the perspective (and the current reality) of a mobile society and of citizens whose everyday life is more and more 'on the move'.

Personal media and connectivity through mobile and ubiquitous computing emphasize the individual-ness of mobile devices. By contrast, references to a strong constitutive social dimension and the re-discovery of a community sense (and of local-ness associated with informational networks) pervade some of the literature on ubiquitous and mobile devices, labelled as 'mobile social software' [cf. Melinger, 2004]. Such references go back to the utopian terms through which new technological systems and infrastructures are described: in the rhetoric, Internetworking is "more direct, participative, democratic, socially engaging, and community oriented" than any other technological infrastructure for communication [Iacono and Kling, 2001: 113].

Furthermore, not only are people mobile, but also cultures can be described as 'on the move' (Urry, 2003). In this respect, the increasing technological mediation of everyday life draws both continuities and discontinuities with previous and current mobilities.

On the one hand, the dis-anchorage from space and time enabled by mobile communication reinforces the perception of ubiquity as "appropriate for an examination of mobile communication. The device is seemingly ubiquitous in its diffusion and in its role as the Swiss army knife of personal technologies" [Ling, 2004: 5].

On the other hand, such a ubiquity, associated with a pervasive diffusion of mobile phones, is very flexible and can be contextualised differently: an example of the 'context-sensitivity' of mobile technologies and artefacts is provided by the possible combination among what Larsen et al. (2005) define 'different mobilities' and the fact that "the mobile phone with SMS text is enabling the flexibilisation of people' s path through time-space (...)" [Urry, 2002: 8].

Different and interdependent mobilities (of people physically travelling, of objects, of information, images and memories, virtual travel on the Internet and communicative-mediated travel; Urry, 2000 and 2003) are differently supported by communicative and technological mediation, with striking combination of mobility and 'immobility', as in the use of ubiquitous computing in the household environment and the renewed emphasis on the home as privileged target for the consumer electronics and media fruition (e.g. attempts to integrate the Internet and television). Furthermore, "family life is becoming plugged into an ever-expanding array of communication technologies that connect families to one another and to the outside world often at great distance. Lives are rarely if ever 'local'" [Larsen et al., 2005: 5].

Then there are (at least) two sides in the discourse of mobility and in the emergence of mobile and ubiquitous technologies. The combination of hypermobility and hypermediatization can result into an increased physical and virtual mobility. Being mobile or not, mobile devices let us afford different kinds of travelling in the information age, recalling what Williams (1974) observed within the diffusion of automobiles and television: a restructured 'mobile privatization', moving towards what we define *mediatized, individual and connected mobility*.

At this stage, we need to move towards the link between discursive practices about mobility and mobile technological artefacts.

4   From ideas to artefacts (and the other way round): back to location?

The three folded model of Iacono and Kling [2001], based on the analytical distinction among technological frames, public discourse and organizational practices, fits the attempt to understand how ideas performed in public discourse come to be translated into technological artefacts: according to Bijker and the SCOT approach [Bijker, 1995], technologies are characterized by interpretative flexibility and constituted as different by relevant social groups who interpret and make sense of them. What is of particular interest with reference to mobile and ubiquitous technology is that these interpretations are totally 'in the making' and they start to draw a path paved of various discursive frames, aimed to establish some favourable links between technological-based networks and social networks and communities. A joint analysis of continuities and break-downs with reference to ideas and artefacts can be drawn in order to understand how and when artefacts come to embed (and support) discursive practices established 'around' them.

"People are able to 'plug into' global networks of information through which they can 'do' to at least certain objects (especially with increased bandwidth) and 'talk' to people without being present in any particular place, without their bodies having to travel. 'Persons' thus occur through various nodes in these multiple networks of communication and mobility. Their body's corporeal location is less relevant in these networks of person-person communication" [Urry, 2002: 8].

This progressive distanciation or separation between physical location and networked communication is one side of mobile and ubiquitous computing. "Mobile phone cultures generate small worlds of perpetual catching up and small talk on the move, blurring distinctions between presence and absence" [Larsen et al., 2005: 50]. On other hand, these small worlds can be supported or enforced by the so called 'location aware technologies' based on specific uses of the mobile infrastructure [cf. www.socialight.net/edu]. These technologies seem to re-orient and anchorage mobility back to physical spaces and location. Design and development of mobilesystems/architectures, in this respect, are exemplary settings for tracing discursive frames linked with local organizational practices. A short review of discourses emerging in the scientific disciplines, professional communities and mass-media advertisement of new mobile services will be proposed in the next section.

The scientific/professional discourse: Technology-driven vs mobile social software perspective

In what direction are discourses and practices on mobile systems and technologies evolving? As discourses are coherent or contradictory traces of embedded organizational practices, it is of the greatest importance to retrieve and retrace discourses in order to understand the most 'local' level in the emergence of new technologies. In this respect, different perspectives of discourse can be identified, layered in the scientific research arena, professional communities and mass-media. It is very important to note that in the discourse about technological infrastructures and devices in general, and about mobile systems in particular, boundaries between scientists, technologists and professional communities linked with specific industries are blurred enough to say that designing mobile and ubiquitous computing systems results from interwoven discursive and organizational practices.

In their review of 105 articles concerning mobile systems development, Hosbond and Jensen [2005] retrieved four perspectives: the 'requirement' perspective, the 'technology' perspective, the 'application' perspective and the 'business' perspective. They conclude noting "the mobility debate so far has been largely technology-driven. The strong focus on technology is an obvious indicator of continuous development and innovation within this field, which reflects somewhat immature technologies, but also emphasizes a strong demand for more robust and flexible technologies" [Hosbond and Jensen, 2005: 11].

On the level of more specific organizational practices, a counter discourse can be retrieved and identified, addressing community and social networking issues rather than the individualizing and personalizing side of mobile and ubiquitous computing. This is "the field of MoSoSo (Mobile Social Software)", which "is evolving quickly, with many new types of applications being developed and deployed. MoSoSo at its most basic level is any software that allows people to connect with others while mobile" [Melinger, 2004a: 1]. This comprises, for example, "a platform that allows people to connect with others in their social network by using mobile telephone handsets in novel ways. Using the current or past location of friends, the (...) platform provides a number of subtle and overt tools which enable unique modes of real-time and time-shifted communication" [http://socialight.net/edu/what.htm].

On other hand, ubiquitous computing goes farther than mobile as "the main challenges in ubiquitous computing originate from integrating large-scale mobility with the pervasive computing functionality. In its ultimate form, ubiquitous computing means any computing device, while moving with us, can build incrementally dynamic models of its various environments and configure its services accordingly. Furthermore, the devices will be able to either 'remember' past environments they operated in, thus helping us to work when we re-enter, or proactively build up services in new environments whenever we enter them" [Lyytinen and Yoo, 2002: 64)]. Such a flexible and 'shapeless' infrastructure, then, will be totally surrounding the everyday life environments and constitutive of them.

However, emphasis on technology rather than society as a recurrent frame of public discourse is not new, neither it is totally new the role played by mass-media in framing the mobile world, society and Internetworking.

Mass-media imaginary and discourse about the mobile world, in fact, reveal a powerful set of stereotypes in delivering the added value of mobile services as devoted to support the individual in his/her social life, to personalize his/her social networks, to bring the world 'around' in the pockets/hands as an extended body. Emphasis on miniaturization and portability of technological devices constitutes a *leitmotiv* of this discourse, which feeds both the layers of public discourse identified (the technology-driven level and the social software level).

In this respect, the Italian context is very interesting with reference not only to the levels of mobile phone diffusion, but also with the symbolic and marketed-to-consumer struggle to enrol new users and expand quality and quantity of mobile services (e.g. TV advertisement especially).

The layers of discourse shortly examined show, on the one hand, a big emphasis on technology as the key-carrier of meaning in practices of mobile systems development (Hosbond and Nielsen, 2005) and, on the other hand, a trend to go back to physical location and afford the re-construction of social connectedness at –a-distance, as in the discourse of mobile social software (Melinger, 2004a and 2004b) This discourse, however, could even be framed as a masked version (ideologically informed) of the technology-driven approach, as it subtly suggests that sociality and community are direct 'emanations' of the mobile software.

5   Politics of signification, inclusion and exclusion as human choice in computerization

"Both the optimistic and the pessimistic stories of computerization are often crafted with the conventions of utopian and anti-utopian writing. The utopian and anti-utopian genres of social analysis are about 500 years old, and predate the social sciences by about 350 years. Authors who write within these genres examine certain kinds of social possibilities, and usually extrapolate beyond contemporary technologies and social relationships. Utopian tales are devised to stimulate hope in future possibilities as well as actions to devise a self-fulfilling prophecy. In contrast, anti-utopian tales are devised to stimulate anger at horrible possibilities and actions to avoid disaster" [Kling, 1996: chapter A section II].

Horrors and hopes can be traced in any technological imagery and public discourse about technologies, in both older and newer media. These attitudes express fear and passion towards embedding a social perspective in narratives of technological development: social expectations framed in public discourse are part of the *politics of signification* carried out and performed by what we could call, with Iacono and Kling [2001] as 'computerization movement activists', or, with Bijker [1995], 'relevant social groups acting in a specific technological frame and constituting it'. Therein, a social informatics perspective deals necessarily with politics of signification: in these politics patterns of action and issues linked with the role of human choice in computerization can be discovered and identified. Mobile and ubiquitous technologies seem to suggest, as in the Internetworking rhetoric [Iacono and Kling, 2001] the utopia of a universal mobile society, where travelling and intermittent co-presence are taken for granted, routinized patterns of action.

However, mobility is neither always a free choice nor is travel 'a fundamental human right' [Kaplan cit. in Urry, 2003] in itself and for all.

Mobility and, correspondingly, immobility, can be coerced or freely chosen (Urry, 2002) and at the same time a 'mobile divide' can be drawn from the apparent hypermobility of contemporary societies, with different possibilities to access and experience mobilities in their mediatized and not-mediatized face.

Who is entitled to mediatized mobility is, often, member of micro communities, or 'mobile elites'. Different communities can aggregate themselves around socio-informational networks where they share specific technological artefacts, services and uses of technologies. These can be variously determined as brand communities (e.g. I-pod users) or loosing-coupled networks of users sharing a common communication model embedded into a specific protocol (e.g. Bluetooth users). Despite the diffusion of the mobile phone and its widespread popularity (now starting and quickly raising in developing countries as new privileged markets for mobile services companies and providers), paths of exclusion and inclusion can be traced at both the level of macro technological infrastructures or architectures, and at the level of e-literacy in using smaller and multifunctional technological devices. On the two sides, different paces and degrees in appropriating technology can be observed. Furthermore, privacy issues seem to constitute the 'horrific' side of mobile and ubiquitous technologies, with the re-discovery of risks of total surveillance and traceability of the 'electronic body'. Permanent connectivity and availability, associated with recording of conversations and messaging under the urgency (and excuse) of international terrorism after September 11th exasperated the emphasis on control and monitoring of communication at a distance. This happens even more with mobile technologies, as "new types of location-aware mobile social software (MoSoSo) applications allow people to develop both weak and strong relationships with others who live and work around them (...) However, location aware MoSoSo applications can bring with them the ability to closely monitor community members and invite unwanted communications, characteristics that often prompt anxieties about intrusions into privacy" [Melinger, 2004b: 1].

In this respect, ubiquity as associated with technologies *anywhere anytime for everybody* hides the (forced) inclusionary path into an invisible network of global surveillance, but also the exclusionary paths which seclude people and communities to coerced (im)mobility and dependence from a thick, seamless web of relations in proximity and distance, or proximity at distance. As Iacono and Kling [2001: 130] concluded, "in their most likely form, the computerization movements of this new century will constitute a conservative transformation reinforcing patterns of an elite-dominated, stratified society". Human choice in computerization has to do with inclusionary and exclusionary politics, performed at different levels. On the level of meanings and symbolic struggles, contending discursive frames orient the miniaturization and portability of technological devices towards individualized or community oriented uses. Discursive frames elaborated in the setting of scientific and professional discourse, as well as in the media, on other hand, contribute to shape ubiquitous technological artefacts in specific directions, to the extent that the mobile phone as object becomes a symbol of fashionable life styles and a medium open towards meaningful practices of consumption and appropriation (cf. Silverstone, 1994) : as it incorporates shared meanings in a specific shape, it can be truly considered a 'cultural object' (Griswold, 1994).

Entering these frames means to recover the mundane root of technological artefacts cultivated and growing through a sociotechnical, 'fully social driven' process. Such a project, we think and claim, is coherent with Kling's constant attention to societal mobilization around technologies.

6   Conclusions

The imperative of mobility and increasing embeddedness of artefacts in the material and immaterial fabric of everyday life were analyzed in this contribution as the starting points to understand mediatization and mobility characterizing contemporary society. Ubiquity as a metaphor and perspective for development of new technological artefacts was de-constructed through the analysis of the technological frame of mobile and ubiquitous computing. Such a frame comprises discursive practices about mobility, ubiquity, miniaturization and other affiliated concepts, which overall depict the 'imaginary in the making' of the 'mobile Internetworking' as a specific sub-culture in computerization movements (cf. Iacono and Kling, 2001). From this analysis, different contending discourses emerged: ubiquity as technology *anywhere, anytime, for everyone* unravels its ideological veil in hiding practices of inclusion and exclusion carried out through politics of signification; both indifference to and awareness of physical location constitute directions for development of mobile systems and architectures; proximity and distance, presence and absence are evoked and enabled by mobile and ubiquitous computing. The way domestication of artefacts proceed is far from indifferent to all this: societal mobilization around technologies always tells us what those technologies will (not) become and, especially, to whom they will (not) deliver their horrors and hopes, beliefs and images, constraints and opportunities.

References

1. P. Berger, and T. Luckmann, *The social construction of reality* (Doubleday, New York, 1967).
2. W.E Bijker, *Of Bycicles, Bakelites and Bulbs* (The MIT Press, Cambridge, 1995).
3. W. Griswold, *Cultures and Societies in a Changing World* (Pine Forge Press, USA London New Dheli, 1994).
4. S. Iacono and R. Kling, in: *Information Technology and Organizational Transformation. History, Rhetoric and Practice*, edited by: J. Yates and J. Van Maanen (Sage Publications, Thousand Oaks:, 2001), pp. 93-135.
5. R. Kling, (ed.), *Computerization and Controversy. Value Conflicts and Social Choices* (Academic Press , San Diego, 1996, 2nd edition).
6. R. Kling, Center for Social Informatics, History of the term (October 10, 2005); http://rkcsi.indiana.edu/article.php/about-social-informatics/35
7. R. Ling, *The Mobile Connection. The Cell Phone's Impact on Society* (Morgan Kauffman Publishers, an Imprint of Elsevier, San Francisco CA, 2004).
8. J. Larsen, J. Urry, and J. Axhausen, Social Networks and Future Mobilities. Report to the UK Department for Transport. Final draft, December 2005; http://www.lancs.ac.uk/fss/sociology/cemore/cemorepublications.htm
9. K. Lyyttinen, and Y. Yoo, Research Commentary: The Next Wave of Nomadic Computing, *Information Systems Research*, 13(4), 377-388 (2002a).
10. K. Lyyttinen, and Y. Yoo, Issues and Challenges in Ubiquitous Computing, *Communications of the ACM*, 45(12), 63-65 (2002b).
11. D. Melinger, Privacy's role in Mobile Social Software for the Urban Community, Paper presented at the 6th International Conference on Ubiquitous Computing, Nottingham, 7-10 September (2004a).
12. D. Melinger, Privacy and Community in the Design of Mobile Social Software, Paper presented at the International Conference on Mobile Communication, Seoul, 18-19 October (2004b).
13. G. Pellegrino, Hypermediatization and Inertia: Patterns of Technological Appropriation between Reproduction and Innovation, Paper presented at the 20th Egos Colloquiuum, Ljubljana, 3-5 July (2004); www.egosnet.org (member area).
14. R. Silverstone, *Television and Everyday Life* (Routledge, London, 1994).
15. Socialight (2004); http://socialight.net/edu/
16. Socialight, What is Socialight (2004); http://socialight.net/edu/what.html
17. J. Urry, *Sociology beyond Society: Mobilities for the 21st Century* (Routledge, London, 2000).
18. J. Urry, Mobility and Proximity, *Sociology*, 36(2) 255-274 (2002), retrieved in http://www.ville-en-mouvement.com/interventions/John_Urry.pdf
19. J . Urry, Mobile Cultures, Paper published by the Department of Sociology, Lancaster University, at http://www.comp.lancs.ac.uk/sociology/papers/Urry-Mobile-Cultures.pdf (2003).
20. M. Weiser, The world is not a desktop, *Interactions*, January, 7-8 (1994).
21. R. Williams, *Television: Technology and Cultural Form* (Fontana, London, 1974).

Firm Information Transparency: Ethical Questions in the Information Age

Antonino Vaccaro, Peter Madsen
IN+ Center for Innovation, Technology and Policy Research, IST Lisbon
and Carnegie Mellon University, USA, vaccaro@andrew.cmu.edu
J. Heinz School of Public Policy and Management and the Center for the
Advancement of Applied Ethics, Carnegie Mellon University, USA
Peter Madsen <pm2n@andrew.cmu.edu>

Abstract. The wide diffusion of information and communication technologies (ICT) over the last few decades has modified the way in which individuals and institutions interact and conduct social and business activities. We analyze the importance of a firm's information transparency, defined as the degree of completeness of information, regarding their own business activities, provided by each company to the market, and the related role of ICT. First, we present a brief historical perspective of information transparency of business organizations. Then, we analyze the actual role and possibilities offered by ICT to contemporary firms and to society. We develop a model that integrates the ethical and economical/financial forces affecting information transparency applying it to the case study of a famous multinational company. Finally, useful insights for scholars and practitioners are presented.

Keywords: Information Ethics, Information Transparency, ICT and Social Change, Business Ethics.

1 Introduction

The recurrent scandals in the industrial and financial sectors that have occurred in the last few decades have given rise to ethical concerns and lower esteem in the public's opinion regarding business practices of contemporary firms. As a consequence, consumers around the world continue to ask for more detailed information about business practices and business ethics.

On the other hand, the introduction and diffusion of information communication technologies (ICT) has caused 'the electronic communication effect' [1]. This is the

Please use the following format when citing this chapter:

Vaccaro, A., Madsen, P., 2006, in IFIP International Federation for Information Processing, Volume 223, Social Informatics: An Information Society for All? In Remembrance of Rob Kling, eds. Berleur, J., Numinen, M. I., Impagliazzo, J., (Boston: Springer), pp. 145–156.

contemporary increase of the amount of information transmitted per unit of time and the reduction of information transmission costs. In particular, the diffusion of web-based technologies can allow corporations to enhance the amount of information concerning their activities transmitted to customers that navigate frequently on the net. As we will see in the following sections, from a conceptual point of view, new virtual technologies could permit the transformation of contemporary firms from opaque to more transparent social institutions. We define a firm's external information transparency as the degree of completeness of information, provided by each company to the market, concerning its business activities[1] [2]. A transparent company is an institution that shares every kind of information concerning its business activities requested by the society. On the contrary, an opaque company prefers not to disclose any kind of information other than that required by national laws (e.g. financial balance sheets, product information, securities filings, etc.).

The possibilities offered by virtual technologies open new solutions to ethical questions concerning the transparency of contemporary companies. Indeed, if ICT could allow the transmission of any kind of information, it is necessary to understand why today the 'civil' society, and in particular customers, receives only a restricted group of information regarding a firm's activities. This theme is of particular interest today for various reasons. First of all, globalization has spaced out the relationships between customers and companies: every person today purchases goods and services from unknown companies that are located thousands miles away and whose activities are regulated by laws of foreign countries. Secondly, individuals of our multi-cultural society can be interested to know whether the goods sold by a company are produced without violating their own ethical and religious beliefs. Third, many consumers' associations around the world (e.g. the Italian As.C.I.I., the American Council on Consumer Interest, the Australian Consumers' Association, etc.) have organized and continue to organize protests and boycotts in order to force companies, in particular multinational corporations, to provide detailed information on how they conduct their business. A very well known example is the case of Nike where the company was constrained to disclose detailed information about the location of its factories described by many as 'sweatshops' and their employees working conditions (e.g. average salary, working hours per day, minimum age requested to be hired, etc.).

In the following sections we will try to introduce the new perspectives offered by the diffusion of ICT and transparency concerns. Based upon Kling's vision of ICT as a 'transformative technology'[2] [3], we are interested to analyze the main socio-economical factors that affect the exploitation of ICT by the society and business organizations in relation to the concerns with transparency.

This paper contributes to the literature in several ways. First of all, grounding on Vaccaro's model (2006) of firms' ICT related ethical concerns, it deepens our understanding of the problems of transparency and contextualizes them within the discipline of business ethics. Secondly, it provides an analysis of the new opportunities and perspectives offered by ICT to contemporary business organizations in order to improve their transparency. Finally, it provides normative indications to practitioners and useful insights to scholars for further research.

The remainder of this paper is divided into four sections. The first presents a brief historical perspective of information transparency in business organizations.

The second contextualizes transparency within the fields of business and information ethics. Section three develops a model that frames the forces affecting the transparency of contemporary firms while the fourth presents a case study analysis and related discussion. Finally, indications for practitioners and insights for further research are proposed.

2   A Brief Historical Perspective of Firm's Information Transparency

The human organization we would consider as the first expression of contemporary firms was the artisan workshop. It has represented in the whole globe a common form of business organization for not less than five millennia. It was the *most transparent* form of business practice in economic history: inside the ancient village everyone knew what was occurring inside the walls of each workshop. Indeed, when ancient villages grew up, a public was born and the public relations of business activities became a reality [4]. Original manuscripts of Medieval and Renaissance periods report artisan laboratories as places opened to the visits of the public [5,6]. Business processes were consequently transparent to everyone inside the community. Individuals that tried to hide their knowledge regarding their working practices were accused of wizardry, imprisoned and/or burned in the village square [7].

The first industrial revolution caused the diffusion of immense business organizations with the concentration of many large groups of workers inside the perimeter of productive plants. This major change in the organization of labor and the raise of competition caused a deep transformation of the relationships between new industrial firms and the world: the factory's walls created a division between society and business organizations [8]. Only workers were allowed to enter into the interior areas of productive plants and consequently the information related to business activities were not directly observable by other member of the society. Historians report to us that for a long period the worst social injustices (e.g. exploitation of children work, inhuman working conditions) were committed and remained hidden within the perimeters of factories [9].

After the first industrial revolution, national governments and inter-governmental associations across national borders tried to improve workers conditions inside business organizations through the creations of specific laws that imposed adequate workplace conditions.

On the other hand, a great part of the information regarding firms' activities continued not to be available for the general citizenry. The legislations of developed countries regulated information regarding business activities and limited how much information could be shared with society. Most of these data are disclosed by firms to the society through balance sheets and through product information instructions and manuals added to the purchased goods. As a consequence, since the early 1970s individuals and citizen organizations have protested against practices of companies that they thought to be unethical. Consumers demonstrated their desire to receive more and more detailed information regarding how companies conduct their business activities and generate their profits. The dawn of the era of 'consumer rights' had occurred.

3   From Traditional to Virtual Transparency Tools: New Perspectives for Contemporary Firms

In the 20th Century, before the advent of the new virtual technologies, the relationship between the firm and the social system was conducted through products and/or services supplied by the firm, direct contacts between customers, suppliers and the firm's workforce, marketing and communication initiatives, and official documents such as balance sheets and financial reports [2]. The diffusion of ICT, and in particular of Internet-based technologies, has, however, modified the interactions between business organizations and the socio-economical environment. Firms started to look at websites as an opportunity to interact with current customers or potential ones. Indeed, today, a growing number of individuals can easily connect to the Net, reach directly the website of a company, read the available information provided on the electronic pages and eventually contact the firms' employees through their email server. This part of the market that frequently uses the Internet and other ICT-based solutions is a very important target of contemporary corporations due to its high financial possibilities and related purchase capabilities.

Consequently Internet based technologies have represented an important driver of change because they lead to firms choosing what kind of information should and should not be available on their websites. In theory, new virtual technologies may allow firms to become completely transparent institutions or *naked corporations* [10]. Indeed, introducing web-cams and microphones in every room of a firm's building, and connecting these systems on a website, could allow monitoring in real time of every workplace activity, conversation or decision taken inside the firm.

In the real world, a large number of companies have not adopted new virtual technologies to transform themselves into completely transparent institutions. In contrast with the rising requests of more transparency provided by individuals and consumers' associations, such as the Nike case, contemporary companies share only a limited set of information regarding their business activities.

We are interested in considering not only the ethical, but also other social and economic components that affect the transparency of contemporary firms. Indeed, the contextual inquires [11] that this work will attempt to raise and answer are: *what are the social, cultural and environmental conditions that affect the ICT-enabled information transparency of contemporary firms? What are the expected results of higher levels of ICT-enabled transparency of business organizations on society?*

We will try to answer such research questions following a four-step conceptual path. First, based upon recent economic and managerial theories of the firm [12, 13], we will identify the economic and financial forces affecting firms' information transparency. In a second step, we will introduce the ethical forces following the indication of Vaccaro's model [2]. As a result, we will present a new framework of the forces that affect firms' information transparency as represented in Figure 1. In the following section we will analyze a case study useful in testing the new model followed by a discussion and some conclusions.

4 Virtual Transparency: Perspectives and Constrains

This section introduces and analyzes the economic/financial and ethical factors affecting the transparency of contemporary firms. This analysis will result in a five-part model presented later.

4.1 Transparency from an Economic and Financial Perspective

The appropriate identification of the economic and financial forces affecting a firms' information transparency should require the definition and contextualization of the firm's specific role inside the economic system and more generally within the society. Among theories that conceptualize business organization in this regard are those that focus upon transaction costs [12, 14], agency theory [13, 15], measurement costs [16], incomplete contracts [17] and knowledge-based resources [18].

We propose a vision of the firm as a natural response of the society to market failures: when a market is not able to provide products and/or services requested by the society, the foundation of a firm represents a solution to supply this need [12]. Firms are created to reduce market transaction costs [12], to exploit economies of scale and scope, to aggregate different and heterogeneous knowledge based resources [18], with the final objective to provide a product and/or a service to society. Moreover, competition guarantees the proliferation of more effective and efficient economic actors while private investors provide the necessary financial support.

Following this perspective three different and contrasting forces affect information transparency of contemporary business organization. The first force is represented by the requests of customers that, as already stated, demand higher levels of information transparency. The second force is represented by the pressure of existent and possible competitors that, in order to improve their market position and power, try to acquire and exploit every useful piece of information from other firms. The third force is represented by the pressure of investors who might choose to modify their financial support to firms' activities reducing both the value of shares and more in general the whole financial capability of the company, if their demands for a more transparent firm are not met.

These three different forces allow us to understand how an 'optimal level' of information transparency could be decided by firms in relation to economic and financial pressures. In order to simplify our analysis, we consider, as a preliminary step, an ideal company that, given specific market conditions and similar productive/technological capabilities available for all competitors, is able to provide optimal service to society and to maximize investors' returns.

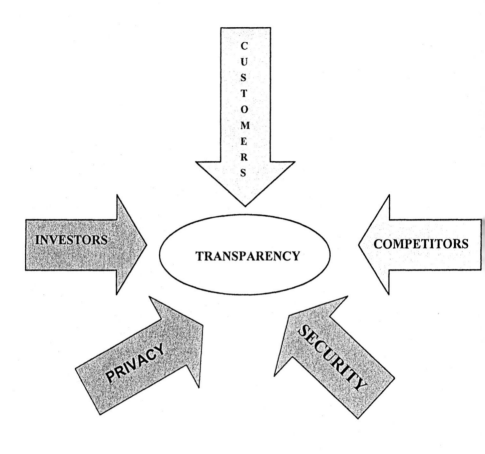

Figure 1: The five forces affecting a firm's information transparency

If we imagine that the second and the third force do not affect the market in which this firm operates, i.e. there is no pressure from existent and possible competitors and none from investors, we should expect a high level of information transparency in our hypothetical firm. Indeed, given two similar products, a customer will choose those provided by a company whose activities are shared with the society instead of those sold by an opaque institution [2]. Consequently, given the absence of the second and third force, every company will try to disclose the highest amount of information in order to maintain the preference of its customers and to gain those of potential ones.

In an opposite situation we could have a market condition in which customers and investors are not interested in a firms' information transparency and each piece of information shared by the firm can be successfully exploited by competitors to improve their comparative position. In this second hypothetical situation, every firm would obviously choose not to share any kind of information because doing so might risk the loss of market position.

Finally, in the case of a market in which there is only the third force, a company will provide a transparency level sufficient to allow investors to control what kind of institution they are financially supporting. The disclosure of a company's information will be in fact associated with the objective to maintain current investors and to attract new ones.

In the real world, companies have to face more complex business conditions. First of all, every company is not sure its service is economically optimal for society because it does not know exactly how effective the operations of other competitors are. This problem is complicated by the fact that different ethical and cultural beliefs can turn on different concepts of 'economical optimality.'

Secondly, firms exploit every kind of useful information of their competitors to improve their market position. An extreme example is reverse engineering in which firms dismantle competitors' products to acquire useful technological information. Consequently, contemporary firms limit the spread of their business data due to the competitors' threat. Finally, there are possible conflicts of interests between customers and investors. The maximization of investors' profits could be in partial conflict with customers' benefits. For example higher levels of product's quality controls can represent a benefit for customers but a decrease of the revenues for investors due to the raise of control costs. The disclosure of information related to quality controls could cause contrasting reaction of customers and investors interested to pursue opposite objectives. Consequently, firms can choose to limit the spread of those pieces of information that can cause incompatible requests of customers and investors.

4.2   The Ethical Concerns

A firm's transparency is conditioned not only by the financial and economical forces that impinge upon it, but also by ethical pressures. Using Vaccaro's model [2], we divided such forces in two main categories, namely, privacy and security. Privacy and security have to do with both individuals that are part of the firm's organization as well as other individuals external to the firm such as customer and suppliers.

Privacy represents an important ethical concern of the Internet era. Indeed, of all the ethical issues associated with the use of ICT, perhaps none has received more media attention [19]. Firm transparency can be affected by privacy requests of employees, customers and suppliers. While ICT can today lead to a complete transparency level for a business organization, this technical possibility cannot be achieved due to the privacy rights of employees. The literature in business ethics and in sociology has widely described the increasing number of privacy rights of employees due to the pressure caused by new ICT [20, 21]. Employees in fact make a claim of privacy principles related to a wide set of information such as salary, medical condition, personal information, working hours, etc. Analogously, customers and suppliers can expect that part of their contractual agreements and activities contracted in with a company will not be made public-ally available and remain a private matter.

Since 9/11, the security concerns of individuals and social institutions have increased greatly around the world. As a consequence, economic and social interactions in the current business environment need to be carefully managed in order to guarantee adequate security to all agents involved in a firms' activities. While customers around the world demand higher levels of firm transparency, it could be claimed that higher levels of transparency could allow other individuals to commit fraudulent or dangerous actions. For example, a nuclear electric-generating facility which has shared detailed information about its productive plants could be attacked easily by terrorists attempting to cause a nuclear disaster. Analogously, unscrupulous parties could exploit detailed personal information of employees that has been shared by a firm for illegal and/or dangerous purposes.

5. Case Study Analysis

The development of the five-part model in the previous section has showed that a level of complete transparency does not *a priori* represent a reasonable choice of contemporary business organizations. Indeed, we demonstrated that companies have to limit the amount of information related to their business activities available in the market in order to defend their competitive position, to manage adequately the relationships with investors, to respect the privacy rights of customers and suppliers and to guarantee the security of individuals and the general public. On the other hand, the continuous demands of customers and the new opportunities offered by ICT suggest that higher levels of information transparency are desirable. We present in this section the case of the Artsana group, a big multi-national company whose transparency level has been changed exploiting the opportunities offered by the Internet-related technologies.

5.1   The Artsana Group

Artsana is a multinational company founded in the 1946 by Piero Catelli in Como, Italy. It currently has a workforce of more than 7000 employees and a worldwide presence in two main market sectors: products for children and for hospitals. In the last decade, this firm has exploited opportunities offered by Internet-based technologies so as to improve the relationship with people throughout the world through a major increase in its level of transparency.

Before the 1990s, communications between Artsana and society were limited. Indeed, the company provided only the mandatory product information in the instructions that were added in a products' pockets. The organization's balance sheet was also a mandatory document, which presented synthetic descriptions of the company's activities and shared outside the firm's internal environment. Today, the group has 26 websites with more than 10.000 web pages that allow users to electronically access detailed information about its products and business practices.

The interviews conducted with one of the top managers of the group confirmed that the transparency of this company is mainly produced by two forces, namely, privacy and customers. Indeed, the investors' force is represented by the three of

Piero Catelli's sons who work inside the company as managers in the General Direction[3]. In other words, investors are not concerned about transparency because all of the information that they need is already available thanks to their position in the Artsana organization. Moreover, transparency is not affected by competitors because product and process technologies relevant for the business activities are protected by patents and, as confirmed by a manager of the organization, there are no *"secrets other than working hard every day"* (Interview, 2006). Finally, Artsana does not manage activities nor does it own any productive plants that can be exploited to endanger individuals or disrupt social security by terrorists. Consequently, the two driving forces that 'shape' Artsana's transparency policy are privacy and customers' demands.

Customers placed strong pressure on Artsana to produce a high level of transparency. During the 1990s numerous companies located in Asia, suppliers of European firms specializing in the commercialization of toys were accused of exploiting children in their productive activities under inhumane working condition. In 1993, various newspapers reported fire of an Asian toys producer's plant, in which 87 employees died and more than 47 were severely hurt due to the lack of an adequate security system. In the following years, various editorials available on the web and letters written by global activists for the respect of human rights accused important multinational companies, an in particular Artsana, to be client of this toy factory and consequently to nourish unethical business activities.

After this tragic event, Artsana decided not only to modify its business activities through the development and following of a rigid code of business ethics and the application of an ethical certification systems for its suppliers (i.e. SA8000 standards), but also it decided to raise its transparency level. The respecting human dignity and social justice and acting with integrity have been an imperative both of the founder and of whole company's workforce[4]. Consequently, more transparency of business practices was established as a good strategy to improve trust and build better relationships with customers, in particular and with society in general.

Since the 1995, the company started to progressively disclose extensive documentations of its products and business activities. The website of the group provides the code of ethics approved by the company's board in 1998, financial reports and also, information regarding the location of plant facilities, working conditions of employees and sub-contractors, etc.[5] Moreover, the company has recently created a specific office that is responsible to answer the questions of customers, and/or potential ones, regarding its products and business practices. Emails and phone-calls directed to the call center located at the group headquarters are the main ways to interact directly with the company. Moreover, it is possible to subscribe to a mailing list in order to receive a monthly email with all the relevant news of the corporation.

Privacy is a value that matters much in such a process of information disclosure. Indeed, the data posted on the group websites have to obey the national privacy laws and in many cases information is provided in aggregated form in order to avoid identification concerns. For example, the Chicco[6] portal supports a newsletter that allows new parents and parents-to-be to exchange information but to do so anonymously without providing any personal information about members and contributors. Analogously, the personal information of customer service employees is protected through email accounts that do not cite their names and surnames.

5.2   Discussion

The Artsana case has offered an interesting example to test the indications of our five-part model and to analyze the opportunities offered by ICT in order to improve the relationship between firms and society. In relation to the firms' transparency concern, this case study suggests that there are two main contributions offered by virtual technologies to our society.

First of all, the Internet has supported the creation of social movements of 'global citizens' that actively apply strong pressures upon companies in order to assure humane working conditions and to promote the following of fundamental sound ethical principles. The websites of these organizations and emails allow the spread of information and personal opinions regarding events occurring around the world today. Contemporary companies consequently have to interact with a *networked society* that is not only more heterogeneous, but also more informed and active against business institutions that operate unethically.

The case of Artsana shows also that Internet-based technologies can effectively support firms to improve their transparency level. Before the 1995, Artsana was an 'opaque' corporation that provided only the information necessary to respect national laws. The scandals that occurred in Asia forced this company to raise its transparency level in order to gain trust with customers and potential ones. Indeed, Artsana's top management recognized the disclosure of information related to the company's products and activities as a strategy to improve the image of the company in the global market. The creation of different websites has allowed Artsana to provide detailed information related to its business while the email supported direct contacts with individuals interested in receiving specific information.

The progressive increase of this company's transparency was enabled by a set of favorable conditions illustrated by our five-part model. The lack of potential security threats, the share ownership concentrated in the Catelli family and the absence of 'company secrets' to protect, have allowed this firm to disclose large volumes of information to society through the successful use of virtual technologies. As already mentioned, customers have represented the driving force behind Artsana's transparency while privacy concerns have limited the disclosure of personal information.

6.   Conclusion

In this paper we have introduced and analyzed concerns associated with the information transparency of contemporary business organizations and the related role of ICT. The development of a five-part model and the analysis of a case study has shown that, while there are ethical and financial/economical forces limiting the spread of information, customers' pressure and the new opportunities offered by the diffusion of ICT can enable higher levels of information transparency in contemporary firms. Information transparency can be exploited in fact by corporations as an opportunity to improve trust and confidence of existent customers and to attract new ones. Our results confirm Kling's analysis of organizations as *'open systems'* [22], i.e. institutions whose behavior is influenced by the relationship that is established with society and its individual members. In this context, ICT play a doubly important role. They widen the horizon of interaction of each firm with the global society allowing contact with distant customers and 'global citizens' to take place. But also, they create the possibility of a networked society in which ethical concerns are shared and promoted as a spontaneous social ethical need. In other words, ICT is transforming society and as a result, a progressive and radical social change can be expected in the future that will see the creation of more transparent markets and more transparent firms in which customers will have more detailed information of a firms' business practices and in which higher levels of interactions will be possible between business organizations and the public.

Acknowledgements

One of the authors is grateful to João César das Neves and to Andrea Adamo for the generous support and suggestions they provided during the development of this paper.

References

1. T. Malone, J. Yates, R. Benjamin, Electronic Markets and electronic hierarchies, *Communication of the ACM*, **30** (6), 484-497 (1987).
2. A. Vaccaro, Privacy, Security and Transparency: ICT-related ethical perspectives and contrasts in contemporary firms, in: *Social Inclusion: Societal and Organizational Implications for Information Systems*, edited by D. Howcroft, E. Trauth, J. I. DeGross , (Springer, New York, forthcoming 2006).
3. R. Kling, Computeration and Social Transformation, *Science, Technology, & Human Values* **16** (3), 342-367 (1991).
4. N.S. Gras, Shifts in Public Relations, *Bulletin of the Business Historical Society*, **19**(4), 97-148 (1945).
5. B. De Dominici, *Vita de Pittori, Scultori e Architetti Napoletani* (Napoli, 1742).
6. T. Garzoni, *La piazza universale di tutte le professioni del mondo* (Venetia,1589).
7. J. Fo, S. Tomat, L. Malucelli, *Il libro nero del cristianesimo*, (Nuovi Mondi Media, Bologna, 2006)
8. P. Deane, *The First Industrial Revolution* (Cambridge University Press, Cambridge, 1979).
9. C. Tuttle, Hard At Work in Factories and Mines: The Economics of Child Labor During the British Industrial Revolution, *International labor and working class history* **59**, 142-145 (2002).
10. D. Tapscott, D. Ricoll, *The Naked Corporation* (Free Press, New York, 2003).

11. R. Kling, What Is Social Informatics and Why Does It Matter?, *D-Lib Magazine,* **5**(1), 1999.
12. R.H. Coase, The Nature of the Firm, *Economica* **4**, 386-405 (1937).
13. B. Holmström, and P. Milgrom, Multitask Principal-Agent Analyses: Incentive Contracts, Asset Ownership, and Job Design, *Journal of Law, Economics, and Organization* **7**, 24-52 (1991).
14. O. E. Williamson, *The Mechanisms of Governance* (Oxford University Press, Oxford, 1986).
15. B. Holmström, Moral Hazard in Teams, *The Bell Journal of Economics,* **13**, 324-340, (1982)
16. Y. Barzel, *Economic Analysis of Property Rights* (Cambridge University Press, Cambridge, 1989).
17. O. Hart, *Firms, Contracts and Financial Structure* (Oxford University Press, Oxford, 1995).
18. C.K. Prahalad, G. Hamel, The Core Competence of the Corporation, *Harvard Business Review,* **6** (May-June), 79-91 (1990).
19. H.T. Tavani, *Ethics and Technology, Ethical Issues in an Age of Information and Communication Technology* (John Wiley & Soons, Inc., Hoboken, 2004)
20. G.T. Marx, Let's Eavesdrop On Managers, *Computerworld* **26**(16), 29 (1992).
21. G. T. Marx, and S. Sherizen, Monitoring on the job: how to protect Privacy as well as Property, *Technology Review,* **89** (Nov-Dec), 63-72 (1986).
22. R. Kling, and T. Jewett, The Social Design of Worklife With Computers and Networks: An Open Natural Systems Perspective, *Advances in Computers* **39**, 239-293 (1994).

---

[1] In the following part of the paper we will refer to it simply as 'transparency,' or 'firms' transparency' or 'external transparency' bearing in mind that we are not interested in analyzing in this work the 'internal transparency' that is *the degree of virtual connectivity (i.e. availability of access through ICT tools) between the workforce and the external environment* [2]

[2] A transformative technology is one that can be exploited by individuals and organizations in order to modify and resolve current problems of society.

[3] In particular, Michele is C.E.O. of the group, Enrico is Account Director, and Francesca is Marketing and Communication Director.

[4] This fact is confirmed by the current financial involvement of Artsana in numerous humanitarian initiatives around the world and by the awards received by Piero Catelli for the ethical excellence of his career as entrepreneur. In particular, the President of the Italian Republic appointed him *Cavaliere del Lavoro,* the most prestigious award provided by the Italian government to entrepreneurs. Moreover, while there are various websites that declare Artsana did not provide any compensation to the families of the victims and to the injured employees of the China factory, an official report of Assogiocattoli, the Italian not-for-profit organization of Italian toys producers, assures that Artsana has created a compensation fund and entrusted Caritas Hong Kong to be responsible for the distribution of the money to the victims.

[5] Gruppo Artsana, Company Profile, Human Resources, http://www.artsana.com/eng/html/company/i_company.htm (May 1st, 2006)

[6] Chicco is one of the most known and successful brands of the Artsana group.

Politics and Law

Databases, Biological Information and Collective Action

Tom Dedeurwaerdere

FNRS, Centre for the Philosophy of Law, University of Louvain (Belgium)
Dedeurwaerdere@cpdr.ucl.ac.be

Abstract. Developments within bioinformatics and software for data exchange in the life sciences raise important new questions for social informatics. In this paper, I analyse the role of property rights in information in directing these technological developments in the direction of certain social values. In particular, I focus on initiatives for networking distributed databases, operating both on a global scale (such as the Global Biodiversity Information Facility) and in more single-issue networks (such as the European Human Frozen Tumour Tissue Bank). Three institutional models for developing such distributed networks for sharing information are presented and briefly discussed.

Keywords: information sharing, social informatics, bioinformatics, database governance, knowledge commons.

1   Introduction

As scientists and user groups become better connected with each other (particularly through the Internet), and as research focuses on issues of global importance (such as climate change, human health and biodiversity) there is a growing need to systematically address data access and sharing issues beyond national jurisdictions and thereby create greater value from international cooperation. The goal should be to ensure that both researchers and the broader public receive the optimum return on public investment, and to build on the value chain of investment in research and research data (Stiglitz *et al.*, 2000).

Integrated and combined access to this multifaceted realm of information opens perspectives for the implementation of new applications. In the field of life sciences, new sets of tools for studying biological building blocks and pathways will lay the foundations for ever more complex future projects. These may include the complete mapping of an organism's protein and metabolism networks, as well as the creation of

---

Please use the following format when citing this chapter:

Dedeurwaerdere, T., 2006, in IFIP International Federation for Information Processing, Volume 223, Social Informatics: An Information Society for All? In Remembrance of Rob Kling, eds. Berleur, J., Numinen, M. I., Impagliazzo, J., (Boston: Springer), pp. 159–169.

biological models that can pave the way for theoretical models on bacterial speciation and its complex ecological dynamics (Gevers *et al.*, submitted), or the development of tools for automated species identification. These tools undoubtedly require access to sets of skills that are not typically encountered among systematists or within the departments and institutions in which the bulk of formal taxonomic identifications are conducted. Developing solid approaches requires new collaborations between microbiologists, engineers, mathematicians, computer scientists and people who have significant knowledge of the legal and socio-economic aspects of sharing biological resources and software tools in the public domain.

These new applications of information technologies within the life sciences raise important questions related to the social embedding of information technologies. i.e. for 'social informatics' (Kling, 1996). Indeed technical choices within the field of bioinformatics also depend on social choices, whether in problems such as the building of genomic sequence databases, the design of persistent numerical identifiers for taxonomic information on living organisms, or the integration of clinical data and images coming from brain research. These technological developments reflect social choices on issues such as the protection of privacy, ownership of life, and bioethics. Moreover, the capacity to make these choices depends increasingly on clarifying the property rights to the information, which define who has the right to decide upon the way it is used, managed and exchanged. Open access to the information and shared ownership has become a key condition for connecting the path of development of information technologies to social values and ethical reflection.

Within the life sciences, initiatives for sharing information through networking distributed databases have emerged, operating both on a global scale (such as the consortium for Common Access to Biological Resources and Information (CABRI), connecting world wide microbiological resources) and in more focused networks (such as the European Human Frozen Tumour Tissue Databank (TuBaFrost)). From a governance perspective, these networks face increasing pressure from the development of global markets. In particular, the introduction of new standards of intellectual property protection during the last twenty years has had a profound impact on the sharing of data and resources in the field of the life sciences. Two of the most influential and widely debated changes in this context are the 1980 Bayh–Dole Act in the US (Rai and Eisenberg, 2003) and, more recently, the 1996 EU Database Directive 96/9/EC (Reichman and Uhlir, 1999). The Bayh–Dole act explicitly gives universities the right to seek patent protection on the results of government-sponsored research and to retain patent ownership. As a consequence, in the period from 1980 to 1992, the number of patents granted per year to universities in the US increased from fewer than 250 to almost 2700 (Rai, 1999). The EC Database Directive 96/9/EC was a landmark decision that lowered the standards of eligibility to database protection. Indeed the Database Directive offered copyright protection to databases that were original in the selection or the arrangement of their contents, but also to non-original databases if it could be shown that there had been a substantial investment in either the obtaining, the verification or the presentation of their contents. This extended protection to library catalogues, for instance, but also to biological information facilities that network existing databases.

In this paper, I will analyse the models for the institutional design of information sharing in the context of global intellectual property rights. In particular, I will rely on contemporary insights from new institutional economics that show the necessity of collective action to deal with both the insufficiencies of market solutions and the limits of the new forms of public regulation (Reichman and Uhlir, 2003; Hess and Ostrom, 2003; 2005a). For instance, within the related field of digital communication, the development of E-print repositories (such as arXiv.org and BioMedCentral) and trusted digital repositories for knowledge of general interest is based on collaboration between groups of scholars and information specialists to build a common knowledge pool. What is new in these initiatives is that researchers are participating in an international epistemic community that is committed to building a global scholarly library – with the aim of obtaining greater joint benefits and reducing their joint harm from the enclosure process. I will build upon these proposals to elaborate a framework for the analysis of institutional choice in the field of the microbiological information commons.

For these reasons I will focus on the following questions:

(1)   What are the characteristics of biological information, as a public good that can be exchanged by networking databases, and what are the related incentive problems for the provision and use of this good (Section 2.1)?

(2)   What institutional solutions for dealing with these complex incentive problems are currently being proposed (Section 2.2)?

(3)   How can we evaluate these propositions from the point of view of their contribution to social informatics (Section 3)?

2   Governance Models for the Microbiological Information Commons

Microbiological information has been characterised as being part of the public domain (Oldham, 2004; Smith *et al.*, 2004), implying appropriate public and regulatory institutions for guaranteeing its provision. However, this characterisation is very broad and, as has been shown in recent research (Kaul *et al.*, 2003), the notion of the public domain covers a heterogeneous set of transaction situations and incentive problems, which demand a more fine-grained approach.

2.1   Microbiological information as a common pool resource

The microbiological information that is managed and exchanged through biological research collections (BRCs) or global information facilities (such as the Global Biodiversity Information Facility) shows characteristics of both public goods and common pool resources. A convenient way to discuss this is to make a distinction between the ideas themselves and the artefacts and facilities through which they are exchanged. In Table 1, I have illustrated these distinctions and the related incentive problems for three components of the knowledge commons: information as an idea; the physical flow units or artefacts through which the information is exchanged; and the resource system or facility storing the ideas and the artefacts (Hess and Ostrom, 2003). Information as an idea clearly has the characteristics of a public good. It is a resource shared by multiple individuals in a non-exclusive way and it is non-depletable. The use of an idea by someone does not subtract from the ability of another individual to use the same idea at the same time. As such, in a similar manner to the self-archiving initiatives in the field of scholarly communications (Hess and Ostrom, 2003), researchers who participate in building global biological information facilities are building a universal public good for which the more people who have access, the greater the benefit to everyone [*ibid.*]. Positive incentives that play a role in self-archiving initiatives, such as the reduction in costs of publication and access, the scientific recognition and credibility that comes with public disclosure, the increased visibility of information, and instant publication and dissemination (Hess and Ostrom, 2005a), have also been documented in the field of the microbiological information commons (Rai, 1999).

	Examples		
	Contribution of information to a global biological information archive	*Participation in the exchange of tumour tissue data*	*Common web server for storing images*
Bio-physical characteristics	FLOW OF IDEAS (KNOWLEDGE ON BIOLOGICAL DIVERSITY)	Flow of artefacts (images)	Facility (physical storage system)
Type of good	Public good	Common pool resource	Common pool resource
Positive incentives	Visibility, public recognition, instant publication	Access to first-hand, high-quality information related to the data	On-line verification of the diagnosis
Perverse incentives	Under-use: low visibility, lack of use	Misuse: use of the data without contributing to the flow, plagiarism, submitting low quality data	Pollution: storing redundant information that takes a lot of memory space

Table 1. Incentive problems for the public good and common pool resource aspects of the microbiological information commons
(Examples adapted from Hess and Ostrom, 2005b, Table 1; for simplicity of presentation, I have merged production and use incentives)

Information as a physical flow unit or artefact has also been characterised as a depletable resource which presents some of the characteristics of a common pool resource. Indeed, the value of information to users is not only related to the opportunities they have to access a stock or pool of accumulated knowledge somewhere in an encyclopaedia or digital repository, but also to the quality of the flow of the information as it is implemented in the artefacts. By exchanging the information, it is consumed, verified, completed and interlinked with other information. It is this complex process of exchanging artefacts and managing the quality of the information flow that makes the information valuable to the users of the common knowledge pool. Management of this flow depends on compliance with a set of rules, such as verification of the quality of information submitted to the common pool, appropriate citation of the source of the information, and tools for cross-linking to the information generated by the user-communities in the field of knowledge concerned. Non-compliance with or violation of these rules harms the access to and use of the common knowledge base, and can lead to the information flow drying up (so rendering the resource depletable).

As mentioned above, sharing microbiological information through microbiological information facilities is a complex endeavour that also involves sharing larger physical resources. For example, the TuBaFrost project (which gathers data on high quality frozen tumour tissue samples with an accurate diagnosis which are stored in major European cancer centres and universities) makes information accessible and searchable through an uncomplicated query system on the Internet. A key physical resource that is shared in the TuBaFrost project is the Nanozoomer, which allows representative histology images to be stored in a central database, enlarged 20x or 40x and accessed through the virtual tumour bank. The advantage is that, through the addition of images to the virtual tumour bank, diagnoses can be verified on line. However, this also creates a depletable resource to be shared, the disk space of the central database.

2.2   Institutional solutions to the incentive problems

In the previous section I discussed some of the incentive problems to be solved in the organisation of data sharing in the microbiological commons. In this section, I will analyse some of the collective arrangements that are currently being considered for dealing with these incentive problems, focusing more particularly on the role of property rights and contractual arrangements.

In the field of microbiological commons, three main institutional solutions have been discussed in the literature: a model of free dissemination and two models based on conditional deposits for commercial and non-commercial use. All three are based on a form of decentralised ownership and include a certain level of collective management and exclusion rights. Such an institutional arrangement for the governance of the information flow is in accordance with the results that have been obtained from case studies within the field of natural resource management. Indeed, these studies show that, to deal with collective action problems within a common pool resource, there have to be common rules (at least for exclusion and management). These rules are necessary in order to delimit the boundaries of the common pool and impose graduated sanctions for non-compliance with the rules of use so as to prevent depletion of the resource.

2.2.1   Facilitating free dissemination with decentralised ownership
In a first model of data sharing, ownership – and hence the right to alienation – remains with the individual data providers. However the providers transfer a part of their management and exclusion rights to a common data portal. Some key features of this first model can be analysed using the Global Biodiversity Facility (GBIF) as an example. In the GBIF, data is provided to a collaborative database from a variety of sources; the database in turn makes the data freely available to non-commercial users, as illustrated in Figure 1. The ownership of the data, and any related conditions on its

use, remain with the original providers. This means that GBIF does not assert any intellectual property rights to the data that is made available through its network. Moreover, all the data is made available on the terms and conditions that data providers have identified in the metadata. However, even though GBIF does not assert any ownership rights, each data provider transfers some of the management and exclusion rights to GBIF as specified in the Memorandum of Understanding establishing the organisation. This transfer agreement allows different incentive problems related to the governance of the information flow as a common pool resource to be dealt with:

1. When registering their services with GBIF, the data provider has to sign the GBIF data sharing agreement. This stipulates that the data provider will make reasonable efforts to ensure that the data are accurate and will include a stable and unique identifier with the data (Articles 1.4. and 1.5. of the *Data Sharing Agreement*).
2. The data provider has to be endorsed by a GBIF participant. GBIF participants are the signatories of the Memorandum of Understanding which established GBIF. Data participants maintain stable computer gateways (the data nodes) that make data available through the GBIF network. The GBIF participants maintain services that enable new and existing data providers in their domain to be integrated within the GBIF network (Articles 1.8. and 2.4. of the *Data Sharing Agreement*).

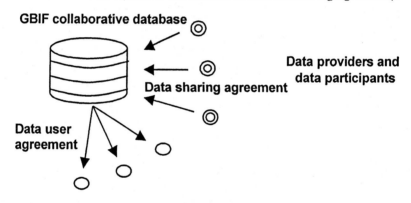

Figure 1. The GBIF model of data sharing

3. The GBIF participants empower the GBIF secretariat to enter into contracts, execute the work programme and maintain central services for the GBIF network. In particular, the GBIF secretariat may provide full or partial data to other users, together with the terms and conditions for use set by the data provider (Article 1.7. of the *Data Sharing Agreement*).
4. Using data through the GBIF network requires agreement to a *Data Use Agreement* when accessing the search engine. This agreement stipulates that users must publicly acknowledge the data providers whose biodiversity data they have used (Article 1.4. of the *Data Use Agreement*).

Through this collective arrangement, GBIF facilitates the free dissemination of biodiversity related data. In practice, GBIF pools data that is, in most cases, already in the public domain or that has been commissioned explicitly for public purposes and can reach a wider audience by being made accessible through the data portal. Elsewhere, more sophisticated two-tiered models have been developed to satisfy both public research interests and commercial opportunities.

2.2.2.   Organising the licensing of data through a collective license organisation

The GBIF model is probably not appropriate for all types of microbiological data sharing. Indeed GBIF covers biodiversity-related data (including substantial microbiological databases) but not the wealth of microbiological data that is relevant for research but not directly relevant for biodiversity conservation purposes (such as plasmids, viruses or human cell lines for cancer research). Moreover, certain types of data are relevant both for public research purposes and private R&D and would benefit from a more coordinated approach to the conditions of data licensing to commercial partners.

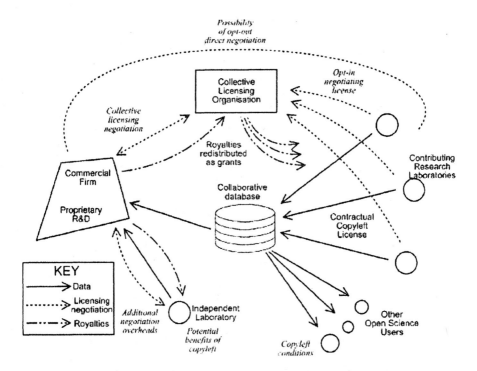

Figure 2. A two-tier system for data sharing based on the transfer of property rights to a collective licensing organisation (Eckersley *et al.*, 2003)

The report of an OECD working group on data sharing in neuro-informatics lists some of the conditions under which a better coordination of the conditions for commercial and non-commercial use of databases is appropriate. For public domain databases and/or in the absence of collective management of the conditions of follow-on use, data sharing does not always guarantee credit to the researchers who originally produced the data, nor provide them with any reward if extensions to their work are commercialised (Eckersley *et al.*, 2003). Moreover, it only provides weak protection against the broader problem of 'patent thickets' (*ibid*).

Under these conditions, the OECD working group advised that different contractual conditions for access to the database be adopted for commercial and non-commercial use. In this model, which is analogous to the dual licensing model employed by some software developers1, non-commercial distribution is permitted by a copyleft license2, with the usual condition that the source of the data must be mentioned (guarantee of credit). Commercial use of the data is only permitted if a specific contract has been negotiated that includes restrictions on this commercial use and specifies a licence fee. Negotiating these ownership licences could be the job of a collective licensing organisation administering the database (Figure 2).

2.2.3 *Organising the licensing of data through agreed contractual templates*
As Reichman and Uhlir (2003) point out, because of the potential problems of leakage (moral hazard) and enforcement (accountability) in collective licensing organisations, the data providers may very well balk at participating in collectively managed collaborative databases. For this reason they propose a model for data sharing that is in many respects similar to the conditional deposits model illustrated in Figure 2, but where the collective licensing organisation is replaced by a 'soft' agreement, which can be a *memorandum* of understanding, a code of conduct, a common prototype or template specifying the way in which contractual relations with private content providers will be entered into (see Figure 3).

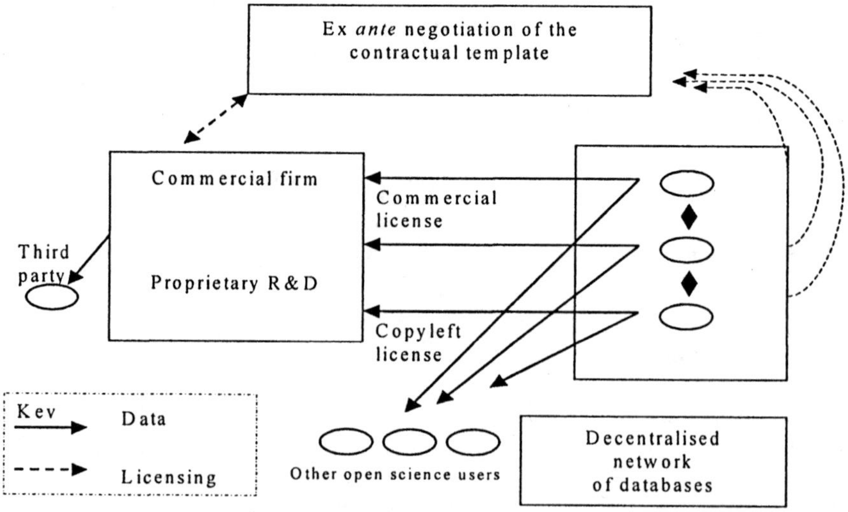

Figure 3. Two-tiered system for data sharing in a decentralised network of providers, based on a multilateral agreement between 'open science' data providers: a copyleft license (for relations with open-science users) and a contractual template (for relations with commercial users) (based on proposals in Reichman and Uhlir, 2003)

Reichman and Uhlir's (2003) proposition is designed to make it possible to restrict the use of basic scientific research data by users who want make a profit from it, or sell it to a third party. In order to prevent a 'race to the bottom' between competing producers of databases in communities that are traditionally dedicated to open science, they propose the adoption of a multilateral negotiated agreement amongst universities and between universities and their funding agencies. These agreements would set the standards for data exchange with other open science users through a kind of copyleft license and the standards for data exchange with commercial users through a common contractual template. To succeed, "these templates must be acceptable to the universities, the funding agencies, the broader scientific community, and the specific sub-committees – all of whom must eventually weigh in to ensure that academics themselves observe the norms that they would thus have collectively implemented" [*ibid.*].

3 Conclusion

The aim of this paper was to discuss a framework for the analysis of the governance of the microbiological information commons, relying on contemporary insights in new institutional economics. I have argued for the importance of considering microbiological databases both as a public good and as a common pool resource, the first referring to them as a common stock of ideas (hence non-subtractable in nature), and the second to the conditions of the organisation of the information flow through the exchange of artefacts and the use of common facilities (resources which are depletable).

Innovative proposals have been made to deal with the complex incentive problems related to the organisation of data sharing, especially in a context where the existing networks have to face increasing pressure from a globalised intellectual property regime. I considered more closely the successful endeavours of the Global Biodiversity Information Facility and the proposals for a two-tiered regime for governing the conditions of follow-on use of the data and related biological resources.

These institutional models offer interesting possibilities for social informatics. As I have argued, retaining some property right in the information, particularly a decision right on the way the information is managed in a certain community, is an important way of embedding the new technologies in the social context. Of course, the question of how these values are put into practice in the different institutional models still has to be evaluated. For instance: do such schemes really prevent enclosure of information in the public domain? do they initiate an effective learning process leading to common beliefs on the social values at stake? The experience of GBIF in this respect is limited. It only connects existing public databases in a distributed network of 'national nodes', without any obligation to decide on a common data policy. The learning that has occurred was mainly technical: through preparatory discussions in OECD, a common data exchange format was agreed upon that benefits the biodiversity conservation community at large. This is an important step forward, but the long-term sustainability of this model, in the absence of a more substantial common policy, can still be questioned. The more centralised propositions by Reichman and the OECD neuro-informatics group go a step further. Indeed, the creation of more integrated institutions allows a set of common values to be implemented. The centralised organisation proposed by the OECD neuro-informatics group has a certain advantage, in that the governing body has to agree on the common management principles. However, more empirical research is needed to evaluate how these different schemes can strike a balance between the requirements of efficient coordination and the effective implementation of their social values.

References

Benkler Y. (1998), The Commons as a Neglected Factor of Information Policy, Remarks at the Telecommunications Policy Research Conference (Sept. 1998), available at http://www.benkler.org/commons.pdf (last visited July 2005).

Eckersley P. Egan G.F., Amari S., Beltrame F., Bennett R., et al. (2003), Neuroscience Data and Tool Sharing, *Neuroinformatics Journal*, Vol. 1 (2), pp.149–165.

Gevers D., Cohan F.M., Lawrence J.G., Spratt B.G., Coenye T., Feil E.J., Stackebrandt E., Van De Peer Y., Vandamme P., Thompson F.L. and Swings J. (submitted). Re-evaluating prokaryotic species. *Nature Reviews Microbiology*.

Hess C. and Ostrom E. (2003), Ideas, Artefacts, and Facilities: Information as a Common-Pool Resource, *Law and Contemporary Problems*, Vol. 66(1/2), pp. 111–146.

Hess C. and Ostrom E. (2005a), A Framework for Analyzing the Knowledge Commons, in Ostrom E. and Hess C. (eds), *Understanding Knowledge as a Commons*, forthcoming.

Hess C. and Ostrom E. (2005b), A Framework for Analyzing Governance and Collective Action in the Microbiological Commons, paper presented at the Workshop on 'Exploring and Exploiting the Microbiological Commons', Brussels, July 7–8, 2005.

Kaul I., Conceiçao P., Le Goulven K. and Mendoza R.U. (eds.) (2003), *Providing Global Public Goods. Managing Globalization*, Oxford University Press, New York/Oxford.

Kling R. (ed.) (1996), *Computerization and Controversy: Value Conflicts and Social Choices*, second edition, Academic Press, New York.

Oldham P. (2004), Global Status and Trends in Intellectual Property Claims: Genomics, Proteomics and Biotechnology, Centre for Economic and Social Aspects of Genomics, 60pp.

Rai A.K. (1999), Regulating Scientific Research: Intellectual Property Rights and The Norms of Science, *Northwest University Law Review*, Vol. 77, pp. 77–152.

Rai A.K. and Eisenberg R.S. (2003), Bayh–Dole Reform and the Progress of Biomedicine, Vol. 66, (1/2), *Law and Contemporary Problems*, pp. 289–314.

Reichman J. (2002), Database Protection in a Global Economy, *Revue Internationale de Droit Economique*, pp. 455–504.

Reichman J. and Uhlir P.F. (1999), Database Protection at the Crossroads: Recent Developments and Their Impact on Science and Technology, *Berkeley Technology Law Journal*, 14, Vol. 793, pp. 799–821.

Reichman J. and Uhlir P.F. (2003), A Contractually Reconstructed Research Commons for Scientific Data in a Highly Protectionist Intellectual Property Environment, *Law and Contemporary Problems*, Vol. 66, pp. 315–440.

Smith R., Thorsteindottir H., Daar S.A. and Singer P.A. (2004), Genomics Knowledge and Equity: A Global Public Goods Perspective on the Patent System, *Bulletin of the World Health Organization*, pp. 384–389.

Stiglitz J., Orszag P.R. and Orszag J.M. (2000), The Role of Government in a Digital Age, Report for the Computer and Communications Industry Association, United States.

1   See, for example, the successful MySQL database software.
2   Under a copyleft regime for software, all users have the right to modify and adapt the program freely, on condition that their resulting development is also made freely available for use and further adaptation. The OECD working group's proposal is to apply the same license provision to the non-commercial use of databases.

Internet-Based Commons of Intellectual Resources: An Exploration of their Variety

Paul B. de Laat

Faculty of Philosophy, University of Groningen,
The Netherlands, P.B.de.Laat@rug.nl

Abstract. During the two last decades, speeded up by the development of the Internet, several types of commons have been opened up for intellectual resources. In this article their variety is being explored as to the kind of resources and the type of regulation involved. The open source software movement initiated the phenomenon, by creating a copyright-based commons of source code that can be labelled 'dynamic': allowing both use and modification of resources. Additionally, such a commons may be either protected from appropriation (by 'copyleft' licensing), or unprotected. Around the year 2000, this approach was generalized by the Creative Commons initiative. In the process they added a 'static' commons, in which only use of resources is allowed. This mould was applied to the sciences and the humanities in particular, and various Open Access initiatives unfolded. A final aspect of copyright-based commons is the distinction between active and passive commons: while the latter is only a site for obtaining resources, the former is also a site for production of new resources by communities of volunteers ('peer production'). Finally, several patent commons are discussed, which mainly aim at preventing patents blocking the further development of science. Throughout, attention is drawn to interrelationships between the various commons.

Keywords: commons, copyright, licenses, open source software, patent

1 Introduction

Both natural and intellectual resources can be held in a commons. That is, according to the common legal definition, everybody is privileged to use them, and nobody has the right to exclude others from use. During the last decades, the commons phenomenon has increasingly attracted attention. This article will focus in particular upon commons of intellectual resources, and their further expansion as facilitated by

Please use the following format when citing this chapter:

de Laat, P., 2006, in IFIP International Federation for Information Processing, Volume 223, Social Informatics: An Information Society for All? In Remembrance of Rob Kling, eds. Berleur, J., Numinen, M. I., Impagliazzo, J., (Boston: Springer), pp. 171–183.

the Internet. I intend to show that talking about the Internet-based commons *in general* is not very helpful. Instead, it is more useful to distinguish between several commons that differ as to the kind of resources and the amount of regulation involved. Throughout it will be argued, that the open source software movement has paved the way, and all subsequent - broader - developments have been modelled upon it.

2   Open Source Software

The term 'intellectual products' may refer to a whole range of creative activities of the human mind: natural and social sciences, technology, the humanities, and art (literature, paintings, photographs, film, music). Expressions of creativity in these domains may enjoy copyright protection (and as a matter of fact, nowadays this protection obtains automatically upon production). Such copyrighted products, by definition, do not constitute a commons accessible for all. Instead, any use or reuse depends on permission of the copyright holders. In the last decades, a remarkable development has taken place. While many producers wanted a more active circulation for the intellectual resources that they created, they invented (legal) mechanisms to allow use and sometimes even modification without previous permission being needed.

It was the movement to liberate software in particular that started this development. In the 1980s already, in pre-Internet times, volunteer software developers were used to exchanging their creations amongst each other, hoping for useful comments, detection of bugs, patches for them, and new features. In this ongoing process, the software involved would become ever better and ever more reliable. This cooperation among 'hackers' (as they call themselves) depended critically upon exchanging the source code of programs as written in one of the available computer languages, as only then a program can be understood and analyzed properly. As soon as source code has been compiled into object code, an unintelligible string of 0s and 1s is the result.

On what terms these programs were made available? Hackers could have opted for releasing their products in the public domain, as for example was the standard procedure for software from US government agencies. This commons, however, was not acceptable to most of them, because they wanted to impose at least some regulations upon fellow hackers. A 'regulated commons' was their preferred choice. One concern, for example, was that the original authorship of pieces of code should remain visible during the ongoing process of source code modification. The approach chosen to actually prescribe regulations was to claim copyright, and on this base write so-called *copyright licenses*. Such licenses typically allow free use and modification of code, as well as (re)distribution of (modified) source code (cf. the open source definition in OSI 1997-2005, for what around the year 2000 came to be christened 'open source licenses'). These regulations, therefore, draw their juridical strength from the combination of copyright law and contract law.

From the very beginning these licenses fell into two separate categories, creating either a commons protected from appropriation, or an unprotected one. Let me explain. One of the oldest licenses is the General Public License (GPL) as formulated by Richard Stallman in the early 1980s, also colloquially referred to as 'copyleft' [FSF/GNU 1989/1991]. It accompanied software packages like his GNU C compiler and GNU Emacs editor. As a more famous example of a later date, the kernel of the Linux operating system carries GPL-terms. The license allows free use, modification and (re-)distribution of code, as any other open source license. In addition, however, any distribution of modified GPL-ed code must carry the GPL again, no other terms of distribution are allowed. More broadly, any program that includes GPL-ed fragments ('a work based on the program') may only be published under GPL-conditions. In this way, an endless cycle governed by the GPL ensues. The license does not, as it is sometimes maintained, preclude composing a modified version in object code and selling it on the market for money. However, any buyer may request access to the program in source code, with a GPL attached. This obligatory offer creates the possibility of retrieving the source code at all times. No branch of the project is permitted to gravitate outside the public view forever. Effectively, this commons is *protected* from private appropriation. In a metaphorical sense, the GPL creates a dam around the lake of source code, preventing irreversible leakage towards lower (commercial) regions. Such a dam is important, while it addresses one of the central problems of a commons: how to maintain the resources in good condition ('provisioning problem')?

On the other hand we find the Berkeley Software Distribution license, dating from the late 1980s, which accompanied the various free Unix-releases. Also the well-known Apache webserver software has evolved under its terms. This license, and others very similar to it, provide the same freedoms as any other open source license (of use, modification and redistribution), while adding no restrictions whatsoever upon the process. Literally everything is allowed, if only the original copyright notices are retained all along (which, by the way, the GPL also requires) [BSD 1998]. So here we have a commons which is *not* protected from 'appropriation': anyone may modify BSD licensed code and sell it in closed form, without being obliged to disclose the source code upon request. As a consequence, a path may branch off ('fork') from the public project and be developed further outside the commons. In terms of the metaphor from above: this lake is not protected by a dam, and the water is free to take its 'natural' course.

In actual fact, some 20 to 30 other open source licenses are in use, as drafted from the 1980s onwards by volunteers, not-for-profit organizations and companies. However, apart from hardly being used, these do not introduce a substantially new type of license. Although minor details of implementation are different, they can be classified as either GPL-like or BSD-like licenses [cf. De Laat 2005]. Protective and non-protective types of open source licenses are the two main classes to be distinguished.

This movement for opening up software is not just a marginal phenomenon. After a slow start in the 1980s, the pace of the movement has been accelerating sharply in the 1990s, mainly because the Internet allows instant reproducibility. The biggest open source platform of today, sourceforge, claims to host over 100,000 projects, populated by over a million participants. Available statistics indicate that the protected commons is the preferred option (79% of packages carry a GPL-like license); the unprotected commons is much smaller (14% of licenses are BSD-like) (figures deduced from sourceforge statistics, as retrieved from http://sourceforge.net/softwaremap/trove_list.php?form_cat=13; cf. De Laat 2005).

As one of the first moves outside the domain of software proper the so-called GNU Free Documentation License (GFDL) deserves to be mentioned here [FSF/GNU 2002]. This license, drafted by the FSF in order to accompany written manuals for GPL-ed software, is similar to the GPL in allowing the free use, modification and redistribution of the texts involved, whether commercially or non-commercially. Any redistribution, furthermore, is to carry the same GFDL terms. So, essentially, this is the GPL for source code transformed to apply to text. Notice that the whole problematic of source code versus object code is absent here. While manuals are simply text, in no need to be compiled, the elaborate provisions as formulated in the GPL to guarantee the return of (updated) source code to the commons are no longer necessary. All modified manuals as published are automatically intelligible. Only a faint echo applies: according to the GFDL, any copy or modification must be 'transparent', not 'opaque': the text must be in a format that allows easy machine manipulation and modification by users.

3   Creative Commons Initiative

The open source movement captured the imagination of many people working outside software. In the sciences, the humanities and art the very same ideas of 'freeing culture' and 'permanent re-use of culture' were taken up. Especially Stallman's ideas about a commons protected against unwanted appropriation acquired many followers. Along the lines of copyleft many academics and artists took to writing down licenses for their specific outputs. Around the turn of the century a series of licenses became drafted: for text generally (Open Content and Open Publication Licenses), for art in general (e.g., the Free Art License), and for media works (e.g., the Design Science License) and music (e.g., the Open Audio License, the Green Open Music License) in particular [cf. Liang 2004].

A more comprehensive approach, however, only came about as a result of the efforts of Creative Commons, a non-profit corporation based at Stanford University. In 2002 they formulated their approach to choosing an appropriate license (information below drawn from http://creativecommons.org). For a license that allows one's work to be freely copied, distributed, displayed and performed, four conditions have to be specified: i) Attribution: whether one requires to be properly credited as the author, or not; ii) Type of use: whether one allows use for non-commercial purposes only, or for any purpose; iii) Derivative works: whether one allows distribution of derivative works, or not; and iv) Type of license: whether derivative works should carry the same license as the original, or any license is allowed.

After the introduction of these licenses nearly every user turned out to require proper attribution. Therefore Creative Commons decided to simplify their approach and declare attribution the default option. As a result, 6 types of license remain (not 8, while the license condition makes no sense if derivations are not allowed): 1) For non-commercial purposes only; no derivative works; 2) For non-commercial purposes only; derivative works allowed, if carrying the same license; 3) For non-commercial purposes only; derivative works allowed with any license; 4) For all purposes; no derivative works; 5) For all purposes; derivative works allowed, if carrying the same license; 6) For all purposes: derivative works allowed with any license. In Table 1 these 6 licenses are listed systematically, together with the abbreviations as used by the Creative Commons corporation.

Table 1. Classification of creative commons licenses and comparison with open source licenses

For non-commercial purposes only	For all purposes
(1) no derivative works ('by-nc-nd')	(4) no derivative works ('by-nd')
(2) derivative works allowed: with same license ('by-nc-sa')	(5) derivative works allowed: with same license ('by-sa')
(3) derivative works allowed: with any license ('by-nc')	(6) derivative works allowed: with any license ('by')

(5) corresponds to GPL-like licenses for software
(6) corresponds to BSD-like licenses for software

This taxonomy is an important step forward for several reasons. For one thing, it is not geared to a specific type of content, but may presumably cover all content. Any text, photograph, film, music, in fact, anything copyrightable can henceforth be licensed properly. Specific licenses as drafted in the past are no longer needed. One exception applies however: because of the distinction between source code and object code, the specific licenses for software - and software manuals - as discussed above remain the preferred choice.

In fact it is useful to compare the commons as created by this corporation, with the commons as opened up by the open source movement. The systems correspond to each other closely. No wonder, as the people behind the creative commons approach draw their inspiration from precisely that movement. The source code commons as protected by the GPL corresponds to license 5, while the unprotected commons carrying BSD-like licenses corresponds to license 6 (as specified above; see Table 1). From Table 1 it can clearly be seen that, on the one hand, the creative commons approach has defined a new type of commons, consisting of content that may be used freely in verbatim form, but not modified or transformed in any way. Such a restrictive commons does not, of course, allow experimentation and innovation too close to the original expression. Therefore I will refer to it as a 'static' commons. For hackers, this is a non-option while the whole point of open source is to create an ongoing cycle of improvements. Nevertheless, such a static commons may be a useful addition, while sometimes creators of content just want their work to be known.

On the other hand, the Stanford approach has introduced a distinction that has always been absent from the mainstream of the open source movement: the distinction between commercial and non-commercial uses of content. Hackers have always been anxious to include participants from all quarters, in order to maximize participation in innovation. Nevertheless, this distinction may appeal to creators of content that want to stay aloof from commercial exploitation.

I shall now proceed to discuss some initiatives that unfolded under this creative commons umbrella, in order to show how the idea of opening up commons has taken root outside the domain of software. These examples are all drawn from the sciences and the humanities. Concerning art, I have not been able to detect significant commons filled with artistic resources. In line with the analysis above, I distinguish between a static commons, a dynamic commons (either protected or unprotected), and the public domain (which is dynamic per definition). All along, commercial and non-commercial purposes will be considered together.

4   Open Access

The 'Open Access Initiative' focuses upon the sciences and the humanities only (the following is based on Suber 2004/5). It strives for open access to this literature through the Internet, which has two main dimensions. On the one hand, access should be *free of charge*. On the other, access should not be encumbered by the usual copyright restrictions, but allow the *free use* of accessed texts. Meetings in Berlin, Bethesda and Budapest of interested participants have produced statements of purpose and intent. The movement may be analyzed as the outcome of conflicting trends [cf. PLOS 2003]. On the one hand, public interest in scientific information seems to be growing, which need could be accommodated by the development of the Internet, allowing easy and instant access. This promise, however, is thwarted by rising prices and 'bundling' of journals that publishers impose upon research libraries. Open Access tries to save this original promise of the Internet.

They propose to 'free' the scientific literature by two main vehicles. First, the initiative pleads for the establishment of open access journals; i.e. fully peer reviewed journals that publish on the Internet without access fee. The cost of publication is shifted from users to producers of content (or their employers like the university) or to funding institutions. Such open access journals may be newly established, or the outcome of conversion of existing subscription-based journals. Secondly, open access archives (or repositories) are being proposed, whether centralized or decentralized, equipped with all available search facilities. Operating without peer review, they are intended to be, one might say, the free abode for *all* scientific output (beside commercial textbooks) in a specific field or setting. For one thing, they are to be the outlet for dissertations, research findings, course materials, data files, and the like. For another, the content of all journals is to be deposited here, both the classically run restricted-access journals and open access journals.

What kinds of commons are opened up by Open Access? They are precisely the regulated ones as proposed by the Creative Commons corporation. The creative commons licenses are explicitly recommended as legal vehicles. Additionally, the public domain is mentioned as a possible option. The Open Access Initiative may be said to embrace the creative commons framework. Nevertheless, ambiguities remain in this respect. Adherents produce confusing statements about the amount of freedom to be allowed. The Budapest Initiative (2002) defined 'open access' as 'free availability on the Internet, permitting any users to read, download, copy, distribute, print, search, or link to the full texts of these articles (...)'. If I interpret this definition as 'allowing *at least* so many freedoms', it refers to all creative commons licenses (the whole of Table 1). Both the Bethesda Statement (April 2003) and the Berlin Declaration (October 2003), however, proposed to grant a broader license 'to copy, use, distribute, transmit and display the work publicly and *to make and distribute derivative works* (...)' [italics added; PdL]. To my view, this clearly represents a 'by' license (license 6, Table 1), allowing anything subject to proper attribution. It seems safe to conclude that a considerable amount of freedom of opinion (or confusion?) is present in the movement. In order to accommodate this variety, in Table 2 Open Access is represented as covering the whole commons spectrum, from a static commons up to the public domain.

Table 2. Various open content initiatives classified according to the domain to which they apply and the type of copyright-based commons created

Copyright-based text commons → Domain ↓	Static (cc-licenses 1 & 4)	Dynamic: Protected (GPL-like, copyleft) (cc-licenses 2 & 5)	Dynamic: Unprotected (BSD-like) (cc-licenses 3 & 6)	Dynamic: Public domain
Software		GNU C compiler *Linux* *Mozilla/Firefox*[•]	*BSD (Unix)* *Apache*	
Software manuals		FSF-manuals		
Sciences and humanities	Open Access	Open Access HapMap (initially)	Open Access PLOS BioMed	Open Access HapMap (ultimately)
Encyclopedias		*Wikipedia*		

[•] Carrying the Mozilla Public License that provides less protection than the GPL.
Italicized initiatives involved in 'peer production'.

Noticeably, not any of these statements makes a point of protecting the commons, a point the open source movement has forcefully called our attention to. Nobody seems particularly worried that the commons may be drained by commercial interests. A reason might be that modified software with a commercial license becomes inscrutable (while in object code), while modified text remains comprehensible. So any modified text taken outside the commons may easily be recovered - not literally of course (copyright preventing), but after rephrasing.

While this movement has been active for several years now, a sizeable number of journals is currently operating along these lines: about 2000 (cf. 'Directory of open access journals', located at http://www.doaj.org). What kind of commons is being instituted by these journals? A (very) rough perusal of editorial licensing policies suggests that most retain copyright, allowing free copying and distribution but no derivative works (sometimes non-commercially only). That is, they effectively implement creative commons licenses 1 and 4 (no derivative works).

Exceptions to this rule, by allowing derivative works, are two well-known initiatives: the non-profit Public Library of Science (PLOS) and the for-profit BioMed Central. PLOS is an organization of scientists and physicians that was launched in 2000 in order to turn their specialist literature into a public resource (all information below retrieved from http://www.plos.org). While their attempts to let existing journals open up their contents to 'free access' in webarchives were hardly successful, they decided to launch their own peer-reviewed journals instead. The first 'PLOS journal', PLOS Biology, appeared in 2003, followed by several others afterwards. For our discussion it is interesting to observe, that PLOS chose the commons with the broadest amount of freedom (apart from the public domain): license 6 ('by' license, see Table 1; Table 2). They did this consciously, while they feel that any risk of plagiarism or misattribution is more than outweighed by potential 'creative uses' of published content. In this vein, they explicitly alert content users to the possibilities of 'reuse and transformation', and 'translation and republication', as long as proper attribution is not neglected (see http://www.plos.org/creative_uses/). The second exception to the rule is BioMed Central (cf. http://www.biomedcentral.com). This for-profit organization focuses upon biomedical research and also issues open access journals, numbering about 130 now. Their copyright policies are similar to PLOS: authors retain copyright, but allow downloading for free as long as users consent to an Attribution License (license 6, Table 1; Table 2).

Before concluding this section on the sciences and the humanities it is illustrative to note a volunteer initiative at its edges: the Wikipedia project (information below retrieved starting from en.wikipedia.org/wiki/Main_Page). It aims at producing a free online encyclopedia. Just like in open source communities, users are invited to turn into producers. Actually, anyone is invited to join and modify existing entries without restrictions. At this time of writing, it boasts of over a million articles (of which 70% in English) and over half a million participants. What kind of commons is involved here? They have chosen the GFDL as discussed above. So here we find a *protected* commons, where modifications are encouraged but only to be redistributed under the same GFDL terms (Table 2). Why this preference for protection? While the Wikipedia itself does not, oddly enough, provide any rationale, I will venture my own explanation. Their output is not software, but pure text or images. Such an output does not need protection per se as explained above. I would argue that another explanation imposes itself: we are dealing here with volunteers, not paid professionals. These would not like to see their creations usurped by commercial producers of encyclopedias, that for example could set up a commercial website featuring a selection of reliable (and possibly upgraded) entries from the Wikipedia, omitting the (as yet) lesser developed sections. Customers would be made to pay for (supposed) reliability and consistency.

5 Active Commons

The foregoing exhausts the new kinds of copyright-based commons that are currently being opened up. One more element, however, needs mentioning. Some of these are promoted with more in mind than just enabling public access. To their proponents, the commons is not only a place for downloading resources, but also for collectively creating new resources from them. An alternative model of knowledge development as carried out by volunteers is the ultimate goal. In Benkler's words: 'peer production of knowledge' that does not rely on markets or managerial hierarchy. Such a commons will be denoted as an 'active' commons (and corresponding instances in Table 2 italicized).

The prototype of this ambition is, again, the open source movement. Source code is being made freely available for all, nowadays mainly on platforms like sourceforge and freshmeat, and routinely downloaded by hundreds or thousands of hackers (depending on the particular project). More than 90% of them will only use the software for their own work or hobbies. But most project leaders hope that a tiny percentage will do more than this, and turn into contributors. Then a cycle may ensue of ever improving public software. Only in this way, of course, popular programs such as Linux, Apache and Mozilla/Firefox could develop into programs of such enormous size (italics in Table 2). During the two decades of open source software (first without, later with the Internet) several instruments of governance have been invented to steer the process of so many volunteers working together across the globe [cf. De Laat 2004]. For one thing, these are technical instruments such as mailing lists, discussion forums, bug-tracking systems, and the concurrent versioning system (CVS) that allows to keep track of contributions by many authors. For another, organizational tools are employed such as introducing a division of tasks and grading of access within a project (a common hierarchy reads: observer, developer, project owner).

This call for a more active commons has not been answered to very frequently outside the domain of software. Open Access efforts are just promoting wider access to resources, to be used by professionals within existing organizations. No alternative paradigm of production is intended. An exception to this rule is, of course, the Wikipedia project (Table 2). Also here, users are invited to turn into contributors, and they seem to do so indeed. In the process, many of the technical instruments from open source software are copied (like the CVS and 'talk pages'). As for a division of roles, initially everyone had immediate change access to articles. Nowadays, in order to meet criticisms of low quality and resolve 'edit wars', its organizers gradually take to the same tool of hierarchy as the open source movement. Sysops (or administrators) have been appointed, who have various powers to try and resolve conflict (deleting articles, (un)freezing pages, (un)blocking user IP addresses). Moreover, the introduction of an editorial board of experts is being discussed that would put an official stamp of approval upon entries ('stable' article versions). So on this platform also, some division of labour seems unescapable.

6   Patent Commons

In this last section I will discuss the spectrum that sometimes haunts the creation of knowledge: patenting. While it obviously does not apply to the humanities or art, in many fields of science and technology patenting has become a standard tool for protecting intellectual property. In some fields the danger is, that patents do no longer seem to promote creativity but stifle it. The main instrument to curb the danger is the creation of pools to which participants contribute their patents in a specific field and license them to each other (or to a third party). Usually patent pools require grant back licenses for improvements of essential patents, in order to reduce the risk of future lawsuits among participants. Let me discuss the cases of software and biotechnology in turn.

As for software, since the early 1990s software-related inventions may apply for a patent. It is estimated that currently, at least in the US, about 20,000 such patents are granted every year. As a result, anyone starting to compose source code is best advised to first perform a patent search and subsequently clear all the necessary rights. Without a search one risks to infringe many patents, and be surprised later on by royalty claims from patent holders. For software developers in bigger organizations this has become a fact of life. All other developers, however, lacking money and search facilities, are perpetually under threat of patents submerging and ruining their efforts.

In particular, this problem has existed for open source software for the last ten years now. Time and again, it is being discussed in those circles how to avert the danger. A tactic under consideration is to let hackers apply for patents themselves, and in the process compose a portfolio of patents that can be used for cross-licensing purposes if need be (just as big firms are used to). This tactic did as yet not materialize, simply because the movement is too loosely structured. Another more unexpected approach *is* materializing, though. Big firms like IBM, HP, and Intel, united in the Open Source Development Labs (OSDL), have been supporting the growth and adoption of Linux for several years now. In August 2005 they announced their 'patent commons project': a central location where patent licenses and patent pledges are to be deposited in support of the open source movement (Table 3; all information below retrieved from http://www.patentcommons.org).

Table 3. Various open patent initiatives classified according to the domain to which they apply

Domain	
Software	OSDL patent commons
Biotechnology	*BiOS protected commons*

Italicized: initiative involved in 'peer production'.

As yet, patents have only been pledged, not licensed. The biggest contributor by far is IBM that committed not to assert 500 named patents against the development, use, or distribution of open source software generally (defined as any software carrying an 'official' open source license). Other firms have contributed much less patents and in a more restricted fashion. RedHat, e.g., will only pledge patents for open source software with a GPL, and Ericsson and Nokia will only pledge some patents for use in the (GPL-ed) Linux kernel specifically. Note that a patent license and a patent pledge differ in a subtle way: in the former case use is legally allowed, while in the latter case users continue to infringe but the patent holder promises not to sue.

As for biotechnology, patenting has been a fact of life much longer. There are some concerns, however, that patents may go too far as far as enabling technologies and genomic data (like sequences of DNA) are involved. Multiple patents that overlap, as well as patents stacking on top of each other may block the very development of science. Fears are that an 'anticommons' may materialize, of multiple owners holding rights of exclusion in a scarce resource [cf. Heller 1998]. Rapid release of genomic data into the public domain (a day or a week after production, but well before any possible analysis by the producers involved) is one type of defense, but increasingly companies seem to be able to develop follow up products that can be patented, effectively precluding use of the underlying public domain data. In response to this pressure, patent pools are being formed. Two initiatives deserve mentioning here.

First, the Canberra based initiative 'Biological Innovation for Open Society' (BiOS) focuses upon biotechnology (information below retrieved from http://www.bios.net/daisy/bios/home.html). According to them, patent portfolios of enabling technologies are to be opened up in a 'protected commons'. Anyone may obtain a royalty-free patent license of pool patents (a 'CAMBIA BiOS license'), on condition that further improvements are shared back to the pool. Patenting is explicitly allowed to go on: licensees may patent both improvements of the enabling technology itself and products based on them. The former kind of patents, however, is not to be asserted against pool members, so effectively being deposited inside the protected pool (not as license but as 'pledge', cf. above). As of today, BiOS has contributed 4 patents to the pool (Table 3). Its originators hope that the Bioforge platform (http://www.bioforge.net/forge/index.jspa) will become a meeting place in cyberspace where collaborative efforts are carried out, similar to sourceforge in open source software. So a community of biotech researchers involved in 'peer production' is the ultimate aim (italics in Table 3).

Secondly, the HapMap initiative deserves mentioning here (information retrieved from http://hapmap.org). This research effort involving institutions from several countries started in 2001 in order to produce a catalog of common genetic variations in human beings across the world. Such a 'HapMap' is useful information for further research linking genetic variants to specific diseases. For this purpose, DNA samples have been collected from populations all over the world. At the end of the project (December 2004), all results have been released in the public domain (Table 2). In the period before this, however, special precautions against appropriation were deemed necessary. The first results were provisionally released under a special copyright license [HapMap 2003]. The main provision was that licensees were not allowed to file patent applications on any so-called 'haplotype' information obtained from the pool, nor on particular uses of such information. Users were to be prevented from being faster than anyone else, incorporating pool data (together with their own data) in a patent application that met with success, and then starting to restrict access by others to the very same data.

What we find here, is a *temporary* commons, of the dynamic and protected variety (Table 2). And indeed, their copyright license is drafted along the lines of the GPL. Similarly, its wordings are comparable to the creative commons license 5: for all purposes, modifications allowed with the same license ('by-sa' license; cf. Table 1). In sum, here we find, instead of a patent pool proper, an unconventional approach to avert the danger of patenting: a (temporary) copyright-based commons of the protected kind.

7   In Conclusion

During the last two decades several kinds of commons for intellectual resources have opened up. The open source movement paved the way for this phenomenon, by creating a commons of source code, based on copyright and contract law. Two kinds of dynamic commons were introduced: one protected from commercial expropriation (regulated by the GPL) and an unprotected one (regulated by BSD-like licenses). Around the turn of the century this movement obtained a broader influence elsewhere: in the sciences, the humanities and art. It was the Creative Commons initiative that formulated a more comprehensive approach to copyright-based commons of text, essentially generalizing the open source typology and adding a static commons in which modification/derivation is not allowed (Table 1). Applications were discussed as implemented by the movement for Open Access in general, and PLOS and BioMed in particular (Table 2). The Wikipedia deserved special mention, as one of the few text-based commons run according to proper 'copyleft' principles. Thereupon, the epithet 'active' was coined for those commons that are not only destined to be a site for consumption but also for production of novel resources. This 'peer production of knowledge' does flourish in open source software communities, but rarely elsewhere. It was argued that in order to function properly, such active commons need instruments of self-governance, like a division of roles.

Finally, patent commons were distinguished. Examples discussed were the mutual pooling of patents on enabling biotechnologies in order to prevent blocking positions (BiOS), and the pooling of software patents on behalf of open source software developers while these lack the means to defend themselves against claims of patent infringement (OSDL pool). The HapMap initiative pioneered another approach to prevent patenting, by ingenuously instituting a copyright-based protected commons of genetic data. The analysis clearly indicated that copyright-based commons and patent commons may be mutually related in various ways. This suggests strongly that, in the future, the various types of commons need to be studied as interrelated phenomena.

References   (Websites mentioned in this article and in the references have all been accessed on 20 December 2005)

BSD, The BSD license (1998). Available at http://www.opensource.org/licenses/bsd-license.php.
P.B. de Laat, Open source software: A case of swift trust?!, *Challenges for the Citizen of the Information Society, Proceedings of the 7th International Conference, ETHICOMP 2004*, edited by T.W. Bynum, N. Pouloudi, S. Rogerson, and Th. Spyrou (University of the Aegean, 2004), pp. 250-265.
P.B. de Laat, Copyright or copyleft? An analysis of property regimes in software development, *Research Policy* 34(10), 1511-1532 (2005).
FSF/GNU, GNU General public license, version 2 (1989/1991). Available at http://www.gnu.org/licenses/gpl.html.
FSF/GNU, GNU Free documentation license, version 1.2 (2002). Available at http://www.gnu.org/licenses/fdl.html.
HapMap, International HapMap Public Access License, version 1.1 (2003). Available at http://www.hapmap.org/cgi-perl/registration.
M.H. Heller, The tragedy of the anticommons: Property in the transition from Marx to markets, *Harvard Law Review* 111(3), 621-688 (1998).
L. Liang, *Guide to open content licenses* (Piet Zwart Institute, Rotterdam, 2004). Available: http://pzwart.wdka.hro.nl/mdr/pubsfolder/opencontentpdf.
OSI, The open source definition, version 1.9 (1997-2005). Available at http://www.opensource.org/docs/definition.php.
PLOS, Open-access publication of medical and scientific research: A PLOS background paper (2003). Available at http://www.plos.org/downloads/oa_background.pdf.
P. Suber, Open Access overview (2004/5). Available at http://www.earlham.edu/~peters/fos/overview.htm.

Virtual Censorship: Controlling the Public Sphere

Mathias Klang
Informatics, IT-University, University of Goteborg, Sweden
klang@ituniv.se,
http://www.ituniv.se/~klang

Abstract: This article deals with online censorship and its relation to user autonomy. By presenting censorship practices and activities of groups helping to circumvent censorship this article shows that the regulation of online material is an ongoing process between the regulator and the regulated. The result of this process is the way in which a society defines itself in terms of a free and vibrant democratic public space.

Keywords: censorship, regulation, public sphere, user autonomy

1 Regulating Disruptive Technology

While the discourse on the regulation and control of technology has an older pedigree [1, 2] much of the discussion in relation to the Internet developed in polemic to Lessig's [3] concept of four modalities of regulation. Murray and Scott [4] further developed Lessig's concepts by in an attempt to create a theory that will encompass the largest range of regulatory strategies and instruments [5].

The incentive to regulate Internet technology has received strong support after the terrorist acts of 9/11, which had a direct affect upon the limitation of online civil liberties. Since then, several governments have moved to implement and extend anti-terror regulation. Hamilton [6] defines three main areas were these activities are taking place (1) the creation of a data retention structure, both at national levels and through international co-operation. This entails the mandatory requirement that Internet Service Providers (ISP) store all user data for specific periods. (2) Online surveillance – regulation in this area is making surveillance technically possible and formally easier. (3) Direct censorship – because "terrorists should not be able freely access sensitive information…" [6].

The desire to control online information stems from the understanding that ICT is a disruptive technology [7]. As such, it is fundamentally altering the way in which

Please use the following format when citing this chapter:

Klang, M., 2006, in IFIP International Federation for Information Processing, Volume 223, Social Informatics: An Information Society for All? In Remembrance of Rob Kling, eds. Berleur, J., Numinen, M. I., Impagliazzo, J., (Boston: Springer), pp. 185–194.

we organize ourselves socially; not all welcome this disruption. This article presents the examples of attempts to regulate online information and reactions to these attempts.

This article begins with an explanation of socio-technical censorship practices, followed by a description of the actions of groups attempting to provide anti-censorship techniques and technology. The discussion shows how the actions of the regulators and regulated form part of a technology negotiation where social groups are attempting to come to terms with the disruptive effects of Internet technology in relation to the democratic ideals of freedom of information and autonomy.

2   Censorship Practice

Internet content filtering is the process of preventing user access to information on the Internet most filtering systems focus on the world wide web by software placed between the user and her Internet connection [8]. For the most part filtering is dependent upon one of three techniques. The different techniques can be used in combination to achieve the desired effect. The processes are known as *blacklisting*, *whitelisting* and *content analysis*. Blacklisting refers to the process whereby lists of unacceptable websites are collected. Once the filtering software is installed, the software will first check to make sure any website requested does not occur on the list of websites collected on the blacklist.

The use of blacklists entails handing over power and decision-making capacity to another agent. Commercial blacklisting products have received a fair amount of criticism for their tendencies to overblock (i.e. to block more access to more information than necessary). A recent study found that in school blocking software "for every web page correctly blocked as advertised, one or more was blocked incorrectly" [9].

Whitelisting is also a process of allowing access to material that has been checked in advance. Under this system, users are permitted access to material that has been approved in advance. This method is more cost efficient in terms of limiting user access to unwanted information. It also is prone to overblocking, i.e. it blocks more information than intended and thus mitigating the potential of the communications technology.

The third form of filtering is content analysis. The concept behind this system is to avoid predefined lists (irrespective of whether they are black or white) and to focus on the actual content of what is viewed. Content analysis works by setting predefined characteristics of the material, which is to be avoided, and allowing software to scan the information for this content prior to delivering it to the user.

If the software is programmed to recognise sexually explicit language and the user attempts to view a page which such content, access to the page will be denied. This system has obvious appeal since it avoids the pitfalls of white & blacklisting. The system brings with it problems of its own. Content analysis is not a substitute for understanding information in context. If keywords are used then sites may be unintentionally blocked. For example, the city of Scunthorpe has been blocked since the word contains within it a four-letter word. Other content analysis systems intended to prevent access to sexually explicit material have blocked sites containing images with large amounts of skin-coloured pixels. These systems have been known to block close up pictures of a non-sexual nature (such as headshots) since the bulk of the image consists of skin-coloured pixels.

State of the art filtering software usually attempts to use a mixture of these three systems and include a level of human activity to 'teach' the filters the items to block and to accept. As these examples have shown, there is no such thing as a system that will not over- or underblock. Therefore, systems will always be either tools of conscious and inadvertent censorship or less than 100% efficient.

In a study conducted by Deibert and Villeneuve [10], they show online censorship activities carried out by 22 states. They divide these censorship activities into three categories (1) comprehensive censorship, (2) distributed censorship, and (3) limited censorship. Comprehensive entails a large-scale censorship activity, distributed censorship refers to a significant amount of censorship performed, and usually the actual act of censorship is delegated to the ISP. Limited censorship refers to, as the name implies, small amounts of censorship.

While there is a great deal of concern about the states who traditionally censor the Internet such as China, Cuba, Myanmar and Turkey etc there are other states which appear on the list which are traditionally not understood to be censorship states. Such states include the USA, France, and Germany. These states rarely receive the same amount of bad publicity for their censorship since it is commonly understood that these states are for freedom of information. It is easy to see how this stance becomes problematic since even these states censor access to information online.

There seems to be two main approaches among States implementing comprehensive censorship practices. Myanmar and Cuba limit access to the Internet by ensuring that only limited numbers of individuals can go online and even those who can may only see approved material – the rest is filtered [10]. China, Saudi Arabia, and Turkey are more permissive when it comes to allowing individual's access to the Internet but the content they are allowed to view is heavily filtered [10]. Additionally these countries attempt to register those who access the Internet through Internet cafés.

Among those who are less ambitious in their filtering activities, we find that ISP's, or in the case of the USA libraries, are required to filter different types of content in an effort to protect certain cultural values. Often the filtering is heavily focused on, but not limited to, preventing pornography. The filtering of dissident and human rights sites follows this in a close second place [10]. Those who filter least, according to Deibert and Villeneuve (2005) are countries like France where courts have ordered Yahoo! to block access to Nazi auction sites, Germany in which certain states require ISPs to block Nazi sites, and Jordan, which blocks the site of arabtimes.com at a national level [10].

What Deibert and Villeneuve's [10] study clearly shows is that it has become increasingly difficult to speak of censorship in terms of them and us. Many states, traditionally accepted as pro-free-speech, censor to a lesser or greater degree. That the more censorship-friendly states such as: Turkey, Cuba and China filter information is not a great surprise. It is important in all these cases to remember that no matter how well planned and organised the system of censorship is – there is no such thing as a perfect system.

Privatized Censorship

While we can understand relatively easily much of the censorship carried out in terms of central powers controlling the flow of information in the attempt to achieve certain political goals, not all Internet censorship follows this pattern. Two main areas of concern, which fall into the category of private censorship, are the role of the Internet Service Provider (ISP) and legislation with a chilling effect [11].

Censorship by ISP can take many forms, but most generally fall into one of two categories. Either the censorship occurs as part of a governmental recommendation or requirement or the censorship is a part of corporate policy – which may in turn be a part of industry self-regulation or simply an individual corporation policy. One example of such as policy is the Public Pledge of Self-Regulation & Professional Ethics for China Internet Industry, which states that the principles of self-regulation and the Internet industry's professional ethics include "...patriotic observance of law, equitableness, trustworthiness and honesty" (Article 3). The duties created by the pledge involve refraining from, and actively monitoring that customers do not, produce, post, or disseminate material that may jeopardize state security and disrupt social stability, contravene laws and regulations and spread superstition and obscenity. One must promptly remove any such material.

The public pledge is written as a one-sided declaration from the corporate actor. This creates the image that the corporate actor has the choice to refrain from signing the document, declaring support for it or implementing it in any manner. The non-implementation of the document is understood to bring with it additional difficulties for companies intending to enter the Chinese Internet market. Therefore, companies follow the Public Pledge, which results in the inspecting and monitoring of national and international sites and blocking access to harmful content as stated by Article 10 of the Public Pledge.

In January 2006, Google launched a local version of its online search engine for China (Google.cn). This version will block 'subversive' content from the Chinese users and therefore help Chinese officials to filter Internet content. Especially since to large degree today any website not listed by search-engines has little chance of users finding it. This addition to the Chinese censorship technology has the effect that even sites which are not caught by the Chinese firewalls [8] can now be excluded since they are not part of the material that can be found when using the search engine. Google made several statements in response to the protests over their actions.

> ...we have agreed to remove certain sensitive information from our search results...This wasn't an easy choice, but in the end, we believe the course of action we've chosen will prove to be the right one...We ultimately reached our decision by asking ourselves...how can we provide the greatest access to information to the greatest number of people? [12]

The threat presented by the privatized censorship of service providers should not be underestimated. Today the online search engines have become the de facto standard for finding online information and online navigation. These search engines are not a form of public good. Many consider the search-engine as a technology and as such neutral. This view omits the fact that the technology exists in a corporate context with a duty to create profit [13]. Despite the search engines role as fundamental infrastructure they are driven by profit motives and therefore no obligation to ensure equal access to information. The effects of privatized censorship are that a greater amount of information becomes unavailable. Once the opposing views are made unavailable, what remains online is a form of consensus. This makes it even more difficult for anyone harboring an opposing view to speak out. In addition to this the harm of privatized censorship is made more grave by the fact that there is little or no information about the censorship rules, therefore the ordinary user cannot be aware of what is censored and therefore cannot realize when she should attempt to circumvent the censorship.

The second category of private censorship is the case of regulation with so called chilling effects, in other words the stated purpose of the regulation is not to limit a certain action (such as free speech) but has that as a negative side effect. This may sometimes fall outside the strict definition of censorship, the effect of legislation, which prevents the ability of communication; it results in the lessened flows of free information. While it is important to mention this topic here, due to space constraints it is not possible to give the topic the attention it truly deserves. Many different bodies of legislative rules may affect the way in which communication occurs. Those that are most common are privacy [14], defamation [15], copyrights [16] and trademarks [17]. The importance of bringing up the topic of the chilling effects of legislation is to underline the difficulties that the communicator faces. The problem is not in the rules but in their interpretation and implementation. When taken at face value the regulations do not vary greatly. One can easily implement their achievements in such a manner as to entirely prevent or cause a chilling effect on the actors.

3   Circumventing Censorship

In an early work on Internet censorship Varlejs [18] discussed which actors were carrying out Internet censorship and for which purposes. Listing actors involved in censorship as governments, academic institutions, religious groups, corporations, media and libraries, Varlejs [18] notes that these actors censor different types of information, for different methods and motivate it through different rationales.

The focus of this work is on Internet content and the limitation or control of the free flow of information it is important to be aware of the technologies of information control available to the controller. The first important difference between the traditional censor and Internet-based censorship is that the information in question has usually already been disseminated. Therefore, the focus is not what we may disseminate but rather how to prevent groups from accessing this information. The main process involved in this activity is one of filtering. The term is aptly chosen since the activity involves allowing the free flow of acceptable material while preventing the harmful content from being accessed.

The evasion of censorship has always been a popular topic [19]. One can almost see this as an escalating race of technology. For every move, the censor carries out to implement new forms of censorship technologies and techniques there is a rapid move towards new and better forms of hidden communication. The advent of the Internet has increased the amount of cheap international communications distributed. The race to censor and to beat the censor has been going on for some time but it is still in its infancy.

Information on censorship evasion also tends to focus on the use of pseudonyms and maintaining a level of secrecy to ensure that if communications are intercepted the communicants will not be able to be identified and punished. There are, naturally, two sides to these arguments. The use of such techniques by those who cause harm is abhorrent while the use of these techniques by those who bravely fight for freedom is praiseworthy. The question then becomes one of degree and definition. Which user causes harm and which users are actually praiseworthy? Much of the activities we deplore today were historically acceptable and there is no reason to think that these decisions have been, or will ever be fixed.

Therefore, censorship becomes a point of view. Those who are against and those who are for are solely demonstrating differences of opinion and serendipity is the only thing that places us on one side of the barrier or the other. This argument from cultural relativism is not an adequate argument to prevent activity on both sides of the fence. Since we may interpret the concept of censorship as a point of view, several actors have been moving towards creating technical anti-censorship devices. The object of these is to help avoid state censorship without detection. One example of such a system is Freenet.

Freenet [20] is software designed to enable the publication and retrieval of Internet based information without fear of censorship and distributed at no cost. This is done by creating a completely decentralised network where information about publishers and consumers of information is anonymous and not stored. The advantages of decentralisation is that no single point controls the network and the advantage of anonymity is that users can depend on the network for communications without fear of advance censorship or post-publishing reprisals. In addition to encryption, communications travel through several nodes to make tracking the information requester more complex. According to the project site, people have downloaded the software several million times and have used it in countries with comprehensive censorship systems.

In addition to the development of technical anti-censorship technologies there have been social actions developed to help with censorship evasion. These have taken the form of publications with the activist as a target audience. The goal is to provide readily available information about censorship and to avoid or mitigate its effects.

The online civil rights organisation Electronic Freedom Frontier (EFF) has produced a guide to ensuring blogging safety that is aimed at ensuring that those who create online information do not meet with negative consequences from employers or state censors. Their advice includes [21] using pseudonyms and limiting the use of identifiable information, promoting the use of 'anonymizing' technologies, and using ping servers to publish information then quickly removing it (the effect is that the information remains on other servers but not on the publishers site). In addition, the advice includes limiting audiences through password-protected sites, avoiding being included in search engines, and registering domain names anonymously.

The EFF has a high reputation for civil liberties work and it has been active online since 1990. The organization has a large audience and deals with a wide range of issues pertaining to online civil liberties. The motivations for producing such documents are to ensure that the individual can act autonomously in providing and receiving information without fear of outside coercion. They write:

> ...we offer a few simple precautions to help you maintain control of your personal privacy so that you can express yourself without facing unjust retaliation. If followed correctly, these protections can save you from embarrassment or just plain weirdness in from of your friends and co-workers. [21]

Hence, the underlying belief is that the individual should have the choice to publish information but this choice or desire is limited by the potential threats the individual faces if such activities are carried out. The EFF publishes several documents of this nature on their website ranging from legal to technical advice intended to empower the individual and provide tools to ensure individual informed choice. In addition, documents such as this also fulfil a political purpose by sustaining and contributing to a larger debate on online freedom.

The EFF takes the civil liberties stance and individual actors provide information without attempting to place their work in a larger ideological context there have also been moves from non-Internet organisations to help circumvent online censorship. One such organisation is Reporters Sans Frontiers (RSF). This organisation focuses on freedom of the press. However, it also has developed an interest in protecting a larger group, namely the non-professional reporter using the Internet to publish and disseminate information online. To this end, RSF has created an anthology [22] that includes introductory texts on information activism with information on topics such as how to get started, which are the best tools and what ethics bloggers should have. In addition to this the handbook gives example cases of what bloggers have been able to achieve before offering concrete advice on anonymous blogging [23] and censorship circumvention [24].

Zuckerman [23] discusses social safety precautions similar to those seen above [21] i.e. using pseudonyms, public computers and anonymous proxies before moving on to the more advanced precautions such as union-routing and using anonymous blog services involving encryption, re-routing and anonymous re-mailers. The main point Zuckerman [23] is attempting to make is that anonymity is possible; however, for each step there is a cost in time or learning required to be able to use the tools. Hence, the trade-off becomes a factor of risk evaluation, knowledge, and time. Depending upon the underlying risk, it may become worthwhile to invest time and energy in learning to use the available tools. Villeneuve's [24] focus is on circumventing online filters, therefore after a brief introduction to filtering he presents a spectrum of circumventing technologies and a methodology for the user in determining the right balance between the users needs and capacities. The results of such an evaluation determine the course of action and the focus needed for developing circumvention methods and avoiding detection. The choice of circumvention method will be based upon factors, such as, number of users, bandwidth availability, point of access, levels of expertise, and the risks being undertaken. Once determined Villenueve [24] presents an array of web-based circumventors, circumvention through proxy servers, tunnelling and the wide-scale anonymous communications systems.

4   Discussion

Autonomy is accepted as a core democratic value and it is often argued that in the absence of compelling evidence to the contrary, everyone should be treated as the best judge of his or her own good or interests [25, 26]. Freedom of information is a fundamental building block in supporting the autonomous actor [27]; therefore the ability to find and communicate information is the basis upon which the democracy is built. This position has been uncontested by most nations for a long time. One may argue that the change is not in the concept but rather in its practice. Prior to the advent of the Internet the ability of the individual to communicate with large groups was not great.

The components defining access to public sphere [28] include (i) physical access, (ii) social access, (iii) access to discussions, and (iv) access to information [29]. Castells [30] presents the idea that the public sphere has, to all intentions and purposes, moved from the physical world to the network. Therefore, it is important to look to those writers who claim that the Internet is the public sphere and then to attempt to understand whether or not the same rules apply to the autonomous participant.

This is the continued negotiation between regulation and technology. This may deal with the adaptation of social behavior (or implementation of technologies) to coincide with regulation or attempts to evade the effects/sanctions prescribed by regulation or the behavior of following the wording of the legislation while ignoring its substance. These negotiated socio-technical solutions attempt to either circumvent regulation completely or at least to cushion its effects.

The issue is one of user autonomy in online environments. The ability to act without coercion or manipulation is vital to democratic participation. This is true even in the online environment. By implementing direct control over Internet content through online content filtering or implementing regulations through industry codes of conducts which require such filtering to be carried out by private actors directly impacts online autonomy. The same can be said of the actions of search engines such as the case of Google.cn, mentioned above, since removing information from the search engines effectively makes the information invisible to the larger public. If the information is not available through search engines it is, for all intents and purposes, not there at all. Without the ability to locate and gather information the individual cannot acquire the adequate information necessary to make autonomous decisions based upon the facts. Therefore through manipulation the public information sphere cannot function.

The promise of efficient communications and the development of the Internet into a public sphere without the limitations inherent in Habermas' [28] model have quickly been proven to be false hopes. Reactions to censorship have caused many to both protest and react towards the threats against online autonomy. These reactions come both in technical solutions and in attempts to educate users on the importance of security and risk awareness to prevent autonomy loss.

5   Conclusion

ICT carries with it many promises for democracy. Despite this, technology is also being implemented to limit the scope of autonomy among ICT users. The present situation is one where many parties are conducting the regulation of online communications and Internet user groups are helping each other communicate and circumvent controls that prevent communication. The result of this negotiation between the regulator and regulated is the development of understanding of information in the digital age.

By understanding online information flows as a disruptive technology it is possible to arrive at a more nuanced understanding of that which is regulated. By recognizing that disruptive technology is as uncontrollable as an 'earthquake' [7] the regulator must understand that suppression is not an adequate solution to the problem.

As this work has shown, the negotiation is an ongoing process without end. Once techniques are developed to block information countermeasures will be devised and implemented. This result of this process is fundamental to the way in which we define the modern democracy.

Bibliography

1.   J. Beniger, *The Control Revolution: Technological and Economic Origins of the Information Society*, Harvard University Press, Cambridge, Mass., 1986.
2.   J. Yates, *Control Through Communication: The Rise of System in American Management*, Johns Hopkins University Press, Baltimore, 1989.
3.   L. Lessig, *Code and Other Laws of Cyberspace*, Basic Books, New York, 1999.
4.   A. Murray, and C. Scott, The Partial Role of Competition in Controlling the New Media, *Proceedings of Competition Law and the New Economy*, University of Leicester, 2001.
5.   R. Brownsword, Code, Control and Choice: Why East is East and West is West, *Legal Studies*, **25** (1), 2005.
6.   S. Hamilton, The War on Terrorism – Towards a 'less free, less choice' Internet for Library Users? *World Library and Information Congress: 69th IFLA General Conference and Council*, 2003.
7.   K. Lyytinen and G. Rose, The Disruptive Nature of IT Innovations: The Case of Internet Computing in Systems Development Organizations, *MIS Quarterly*, **27** (4), 2003.
8.   J. Zittrain, and B. Edelman, Internet Filtering in China, *IEEE Internet Computing*, **7**(2), 2003.

9. EFF & OPG, Internet Blocking in Public Schools: A Study on Internet Access in Educational Institutions, Report from the Electronic Frontier Foundation (EFF) and the Online Policy Group (OPG), Version 1.1 of 26 June 2003.
10. R. Deibert and N. Villeneuve, Firewalls and Power: An Overview of Global State Censorship of the Internet, in *Human Rights in the Digital Age* edited by M. Klang and A. Murray, Glasshouse Press, London, 2005.
11. J. Boyle, *Shamans, Software & Spleen: Law and the Construction of the Information Society*, Harvard University Press, Cambridge, Mass. 1996.
12. A. McLaughlin, Google in China, in *Google Corporate Blog - Googler insights into product and technology news and our culture*, 27 January. 2006, http://googleblog.blogspot.com/2006/01/google-in-china.html – consulted 1 April 2006.
13. M. Friedman, The Social Responsibility of Business is to Increase Its Profits, *New York Times Magazine*, 1 September 1970.
14. N. Taylor, State Surveillance and the Right to Privacy, *Surveillance & Society* 1(1): 66-85, 2002.
15. C. Dent and A. Kenyon, Defamation Law's Chilling Effect: A Comparative Content Analysis of Australian and US Newspapers, *Media & Arts Law Review*, 9(2): 89-112, 2004.
16. M. Heins, The Progress of Science and Useful Arts: Why copyright today threatens intellectual freedom, Free Expression Policy Project (policy paper), 2003.
17. S. Dogan, and M. Lemley, Trademarks and Consumer Search Costs on the Internet, 41 *Houston Law Review:* 777-838, 2004.
18. J. Varlejs, Who Censors the Internet and Why? *Proceedings of Freedom of Expression, Censorship and Libraries*, Riga, Latvia, October 14-17, 1998.
19. S. Curry Jansen, *Censorship: The Knot that Binds Power and Knowledge*, Oxford University Press, Oxford, 1991.
20. I. Clarke, and O. Sandberg, Routing in the Dark – Scalable Searches in Dark Peer to Peer Networks *Defcon 13*, Las Vegas, July 2005.
21. EFF, How to Blog Safely (About Work or Anything Else), Electronic Frontier Foundation Report, 2005.
22. J. Pain, *Handbook for Bloggers and Cyber-Dissidents*, Reporters Without Borders, 2005.
23. E. Zuckerman, How to Blog Anonymously, in *Handbook for Bloggers and Cyber-Dissidents*, Reporters Without Borders 2005.
24. Villeneuve, N. (2005) Technical Ways to Get Around Censorship, in *Handbook for Bloggers and Cyber-Dissidents*, edited by J. Pain Reporters Without Borders, 2005.
25. R. A. Dahl, *On Democracy*, Yale University Press, New Haven, 1998.
26. T. Scanlon, A Theory of Freedom of Expression in *The Philosophy of Law*, edited by R. Dworkin, Oxford University Press, Oxford, 1977.
27. G. Dworkin, *The Theory and Practice of Autonomy*, Cambridge University Press, Cambridge, 1988.
28. J. Habermas, *The Structural Transformation of the Public Sphere: An Inquiry into a Category of Bourgeois Society*, translated by B. Thomas, MIT Press, Cambridge, Mass., 1989.
29. S. Carr, M. Francis, L. G. Rivlin, and A. M. Stone, *Public Space*, Cambridge University Press, Cambridge, 1992.
30. M. Castells, *The information Age: Economy, Society, and Culture*, Volume 1: *The Rise of the Network Society*, Blackwell, Oxford, 1996.

Communicating Information Society Related RTD and Deployment Results in Support of EU Public Policies

Vasileios Laopodis
Innopolis: Centre for Innovation and Culture
International non-profit organization, Athens, Greece
vasileios.laopodis@gmail.com, http://www.innopolis.org

Abstract. The aim of this paper is to discuss issues related to communication and exploitation of Information Society related project results emanating from RTD and deployment projects funded by EU programmes such as IST programme, eTen, eContent and eContent plus etc. In particular it will examine how these results may impact other major EU policies e.g. public health, environment, education etc. First, it presents the different EU programmes and initiatives aiming at greater economic growth, sustainable development and social cohesion through ICTs and their pervasive role in economy and society. Then it discusses the role that communication of RTD results may have on transferring knowledge, influencing action and more important creating public appreciation of the benefits obtained. To illustrate this dimension it presents in detail the 'Information Society Policy Link' initiative of Information Society and Media Directorate-General (DG INFSO) and its first collection of successful project results (policy cases) having positively impacted different EU policy areas and in particular Environmental policies. Finally it draws some conclusions regarding the inclusion of such approaches for effective dissemination of research and deployment results in the EU funded programmes as well as in national initiatives.

Keywords: Information Society Policy Link; ICTs; Information Society; RTD policy making; Environment

1 From RTD Results to Policy Making: the Case of ICT

Information and Communication Technologies (ICTs) are of crucial importance for Europeans. They are 'breakthrough technology', similar to the steam engine and electricity, that will have a major impact on how we live and work over the next century. They are therefore fundamental to achieving the EU's 'Lisbon goal' of greater

Please use the following format when citing this chapter:

Laopodis, V., 2006, in IFIP International Federation for Information Processing, Volume 223, Social Informatics: An Information Society for All? In Remembrance of Rob Kling, eds. Berleur, J., Numinen, M. I., Impagliazzo, J., (Boston: Springer), pp. 195–207.

economic growth, sustainable development and social cohesion. Consequently, the European Union devotes considerable effort to Information Society related actions.

For instance, Information Society Technologies (IST) research programme [1] has been the largest thematic priority in the EU's Fifth (1998-2002) and Sixth (2002-2006) Framework Research Programmes. Together they represent an investment of over €7bn in IST research, and are complemented by programmes such as eContent (€100m) and eTen (€315m), which focus on digital content and eServices deployment respectively. A range of policies also aims to ensure that Europe exploits the possibilities offered by the Information Society. The main components are: eGovernment, eHealth, eInclusion, eLearning, eBusiness, Security — cyber crime, Broadband, eSafety, Safer Internet Programme.

Fig. 1 Integrated process for assessing and disseminating RTD and deployment EU funded results in the area of Information Society and Media.

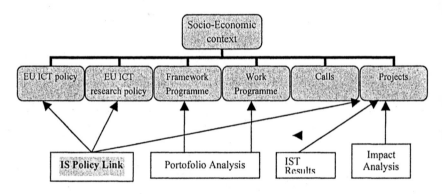

The projects funded by these programmes offer benefits to all areas of Europe's economy and society. To fully realize these benefits, the technologies on the one hand, need to be linked closely to European policy-making in the relevant areas, and on the other ensure that the results are used as quickly as economically justifiable for the benefit of EU citizens and the EU economy. *Effective communication is essential, both in transferring knowledge and influencing action.*

On the other hand there is a need to ensure that the flow of R&D funding is sustained by *creating public appreciation of the benefits obtained.* Such an action also demands effective communication to help recipients become aware about new technological breakthroughs facilitating our life but also about potential dangers and ways to prevent from possible negative effects.

Passing the right message to the right people: For each of these objectives there is a need for a professional approach for a communication strategy. This strategy will analyse the target audiences and communication channels and it will define appropriate sub-objectives, communication messages, and techniques. In our view current efforts do not address these issues adequately.

The diverse nature of the R&D projects supported within the Framework Programmes means that different projects require different approaches. While some projects will produce results that are quickly obvious to end users in products or services, others will mainly affect industrial or commercial processes or components. Communication strategies need to take account of these differences and different target groups and stakeholders: networks, clusters and EU industrial groupings as well as the public.

Similarly, fostering public appreciation is not a task for which a single 'one size fits all' approach should be expected. Different types of result are impressive for different groups, and the diffusion of attitudes within a population operates differently both for different ideas and for different cultures. The existing state of public opinion is also a factor to be taken into account when devising strategies, and this will introduce inter-country differences.

We feel that applications of EU R&D results, creating networks and leading to products and services that are in wide public use, represent an area in which strategies for uptake and strategies for public appreciation can overlap. This needs to be investigated to determine the full scale of the opportunity.

There is scope for both direct promotion and influencing and for indirect action, allowing the message to become apparent through the actions of third parties. The underlying perception is that citizens who are alerted to the developments which the EU R&D programmes are aiming at — and are delivering as time goes on — will be affected in three key ways:

- by coming to appreciate the case for EU R&D
- by exerting market pull which speeds up the adoption of future developments
- by generating a constituency for the adoption of Framework Programme results by Commission policy departments

2   Integrated Process for Disseminating ICT Research and Deployment Results

The study and close monitoring of research and deployment projects results has always been an important issue for policy makers in Information Society. At EU level and in particular in the Information Society and Media DG, a fully integrated process has been developed by the strategy and policy for ICT research unit (DG INFSO C.2) with main components the following projects and framework contracts: Integrated Programme Portfolio Analysis (IPPA); Impact Analysis. On the other hand there exist initiatives focusing on broader dissemination and reinforcing exploitation of ICT related research and deployment activities, notably: IST Results [2]; and in 2004 the Information Society Policy Link initiative [3].

Figure 1 presents the framework for such synergies and the level of intervention of each one of them.

2.1   IST Results: Key Part of an Integrated Process

The objective of this approach is to seek for synergies among these actions.

- Impact Analysis is an ex-post assessment of programme/projects results for families of programmes / projects e.g. IST, Esprit IV, ACTS and TAP) in one or more particular areas e.g. 'Health Applications' 'Mobile Communications and Systems' and 'Microelectronics and Microsystems'.
- IPPA is an analysis of the focus of the different RTD projects as they are launched) are part of a complementary set of activities contributing to strategic analysis and communication while IPPA is a rolling process which can also contribute to development of synergies within the IST Programme.

- IST Results is an online editorial service whose objectives are to raise the visibility of IST-funded research results, to support projects' access to markets and encourage uptake of innovations, and to raise awareness of the IST Programme and its activities.

   For achieving this goal IST Results initiative has a number of deliverables to different target audiences: Feature Articles on specific FP5 and FP6 IST projects, Regular News in Brief on ICT-related topics, Weekly E-Bulletin / customisable Email Alerts, Events Calendar covering IST project events, Dedicated Press Desk and Investors Room, Syndicated content via press wires and RSS.

   Target Audiences vary from:
- New Technology Users (enterprises of all sizes, public authorities)
- Intermediaries / Information Relays
- Investors / Technology Brokers
- Research Community
- Press / Media, and,
- Internal EU audiences (POs, IST projects, other DGs).

2.2   Looking for Synergies

There are several links among the above initiatives and projects, which can be summarised as follows:
- IPPA and IST Results provide an essential input to Impact Analysis
- IST Results can carry out data collection and editing which is essential both for the dissemination of results (current IST Results) and IS Policy Link initiative
- IPPA and Impact Analysis should be more 'rigorous' and systematic while IST Results and IS Policy Link can be more punctual and more focused on success stories and showcases within a strong PR perspective
- IPPA, IST Results, IS Policy Link and Impact Analysis contribute together to the development of EU ICT research policy

3   Information Society Policy Link

3.1   Description of the Initiative

Information Society promises potentially significant benefits throughout Europe's economy and society. These benefits will not be realized completely, however, if the technologies are not linked closely to European policymaking in the relevant areas.

   Among the numerous EU awareness raising and promotions actions regarding ICT research and its impact the Information Society Policy Link initiative [3] of Information Society & Media DG to identify and reinforce links between its projects and relevant EU policies launched in 2004, is linking Information Society projects with relevant European policies as diverse as environmental protection, security and public health [1].

   Hence 'Information Society Policy Link' where these cutting-edge projects are connected to the relevant policies, helping Europe both better implements today's policies and ensure that policy development takes the possibilities offered by ICTs into account.

   This is a targeted initiative to EU Policy Makers started mid 2004 with the aim to improve co-operation between DG Information Society and Media and all other policy DGs, EU institutions as well as Public Administrations in Member States.

The approach selected is to proceed to by linking projects results from INFSO-funded actions (e.g. IST, eTen, eContent) to EU policy makers, thereby bringing together the major stakeholders.

Fig.2 The Information Society Policy Link multipartite collaboration

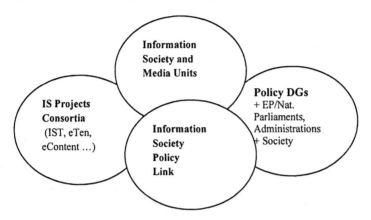

The Figure 2 illustrates the multipartite collaboration where all main actors such as EU policy makers; INFSO Units; INFSO funded projects consortia (under programmes such as: Information Society Technology – IST, European Trans European Networks – eTen, Digital Content (eContent and eContentplus) are involved with major beneficiaries EC policy DGs/services (main target), other EU institutions (in particular EP), Agencies National Parliaments & Member States administrations.

3.2 Impact of ICT Research Projects on Other EU Policy Areas

The pilot phase of this initiative ended in June 2005 identified ~ 200 Policy Cases (promising projects) grouped in six categories covering 20 European Union Policy Areas

European Society: Culture & Multilingualism; Education; Employment & Social Affairs; Health; E-Inclusion

Governance: E-Government & E-Democracy; Regional Policy; Security & Justice; Sustainable Development; Environment; Energy & Transport; Agriculture & Fisheries

Competitiveness: Enterprise Policy; Industrial Policy; Single Market

Research & Innovation: Information Society; Research & Technology; Standardization

International Relations: International Community; (External Trade, External Relations, Development, Humanitarian Aid)

To demonstrate the impact of DG Information Society and Media funded ICT research and development projects on specific EU public policies we discuss below the case of EU environmental policy where ICTs could be used for policy purposes.

4   Impact of ICTs on other EU Polices: The Case of Environmental Policy

4.1   Challenges for the Environment

Environment constitutes one of the major EU policy priorities. Protecting our environment is essential for the quality of life of current and future generations. While environmental protection is not synonymous with sustainable development, it is a key component and serves to emphasize the fact that environmental considerations should be an integral part of other policy objectives in areas such as competitiveness, innovation, inclusion, health and security. Access to and exploitation of high-quality information is essential to our ability to safeguard the environment. There is paradox here in that many environmental theories, assumptions and models are currently based on very limited amounts of data. Better identification and exploitation of environmental data sources is a prosperous field for ICTs applications for improving our understanding of the environment.

Management of natural resources presents another key challenge. It is widely recognised that the current pace of world population and economic growth cannot be sustained. The combination of resource exhaustion and pollution threaten widespread degradation of our physical environment. The gross inequality of wealth distribution, where 20% of the world's population consumes 80% of its resources, is also unsustainable because of the tensions and threats it raises for global security. We need to address both the absolute increases in resource consumption and the relative inequalities between the developed and developing worlds.

The Information Society has been playing an important role in environmental protection and sustainable development. New technologies and organisational structures will reduce the environmental impact of industry and society, improve our understanding of our environment and provide us with the information we need to protect our world for future generations.

Sustainable development has been a central EU priority for several years and was articulated in an EU strategy agreed at the Göthenburg Summit in June 2001. Since then, environmental protection and sustainable development have been 'mainstreamed' throughout the EU's policies and activities.

The cornerstone of the EU's environmental policy is Environment 2010: Our Future, Our Choice, and the EU's Sixth Environment Action Programme [4] covering the period 2001–2010. The Programme identifies four thematic priorities to be tackled over the current decade:

- Climate change;
- Nature and biodiversity;
- Environment, health and quality of life;
- Natural resources and waste.

4.2   Where the Information Society Meets the Environment

The 6th Environmental Action Programme provides the environmental component of the Community's sustainable development strategy, placing the EU's environmental plans in a broad perspective, considering economic and social conditions. It also makes the link between environment and European objectives for growth and competitiveness.

To further focus stakeholders' efforts, seven thematic strategies have been developed, each following a common and incremental approach towards policy action and proposals. These thematic strategies cover: air pollution; soil protection; protection and conservation of the marine environment; sustainable use of pesticides; urban environment; sustainable use of natural resources; and waste recycling.

The Information Society can support these goals in many ways, providing key building blocks for putting the sustainable development principle into action. Connecting cutting-edge Information Society projects to relevant environmental policies will therefore both help Europe meet its environmental and sustainability goals and stimulate growth and innovation. A wide range of EU policies and activities are already applying Information Society technologies to help us better understand our environment and how we are affecting it.

Good communications and IT support also play a life-saving role in crisis management.

Key initiatives are:

* *Galileo:* a satellite navigation system being supported jointly by the European Union and the European Space Agency (ESA), which will have a substantial impact on our understanding of the environment as well as contribute to other sectors such as agriculture, fisheries and transport.
* *Global Monitoring for Environment and Security (GMES):* another joint initiative between the EU and ESA to strengthen the acquisition and integration of high-quality EU environmental, geographical and socio-economic data. It will help improve policymaking from local to global level.
* *INfrastructure for SPatial InfoRmation in Europe (INSPIRE):* an initiative of the European Commission with Member States to improve access to high quality geo-spatial information.

Under Framework Programme 6, IST research activities in the field of environmental applications focus on the management of environmental risk due to natural hazards, industrial accidents or civil security events. Activities cover two phases: the first one covering the monitoring, planning, forecasting, preparedness and recovery phases; and the second dealing mainly with the alert and response phase. ICT for Environmental Risk Management constitute an important action whose objectives are:

(i) to improve risk planning and forecasting by the development of harmonised geo-spatial information to maintain vulnerability information and allow for managing inter-related risks (domino effects)

(ii) to improve the crisis management operation by addressing the interoperability of civil protection equipment allowing for joint intervention in case of major disasters, and

(iii) to develop new approaches for the deployment of in-situ sensor networks and bridge the gap between in situ and remote sensing observation in the context of the Global Monitoring for Environment and Security initiative and of the proposed INPIRE directive.

Key technology areas being addressed in the research include:

* Sensors with communication and location capabilities;
* Tools for modelling, simulation, decision support and visualisation, including integration of geo-spatial data;
* Service architectures and platforms for environmental and crisis management based on open standards. Interoperability of equipment and systems is a key concern in this field. IST research promotes the development of open platforms that support the evolution towards network-centric environmental and crisis management solutions.

Environmental applications can also be found in other Information Society and Media funded Activities such as a) the eTEN Programme, primarily for the practical realisation of eEurope's objectives on eServices. Projects address the deployment of environmental applications and services as one of several areas of common interest for online public services; b) the eContent programme which is a market-oriented programme supporting the production, use and distribution of European digital content, including its linguistic diversity. Access to and use of geographical information is a key theme, where environment and risk management are important end-user applications. Geographical and spatial data remains a key priority under the follow-on programme, eContentplus (2005-2008).

5.1   4.3   Current R&D Activities in ICT and Environment

Risk Planning and Forecasting
Until recently risk management components were developed independently by a vast range of institutions and organisations. Exchange of relevant information needed in dealing with risk is too often hindered by administrative and legal boundaries as well as lack of interoperability on the technical side. Recently, the Commission proposed a new regulation, which aims at harmonising geo-spatial information across the EU called INSPIRE (www.ec-gis.org/e-esdi/). This offers a unique opportunity for a major overhaul in disaster preparedness, contingency planning as well as community involvement in risk reduction. Current projects such as ORCHESTRA (www.euorchestra.org) and WIN (www.win-eu.org) are working on service architectures for risk management based on open standards and fully compliant with the INSPIRE regulation (see also Table 1).

This approach should not only dramatically reduce the cost of building and maintaining risk management applications, but it will also allow for the appropriate handling of systemic risk or domino effects.

Crisis Management Operations
It appeared that civil protection authorities did not benefit as much as other professionals from the new Information and Communication Technologies. Most of these public bodies are poorly equipped, and since this market is rather small, providers companies are slow to invest in up-to-date applications and equipment. This was the one of the reasons for the EU to promote this field. It was also perceived as an opportunity to improve equipment *interoperability*, to allow different *emergency actors*, possibly belonging to different regional or national European authorities, to work jointly in case of large-scale disasters.

Crisis management operations are based on a three-level architecture concept: the coordination and command centre supported by function-specific control rooms, the mobile command centres, and the field crew. The function-specific control rooms host the local management and interfaces with auxiliary functions (technical and scientific support, short-term forecasting, meteorological office, emergency health care, public utilities, damage assessment, etc.). The reporting is made to the upper level, the coordination centre, which is located on the local, regional or national government premises, depending on the size of the crises, with a link to the crisis centre of the EC in case of major disaster.

Priorities for Future Work
Future research will focus on the integration of a wide range of sensors (in-situ, airborne, and satellite) to provide full information awareness for risk planning and

emergency management. It will also promote the integration of secure, dependable public safety communication systems including ad-hoc broadband networks for emergency operations and alert networks.

To demonstrate its particular interest on the subject, In February 2005, Information and Media DG established a new Unit *ICT for the Environment* in order to address more efficiently ICT research related to environmental challenge

5   Information Society Policy Link: Concrete results related to Environment

On the initiative web site [3] a number of selected Policy cases are demonstrated for all areas including EU Environment policies. A detailed presentation of the selected Policy Cases is given on Table 1. For each policy case are indicated the following elements:

- Project Identification (name, EC code, webpage);
- Policy Area (policy domain e.g. air quality for environmental policy);
- Related policy measure (EU major programmes, references to EU Communications, Directives, Ministerial conferences proceedings etc.);
- Beneficiaries (in both EU and national/regional level);
- Expected impact (concrete impact on policy making or policy monitoring process).

Concrete (Results Policy Cases) Related to Environment

Table 1 presents a synopsis of Information Society projects impacting EU Environmental Policy identified and analyzed in 2004-2005.

Table 1: Information Society projects impacting EU Environmental Policy
Part I: Policy Area and Related policy Measure

Project Identification	Policy Area	Related policy measure:
APNEE-TU IST-2001-34154 (FP5) www.apnee.org/en/index.htm	Air quality Early warning of environmental hazards	Communication on Clean Air for Europe (CAFE) Programme (COM(2001 245 final); Framework Directive 96/62/EC on ambient air quality assessment and management; Decision 97/101/EC on exchange of information and data on ambient air quality
DISMAR: IST-2001-37657 (FP5) Web:www.nersc.no/Projects/ dismar	Marine protection Open standards for marine risk management	INSPIRE initiative; Decision No 2850 of 20/12/2000 on cooperation in the field of accidental or deliberate marine; Pollution
EGERIS: IST-2000-28345 (FP5) Web: www.egeris.org	Risk management	INSPIRE initiative; Galileo Joined-up emergency response
Project Identification	Policy Area	Related policy measure:
HARMONOISE: IST-	Noise	Directive 2002/49/EC on the

2000-28419 (FP5) Web: www.harmonoise.nl	One voice on noise assessment	Assessment and Management of Environmental Noise
HEAVEN: IST-1999-11244 (FP5) Web: http://heaven.rec.org	Air quality HEAVEN controlling pollution through real time traffic management	Clean Air for Europe Programme (CAFÉ) Directive on Air Quality Assessment and Management (Framework Directive) (1996/62/EC) and associated Daughter Directives Directive on the Assessment and Management of Environmental Noise (2002/49/EC)
MINEO: IST-1999-10337 (FP5) Web: www.brgm.fr/mineo	Land use MINEO: Mitigating mining impacts	Communication: Towards a Thematic Strategy on the Urban Environment (COM(2004)60); Directives on environmental impact assessment and land use
ORCHESTRA IST-2002-511678 (FP6) Web: www.eu-orchestra.org	Risk management for Europe	INSPIRE initiative Global Monitoring for Environment & Security (GMES)
OSIRIS: IST-1999-11598 (FP5) Web: www.ist-osiris.org	Civil protection Timely responses to flood risks	Communication: Reinforcing the Civil Protection Capacity of the European Union (COM(2004) 200)
SUMARE: IST-1999-10836 (FP5) Web: www.mumm.ac.be/ SUMARE	Marine protection Sustainable marine environments	The Water Framework Directive 2000/60/EC; Directive on Quality of Bathing Water (COM(2002)581)
eSEVESO (eTEN) Web: www.e-seveso.net	Chemicals cost-effective compliance	Directive on the Control of Major-Accident Hazards (96/82/EC)-(the 'Seveso II Directive'); EU Proposal on Chemicals Policy (REACH)

Table 1: Part II (Beneficiaries and Expected impact)

Project Identification	Beneficiaries	Expected impact
APNEE-TU IST-2001-34154 (FP5) www.apnee.org/en/index.htm	Environmental agencies; meteorological services; local administrations	Ability to 'narrowcast' environmental warnings or advice to citizens most at risk
DISMAR: IST-2001-37657 (FP5) Web:www.nersc.no/Projects / dismar	: Environmental agencies and civil protection authorities	Better monitoring and management of marine environments
EGERIS: IST-2000-28345 (FP5) Web: www.egeris.org	Civil protection & emergency services	More effective management of civil emergencies and disaster response
HARMONOISE: IST-2000-28419 (FP5) Web: www.harmonoise.nl	Environmental regulators; citizens	Harmonised approach to the assessment of environmental noise levels

HEAVEN: IST-1999-11244 (FP5) Web: http://heaven.rec.org	Municipal & local administrations responsible for	Monitoring of vehicle related pollution in near real-time and prediction of future trends
MINEO: IST-1999-10337 (FP5) Web: www.brgm.fr/mineo	Local administrators; environmental regulators, industry	Better assessment of environmental status and impact in European mining areas, as well as applications to other environmental problems
ORCHESTRA IST-2002-511678 (FP6) Web: www.eu-orchestra.org	Civil protection authorities, environmental agencies	More effective trans-boundary risk management
OSIRIS: IST-1999-11598 (FP5) Web: www.ist-osiris.org	Flood prevention authorities; citizens in flood-prone areas	More effective management of flood risks and inundation events
SUMARE: IST-1999-10836 (FP5) Web: www.mumm.ac.be/ SUMARE	Environmental agencies; marine industries	Better and more detailed monitoring of marine environments
eSEVESO (eTEN) Web: www.e-seveso.net	Industry, especially SMEs; regulatory authorities	More cost-effective compliance with EU legislation

6   Information Society Policy Link: The next steps

In order to better demonstrate impact of IS projects and initiatives on other EU policy areas the instrument of Policy Interfaces and Policy Workshops have been launched in 2005. Policy Interfaces are structured meeting between Information Society and Media Directorate-General and other EU services with the aim to inform Policy DGs about INFSO plans for RTD activities in ICT, listen to their specific requirements for ICT research and ensure that results from INFSO-funded research projects and other activities can support the implementation of EU policies to the fullest possible extent.

Under this framework IS Policy Workshops i.e. a *working event/conference on a particular theme* are organized in cooperation with INFSO units, one or more thematic sub -groups or DGs. First themes proposed are: Employability of ICT Professionals, Beyond the Internet, E-resources for SMEs, E-Collaboration for Public Administrations, eInclusion / eUser workshops.

The next phases of the Information Society Policy Link initiative will focus on three areas:

- Refinement of existing cases e.g. review existing data collections — revisit findings (FP5); processing new information (mainly 1ST FP6; eTen; eContent); new wave of Policy Cases for each of 20 thematic areas
- Expansion of coverage by establishing contacts with remaining DGs and run Policy Interface meetings with DGs; launch special actions for EP & pilot National Parliaments, MS Administrations
- Promotion and in particular disseminate first findings to EU policy makers; Targeted promotions campaign; Launch new publications on new Policy

areas and cases; Organize a number of IS Policy Workshops; Pilot actions for MEP, Nat. Parliaments and Administrations

Furthermore synergies will be sought between DG INFSO coordinated related information services and projects such as IST results and Information Society Policy Link and targeted promotional efforts to increase societal awareness on impact of ICTs in economy and society.

7   Conclusions

The European Commission is supporting ICT research since 20 years with considerable resources devoted not only on IT technologies and communications but also to important applications notably in the areas of Public Health and Environment. Project results from the most recent Framework Programmes (FP4 and beyond) have demonstrated that even if selected on their policy relevance but mainly for its scientific merit, numerous ICT EU funded projects have considerable impact on other EU policies such as public health, environment, security, regional policy etc.

The first results of the DG Information Society and Media Information Society Policy Link initiative show that practically all policy areas could benefit from such project results in particular in integrating new concepts in coming policy initiatives, monitoring the implementation of existing regulation e.g. pollution levels, biometric controls etc. Communication and awareness raising actions should be reinforced in order to inform policy makers at all levels and influence the decision making process.

EU is devoting now a lot of resources on RTD and deployment actions impacting all policies and environment in particular. It is supporting the implementation of the research results through various initiatives such as eEurope, specific deployment actions, Action plans and Communications, Ministerial and high-level conferences and policies related to beneficial take-up ICTs. Information Society and Media Directorate-General in close cooperation with other EC services also contributes to major EU environment related large scale activities such as GMES and INSPIRE.

Regarding environment and ICT future research will focus on the integration of wide range sensors (in-situ, airborne, and satellite) to provide full information awareness for risk planning and emergency management. It will also promote the integration of secure, dependable public safety communication systems including ad-hoc broadband networks for emergency operations and alert networks. Finally, Information Society Policy Link initiative will in the near future intensify efforts to cover the whole spectrum of EU policies with meaningful policy cases – promising ICT project results positively impacting all EU policy areas.

References

1. IS Portal: http://europa.eu.int/information_society: Information on all policy initiatives and actions covering the Information Society and Media area.
2. IST Results: http://istresults.cordis.lu/index.cfm: Information service promoting RTD results emanating from the IST programme
3. ISPL: http://europa.eu.int/information_society/activities/policy_link/index_en.htm
4. 6th EAP: http://europa.eu.int/comm/dgs/environment/index_en.htm

Abbreviations

EU: European Union; EC: European Commission;
ICT or ICTs: Information and Communications Technologies
DG INFSO: Information Society and Media Directorate-General
RTD: Research and Technological Development
MI: Medical Informatics
IST: Information Society Technologies (research programme)
FP: Framework Research
EP: European Parliament
DG: Directorate-General
ESA: European Space
INSPIRE (INfrastructure for SPatial InfoRmation in Europe)
Environment 2010: Our Future, Our Choice
Environment Action Programme (EAP)

Acknowledgements

We cordially thank our colleagues in DG Information Society and Media, C.2 Unit: Strategy and Policy for ICT research and other thematic Units (G.5: ICT for Environment) for their contributions in this paper.

Consumer Models in the Encounter between Supply and Demand of Electronic Administration

Françoise Massit-Folléa, Cécile Méadel
Laboratoire C2SO – Ecole Normale Supérieure – Lettres et Sciences
humaines, Lyon, France ; francoise.massit@club-internet.fr
Centre de sociologie de l'innovation, Ecole des Mines, CNRS, Paris,
France; cecile.meadel@ensmp.fr

Abstract. In the modernization process of public administration, information technologies are used as a tool to transform both its practices and its relations with its users. The new user-centric pattern comes from the market world: Customer Relationship Management becomes Citizen Relationship Management. Are the devices and tools of e-commerce convenient with the goals and practices of e-administration? Analyzing characters such as identification, deliberation, personalization and trust building reveals the limits of such a comparison and the need for a renewal of mediation functions between public and private spheres.

Keywords: customer, citizen, e-commerce, e-administration, devices, mediation

1 Introduction

According to the participants at a Round Table of the Telecommunications Observatory (Observatoire des Télécommunications dans la ville) in 2003: 'To meet the administered citizen's needs, Citizen Relationship Management has to be set up', along the same lines as Customer Relationship Management. 'This approach overturns the traditional logic of administration and focuses on the quality of the service as well as reception, assistance and the handling of complaints […] It is no longer the citizen who makes an effort to reach the administration but the administration that is put at the citizen's service'. Citizen relationship management 'primarily concerns the organization of channels of information and communication around citizens' needs, especially by multiplying the channels and restructuring

Please use the following format when citing this chapter:

Massit-Folléa, F., Méadel, C., 2006, in IFIP International Federation for Information Processing, Volume 223, Social Informatics: An Information Society for All? In Remembrance of Rob Kling, eds. Berleur, J., Numinen, M. I., Impagliazzo, J., (Boston: Springer), pp. 209–217.

information systems [...], by taking into account legislative, financial and human constraints and imperatives in terms of public service and equality in the treatment of users [...], in the implementation of a whole range of tools (call centers, pagers, SMS, websites, automatic message or email management, etc.)' [1]

This is not relevant only to France. According to the Austrian chairwoman of TeleCities interviewed in 2003, 'E-administration is based on the transformation of the citizen into a consumer [sic]. In North America these forms of electronic governance are part of a more general movement of transformation of the administration (New Public Management) and the challenging of its role in supporting the welfare state. Public management is evaluated above all in terms of its capacity to produce quantifiable results [2]. Everywhere, we see that public administration seems to use information technologies as a tool to transform both its practices and its relations with its users. Its ambition is to become 'user-centric'.

Under what conditions can an approach conceived of in a market perspective be adapted to the relationship between citizens and their administration? This type of approach implicitly contains some serious assumptions: the administration has to be more efficient, and 'commodifying' relations can contribute towards that; the citizen is defined in terms no longer of rights and duties but of needs; finally – and this is not the smallest difficulty – this policy of commodification of the relationship can be applied to everything affecting the information of citizens.

The subject under study in this paper is a few number of devices set up on e-administration sites. We focus on these devices rather than on the sites themselves since as we are less interested in the content – which simply consists of on-line copies of the data sheets of public services – than in the devices that form a particular type of link with the user and are designed to induce a behavior, obtain an opinion, prompt a response, and so on. These devices will be compared to the discourses of the website managers by way of several types of question.

- What assumptions are made on the citizen's competencies and expectations?
- What types of device are produced and to what extent do they draw on the logic of commercial relationships?
- What conception of the service is implemented in the concrete devices set up to create the relationship? What is the administration's position?
- What means does the e-administration have to verify the relevance of its hypotheses?
- What types of relationship are enabled by the devices?

The aim is to test a very common assumption that, whereas e-commerce invents new consumer figures (communities, education, enlightened choices, etc.), e-administration gives preference to the front office and remains in a supply logic wrapped in a new technical appearance.

At this stage of the research, almost six months before the conference, we can only clarify the issue. The goal of this preliminary paper is to improve our hypotheses. The results of our fieldwork and the validation of the hypotheses will be presented at the conference.

Why Talk of e-Administration?

What is e-administration? First, it is an appendage of the State. Under certain conditions it shares its missions and concretizes its transformations. In the wake of WWII, the State (particularly the French State) became a supplier not only of rules and services in the general interest but also of products in the strict sense of the term (public or nationalized enterprises for the production and distribution of energy, transport, cars, etc.). Despite significant structural upheavals (for instance, the end of state monopolies), the objects concerned by e-administration still bear the marks of this trend. Use of the term therefore encompasses diverse figures and publics.

The term e-administration also covers very different spaces, which differ by their legal status, funding system, management practices, etc.: the agency with a public service mission (such as dealing with the unemployed); the local authority that produces public and political communication on town life; the legal information service; the institution with a semi-commercial mission (e.g. the postal bank), and so on.

This heterogeneity of missions relates to a wide diversity of publics. In overlapping organizational contexts (the 'administration user' being the taxpayer, the victim or culprit in a court case, the schoolchild's parent, the council housing tenant, the customer of postal services or public transport, the voter for various authorities, the Internet user testing online procedures, etc.), highly variable possibilities of 'transaction' frame the addressee's margin of maneuver. Between the citizen's duties and the user's rights there exist different levels of intervention that the e-administration ought to take into account. The first clarification therefore has to be made in relation to the type of mission that the issuer of an e-administration proposal has to fulfill, and possibly in relation to its legal form (administration of the state, public institution with different 'statuses', public service agency or subsidized representative). This enables the various communication figures in question to be distinguished.

The diversity of publics, missions and users concerned has not prevented large-scale compulsory mobilization around the common notion of e-administration. Sites, applications and tools have proliferated [3]. This has also entailed many questions on the grounds for this type of transformation of communication formats and its impacts. In France, over half a dozen public reports have been commissioned since 2000, that question the forms of citizenship at work in such applications [4] [5], and the trend is the same all over Europe [6] [7].

The unified representation of the citizen as a cell of the social body still prevails in a traditional – centralized, hierarchical, sectoral, anonymous – functioning of state services. The citizen is a 'subject' (to taxes, until recently to military service, to compulsory schooling, etc.). He or she is the motive for public action but is kept far from the definition of goals and the implementation of means. This model is useful for its integrating function that transcends social peculiarities. By contrast, the 'client approach', increasingly present in the preoccupations of public producers of goods and services, implies: a segmentation of the supply – which takes into account the client's interests, competencies, financial or other capacities –; a relative freedom of choice – which almost always leaves an alternative to the consumer but urges the firm to emphasize the specificity of its product or service or even to make it irreplaceable –; and finally, a form of constitution of the social link by aggregation of shared interests and no longer on an abstract uniform republican base.

Our objective is not to add an additional evaluation of the work and results of e-administration to an already long list[1]. It is rather to examine the proposed devices and to take literally the notion of 'citizen relationship management' in order to understand how it operates and what type of e-citizen figure is constructed. The devices of sites that will serve as a field for observation will be analyzed by comparison with the characterization that we give here of commercial spaces of interaction.

2   Characterization of the Market-Citizen Relationship

To ensure that supply corresponds to demand (chap. 2 [8]), e-commerce makes a number of assumptions about its customers, which it tests in many ways. The strategies are diverse: it can bargain on communities of experience, play the critical intermediary card, aim for the consumer's rationality (by comparative prices), etc. In any case, it transforms the way in which the relationship with customers is traditionally established in its field of activity. It therefore simultaneously has to redefine the service that it proposes. At this stage, four ways of analyzing the relationship with users have been selected:
-    What means are made available to the user to relate to the proposed device?
-    What type of interaction is organized?
-    Under what conditions and with which participants?
-    Is the user identified as a particular individual or a non-particularized visitor? In the former case, what forms of personalization are organized?
-    How does the device create trust?

2.1   Identification in Space / in the Device

What competencies does the device assume users to have? In particular, in what space does it presume users think they are? To what extent do users participate in the construction of their demand? Do they have to correspond to a pre-established offer or is there some leeway?

In the e-commerce context, the prevailing model (at least in these early days of e-commerce) is the supermarket. Products are arranged on 'shelves' and by types of product and brand. Wandering around the supermarket is evoked by scroll-down menus, which present products by type. Each pause marks the entry into an aisle where the space is again divided up. The model is that of the rational consumer whose decisions are enlightened, but where impulsive buying is made possible by a series of commercial propositions 'slipped in' alongside the main pages (the key argument being the promotional character of the proposition).

---

[1]   Especially since the agency in charge of these issues (the ADAE) has already done a large amount of work on the subject: http//www.adae.gouv.fr/adele/

In the case of public sites, the competencies that users are expected to have depend on the field in which the public actor operates[9] [10]. On the site of the ANPE, the French national employment agency (Agence nationale pour l'emploi), the reference is that of job advertisements. Job offers and adverts by job seekers are presented in two different, parallel or successive but unrelated spaces. Each actor knows what he or she is looking for; there is no possible move in qualifications. This is the traditional space of supply and demand of jobs that probably supports the current organization of the labor market [11].

The user figures for whom the public sites cater are often diverse: users seeking information or wanting to communicate with an administrative service, file a complaint, understand the functioning of a benefit, and so on. To what extent can these sites provide such diverse questions? This point, even by leaving aside the digital divide, relates directly to the problem of equality in citizens' information. Considering the complexity of administrative processes, do these sites enlighten the information of all citizens or do they worsen inequalities?

Promoting e-administration usually reveals a concern for rationalization and saving money. For instance, the national portal 'service-public.fr' has been adapted as 'service-public-local.fr', designed for web sites of local authorities. With the same headings, which is good for ergonomics and routine training. However, it misses the point that the relationship between the administration and its users is not the same depending on the lifetimes, the degrees of intensity in demand or the relevance of the situation. Consequently, such initiatives have a paradoxical outcome: the main challenge is on the back-office, with the necessity of interconnecting data and services; the main effort is expected – and scarcely met - in the mediation, or intermediation, process.

2.2   Interaction and Deliberation

One of the noteworthy characteristics of e-commerce sites is the way in which they organize forms of interaction between suppliers and customers, and among customers themselves, by providing a range of devices. At least three levels of increasingly intense interaction can be distinguished: answering consumers' questions, making these interactions public, and organizing interactions among consumers. This takes place via a series of devices, including FAQs, forums, 'community' sites, and so on. Until now, in certain cases, this has gone as far as the creation of 'communities' of users or consumers.

E-traders are also configured as intermediaries and, in a number of services, tend to move into the background or at least not to be the only ones motivating purchases. For example, they may share assessments of goods with the web users. They thus tend to establish a collective that will, in a sense, bypass them, although with their consent. As certain promoters of e-administration projects claim, these two characteristics are transposable onto sites intended for relations with the administration.

However, contrary to e-government defenders' assertions, 'User of public services' is currently considered to be a single person (asking to be informed, to be put in contact, or to receive redress for a grievance). When he simply expresses a specific viewpoint or a personal belief, and most of all when he fits into public policy issues as a collective body, he or she becomes a source of problems for the civil servants, who are not prepared to deal properly with users that are reluctant or who demand change too much.

This relates to two types of question: one on the common constitution of points of view; the other on relations with decision-makers or the organization.

When a device authorizes the user to express his beliefs, his needs, his questions, or even his criticism, from what point do the participants in these discussion areas construct a collective place for debate and interaction, or even a common opinion? When, or under what conditions, do the various individual messages go beyond and embody a collective advice? On the City of Paris site, for example, the addition of opinions is an explicitly sought-after objective since the preferred – in fact the only – form of interaction is consultation of Internet users by way of an opinion poll. But the feedback improvements are left to the site managers' good will, without any transparency...

What are the impacts on decision-making? Commercial sites can mobilize their consumers to transform their offer, or alter their communication tools. But in order to do so they have to allocate particular resources to the task of answering consumers' questions and monitoring their interactions or involving themselves in those interactions. The objective is very simple: go on with business. For public websites, the objectives are much more complex: to give certified information, to open an interaction delimited by legal constraints, to enforce requirements in the question-answer process (deadline, conformity, identification, etc.). The assessment of success or failure is far less direct for e-administration, and measures are difficult to interpret. But if there is a bug, unpleasant consequences can occur in terms of control or sanction, and probably first of all on users!

2.3   Personalizing the Demand

Concerned about retaining their customers and increasing consumption levels, commercial sites set up devices enabling them to personalize their customer relationships: identification of consumer profile, records of former purchases, various advantages related to loyalty, and so on. Customers are identified both by their past (what they have consumed and even what interests them), by their abilities and by their behavior (e.g. e-Bay's reputation index [12]). They may, for instance, be welcomed with messages related to former sessions, or have a so-called 'personal' space.

This approach by differentiation and personalization of users is more recent in the public sector. Unlike traditional practices in the French civil service, new modes of organization have been introduced to put an end to agents' anonymity and to personalize the reception of users, trying to reconfigure the organization of services according to the citizen and no longer according to the bureaucratic territories; for example, the notion of a 'single front office' in which the citizen is considered as a whole, encompassing all his or her relations with the various public institutions. A project of website named 'my-service-public.fr' has been under testing for several years. Yet even though this personalization is a response to certain demands by citizens [13], it poses specific problems in the public service insofar as it has to be consistent with the basic principles of equality, neutrality and continuity.

On administrative sites, we find devices that allow forms of personalization of the service. For instance, on the ANPE site, the job seeker has to create a personal space in which to save advertisements of interest, his or her CV, etc. The same applies to employers. But this space is simply an archive accessible only to that person that has been pre-formatted to a large degree by the service. This raises questions on the specific characteristics of this form of personalization of the service and on the way in which it may be redefined.

Two patterns are competing. In the 'new public management' design, "the idea of a plural citizen related both politically and economically to the public sector is replaced with the idea of a customer being motivated only by a direct and immediate exchange with it" [14]. In the 'democratic governance' design, the solution is to be found not in efficiency but in active participation from one side, true accountability for the other side. Both actors are asked to become co-designers of the public service.

There are also other questions relating to the personalization issue. Both on commercial sites and on e-administration sites, questions are raised concerning the protection of personal data.

How is this addressed? Who guarantees that individuals are protected? What redress procedure is provided for?

2.4   Trust and Security

One of the crucial problems encountered by commercial sites is trust in the device. How can a remote service be provided, with people who are often new actors and sometimes anonymous (on platforms of interaction between private individuals)? A range of devices has been set up by sites to provide users or consumers with elements of assessment: identification of firms, clarification of modes of functioning, existence of a procedure for redress, etc.

Transparency is one of the means mobilized to nurture trust. For instance, e-Bay organizes a high level of transparency between sellers and buyers. The reputation of an 'e-bayer' is the sum of opinions of others on the transactions in which he or she has been involved (called the evaluation profile). His or her career is the list of goods that he or she has sold or bought, and of the 'e-bayers' with whom he or she has concluded a transaction. This transparency is nevertheless possible only with the agreement and participation of those concerned and is obtained only when they have a shared objective (e.g. organizing the security of transactions).

This transparency is also highlighted by new public management, but is it really the same thing? Probably not. The transparency in e-government faces the everlasting process of modernization of the public sector, with numerous territorial and political layers. And, on the user's side, reluctance or resistance appear to being 'captured' in interconnected files related to the control powers of the State.

Moreover, the benefits of public policies apply whether to a public service consumer, or to a public space citizen: administration managers are so devoted to e-modernization that they cannot comprehend and thus cannot solve this dichotomy.

The challenge could be in redesigning the concept of 'public service' and in activating a more collaborative behavior in its users.

3   To conclude

What questions derived from Customer Relationship Management enable us to understand the change under way as the administration goes online? For as we have seen, the issue here is not just about simplifying procedures, cost-cutting or saving the time of citizens and civil servants. In a broader sense, the objective is to reconfigure the administration so that it places the citizen at the center of its preoccupations, in other words, so that its quick and good response to citizens' requests are the measure of an administration's success. The comparison with e-commerce highlights, in a particularly stark manner, the importance of useful mediation in developing such services. It is not enough for any service to just combine a device, no matter how sophisticated, and an agent, no matter how competent; the interaction between supply and demand assumes a series of tests that enable the supply (or offer) to be modified and the demand to be adjusted. In conclusion, we will note the most significant forms of this mediation.

The web user is not an isolated individual, but an actor in society, connected to numerous groups, informed and influenced by diverse viewpoints. Prescribing agents have helped him to forge his judgment – the more competent he is and hence the more capable of identifying and increasing these agents, the more numerous they become. On certain sites, this notion of prescriber is instrumentalized, as the prescribers' opinions are gathered, solicited and capitalized upon, often on a voluntary basis [15], in order to help to describe products for the greater good of the site and its customers.

Nor is the web user in front of his computer necessarily isolated in consulting the web; his learning has quite often taken place in part in a collective setting, as has his behavior in front of the device [10]. Sites take into account this common way of acting by making group behavior possible and favoring the constitution of groups of uses, but also by making visible the shared nature of certain ways of doing things.

What are the alternatives to supply?

The transaction can fail and then the question of possible recourse is raised: what enables the 'lost' web user to be reconnected to his supplier, or by the same token, what connects the service to the client? Indicating one's location and opening a space of interaction with the supplier are part of building a relationship of trust and therefore contribute to redefining the interaction between supply and demand.

To what degree can e-administration use such forms of mediation, or rather, to what extent can e-administration take place *via* these forms of mediation? The field research is expected to provide critical feedback on the innovations of e-administration and to analyze its link with democratic practices in the digital age.

References

1. H. Lambling, La gestion de la relation citoyen : les TIC à l'écoute et au service des territoires. (2003).
2. J.-E. Lane, *Public Sector Reform. Rationale, Trends and Problems*, London: Sage, 1998.
3. D. Alcaud and A. Lakel, Les nouveaux 'visages' de l'administration sur Internet : pour une évaluation des sites publics de l'Etat. *Revue française d'administration publique.* **110**, 2004.
4. M. Chauvière and J.-T. Godbout, *Les usagers entre marché et citoyenneté,* Paris: L'Harmattan, 1992.
5. B. de Quatrebarbes, *Usagers ou clients : marketing et qualité dans les services publics,* Paris: Ed. d'Organisation, 1996.
6. C. G. E. Young, *Online Availability of Public Services: How Does Europe Progress?* Brussels: European Commission DG Information Society, 2004. europa.eu.int/information_society/eeurope/2005/doc/highlights/whats_new/capgemini4.pdf.
7. G. García-Arribas and F. López-Crespo, Presentation. Landscape of e-Government at the Dawn of the 21st Century –. *Upgrade. The European Journal for the Informatics Professional.* **IV**(2), 2003. http://www.upgrade-cepis.org.
8. F. Massit-Folléa (ed.), Internet Governance: Common fact and rights., 2005. http://www.voxinternet.org/
9. Services publics : questions de communication et de management. *Revue Etudes de communication.* **23**, 2001.
10. R. Suire, Encastrement social et usages d'Internet: le cas du commerce et de l'administration électronique. *Cahier de recherche Marsouin.* Mai (5), 2005. http://www.marsouin.org/article.php3?id_article=49.
11. E. Marchal, K. Mellet and G. Rieucau, *Job Board Toolkits: Internet Matchmaking and the Transformation of Help-Wanted Ads,* Noisy-le-Grand: Centre d'études de l'emploi, 2005. http://www.cee-recherche.fr/fr/c_pub3.htm.
12. C. Méadel, La qualification croisée des biens et des services ou le marché ebay. *Hermès.* **44**, 2006.
13. *Survey: Usages et attentes en matière de services publics sur l'Internet. France, Europe,* Paris: Capgemini et TNS Sofres, 2005.
14. J.-P. Villeneuve, Citoyens, clients et usagers face à l'administration publique Les balises d'une relation difficile. *Working paper de l'IDHEA.* **6**, 2005.
15. M. Gensollen, Internet: Marché électronique ou réseaux commerciaux ? *Revue économique.* **52** (Hors série octobre 2001): p. 137-161. http://www.brousseau.info/semnum/pdf/2003-01-06_Gensollen.pdf.

Sustainability and the Information Society

Christian Fuchs
ICT&S Center: Advanced Studies and Research in Information and
Communication Technologies & Society, University of Salzburg, Austria,
christian.fuchs@sbg.ac.at

Abstract. The aim of this paper is to discuss the notion of sustainability in relationship to the idea of the information society. In the first part the relationship is on ecological aspects of a sustainable information society. In the second and third part of this paper I introduce a broad notion of sustainability that consists of multiple dimensions. The concept of a sustainable information society is developed, it is conceived as a society in which new information- and communication technologies (ICTs) and knowledge are used in order to advance a good-life for all individuals of current and future generations. This idea is conceived in a multidimensional way, identifying ecological, technological, economic, political, and cultural aspects and problems.

Keywords: sustainable information society, sustainability

1 ICTs and Ecological Sustainability

Related to the rising production, use, and diffusion of ICTs there are a lot of hopes, dreams, and myths. This also applies for the ecological subsystem of society where discussions focus on the question if ICTs can advance ecological sustainability, i.e. biological diversity and environmental protection. "Our contention is that, as ICT becomes more sophisticated and more embedded in our organizational structures and everyday life, we are in a better position than ever before to make sustainable development work" [1: p. 5]. I don't think that ICTs automatically advance ecological sustainability, but that ICTs pose both new opportunities and risks for the ecosphere. There is a positive and a negative tendency: ICTs allow the reduction of travelling by doing parts of necessary communications online, it is a medium of ecological communication and the communication and co-operation of the ecological protest movement, but it also contributes to ecological degradation e.g. in the form of computer scrap and the waste and emissions generated in production processes of

Please use the following format when citing this chapter:

Fuchs, C., 2006, in IFIP International Federation for Information Processing, Volume 223, Social Informatics: An Information Society for All? In Remembrance of Rob Kling, eds. Berleur, J., Numinen, M. I., Impagliazzo, J., (Boston: Springer),
pp. 219–230.

ICTs. I will discuss the implications of ICTs for sustainability in the areas of transport, business, ecological activism, and developing countries.

The question is whether private and business Internet communication automatically reduces the need for travelling. This can be the case if people consciously choose to avoid unnecessary travelling and transport by plane and car, but Internet communication also makes it easier to connect people globally and to initiate and maintain social relationships and hence it can also raise the desire or need to meet people face to face more frequently.

Some scientists argue that due to the fact that telework allows knowledge workers to overcome spatio-temporal distances and to work from home the need for transport and hence environmental pollution would be reduced. The same argument can be employed for teleconferencing saying that by substituting personal meetings by teleconferences travelling can be reduced. But teleworkers normally don't work full time at home because they need to stay connected personally and face to face with their social work environment, the number of teleworkers is generally relatively low (in Europe the share of teleworkers in the total labour force ranges from less than 2 per cent to more than 10 per cent, [cf. 9: p. 9])), travelling to work produces only a relatively small share of total carbon dioxide emissions, and working from home doesn't automatically imply less transport because online work can produce new contacts that might generate the need for meeting people personally. Working at home can have negative environmental effects, e.g. people can't go shopping on the way home from work, but might take an extra trip by car from home to shops and supermarkets.

Companies often paint an optimistic picture of the effects of teleworking on the ecosystem, but studies show that although teleworkers frequently reduce their commuting distances "the overall distance travelled for commuting is growing though not very fast. That the last three years represent the highest figures, does not support the thesis which suggests that transport savings have been made because of telework" [9: p. 26]. The European reality seems to be that telework and teleconferencing are simply too unimportant for having positive effects on transport savings and that there are rebound effects from online communication on the increase of travelling. About 5 per cent of the labour force in Europe can be considered as teleworkers, roughly 10 per cent of the working days of the complete European labour force can be considered as home-based telework [9: p. 52]. The result of another study is that "homeworkers are spending more time travelling than conventional workers" [7].

Telework and teleconferences certainly pose an opportunity for reducing travelling, but this opportunity has thus far not been adequately realized. What is needed is a conscious commitment of business and individuals to reduce the amount of travels by car and plane. ICTs alone don't solve the problem. The reality of work and life today is that in a flexible economy and society individuals have to be flexible and have to travel long-distances in order to maintain work-related and private social relationships.

Some scientists argue that the shift from the 'industrial society' to the 'information society' means that the economy becomes less resource-intensive and that hence there is a 'dematerialization' of production that creates a 'weightless economy' that advances ecological sustainability The argument here is that knowledge-based industries and services are less resource intensive than industrial production, that ICTs can reduce negative environmental impacts of traditional industries by allowing more efficient ways of production and distribution, that certain products and services could be dematerialized/virtualized which would reduce their environmental impact, that such goods are traded and transported over the Internet which would reduce the amount of physical transport, and that ICTs can increase the efficiency of transportation.

The reality of dematerialization seems to be that fully virtualized products and the ICT sector constitute only a small portion of the economy, that the total resource use of the economy is constantly rising, and that hence thus far there has not been a massive 'greening' of production and consumption induced by knowledge products and ICT [6, 15]. It is not true that "economic value is dematerialising" [3: p.1]. Postindustrial capitalism as a dematerialized ecologically sustainable economy is a myth. Alain Touraine has argued in this context that the information society is a 'hyperindustrial society' [11]. It is not a new society that is characterized by immaterial goods, but a new phase of development of capitalism that is both continuity and discontinuity of industrial capitalism and has emergent qualities such as the central importance of cognitive, communicative, and co-operative labour.

The knowledge economy is not an economy of invisible and intangible goods, there indeed are many physical information commodities that are transported and sold. Another argument is that certain products and services can be entirely virtualized and transported in digital format over the Internet and that hence material and energy savings can be made. If music, books, newspapers, and journals are distributed in digital format online resource savings in production and distribution can be made. Also new flexible production technologies that are based on just-in-time-production (e.g. books on demand) allow resource savings. But almost no one wants to read a book or a whole newspaper online because it is not very comfortable to read on screen, therefore many people print out articles or whole books which results in a high consumption of paper, toner, and ink. There are certain alternatives such as e-paper that can be reused, but companies thus far have not widely supported reusable or eco-friendly equipment (such as e-paper, the 'green PC', or refillable ink cartridges for printers) because reusable computer equipment is not only less resource-intensive, but might in the long-term also be less profitable. Thus far companies have not much supported the development of ecologically sustainable ICT equipment. The use of recyclable and reusable equipment could indeed reduce the environmental impact of ICTs, but for doing so the logic of capital accumulation needs to be subordinated under ecological and social awareness. The relationship of ICTs and sustainability is not only a question of ethical consumerism, but also one of corporate social and ecological responsibility. In capitalism not those technologies that most benefit society and ecology are promoted, but those that enable capital accumulation. Hence it is e.g. not solar or wind energy or the reusable computer that are promoted, but nuclear energy, fossil fuels, the automobile, and non-renewable computer equipment. As long as a company is profitable, it might be open-minded for ecological and social goals, but capitalism is based on competition and economic crisis is an inherent feature of the system, hence in the end in many cases the logic of profit will outstrip social and ecological awareness.

For ecological sustainability we don't necessarily have to slow down technological progress, but the way hardware is manufactured and diffused surely have to change because millions of people continuing to buy a whole new computer each two or three years is detrimental to reaching ecological goals. One should also add that ICTs are industrial products, their production and disposal generates waste and emissions. Environmental performance assessments of computer technologies show that the latter doesn't heavily reduce material outputs, the production of one PC requires 16-19 tonnes of material resources and more than 5000 kWh energy, the emission of the production of one piece include 60 kg waste, 1850 kg carbon dioxide, 2 kg sulfur dioxide, and 1 kg nitrogen oxide [5]. The knowledge society is not an immaterial society, but a new phase in the material reality of capitalism. It requires a large material infrastructures made up by computers, periphery, servers, routers, switches, network cables, etc. The hardware industry makes profit by selling computers and periphery. If computers were used for a longer time or if it were increasingly possible to renew only certain parts in order to come up to date with technological progress and not having to buy a whole new computer, environmental improvements could indeed be made. But his would require a step away from the logic of profitability towards the logic of ecological sustainability. Hence it would mean to accept lower profits in order to protect the environment. Such moves are possible, but they contradict the dominant economic logic. If corporate social responsibility shall not only be ideology, corporations must be ready to go beyond and to question to a certain extent capitalist logic.

There are technological possibilities to reduce the energy consumption of television sets and monitors (by using LCD monitors and television sets and selling such machines at reasonable prices) as well as computers (by including components that automatically detach computers from energy supply if they are not used for a certain time, Switched Mode Power Supply). But the interests of the energy industry might be detrimental to establishing 'green ICTs' because high amounts of energy use mean high profits, what is needed are political pressure and unified laws that define minimum standards of energy efficiency of ICTs and require producers to include energy consumption labels on ICTs. This might have negative consequences on profitability, but if sustainability shall be achieved the domination of society by economic logic must be challenged.

2   Towards a Sustainable Information Society?

An anticipation of the idea of sustainable development can be found in Marx's writings. He argues that in communism the globe must be improved by human beings and passed on to succeeding generations in such a condition. "From the standpoint of a higher economic form of society, private ownership of the globe by single individuals will appear quite as absurd as private ownership of one man by another. Even a whole society, a nation, or even all simultaneously existing societies taken together, are not the owners of the globe. They are only its possessors, its usufructuaries, and, like *boni patres familias,* they must hand it down to succeeding generations in an improved condition" [8: p. 784]. If one compares this passage to the most common definition of sustainable development by the Brundtland Commission – "Sustainable development is development that meets the needs of the present without compromising the ability of future generations to meet their own needs" [14: p. 43] – one finds a striking concurrence.

In 1992 the UN Conference on Environment and Development ('Earth Summit') took place in Rio de Janeiro, Brazil, where for the first time heads of state from all over the world gathered to discuss problems of sustainability. At the Earth Summit all participating countries agreed to the Rio Declaration on Environment and Development that put forward 27 principles for the future that can help in achieving sustainable development. The discourse on sustainable development shows a shift from the view of nature as an enemy that must be controlled to a view that considers nature as an important pre-condition of human existence that must be treated carefully. In 2002 the World Summit on Sustainable Development (WSSD) conference was held in Johannesburg with the intention of having a review ten years after the 1992 Rio Earth Summit. The outcomes include a Plan of Implementation and the Johannesburg Declaration on Sustainable Development [16]. Whereas the Earth Summit focused on the environmental issues of sustainability, the WSSD conference more effectively integrated economic and equity issues into the discussion.

In the discourse on sustainability there has been a shift from a focus on ecological issues towards the inclusion of broader societal issues. The 'triangle of sustainability' introduced by the World Bank has been very important in shifting discussion on sustainability from purely ecological aspects towards more integrative concepts. Ismail Serageldin, then vice-president of the World Bank, identified an economic, a social, and an ecological dimension of sustainability. "It is not surprising that these concerns reflect the three sides of what I have called the 'triangle of sustainability' - its economic, social, and ecological dimensions" [10: p. 17]. It has now become very common to identify an ecological, an economic, a social, and an institutional dimension of sustainability (as e.g. the EU and the UN do). "At the time of Rio, sustainable development was mainly about protecting nature, but now, in the wake of Johannesburg, it is first and foremost about protecting people" [16: p. 22].

In the relationship of nature and society human beings and groups act as subjects that appropriate and change nature in different ways. Although nature is active itself (it produces itself permanently in autopoietic cycles), it is an objective structure in society that is changed by man and enables the latter's activity. Hence one can conceive human individuals and groups as subjects and natural resources as objects in the nature-society-relationship. One can distinguish four types of sustainability concepts based on where in the nature-society-relationship they locate sustainability. Ecological reductionistic approaches define sustainability primarily in ecological terms, social projectionism considers sustainability as a quality of social systems, dualistic approaches speak of both a sustainable ecology and a sustainable society, but they consider both realms to be independent. Ecological reductionism ignores social aspects of sustainability such as wealth, participation, and wisdom, social projectionism is ignorant of the relative autonomy of nature, dualistic approaches ignore the interconnectedness and interdependence of nature and society. Dialectical approaches on sustainability try to solve the problems of these concepts by arguing that societal sustainability requires ecological sustainability and ecological sustainability societal sustainability, the two systems mutually enhance each other.

Table 1. A Typology of Approaches on Sustainability

Approach	Nature (Object)	Society (Subject)
Ecological Reductionism	Sustainability of Nature	
Social Projectionism		Sustainability of Society
Dualism	Sustainability of Nature	Sustainability of Society
Dialectic Thinking	Interconnected Sustainability of Nature and Society	

Both nature and society are self-organizing systems in the sense that they permanently produce themselves, i.e. their elements and unity, they are self-maintaining, self-reproducing, and (in the case of society) self-reflecting. Nature is made up of eco-systems that permanently reproduce themselves, they are living, autopoietic systems that permanently reproduce their elements and their unity. If man negatively influences nature by depleting and polluting natural resources, ecosystems are no longer able to autopoietically reproduce themselves and break down. Hence their processes of reproduction and differentiation come to a halt. Ecological sustainability means that humans appropriate nature in a way that allows ecological diversity, i.e. the autopoiesis of nature can develop in such a way that nature flourishes, reproduces its subsystems, differentiates itself and produces new qualities, i.e. new ecological life forms and subsystems.

Social systems and society are self-organizing in the sense that there is a permanent mutual production of social structures and practices of human actors. These processes are goal-oriented, i.e. humans have the ability to identify and anticipate different paths of development, to judge which ones they consider as desirable and to act according to these wishes, values, and desires. Societal sustainability is based on the desire of all human beings to live in a fair, just, and beautiful society. Sustainability in general means a good life for all. Society is made up of different, interconnected subsystems: ecology, technology, economy, polity, and culture. Sustainability is a desirable aspect that humans strive for in all of these subsystems. A sustainable society encompasses ecological diversity, technological usability, economic wealth, political participation, and cultural wisdom. Usability means that technologies are designed in a user-friendly way and support humans in achieving their goals more easily. Economic wealth means that basic needs and social security should be provided for all human beings. Political participation requires a distribution of power that enables humans to adequately influence those decisions that affect them. A culturally wise society is one that is critical, self-reflective, allows a plurality of life-styles, meanings, ways of life, and values that complement each other (unity in diversity) and finds ways to solve and manage its problems in a way that brings advantages for all. Culture is made up by various subsystems such as the mass media, science, art, education, ethics/belief systems, medicine, sports, and the system of social relationships. In these systems cultural sustainability, i.e. wisdom, has different meanings such as wise knowledge and media (mass media), truth (science), beauty and imagination (art), literacy and good skills (education), openness and unity in diversity of values and rights (ethics), health (medicine), fitness (sports), love and understanding (social relationships). In a dialectical approach on sustainability ecological sustainability is based on social sustainability and vice versa, i.e. biological diversity is best advanced by a society where we finds technological usability, economic wealth for all (i.e. a rather symmetrical distribution of wealth), political participation for all, and cultural wisdom and a biological rich and diverse ecosystem is a life-support system that is a good foundation for a socially sustainable society where one finds social systems that are usable, wealthy, participatory, and wise. An unsustainable ecosystem advances an unsustainable society and vice versa: If man pollutes nature and depletes non-renewable natural resources problems, i.e. if he creates an unhealthy environment, problems such as poverty, war, totalitarianism, extremism, violence, crime, etc. are more likely to occur. The other way round a society that is shaken by poverty, war, a lack of democracy and plurality, etc. is more likely to pollute and deplete nature. This can result in a vicious cycle where nature and society are connected in negative feedback loops that have destructive effects for both systems. If nature and society are connected in sustainable ways there can be positive feedback loops that enable both systems to flourish and to develop in sustainable ways. Sustainable development of the ecosystem means that it increases its diversity and reproduces itself, sustainable development of the socio-sphere means that it increases wealth for all, fosters technological progress that benefits all, and enhances participation and wisdom for all. In a sustainable society social structures such as technology, property/use values, power, and knowledge/meaning are produced and enhanced in ways that benefit all human beings, the self-organization cycles of a sustainable society develop in such a way that a good life for all is possible, the self-organization of the ecosystem and the self-organization of the socio-sphere positively influence each other.

Table 2. Dimensions of Sustainability

Dimension	Quality
Ecological Sustainability	Biological Diversity
Technological Sustainability	Usability
Economic Sustainability	Wealth for All
Political Sustainability	Participation of All
Cultural Sustainability	Wisdom
Sustainability of:	
Mass Media	Wise Knowledge and Media
Science	Truth
Art	Beauty and Imagination
Education	Literacy and Good Skills
Ethics	Openness, Unity in Diversity of Values and Rights
Medicine	Health
Sports	Fitness
Social Relationships	Love and Understanding

Modern industrialism is unsustainable in two ways: 1. Accumulation processes result in the depletion of non-renewable natural resources, limits to extraction and accumulation are herewith created. 2. Economic production and consumption result in residues of goods that are shoved into nature by society in the form of waste. Hence ecological degradation includes both depletion and pollution. Based on figure 3 one can describe ecological degradation as a double process of the depletion of nature (in the direction where nature is appropriated by society) and the pollution of nature by society (in the direction where society transforms nature) (cf. fig. 3). Unsustainable ecological development is a process where depletion and pollution of nature by society cause the breakdown of more and more material (living and non-living) cycles of self-organization in nature and create threats to the survival of the whole eco-system that forms the material foundation of society. Hence the destruction of nature also threatens the survival of society and humankind.

Fig. 1. Unsustainable ecological development

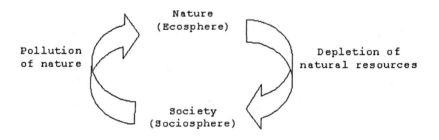

3   Measuring the Sustainability of the Information Society

The shift towards the knowledge-based society has resulted in an increasing orientation of empirical sociological research and statistical analysis towards developing statistical indicators of the knowledge-based character of the economy and society. In order to benchmark the success of the member states in achieving the goals defined in the eEurope action plans the European Council has defined main indicators plus supplementary indicators in the areas of 1. Citizens' access to and use of the Internet, 2. Enterprises' access to and use of ICTs, 3. Internet access costs, 4. eGovernment, 5. eLearning, 6. eHealth, 7.Buying and selling on-line, 8. eBusiness readiness, 9. Internet users' experiences and usage regarding ICT-security, 10. Broadband penetration [2]. There are 16 policy indicators and 25 supplementary indicators. For benchmarking eEurope 2002 there were 23 indicators. There was a World Summit of the Information Society (WSIS) thematic meeting on 'Measuring the Information Society' from February 7-9, 2005 in Geneva in which possibilities for an international unification of information society indicators were discussed. The final conclusions suggest 42 indicators in 3 areas: 1. Infrastructure and access, 2. Access and use of ICTs by households and individuals, 3. Access and use of ICTS by businesses [17].

Sustainability indicators such as the Ecological Footprint, the Pilot Environmental Sustainability Index, the Living Planet Index, the early OECD core set of environmental indicators, Eurostat Environmental Pressure Indicators, and Material Flow Analyses focus on the ecological dimension of sustainability. Many of these indicators are based on the OECD's Pressure-State-Response (PSR) model that assumes that human activities exert pressures on the environment that change the latter's state which results in responses of society in the form of policy measures.

The discourse on sustainability has shifted from an early ecological focus towards the inclusion of economic, political, cultural, and social issues. Hence there are not only ecological indicators, but also ones that try to cover the whole bandwidth of societal issues concerning sustainability. Such broad indicators of sustainability covering a wide range of topics and societal areas are e.g. the United Nations Commission of Sustainable Development's (UNCSD) set of indicators of sustainable development, Eurostat sustainability indicators, the World Development Indicators that are based on the Millennium Declaration, the sustainability indicators suggested by the Wuppertal Institute, the Genuine Progress Indicator, and the Barometer of Sustainability.

In 1996 the United Nations Commission on Sustainable Development (UNCSD) developed a list of 134 indicators of sustainability [12]. Later the UNCSD chose to classify indicators according to thematic areas. A working list of 134 indicators was selected and 22 countries volunteered to test their applicability. The goal for 2001 was the development of a standardized set of indicators available as a tool to measure progress towards sustainable development. As such a standardization the United Nations Division for Sustainable Development [13] suggests a total of 57 indicators in four key areas: social, economic, environmental, institutional. Based on the UN indicators Eurostat [4] developed 64 indicators of sustainability in the same four main areas as UNDSD..

There are both indicators for measuring the information society and sustainability. But there is a lack of attempts trying to measure the progress towards a sustainable information society. If we assume that important societal changes are taking place and affecting all realms of society that are due to the increasing importance of information, ICTs, networks, and globalization, it is not sufficing to measure the degree to which society is an information society, but one also should develop indicators that show to which degree we live in a sustainable information society that provides human well-being and ecological diversity. The task of a theory of the information society is on the one hand to discuss and advance essence, principles, and dynamics of the new societal formation, and on the other hand to identify aspects and indicators of sustainability that allows stakeholders to develop guidelines for advancing the sustainable character of the information society. The information society indicators that are currently used and discussed focus on quantifying the production, diffusion, and use of ICTs in society, but they frequently lack an explicit inclusion of sustainability issues. Approaches on measuring sustainability discuss broad societal issues, but they frequently lack taking adequately into account issues of information and ICTs. Some of them simply ignore such topics, others only include measurements of computer and Internet diffusion in society. The task at hand is to identify principles, tendencies, opportunities, risks, dimensions, and indicators of a sustainable information society, to assess and develop ideas of how to use information and ICTs in such a way that ecological, economic, social, and institutional sustainability can be advanced, and to work out indicators for measuring the degrees of sustainability of the various dimensions of the information society.

During the last decade there has been a shift from considering sustainability as a purely ecological concept to defining it in broader societal terms. Hence the discourse on ICT, knowledge, and sustainability shouldn't halt at ecological issues. I have argued that there are ecological, technological, economic, political, and cultural aspects of sustainability and that goals of sustainability are biological diversity, technological usability, economic wealth for all, political participation and justice for all, and cultural wisdom and unity in diversity management. Information and ICTs pose both new opportunities and risks in all of these subsystems of society, it is antagonistic and produces in parallel various tendencies that run counter to and contradict each other. Table 3 identifies opportunities and risks of the various dimensions of the information society. A sustainable information society is one that advances such opportunities and minimizes risks.

Depending on how ICTs are socially designed and applied they can have positive and/or negative effects on society. There are enabling and constraining tendencies of ICTs and information in society and ecology today, it is a political task to advance and realize opportunities and to avoid risks that are related to ICTs.

Table 3. Dimensions of the Sustainability of the Information Society

Dimension	Quality	ICT- and Information-related Opportunities and Risks
Ecological Sustainability	Biological Diversity	Ecologically sustainable vs. ecologically destructive ICTs
Technological Sustainability	Usability	User-oriented, user-friendly, enabling vs. Unusable, constraining ICTs
Economic Sustainability	Wealth for All	Free knowledge and ICTs vs. Knowledge and ICTs as commodity and private property
Political Sustainability	Participation of All	Participation vs. Control enabled by ICTs
Cultural Sustainability Sustainability of:	Wisdom	Wisdom vs. False Consciousness advanced by ICTs
Mass Media	Wise Knowledge and Media	Participatory, wise Online-Journalism vs. Manipulative, one-dimensional Online-Journalism
Science	Truth	Speed vs. Quality of E-Science
Art	Beauty and Imagination	Aura Gain and participatory art vs. Aura and authenticity loss of

		works of art in cyberspace
Education	Literacy and Good Skills	Co-operative vs. Individualized E-Learning
Ethics	Openness, Unity in Diversity of Values and Rights	Open VS. Fundamental values communicated in cyberspace and by cyberethics
Medicine	Health	Positive vs. Negative effects of ICTs on health
Sports	Fitness	Advancement/socialization vs. limitation/individualization of physical activity and games
Social Relationships	Love and Understanding	Cyberlove vs. Cyberhate

4 Conclusion

The modern mode of production that is based on the logic of accumulation has produced unsustainable patterns of development that continue to shape the information society. The emergence of the information society has put forward both new opportunities and risks for sustainable development. A theory of the information society should help analyzing and identifying risks, opportunities, and choices. For doing so a multidimensional concept of sustainability and the sustainable information society as well as concepts for indicators that measure the degree to which a sustainable information society has been achieved are necessary and foundations of such an approach and research-program have been suggested in this paper.

A sustainable information society is a society in which knowledge and the usage of new, computer-based, networked information and communication technologies (ICTs) advance a good life for all individuals belonging to current and future generations. This notion is multidimensional and suggests that ICTs and knowledge should help humans and society in achieving biological diversity (ecological sustainability), usability of technologies (technological sustainability), wealth for all, (economic sustainability), participation of all (political sustainability), and wisdom (cultural sustainability). In the cultural realm there are several sub goals of sustainability, wisdom contains wise media, truth, beauty and imagination, literacy and good skills, unity in diversity, health, fitness, love and understanding that should be supported by knowledge and ICTs.

References

1. V. Alakeson, T. Aldrich, J. Goodman, and B. Jorgensen, *Making the Net Work. Sustainable Development in a Digital Society* Forum for the Future, Teddington, 2003.

230   Christian Fuchs

2. Council of the European Union, *Legislative Acts and other Instruments: Council Resolution on the Implementation of the eEurope 2005 Action Plan*. Council of the European Union, Brussels, 2003.
3. D. Coyle, *The Weightless World. Strategies for Managing the Digital Economy*, Capstone, London, 1997.
4. Eurostat (2001) Measuring Progress Towards a More Sustainable Europe. Proposed Indicators for Sustainable Development. Luxembourg. Office for Official Publications of the European Communities.
5. A. Grote, Grüne Rechnung. Das Produkt Computer in der Ökobilanz, *CT*. 10(1996).
6. M. Kuhndt et al., *Project Theme Report: Virtual Dematerialisation. eBusiness and Factor X*. 2003. Online:
   http://www.digital-eu.org/uploadstore/theme_reports/dematerial_report.pdf
7. Piercarlo Marletta et al., *The Environmental Impact of ISTs. E-Living Project Report.* 2004.
   Online: http://www.eurescom.de/e-living/deliverables/e-liv-D14-Ch3-Environment.pdf
8. K. Marx, *Das Kapital. Band 3*. MEW Vol. 25, Dietz, Berlin, 1894.
9. K.O. Schallaböck et al., *Telework and Sustainable Development*. 2003. Online:
   http://www.forumforthefuture.org.uk/uploadstore/GeSI_case_study.pdf
10. I. Serageldin, *The Human Face of the Urban Environment*,. in: Proceedings of the Second Annual World Bank Conference on Environmentally Sustainable Development: The Human Face of the Urban Environment, edited by I. Serageldin, World Bank, Washington, D.C., 1995, pp. 16-20.
11. A. Touraine, *Return of the Actor*, University of Minnesota Press, Minneapolis, 1988.
12. United Nations Commission for Sustainable Development (UNCSD), *Indicators of Sustainable Development Framework and Methodologies,* United Nations, New York, 1996.
13. United Nations Division for Sustainable Development (UNDSD), *Indicators of Sustainable Development: Guidelines and Methodologies*, United Nations, New York, 2001.
14. World Commission on Environment and Development (WCED), *Our Common Future*, Oxford University Press, Oxford, 1987.
15. World Resource Institute (WRI), *The Weight of Nations. Material Outflows from Industrial Economies. Developing Environmental Indicators*, WRI, Washington, D.C., 2000.
16. World Summit on Sustainable Development, *The Jo'burg Memo. Fairness in a Fragile World*, Heinrich Böll Foundation, Berlin, 2000.
17. World Summit on the Information Society (WSIS), *WSIS Thematic Meeting on 'Measuring the Information Society'. Geneva, 7-9 February 2005*. Online:
   http://www.itu.int/wsis/docs2/thematic/unctad/final-conclusions.PDF

Information Society and ICT Policies

The Production of Service in the Digital City: A Social Informatics Inquiry

Elisabeth Davenport, Keith Horton
School of Computing, Napier University, Edinburgh, UK
e.davenport@napier.ac.uk; k.Horton@napier.ac.uk

Abstract. The authors discuss eGovernment as a computerization movement, and present a case study of a small project that was part of a modernising government initiative in a UK municipality. The case is analysed by means of an analytic construct, the technological action frame or TAF, that was developed by Iacono and Kling in 1998. This socio-technical approach provides distinctive insights at a number of different organizational levels.

Keywords: eGovernment, web of computing, computerization movement, technological action frame

1   Introduction

Though a human focus features strongly in the discourse of digital cities and e-government, we suggest that the notion is ambivalent. An extensive literature gives accounts of the technical infrastructure, and the design rationale for augmentation, but fails to explore in detail the work of maintaining and managing the multiple layers of infrastructure that must be installed to meet the challenges of public service delivery. This hidden articulation work is in the hands of municipal officers whose agency is opaque. In contrast, consumer agency ('empowerment') is highly visible in digital city discourse, and, thereby, the agency of producers of commodities and services that satisfy consumer desire. Empowerment is also addressed in the context of civic communities, where agency is presented in terms of participation and membership. In both these cases (consumer and community), a utopian version of agency prevails, emphasising augmentation and engagement, increased opportunity and choice, and strength through cohesion.

However, in the digital city, as in any technology implementation, the infrastructure that 'empowers' or 'augments' one group may disempower others, or empower them in ways that they have not sought, though these anomalies and discrepancies are smoothed over in official versions of development. In the text that

Please use the following format when citing this chapter:

Davenport, E., Horton, K., 2006, in IFIP International Federation for Information Processing, Volume 223, Social Informatics: An Information Society for All? In Remembrance of Rob Kling, eds. Berleur, J., Numinen, M. I., Impagliazzo, J., (Boston: Springer), pp. 233–242.

follows, we present the case of a group of municipal service workers whose work has been transformed in a series of digital city projects financed by national 'e-government' funding. We track the ambivalent agency of this group using a social informatics lens, computerization movements, that was developed in a series of studies by Kling and his colleagues (e.g. Kling & Iacono 1994; Iacono & Kling, 1998) for twenty years or so.

2   eGovernment as a Computerization Movement

Choices and decisions surrounding information technology acquisition and configuration are rarely straightforward, but in the UK public sector these can often involve the spending of hundreds of thousands, or millions of pounds over the course of a project. There is considerable scrutiny and reporting of such practice, often unfavourably. Increasingly, public services are faced with tasks involving information service integration, which in essence is concerned with addressing complex technology needs with particular configurations of technologies that reflect, and are reflected in the socially and historically situated nature of the proposed usage (Fleck, 1993). This is not acknowledged however in the rhetoric of integration that drives projects, and that is premised on the deterministic assertion that institutional activity can be 'modernised' through the introduction of ICTs (Cabinet Office, 1999).

A national agenda for e-government in the UK has emerged from two historical trends. The first is a privatization movement that has evolved over almost twenty years, starting with the publication of a UK government report in 1986 that paved the way for the privatisation of government data, and the establishment of an industry-government nexus that has continued to expand under both Conservative and New Labour administrations. In addition, an uncompromising deployment of e-commerce and business models and applications has produced a service ecology dedicated to improved efficiency and quality of service which can as easily support private as it does public administration. E-government in the UK thus promotes itself as process-oriented and customer-focused. The second trend is modernisation, a policy that also emerged in the 1980s and seeks to ensure that public services are 'joined up' and strategic, 'responsive to citizens', and 'high quality and efficient' (Cabinet Office, 1999).

Such utopian visions are characteristic of computerization movements (CMs), the powerful social informatics concept that is introduced above. The studies of technology in organizations that underpinned the evolution of the concept shared a common feature – a dissonance between the expected and the actual outcome of projects. This could be explained, suggested Kling and Iacono (1994), by the fact that the goals of many projects were ideological as much as technical, with systems seen as 'instruments to bring about a new social order'. CMs 'communicate key ideological beliefs about the favourable links between computerization and a preferred social order which helps legitimate relatively high levels of computing investment for many potential adopters. These ideologies also set adopters' expectations about what they should use computing for and how they should organize access to it' (Kling and Iacono, 1994, p. 3). In addition to articulating ideologies, CMs are a means of setting agendas. Kling and Iacono present a number of societal computing initiatives as examples of CMs – artificial intelligence, home computing and remote working.

As we note above, e-government projects in the UK are driven by two ideologies, privatisation and modernisation. These are tightly coupled through what are known as 'public private partnerships', whereby design and implementation are outsourced to commercial companies. Along with central government, they are key players in setting an agenda for modernising government. Design and implementation reinforce the ideology of efficiency by employing standardised proprietary protocols that pay scant attention to participative requirements analysis, and smooth the lumpy texture of organizational social life, leaving little or no room for the negotiation and adjustments that collaboration inevitably requires (Davenport, 2004). The elision of the local and the social is consolidated in norms for evaluation within project planning protocols, as these are rigorously constrained to address the validation of pre-scribed functions and features. Emergent and contingent localised behaviour is thus construed as problematic – the phenomenon of the 'problematization of the user', explored in depth by Lamb and Kling (2003)[1]. In addition, the current trend in e-government (and organisational computing generally) is to assemble components designed and validated elsewhere – these exogenous assemblages have emergent local effects that are not acknowledged in the utopian planning stages of project planning.

The original completion date for the construction of an integrated UK infrastructure (all services integrated by 2005) has not been fully achieved, and there have been repeated over-runs in terms of time and budgets. Yet, puzzlingly, contracts have continued to be awarded to a small group of providers, few of whom have been called publicly to account. We suggest that the puzzle can be explained with a detailed CM analysis, using one of Iacono and Kling's (1998) key concepts, the technological action frame.

3   Technological Action Frames

According to Iacono and Kling (1998), 'participants in computerization movements build up frames in their public discourses that indicate favourable links between internetworking and a new, preferred social order...changes in worklife are shaped (but not determined) by the prevalent discourses informing new technologies and the practices that emerge around them in actual workplaces' (p. 4). They describe this phenomenon as a technological action frame (TAF). This notion is an amalgam of two concepts. The first is the sociological concept of framing, presented by Goffman in 1974 and elaborated by analysts of social movements such as Snow and Benford (1992), who present 'collective action frames' (CAF) as a political instrument, a means of aligning support and resources, and consolidating power. CAFs specify what is in the frame and what is out of the frame – one set of meanings rather than another is conveyed, or one story rather than another is told; CAFs are thus is 'more agentic and contentious' (Snow, 2004) than everyday interpretive frames. The second feeder concept is the 'technological frame' (TF) developed in the socio-technical analyses of Bijker (1997) and Orlikowski and Gash (1994) to explain ways in which technology is perceived and appropriated in different contexts. Technological frames are an effective unit of analysis that supports explanation of the unintended consequences of organizational computing. The TAF, according to Iacono and Kling, combines the explanatory power of TFs and political power of CAFs and explains how groups achieve authority and legitimacy, and marginalise opponents. A strong TAF, or 'master frame' stabilizes a set of key meanings for a focal technology' (Iacono and Kling, 1998, p. 8).

As we note above, the provision of e-government services in the UK is dominated by a few very strong players who have links to the relevant networks in central government, local government, private sector vendors and consultants, and citizen groups. This elitism is manifest in the small and oligopolistic market that has developed for e-government service implementation, where repeated contracts are awarded to large corporate developers whose previous contracts have not been delivered either to budget, nor on time or to a performance standard that satisfies agreed criteria.[2] Members of the elite group share and maintain the master frame, a 'winning' discourse that draws its strength by association with proven players, who offer 'integrated off-the-shelf solutions' in the form of implementation plus training and economies of scale that undercut the costs of those involved in detailed local user requirement analysis.[3] In the case study that follows we explore 'mobile working', the most recent of a series of modernization initiatives in a small municipal service group.

4   The Rapid Response Team Case Study

The case that is reported here is not untypical of many ICT initiatives in UK municipalities where a local council seeks to embrace the modernising of its activities through the utilisation of, in this instance mobile, ICTs. The Council in this case (a Scottish municipality) aimed to have "30% of peripatetic staff ... mobile working by 2005" (Council, 2004). Whilst this broad aim was 'at the back of the mind'[4] of some senior staff with an interest in ICT utilisation, it was the unforeseen availability of £200,000 that prompted the decision to introduce mobile ICTs into several areas of work. (This is an example of the opportunism that sometimes consolidates collective framing). Negotiations with the council's outsourcing partner (one of the big consulting firms that constitute the elite in UK e-government contract work), with whom the council have a ten year partnership agreement for provision of ICT services, led to the identification of both technologies and services that could be introduced. Discussions within the council management team identified the areas work to which the new ICTs could best be applied.

One of the areas identified was a social services rapid response team. The Rapid Response Team (RRT) is a small unit of six people who normally operate in pairs, and are responsible for community care. They work with clients, often at short notice, to provide support services and equipment that will allow the client to remain living within the community (as opposed to moving into a hospital, or other form of institutional care facility. In spring 2004 we were invited to undertake a quick and dirty evaluation of a pilot project to assess the potential of mobile technologies in the RRT. Team members were issued with notebook and tablet PCs, and given access to a (limited) number of information services, and canvassed for their opinions. Our study ended at the beginning of 2005.

4.1. The Official Version

According to the vendors and the council policy-making team, the project was a success. After the six month pilot study, an evaluation was undertaken by the outsource partner, and published (internally only). In terms of CM analysis, this can be seen as the confirmation of a TAF (modernization, efficiency) by the dominant stakeholders in the project. The criteria in the evaluation were restricted (a typical manoeuvre in the discourse of justification in computerization movements), having been defined by the outsource partner, and evaluation focused solely on the Return on Investment. The outcome of this evaluation was the calculation of a time saving of 10.4%, and a net 'productivity saving' of £2280 per worker per annum. This evaluation document directly supported the ideology of modernization – it described a 'successful' pilot project, with a demonstrable financial benefit. The document was circulated within the council, and played an important part of the discussion of an extended roll-out of mobile technologies, and integration of information services across further groups within the council.

4.2. The View from the Ground

But the story from the frontline was different. In our 'unofficial' evaluation, members of the RRT raised a number of 'issues and concerns' (Kling & Scacchi, 1982). The first of these was technology. There were significant differences in the experiences with the technologies used (from three different suppliers). Frontline RRT workers liked the functionality on offer, though perceptions of reliability and battery life were a key factor in determining whether a technology was used in the field, as they would not take the chance of a technology failure impairing the interaction between themselves and their clients. The ability to utilise the mobile technologies with the client in-situ, was viewed as providing a speedier, and thus enhanced level of service (i.e. enabling more people to be independent in the community). The official evaluation did not pick this up: the criteria used by RRT members (client and human-centred) were outside the frame of cost efficiency. But though mobile technology was accepted in principle, there were problems with integrating information services. The issue here was the importance of access to both key information (e.g. client file, stores), as well as to communication services (e.g. email, fax) for mobile working to be feasible. In addition, it was not possible to utilise electronic versions of the forms that RRT members had to complete and share with other agencies, noting that it was "a shame that no-one had ever thought about using the forms electronically or delivering them electronically when they were designed ... which seems crazy".

Contrary to comments made in the official evaluation of the pilot project (Evaluation Paper, issue 1.0, p.51), there was a perception in the RRT that the technology was "a solution thrown over the wall". This was reinforced by perceived lack of consultation about process, as well as about technology requirements. Lack of training in the early stages meant that technology functions were not maximised. This reflected a general disquiet about the consultation that had taken place, with Team members commenting for example, "They did it back to front ... it would have been nice if they'd asked us what we needed, but instead they imposed it on us".

Frontline workers were frustrated by the lack of attention to a complex of work practices that is characteristic of RRT work, or what may be described as the 'production lattice' (Kling & Scacchi, 1982) of service delivery. Though the mobile technology enabled some *remote* working (i.e. undertaking a task from a 'remote' location) ultimately, the RRT's activities remained unaffected by the introduction of the mobile technology. While access to the mobile technologies meant that RRT members felt able to meet up with their own team, and other team members while out of the office (e.g. a client's home to complete an ABC form), this did not affect significantly the time they spent in/away from the office. RRT members spend only 50% of their time on Rapid Response duties: the other 50% of their duties ('picking up cases' within the office) was not affected by the project.

Historically, the social work team has worked from a local council office, where cases are picked up and discussed, where expert judgment is exercised, and where much of the coordination of services from different agencies is arranged. Work in the office is interspersed with home visits, where initial assessment can be discussed with colleagues back at the office before a plan of action is agreed. Traditionally, one might say, a response by the RRT is 'configured' in the office after a more or less lengthy series of moves and deliberations. The response team are qualified professionals, and office meetings are also occasions for exchanging and updating knowledge, alerting colleagues to new developments, and discussing client circumstances 'off the record'. The mobile initiative will diminish information exchange in the team, as it is intended to shift this part of the process to the client's home, where an individual client and one, or two individual team members can configure what is required on the spot, in a process of in situ consultation and coordination. The configuration that is agreed will be entered on the relevant form, and activates a series of data transactions – the configuration is compiled, the relevant resources are coordinated and a response is composed that indicates what will arrive when. While this may 'augment' service for an individual client, as they may be given material support sooner by means of the digital service than in the traditional service, we suggest that understanding of service across the community may be diminished.

5   Discussion

We suggest that an important question that is rarely asked in the context of modernisation and visions of virtual services in e-government is 'where and when and by whom does a response get made'. Such issues of material realisation underlie the effective exploration of agency. Those who commission and design virtual services (for example, senior service managers) will respond: 'by means of an integrated transaction process that is mostly handled within an IS'. This fits well with the TAF that drives prevailing policy in the municipality, a response, as we imply above, to a mandatory UK 'modernising government' initiative, which has introduced the dehumanized concept of the 'managed citizen' into council thinking. The management of citizens is achieved by means of process modelling that combines representation of services and representation of individual profiles. There is little room in this componential model to apply the collaborative knowledge of grounded professionals (the output of sometimes messy and contested negotiations and consultations in the RRT office), as it is premised on the satisfaction of an abstract profile of consumer 'needs' The TAF or master frame takes little account of the micro-geography of expert social care work, as the 'workers' are modelled as ancillaries, whose location when they input, retrieve or report is of little interest.

If the question is asked of the frontline social care workers, the response comes from a different frame, one that is based on humanistic notions of interaction, solidarity and shared practice. From this perspective, the response emerges over time (one might compare the 'process' and 'human' versions of rapid response with 'fast' and 'slow' food), and happens in multiple locations where people interact, in the 'interspaces' (Crabtree, 2000) between technologies. It is supported by a number of activities and events, more or less computerised (some data is entered into databases, some is held in notebooks and folders of case notes) and more or less mediated (by e-mail, telephone). The communal office is the primary site for picking up cases, and checking on their progress, and eliciting help from colleagues when cases get out of hand. Places in the sense of 'articulated moments in networks of social relations and understandings' (Massey, 1993) are thus important in the work of the RRT, as the 'response' is a socio-technical interaction, not merely a computerised transaction. This frame was not, at the time of our inquiry, politicized, and thus conferred little power on those adhering to it.

However, the 'process imperative' that characterises modernising government initiatives across the UK is closely coupled with visions of the elision of space: it is quite literally 'utopian'. The mobilisation project is not exempt, as the city council intends to make savings on real estate by closing some local social services offices. Some RRT members may become migrant or nomadic workers who must find space where they can, and operate as dispatchers rather than flexible specialists; they will occupy the 'non-spaces' (Auge, 1995) that characterized the late twentieth century; malls, cafes, car parks, where memory has no purchase and transience is the prevailing experience (This vision may be compared with that of Iacono and Kling in a discussion of the 'death of distance' TAF, 1998, p. 14). If this scenario is realized, it may be that RRT members will mobilize support from their professional bodies and their trade unions and from a competing action frame.

6   Conclusion

Our starting point in this paper was the unequal and shifting nature of power in the digital service arena. We have briefly presented the positions of two of the agents involved in an e-government pilot study (senior managers and social care workers in the form of the rapid response team and the council information services directorate). To explain the happenings in the case that we present above, a CM framework using TAF analysis provided insights at different levels of organization[5].Firstly, TAF helped us clarify the dynamics of implementation in a way that a less ambitious TF analysis would not have achieved. If the case is seen as a specific example of a computerization movement (e-government), where a master TAF is at work then some puzzling features can be explained. These include the lack of local requirements analysis and the arbitrary provision of functionality in the pilot project for 'mobile working'.

Secondly, by focusing on what is outside the TAF, a researcher or manager can find out where and why resistance happens in the form of tweaking and work-arounds. Such apparent inefficiencies may contribute to effective service, and can be grounds for negotiation and development. Thirdly, a CM/TAF approach embeds the case in a historical trajectory of government computing initiatives over a period of 20 years, that in aggregate, constitute the master frame of' modernising government'/'e-government'. At this macro-level, CMs are an arena for contests about societal values and knowledge, where, for example, cost accounting competes with professional expert judgment as a measure of good service. In the case presented here, the marginalisation of local practitioner knowledge and practice is an instance of a societal phenomenon - an analogous conflict between cost accounting, ICT investment and expert knowledge is currently visible in the UK's health service. In the case presented here, such a macro-level epistemological contest may be a significant issue in any extended roll-out of mobile technologies.

Full 'mobilization' of the rapid response team will implicate a larger group of players; the council social services IT department; the social services directorate; the council leaders; the national health service (including: hospital trust managers; hospital trust IT departments; general practitioners); the outsource partner; the government (through policy initiatives); the providers of prostheses and other material aids to the housebound. We may therefore, tentatively, begin to ask whether more penetrating questions should be asked by those commissioning (and those investigating) service projects in digital cities – not 'How can we integrate service provision and save money and time?' but, 'Where and when does service happen? In whose interest? Who benefits, and how? Who loses, and how?' We suggest that a TAF analysis is an appropriate way to answer such questions.

Acknowledgments

We wish to acknowledge the help of anonymous interviewees in our fieldwork, and feedback from participants in a workshop on Digital Cities at the Communities and Technology meeting in Milan in June 2005 where an early version of this paper was presented.

References

Auge, M. (1995) Non-Places: Introduction to Anthropology of Supermodernity, Verso, London
Bijker, W (1997) Of bicycles, bakelites and bulbs: toward a theory of socio-technical change. Cambridge MA: MIT Press.
Cabinet Office (1999) Modernising Government. London: HMSO
City Council (2004). Internal document

Crabtree, A. (2000) Remarks on the social organization of space and place. Journal of Mundane behaviour, at www.mundanebehavior.org/issues/v1n1/crabtree.htm (Last consulted 31 March 2006)

Davenport, E. (2004). Project management and the elision of the social. In K. Horton & E.Davenport (Eds), Understanding socio-technical action. Abstracts of a Workshop in School of Computing, Napier University, June 2003. Edinburgh: Napier University

Evaluation document. Council, 2004.

Fleck J (1993) Configurations: crystallizing contingency. International Journal of Human Factors in Manufacturing. 3, 1, 15-36.

Goffman, E. (1974). Frame analysis: an essay on the organization of experience. New York: Harper and Row.

Horton, K., Davenport, E. and Wood-Harper, T. (2005) Exploring socio-technical interaction with Rob Kling: five big ideas. Information, technology and people, 18(1), 52-67.

Iacono, S. and Kling, R. (1998) Computerization movements: the rise of the Internet and distant forms of work.. At http://rkcsi.indiana.edu/archive/kling/pubs/ Kling_comp.htm (Last consulted 27 March 2006)

Kling, R. & Iacono, S. (1994). Computerization movements and the mobilization of support for computerization. Retrieved 12 February 2005 from http://www.slis.indian.edu/faculty/kling/pubs/MOBIL94C.htm (Last consulted 23 March 2006)

Kling, R. & Scacchi, W. (1982). The web of computing: computer technology as social organization. Advances in Computers, 21, 1–90.

Lamb, R. & Kling, R. (2003). Reconceptualizing Users as Social Actors in Information Systems Research. MIS Quarterly, 27(2), 197-235.

Massey, D B (1993) Power-geometry and a progressive sense of place. In Bird, J. et al. (eds.) Mapping the futures: local cultures, global change London: Routledge, 59 – 69.

Massey, D B (1993) Power-geometry and a progressive sense of place. In Bird, J. et al. (eds.) Mapping the futures: local cultures, global change London: Routledge, 59 – 69.

Orlikowski, W.J. & Gash D.C. (1994). Technological frames: making sense of information technology in organizations. ACM Transactions on Information Systems, 12 (2), 174-207.

Snow, D. (2004). Framing processes, ideology and discursive fields. In D. Snow, S. Soule & D. Kriesi (Eds.), Blackwell companion to social movements (pp. 380-412). Oxford: Blackwell.

Snow, D. & Benford, R. (1988) Ideology, frame resonance and participant mobilization. International Social Movement Research, 1, 197–217.

UK Cabinet Office. (1999). Modernising government. (Command paper) London: the Stationery Office. http://www.official-documents.co.uk/document/cm43/4310.htm (Last consulted 25 February 2005)

---

[1] These issues observations have also been explored by SST and CSCW analysts; see contributions to Luff, Hindmarsh &Heath, 1997).

[2] Under European Union procurement rules, past performance cannot be considered when awarding public sector contracts.

[3] User requirements analysis is an atavistic presence, however, in most of the approved methodologies for e-government systems development and design (it is, for example, a

staple component of project management protocols in UK public sector (PRINCE2) and EC 5th and 6th Framework projects).

[4] Interview with an informant.

[5] Such multilevel rich explanation was a feature of Kling's work throughout his working life. The basis format for this 'web of computing' approach is provided in Kling & Scacchi, 1982. And see Horton et al., 2005.

The Social Informatics of the Internet:
An Ecology of Games

William H. Dutton[1]
Oxford Internet Institute, University of Oxford, U.K.
Director@oii.ox.ac.uk

Abstract. Key insights revealed by social informatics studies have come from the new light they have shone on the social dynamics underlying broad changes tied to technological innovations. In particular, they have shown how major developments in computing and other information and communication technologies (ICTs), such as the Internet, are often the outcome of complementary or conflicting social movements, and their intersections. This paper focuses on an important supportive and complementary framework that helps to further understanding of these social dynamics: the concept of an 'ecology of games'. The focus of this approach is on examining the unfolding interaction of various actors pursuing a diverse array of goals and objectives in a variety of interrelated arenas where everyday and strategic decisions are taken about whether to use – or not use – various ICTs.

Keywords: Social shaping of technology, social informatics, computerization movements, ecology of games, Internet, information and communication technologies, Internet governance.

1 Introduction

A key contribution of social informatics to enhancing understanding of the social dynamics that translate a landmark technical innovation into a breakthrough in real-world contexts has been the way it has connected technical innovation to social change by showing that computerization movements, such as personal computing, should be understood as social movements [1]. As Kling and Iacono [2] commented, computerization movements "communicate key ideological beliefs about the favourable links between computerization and a preferred social order ...".

This conception provides an important advance over a narrow technological focus on innovation because it demonstrates how the nature of technologies and the outcomes of their use are 'socially shaped' by, and inseparable from, the economic,

Please use the following format when citing this chapter:

Dutton, W. H., 2006, in IFIP International Federation for Information Processing, Volume 223, Social Informatics: An Information Society for All? In Remembrance of Rob Kling, eds. Berleur, J., Numinen, M. I., Impagliazzo, J., (Boston: Springer), pp. 243–253.

social, institutional and policy contexts in which the technologies are designed, developed, and used (see also [3]). Multidisciplinary social informatics researchers have placed the users of computers and related ICTs and the social contexts of their use at the centre of their enquiries and analysis. This has helped to illuminate, for example, how the Internet and its applications, such as the Web log 'blogging revolution', are more than only a technical innovation – they are social phenomena that have emerged and grown because of their relevance to people's lives.

An earlier example of a computerization movement was the way personal computers (PCs) were initially developed in the late 1970s by 'home brewing' do-it-yourself technical entrepreneurs. Initial attempts by managers and professionals to introduce PCs into the workplace were actively discouraged as being institutionally counter-productive until, fuelled by experiences with home-based PCs that seemed more beneficial than corporate systems, there was a groundswell of grassroots demand for PCs within organizations. On the other hand, top-down initiatives to promote a breakthrough, such as frequent government and industry attempts to encourage use of the videophone, have been rejected by users who couldn't see their relevance to their lives [4].

Such insights also help to explain how technologies enable people to reshape fundamentally how they do things, for instance in using the Internet to reconfigure how they gain access to other people and to information, services, and technologies [4]. They also demonstrate that major developments like the Internet are not the outcome of a single social movement, but are tied to several intersecting social, technical, regulatory, political, and other movements and counter-movements

This paper argues that it would be useful to embed these different conceptions of social movements, technical invention and public policy within a larger framework of action represented by the concept of an the 'ecology of games'. Within this, computerization developments can be understood as the outcome of the unfolding interaction of various actors pursuing a diverse array of goals and objectives. This approach is proposed as a useful integrative framework within which to analyze the co-evolution of economic, cultural, organizational, legal, and other intertwined dimensions of social transformations associated with technological change.

2   The Ecology of Games

2.1   Defining the Concept

The ecology of games framework explored in this paper depicts a wide system of social, institutional, and technological action and interaction composed of two or more separate but interdependent 'games' [4]. Here, a game is defined as an arena of competition and cooperation, with each game structured by a set of rules and assumptions about the strategies used by players to achieve a particular set of objectives. The rules, strategies, and players in different games offering a 'grammar' for describing the system of action shaping technological change in the overall ecology. All games share several key attributes.

First, each game has a set of goals, purposes or objectives (e.g. a bureaucrat within a regulation game might seek to avoid conflict), with some games having multiple objectives (e.g. a telecommunication regulator in a European Union member state seeking to enhance industrial competitiveness in that country while promoting the harmonization of open networking standards across the EU). In addition, a game has a set of prizes (e.g. a higher salary or larger office for a bureaucrat who achieves the goal of resolving conflict).

Games also have rules that govern the strategies or moves open to players (e.g. in a regulation game governed in part by administrative law, there could be guidelines on the need to make rules public and fair, although in some games played for private and other interests the rules may not need to be public or fair). Rules may change over time, and there may not even be consensus on a definition of the rules [5]. Finally, a game has a set of players. These are defined by the fact that they interact in competition or cooperation with one another in pursuing a game's objectives (e.g. a regulatory game incorporates bureaucrats, legislators, and regulated firms and industries, as well as the possible involvement of the public, courts, and other actors).

In such an ecology, individual games can be interrelated in several ways. Some players might simultaneously participate in different games, and some might transfer from one game to another. Moves or actions made in one game can affect the play of others. Also, the outcome of one game might affect the rules or play of another. Players might be able to anticipate a range of strategies open to individuals, organizations or other actors if they know what roles those actors play in the game(s) most central to them. Conversely, when the actions of players appear irrational, it is likely that the observer does not know the rules and contexts of the games in which players are most centrally involved (e.g. that the players' moves in one game might be constrained by their moves within other games). This can help to reveal the dynamics of technical, social, and policy choices shaping the development of technological innovations and outcomes tied to their use.

In the approach discussed in this paper, it is important to note that the terms 'game' and 'ecology of games' are not employed in a formal game theoretic sense, as has been used for example in formal game theory (e.g. [6])The 'grammar' of the games employed here is less precise and rigid, used as sensitizing concepts, but nonetheless of equivalent value in simplifying and revealing the complexity of the underlying dynamics of the interplay between interrelated and continuously co-evolving social, institutional, and policy arenas.

2.2   Background and Benefits for ICT-related Policy and Practice

The framework of an ecology of games as developed here first emerged in a field far from innovation in ICTs. In the 1950s, Norton Long [7] used the idea to provide a new perspective on the pluralist versus elitist debate over who governs local communities. Previously, most such theorists viewed policy making as an isolated game in which all players seek to shape policy within the rules defined by the political and economic system. Long claimed that local events are generally governed neither in rational-comprehensive ways nor by a pluralistic set of elites or a more networked economic elite. Instead of primarily being concerned with governing the community, as both pluralist and elite theorists assumed, major players were as much – or more – focused on such matters as being elected to the city council, developing land, creating a general plan or finding a decent home. To understand the behaviour of these players, it was therefore useful to think of them as candidates for the council, land developers, planners, and house hunters, rather than people only or even primarily seeking to govern their community.

The development of communities could then be understood as the consequence of an unfolding history of events driven by often unplanned and unanticipated interactions among individuals playing relatively independent games, in which they most often make decisions as the occupant of a particular role within a specific game, rather than as individuals making decisions about the larger community. Thus, the evolution of local communities might be viewed as the outcome of a history of separate but interdependent games that give 'a sense of purpose and a role' and offer 'a set of strategies and tactics' [7: 252]. Long [7] identified local communities as the 'territory' of a game, but in the approach discussed here the arena in which games are played could also be a household, a locale, a firm, non-governmental organization (NGO), government department, region, nation or global body.

Since Long published these ideas, although elitist and pluralist debates have been sustained they have also been overtaken by new perspectives on power and public policy. Nevertheless, the ecology of games continues to offer a viable alternative to prevailing theoretical perspectives, for example by providing a heuristically rich and useful framework for understanding the dynamics of decision-making in technology and public policy in a wide range of areas [4, 8, 9].

Within this framework, structural, and institutional factors can be linked to the behaviour of actors by the manner in which they help to define the goals or rules of particular games. For instance, the separation of powers distinguishes the rules of some games shaping communication policy in the US from those in parliamentary democracies like the UK [4]. It is in such ways that the ecology of games can help to bridge levels of analysis in social and policy sciences.

3   Games Shaping the Internet

The value of the ecology of games approach can be illustrated through the Internet phenomenon, which encompasses some of the most important ICT-oriented social movements of recent times. This perspective reveals that a complex innovation like the Internet's 'network of networks' is best viewed as the outcome of actions and interactions in an ecology in which specific actors seek to achieve their own goals within one or more separate but interrelated games. The search for a single source of invention or governance of the phenomenon can then be seen to be a misdirected exercise.

The ecology of games view helps to explain how direction of technological change is shaped by the unfolding consequences of strategic choices about matters more directly significant to the actors than those related to specific technical choices. For example, although much has been written about the invention of the Internet in terms of the relative contributions of different innovations, groups, organizations, and technical advances (e.g. [10-11]), it actually emerged through the interaction of different advances across different sectors, made by a variety of individuals, groups, and organizations with different aims and objectives. Significant social movements, such as the Internet Society (ISOC)[2], developed around the team within the US Department of Defense's Advanced Research Project Agency (ARPA) that developed the ARPANET network in the 1960s, initially as an experiment to link together only a few small computers but which laid the foundations that still underpin the Internet's infrastructure that now interconnects vast numbers of computers around the world.

Social movements have also formed around other Internet-related innovations. For instance, the Web in its current form emerged from a set of networking projects at the European Laboratory for Particle Physics (CERN) in Switzerland, with Tim Berners-Lee [12] as a key driving force. However, its design and cultural ethos was strongly influenced by an earlier hypertext design concepts inspired by Ted Nelson's visionary work on the Xanadu project [13], which in turn drew on Douglas Engelbart's 'oN-Line System' (NLS) at Stanford Research Institute that aimed to make computers a more useful tool to help people think and work. The rise of computerization movements around open source software [14-15] and a 'creative commons'[3] of more flexible copyright licences have also been facilitated by the Internet and Web. The origins and development of these movements were distinct from efforts to invent the Internet, but have become interwoven with the evolving culture of Internet producers and users. The Internet and Web continue to be shaped by contributions from a vast number of users embedded within a variety of games.

This illustrates how the growth of the Internet from an experimental network within an ecology of defence, public policy, and technical innovation games to become today's worldwide phenomenon did not happen just because a few people turned bright ideas into practical systems. It resulted from a huge number of players in intertwined academic, commercial, technical, industrial, and other games making decisions about how specific aspects of the Internet should be designed, developed, used, or governed. Each decision met goals and made sense within different arenas, and the interaction between choices in each game combined to create the 21st Century phenomenon represented by the Internet and related ICTs. The developments in broadband and Internet governance discussed in the next two subsections further illustrate the value of an analysis of Internet-related activities based on the ecology of games concept.

3.1   Games Relating to Broadband Internet Infrastructures and Services

Delivering to Internet users the advantages of having 'always on' high speed broadband access to multimedia content whenever and wherever they want has been a key goal in overlapping sets of telecommunications, media, regulatory, and policy 'broadband Internet games' (see Table 1). In the economic development game in this table, governments, and other agencies around the world have typically seen broadband as a means of reaching key economic and industrial competitiveness goals [16], with overall economic growth a main prize. In developing countries, NGOs, and local activists often play a strong role in a variation on this game, where the rules take account of lower levels of existing telecommunications infrastructure, skills, and financial resources. Activists in local communities throughout the world have also been influential in their own communitarian broadband games, for example in the promotion of free or low cost access to a creative commons. At the same time, commercial and professional players in the content provision game seek to maximize their profits in competition with each other and with other content providers, such as bloggers, offering free or low price alternative channels. Telecommunication regulation and broadband supplier games are also crucial influences on the other broadband Internet games in Table 1.

Table 1. Illustrative Broadband Internet Games

Game	Main players	Goals and objectives
Economic development	Governments, public agencies, investors.	Players build broadband infrastructures to attract business, investment, and jobs to localities, nations, and regions.
Developing country	Governments, NGOs, local activists, investors, local Internet content and service providers.	Players seek to close social and economic divides in developing countries using widely available broadband infrastructures.
Communitarian	Neighbourhoods, community groups, Internet enthusiasts.	Individuals and groups seek free or low-cost open access to broadband Internet, including competing with commercial players.
Telecommunication Regulation	Telecommunications firms, regulators, investors, consumers.	Regulators umpire moves of competing firms, taking account of conflicting and complementary goals of players.
Broadband suppliers	Traditional telephone companies using Direct Subscriber Line (DSL) digital adaptation of existing lines, cable TV firms, wireless, and other vendors	Suppliers compete for shares in a market, where DSL and cable vendors have often been the main broadband players winning lines into homes and offices.
Content provision	Media giants v. Internet entrepreneurs; media novices and non-profit content producers v. professionals.	Established and emerging producers of Internet content compete to reach audiences.

Source: Dutton et al. [16: 54, Table 4].

Broadband Internet could change the rules of some media games, for instance through outcomes from the continuing attempts to build new forms of integrated multimedia operations by exploiting technical digital convergence, such as voice and video services delivered over the Internet. Cultural and policy contexts also matter to outcomes of these kinds of games. For instance, in some countries the provision of a multimedia package that mixes television, telephony, and broadband Internet services involve a number of regulatory games within and between different institutions responsible for different media; in others, just one regulator covers many old and new media, such as the UK Office of Communication (Ofcom) formed in 2003 to cover telecommunication, broadcasting and print industries. Certain governments have a strong general anti-monopoly agenda backed by legislation, even though the digital convergence of different media makes it harder to define the precise boundaries of ICT and media marketplaces within which one player can be said to be over-dominant. Other countries see these industries as being either part of an economic game that is best left to market forces or, conversely, wish to place them under state control. In addition, goals set for regulators vary according to the particular political and economic policies being pursued.

Important social movements and initiatives that have developed around broadband Internet included the WiFi (Wireless Fidelity) grassroots nourishment of local wireless-based computer networks [9] and the peer-to-peer (P2P) file sharing used in key music distribution services. Broadband Internet can also open up new roles for those who have been communicatively empowered by broadband access, as when media consumers become media producers by setting up Websites offering their own blogs, online news media, and discussion forums.

3.2   Internet Governance Games

The ecology of games viewpoint can assist the reassessment and rethinking of appropriate Internet governance institutions and mechanisms to take account of the network's rapid global expansion and significance. Despite the development of an increasingly well informed debate on this issue, discussion on Internet governance often seems to stumble over the notion that 'someone' or 'some body' can govern it [17]. However, the Internet community, policy makers, and the public at large are divided about who, if anyone, should be involved in such regulation. This is illustrated in an Oxford Internet Survey (OxIS) conducted in 2005 by the Oxford Internet Institute (OII), which found that Internet users in Britain are not predominantly pro- or anti-government regulation of the Internet – they are divided. Most (45%) survey respondents did not know or were undecided while roughly equal numbers were pro- and anti-regulation by governments [18].

To some involved in Internet development, provision and use, the word 'governance' conjures up the unwelcome notion of governments moving into a thriving arena that has been fostered by seemingly ungoverned entrepreneurial and technical ingenuity. This raises the spectre of killing the vitality of the Internet through governmental, administrative, political, industrial, and legal barriers to technical innovation. On the other hand, there are those who contend that there has always been some form of Internet governance, although this has been highly informal and non-governmental, and that more national and international public oversight and regulation is essential because of the Internet's growing significance in most sectors of society worldwide.

Difficulties in resolving such conflicting views, interests, and goals is reflected in the final report of the United Nation's Working Group on Internet Governance (WGIG), which recommended 'the creation of a new space [a 'Forum'] for dialogue for all stakeholders on an equal footing on all Internet governance-related issues' [19]. It offered a number of options for consideration, rather than a specific recommended route to global governance of the Internet, and concluded [19: 12]: "The organizational form for the governance function will be multilateral, transparent, and democratic, with the full involvement of Governments, the private sector, civil society, and international organizations."

This indicates that the governance of the Internet is most appropriately viewed not as something capable of being in the control of any one set of actors but as the outcome of an ecology of games, as illustrated by the Internet governance games summarized in Table 2. For instance, the management and operation of the Internet is greatly affected by the system of allocating and managing names and numbers used within the Internet's infrastructure, such as Web domain names and e-mail addresses. Key players in this game included the non-profit Internet Corporation for Assigned Names and Numbers (ICANN), commercial Internet service providers (ISPs), registries, and users. Substantial commercial, personal, and national interests and convenience are at stake in these games, so great store is placed by most actors on establishing rules that create a fair playing field, without an over-dominance by particular vested interests.

Table 2. A Few Selected Games and Players Shaping Internet Governance

Game	Main players	Goals and objectives
Names and numbers	Individual experts, ICANN, Registries, ISPs, users.	Obtain, sell, and allocate domain names, addresses, etc. to identify sites, users, etc.
Standards	Standards-setting bodies, World Wide Web Consortium (W3C), Internet Engineering Task Force (IETF).	Efforts to establish and propagate standards for the Internet.
Jurisdictional 'turf struggles'	ICANN, International Telecommunication Union (ITU), UN, national governments.	National actors participate in Internet governance bodies to gain or retain national control over policy (e.g. by filtering Internet traffic or gaining access to encrypted data for security reasons).
Political speech, freedom of expression	Media rights advocates, activists, politicians, news media, governments, writers, artists, censors.	Individuals and organizations aim to facilitate or constrain flows of information, political views, and creative works.

Interactions between a growing number of players in the kinds of games shown in Table 2 are making it harder to reach technical agreements, which is increasing the difficulty of implementing core technical changes to Internet protocols and infrastructure [20]. For instance, until the late 1990s such changes could be determined largely by a relatively small group of public-spirited and mutually-trusting experts in a relatively simple ecology of Internet-related games. The escalation since then in the number of players with an interest in the Internet is shown by more recent meetings of about 2000 members of the IETF, the international community of network specialists concerned with the evolution and smooth operation of the Internet. An even greater challenge is getting a technical decision adopted on the millions of computers linked to the Net once a decision is taken because there are a growing range of technical barriers to core innovations, such as firewalls, and decisions in each specialist arena of expertise overlap and intermesh in highly complex and often conflictual ways with decisions by actors in other key arenas, for example in challenging users' investment in older technologies and skills that might need to be replaced.

The ecology of games perspective therefore shows that not only is there unlikely to be a central source of Internet governance, but that very few people or organizations are actually seeking to govern the Internet as such. Instead, most actors try to win more focused prizes, for instance developing a market for registering names and numbers, keeping a bank's computer system secure from hackers, avoiding spam e-mails, and so on. Governance of the Internet can then be understood as the outcome of a variety of choices made by many different players involved in many separate but interdependent policy games or areas of activity. By decomposing or unpacking this complex ecology, policy makers and activists can better focus on the objectives, rules, and strategies of specific games that drive particular players, while also recognizing that each game is being played within a much larger system of action in which the play and outcomes of any one game can reshape the outcomes of other games.

4   Conclusion: Understanding How the Future Unfolds

The notion of an ecology of games outlined in this paper places the computerization movements concept within a larger system of action in order to offer a framework for thinking about the highly complex entwining of social, technical, organizational, governance, and other forces that shape the emergence of changes tied to the increasingly ubiquitous use of the Internet and related ICTs. At the same time, it embeds many ideas from the computerization movement concept and reinforces the value of its central illumination of the ways in which the motivations and actions of people and organizations in particular social contexts shape the ultimate design and impacts of the technology and related policies in real-world settings.

The ecology of games also recognizes the significance of many technical inventions and new ideas that may fail to kindle social movements. Its emphasis on the potential for unanticipated, unplanned developments raises doubts about perspectives on technological change, such as the 'single inventor' thesis, that posit a more governed, isolated, and predictable system of action. This helps to explain why accurate prediction is likely to elude those involved in technology and policy studies who seek to attain this goal. It also challenges some traditional tenets of structural and institutional explanations of social and political orders.

However, this framework strongly supports the thrust of the kind of institutional perspective developed by March and Olsen [21: 9), who argue that the long-run development of political institutions 'is less a product of intentions, plans, and consistent decisions than incremental adaptation to changing problems with available solutions within gradually evolving structures of meaning' (see also [22-24]). Policy-makers and many technologists might like to deal with more predictable outcomes, but the real world is far more 'messy' than indicated in narratives telling stories of the inevitable, unfolding paths towards a future carved out by heroic inventors and their technologic swords. In reality, those swords are two edged, for example with the same Internet delivery mechanisms carrying software viruses, spam, and paedophile contacts as well as the communication, educational, news, and entertainment channels that enhance people's lives. Actual outcomes are also determined by a multitude of people making small and large strategic decisions every day about whether or not to use the Internet or other ICTs.

Major upheavals in industry sectors, the opening of significant new patterns of domestic and working life and shake-ups in major policy sectors, such as Internet governance, are often created by using technological developments that few, if any, have predicted well in advance. The examples related to the Internet given in this paper illustrate the value of the ecology of games framework in analysing the ways inventions, new ideas, and myriad choices by consumers and users contribute to such transformations.

References

1. R. Kling, Computing as an Occasion for Social Control, *Journal of Social Issues*, **49**(1), 77-96 (1984).
2. R. Kling and S. Iacono, Computerization Movements and the Mobilization of Support for Computerization, in L. Starr, (ed.), *Ecologies of Knowledge*, SUNY Press, New York, 1994, pp. 119-153.
3. D. MacKenzie and J. Wajcman (eds.), *The Social Shaping of Technology*, Open University Press, Milton Keynes, 1999.
4. W. H. Dutton, *Society on the Line: Information Politics in the Digital Age*, Oxford University Press, Oxford, 1999.
5. M. Crozier and E. Friedland, *Actors and Systems*, University of Chicago Press, 1980, Chicago.
6. Luce, R. D., & Raiffa, H. *Games and Decisions: Introduction and Critical Survey*, New York: John Wiley, 1957.
7. N. E. Long, The Local Community as an Ecology of Games, *American Journal of Sociology*, **64** (November), 251-261 (1958).
8. T. Vedel and W. H. Dutton, New Media Politics: Shaping Cable Television Policy in France, *Media, Culture and Society*, **12**, 491-552 (1990).
9. W. H. Dutton, *Social Transformation in an Information Society: Rethinking Access to You and the World*, UNESCO Publications for the World Summit on the Information Society, Paris, 2004.
10. M. Castells, *The Internet Galaxy: Reflections on the Internet, Business, and Society*, Oxford University Press, Oxford, 2001.
11. B. M. Leiner, V. G. Cerf, D. D. Clark, R. E. Kahn, L. Kleinrock, D. C. Lynch, J. Postel, L. G. Roberts, and S. Wolff, 'A Brief History of the Internet', 2005; http://www.isoc.org/Internet/history/brief.shtml [accessed 28 February 2006].

12. T. Berners-Lee, *Weaving the Web: The Origins and Future of the World Wide Web*, Orion Books, London, 1999.
13. T. Nelson, *Literary Machines*, Mindful, Swarthmore, PA, 1987.
14. S. Weber, *The Success of Open Source*, Harvard University Press, Cambridge, MA, 2004.
15. M. S. Elliot and W. Scacchi, Mobilization of Software Developers: The Free Software Movement, *Information, Technology and People*, forthcoming; open source draft available at http://opensource.mit.edu/papers/elliottscacchi2.pdf [accessed 28 February 2006].
16. W. H. Dutton, S. E. Gillett, L. W. McKnight, and M. Peltu, *Broadband Internet: The Power to Reconfigure Access. OII Forum Discussion Paper No. 1*, Oxford Internet Institute, University of Oxford, Oxford, 2003; http://www.oii.ox.ac.uk/resources/publications/FD1.pdf [accessed 12 February 2006].
17. W. H. Dutton and M. Peltu, *The Emerging Internet Governance Mosaic: Connecting the Pieces, OII Forum Discussion Paper No. 5*, Oxford Internet Institute, Oxford, 2005; http://www.oii.ox.ac.uk/resources/publications/FD5.pdf [accessed 28 February 2006].
18. W. H. Dutton, C. di Gennaro, and A. M. Hargrave, *The Internet in Britain: The Oxford Internet Study (OxIS), May 2005*, Oxford Internet Institute, Oxford, 2005; http://www.oii.ox.ac.uk/research/oxis/oxis2005_report.pdf [accessed 28 February 2006].
19. WGIG, *Report of the Working Group on Internet Governance*, United Nations, Geneva, 2005; http://www.wgig.org [accessed 28 February 2006].
20. W. H. Dutton, Can the Internet Survive? Why Your Decisions Matter, *Nominet.uk News*, 2004; http://www.nominetnews.org.uk/dec04/debate.php [accessed 28 February 2006].
21. J. G. March and J. P. Olson, *Rediscovering Institutions*, The Free Press, New York, 1989.
22. M. D. Cohen, J. G. March, and J. P. Olson, A Garbage Can Model of Organizational Choice, *Administrative Science Quarterly*, 17, 1-25 (1972).
23. J. G. March and J. P. Olson, The New Institutionalism, *American Political Science Review*, 78(3), 734-749 (1984).
24. R. Lane, Concrete Theory: An Emerging Political Method, *American Political Science Review*, 84(3), 927-940 (1990).

Notes

[1] My thanks to several anonymous reviewers for their helpful comments on an earlier draft, and to Malcolm Peltu for his assistance in editing the final manuscript.

[2] A major international association of people championing the Internet, with more than 20,000 members in over 180 countries (see http://www.isoc.org [accessed 21 January 2006]).

[3] See http://creativecommons.org [accessed 21 January 2006].

Enhancing Human Choice
by Information Technologies

Tanja Urbancic, Olga Stepankova, and Nada Lavrac
Nova Gorica Polytehnic, Slovenia; tanja.urbancic@p-ng.si
Jozef Stefan Institute, Ljubljana, Slovenia; nada.lavrac@ijs.si
Czech Technical University, Prague, Czech Republic;
step@labe.felk.cvut.cz

Abstract The paper discusses what the research community in the field of information technologies can do to improve quality of life by offering more alternatives both to individuals and to the society. Moreover, attention is given to the present IT tools which can be used to support decision making and choice among possible alternatives in complex settings. The role of ITs in achieving this goal is explained and illustrated by examples in different fields, including environmental decision-making and health care. Enhanced possibilities of choice in collaborative settings supported by new media and computer networks are also shown. Besides the role of ITs that support this enhancement, the importance of non-technological aspects is presented with special emphasis on responsibility and network intelligence.

Keywords: human choice, human-computer interface, data mining, collaborative decision-making, networked organizations.

1   Introduction

The responsibility of science and technology towards the society has increasing importance, since accumulated consequences of short-sighted decisions and actions of the human race in the past make it more and more difficult to bring things into balance [McKibben, 2004]. An important step was done by [Bruntland, 1987] that introduced the notion of sustainable development and put it as a central question of our time. In 1999, ICSU/UNESCO World conference on Science, Budapest stated explicitly that science should be for knowledge, peace, development and society. Also declarations of IT professional communities are in accordance with this see for example the ACM Ethical Code from 1993. This code requires from ACM members,

---

Please use the following format when citing this chapter:

Urbancic, T., Stepankova, O., Lavrac, N., 2006, in IFIP International Federation for Information Processing, Volume 223, Social Informatics: An Information Society for All? In Remembrance of Rob Kling, eds. Berleur, J., Numinen, M. I., Impagliazzo, J., (Boston: Springer), pp. 255–264.

among other, also to improve public understanding of computing and its consequences, and to design and build information systems which enhance the quality of working life [Kling, 1994]. Recent development proved that ITs are able to offer lot of support to each of us as an individual (a citizen or a professional) as well as to society as a whole. Due to Internet we are able to remain in contact with our family and friends at the far ends of the Earth as well as to find lot of up-to-date information, provided the following conditions hold: we have access to Internet, we are aware of the necessary technology, we can and we know how to use it. Internet represents a novel phenomenon, which can significantly change our life and improve functioning of our society, provided these three conditions are ensured. An obvious first step towards this goal is to guarantee geographical coverage by Internet. But this is not enough since there are many additional obstacles due to which IT is not directly available to everyone. Official resources confirm that only in Europe there is more that half million of people who cannot make use of mouse as a standard PC user interface due to their physical handicap. Number of challenged persons who need some sort of support in order to get access to Internet is even much higher since they represent at least 5% of present population. Of course, it is important to support development of better technical means fine-tuned to the needs of their users. But even that is not enough, since there are many additional economic and social reasons which hinder entrance of modern IT into various segments of society (e.g. in elderly population). and that is why the decision-makers stress the need to wipe off 'digital divide'.

We have to be aware of many more ways how present technology can impact or improve conditions of many individuals. In the second half of the 20th century there have appeared numerous technical devices (pacemakers, hearing aids, artificial kidney, etc.), which can significantly change quality of life of people whose health status cannot be described as average. Often, these solutions help to overcome difficulties and challenges which have been up to now considered as impassable: in laboratories of universities there are tested new devices which make up for various deficiencies, e.g. limited ability to move, to see, to hear or to remember. Unfortunately, most of these handy solutions are too expensive or too demanding (e.g. requiring invasive treatment of the patient or setting too much constraints on his/her behaviour) to become an available and attractive alternative for everyone who could benefit from it. That is why it is important to proceed one step further and insist on the need to design *affordable solutions* for the considered problems. We believe this can be achieved in many cases by combining means offered by new technical tools, information and communication technologies (ICT) and artificial intelligence.

In the global world, it is important to help humans in making wise choices, based on the best information and knowledge available. More knowledge means better choice, and good choice means one that is more in alignment with the long-term goals of human society.

In this respect, besides providing access to enormous amount of information at the World Wide Web any time from any place, information technologies are ready to help us in improving conditions of many individuals and of society as such
-    by enhancing human potential of challenged persons through *affordable solutions* which let them overcome their handicap and ensure additional

alternatives including those one could otherwise not be aware of, or one would not be able to explore,

- by *helping to extract more knowledge from available data* about the situation and to design various alternatives, giving foundation for better decision-making,
- by *supporting decision-making process* in complex situations,
- by enabling *cooperative settings*.

In the following sections, we discuss each of these possibilities in more detail. They are illustrated and commented through examples originating in personal experience of the authors and their co-workers from the research laboratories at the Department of Knowledge Technologies at the Jozef Stefan Institute, Ljubljana, at the Nova Gorica Polytechnic, and at the Department of Cybernetics of the Faculty of Electrical Engineering at the Czech Technical University, Prague.

2   Offering New alternatives: Man-Computer Interaction for Handicapped People

It is no doubt that there are many health problems we are not able to treat. Other problems can be improved by application of most sophisticated technology – this is the case of deficiencies related to some cognitive functions. After years of research cochlear implant is produced in massive scale now, it became an affordable tool and there are thousands of its users who enjoy its positive impact on their life [Chorost, 2005].

But sometimes the present technology is ready to be applied in much simpler way provided the scientists are able to identify the need and recognize the opportunity. Let us describe one of the affordable solutions, which was designed and developed at the Department of Cybernetics in Prague. It is the device I4Control⁾ [Fejtova and Fejt, 2005], a new computer periphery awarded the IST Prize 2006 (for details see *http://cyber.felk.cvut.cz/i4c/en_system.html*). I4Control⁾ emulates the computer mouse – its distinguishing feature is the way it is controlled: while actuators of computer mouse are fingers this periphery reacts to the movements of eyes of its user. This feature makes it most useful to everyone who cannot use a keyboard or a traditional PC mouse to control a computer. This might be the case of people who lost their hands in an accident or patients with cerebral palsy who cannot move at all. For the last type of patients communication based on eye movements remains the only option. The user of I4Control⁾ gets direct access to everything, what can be controlled by the PC mouse. Namely, this is the case of a software keyboard, which is nowadays a common part of an operating system. Consequently the I4Control⁾ user is ready to type using the software keyboard and he/she can write the text documents, send the e-mails, brows the web pages, etc. There are even cases when this device becomes a unique mediator between the paralyzed person and its environment (e.g. when the person cannot speak).

The main advantage of the I4Control⁾ solution is that it represents a technological solution, which is safe and available to everyone – it meets the demands of democratic AI. It can be produced in mass and nearly everybody can learn to use it. The device proved to be very well accepted by handicapped persons (e.g. a boy who lost both hands as a result of an accident or a boy with myopathy) who have learned to use it quickly [Fejtova et al., 2005]. An important feature is that the used I4Control⁾ hardware is based on easily available and financially not demanding off-the-shelf components which are assembled into a simple, mobile, efficient and fault tolerant product with good resolution which can be easily installed at home of its user. The resulting computer periphery is not the first device ensuring gaze-based man-computer interaction. Certainly, it is the first one, which offers following significant advantages to its users:

- it does not pose on them any unnatural constraints: the user does not have to remain fixed in a single position (so that it does not interfere with his/her usual habits),
- the device is as easy to operate as glasses (it is absolutely non-invasive – there is no need to glue special marks etc.),
- it has affordable price and it is simple to install, moreover, the user needs no demanding instruction. The resulting periphery enables physically handicapped users to communicate with their environment or even work or study on their own.

3   Getting More Knowledge from Data: Examples in Health Care

Effective medical prevention and good access to health care resources are among the most important issues that contribute to the citizens' welfare and quality of life. As such, these issues have an important place in strategic plans at the level of regions, countries and even broader. In The European Health Report from 2002, WHO gives guidelines for assessment of national health systems, stating explicitly their objectives: good health of population, good availability and accessibility of health care services for patients and fair distribution of financial burdens of health care services.

Data collected in enormous quantities by medical institutions and governmental institutions responsible for public health care can serve as a valuable source of evidence that should be taken into account when deciding about priorities to be included into strategic plans, or when deciding about specific measures to solve a particular problem.

Data mining methods [Fayyad et al., 1996] [Han and Kamber, 2001] have big potential to support abovementioned activities and have already proved to be useful in many applications.

An example that offers a direct connection to the enhancement of choice is described in [Gamberger et al., 2003]. The authors use data mining for coronary heart disease (CHD) risk group detection. CHD is one of the world's most frequent causes of mortality and an important problem in medical practice. We know a lot about CHD risk factors and one concept of CHD prevention is general education of the whole population about them, especially about those related to life-style factors. Interestingly, the practical influence of this concept is estimated as small because people are not ready to accept the suggestions seriously before the occurrence of first actual signs of disease. (So we should not simplify and believe that problems are solved if people have information and possibility of choice.) Therefore, it is very important to apply the second concept, namely risk factor screening in general practice by data collection performed in three different stages: anamnestic information, laboratory tests and ECG at rest tests. The problem appears mostly in cases with slightly abnormal values and in cases of combinations of different risk factors. Gamberger, Lavrac and Krsti_ used data collected at the Institute for Cardiovascular Prevention and Rehabilitation in Zagreb, Croatia, as a basis for detecting patients at risk. They used the interactive Data Mining Server (DMS) available on-line for public use at *http://dms.irb.hr* and discovered several relatively simple rules that can either help in deciding whether a particular person needs further medical testing, or to efficiently organize systematic prevention testing to subpopulations in which proportionally many CHD patients can be expected. In this case, the results of data mining can directly support professional decision-making of medical doctors. The rules are simple enough also to be publicly announced together with a call to people who recognize themselves as being at risk to come for further tests, but of course, this should be done with precaution. Also, we should not expect that people will suddenly change their behavior and follow the recommendations, but this should not prevent anybody from giving them information and possibility to choose how they will react.

Another example of obtaining useful information from data in the field of public health care is presented in [Lavrac et al., 2005]. In this case, data mining and statistical techniques were used to analyze data collected by Celje regional Public Health Institute, in order to address the problem of relatively big differences in directing patients from primary health centres to specialists. The results of data mining were used for a more elaborate study using decision support techniques [Mallach, 2000]. The objective was to detect local communities that are underserved concerning general practice health care. The resulting representation was well accepted by the experts, as it clearly shows the distribution of the availability of health care resources for patients from different communities. The study later continued by the analysis of causes for different availability and accessibility of services, and has been recently completed for two additional regions within a project for the Slovenian Ministry of Health, in which also secondary level of health care (specialists and hospitals) was analyzed in a similar way. The analysis provides information needed for planning the health care providers network in accordance with the strategic goals of equal availability and accessibility of services for everybody.

4   Supporting Collaborative Decision-Making: An Example in Environmental Planning

There is no general consensus about how and to which extent public opinion should be taken into account in environmental decision-making. There are arguments that people don't have enough knowledge to predict the consequences of certain decisions, so their involvement would bring noise and bias into the decision-making process. On the other hand, environmental decisions may deal with questions that even experts cannot answer with certainty. What is certain is that laymen in each specific case will carry the burden of potential environmental damage, and this is why they should be involved in the decision-making process in spite of the issue of different and very often opposing interests and value systems. It is becoming clear that the assurance of a fair distribution of benefits and costs among different social groups is not just scientific, but also a social issue [Bedau, 1991].

The problem remains how to assure that a collaborative decision-making process in such a heterogeneous group of experts, local authorities and public would still lead to an operational result. In [Kontic et al., 2006] it was shown that a method of multi-attribute decision modelling used in DEX [Bohanec and Rajkovic, 1990] offers a good foundation for a collaborative decision-making process in such cases, providing that the process is led by a skilled and knowledgeable moderator. DEX is a decision support system that has proved to be useful in many real life applications [Bohanec and Rajkovic, 1999].

The method was tested in a collaborative decision-making setting [Kontic et al., 2006] at a workshop simulating a situation of selecting a site for a low and intermediate level radioactive waste repository in Slovenia. The participants were first equipped with basic knowledge and understanding of the method, and then exposed to problem-solving in groups that simulated realistic situation in which different backgrounds and interests had to be taken into account. The results show that due to the well defined procedures that guided the decision-making process, the participants were able to end up with surprisingly complex and fully reasonable decision models. This opens new perspectives in the practice of decision-making and offers new views on the dilemmas about public involvement in the evaluation of alternatives and decision-making in delicate and complex environmental domains.

5   Enabling Cooperative Settings: A SolEuNet Example and Lessons Learned

New media and computer networks enable business, medicine, science etc. to be done in a collaborative setting with no geographical boarders, resulting in eBusiness, eMedicine, eScience. Networked organizations are becoming increasingly important. Their activities are facilitated by the use of shared infrastructure and standards, decreasing risk and costs. A specific form of networked organizations in a virtual enterprise [Camarinha-Matos and Afsarmanesh, 2003] in which a group of organizations or individuals join voluntarily to share their knowledge and resources in order to better respond to a particular business opportunity through collaborative work, supported by information and communication technologies. Having such a possibility greatly increases possibilities of choice since one can choose their co-workers across organizational and geographical boarders, having in mind in the first place their competences to accomplish a task. Group work support systems provide technical infrastructure, so in principle, could we now work successfully with anybody in the world?

Things again are not so simple. Kling and Lamb [2000] draw attention to the fact that interorganizational computer networks are also social networks in which relationships are complex, dynamic, negotiated and interdependent. They claim that needed organizational changes when 'going digital' are often neglected and refer to them as to 'hidden costs of computing'. We experienced this in a virtual enterprise SolEuNet (*http://soleunet.ijs.si*) in which 12 academic and business partners from 7 European countries joined their forces with the aim of offering their data mining and decision support expertise to the European market. Collaborative work of geographically dispersed teams had very well established Internet support and infrastructure [Jorge et al, 2003], the participants were professional experts and really devoted to the project. However, since engineering side of the project did not have a suitable counterpart at the organizational side, the organizational model evolved through different stages mainly on the basis of lessons learned during the project, including 'discovery' of the danger of information asymmetries, the importance of the IPR issues and the key role of building trust among the partners of the network [Lavrac and Urbancic, 2003]. The main direction of these changes was towards more flexibility, as in the final model, every partner of the network was given the opportunity to be the net broker in particular projects. This resulted in enhanced choice for project partners and consequently in less tensions between them.

The need of additional efforts in knowledge management [Smith and Farquhar, 2000] had to be fulfilled since in such a model, information and knowledge needed for a role of a net broker had to be organized, stored and maintained in a way that made it accessible to all partners [Jermol et al., 2004]. One of the lessons learned was that trust modelling and management should be a part of knowledge management when establishing and managing a virtual enterprise. Social network analysis as an established research field aimed at modelling social network phenomena [Wasserman and Faust, 1998] can well be used as a basis for trust modelling.

Finally, partners had to face a psychological challenge of shifting from the culture of the enterprise and the motivation of the individual towards the network culture in which sharing knowledge does not mean losing, but gaining. The concept of network intelligence as a capability of going beyond the fixed individual identity by dialogue, mutuality and trust [Palmer, 1998] is an unavoidable counterpart to technological preconditions of networked organizations. Building this kind of intelligence is a long-lasting, but very important process that should be strongly encouraged in the society, starting with education system, which, unfortunately, still strongly favourites individual competition over cooperation.

6   Conclusion

Enhancing human choice by technical means is important, but not sufficient for increased quality of life in the society. A decision will be in long term a good one if the process of decision-making enables cooperation of groups with different interests and is done with the responsibility towards those that can not speak for themselves but will be affected by the results of decisions (like future generations, people underprivileged due to their health or social status, etc.). Advances in science and technology should go hand in hand with human rights, moral issues, tolerance and responsibility.

Those that want more 'down-to-earth' reasons should bear in mind that science is mostly paid by the money that comes from taxpayers. If not for other reasons, this is why scientific community should act with a responsibility towards their needs. There is a problem due to the fact that consequences of discoveries can show up later and the history has shown that the same scientific result can be used for good or for bad. This cannot be prevented by science itself, because it will always be pushed also by pure curiosity and a wish to broaden the limits of current knowledge. What can be done by researchers with a sensitivity for social needs is to think about possible consequences of their work and to show possible benefits for the society whenever possible. Also, they should report about their work and results to a wider community, not only to their professional colleagues, explaining them in an understandable way and showing the ways the developed methods and research results can serve the goals of society. Researchers usually don't like this kind of activities, because they are time consuming and at the first glance, they don't add to their professional credit. However, things are changing. European commission requires serious justifications about expected benefits for society already at the point of project proposal submission. Also, besides technical results of a project, dissemination of results is getting increasing importance and recognition. European community as well as other bodies financing research can do a lot also when setting the priorities in their calls for proposals since in the end, the majority of research stream will go where the money will be.

To achieve the upper mentioned goals many issues will have to be considered and resolved. Designing affordable solutions represents not only a challenge to technology but it sets even new questions to the way our society operates. Let us mention the problem related to intellectual properties (IP) protection. To protect IP rights is rather expensive. How the designer of a handy affordable solution should proceed when he or she wants to make sure that the product can be produced as cheaply as possible? Is it necessary to worry about the IP rights protection at all? If one decides that he/she can do without, there is a danger that someone else can claim the IP rights and then become a monopolistic provider of a device, which will be delivered to the market for unreasonably high prise. Where to get money for appropriate protection of such products? Fortunately, in the case of software using the Open Source technology can prevent this problem. But there is no reasonable solution for HW products. Surprisingly, there are no funds to ensure IP protection for products created under support of different research grants.

So, how to achieve 'People in the first place' and 'for everybody' in the information society?
-    By making information and knowledge widely accessible.
-    By special care for challenged groups: adding them to be as independent as possible, to learn and live in accordance with their best abilities.
-    By all people, especially those having knowledge and power, becoming 'network intelligent', i.e. understanding that sharing means gaining, not losing. Recognizing that everything is connected in a modern world, and that everybody

has a responsibility towards other people, especially towards those that cannot speak for themselves.

- By giving credit to researchers communicating with the public. This helps in developing a sense of interconnection and responsibility.

As researchers in the IT field, we have the opportunity to focus our work towards achievements that increase quality of life in the society by offering more choice to everybody. Will we take it? And what about the society? Will it be able to create such an environment where science and technology can quickly offer all its results to the benefit of those who need it? It is not ICT itself who can offer adequate solutions for these problems. The topic calls for serious interdisciplinary dialog involving representatives of technology and humanities.

Acknowledgements

When writing the paper, the authors have been partially supported by the bilateral SI-CZ grants 08-2004-05 *Knowledge management in medicine and health care* and *21/2006-2007 Knowledge technologies in medicine and health care.*

References

1. H.A. Bedau, Ethical Aspects of Environmental Decision-Making, in: *Environmental Decision-Making: A Multidisciplinary Perspective*, edited by H.A. Bedau, Van Nostrand Reinhold, New York, 1991, pp. 176-179.
2. M. Bohanec and V. Rajkovic, DEX: An Expert-System Shell for Decision Support, *Sistemica*, 1(1), 145-157 (1990).
3. M. Bohanec and V. Rajkovic, Multi-Attribute Decision Modelling: Industrial Applications of DEX, *Informatica* 23, 487-491 (1999)
4. G. Bruntland, editor, *Our common future: The World Commission on Environment and Development*, Oxford University Press, 1987.
5. L.M. Camarinha-Matos and H. Afsarmanesh, Elements of a base VE infrastructure, *Journal of Computers in Industry*, 51(2), 139-163 (2003).
6. M. Chorost, M. (2005) *Rebuilt: How becoming part computer made me more human*, Houghton Mifflin Company, 2005.
7. U. Fayyad, G. Piatetski-Shapiro, P. Smith and R. Uthurusamy, editors, *Advances in Knowledge Discovery and Data Mining*, MIT Press, Cambridge, MA, 1996.
8. M. Fejtova and J. Fejt, (2005): System I4CONTROL®: The Eye as a New Computer Periphery, in: The 3rd European Medical and Biological Engineering Conference EMBEC'05 [CD-ROM], Prague, 2005, vol. 11, pp. 1727-1983.
9. M. Fejtova, J. Fejt and O. Stepankova, Towards society of wisdom, in: Interdisciplinary Aspects of Human-Machine Co-existence and Co-operation, edited by V. Marik, P. Jacovkis, O. Stepankova and J. Klema, Czech Technical University Prague, 2005, pp. 253-261.

10. D. Gamberger, G. Krstacic and N. Lavrac, Active subgroup mining: A case study in coronary heart disease risk group detection, *Artificial Intelligence in Medicine*, **28**, 27-57 (2003).

11. J. Han and M. Kamber, *Data Mining: Concepts and Techniques*, Morgan Kaufmann, San Francisco, 2001.

12. ICSU/UNESCO World conference on Science, Budapest (1999) Science agenda – framework for action, (November 15, 2005).
    http://www.unesco.org/science/wcs/eng/framework.htm

13. M. Jermol, N. Lavrac and T. Urbancic, Managing business intelligence in a virtual enterprise: a case study and knowledge management lessons learned, *Journal of intelligent and fuzzy systems*, vol. 14, pp. 121-136 (2004).

14. A. Jorge, D. Bojadziev, M.A. Alves, O. Stepankova, D. Mladenic, J. Palous, P. Flach and J. Petrak, Internet support to collaboration: A knowledge management and organizational memory view, in: *Data mining and decision support: integration and collaboration*, edited by D. Mladenic, N. Lavrac, M. Bohanec and S. Moyle, The Kluwer international series in engineering and computer science, SECS 745, Kluwer Academic Publishers, Boston, Dordrecht, London, 2003, pp. 247-259.

15. R. Kling, Fair information practices with computer supported cooperative work, *Computer-Mediated Communication Magazine*, 1(2), p. 5 (1994).

16. R. Kling and R. Lamb, IT and organizational change in digital economies: A socio-technical approach, in: *Understanding the Digital Economy – Data, Tools and Research*, edited by B. Kahin and E. Brynjolfsson, The MIT Press, 2000.

17. B. Kontic, M. Bohanec and T. Urbancic, An experiment in participative environmental decision making, *The Environmentalist*, **26**, 5-15 (2006).

18. N. Lavrac, M. Bohanec, A. Pur, B. Cestnik, M. Jermol, T. Urbancic, M. Debeljak, B. Kavsek, T. Kopac, Resource modelling and analysis of regional public health care data by means of knowledge technologies, in: *Proceedings of the 10th Conference on Artificial Intelligence in Medicine*, AIME 2005, Aberdeen, UK, July 23-27, 2005, edited by S. Miksch, J. Hunter and E. Keravnou, Springer, Berlin, Heidelberg, New York, 2005, pp. 414-418.

19. N. Lavrac and T. Urbancic, Mind the gap: Academia-business partnership models and e-collaboration lessons learned, in: *Data mining and decision support: integration and collaboration*, edited by D. Mladeni_, N. Lavrac, M. Bohanec and S. Moyle, The Kluwer international series in engineering and computer science, SECS 745, Kluwer Academic Publishers, Boston, Dordrecht, London, 2003, pp. 261-269.

20. E.G. Mallach, *Decision Support and Data Warehouse Systems*, McGraw-Hill, 2000.

21. B. McKibben, *Enough: Staying Human in an Engineered Age*, Owl Books, 2004.

22. J. Palmer, The Human Organization, *Journal of Knowledge Management*, 1(4) Number 4, 294-307 (1998).

23. R.G. Smith and A. Farquhar, The Road Ahead for Knowledge Management: An AI Perspective. *AI Magazine*, **21**(4), 17-40 (2000).

24. The European Health Report, Health Systems Performance Assessment Methods, Annex 1 (November 15, 2005); http://www.euro.who.int/document/e76907.pdf

25. S. Wasserman and K. Faust, *Social Network Analysis. Methods and applications*, Cambridge University Press, 1998.

User's Knights in Shining Armour?

Katarina Lindblad-Gidlund
Department of Information Technology and Media
Mid Sweden University, Sweden; katarina.lindblad-gidlund@miun.se

Abstract. The aim of this article is to address the relation between a user-centred objective and social constructionism and the possibility to refine user-centred fundamentals by enhancing the awareness of the relation between humans and the constructed environment. Through social constructionism we could enter a bit deeper into questions like; (1) reality's subjective character especially concerning technology development, (2) the importance of a power analysis while creating technological artefacts, (3) the importance of analysing our own role in technology's construction and (3) we are made aware of the importance of how technology is communicated to others. The article is in a way an extension of an argument put forward by Jacob Nielsen about usability as empiricism and/or ideology.

Keywords: user-centered objectives, theoretical standing points, social constructionism, user advocacy.

1 Introduction

In June 2005, the usability profile Jakob Nielsen (2005) wrote in his alert box the following. "There's a duality to usability. On the one hand, it's a quality assurance methodology that tells you what works and what doesn't work in the field of user experience. On the other hand, usability is a belief system that aims to ensure human mastery of the constructed environment."

Nielsen then explains this further by an interesting distinction between usability as empiricism and usability as ideology. Where usability as empiricism roughly could be described as "conclusions and recommendations [that] are grounded in what is empirically observed in the real world" and that these should "determine what works and what doesn't". Usability as ideology on the other hand could be described as a belief in a certain specialized types of human rights:

- The right of people to be superior to technology. If there is a conflict between technology and people, then technology must change.

Please use the following format when citing this chapter:

Lindblad-Gidlund, K., 2006, in IFIP International Federation for Information Processing, Volume 223, Social Informatics: An Information Society for All? In Remembrance of Rob Kling, eds. Berleur, J., Numinen, M. I., Impagliazzo, J., (Boston: Springer), pp. 265–278.

- The right of empowerment. Users should understand what is happening and be capable of controlling the outcome.
- The right to simplicity. Users should get their way with computers without excessive hassle.
- The right of people to have their time respected. Awkward user interfaces waste valuable time.

And "if designers and project managers do not believe in the usability ideology, why would they implement usability's empirical findings? After all, if you don't want to make things easy, knowing how to make them easy is irrelevant." (Ibid.)

This article will draw heavily on Nielsen's declaration but the text is not to be understood as a critique of the usability field (as practitioners only with no ideological base), neither is it its aim to present a study of the field which shows how many pure empiricists or pure ideologists there are. The aim of the article is rather to go further with Nielsen's thought about the close relationship between usability as knowledge about what works and what does not and usability as ideology i.e. a belief system to ensure human mastery of the constructed environment. It will do so by trying and confronting Nielsen's arguments with one of the most widespread theoretical bases to analyse human mastery of the constructed environment, social constructionism. The article's underlying hypothesis is that our basic outlook affects the information systems we create. In the same way as teachers constantly confronted their basic views on human beings and the fundamentals of pedagogy, developers, and producers of information systems should be made aware of their view on the relation between humans and the constructed reality since it influences many choices we make during the developing process.

However, the headline, *User's knights in shining armour?*, could definitely be interpreted as provocative since the question mark implies that it might not always be the case that the first priority is to defend the user(s) when using and implementing user-centred methods and models. However, the reason for starting with such a question is rather to point out that there might exist differences in degrees of motivation and that it could be rewarding to declare openly one's starting point and priorities at least to oneself. And again, to bounce one's understanding against social constructionism is in this article proposed to be constructive to get in touch with these starting points and find out whether my decisions in the design process stems from the understanding that there exists a human mastery of the constructed environment or not.

2   Usability and Other User-Centred Objectives

One side of tackling user-centred objectives is to try to deal with the inequalities of the distribution of the positive and negative parts of the technological development. Who enjoys the positive sides/or suffers the negative sides of technological development? Closely connected to these questions is critical analysis since a core issue in critical analysis is to identify and question inequalities (hidden agendas) and create tools for the emancipation of the oppressed. The critical societal analysis leans on key terms such as values, equality, care, democracy, and efficiency (that already appear in the texts by Horkheimer & Adorno (1981), Adorno (1987), and Marcuse (1941) i.e. the leading theorists of the Frankfurt school). This is however not at all an unexplored area in IS research, particularly not in Scandinavia where several attempts have been made to democratise the information technological development (see for example Bansler 1989 about the critical tradition in Scandinavian research in systems development). What they call the 'Scandinavian approach' (see for example Bødker, Knudsen, Kyng, Ehn & Madsen 1988, or Bjerknes & Bratteteig 1987) is very much concerned with methods to support democratisation (participatory/cooperative design) in the workplace. By inviting the users-to-be to different steps of the system developing process, they strive for a better quality of work i.e. working life democracy.

The Scandinavian approach or 'participatory design' (PD) has however recently been discussed (Beck 2002, Kanstrup 2003, Dittrich 2003, Bødker 2003) as possibly outdated, though not in Scandinavia. Beck argues that it still has potential in the area of analysing the political (and ethical) dimensions and identifying dominance patterns. This approach partly rests on the work of Bjerknes & Bratteteig who in 1995 addressed the topic when arguing the re-introduction of the political dimension1. However, Kanstrup argues that the political is not missing in contemporary PD; it is rather inherent and constantly present even if it is not articulated (Kanstrup 2003: 81). According to Beck "understanding the multiple ties that link computer (in its variety of senses) with dominance (in its variety of senses) would be one of two pillars of a rejuvenated PD" (Beck 2002:85) and ends with the statement that "the project of PD is needed more than ever" (ibid. 2002:89). However, Bødker responds by stating that "in order for the questioning to have a constructive impact on people's life with technology it is important that we do not only challenge, but offer alternatives as well" (Bødker 2003:89). Furthermore, by doing so one returns to the techniques (design methods) to create real alternatives for the users to choose from and not only creating ideological standpoints.

Bødker's comment on this matter relates to what might be described/labelled as user-centred design *methodologies*. 'User-centred' is here used as a label of the more practical field of creating design methods which explicitly put the user in the centre of their activities. It includes user-centred design (UCD) (as in Vredenburg, Isensee & Righi 2001) but it is not totally defined by it. In this context, user-centred design methodologies could be found in participatory design as well as in human-computer-interaction (HCI).

At the NordiCHI -04 conference, however, Kanstrup together with Iversen and Petersen (Iversen, Petersen & Kanstrup 2004) addressed the same question from a slightly different perspective by stating that the original Utopian ideals of co-operative design are now facing new challenges since today technology is spread into domestic and non-professional practices (ibid 2004:171). Kanstrup et al. argue that today we need "to develop a better understanding of what 'use quality' means in everyday life" (ibid. 2004:174). "Quality of work is now replaced by a concern with quality in life, and democracy is replaced by concerns with consumer power..." (Ibid. 2004:177). The key principles that should be highlighted according to Kanstrup et al. are *democracy, emancipation* and *quality*.

What is touched upon here are questions also addressed by Rob Kling (starting in 1977) in what is nowadays defined as *social informatics* i.e. "the interdisciplinary study of the design, uses and consequences of ICT's that takes into account their interaction with institutional and cultural contexts" (Kling, Crawford, Rosenbaum, Sawyer and Weisband 1998). Social informatics comprises normative, analytical, and critical orientations combined in a specific context/study (it is as such characterised by its problems rather than by the theories or methods used in a research study). By doing so, social informatics combines critical analysis and social constructionistic ideas2.

As mentioned above, there are several theories, methodologies and instruments in IS such as access theories, digital divide, diffusion, user-centred design, participatory design, and usability that aim at protecting the user's/human's interests. In different forms, they all emphasise the importance of bringing the user/human into the design process, making technology use-worthy and/or see the equal distribution of information technology. From different perspectives, they narrow themselves the user and her/his perceptions and experiences of information technology. Some are more theoretical, and others are more practical oriented, but all are contributors to the field of creating more user-centred information systems.

So far so good, but, according to Nielsen, the problem occurs when there develops a conflict of interest in hands on situations, when high ideals clash with prerequisites in practice. We sometimes place users' needs against organisational requests such as financial realities and time-schedules (or maybe even against designers' ideals of what is beautiful or attractive designs). In these situations, we start to negotiate with one's beliefs, which could be acceptable as long as one is aware of the negotiating process and its consequences and takes responsibility for one's choices, decisions, and actions.

It is when this negotiating process is repressed or, as sometimes, totally absent, (since other needs than the users' are predominant) it is reasonable to put the question forward; that is, are we really the *users' knights in shining armour?* If we are, what does it mean? In what way do we defend and protect the users? Or maybe, the answer is that we should create environments where there are no need to defend or protect the users since they are able to do that themselves? Moreover, underpinning it all, when faced with a situation with conflicts of interests, do or choices, decisions, and actions rest on a belief system of human mastery of the constructed environment that could support democratic decisions?

3   Human Mastery of the Constructed Environment

In 1966, the sociologists Peter Berger and Thomas Luckmann (1967) wrote "The Social Construction of Reality, A Treatise in the Sociology of Knowledge" where they formulated a theoretical structure to the understanding of how the reality we live in is constructed, reconstructed, and transformed by the usage of sociology of knowledge3. Since then, authors often quoted and used their text in several different contexts. However, in the this article the most interesting part is the way Berger & Luckmann managed to describe the complex relationship between the subjective and the objective. The approach touches upon our (as humans) possible mastery of the *constructed* environment (which is also the reason for going back to the original source instead of using the numerous interpretations and further developments that have been made since then (starting with Bijker, Hughes & Pinch 1987). The point in this text is to return to the more philosophical issue of reality (knowledge) construction to provide tools for an ideological standpoint.

It is necessary to point out clearly, as Berger & Luckmann do, that their contribution is not an ontological one4. That is, they do not state the ontological status of our perceived reality; they merely try to explain how reality, at the same time, could act as an impediment to our actions and because of our actions. Furthermore, the reality they are referring to is the reality of everyday life experienced by ordinary inhabitants of it, it is not the philosophical and theoretically burdened reality of academicians. Their interest is strictly sociological and stems from what they see as evident; reality's social relativity.

How then is Nielsen's discussion about the relation between empiricism and ideology in usability related to Berger & Luckmann's view on reality as both subjective and objective? Why is it interesting to return to the classics?

What is argued here is that the *dynamic* between subjective and objective reality, which Berger & Luckmann so successfully and logically point out, could serve as a returning point to hold on to in the critical moments mentioned above where other objectives (such as time-schedules, financial limits etc.) appear to be untouchable and impossible to alter. An awareness of every individual's possibility and responsibility in the creation of new 'realities' other individuals are forced to adjust to.

According to Berger and Luckmann the knowledge of every-day life guides our conduct and is taken for granted as reality and it is exactly this kind of knowledge that sociologists (and hopefully also other disciplines) should take as the object of analysis and attempt to clarify. The knowledge originates from thoughts and actions and we maintain it as reality. That is, it becomes "the objectivations of subjective processes (and meanings) by which the *inter*subjective common-sense world is constructed" (ibid. p. 34). Moreover, it is exactly in this 'taken for granted-ness' where lies the possibility to make a change while such objectivations are co-constructed in subjective processes.

What is suggested here is that there are methods or rather processes available (resting on social constructionism) to enhance awareness of one's basic outlook and by such challenge what might be taken for granted and open op for a continuum of Nielsen's argument, "to ensure human mastery of constructed environment":
1.   The possibility to reconstruct (from acknowledgment)
2.   The importance of communication in the construction of the environment
3.   The danger of habitualisation
4.   'The bigger stick' aspect
5.   Upgrading of the 'user' through enhanced contextuality
6.   The dynamic and hopeful process of socialization
7.   Understanding the dialectic through 'focus point'

3.1   The Possibility to Reconstruct (From Acknowledgment of Reality's Partly Constructive Character)

As mentioned above, according to Berger & Luckmann, the analytical object of sociology of knowledge is the reality of *everyday life* since there is no other reality that is as empirically grounded (as a contrast to the philosophically or scientifically logic reality). The reality of everyday life has a 'taken-for-granted character' and we tend to accept it quite easily. We seldom argue whether the rules for attending a football game (such as paying a fee) exist or not, they just do, and we experience them very concretely. It is in a way self-evident. Furthermore, we quite often experience it as independent of our apprehensions that is exactly the core of the argument in bringing social constructivism as a returning point for user-centred IS. Our perception of reality is more relative to the dialectic construction process than we have the strength to admit in the 'critical moments'. As such, it is already objectified, "constituted by an order of objects that have been designated as objects before my appearance on the scene" (ibid. p. 35). These objects and their inner logic and order remain unproblematic and undisputed until further notice, that is, until its continuity is interrupted by the appearance of a problem. Only then, do we *pay attention to their construction and attempt to understand and possibly reconstruct the logic of the perceived reality.* The thing is that the problem might not focus upon, might be in terms of minor importance, and sometimes someone needs to address the problem and claim its importance. If we for example view non-use of our information systems as the result of incompetent users we might address some parts of the problem while others are missed out, such as the possibility that the information systems is badly constructed to meet the users' needs.

3.2   The Importance of Communication in the Construction of the Environment

Our reality of everyday life is according to Berger & Luckmann interpreted, communicated, and made real and objective in many forms. In addition, the most common sign system, which makes this intersubjectivity obvious, is our vocal sign system, language. Language provides us with the necessary objectifications and order; it is 'the realissimum of my consciousness'.... It constantly proves itself as an intersubjective world, "I know that there is an ongoing correspondence between my meanings and their meanings in this world, that we share a common sense about its reality" (ibid. p. 37). As such, the function of language is 'translation and interpretation' since when we experience something we try to describe these experiences to others and when doing this we also try to make them fit into the existing reality. They need to make-sense in some way or another and while trying to ascribe them meaning they become more real as we communicate them with others. *This is especially important to have in mind trying to communicate information technology, due to its sometimes abstract and unintelligible character.*

As user-centred IS designers we should look after that it is communicated in an as non-power coloured way as possible.

3.3 The danger of habitualisation

Furthermore, sometimes we encounter these different forms of experiences of reality as more objective and static. We understand them as independent of our own wishes and actions and we sometimes even refer to them as impediments to our actions. The easiest way to explain the construction of such objective reality is to refer to *habitualisation*. Habitualisation is a way of saving ourselves much mental processing and effort. If we should, in every new encounter, totally unprejudiced, try to capture the new situation, its surroundings, and its inhabitants it would be almost impossible. There would be too many impressions to process and too many decisions to make. Instead, we save time and effort by making 'typifications' and create habits, both regarding situations and individuals. These 'typifications' and habits narrow possible choices; they remove great amounts of tension and as such provide psychological relief.

This is another area which could be rewarding for user-centred IS to keep in mind; *what might save resources in the short run might create problems in the next step since 'typifications' seldom exist other than just 'typifications' with no exact reference in reality*. They are indeed very attractive to use in design-processes since they provide generalisations and order but in the end, they have a tendency to fail. Furthermore, diverging from them are energy consuming and implies a great amount of courage since diverging also creates a feeling of loss of control and meaning.

So what's the point of doing it? If we, in some way or another, are a part of the construction of reality, for example in designing a public information system handling parent insurances it might be rewarding to test and analyse what is perceived as natural. Even though mostly women/mothers use parent insurance, we should be aware that we are passing on a perceived reality by constructing the system to mostly deal with women. We do have an opportunity to make humans masters of the constructed environment by adding men into the system.

3.4 'The bigger stick' aspect

We can further explain this aspect by the fact that no socialisation is ever completely successful; because of that, the symbolic universe (a level of legitimation of what one perceives as objective) needs constant maintenance (through mythology, theology, philosophy, and science). We could describe both the maintenance and the definition process from a power analytical point of view. That is, "he who has the bigger stick has the better chance of imposing his definition of reality" (ibid. p. 127). Hence, it is important to ask the question 'Says who?' and analyse the preferences behind the statements put forward. To "understand the state of the socially constructed universe at any given time, or its change over time, one must understand the social organization that permits the definers to do their defining" (ibid. p. 134). Therefore, for a user-centred IS *it is very important that while defining a part of a reality, for example an organisational structure or a pedagogical process, have the power analysis perspective in mind to not only reproduce what is most easily perceived.*

3.5 Upgrading of the 'User' through Enhanced Contextuality

According to Berger and Luckmann the identity-forming process is a social process. Our identity is dependent on our social context: "once crystallized, it is maintained, modified, or even reshaped by social relations" (ibid. p. 194). Different social contexts form different identity *types* and these types of identities appear in individual cases and described within certain societies, such as 'the polite Englishman' or 'the western intellectual middle-class woman'. In addition, these identity types are social products to court. Nevertheless, it is thus important to note, that societies do not form *identities*. Identities are always unique and we can never typify them. Berger and Luckmann do not openly discuss the difference between nature, society, and identity when it comes to uniqueness but they only stress this fact on behalf of identity. Nature is something 'outside us', society is something in-between (outside and inside) and finally, identity is 'inside' and as such partly untouchable to other subjects when it comes to understanding it.

This inability to gain full insight into another subject's reality does have implications for our mutual reciprocity. When trying to investigate this further, it is thus necessary to have a strong methodological contextual connection to the social structure, where we shape the self within. The image of what is reality and what should be preserved as reality is mediated through communication and the use of language is the most important vehicle of reality-maintenance (and therefore also investigations about reality5). We communicate with each other to create a structure to use both in routine cases and in cases of crisis.

We might even misinterpret an individual for lacking a sense of reality if we do not take into consideration the reality within which he or she is formed. This is also applicable to the situation when trying to understand the possible user(s) of a system, *it is never possible to totally understand the user but since we are trying any way we should always have the contextuality in mind. Especially non-users are often seen as hard to understand but is this only an effect of lack of contextuality?*

3.6 The Dynamic and Hopeful Process of Socialisation

According to Berger & Luckmann (among others such as Mead), the contextuality is imprinted in our subjective reality through different processes such as *primary* and *secondary socialisation*. When a child is born, he or she is born *into* an already existing reality that (most usually) his or her parents and a few others present and mediate to him or her. We refer to these persons as *significant others* since they become very important for the child's identity forming process and the situation is highly charged emotionally. Later on the child will take on the roles and attitudes of the significant other and bill begin to internalise them and make them his/her own.

Finally, he/she will be capable of making abstractions from these roles and attitudes (called *generalised others*).

These abstractions serve as self-controlling and restricting. He/she knows what is right without asking or being shown it since he/she could imagine what the significant others would say.

Therefore, socialisation is a continuously ongoing process. Even though primary socialisation is more routed in our identity and, because of that, harder to displace, it is exposed to subsequent change. We are constantly facing new sectors of the objective world of society called *secondary socialisation*. It is not necessarily replacing already existing conceptions; however, it could be widening the ones we already possess. The conceptions transmitted to us in early childhood also appear as almost unconscious apprehensions but the ones presented later in life are more mentally processed and challenged. Nevertheless, the above implies the possibility that we can transform subjective reality and such transformations, called alternations, require processes of re-socialisation.

By acknowledging and keeping in mind the primary and secondary socialisation, we could understand several layers of use and non-use in terms of contextuality. *It matters how we are introduced to information technology, who the 'introducers' are and (which is a comforting thought) it is never to last to make a second impression (only so much harder).* If our identity indicates we are computer-illiterate because early in life we were given that role in our family (maybe due to gender or age), it is likely that we are viewing ourselves in that manner fifty years later in a work situation. Moreover, not addressing the condition, this image will last. If we want to change the condition (for whatever reason), we have to start with acknowledging its existence. As user-centred IS designers this is important knowledge and we should not belittle it.

3.7 Understanding the Dialectic through 'Focus point'

And finally, "it is important to emphasize that the relationships between man [woman], the producer, and the social world, his [her] product, is and remains a *dialectical* one. That is, man [woman] (not, of course, in isolation but in his [her] collectivities) and his [her] social world interact with each other. The product acts back upon the producer." (Berger & Luckmann 1967:78-79) And when then making an analysis, the dialectical nature of this relationship makes it impossible to single out a starting point and claim something has priority over another. Instead, the only possibility is to *single out a focus point (see figure 1 below) and say that "this is where this analysis take place" and "these are the prerequisites we are facing at this moment".* The analysis will then regard what the individual claim is his or her experiences and describes the experience as his or her reality. Later, he or she would describe what happens from that moment and then forward.

Nevertheless, we often perceive human phenomena as if they were "non-human or possibly supra-human" (ibid. page 107). *We forget our own authorship of the human world and the dialectic between ourselves as producers and our products are lost to consciousness.*

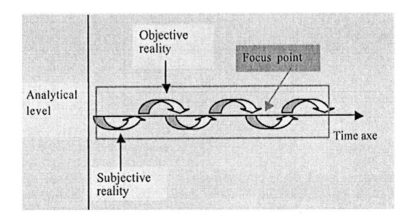

Figure 1: Social Constructionism: The Dialectical Relationship between Objective and Subjective Reality (Lindblad-Gidlund, 2005)

4   Challenged and Made Aware of One's Basic Outlook and its Consequences for One's Choices, Decisions and Actions

The *dynamic* component described is the most important reason for giving space to this theoretical area because it is possible to explain and focus always on our own status in reality. *We are neither totally free nor totally controlled, but if we want to make a change we will have to engage in understanding and questioning what is perceived as objective.* So, if the technological development is not satisfactory to us, we could, by putting some effort into it, question the relations and analyse the 'habitualisations' and alter it (even thought we have to be aware of the time-variable, some changes might take such a long time as we might experience them as almost unchangeable). At this point, Berger & Luckmann would parallel the work of Jacques Ellul; he states that technological development is not objective reality (even though the products we already have produced are covered by what Berger & Luckmann would call the everyday reality, ipso facto) as it is untouchable to us. It is the product of our continuous social constructing process and the only way to change the technological development in the way we want it to be changed is to become aware and take an active part in its construction.

However, for those who, for different reasons, cannot take an active part in its construction, they need *knights in shining armours*. These knights have several tasks, but two of the most important one's are (1) to defend the non-users so that they are not only disregarded as 'bad users' and (2) to act as user advocates to strengthen the voice of the users in the construction of their information technological reality. For the first task, Wyatt, Thomas & Terranova (2002) (among others) claim that not only could people reject non-users as irrational, they might actually have rational and logical reasons for choosing to use information technology. For the second task, Oudshoorn and Pinch (2003) openly declare that it is 'a complicated endeavour'. However, as Epstein points out, there is a complex configuration of power and knowledge 'involved in configuring user identities'. These tend to be the way (up until now) we speak on behalf of the users.

In the beginning of this article, we presented Nielsen's proposal of a belief in certain specialized types of human rights (an ideology of usability). The proposal claims that people should be superior to technology, people should understand technology, and as such, people should be able to control the outcome. In relation to that philosophy, Nielsen touched upon an interesting idea, namely, that while being usability professionals, *a more profound understanding about one's fundamentals or basic outlook is important*. In addition, this article has tried to show how social constructionism could serve as a source to help examine the relation between humans and the construction of reality; it also showed the need to create a deeper awareness that could be of assistance to one's decisions, choices, and actions as a creator and producer of information systems.

References

Adorno, T W (1987) *Kritisk teori: En introduktion* (edited by John Burrill), Göteborg, Daidalos

Bansler, J (1989) Systems development Research in Scandinavia: Three theoretical schools, in *Scandinavian Journal of Information Systems*, Vol. 1, pp. 3-20

Beck, E (2002) P for Political, Participation is Not Enough, in *Scandinavian Journal of Information Systems*, Vol. 14, pp. 77-92

Berger, P & Luckmann, T (1967) *The Social Construction of Reality*, London, Penguin Books

Bijker, W, Hughes, T & Pinch T (1987) *The Social Construction of Technological Systems*, Cambridge, Massachusetts, The MIT Press

Bjerknes, G & Bratteteig, T (1987) *Implementing and idea – cooperation and construction in the Florence project*, Florence report no. 3, Department of Informatics, University of Oslo

Bjerknes, G & Bratteteig, T (1995) User Participation and Democracy: A Discussion of Scandinavian Research on System Development in *Scandinavian Journal of Information Systems*, Vol. 7 (1), pp. 73-98

Bødker, S, Knudsen, J L, Kyng, M, Ehn, P & Madsen K H (1988) *Computer Support for Cooperative Design*, Proceedings of the 1988 ACM Conference on Computer-supported cooperative work

Bødker, S (2003) A for Alternatives, in *Scandinavian Journal of Information Systems*, Vol. 15, pp. 87-89

Dittrich, Y (2003) We are not yet there!, in *Scandinavian Journal of Information Systems*, Vol. 15, pp. 91-94

Feenberg, A (2000) Constructivism and Technology Critique: Replies to Critics, *Inquiry*, Vol. 43, Issue 2, June 2000, pp. 225-238, London, Routledge

Horkheimer M & Adorno T W (1981) *Upplysningens dialektik: filosofiska fragment*, translated by Lars Bjurman & Karl Henning Wijmark, Göteborg, Daidalos

Iversen, O S, Kanstrup, A M, Petersen, M G (2004) *A visit to the 'new Utopia': revitalizing democracy, emancipation and quality in co-operative design*, Proceedings of the third Nordic conference on Human-computer interaction NordiCHI '04

Nielsen, J (2005) https://www.useit.com/alertbox/20050627.html (2005-06-30)

Kanstrup, A M (2003) D for Democracy, in *Scandinavian Journal of Information Systems*, Vol. 15, pp. 81-85

Kling, R, Crawford, H, Rosenbaum, H, Sawyer, W & Weisband, S (1998) *Learning from Social Informatics: Information and Communication Technologies in Human Contexts*, Center for Social Informatics, Indiana University

Mannheim, K (1936) *Ideology and Utopia*, London, Routledge & Paul Kegan

Månsson, P (1991) *Moderna samhällsteorier, Traditioner, riktningar och teoretiker*, Stockholm, Prisma

Marcuse, H (1941) *Reason and Revolution: Hegel and the Rise of Social Theory*, London, Oxford University Press

Oudshoorn, N & Pinch T (2003), *How users matter: The co-construction of users and technology*, New Baskerville, MIT Press

Scheler, M (1960) *Die Wissensformen und die Gesellschaft*, Francke, Bern

Winner, L (1994) Political Artifacts in Scandinavia: An American Perspective, in Scandinavian Journal of Information Systems, Vol. 6 (2) , pp. 85-94

Vredenburg, K, Isensee, S, & Righi, C 2001 User-centred Design: An Integrated Approach with Cdrom, Upper Ssaddle River, NJ, USA, Prentice Hall PTR

Wyatt, W, Thomas, G & Terranova, T (2002) They came, they surfed, they went back to the beach: conceptualising use and non-use of the Internet, in *Virtual Society?* Ed. Woolgar S, Oxford University Press

Notes

---

1   It is thus possible to say that that would be a not insignificant change from the original idea of incorporating the user into the design process to secure better systems and a higher quality of work. Becks' proposal also contains a slight shift in level of analysis from organisational to societal in order to be political. It also suggests a shift from techniques (design methods) to ideological analysis (ethical values), furthermore it stresses the fact that the workers have become consumers and as such are difficult to incorporate.

2   But since authorities such as Langdon Winner describe academics concluding that people have a choice in the social construction of technology as "extremely comforting, almost (yawn) sleep inducing" due to its too relativistic character (Winner 1994:90) it is comforting that yet another authority, Andrew Feenberg, on the other hand claims that it is definitely possible to combine constructionism and technology critique and goes even further by saying that it is equally possible to use constructionist analysis at the same time as ontological essentialism, it all depends

on how deep you use each standpoint2 (Feenberg 2000). Feenberg finds social constructionism interesting due to the "tools they give us for interpreting technology and its place in the social world" (ibid. 2000:229). At the same time Feenberg talks about primary and secondary instrumentalizations where technology turns into something real and inseparable from the essence of technology (even if every technological essence from the beginning is inseparable from human activity). Feenberg concludes by stating that he "combines essentialist insights into the technical orientation toward the world with constructivist insights into the social nature of technology" (ibid. 2000:233). "I believe that both essentialism and constructivism have something to contribute to our understanding of technology... The problem is to combine their insights in a theory that bridges the theoretical gaps between traditions and the cultural gaps between their practitioners" (ibid. 2000:236).

3   A thorough and illuminating description of the sociology of knowledge is made by Rigné in Månsson 1991, but Berger & Luckmann themselves defined it as follows "The sociology of knowledge is concerned with the relationship between human thought and the social context within which it arises" (Berger &Luckmann 1967:16).

4   Berger & Luckmann start their journey by stating that: "reality is socially constructed" and define reality as "a quality appertaining to phenomena that we recognize as having a being independent of our own volition (we cannot 'wish them away')" (ibid. page 13). These two statements point in two directions: reality's social relativity but also its existence *ipso facto*. The explanation behind the statement of reality's social relativity is that reality is dependent on its social contexts. What we may perceive as reality in wealthy western societies might not be the same reality perceived in a poorly developed society and this is especially evident in the social foundations of values and worldviews4. Berger & Luckmann refer to Scheler's (1960) 'relative-natural world-view' to emphasise that "human knowledge is given in a society as an *a priori* to individual experience, providing the latter with its order of meaning. This order, although it is relative to a particular socio-historical situation, appears to the individual as the natural way of looking at the world" (ibid. page 20). They continue by referring to Karl Mannheim's (1936) 'relationism' which is not "a capitulation of thought before the socio-historical relativities, but a sober recognition that knowledge must always be knowledge from a certain position" (Berger & Luckmann 1967:22). But, as mentioned above: reality's social relativity is not dominant over its existence. It is necessary to draw attention to that it is not a form of post-modernism or relativism where reality is nothing but the perceived, quite the opposite, Berger and Luckmann often point out that there exists an every-day reality *ipso facto*, the point here is rather the focus on the *construction* of this reality. Berger and Luckmann do not aim to describe or investigate, philosophically, reality's ontological status, their aim is to try to explain how this reality is constructed and reconstructed. As Berger and Luckmann state : "Society does indeed possess objective facticity. And society is indeed built up by activity that expresses subjective meaning". They continue by claiming that these two statements are not contradictory because "It is precisely the dual character of society in terms of objective facticity and subjective meaning that makes its 'reality *sui generis*'.

5   This statement has methodological implications and possibilities. If language is the most important instrument of reality mediation then it might possible, through language, to unfold and uncover the reality we perceive and construct. This implies that it is thus possible to reach some knowledge about another person's subjective reality.

Models of Democracy and the Design of Slovenian Political Party Web Sites

Simon Delakorda
Faculty of Social Sciences, University of Ljubljana, Slovenia,
simon.delakorda@guest.arnes.si

Abstract. Web sites of Slovenian political parties do not fully exploit the Internet's potential for interactive and deliberative communication on political issues with citizens, because they favour a competitive-elitist perception of democracy. As result, political party's web sites are mainly used for political mobilization, agitation in persuasion. Supporting this model of democracy via web pages enables political parties to strengthen their position of power and control in decision-making process, to legitimise a hegemonic position of representative democracy within political system, to impose the perception of citizens as consumers of political information and to provide democratic legitimization for capitalist mode of production. In order to strengthen citizen's e-participation on political issues, a conceptual shift in designing political party's web sites according to participatory and deliberative model of democracy is needed.

Keywords: Political parties, Web sites, Electronic democracy, Citizens, Slovenia

1 Introduction

There is a wide recognition among authors that Internet is playing an increasingly important role in party politics [Vreg, 2000; Selm, Jankowski and Tsaliki, 2001; Norris, 2003; Gibson, Lusoli and Ward, 2003]. Political parties in western democracies have recognized the importance of Internet technology in improving their communication strategies, political mobilization and information delivery. On the other hand, many authors argue [Nixon and Johansson, 1998; Becker and Slaton, 2000; Franz, 2000] that the web sites of political parties do not fully exploit the potential of the Internet for participatory means. Although different authors provide different explanations for this phenomena (e.g., balance of power, lack of interest,

Please use the following format when citing this chapter:

Delakorda, S., 2006, in IFIP International Federation for Information Processing, Volume 223, Social Informatics: An Information Society for All? In Remembrance of Rob Kling, eds. Berleur, J., Numinen, M. I., Impagliazzo, J., (Boston: Springer), pp. 279–295.

lack of knowledge and resources, fear of mass participation, strive for control), a substantial amount of the existing analysis [Vreg, 2000; Nixon and Johansson, 1998] lacks theoretical background that would help to explain why political parties are not prone to use the Internet to stimulate interactive political communication with citizens on public issues.

My underlying assumption is that web sites of Slovenian political parties do not fully exploit the Internet's potential for interactive communication because they favour an elitist-competitive perception of democracy. This perception emphasizes central role of political parties and leaders and recognises elections of representatives as the most important operation of political system [Van Dijk, 1996:48]. Political parties are perceived as intermediates between state and citizens, as the main actor during elections, as important factor in the process of political socialization and as formal executive control over decision-making and formulation of public policy [Della Porta, 2003: 120-121]. Those functions are in line with a representative type of democracy, which according to Van Dijk (ibid.) does not favour wider and direct participation of electorate in decision-making process. Therefore, supporting an elitist-competitive model of democracy via Internet communication and web pages enables political parties to strengthen their position of power and control in democratic process, to legitimize hegemonic position of representative democracy within political systems and to impose the perception of citizens as consumers of political information. What is more, political parties are forced to reproduce this model of democracy in order to provide democratic legitimization for capitalist mode of production [Offe, 1988: 59-61]. As a result, there is little reason for political parties to promote participation and deliberative democracy [Perczynski, 2003] via Internet communication.

On the other hand, a substantial amount of academic analysis is concerned with the democratic deficit of the present form of democracy in Slovenia [Bernik, 2002; Makarovic, 2002; Vodopivec et al., 2002]. Most important causes for the decline of political participation by citizens in Slovenia are: consolidation of representative democracy, instrumental understanding of democracy and relatively satisfactory economic and social situation [Makarovic, 2002: 77-84]. On the other hand, problems with political party's arrogance, clientelism, and ambition to regulate public life (centralization and hierarchy) are resulting in lower quality of governance and stressing the need for more direct democracy [Rus, 2002: 25]. Combining with traditional rejection of their mobilization role by Slovenian citizens, political parties rate among the least trustful institutions in Slovenia. One way to deal with representative democratic deficit (i.e. strengthen legitimacy of political parties) in western political systems is by enriching public debate on political issues and by allowing citizens to directly participate in democratic decision-making using Internet technology (parties web sites) [Fishkin, 2000]. In that manner Nixon and Johansson (1998: 135) are using the term discursive democracy to describe discussion and interaction between individual citizens that may support more consensual forms of decision-making. It implies an engagement or involvement in politics that refutes the notion of a passive consumption of 'top down' delivered political views, in favour of »bottom up« discursive interaction in which citizens not only consume, but also play, a part in the creation of politics. Those ideas were implemented in various concepts of electronic, digital, cyber and teledemocracy [Grossman, 1995; Hagen, 1996; Tsagarousianou, 1998; Becker and Slaton, 2000; Hague and Loader; 2001].

My basic intention in this paper is to provide limited empirical contribution to existing interpretation of political science web sites analyses in what I call an *e-party dilemma* - improving political party's web sites information delivery but not improving citizen's e-participation in decision making. Slovenian political party's web sites will be analysed in terms of various e-democracy techniques they provide in order to enable interactive in inclusive online communication with citizens on public issues. Frequency and type of different e-democracy techniques will examine my assumption whether Slovenian political party's web sites are designed according to elitist-competitive democracy or not. This will further lead to conclusion whether the one way communication flow of web sites contributes to reduction of the democratic deficit of representative democracy in Slovenia and how the web sites should be conceptually improved in order to enrich public debate on political issues by allowing them to directly participate in democratic decision-making.

2   Theoretical Framework

2.1   Models of Political Democracy

In order to establish proper operational framework for empirical web sites analysis, I created an analytical model combining Van Dijk's typology of political democracy with Trechsel's typology of e-democracy techniques (see Chapter 3 for more details).

Jan A.G. M. van Dijk [1996: 47-52] draws very clear links between the models of democracy and ICT (information-communication technology) usage for strengthening citizen's participation. Van Dijk distinguishes among five models of democracy and their distinctive understanding of e-participation: legalist democracy, competitive democracy, plebiscitary democracy, pluralist democracy and participatory democracy[1].

2.1.1 Competitive-Elitist Model of Democracy
In this model, the use of ICT instruments is focused on elections and information campaigns. Political elites directly address selected target groups of voters via one way mass and modern public information systems that relay differentiated political messages. The interested public, which is understood as a fragmented electoral body of political leaders and parties, must have access to the information, views, opinions and conduct of its elected leaders and representatives. Other ICT instruments intended for conversation and registration (debate forums, e-conferences) are used only if they are of benefit to the political leadership. The use of these instruments can be misleading, because it can make us believe that the model in question is direct democracy, which is not true.

2.1.2 Legal Model of Democracy

From the point of view of legal model, the role of ICT in a political system is limited to remedying the fundamental problem of the existing political system - information deficit. Information deficit is generated at three levels: information shortage of the political system caused by bureaucratic barriers, an insufficient flow of information between the government/administration and citizens and unsuitable information distribution resulting in difficult situation in the system of checks and balances. ICT is used to tackle an information deficit by means of a computer-supported information systems, information centres, public services and computer-supported enquiries by citizens. These aplications facilitate greater transparency in the functioning of the political system, which should tackle the problem of information complexity and shortage. The ICT instruments that are rejected or not trusted are e-referendums, e-debates among citizens and e-conferences.

2.1.3 Pluralist Model of Democracy

Two ICT features are relevant for this model of democracy: 1) a multiple political information chanells and debate systems that allow conversation within an organisation and between an organisation and citizens; 2) access to interactive communication networks that support the network concept of politics. Consequently, ICT systems are used within and among civil society organisations to establish databases, to voice opinion and take part in the debate. In addition mass and public information systems, registering systems and various computer-supported lists and reviews of organisations and institutions are generated. The preferred ICT instruments are e-mail, discussion lists, teleconferences and support systems for debates on both complex issues.

2.1.4 Plebiscitary Model of Democracy

This model favours establishment of direct democracy in a large and complex societies (teledemocracy). Decision-making in a political system was to be replaced with a constant registration of the will of individual citizens. Consequently, registration systems of elections and opinions (tele-elections, referendums and e-assemblies) of citizens are favoured. To these are occasionally added conversation instruments, such as electronic town halls, teleconferences, etc. Even consultation instruments are not ignored, facilitating communication between citizens and mass and public information systems. Information delivery instruments and those that are controlled by institutional politics are mistrusted.

2.1.5 Participatory model of democracy

ICT instruments that can offer information and support for citizen activism are central. Computerised information campaigns and public information systems must be suitably structured and accessible all in order to open up the political system and make its functioning transparently. User-friendly new media and electronic discussion instruments are tools for opinion forming, learning and active participation. Notice-board lists in computer networks, teleconferences and electronic town halls are only welcome in the participatory model if participatory processes are not reserved for social and intellectual elites and if they are designed to suit discussion instruments.

2.2   eDemocracy Techniques

Alexandre H. Trechsel [2002: 43] defines e-democracy as "all electronic means of communication that enable/empower citizens in their efforts to hold rulers/politicians accountable for their actions in the public realm. Depending on the aspect of democracy being promoted, e-democracy can employ different techniques: (1) for increasing the transparency of the political process; (2) for enhancing the direct involvement and participation of citizens; and, (3) improving the quality of opinion formation by opening new spaces of information and deliberation."
    Trechsel (2002: 45-51) defines each technique further as:

2.2.1 Techniques for Increasing Transparency
Basically it refers to e-access, defined as the use of the Internet to improve electronic access to official documents and to political information that will enhance the transparency of the political process and the quality of opinion formation leading to a greater political involvement of citizens.

2.2.2 Techniques for increasing participation
They include applications of e-consultation, e-petition, e-polling and e-voting. *E-consultation* refers to the use of the Internet to disseminate to the wider public, experts and interest groups developments in a policy field and invite them to respond. *E-petition* uses the Internet to enable citizens to initiate a petition on a public issue, invite others to signal their support and finally submit their petition. *E-polling* refers to the use of the Internet for providing citizens (or a sample thereof) with a tool that allows them to express their opinions on a public issue and to measure public opinion. E-voting can be separated in two models. The first model simply replaces existing paper ballots with a machine that records votes locally then transfers those votes via the Internet to election headquarters. In the second model voters are offered the possibility of voting from any terminal or computer connected to the Internet to cast their vote. E-voting can be further distinguish between *e-referendum*, where citizens are offered to vote online on a specific public issue to be adopted and *e-election* which relates to the use of the Internet for casting a ballot that is transmitted to electoral officials via the Internet. In the case of e-elections within parties, e.g. for primaries or for electing party leaders, the vote is transmitted via the Internet to party officials.

2.2.3 Techniques for Promoting New Spaces of Deliberation
Are focusing on the development of an *e-forum*. This e-technique provides citizens with an online tool that allows them to exchange and share respective political opinions among themselves. The aspiration of e-democracy advocates is that e-forums will enhance the process of citizen's opinion formation through their deliberative engagement.

3   Analytical Model

A distinctive connection between Van Dijk's models of political democracy and Trechsel's e-democracy techniques can be illustrated by table 1:

This disposition will be used as an analytical model for analysing Slovenian political party's web sites. For example: if a certain Slovenian political party web site employs e-democracy techniques of e-access, e-poll and e-voting, it would mean, that the web site is conceptually designed according to competitive-elitist model of democracy. And opposite, if a web site employs techniques of e-petition, e-forum and e-consultation, it would mean that the web site is based on participatory model of democracy. In case, party's web site employs combination of various e-democracy techniques, this would suggest that the web site is designed according to various models of democracy.

Table 1. E-democracy techniques favoured by models of political democracy

		Models of democracy				
		Elitist-competitive	Legalist	Pluralist	Plebiscitary	Participatory
e-democracy techniques	e-access		x	x	x	x
	e-petition				x	x
	e-consultation	x	x	x		x
	e-voting	x			x	
	e-referendum				x	
	e-forum	x		x		x
	e-poll	x	x		x	

4   Empirical Analysis

4.1   Analysis of Slovenian Political Parties Web Sites

Empirical analysis consists of three stages. At the first stage I used web browsers to identify the 'Universe' of the web sites of registered Slovenian political parties. At the second stage instrumental analysis of electronic democracy techniques was conducted on identified political party's websites as suggested by analytical model. In final stage of empirical research, collected data were analysed in order to test research assumptions raised in this paper.

4.2   Identifying the Registered Slovenian Political Parties

According to the official list of registered political parties[2] held by Ministry of Internal Affairs of Republic of Slovenia (MNZ RS)[3], 39 political parties were registered in Slovenia on 12.7.2004. Of which there are 8 parties that constitute present National assembly (parliament) and 31 parties that are non parliamentary.

By using combination of Slovenian search engines www.najdi.si, www.slowwwenia.com and www.matkurja.com/ we were able to identify 22 political parties' websites out of 39. 8 of them belong to parliamentary and 14 belong to registered political parties (see Appendix for more details). One registered political party website was not accessible. This means that 56 % of registered political parties in Slovenia have their own web site. As a result the 'universe' of registered Slovenian political party's web sites consists of 21 sites (Table no. 2).

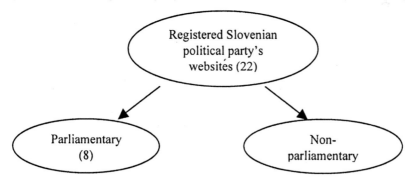

Figure 1 The 'universe' of Slovenian political party's websites as located by web browsers www.najdi.si, www.slowwwenia.com and www.matkurja.com/ during 15th -18th of March 2004 and supplemented on 27th of July 2004.

4.3   Frequency and Types of Electronic Democracy Techniques

Analysis of e-democracy techniques, as suggested by analytical model, was conducted on 21 web sites since one was no accessible. Tables, 2, 3 and 4 are presenting the performed analysis.

Table 2 shows that all political parties with web sites provided kind of information on party activities, members, issues, events etc. Less than half of web sites provided e-poll[4] application on current political issues and standings. One third of web sites also had e-forum[5] application, which enables users to express their positions, comments and standing on certain political issues.

Table 2. Frequency of provided on Slovenian political parties web sites

E-democracy techniques	e-access	e-poll	e-petition	e-forum	e-consultation	e-election	e-referendum
Number of websites	21	9	none	7	none	none	none

Slovenian political party's web sites do not hold e-petition, e-consultation, e-election and e-referendum applications. Those e-democracy techniques are currently not available to Slovenian Internet users.

Table 3. E-Democracy Tolls Comparison Between Parliamentary and Non Parliamentary Political Party's Web Sites

	e-access	e-poll	e-petition	e-forum	e-consultation	e-election	e-referendum
Parliamentary web sites	8	6	none	4	none	none	none
Non-parliamentary	13	3	none	3	none	none	none

Based on empirical frequency of e-democracy tolls provided by Slovenian political party's web sites, it is safe to claim that parties are not using all participatory possibilities provided by Internet technology. As noted, they focus mainly on policy information delivery, issues promotion, campaigning, presenting party leaders activities etc. As result, e-access tool is most common web sites application. On the other hand, interactive communication with publics and citizens is facing serious deficiency. Although web sites provide very simple e-polling and e-forum applications to some degree, they use in traditional way. Consequently e-forums do not enable deliberative, moderated and focused conversation on political issues that would create qualitative public opinion. Similar case is with e-polls, which provide no representative and deliberative public opinion on often trivial political issues (expressing party support, evaluating political decision made by political authorities etc).

As noticed, web sites are clearly missing participatory e-democracy techniques such as e-consultation and e-petition, which would enable party members, and voters to direct influence party politics, programmes, policy and law proposals. Same counts for plebiscitary e-democracy applications such as e-voting or e-referendum.

Comparing parliamentary and non parliamentary political parties e-democracy application frequency on their respective web sites it is clear that parliamentary actors are putting greater emphasis concerning information and communication performance and activities. Most of parliamentary parties have e-poll application in contrast to less than third of non-parliamentary. Half of parliamentary parties have e-forum application in contrast to less than of non-parliamentary.

These results suggest that stronger, bigger and parties within parliament are more eager to provide interactive relationship with voters and citizens and to enable information delivery to public.

Table 4. E-democracy Techniques Comparison Among Single Registered Political Parties

Political party	e-access	e-poll	e-petition	e-forum	e-consultation	e-election	e-referendum	N/A
1. Active Slovenia (AS)	x	x						
2. Association for Primorska Region (ZZP)	x							
3. Association of Independents of Slovenia (ZNS)	x							
4. Democratic Pensioners Party (DESUS)	x	x						
5. Slovenian Democrats (DS)	x							
6. Voice of Women (GZS)	x							
7. Communist Party of Slovenia (KPS)	x							
8. Liberal Democracy of Slovenia (LDS)	x	x						

9. New Democracy of Slovenia (NDS)	x			
10. New Slovenia - Christian People's Party (NSi)	x	x	x	
11. New Party (NS)				x
12. Progressive party (PS)	x		x	
13. Republicans of Slovenia (RS)	x			
14. Slovenia is ours (SJN)	x	x	x	
15. Slovenian National Party (SNS)	x	x		
16. Slovenian People's Party (SLS)	x	x	x	
17. Slovenian Democratic Party (SDS)	x	x	x	
18. Ecological Movement of Slovenia (SEG	x	x	x	
19. Youth Party of Slovenia (SMS)	x		x	
20. Slovenian Nation's Party (SSN)	x			
21. United List of Social Democrats (ZLDS)	x			
22. Greens of Slovenia (ZS)	x			

5   Results

Although providing basic theoretical framework and limited empirical data collection, answering research assumptions raised in this paper seems rather difficult. The general research assumption whether web sites of Slovenian political parties are designed according to the elitist-competitive model of democracy, is supported by empirical findings. In general, web sites provided only three distinctive e-democracy techniques: e-access (information delivery), e-poll (public opinion measurement) and e-forum (creating and expressing political standings). According to theoretical framework and analytical model, those applications present central elements of competitive-elitist model of democracy. E-voting was the only one application, suitable to this model, which was not identified during web sites analysis.

Second assumption, whether web sites more often employ one way political information and promotion flows than interactive e-democracy techniques is also confirmed by empirical findings. E-access and e-poll applications present, according by frequency, most common communication flow between Slovenian political parties web sites and Internet users. Those applications, supplemented by e-questionnaires and e-comments options represent typical one-way communication flow which dominates political party's web sphere. On the other hand, web sites also employ substantive amount of various interactive communication flows such as e-forums and chat rooms. Although such applications do provide some degree of two-way communication between Internet users and political parties, but are limited to informal, non-biding and trivial conversation and opinion exchange among Internet users itself. As a result, interactivity on web sites does not support public participation in deliberative decision-making, but rather in sharing already established political standings among Internet users.

The last assumption whether Slovenian political parties web sites contribute to reduction of the democratic deficit of representative democracy in Slovenia, can is both supported and rejected. Firstly, it can be supported because important part of democratic deficit of representative democracy, especially its competitive-elitist and legalist perception as defined by Van Dijk (1996), consists of information deficit that causes transparency in efficiency problems of a current political system. All consulted web sites provided variety of information concerning policy and legislative process within parliament, parties activities and work, positions and standing to certain issues, political programmes etc. Since extensive information delivery enables voters and citizens to form and express public opinion, to receive insight in political arena and consequently control and evaluate their political representatives[6], it safe to say that web sites contribute to reduction of democratic deficit by enabling e-access technique. By enabling e-poll and e-forum applications, web sites also contribute to formulating and expressing public opinion on public issues which can help reducing democratic deficit in terms of citizen's political socialisation and education. As already mentioned, since political parties do not use those applications in deliberative and discursive way, further democratic effect is questionable. Secondly, the assumption that Slovenian political parties web sites contribute to reduction of the democratic deficit can be rejected, because they do not support any e-consultation or e-petition techniques. In theory, important part of representative democratic deficit consist of participation deficit [Becker and Slaton, 2000] which indicates lack of communication channels that enable citizens to directly influence political decisions such as legislation and policy documents (strategies, programmes, plans). At the level of political party's role in representative democracy this would mean that citizens take part in decision-making concerning party's legislation and policy proposals which are then decided in parliament. As already mentioned, no Slovenian political party's web site provided any e-democracy technique that would support deliberative electronic participation such as e-consultation and e-petition[7], which are according to Trechsel (2002: 47-49) designed for increasing public participation in certain policy filed by initiating or responding on policy and legislative proposals. Since party's web sites currently provide only simple and traditional techniques for gathering public opinion (e-polls, e-questionnaires, e-comments etc.), Slovenian citizens can not directly influence party politics thorough moderated and continual e-consultations. As result web sites do not contribute to reduction of democratic deficit in terms of participatory democracy.

6   Conclusion

E-democracy techniques analysis on Slovenian political party's web sites shows, that in terms of reducing democratic deficit, promoting public participation and deliberative democracy development in Slovenia, there are still a lot of opportunities that remain unchallenged[8]. Electronic communication flows between parties web sites and Slovenian citizens are designed according to competitive-elitist model of democracy as defined by Van Dijk, (1996: 48), which favors one-way information delivery on political issues, political campaigns and expressing political standings. At the application end, this model clearly favors e-access, e-poll and e-forum techniques that dominate party's web sites. Political communication between citizens and Slovenian political parties is based on using the Internet for election and information campaigns, political mobilization and persuasion, promotion, debating and foremost as efficient tool of public relations. Most of the political party's information provided is one-way, top-down, party to voter rather than two-way interactive communication. By employing limited selection of e-democracy techniques on their web sites, Slovenian political parties fail to play a leading role in the diffusion of new technologies for participatory ends and providing direction for civic political action in order to implement idea of digital democracy. Since their web sites do not support e-consultation and e-petition tools, they also fail to involve Internet users in deliberative and interactive participation on policy and law proposals. Parties do not tend to rally widen participation extensively, nor do established electronic channels necessarily empower ordinary citizens since such channels rarely play a formal role in decision-making and for a large part are controlled by parties elites. They tend to use Internet for involving voters in ways that are largely beneficial to the parties' own promotion. As such citizens are reduced on passive consummation of political information, rather than creating own political standings and applying them in political decisions. At the end, party's web sites do not favor active citizen ideal. As labeled by Becker and Slaton (2000: 140): "They are, in our view, cyberpolitics – as-usual. And since politics-as-usual, in our view, is dis-empowering to say the least, emulating it on the Web does not change anything for the better. Actually, such web sites are akin to public relations-they aim to shore up, reinforce, and cyber legitimize a system that specializes in creation the »necessary illusions« so vital to the status quo."

Regarding those assumptions, further steps should be reconsidered when upgrading web sites in order to enrich public debate on political issues and to allow citizens to directly participate in democratic decision-making. Firstly, it is necessary to adopt conceptual shift in designing web sites. They should be designed according to models of democracy, which favor greater and wider public participation. At the structural level, conceptual shift should result in adopting participatory model of democracy according to Van Dijk's typology and model of associative democracy as suggested by Perczynski (2001). Consequently, e-democracy tools deriving from participatory model, e-consultation and e-poll, should be applied on web sites. Secondly, from procedural level, interactive part of web sites communication (e-forums and e-consultations) should be grounded in deliberative democracy as suggested by Fishkin (2000), which provides standards for focused, moderated and creative decision-making on political issues. Adopting such conceptual changes in political party's web sites design would contribute to more transparent, informed, deliberative, democratic and legitimate decisions within representative democracy and helping to reduce participatory democratic deficit. But on the other hand it would also shift the balance of power within parties from higher levels to those at the button of decision-making. Thirdly, for this reason it is necessary to promote successful practices of e-democracy cases in Slovenia, which would consequently lead to much needed change in political culture. Only when recognizing advantages from participatory usage of Internet for democracy development and consequently recognizing their own benefits, political parties will start to redesign their web sites, which would lead to further diminishing of democratic deficit in Slovenia.

Current Slovenian political party's web sites present proper foundation for suggested conceptual upgrade. In order to result from upgrade, it is important that legal institutions and policy-making practices adopt e-participation as legitimate and legal part of decision-making procedure. This can not be achieved without changes in political culture and governing style, upon which representative democracy in Slovenia is currently based. As noted by Andrej A. Luksic (2003: 26): "Using current efforts, Slovenia achieved informatization level of information society. But now process of its 'communicatization' awaits, as next level in development of information society. Supported by 'communicatization', the process of democratization of democracy can yet begin."

References

1. Becker, Theodore Lewis / Slaton, Christa Daryl (2000) The Future of Teledemocracy. Westport (Conn.), London: Praeger.
2. Bellamy, C. / Taylor, John A. (1998) Governing in the information age. Buckingham.
3. Bernik, Ivan / Uhan, Samo (2002) Koliko nezadovoljstva lahko prenese mlada demokracija? V N. Tos / I. Bernik (ur.) Demokracija v Slovenij, 113-138. Ljubljana: FDV, IDV, Center za raziskovanje javnega mnenja in mnozicnih komunikacij.

4. Center za raziskave javnega mnenja in mnozicnih komunikacij (CJMMK): *Slovenian public oppinion – Politbarometer (May 2004)*. [URL:http://e-uprava.gov.si/ispo/politbarometer/prikaz.ispo?vprKey=120&pregled=0], (25.5.2004).

5. Coleman, S. (2004) Connecting Parliament to the Pubic via the Internet. *Information, Communication & Society*. Vol. 7, No. 1, pp. 1–22.

6. Delakorda, Simon (2003) Elektronska demokracija v refleksiji izbranih politoloskih kategorij: politicne participacije, politicne moci in politicne akcije. In Andrej A. Luksic / Tanja Oblak (ed.), *S poti v digitalno demokracijo*, 87-104. Ljubljana: Fakulteta za druzbene vede.

7. Della Porta, D. (2003) *Temelji politicne znanosti*. Ljubljana: Sophia.

8. Donk, Wim van de (2004) *Cyberprotest: new media, citizens, and social movements*. London, New York: Routledge.

9. Fishkin, James (2000) *Virtual Democratic Possibilities: Prospects for Internet Democracy*, Department of Government, University of Texas at Austin. [URL:http://cdd.stanford.edu/research/papers/brazil_paper.pdf], (5.5.2004).

10. Franz, Damjan (2002) *Theoretical and Empirical Aspects of Digital Democracy with the Focus on Slovenia*. Presented at the Euricom Colloquium: Electronic Networks & Democracy, 9-12 October 2002.

11. Gibson, Rachel Kay / Römmele, Andrea / Ward, Stephen J. (2004) *Electronic democracy: mobilisation, organisation and participation via new ICTs*. London, New York: Routledge.

12. Grossman, Lawrence K. (1995): *The electronic republic: reshaping democracy in the information age*. New York: Viking.

13. Hagen, Martin (1996) A Road to Electronic Democracy? Politische Theorie, Politik und der Information Superhighway in den USA in Hans J. Kleinsteuber (ur.) 1996: *Der Information Superhighway*. Opladen: Westdeutscher Verlag, str. 63-85. [URL:http://www.uni-giessen.de/fb03/vinci/labore/netz/hag_en.htm], (15.5.2004).

14. Hague, Barry N. / Loader, Brian D. (2001). *Digital democracy: discourse and decision making in the Information Age*. London, New York: Routledge.

15. Luksic, Andrej (2003) Hermesovi obrazi demokracije. In Andrej A. Luksic / Tanja Oblak (ed.), *S poti v digitalno demokracijo*, 11-33. Ljubljana: Fakulteta za druzbene vede.

16. Makarovic, Matej (2002) Politicna participacija v desetletju demokratizacije. V N. Tos / I. Bernik (ur.) *Demokracija v Sloveniji*, 65-87. Ljubljana: FDV, IDV, Center za raziskovanje javnega mnenja in mnozicnih komunikacij.

17. Neumann, Franz (1950) Politicka znanost u demokraciji. *Treci program*, st. 64 (1985), str. 363-378.

18. Nixon, P., / H. Johansson (2001). Transparency through Technology: The Internet and Political Parties. In B. Hague / B. Loader (ed.), *Digital democracy: discourse and decision making in the Information Age*, 135-153. London, New York: Routledge.

19. Norris, P. (2003) Preaching to the Converted: Pluralism, Participation and Party Web Sites. *Party Politics* 9(1): 21-45.

20. Oblak, Tanja (2003) *Izzivi e-demokracije*. Ljubljana: Fakulteta za druzbene vede.

21. Offe, Claus (1985) *Druzbena moc in politicna oblast: protislovja kapitalisticne demokracije: razprave o politicni sociologiji poznega kapitalizma*. Delavska enotnost. Ljubljana.
22. Perczynski P. (2001) Associo-deliberative democracy and qualitative participation. In Hirst, Paul / Bader, Veit-Michael (ed.), *Associative democracy: The Real Third Way*, 71-84. London, Portland (OR): F. Cass.
23. Van Dijk, Jan A.G.M, (1996) Models of Democracy - Behind the Design and Use of New Media in Politics. *Javnost* 3(1), 43-56.
24. Van Selm, M., Jankowski N.W., Tsaliki, L. (2001). *Political Parties Online: An Examination of Electronic Democracy on Three Dutch Political Party Web Sites*. Paper presented at Euricom Colloquium: E-Networks & Democratic Life (Piran, Slovenia).
25. Trechsel, Alexandre H. (et al.) (2003) *Evaluation of the use of new technologies in order to facilitate democracy in Europe: e-democratizing the parliaments and parties of Europe*. Geneve: Research and Documentation Centre on Direct Democracy.
26. Tsagarousianou, Roza / Tambini, Damian / Bryan, Cathy (1998) *Cyberdemocracy: technology, cities and civic networks*. London, New York: Routledge.
27. Vreg, France (2001) Globalizacija in elektronska demokracija. *Teorija in praksa* 38 (1), 5-28.
28. Vintar, Mirko / Decman, Mitja / Kunstelj, Mateja (1999) Telematics and the Service of Democracy: The Slovenian Parliament and Other Slovenian Public Institutions on the Internet. *Parliamentary Affairs* 52, 3, 451-463.
29. Vodopivec, Franc / Ursic, Sonja / Franko, Maja (2002) Vec neposredne demokracije v Sloveniji – da ali ne. *Novi trendi v javnem menedzmentu*: predavanje 17. aprila 2002: zbornik referatov in razprav. Ljubljana: Drzavni svet Republike Slovenije.
30. Ward, S., Gibson, R. K., and Lusoli, W. (2003) Participation and Mobilisation Online: Hype, Hope and Reality. *Parliamentary Affairs* 56(3): 652-668.

Appendix

A list of identified political parties web sites:

a) *Parliamentary*[9] (consulted on 15th -18th of March 2004 and supplemented on 27th of July 2004)

http://www.lds.si/ *Liberalna demokracija Slovenije (LDS)*; Liberal Democracy of Slovenia

http://www.zlsd.si/ *Zdruzena lista socialnih demokratov (ZLSD)*; United List of Social Democrats

http://www.sls.si/ *Slovenska ljudska stranka (SLS)*; Slovenian People's Party

http://www.desus.si/ *Demokraticna stranka upokojencev Slovenije (DeSUS)*; Democratic Pensioners Party

http://www.sds.si/ *Slovenska demokratska stranka (SDS)*; Slovenian Democratic Party

http://www.sns.si/ *Slovenska nacionalna stranka (SNS)*; Slovenian National Party

http://www.nsi.si/ *Nova Slovenija - Krscanska ljudska stranka (NSi)*; New Slovenia - Christian People's Party http://www.sms.si/ *Stranka mladih Slovenije (SMS)*; Youth Party of Slovenia

b) *Non-parliamentary* (consulted 15th -18th of March 2004 and supplemented on 27th of July 2004)

http://www.zeleni.si/ *Zeleni Slovenije (ZS)*; Greens of Slovenia
http://www.sgn.net/~zoranp/ds/stranka.htm *Demokratska stranka Slovenije (DS)*; Slovenian Democrats
http://www.glaszensk.si/ *Glas zensk Slovenije (GZS)*; Voice of Women
http://users.volja.net/mrmilan/kps.htm *Komunisticna partija Slovenije (KPS)*; Communist Party of Slovenia
http://www.republikanci.si/ *Republikanci Slovenije (RS)*; Republicans of Slovenia
http://www.seg.si/slo/ *Stranka ekoloskih gibanj Slovenije (SEG)*; Ecological Movement of Slovenia
http://zzpkp.naspletu.com/ *Zveza za Primorsko (ZZP)*; Association for Primorska Region
http://freeweb.siol.net/insignij/firme/ssn/program.htm *Stranka Slovenskega naroda (SSN)*; Slovenian Nation's Party
http://www.nds.si/nds.php *Nova demokracija Slovenije (NDS);* New Democracy of Slovenia
http://www.aktivnaslovenija.si/ Aktivna Slovenija (AS); Active Slovenia
http://www.sjn.si/ Slovenija je nasa (SJN); Slovenia is ours
http://www.zveza-zns.si/ Zveza neodvisnih Slovenije (ZNS); Association of Independents of Slovenia
http://www.progresivna-stranka.si/ *Progresivna stranka (PS)*; Progressive party
http://www.nova-stranka.si/ *Nova stranka (NS)*; New Party (web link is not working)

---

[1]   It is important to realise that these models are theoretical constructions. In fact they are ideal types. In the reality of political systems and views several of them can be combined, often in contradictory ways (Van Dijk, 1996: 46)

[2]   Every political system of parliamentary democracy also has non-registered political parties (usually minor, non-influential, publicly unknown and locally based). Since official data on their number and names does not exist in Slovenia we excluded them from empirical research.

[3]   Ministry of Internal Affairs of Republic of Slovenia (MNZ RS): http://www.mnz.si/si/urupnot.php?men=menu/M1324.inc&tekst=Seznam%20politi_nih%20strank&d at= upl/uru pnot/stranke.htm

[4]   As noted during research, those e-poll applications are usually design in order to get already formed public opinion standing (similar to TV or news papers polls) and not to identify public opinion that derives from deliberative public debate or consultation.

[5]   As noted, those forums were not design in order to enable focused, moderated and deliberated public debate on certain political issue which would result in qualitive public oppinion formation. Contrary to discursive usage of this e-democracy tool, political parties e-forums mainly are understood as public place for expresing individual and plain political positions, attacking political opponents, advertising political ideologies and engaging in fruitless personal debates.

[6]   At this point we are not discussing friendlines of information delivery and quality of information itself.

[7]   In some cases parties web sites provided sort of possibilities for citizens to directly express and consult their standings with political parties and their leaders but they were rather informal, non deliberative and non binding. For example governmental party LDS (Liberal Democracy of Slovenia) enabled citizens to fulfill e-questionnaire on priorities concerning future development of Slovenia and provided informal chat room application between party leaders and citizens http://www.lds.si/kiosk.cp2 (consulted on 27th of July 2004). Parliamentary parties such as SLS (Slovenian People's Party), NSi (New Slovenia - Christian People's Party), SNS (Slovenian National Party) and ZLDS (United List of Social Democrats) enabled citizens to publicly comment news, statement and articles provided on parties web sites. Parliamentary opposition party SDS (Slovenian Democratic Party) also provided possibility to comment members of parliament statements in documents from parliamentary sessions http://seja.sds.si/ (consulted on 27th of July 2004).

[8]   See also Franz (2003)

[9]   http://www.uvi.si/slo/slovenija/naslovi-povezave/stranke/ List of Slovenian parliamentary political parties web sites (consulted on 15th of March 2004)

ICT in Medicine and Health Care: Assessing Social, Ethical and Legal Issues

Goran Collste, Penny Duquenoy, Carlisle George, Karin Hedström,
Kai Kimppa, Emilio Mordini
Linkoping University, Sweden, gorco@cte.org.liu.se
Middlesex University, UK, p.duquenoy@mdx.ac.uk
Middlesex University, UK, c.george@mdx.ac.uk
Örebro University, Sweden, karin.hedstrom@esi.oru.se
University of Turku, Finland, kakimppa@it.utu.fi
Centre for Science, Society and Citizenship, Italy, e.mordini@bioethics.it

Abstract. Continuous developments in information and communication technologies (ICT) have resulted in an increasing use of these technologies in the practice of medicine and in the provision of medical care. This paper presents a series of perspectives from different areas of expertise on some of the ways in which ICT has changed the social picture in respect of the practice of medicine. The aim of the paper is to provide a context for further debate, in the form of a Panel Session, where the issue of Human Choice and Computing can be discussed with reference to a set of specific scenarios. The authors of this paper represent a wide variety of disciplines including law, ethics, medicine, philosophy and computer science, thus bringing a broad perspective to begin the discussions. The aim of the session is to provoke further discussion, encouraging input from other disciplines respresented by the participants, with a view to identifying the level of human choice in a social arena, which has at its heart a vulnerable community. In this environment, and in this era, the 'social' in social informatics has never been more important.

Keywords: social impact, medical informatics, online healthcare.

1 Overview

Continuous developments in information and communication technologies (ICT) - including the Internet, ambient devices, and intelligent computer systems - have resulted in an increasing use of these technologies in the practice of medicine and in

Please use the following format when citing this chapter:

Collste, G., Dequenoy, P., George, C., Hedström, K., Kimppa, K., Mordini, E., 2006, in IFIP International Federation for Information Processing, Volume 223, Social Informatics: An Information Society for All? In Remembrance of Rob Kling, eds. Berleur, J., Numinen, M. I., Impagliazzo, J., (Boston: Springer), pp. 297–308.

the provision of medical care. This has led to new concerns regarding the social impact of technology in medicine. Such concerns range from how information technology has changed the practice of medicine and the resulting social consequences, to how the practice of medicine responds to the increasing pervasiveness of technology in our daily lives. The aim of this panel discussion is to identify, review, analyse and debate the social impact of ICT on the practice of medicine. It will focus on various topics such as online medical consultations, online pharmacies, telemedicine, medical information systems, intelligent and ambient medical technologies, and patient autonomy among others. Within all of these topics the central theme of human choice is evident. In some cases technology appears to offer individuals greater choice (for example, online medical consultations, pharmacies, and appliances in the home) and in others the move to technology may constrain individual choice in the practice of health care.

The primary objective of the panel session is to identify the extent to which human choice is encouraged, or diminished, as a consequence of introducing ICT to this specific area. The discussions may reveal that in the health-care field, where the impact of technology can bring both huge benefits and potential disasters, critical choices have to be made. In meeting this objective, and in order to gain a broad perspective, the panel will draw on the expertise of a wide variety of disciplines including law, ethics, medicine, philosophy and computer science. Members will present the current state of affairs from their different perspectives and also comment on possible developments in the future (e.g. electronic implants).

In the following sections the Panel Members describe the areas of their own particular concerns in respect of ICT and the health-care domain, and thus give context to the discussions that all authors hope will form the basis of the session.

2   Position Statements

2.1   Goran Collste

Professor of Applied Ethics Centre for Applied Ethics, Linköping University, Sweden

Ethics of e-medicine
The Internet is more and more used for providing medical information, medical consultation and drug prescriptions. Medical information can be found on an increasing number of medical information site[1], [Parker & Muir Gray, 2001; Garpenby & Hisberg, 2000] patients can consult doctors on line, patients can get access to their medical record through Internet and drugs can be bought on line. Hence, health care is going through a transformation due to different applications of e-medicine.

E-medicine has a number of possible benefits. Patients (and prospective patients) can be better informed about illnesses, drugs and possible treatments. Through consulting an Internet-doctor patients can get a second opinion and become less dependent on local health care. Access to the medical record can give the patients quick and accurate information about their health status. These gains are also important from an ethical point of view. For example, one condition for realising the nowadays highly regarded principle of autonomy in health care is that patients are well informed [Beauchamp & Childress, 1989].

However, it is also possible to envisage a number of ethical problems related to the new development. Internet is a source of medical information but more information is not necessarily beneficial for moral autonomy. Information must be objective as well as comprehended and understood. Do the information sites live up to standards of accuracy and relevance? Pharmaceutical companies own many sites. How does this fact affect objectivity and impartiality? [Silberg, Lundberg & Musacchio, 1997].

The possibility to consult a doctor on line will have implications for the patient-doctor relationship. The medical encounter has for many years been an issue for discussions in medical ethics [Pellegrino & Thomasma, 1981]. The relation between doctor and patient is embedded by values of commitment, trust, privacy, confidentiality and responsibility. One can distinguish between different kinds of relationship like, for example, dialogical, instrumental and contractual. In connection to the new possibility of consultation on the Internet one can ask what kind of relation will be established between patient and doctor on line.

A system for an Internet-based patient portal is tried out in Swedish health care. Through the system a patient can get direct access to his/her own medical record. How will this possibility influence the quality of the medical record? Will it perhaps imply that the doctor may leave out some sensitive or harmful information about the patient?

Prescription of drugs is in many countries surrounded by restrictions motivated by solicitude for the patient and avoidance of abuse. Such a policy of weak paternalistic restrictions has a moral basis in principles of non-maleficence and beneficence. The unrestricted marketing of drugs on the Internet runs the risk of undermining this policy.

Common to most kinds of e-medicine is the transcendence of borders. Neither are Internet-based sources of medical information nor Internet-mediated medical consultation restricted to one nation or to one culture. As a consequence the culturally bound values that surround health care are challenged. Hence, the issue of how e-medicine can be ethically assessed must also take the fact of ethical pluralism into consideration.

2.2 Penny Duquenoy

Senior Lecturer in Computing and Ethics, Middlesex University, The Burroughs, London, UK

Technology and the self-help patient: issues of competence and understanding
There is an increasing trend towards utilising the latest developments in technology to facilitate patient self-help and health management. The combination of intelligent systems, hand-held devices and mobile technologies offer a range of applications designed to support patients' independent lifestyles whilst maintaining contact with

healthcare professionals. Some current examples are: self-monitoring of sugar levels for people with diabetes, together with data link via mobile phone to the medical practitioner [Fleming, 2005]; intelligent monitoring devices in the home for people with potential cognitive difficulties (for example, the elderly) that will alert remote carers [Pollack, 2005]; intelligent materials (used as clothing) that can monitor "vital health data, communicate with remote health centres and present data in a variety of formats for further analysis by doctors and researchers" (EU Project).

These applications are to be applauded in their concept, which is to allow patients the opportunity of living a 'normal' life. In some cases, the diabetes self-management system for example, empowering the patient by showing them patterns of sugar levels, so they can recognise and adapt their habits appropriately. The benefits to the healthcare profession are in allowing monitoring of the patients' condition without the need for physical presence.

However, while these systems help to 'manage' a health situation, they can also reduce patient autonomy. Where technology is employed, and where individuals using this technology are ignorant of how the technology works, it is arguable to what extent they can be said to be 'informed' or in control. The patient is likely to be (in computing science terms) a 'novice user'. That is, a user with little comprehension of how the device works, and its possible consequences. Although there has been, and still is, a great deal of research in the field of usability and computing it is, in most cases, conducted with the 'average' user in mind. We should bear in mind though, that where technology is employed in the medical field, the patient who is the user is likely to be not only a novice, but may have additional difficulties in using technology as a result of either physical or cognitive difficulties.

The patient group represents a particularly vulnerable community, for which competence levels may vary – not only between one individual and another, but also for any one individual over a period of time. For example, the patient may have an illness that affects their cognitive ability at different times (the diabetes patient, for instance). A deficit in cognitive performance may have an adverse effect on their ability to effectively use the technology provided, with possibly disastrous consequences.

A rather less visible concern is where intelligent devices are used in patient care. If these devices are making decisions regarding the health status of the patient (as in the intelligent clothing example), questions relating to decision-making processes must be investigated. If future devices incorporate decision-making methods (such as from Artificial Intelligence, and/or multi-agent systems) it is important to know the basis on which the decisions are being made. Can we be sure, for example, that the data, which informs the decision, is accurate? Some thought should also be given to what constitutes a 'decision' – this is particularly relevant in terms of patient personal data, whereby the Data Subject has "The right to prevent decision making solely by automatic means" (UK Data Protection Act).

Incorporating complex technological systems into the healthcare picture, and in particular placing these systems in the hands of the patients, creates a tension. On the one hand the systems are aimed at benefiting the patient, and on the other they place an extra burden on the patient in terms of technological understanding and management.

From the point of view of the health-care professional, how are they to ascertain 'informed consent' if the patient does not understand how the technology works, or its possible consequences? Will the technology have to be explained to patients, together with all the implications of data transfer and medical impact (in the physiological sense). What are the criteria for informed consent? Should a list be devised? How will it be judged that such consent has been given (and that the patient fully understands the information that has been given)?

Whilst these technologies may be welcomed by practitioners and patients alike, offering increased levels of independence for some health conditions, that independence carries further responsibilities. The patient needs to understand not only the operation of the technology with regard to their own condition, but also in relation to the wider world. Modern devices can have an impact on other devices, as the following 'safety information' [Nokia, 2005] makes clear:

"Operation of any radio transmitting equipment, including wireless phones, may interfere with the functionality of inadequately protected medical devices. Consult a physician or the manufacturer of the medical device to determine if they are adequately shielded from external RF energy or if you have any questions. Switch off your device in health care facilities ...

Pacemaker manufacturers recommend that a minimum separation of 15.3cm be maintained between a wireless phone and a pacemaker to avoid potential interference ... If you have any reason to suspect that interference is taking place, switch off your device immediately.

Hearing aids: some digital wireless devices may interfere with some hearing aids. If interference occurs, consult your service provider ..."

[Source: instruction booklet provided with Nokia 6680, November 2005.]

Note how it is the user who has to (a) understand and know that their device (in this case an ordinary mobile phone) may cause problems, and (b) take steps to deal with it (consult their physician, manufacturer, or service provider, or switch it off). If hand-held devices are to be used for self-management of health care the problems of radio transmission outlined above could well apply – not just to the patient, but also to others in their vicinity. In the case of the mobile phone extract quoted above the responsibility is on the user, and it should be remembered that our user – the patient – is by definition unwell. They may find it difficult to cope, both with the information received and with managing their devices, thus increasing stress. Further work is needed to assess the capability of patients (and healthcare professionals) in using the new technologies, to determine appropriate levels of training, and above all to recognise that technology may not be the best answer for all patients.

2.3 Carlisle George

Barrister and Senior Lecturer in Computing and IT Regulation, Middlesex University, The Burroughs, London

ICT in healthcare: some legal concerns

Information and communication (ICT) technologies in medicine and medical care arguably bring benefits to medical practitioners and patients [e.g. see Hodge et al, 1999]. There are, however, many legal concerns about the use and operation of these technologies which include the Internet (e.g. online pharmacies, telemedicine, email) and information systems (e.g. computerised databases holding electronic patient records and other medical data). This discussion will focus on some legal issues related to use of these two technologies.

The Internet is increasingly being used to provide healthcare, in various ways including the operation of Internet Pharmacies. An important legal concern with Internet Pharmacies is whether medical practitioners and pharmacists providing online/distant services are licensed to practice their respective professions in the respective jurisdictions where they and their patients are located. Related to this is issue is whether drugs offered to patients are legally approved in the jurisdiction where the patient is located. Internet Pharmacies also provide online consultations (via online questionnaires), which are used as a basis for issuing prescriptions and selling prescription drugs. The writing of prescriptions via online consultation raises important legal issues especially related to confidentiality and civil liability for medical malpractice should something go wrong [Kahn et al, 2000]. With regard to confidentiality, information given for online consultations may be prone to be seen by people other then the consulting doctor, unless strict security and protocols are in place. Patients may have no way of knowing whether or not such breaches have occurred and hence may not be able to address them. With regard to civil liability, it may be difficult to clearly establish malpractice where an online prescription is issued. This is because whereas in a traditional doctor-patient relationship a clear duty of care exists, it is debatable whether a doctor who prescribes medication online (without any direct verbal or physical contact with a patient), forms a doctor-patient relationship and therefore attracts a duty of care [Kahn et al, 2000]. In view of the above, can online patients, legally address issues of medical malpractice, especially where the medical practitioner is located in a distant nation state? If not, what legal mechanisms need to be put in place to address this issue?

Telemedicine involves the use of ICT to deliver health care (information and services) to patients separated (from medical providers) by geographic boundaries [Bashshur, 1995]. A main legal concern with telemedicine is the issue of jurisdiction in terms of (a) whether a medical provider has the necessary license to practice in the jurisdiction where he/she is situated and also where the patient is situated; (b) determining the procedural issue of where an action can be brought against a medical provider for malpractice. Within the EU jurisdiction is addressed by the Brussels Regulation, which determines where actions in tort and contact can commence, however, this may be more difficult to resolve where countries not governed by the Brussels Regulation are involved. Another legal concern is the possible liability for malpractice for either transmitting or receiving an inaccurate telemedical opinion [Hodge et al, 1999]. This raises issues such as: the timing and nature of the doctor-patient relationship; and the reliability of technology used in telemedicine. How can one legally determine when a doctor-patient relationship begins and the extent of the duty of care owed to the patient? How can one legally address errors which may be due to either (or a combination of) the doctor's medical competence, the failure to use the technology properly or the failure/reliability of the technology itself? One electronic technology used in telemedicine is email. Use of email in telemedicine raises the legal issue of doctor-patient confidentiality among other issues [see Spielberg, 1998] since a doctor has a duty to keep all patient information confident. Emails are subject to being intercepted during transmission and can be read by others having access to the doctor's mailbox. Such privacy breaches are usually very difficult to prosecute due to the need for adequate evidence (such as security trails). The contents of emails can also form part of a patient's medical record and emails are recoverable from servers even when deleted. Are patients adequately informed of the potential issues regarding email communication? Who is responsible for compensating the patient if email correspondence is compromised during transmission?

Information systems in healthcare are often used to store, access and transmit electronic medical data. These activities include implementing computerised databases and facilitating data exchange. Compared to physical records, electronic records can be easily accessed (by many people in different locations), searched, changed, copied and transmitted across networks. Also, inadequate security can result in unauthorised access and interception of communications (especially email). The above raises many legal concerns such as maintaining the: privacy of patient (identifiable) data; quality and reliability of patient data; and confidentiality (obligation in both tort and contract) of patient information [Hodge et al, 1999].

The protection of medical data is extremely important since unauthorised access, modification or disclosure can adversely affect a patient (e.g. wrong treatment, stigmatisation, discrimination). In the European Union (EU), personal data (collected from a 'data subject') is protected under data protection legislation, which address issues such as subjects' rights regarding disclosure of personal data, limitations on disclosure without consent, duty to maintain accuracy and integrity of personal data, the provision of adequate security against unauthorised access of personal data, and strict conditions for the transfer of personal data outside the EU. The effectiveness of EU data protection law, however, must be examined in light of the many exceptions which are given in the Act. For example under the United Kingdom (UK) Data Protection Act 1998 (which implements EU legislation), 'sensitive personal data' (which includes medical records, racial origin, criminal records among others) must not be processed without the explicit consent of data subject. The law, however, makes an exemption to this requirement where the processing of data is necessary for medical purposes and is carried out by a health professional or anyone owing a duty of confidentiality (*Data Protection (Processing of Sensitive Personal Data) Order 2000, Article 8(5))*. This exemption clearly introduces a weakening of subjects' rights since the 'processing' of data includes a variety of activities such as amending, augmenting, deleting, re-arranging and extracting information (*Data Protection Act 1998, Section 1(7))*. While this is counterbalanced by the lawful provision of subject access to medical records in the 1998 Act, the law also exempts the grant of access, if in the opinion of a relevant health professional such access would result in serious physical or mental harm to the data subject or any other person (*The Data Protection (Subject Access Modification) (Health) Order 2000*). Does UK/EU data protection legislation provide the right balance between patients' rights and the needs of the medical profession? Should patients have an absolute legal right to their records?

2.4 Karin Hedström

Senior Lecturer, Department of Informatics, Orebro University, Sweden.

IT as a prerequisite for the realization of care services

Earlier research of IT in elderly care has often viewed IT as a tool for administration and management [e.g. Beck, 1997], and not as a way of providing support that facilitates the care worker's meeting with the elderly. This is in line with the prevalent view of administrative tasks in elderly care, where it is common, notably in organization wide IT systems, to separate administrative tasks and care activates. Administration and the use of IT systems for coordination and administration are frequently viewed as an obstacle that prevents care workers from doing their 'real job'. Administration is not always well integrated in the care related activities and thus not seen as part of the care work. Administrative tasks as well as its tools are often treated and viewed as separate from the core of care work. Administration is seen as a negative activity that takes time from the 'real work'.

IT systems and administration are often seen as separate from the care giving organisation, and care professionals are furthermore often forced to prioritize administrative tasks on the expense of more care related tasks, with antagonism against the new IT system as a consequence [see also Wilson, 2002]. Care tasks and administrative tasks are often inadequately integrated, both in relation to the care worker's professional role and the content of care work.

To use the concept 'administration', instead of for instance 'information transfer' or 'communication', which describes the functions of the IT systems in elderly care more accurate, indicates alienation and distancing. To 'administer' is often, by the care workers, viewed as a destructive activity, even though it mostly involves necessary tasks such as to be informed and inform others. Care work requires sufficient and accurate information, which makes administration, in the form of communication and knowledge transfer, vital. To communicate, orally or via documents or tools such as IT systems, is necessary in order to provide safe and high quality care. Why is administration seen as such a negative work task? And why are there still so many 'failed' IT systems in healthcare? Another interesting question is the role of the care professional in relation to IT? What is it to produce care services? What is included and what is the role of the care professional?

2.5 Kai Kimppa and Janne Lathtiranta

Kai Kimppa: Lecturer, Department of Information Technology, University of Turku and Turku Centre for Computer Science (TUCS/LABORIS) focusing on the ethical aspects of ISs.

Janne Lahtiranta: Research Associate, Turku Centre for Computer Science (TUCS/HMII), Finland, focusing on health and medical informatics.

Health and Medical Informatics and Responsibility: What are the Roles of Anthropomorphism and Informed Consent in a Distributed World?
Anthropomorphism, or humanisation, of the artefacts of ICT used in medicine and health care, has an impact on the relationship between the patient and the health care professional [Lahtiranta & Kimppa, 2004]. Anthropomorphism can manifest in many different ways: the artefacts can be designed to interact with the user in a human-like manner, or the artefacts can encapsulate the decision making process behind a result or recommendation, creating an illusion that the information is provided by a human expert and not by, for example, some medical instrument or application. In addition, the artefacts are often anthropomorphised by the users themselves, it is not uncommon to hear a user to blame a system or application by saying 'it is not my fault - the machine did it!'

The decisions originating from an artefact of ICT used in medicine or in health care should be analyzed by a trained professional(s) and in practice never relied upon automatically. This is usually the case, but there are situations where it is nearly impossible for the verification process to be executed by a human. For example, in calculation-intensive work the verification is sometimes beyond human capabilities. The artefact could also be implemented in such fashion that the professional is intentionally removed from the decision making process, such as with certain 'black-box applications' used in diabetes. These applications analyze patient's condition, calculate and ration the medication to be applied by the patient automatically.

The fact that the artefacts of ICT used in health care or medicine are used to overcome geographical distances and cultural barriers creates a problematic situation. First, this brings forth an issue of who (or even what) answers to the consultation request. Second, it raises the question of relevant authority; the answer may originate from a location which belongs to a completely different jurisdiction from the one the request was submitted. Should a problem arise with the given treatment, which legislation is to be used? Third, reliance to the given advice, or overriding advice of a health care professional with it, could lead to problems. If the professional relies to the advice and the treatment is not successful, this can be pointed out and the professional could be accused of over-relying on the advice. On the other hand, should the health care professional choose to override the advice because of their professional expertise, the system typically can be shown to be consulted, and overwritten, and a malpractice suit be brought forth. These kinds of reliability problems are not just a matter of possibly near-future expert systems based on artificial intelligence technologies, but more closely to the everyday hospital information systems, if the source of the advice is not known or it is obscure by nature.

If the health care professional cannot always be aware of the source of information, consultation or recommendation, how could the patient? With who (or what) does the patient-health care professional form a relationship? Surely not with an artefact of ICT. With the party responsible of implementing the original health care procedures on the artefact? With the party who decided that this kind of artefact could be utilized in this particular situation? What kind of (informed) consent issues should be taken into account? These questions are more current now than ever before due to the ongoing health care paradigm shift in the western highly industrialized countries where responsibility of one's personal care is becoming more and more one's personal matter.

2.6 Emilio Mordini

Medical doctor and Coordinator of the EU funded project BITE – Biometric Identification Technology Ethics (www.biteproject.org).

Automatic Identification Technology in Medical and Social Care
Accurate identification and verification of identity is important at many levels in social and medical care. First the need to administrate scarce resources in social and medical care creates an imperative to avoid the illicit use of social welfare and medical support. Within a few decades, nearly half the European population will be at retirement age or beyond, placing a great burden on the European economy. Identification technologies will increasingly play a critical role as a gatekeeper of future healthcare and social services. Departments in charge of social assistance in countries like Spain and the Netherlands are already launching programmes for detecting and preventing duplicate benefits. This is a kind of fraud that involves the collection of more benefits than one is entitled to, by entering the program under two or more identities. A wide consensus appears to exist concerning the high levels of this type of fraud, and heighten the urgency for establishing new identification practices. It is claimed that the introduction of identification / verification of identity technologies would result in billions of savings on public spending. Unauthorized use of assistance programmes (e.g., heroin addicts who participate in methadone maintenance plans) could be tackled by using automatic systems for identification (both to authenticate people and to track medications, for instance by using RFID or other electronic tags). In addition, people are accessing more and more social services over the Web; for this to be secure, establishing people's identity is essential. Finally, among the most important healthcare issues that directly affect patient safety and quality of care are the ability to correctly identify patients and to confirm the accurate delivery of clinical services for those patients. In health care we need to know that the clinician is administering the right medication to the right patient, each and every time. Identification technologies such as biometrics and RFID are already in use to identify and track special categories of patients in hospitals. Pilots are in progress in Italy, Spain and the Netherlands. RFID has been in use since 2004 in California to track organs for transplants. Concerns have been raised about the ethical and social implications of identification technologies, when they touch areas of personal life where one would not ordinarily expect to be identified and tracked, such as healthcare and social services. In this area, individuals must face a decision to trade their personal data for gain, affecting the balance between ease of use and levels of security and protection of privacy. Citizens often must waive their data protection rights if they wish to receive many services. This is not purely a privacy issue, because it involves important ethical questions, such as the conflict between the individual's autonomy and social pressure. On the other hand, there is also a conflict between personal freedom to trade one's personal data and what society at large considers desirable or ethically acceptable in this field.

3   Conclusion

The position statements above have focused on various perspectives on ICT in medicine and health care. They are a critical reflection on aspects of the politics of the information society, because they discuss important issues regarding the effect of information technology use on the individual and society as a whole. They also focus on the common theme of 'human choice' whether viewed from an ethical, legal or social dimension. It is hoped that the contributions will provide a springboard for interesting discussions which will bear fruitful solutions to address some of the concerns raised.

References

Bashshur, L (1995) On the definition and evaluation of telemedicine. *Telemed J* 1995; 1:19-30.

Beauchamp, T L & Childress, J F, (1989). *Principles of Biomedical Ethics*, Oxford: Oxford University Press

Beck, E. (1997). Managing Diffracted Rationalities: IT in a Home Assistance Service. *Technology and Democracy: Gender, Technology and Politics in Transition?* Moser, I. and Aas, G.H., Eds, Centre for Technology and Culture, University of Oslo, Oslo: 109-132.

EU Project: WEALTHY. Source: Virtual Medical Worlds, Monthly Newsletter. http://www.hoise.com/vmw/05/articles/vmw/LV-VM-06-05-37.html. (06/12/2005)

Fleming, Nic. 'Mobile phone link reduces chance of diabetes problems' 29/08/2005 at http://www.telegraph.co.uk/news. (06/12/2005)

Garpenby, P & Hisberg, M, 2000, *Hälsoinformation idag och imorgon,* CMT Rapport 2000:3, Linköpings universitet, Linköping (unpublished)

Hodge, J, Gostin, L and Jacobson, P (1999). Legal issues concerning electronic Health information: Privacy, Quality and Liability. *JAMA* October 20, 1999, Vol 282, No 15.

Kahan, S, Seftel A and Resnick, M (2000) Sildenafil and the Internet. *The Journal of Urology,* Vol. 163, 919-923, March 2000

Lahtiranta, J. & Kimppa, K. (2004) Telemedicine and responsibility: why anthropomorphism and consent issues muddle the picture. *The 5th International We-B (Working For E-Business) conference*, 25-26 November, Perth, Western Australia.

Parker, M & Muir Gray, J A (2001). What is the role of clinical ethics support in the era of e-medicine?, *Journal of Medical Ethics,* 2001; 27, suppl I:i 33-35

Pellegrino, E D & Thomasma, D C, 1981 *A Philosophical Basis of Medical Practice*, Oxford, Oxford University Press

Pollack, Martha E. (2005) 'Intelligent Technology for an Aging Population' *AI Magazine*, Vol.26:2, Summer 2005.

Silberg, W M, Lundberg, G D, Musacchio, R A (1997) Assessing, Controlling, and Assuring the Quality of Medical Information on the Internet, *Journal of American Medical Association*, 277:1244-1245

Spielberg, A (1998) On Call and Online, *JAMA* October 21, 1998, Vol 280, No 15.

Wilson, M. (2002). 'Making nursing visible? Gender, technology and the care plan as script.' *Information Technology & People* 15(2): 139-158.

Notes

---

[1]   There are currently between 15,000 and 100,000 health-related sites in Great Britain and they have been visited by approximately 30 million people. A Swedish survey showed that of those that accessed the Internet, about 20% had been looking for health-related information (see Parker & Muir Gray, 2001; Garpenby & Hisberg, 2000).

Internet in the Street Project: Helping the Extremely Poor to Enter the Information Society

Corinne Chevrot, Emmanuelle Comtat, Gwenaël Navarette, Bruno Oudet,
Jean-Pierre Pinet
ATD Quart Monde France,
jeanpierre.pinet@atd-quartmonde.org, http://www.atd-quartmonde.o
Leibniz Laboratory, University of Grenoble, France,
bruno.oudet@imag.fr, http://www-leibniz.imag.fr

Abstract. The most common measures so far to reduce the digital divide has been the development of telecentres (Internet public access points) that provide Internet access and specific training. However, the extremely poor very rarely enter the telecentres. In this paper, we propose a more specific approach suited to this population. We first describe the social-digital exclusion process facing the extremely poor, its inputs, its outputs, and our approach to help the poor to start to integrate the information society. We then present stories collected during our field actions in our *Internet in the street* project. We conclude by presenting what we have learnt so far.

Keywords: digital divide, extremely poor

1   Introduction

It is now obvious that what we call the information society will have a growing impact on communication, education, knowledge acquisition and the development of social relations. It is thus a matter of respect of human rights to work so that we leave no one behind, especially the persons who may need it most. Among those experiencing exclusion are illiterate populations, people with disabilities, inhabitants in remote areas and the extremely poor. In the literature, the gap that exists between communities taking advantages of the information society and those excluded from it called the digital divide [1]. Numerous actions have been proposed to reduce the digital divide during the United Nations Word Summit on the Information Society in Geneva (2003) [2] and Tunis (2005) [3]. The Digital Divide Network [4] coordinated

Please use the following format when citing this chapter:

Chevrot, C., Comtat, E., Navarette, G., Oudet, B., Pinet, J.-P., 2006, in IFIP International Federation for Information Processing, Volume 223, Social Informatics: An Information Society for All? In Remembrance of Rob Kling, eds. Berleur, J., Numinen, M. I., Impagliazzo, J., (Boston: Springer), pp. 309–318.

by Andy Carvin is the online forum where one can share experiences and knowledge on the subject.

In the digital divide debate, we can distinguish at least two schools of thought. One school embraces the working of the market forces to close progressively the digital divide; organizing and encouraging a true competition and providing training will do the job. For others, the digital divide is not an isolated symptom; it is just another expression of the social divides facing society. Fighting against the digital divide implies undertaking actions to reduce social exclusions. This second approach is the one retained by the eEurope Advisory Group in its July 2005 report [5].

The project presented in this paper is in line with this second approach. Our objective is the reduction of the digital divide for the extremely poor. These persons are in 'chronic poverty and lack of basic security'. They are also "Geographically segregated and socially isolated, they are cut off from the cultural, political and civil life of the country" [6]. We cannot reach the extremely poor via a top-down approach. It requires a collaborative approach that embraces the notion, 'let us learn together what Internet can bring in your daily life'. While working with the extremely poor we cannot avoid basic questions. Why are we emphasizing the use of Internet for the very poor? Don't the poor have other priorities such as finding jobs, keeping their families together? In truth, the poor themselves must provide answers to these questions. "The best informed experts on poverty are the poor". [6]

We first describe what we call the social-digital exclusion process facing the extremely poor: its inputs (causes), its outputs (consequences) and our approach to help the poorest to start to take advantage of the Information Society. We then present the Internet in the street project and our approach before telling stories collected during our action in the field. We conclude by presenting what we have learnt so far.

2   The Social-Digital Exclusion Process

Table 1 lists the inputs and the outputs of the social-digital exclusion process.

Table 1.   Inputs and outputs of the social-digital exclusion process

INPUTS Barriers to entry	OUTPUTS Participation to the IS
access to equipment	access to information
access to the net	communication
know-how	access to opportunities (employment,)
Illiteracy	access to knowledge (training…)
fear of the unknown, of ICT's impact	access to collective work, networking
lack of quality, culturally relevant content	creation of relevant content
Motivation	participation in the democratic process
feeling of exclusion	
existing social networks	

2.1 The Inputs

Lack of access to equipment and to the net is of course a factor of exclusion of the Information Society. The world devotes much effort to reduce these two sources of exclusion. The computer + connectivity mix is however not sufficient. They are other major causes to the exclusion process. The lack of expertise to use a computer is one of them. Much work remains to simplify the computer interface, to make it more easily accessible and user friendly.

'I am not intelligent enough to use a computer' 'I am a hand worker, it is not for me' are reaction we often hear. This reaction concern more than just basic ICT literacy or general literacy, as well as not understanding ICT's relevance in improving their quality of life.

The lack of motivation is another important obstacle. The very poor families are often facing difficult situations. Their interest for using Internet such as discovering images from their homeland, sending messages can disappear suddenly when they face problems that take their full attention.

The feeling of exclusion - 'it's not for me' - is another major obstacle. The majority of the persons we are meeting in our project have a strong feeling that the 'outside world' is not accessible. One person told us that the only places outside their homes where they felt safe are the shopping centers because they are looked upon as potential customers and not as strangers. The feeling of exclusion has its own dynamic: it increases with the development of the Information Society. In the 1980's, a very poor person said to Father Joseph Wresinski, the founder of ATD Fourth World movement 'I don't know to read, but I think that it will be even worst with Informatics'. The very poor realized at that time that this was a new important challenge facing them, and they felt excluded from this new world. The very poor social links are generally limited to their families and to their immediate neighborhood. Compared to others, they have more difficulties to realize that the Internet can help to develop social relations. Migrants are an exception, though, because they often perceive the benefits of email and the web to keep contact with their homeland.

In our project, it is relatively easy to bypass the material obstacles, and we are relatively successful in providing the sufficient knowledge to use the computer. What is very time consuming is the required human investment. The socioeconomic situation of the poor has deteriorated for such a long time that the action team needs first to rebuild the trusted relationship between the people they meet and themselves. It takes even more time to reconcile the extremely poor with their social environment (schools, libraries, and administration), overcoming racism, social exclusion, and creating relationship.

We also realize that our effort can be easily interrupted or even destroyed. For example, the relations with a group of people living in mobile homes were interrupted because an expulsion decision from the living quarter was decided during the summer 2005 by the local administration. Extreme poverty and social exclusion are like waves that unceasingly come to erase the sand castle built on the beach.

2.2 The Process: Moving from 'Digital Exclusion' to 'Participant in the Knowledge Society'

In the heart of the process are the commitments of persons from the civil society who are external to the world of extreme poverty. By the word commitment, we point at these voluntary acts of working with very poor populations despite all the many challenges associated with working in overcoming these situations.

Nevertheless, the commitments are not sufficient. We should create situations where the social links are restored, where the people we met have the possibility of meeting others with whom, thereafter, they will be able to interact over the Internet. For example, a person once active in our project in the Paris suburbs area left for Algeria. She started email exchanges with the poor communities she had encountered in Paris. Another example is a person who, touched by the situation of prisoners in Ivory Coast, started to send postcards to a volunteer working in that prison. This volunteer was later assigned to Bangui, in Central Africa, and the dialogue quite naturally continued with email.

A third aspect is the necessity of implying the very poor in the creation of robust, relevant content for the web. One of the obvious reasons for which a certain number of people do not use information and communication technologies is that they do not find content that interesting or relevant to them. Helping people to develop content to the Net contributes to fighting digital exclusion.

2.3 The Outputs

The outputs appear in Column 2 of Table1. We need to emphasize that these persons are facing many difficulties that are far away from the digital world. The Internet is not the sole solution to their problems. We thus have always to look for digital outputs that can be of interest to them.

One of the objectives currently put forward by UNESCO in its Community Multimedia Centers program [7] is to initiate changes that will increase the level of income of the community. This program stresses the potential economic impact on the poor communities, their access to their own rights and their cultural development. Nevertheless, does this approach have an impact on those *who are excluded from their community*?

We have always to remember that the inclusion into the information society is only one little contribution to the difficulties facing the very poor. It is a true challenge to develop a dynamic that can bring concrete benefits. For example, many Roma from Romania do not have the necessary documents to stay legally in France, despite the fact they will become European citizen in 2007. Their situation as illegal immigrants prevents them to have access to employment, healthcare, and even to school for their children. Unfortunately, this is a matter of political decision making which is outside the Internet domain even if Internet can be used to draw public attention on these situations.

3   The 'Internet in the Street' Project

In France as in other countries, many efforts are devoted to reduce the digital divide. They focus on providing computer and Internet access, as well as training. A recent report [8] on the public access point in the Ile de France region provides a good presentation on what is currently happening. A department within the French Ministry of Education is in charge of the follow-up of the public telecentres [9]. We can find a description on the ongoing research on the digital divide in [10].

Several initiatives were launched recently with objectives close to the ones of our project: in Paris, the telecentre in the Emmaüs NGO Agora [11], 'Le dire pour agir' web site of the Secours Populaire Français [12], 'paroles de rue', web site of the NGO 'aux captifs la liberation' [13] and 'Couleur Quartier' in Brest [14].

The 'Internet in the Street' project [15] was launched at the end of 2004. Its goal is to conduct research to study how the Internet can help to create or restore the socials links for very poor communities. We choose the 'Internet in the Street' appellation to refer to the library in the street, which is an on going ATD Fourth World project for many years. In addition, we wanted the project to be a continuation of 'computer in the street' projects that the ATD Fourth World carried out with children in the 1980s [16]. In our project, we focus on helping adults, who generally are not as receptive to technology as young people.

The research team in the field consists of three volunteers (name given to ATD Fourth World full time collaborators). Two researchers in Grenoble are in charge of the follow-up and of the links with the scientific world. We keep two web sites: one blog [17] and a web site open to various contributions and testimony [18]. We have weekly exchanges through a mailing list and we meet once a month in Paris. We hold in June and in October seminars with the team of the PSAUME project [19] that is studying how to reach the excluded persons in the Brest region.

The ATD volunteers have the same equipment: a computer with only one battery (access to electricity is still a problem), a card for multiple wireless accesses to the Internet (WIFI, GPRS, 3G, and EDGE), a color printer with battery, a digital camera.

Despite the title of our project, only one volunteer had spent a limited part of her time in the street with a computer to reach homeless persons. The action toward homeless takes place more easily 'under a roof' in places where they usually go by for a coffee, getting their postal mail. Two volunteers meet the very poor in their living quarters, mostly mobile homes or very low-rent apartments. All the volunteers have the same approach: they go to meet extremely poor people in their living places.

3.1   The Approach: Collaborative Learning with the Very Poor

It has been a long working tradition of ATD-Fourth World volunteers to learn in the field together with the very poor [20]. This approach of ethnographic nature observes and contributes to practices of everyday life. This contributes to a long immersion in the field and differs from the classical top-down research where the scientist puts forth assumptions and seeks to check them. In our project, we observe what the persons we meet consider as 'successful' actions; we then collect them and try to make sense of them [21].

3.2   Collected Stories

One of the main outputs of our project is the collection of stories written in our blog after our field work [17]. They are 'success stories' for people we meet: they express their way of finding a place in society. Based on these stories we shall provide in our final project report concrete suggestions for other NGO's willing to help the extremely poor persons to take advantage of the Information Society.

Voice over Internet
A volunteer tested voice communication by Internet with families in mobile homes using Skype. The objective was to speak to a person who visited their families last year. During the conversation a connected Romanian friend sought to speak to this volunteer. It was impressive for these families in the Val d'Oise (a remote suburb of Paris) to realize that they were able to speak with somebody living in Romania, only with this computer.

Information on the floods back home
From the very start of the project, Rrom families have shown great interest in obtaining news from their home country. At nearly each meeting, we look at newspapers online. Sometimes, we print an article that makes the tour of the camp. Since the beginning of the summer, a succession of floods had damaged Romania. They were all anxious for their families. This time, the newspaper posted a gallery of photographs on the floods in New Orleans. The person who was in front of the screen took much time to look at each photograph, asked the volunteer to translate the English legend. It was not simple curiosity; the expression was the glance of a person who knew the misfortune that strikes the poorest people. The Internet can reinforce people's compassion for others.

Looking for a job
A volunteer met in a community center a person living in the street. This person shared how invaluable Internet was in his search for jobs. He sent its Curriculum vitae, motivation letter by Internet to the e-mail address indicated on the job offers of the ANPE (the national agency in France in charge) web site, saving on post, train, and subway travel expenses. He noticed that companies quickly answer his mail whether it was negative or positive which is usually not the case when you contact the Company by postal mail. You also do not show them that you do not posses a permanent address, which is important for people combating homelessness. He found some short time jobs by this way.

Obtaining ID papers using the Internet
One person a volunteer have been meeting for months did not have his French national ID card, despite of the fact that he was born as a French citizen. He has been reluctant to contact the administration due to his others difficulties: living in a mobile home, isolated from the outside world. With the volunteer, they had already

gone together to fulfill a few administrative procedures. He had gone to the town hall on several occasions, in vain, unable to get his new ID card for lack of the necessary papers. He had lost hope of obtaining it. They started our search on Internet and filled an electronic form for getting a copy of his birth certificate. He obtained it by postal mail within two days without having to pay for a stamp. It gave him the feeling that finally he will be able to reach his goal. He now has his ID card, which gives him motivation for applying to a driving license.

Taking a picture and printing it: a simple application to develop social links
In mid-September of 2005, a volunteer visited the Rrom families. They have recently been working on taking pictures. However, this time, it was a veritable festival! Inside the mobile home, ten people were around the computer and the printer. We printed on A4 page a picture taken during our last meeting: it was almost 'magic' to them. Then, there was this 'old' digital camera, found somewhere, for which I had never succeeded in finding the driver. By chance with my flash reader, I was able to 'extract' and print the pictures. The pictures made the tour of the camps. The young person that returned them to me then had an idea: "I will send the camera to my mother who is still in my country. She will take photographs, and specially the one of my son whom I have not seen any more for two years. He was five years old when I left him. She will return the camera to me, and we will print them here."

Side effects
Even while paying attention, we do not always realize the type of change we are initiating. Recently, at the time of a meeting with other volunteers in the field, one of them told us: "You do not imagine what you initiated with your Internet. Mr. X (out of the employment world for a long time) gets up generally very late. As he knows that you are coming, he gets up earlier seeking an activity, a work to make him busy when you arrive". Within the framework of our cultural activities with children, it has been difficult to tackle the question of administrative papers with the parents, and especially with the men. With the help of our computer we carry to their homes, we can speak more easily about their papers.

These stories clearly validate the exclusion process presented in Table 1. We are very far from a simple digital divide process. Providing computers, access, and basic training is not sufficient; we need to bring IT to the very poor at the point that is the closest both to their living quarters and to their places of employment. By doing so we fight against their feeling of exclusion, we help them to recover confidence, starting a dynamic process that could help them to better face their difficult and delicate situations.

4   What Have We Learnt So Far?

We provide below a first list of findings after one and half year of this experimental project.
- Even if they do not constitute major obstacles, we should not neglect common technical problems: batteries, wireless access to the Internet, maintenance of the

machines, need for working under XP or equivalent (our 3G card recognizes only XP system). During several weeks the project was delayed (and is still) because one or the other component was deficient;

- The presence of a laptop computer facilitates contact with the people who live on the street. However, volunteers can intervene only after introduced by an already accepted and trusted person. It takes time and energy to make this acquaintance. The length of time to do so varies according to social backgrounds... In our case, the presence of the computer helps and some time shortens the time necessary to establish the contact.
- The computer brings in some way a 'neutral ground' that allows people with different history to begin exchanges. People living in the street feel the arrival of the ATD volunteer with a computer is a proof of confidence and of recognition. They also can discover the Internet, about which they have often heard on TV. The Internet is a good subject for introductions and launching discussions.
- We have always to be attentive to the concerns of the people we meet. People are often more demanding discussion than Internet use.
- People living in the street have very different sensibility and knowledge on the use of the computer due to their history. One can find in the street other persons who are able to help the ATD volunteer in the discovery and training of their companions.
- Once a relationship occurs, the dynamics can lead in unforeseeable directions. For example, as a by-product of our work we were able to convince NGO leaders who were very reluctant regarding our work. (They said it was a luxury that poor persons did not need!) Eventually, they became Internet pushers.
- The most popular applications: taking and printing pictures, finding news and writing to the family at home, help to obtain administrative papers, contributions to content on the web.
- We succeeded in creating relationships with libraries and NGOs, but we are also facing the lack of training of their staff to accept in their activities extremely poor people.
- After a time of discovery and learning on computer and Internet with extremely poor people, we continue our visits. Some ask us to participate to other activities. Because of the acquired trust, others ask us to undertake a more collective action.

5   Conclusion

Despite the overall growth of per capita incomes, the numbers of families facing chronic poverty in the wealthiest countries is increasing. To this population the development of the information society is an additional source of exclusion, as long as they too lack access and the skills to participate effectively. The fight against this new source of exclusion requires a lengthy, ongoing effort. In our project, we have been working for a short period of time (sixteen months in a very slow moving process) with a limited number of persons. Getting in contact with the poorest person, acquiring their trust, finding common ground of interest is a lengthy and delicate progress. Moreover, we faced a permanent obstacle: Individuals and families who are trying to deal with an accumulation of poverty-related problems can think of little else but meeting their basic needs [6]. We have to show concrete, real, and personal examples of what the Internet can bring to low-income communities. However, by doing so we are able to point to difficulties encountered by other excluded populations, including illiterate populations, the unemployed, senior citizens, and people with disabilities.

In the following months, we plan to complement our individual approach (one person, one family, a few persons in a camp) with a collective training closer to the one provided at telecentres. The group attending the training will be a combination of ATD Fourth World members and extremely poor persons keeping on the approach of collaborative learning. Our findings will complement the ones presented in this paper.

References

1. Digital divide, http://en.wikipedia.org/wiki/Digital_divide [3/29/2006]
2. WSIS Geneva Plan of Action, http://www.itu.int/wsis/docs/geneva/official/poa.html [3/29/2006]
3. WSIS Tunis Commitment and Tunis Agenda for the Information Society, http://www.itu.int/wsis/documents/index2.html [3/29/2006]
4. The Digital Divide Network, http://www.digitaldivide.net [3/29/2006]
5. eEurope Advisory Group, e-Inclusion: New challenges and policy recommendations, July 2005, http://europa.eu.int/information_society/eeurope/2005/all_about/advisory_group/documents/index_en.htm [3/29/2006]
6. Joseph Wresinski, Chronic Poverty and Lack of Basic Security, Report of the Economic and Social Council of France, 1987. http://www.atd-quartmonde.org/intern/fondam/Wres_JO87en.pdf [3/29/2006]
7. The UNESCO Community Media Centres, http://www.unesco.org/webworld/cmc [3/29/2006]
8. Etat des lieux du web public communal en 2005, ARTESI, http://www.artesi.artesi-idf.com/public/anv/dossier.tpl?preview=1&nolog&id=10933 [3/29/2006]
9. Délégation aux usages de l'Internet , Qu'est ce qu'un espace public numérique?, http://delegation.Internet.gouv.fr/netpublic/index.htm [3/29/2006]
10. Alain Rallet (Editeur) La fracture numérique, Revue Réseaux , 22/127-128 (2005)
11. Bilan d'activités des 18 premiers mois du cyberespace Agora-Emmaus, paris, http://www.a-brest.net/article1530.html [3/29/2006]
12. 'Le dire pour agir' website, http://www.ledirepouragir.net [3/29/2006]
13. Paroles de rue website, http://www.captifs.asso.fr/parolesrue/index.html [3/29/2006]
14. 'Couleur quartier' website, http://www.couleurquartier.infini.fr/ [3/29/2006]
15. The Internet in the street project, http://reso.blogs.com/crealiens/Usesofinternet.rtf [3/29/2006]
16. Bruno Tardieu, High Technology and Low-Income Communities: Prospects for the positive use of advanced Information Technology, 1985 MIT seminar on High Technologies and Low income,

http://www.mit.edu/afs/athena/org/s/sap/www/colloquium96/papers/12tardieu.html
[3/29/2006]
17. The Internet in the street blog, http://reso.blogs.com/crealiens, [3/29/2006]
18. The Internet in the street expression space, http://www.carnet-expression.org/ [3/29/2006]
19. Le site du projet PSAUME 'Populations Socialement défavorisées : Analyse des Usages et
    des Moyens de les Étendre', http://www.psaume.infini.fr/ [3/29/2006]
20. « Le croisement des savoirs : quand le Quart Monde et l'Université pensent ensemble »
    Collection Des Livres contre la misère, Éditions de l'Atelier/ Éditions Quart Monde, 1999
21. Jona Rosenfeld, Emergence from extreme poverty, editions Quart Monde, 1989,
    http://www.editionsquartmonde.org/live/detail_produit.php?parm_produit=149&parm_cat
    =98-NOUV&mots=emergence [3/17/2006]

ICT and Free Open Source Software in Developing Countries

Pia Krakowski

School of Economics and Commercial Law, University of Gothenburg,
Sweden, pia.krakowski@gmail.com

Abstract: The topic of this essay is if and how the use of information and communications technologies, (ICT), as well as the use of free open source software, can change the prerequisites of third world countries. Many people consider that the Internet is not only access to unlimited information, but also has a potential to make a difference in the development of human rights and democracy. Information and communications technologies, free software, and open source have a big role to play in this context. The importance of access is an issue: one tends to focus mainly on the physical access, which is only a small part in this connection. There are other types of limitations to access: the technology should be appropriate, be affordable, and a political will to provide all citizens with equal possibilities should support the introduction of the technologies. Who has access to these new technologies? Who does not have such access? Finally, we discuss a field study of an open source project in Namibia and their conclusions.

Keywords: access, digital divide, ICT, free open source software, developing countries

This essay assumes certain basic knowledge in the subject of free software, open source, and Information and Communication Technology. It is not the purpose to explain these concepts, ideas, and theories in this essay; we assume that the reader knows the background to different philosophies within the subject before reading the text below.

Common abbreviations that are used are:

FLOSS Free/Libre and Open Source Software
FOSS   Free Open Source Software
FSF   Free Software Foundation
ICT   Information and Communication Technology
IT   Information Technology

Please use the following format when citing this chapter:

Krakowski, P., 2006, in IFIP International Federation for Information Processing, Volume 223, Social Informatics: An Information Society for All? In Remembrance of Rob Kling, eds. Berleur, J., Numinen, M. I., Impagliazzo, J., (Boston: Springer), pp. 319–330.

OSS   Open Source Software
SNN   SchoolNet Namibia
TCO   Total Cost of Ownership

1   Introduction

The world is unfair. Some countries have stable economies and are at the forefront of the technical development; others are deeply in debt and have populations suffering from famine, disease, and poor economical and educational conditions. The gap between the industrialized world and the developing countries is still very large and if one studies in particular the information technological prerequisites the differences are enormous. What one in Sweden take for granted, there is at other places a lack of awareness about; at the same time as we discuss the speed of the broadband, large parts of the world still don't have a phone line connected into the village.

According to Statistiska Centralbyrån (Statistical Central Bureau), SCB, 82% of Sweden's population between the ages 16 and 74 had used the Internet in 2004. Disregarding the oldest people in the investigation, 55-74 years of age, the national average is about 90% [SCB, 2005-10-17]. This is a huge number if you compare it to rest of the world. According to the UN report *E-commerce and development report 2004* [UNCTAD, 2005-10-17] 12% (about 676 million people) of the world's population had Internet access by the end of 2003, which was an increase by 50 million people in comparison with the year before (2002). The largest part of this increase, 75%, took place in the developing world. Even if the number of Internet users is increasing in the developing countries, a few countries stand for the largest increase. China, Korea, India, Brazil, and Mexico inhabit 62% of all Internet users in third world countries [UNCTAD, 2005-10-17]. Africa has 12 million Internet users compared to North America's 175 million [UNCTAD, 2005-10-17] or Europe's 188 million users [UNCTAD, 2005-10-17]. Africa has slightly more Internet users then all the population of Oceana counted together (Australia, New Zeeland et cetera), about 12 million inhabitants [UNCTAD, 2005-10-17].

Can the introduction of free and open source software and the use of ICT in any way change the prerequisites of the developing countries? In what ways can free software, open source, and ICT change the development of a country? Is it the software that is the main need in focus for the developing world, or is it something else? Are the opinions about free and open software and ICT the same in the industrialized and the developing world?

This essay intends to give an overview of the different problems and possibilities with ICT and free and open software, and highlights the research and discussions under debate now. Further, we present a comparison between the political views of the subject in Europe and Africa. In addition, we provide a short summary and discussion about a Swedish study made in Namibia, performed by two students from the Department of Informatics at the University of Gothenburg.

2   Theory

The theory model of this essay is inductive, which in this context means that the author tried to derive general principles from known facts. Theories about ICT and the use of FOSS connect to a real life example in the description of the Namibia case study. This being a short essay, we should accept the reliability of the results with some reservations.

In what ways can ICTs matter in the context of developing countries? Many people consider, and the UN with them, that ICT can play an enormously big role for the development of the non-industrialized world. In the report *E-commerce and development report 2004*, the UN writes, "Information and communications technologies have considerable potential to promote development and economic growth. (...) In the hands of developing countries, (...) the use of ICTs can bring impressive gains in employment, gender equality and standards of living." [UNCTAD, 2005-10-17].

In this essay, the author will try to support the theory that the use of ICT and free open source software can change the prerequisites of developing countries. One of the arguments for this claim is the noted success of the Swedish government's commitment to enable Internet access for all its citizens. This is a good example of the need for a strong political will to enable the evolvement for any country to enter the IT era; it is also a good example of how one can decrease the digital divide within a country. Can you apply the example above from a western industrialized nation to the situation of the developing world? It is certainly not applicable to 100%, but this is where the importance of FOSS comes in. Free and open source software enables a cheaper way to introduce information and communication technologies to citizens of the developing world and by doing so, reducing the digital divide between and within these countries.

3   Discussion

3.1   General

The discussion of the importance of ICT and free software and its possibility to affect the conditions for many of the world's underdeveloped countries is a constant topic in many forums. Where large companies see disadvantages and feel the competition from the free software advocates, others mean that ICT and free software opens up for the possibilities for countries to give their inhabitants access to computers, applications and above all, the Internet. The Internet is not only the access to unlimited information, but also has a potential to make a difference in the development of human rights and democracy. Some mean that ICT, free software, and open source have a big role to play in this context. The website <www.bridges.org> is an organization that strives to give more people the possibility and access to ICT in developing countries. They are working with reducing what people call the digital divide between countries. With the concept of the digital divide, one can shortly say that it means the difference between the ones that have access to ICT and the ones that do not. On the Bridges website, one can read reports about different projects illustrating the use of open source software in different contexts to prepare developing countries for the possibilities of ICT. Bridges shows that free and open source software during the last couple of years have become a relevant alternative to non-free software[1] for countries that cannot afford to pay expensive licenses fees.

Bridges has recently published the report *Free/open source software (FOSS) policy in Africa: A toolkit for policy-makers and practitioners* at their website [bridges.org1, 2005-10-16]. The report is a support for governments that "... are investigating whether and how they can integrate FOSS into their strategies for social and economic development". The report discusses the African nations' attitudes against FOSS and it indicates that so far no African country has formulated a strategy that is in strong favor of FOSS as, for example, Brazil, Peru, and Malaysia have done. However, we note that several countries have at least started the work. The country that has reached the furthest with ICT in Africa is South Africa. The South Africa government has issued a policy regarding open source software (OSS), where it says that: "Government will implement OSS where analysis shows it to be the appropriate option. The primary criteria for selecting software solutions will remain the improvement of efficiency, effectiveness, and economy of service delivery by Government to its citizens. OSS offers significant indirect advantages. Where the direct advantages and disadvantages of OSS and PS (Proprietary Software) are equally strong and where circumstances in the specific situation do not render it inappropriate, opting for OSS will be preferable [bridges.org1, 2005-10-16]. Namibia, where a field study will be discussed later on in the essay, has a relatively large amount of FOSS related activities and users, where among others the organization SchoolNet Namibia (SNN) are leading a big campaign to install computers and free open source software's on schools all over the country.

3.2   Europe: Pragmatic and Social Reasons

Regarding Europe Rishab Aiyer Gosh recently published a report about the European Unions' attitude against FOSS, *The European Politics of F/OSS Adoption*. The report formed a port of a larger collection of reports published by the Social Science Research Council (SSRC), a New York based, independent organization of researchers and experts effective within different subject areas, such for example how ICT can be used to change the society and the conditions for its citizens [Gosh, 2005-10-18]. The report discusses several practical example of different FOSS projects and strategies, as for example the German city of Munich's' commitment to Linux, called LiMux. Rishab Aiyer Gosh means that there are two big reasons for the positive attitude within EU against FOSS, one more pragmatical with lower costs, better security and independence from individual suppliers, and a more social perspective where it is regarded that free software gives more freedom and local control and strengthens then democracy [Gosh, 2005-10-18]. Especially for government organizations, the possibility to change and configure the software without surveillance from the supplier is of major significance; one does not want to be dependent on certain large American companies. Gosh quotes Microsoft's Jim

Allchin that with his clearly nationalistic approach can make any government wonder what they install in their networks: "I'm an American, I believe in the American Way. I worry if the government encourages free software, and I don't think we've done enough education of policy makers to understand the threat" [Gosh, 2005-10-18]. Another factor Gosh emphasizes is the constraint to use some companies' software to be compliant with other organizations, to upgrade when other organizations upgrade, and forced to use the same companies' byproducts, because otherwise, the formats do not support each other. One has, to put it briefly, no freedom of choice. Because patent protected software, *proprietary software*, does not allow a manipulation of the source code, nor make the code public, the free software advocates cannot control how the proprietary code acts or process the data the proprietary software produces. Thus one cannot fully be compatible with the patent protected applications neither compete with the software's that can, i.e. software's that are owned by the same companies. The suppliers then create a company based de facto standard and ensure their position on the market [Gosh, 2005-10-18].

3.3   Third world: piracy, cost- and security reasons

The Finland based researcher Niranjan Rajani has studied the importance of Free/Libre and Open Source Software (FLOSS) for developing countries [Rajani, 2005-10-17]. In his report, *Free as in Education: Significance of the Free/Libre and Open Source Software for Developing Countries*, Rajani discusses the right to education in comparison to the right to free software. Where the Free Software Foundation (FSF) says: "'Free software' is a matter of liberty, not price.

To understand the concept, you should think of 'free' as in 'free speech', not as in 'free beer'. [FSF, 2005-10-17] Rajani makes an addition statement and indicates that the price, despite what FSF says, is relevant in the case of developing countries. Rajani states, "From the point of view of the developing countries, we would argue that though the freedom is of paramount importance in more than one way, the price aspect is also very important, without which developing nations would not be able to significantly meet the challenges of the computer age. In fact, the Freedom aspect can be seen in terms of 'free education', which ought to be free in terms of *freedom* as well as *price*." [Rajani, 2005-10-17]. The reasoning of Rajani is not a matter of course. In Sweden, education is free and relatively open and objective, a condition that is not obvious in many other parts of the world. Rajani takes Saudi Arabia as an example, where he means that even though the education is free, free meaning gratis, it is not open and objective – *free and independent* – but strictly regulated.

We can relate the analysis of Rishab Aiyer Goshs in *The European Politics of F/OSS Adoption* about the reasons for Europe having a positive attitude to FOSS to Rajani's discussion about the developing countries premier arguments to use FLOSS[2]. The logic of both the researchers follows the same line. Rajani notes the following three important reasons in *Free as in Education: Significance of the Free/Libre and Open Source Software for Developing Countries* for why developing countries should consider using free software [Rajani, 2005-10-17]:

1.   Lower Cost
2.   The Anti-Piracy Campaign

3.   Security and Technological Independence

First, the cost to migrate today's non-free systems to free software does not exceed the cost for the patent protected software licenses. Secondly, in many developing countries people can use illegal copies and do not have to pay any license fees. The severe pressure from the U.S, where the largest software companies are based, forces many countries to realize that this cannot go on any longer. Free and open software can be an alternative for developing countries that cannot afford to pay expensive license fees. Third, many countries consider frightening the U.S. world domination on the software market. By taking control over the software, one prevents unwelcome installation of spy programs on one's software.

Further, Rajani describes one more factor: the aspect of language. Much non-free software is released in a limited number of language variations as English, Spanish or for that matter, Swedish. African languages are not top priority. Here, free software can contribute with a number different products and adaptations to local languages. Ubuntu is an African adjusted Linux distribution that tries to set things right regarding the language problem. On Ubuntu's website they say among other things that: "software tools should be usable by people in their local language" [Ubuntu1, 2006-04-22]. The Ubuntu Linux distribution is an excellent alternative, if you compare it with Rajani's three reasons one should consider migrating to free software: the operating system is free ("Ubuntu will always be free of charge"). In addition, it supplies the source code for modification ("You have the right to modify your software until it works the way you want it to"), [Ubuntu2, 2006-04-22].[3]

3.4   What does real access mean?

The organization <www.bridges.org> focuses a lot on the concept of *real access* [bridges.org2, 2005-10-16]. They mean that real access is much more than just the physical access: "Providing access to technology is critical, but it must be about more than just physical access. Computers and connections are insufficient if the technology is not used effectively because it is not affordable; if people do not understand how to put it to use or if they are discouraged from using it; or if the local economy cannot sustain its use." Just because some free software is gratis, it does not mean that it solves the problem with the digital divide; the digital divide includes so much more. According to Bridges, Africa has for example "only 0.25% of all Internet hosts in the world, and that percentage is decreasing" [bridges.org2, 2005-10-16]. In some third world countries, one lacks the basic, fundamental ICT infrastructure. Except for the physical ICT infrastructure, Bridges shows that the installation and use of correct and appropriate technology is also very important to consider. They have set up twelve criteria for what *real access* means and by comparing the reality of the citizens against these criteria, one can decide whether people have or have not *real access* to ICT; that is, "access that goes beyond just physical access and makes it possible for people to use technology effectively to improve their lives."

We can summarize these criteria with the following key words:
-    Physical access
-    Appropriate technology

- Affordability
- Capacity
- Relevant content
- Integration
- Socio-cultural factors
- Trust
- Legal and regulatory framework
- Local economic environment
- Macro-economic environment
- Political will

Bridges simply implies that we should adjust technology to human beings and their needs, not the other way around. However, at the same time, one should inform people about the advantages and the future prospects of information and communication technologies. At government level, one must conduct a political debate that promotes ICT and FOSS and that tries to give all citizens of a society the possibility to take part of the global information society. The purpose of the Internet is not only for the well educated classes that work in offices in the big cities, but also for less fortunate citizens in a society. With the idea of *affordability*, Bridges want to illustrate the significance of the economical factor. The average American Internet user spends about 1.2% of their average income on their Internet access. In comparison with countries of smaller means like for example Madagascar (614% of the average income), Nepal (278% of the average income), Bangladesh (191% of the average income), or Sri Lanka (60% of the average income) the differences, and for that matter the possibilities, are enormous [bridges.org2, 2005-10-16]. If considering Sweden as a positive example, one can note that the municipalities committed themselves very early to provide the community with Internet-connected libraries, where all citizens could have access to computers and surf the Internet gratis. This is just the needed strategy, according to Bridges, a political will to provide all citizens with equal possibilities.

3.5   Local Development

The absence of ICT infrastructure implies other limitations beside that you are deprived from the possibility to take part to the global information society. The development of local open and free software cannot take place without basic fundamental ICT infrastructure. Sometimes one can hear critical voices regarding why so little open source software development takes part in developing countries. Nevertheless, the arguments are a bit contradicting. A large part of the culture surrounding open source and the development of free software depend on common, repeatedly developing activities where people from all over the world contribute with the help of Internet. Eric Raymond in his famous (in open source circles) article *The Cathedral and the Bazaar* writes "cheap Internet was a necessary condition for the Linux model to evolve..." [Raymond, 2006-04-22]. As shown, the possibility to constant Internet access is not a matter worldwide.

3.6   A simple investigation

The website <http://sourceforge.net/> is the world's largest website for developers working with open source and free software. They have over 100,000 projects and over one million registered users. Here one can host one's open source project and take part in the development of thousands of others. Here you can of course also download other open source applications.

Making a simple investigation of which types of projects are operating at Sourceforge right now [Sourceforge, 2005-10-18], by searching on the website on a number of selected key words such as Africa, Europe, and America, one can easily reveal what types of open source projects that occur at different places in the world.

Using the key word *Africa* gives you a number of now ongoing projects, of which quite a few school projects, plus a couple of games. For instance, you get these two below descriptions of projects within the educational area:

Edu-SLUG   "Edu-SLUG is the educational software part of SLUG, the Schools Linux User Group in South Africa. SLUG installs low-cost Linux networks at schools. Edu-SLUG aims to produce software to aid teachers in education using the Outcomes Based Education system."

OpenSchool   The aim of this project is to create local educational content for Southern Africa, applying Open Source principles and engaging South Africans from disadvantaged backgrounds in the Information Society, thus contributing to an improved understanding of Op.

On the key word *Europe*, you get quite a few games, game consoles, stock software, development tools, and software to search for cheap airline tickets.

On the key word *America*, you get several games, development tools, and a web portal for students to exchange books.

None of the two last key words (Europe, America) resulted in a project that was about education, or that gave people access to education or information. Admittedly, you obtained a website for exchanging books among students though it could have been a website for exchanging any books what so ever. It did not have anything to do with the education system. This investigation is of course not very scientific and has very limited reliability. Nevertheless, it still says something about the type of open source projects carried out in the world. It says something about the different types of needs people have in different places.

4   Example

4.1   Introduction of case study

Two students, Carolina Hafström and Jessica Hofbauer of the Department of Informatics (at the School of Economic and Commercial Law, University of Gothenburg, Sweden), did their master theses as a field study in Namibia [Hafström, Hofbauer, 2005-10-16]. Their focus was to study which factors were critical for a successful IT-adaptation in a developing country. They stayed a month in Namibia and they did their field study at SchoolNet. The students observed and interviewed the people involved in the project. SchoolNet is an organization that works to provide all Namibian schools with computers and Internet access by the use of donated computers and open source software [SchoolNet, 2005-10-16]. The goal of Hafström and Hofbauer's study was to investigate whether or not the users accepted well the open source technology.

4.2 Discussion and result of case study

Hafström and Hofbauer found out that large parts of Rajani's argumentation was correct in the case of Namibia, and they could also add one additional factor: the cost of maintenance and operation. In their interviews, they found that the opinion at SchoolNet was that the maintenance and operational costs for commercial products such as for Microsoft Windows, was larger than they were for the open source products they had chosen (SUSE Linux). The operational security was higher because it was more stable, which also made it cheaper. This fact lowered the total TCO (total cost of ownership) for the ICT. Furthermore, Hafström and Hofbauer confirmed their thesis that if there were a possibility to have software, the preference was to have it in one's local language. At SchoolNet, many realized that they could easily translate and configure the software to the local language if they wanted. However, many also said that they did not find this necessary since English is Namibia's official language.

Another advantage other than language with free software is the possibility to develop new and better versions of an application or adjust to local customs and practices. The SchoolNet coworkers considered this a great advantage in comparison with non-free software. The Western world mostly develops non-free software for its western culture. For example, software used in American schools does not provide for the needs of pupils in Namibia. They gave an example: most Namibians do not eat bread or sandwiches in the way American or Western people do; many Namibians have never heard of the word 'sandwich'. Still they must learn English words such as 'peanut butter and jelly sandwich' because they use software created for American children [Hafström, Hofbauer, 2005-10-16].

Which were the biggest difficulties in the case of Namibia? According to Hafström and Hofbauer the main problem was the short supply of an educated workforce. Namibia suffers, as many other developing countries, of *brain drain*; the best-educated people leave the country to find work where the possibilities are better. Even if SchoolNet succeeded in installing and operating Linux, they said that when they encountered problems, they had a difficult time solving them. It was difficult to get local support.

One of the conditions Hafström and Hofbauer found to be critical for a successful IT-adaptation was physical access; that is, the region needed a well functioning IT infrastructure. "Physical access is a key factor for a successful implementation and it is therefore important to control that the existing infrastructure meets the demands." [Hafström, Hofbauer, 2005-10-16]. They support the Bridges opinion of the importance of a well-built ICT infrastructure. When comparing their conclusions against the twelve critical factors Bridges presented to fulfill real access, you could see agreement on most levels. Hafström and Hofbauer end their study by presenting the following eight important factors for a successful IT-adaptation in a developing country [Hafström, Hofbauer, 2005-10-16]:

- The technology must address real, *experienced problems* in the country.
- The technology must *make sense* for the people that are going to use it.
- The technology must provide *sustainable solutions*. The software cannot be outdated and demand upgrades every year.
- The essential *physical infrastructure* must be installed and the citizens must be able to *afford it*.
- It is important to realize the *importance of local champions* that use the technology and can act as models.
- The importance to focus on the *right target group*.
- The importance that technology is implemented to solve *people's problems*, not to increase them.
- The importance to focus and understand *structures and attitudes* in a society; people are likely to follow official institution's lead.

5   Conclusions

By way of introduction, one may ask some questions such as:

Can the introduction of free and open source software and the use of ICT in any way change the prerequisites of the developing countries?

In what ways can free software, open source, and ICT change the development of a country?

Is it the software that is the main need in focus for the developing world, or is it something else?

Are the opinions about free and open software and ICT the same in the industrialized and the developing world?

Depending on which country in the developing world you reference, they have different needs depending on the given basic conditions. A lesson learned is that discussions regarding the possibilities of free software and open source are a bit dashed when one realizes that at many places there is a need for ICT on a much lower level—a need for first filling the basic prerequisites. Of what use is free software if people cannot afford Internet access, or even worse, if there is no Internet access available or no computer or electrical power exists.

If one assumes the fulfillment of the basic conditions for ICT, one can notice several examples where free and open software can contribute to development. A school can have access to word processing editors free of cost instead of buying equivalent software for expensive licensing money (for example, Open-Office in contrast to Microsoft Office), you can adjust applications so they fit local customs and practices instead of something that is adjusted for an American or at least for a Western market. The most basic condition is the use of a free operating system instead of one that costs money, and by so, renders possible the use of computers

Another important aspect on advantages of free software is that they usually do not demand the newest or best hardware. Companies release new versions of software's continually that demands better and better hardware. Developing countries cannot count on a constant flow of used hardware to them, or for that matter, buy it themselves. System developers in Western countries do not as much have to take computer memory or CPU load into consideration when programming applications as developers using hardware from the eighties or nineties. The West regards hardware relatively inexpensive, a fact that is not applicable in the rest of the world. Developing countries need stable applications that work without constant upgrade, neither of the hardware nor the software.

It is difficult to say in general that the opinions regarding free and open software and ICT differentiates between the developing and industrial countries. If you compare individual developers the attitude positive for the most part, but it does not mean that you develop the same things. Programmers in the West do not have to develop applications as a support for education. These types of applications are already in place. Then of course, you could always *choose* to do so if desired. For many programmers and users in developing countries, the situation is very different, especially when no possibility exists to buy applications (as for instance Microsoft Office due to the licensing fees). You *must* use FOSS software if you do not want to generate illegal copies.

Still, the good will of individual programmers or project team members is not enough. For FOSS to succeed in the developing world, one must have support at government level, as has happened in for instance Brazil, Peru, and Malaysia. FOSS demands existing ICT infrastructure, an infrastructure in which individual governments must invest. Only then can one fully succeed.

References

[bridges.org1, 2005-10-16]. *Free/open source software (FOSS) policy in Africa: A toolkit for policy-makers and practitioners*, bridges.org and the Collaboration on International ICT Policy for East and Southern Africa (CIPESA) 10 August 2005, http://www.bridges.org/foss/FOSSPolicyToolkit_10Aug05.pdf. p. 8.

[bridges.org2, 2005-10-16], http://www.bridges.org/digitaldivide/realaccess.html.

[FSF, 2005-10-17], Free Software Foundation, http://www.fsf.org/licensing/essays/free-sw.html.

[Gosh, 2005-10-18], Gosh, Rishab Aiyer, in *The Politics of Open Source Adoption*, The European Politics of F/OSS Adoption, edited by Joe Karaganis and Robert Latham. Social Science Research Council (SSRC), Version 1.0, May 2005, http://www.ssrc.org/programs/ccit/publications/POSA1.0.pdf, pp. 14-15.

[Hafström, Hofbauer, 2006-04-22], Hafström, Carolina and Hofbauer, Jessica. *IT Adoption in Developing Countries*, Department of Informatics, School of Economics and Commercial Law, University of Gothenburg, 2004, http://www.handels.gu.se/epc/archive/00003927/01/Nr%5F39%5FCH%2CJH.pdf, pp.50-64.

[Rajani, 2006-04-22], Rajani, Niranjan. *Free as in Education – Significance of the Free/Libre and Open Source Software for Developing Countries*, Ministry for Foreign Affairs, (Helsinki, Finland. 2002/2003), http://www.maailma.kaapeli.fi/FLOSS_for_dev.html, chapter 1, chapter 6.

[Raymond, 2006-04-22], Raymond, Erik. *The Cathedral and the Bazaar*, 2002. Version 3.0, 2002/08/02, http://www.catb.org/%7Eesr/writings/cathedral-bazaar/cathedral-bazaar/ar01s11.html.

[SchoolNet, 2005-10-16], SchoolNet Namibia, http://www.schoolnet.na/about/history.html.

[Sourceforge, 2005-10-18], http://sourceforge.net/.

[SCB, 2005-10-17], Statistical Central Bureau SCB, http://www.scb.se/templates/tableOrChart____112387.asp.

[Ubuntu1, 2006-04-22], http://www.ubuntu.com/.

[Ubuntu2, 2006-04-22], http://www.ubuntulinux.org/.

[UNCTAD, 2005-10-17], United Nations Conference on Trade and Development. *E-commerce and development report 2004*, Internet edition, prepared by the UNCTAD secretariat. United Nations, New York and Geneva, 2004, http://www.unctad.org/en/docs/ecdr2004_en.pdf, pp. 1-32.

---

[1]   For a discussion regarding the idea of non-free, please refer to http://www.gnu.org/philosophy/words-to-avoid.html#Commercial. In this context non-free is used instead of the more common, but incorrect word, commercial (as in commercial software). A commercial software can be both free and non-free, therefore the careful distinction between the both.

[2]   The words FOSS and FLOSS are both used because the two researchers in their texts use the words respectively, FOSS is used by Rishab Aiyer Gosh, and FLOSS is used by Niranjan Rajani. Not for any other reason.

[3]   To read more about the Ubuntu Linux license rules, please refer to: http://www.ubuntu.com/ubuntu/licensing/document_view.

Economic, Organizational, and Technical Issues

Knowledge, Work and Subject in Informational Capitalism

Rudi Schmiede
Technische Universität Darmstadt, Institut für Soziologie
schmiede@ifs.tu-darmstadt.de
http://www.ifs.tu-darmstadt.de/85/

Abstract. With the development of informational capitalism and the network society, globalization and informatization play an increasingly crucial role for understanding technology and society. Informatization describes a qualitative leap in technology development which opens up new dimensions of productivity by information modelling on the one hand, but which demands new forms of knowledge of information workers on the other hand. Work is becoming more flexible, but also more precarious and more polarized socially. These tendencies create a contradictory situation for the subject: formalization and new scopes of autonomy exist side by side. This constellation allows for new approaches to the social shaping of technologies. But they presuppose a fundamental change in attitude by both, system developers and social scientists.

Keywords: Information Society; informational capitalism; informatization; network society; flexible work; digital divide; knowledge; shaping technology

1   Introduction

The fact that the informatization of work comprehensively and lastingly influences the latter has meanwhile become general knowledge, apart from the term itself.[1] The fact that this process is an essential feature of a society changing fundamentally is less common, sometimes even contested. The organizers of the conference which was the origin of this paper[2], even when formulating their headline, started out from their definite conviction that this internal structural connection exists and is highly significant for an appropriate way of understanding today's society and its tendencies of development. It is expressed by the concept of 'informational capitalism', as coined by Manuel Castells, of informatized capitalism, and of the network society [Castells 2001] whose differentia specifica will thus be sketched in the first paragraph (2). Together with an extended qualitative way of understanding the

Please use the following format when citing this chapter:

Schmiede, R., 2006, in IFIP International Federation for Information Processing, Volume 223, Social Informatics: An Information Society for All? In Remembrance of Rob Kling, eds. Berleur, J., Numinen, M. I., Impagliazzo, J., (Boston: Springer), pp. 333–354.

process of informatization as creating a redoubled world of the 'second nature', which will be the subject of the then following paragraph (3), a theoretical framework is thus offered, within which many of the loose ends presented in this debate may be tied together. The current social change is not only connected to a clear quantitative extension of informational work but even more perceptible are its qualitative changes which can be observed with work itself, with the ways in which it is organized, and on the social level as a tendency towards 'social digital divide' (4). However, informatization is not a linear tendency but contradictory in itself: it needs extended subjective ingredients and interpretations which in each case newly define themselves to generate knowledge from it and thus make it useful for a purposeful practice; the fact that the term 'information society' is gradually replaced by 'knowledge society' is an indication of the increasing awareness of this shift. Information and knowledge, knowledge and not-knowing form an internal unity (5). From this tension between information and knowledge, between formalization and subjectivity there finally result leeways for the subject and thus leeways for the shaping of technology and organization. Their perspectives will be discussed in the final paragraph (6).

2   Informational Capitalism and Network Society

The process of informatizing and the diagnosis of a fundamental social change were most explicitly and most extensively related to each other by Manuel Castells in his theory of 'informational capitalism' and the rise of the 'network society' which is connected to it. However, he is not at all the only author to see a close ,connection between the development and spread of IC-technologies and social changes, i. e. parallel developments in the fields of economy, technology, society, and politics; the formation of concepts like 'digital capitalism', 'knowledge capitalism', or 'high-tech capitalism' are indications of this connection.[3] The central ideas of these analyses, the emphasis being on Castells' theory, are as follows: with the world economic crisis of the mid-70ies of the 20th century, which only at first sight was an 'oil crisis', the long age of mass production highly based on the division of labour and standardization – which was marked by its Taylorist and Fordist technological-organizational basis as well as by the enduring Keynesian-based state intervention into the economy – reached the end of its development possibilities. What are the new aspects that justify speaking of a break of ages?

Two answers – not at all belonging to each other intentionally but practically and in respect of their consequences complementary – to this crises have developed: globalization and informatization of economy and society. Even if or just because *globalization* is a common catchphrase these days, it is worth the effort to name its most important dimensions. Since the end of the 70ies we have been able to observe a clearly intensified competition on the worldwide markets and as a result also on the national goods and financial markets. At the same time the latter have changed their structure: worldwide differentiated and specialized sub-markets have developed and pushed through; they are the arena for increased competition. Trans-national companies have become decisive actors in many of these markets. Although the national states are still the dominating political organizational form of societies [Bielefeld, 2003], nevertheless the national state erodes particularly in the area of economic policies, national economies find themselves being increasingly bound in trans-national goods, financial and labour markets. Clear neo-liberal tendencies of de-regulation increase the influence of economy at all levels, in many cases they make social and political action a subject of their hegemony.[4] Not surprisingly, these processes come along nationally and internationally with social differentiation and polarization, i. e. a renewed increase of social inequality.

Apart from this external dimension which is directed towards the national and international markets, there is a second, internal, and equally important effect of globalization which is directed at companies and organizations. Appropriate to the external hegemony of economy there is an internal and new direct influence of economy which is perceived in many ways. The first clearly visible and publicly perceived step of this change was the spread of models of 'lean production' and 'lean administration' following the Japanese example after the end of the 80ies in Germany (in the USA and Great Britain some years earlier). This means on the one hand de-centralizing moments of labour and company organization: the move of leeways of flexibility, but also the shifting of responsibility towards the single labourer, the team, or the department. Its equivalence is the thinning-out of the middle levels of hierarchy, by help of which more direct information and decision chains are created. Already a part of this system was also the direct and constant comparison to parallel processes, to increase transparency and stimulate competition for the best ways and the least amount of time and costs; continuous quality control has since become a common practice of a whole lot of companies.[5] These elements are completed by the purposeful re-organization of logistic chains being orientated towards the optimization of the processes of the dominating companies, in the words of a popular manager-slogan: 'concentrating on core competencies' provided starting points and examples of the general re-organization of economy. Along this guideline both a new international division of labour with strongly differentiated, specialized, and flexible markets and new forms of the division of labour in product markets and in branches in the form of company networks, network or virtual companies, i. e. 'horizontal' organizations (Castells), emerged.

However, these organizational aspects of de-centralization should not be taken for the whole: regarding the dimensions of capital concentration, financial control, or the economic and political power of the companies, centralization goes on incessantly. This is not only true for producing or services companies but even more for purely financial service corporations. In a certain sense, the finance-capitalist origins of globalization catch up again with the sphere of real production and services and structure them: the orientation towards the short-term goals of 'shareholder value' makes corporations, even the big and biggest ones, newly dependent upon global capital flows. Financial and finance policy centralization together with organizational de-centralization are typical for globalized companies; the company's limits are of virtual, financial nature, they are not any more the traditional factory walls or fences.

Network structures do not only play an increasing role in and among companies but they also occur throughout other parts of society. As the appropriate literature shows, they are found just as well in communal ways of co-existence, in the structures of communication and decision in the political field, and in the informal ways of cooperation in all parts of society. They seem to be a general way of organizing social relationships, appropriate to highly changeable and complex structures. Networks are not – just as it was the case with the traditional bureaucratic-hierarchical kinds of companies of the past – per se the adequate way of organizing capitalist business. In our opinion, the fact that they more and more push through and so to speak become a paradigm of modern organizing is due to network structures allowing for the immediacy of economic influences on the one hand but also the uncertainty of individual action on the other hand, as necessary for a way of doing business increasingly orientated not any more towards execution but towards the result. According to the number and strength of their knots and to increasing or decreasing effects, networks open up several possibilities to reach a goal or another place. Under today's conditions of increased economic and social complexity and appropriate increases in insecurity they allow for the extent of individuality, also of individual responsibility, which make the most extensive inclusion of the individual into added-value chains possible. The network-shaped economy – as Castells impressingly shows by the case of the amalgamization of traditional social and family network-structures and most modern capitalism in South East Asia – also results in forms of a network society.

To avoid misunderstandings: currently the empirically found organizational shape of production and service organizations is a colourful mixture of old and new models. Forms of flexible project organization or even of virtual companies are contrasted by attempts at re-Taylorizing and enduring large flow technologies. Nevertheless, the sketched tendency of finer granulating and growing importance of market-economic structures is obvious. Also the still existing companies producing by large-scale technologies find themselves being under the pressure of developing towards technological and organizational de-centralization to be able to survive as financially highly centralized company-units. Today's information and communication technologies, which provide the technological basis for international capitalism, play a key-role for these diverging development tendencies of value and production economy.

3   The Informatization of Economy and Society

Informatization – the second answer to the world economic crisis of the Seventies and the end of the age of Taylorist and Fordist mass production as indicated by it – does not only and not primarily mean the ubiquitous spread of digital information and communication technologies but first of all their qualitative increase of significance. But despite the popularization of the concept of information induced by the mass spread of computers we must not deceive ourselves about the fact that neither information nor information technology are new for the predominant way of production; they have accompanied capitalism right from its beginnings. The first manifestation of the abstracting information, which doubles reality in the form of a model, is double-entry bookkeeping which, as it is well-known, was developed in Northern Italy in the 13th and 14th centuries, that is during the first, short peak of a commercial capitalism which also came up against the limiting factors of modern production. The different systems of bookkeeping; card systems which have gained increased significance since the spread of the piece-work system after the end of the 19th century; the collecting of information in personnel accounting and calculation offices; the development of filing systems, record systems, index card-techniques, registries etc.; finally the technologies for copying, spread and evaluation of information like typewriters, stencil and repro processes, pneumatic dispatch systems, telegraph, telex, calculators, Hollerith machines which preceded the computer, make clear that the history of the capitalist way of production was at the same time a history of the increasing significance of information and communication and the development of the appropriate technologies.[6]

Thus, what is new about the digital information and communication technologies? What gives us the right to speak of a new kind of informatization, which is the technological basis of informational capitalism? It is three fundamental, technological features of IC-technologies, resulting in several consequences. First, computer technology is different from all preceding technologies – which all were auxiliaries for solving particular tasks, i. e. were special machines – due to the fact that the computer is a 'universal machine' [Krämer, 1988; Krämer, 1989, 38-52; Heintz, 1993] which – as being programme-controlled – may be used for any task. As it is the objectification of a general, symbolic machine, it can also work on the universe of symbolic models and worlds. Although this machine needs an input from the real world and must give back its output to the real world to fulfil its purpose within the context of the system as a whole, within the redoubled world of working on and processing symbols it is free of these limits and open to any step of work.

This leads us to the second fundamental feature of IC-technologies: they are not anymore primarily a tool for supporting solutions located outside of their tasks but they are a part of a whole process, of a system. On the one hand, the 'autonomization of the machine system' [Holling and Kempin, 1989, 139 sq.] includes enormous dangers of subjecting the individual to a seemingly inevitable technological process and is perceived in the contexts of work and everyday life as deeply influential omnipresence of the IC-technologies. On the other hand, however – and this was and still is the condition for its pushing through and its central role in current capitalism – due to just this nature it offers a gigantic new potential of productivity: in the redoubled second world of information a growing number of material processes can be modelled, calculated, simulated by all its variants, calculated regarding their mechanic, chemical, biological, or electronic effects. Increasing shares of the changing and designing work of the real world are shifted towards the world of information and are carried out there in a virtual way. To have it more theoretically: innovations are generated and again used for innovations in a cumulative feedback context. The IC-technologies have become reflexive: facts and contexts are understood to be informational processes right from the beginning and are formulated and modelled appropriately; they are the starting point of processes of reorganization and technologization. What is new is the 'technology-based, media-mediated ability of changing knowledge'. The complete technologization of knowledge in its informational form is the step from conventional mechanization towards informatization [Spinner, 1998, 63, 75)]. The strategies of productivity competition, which still is the economic basis of capitalist production, have shifted from material production, which more and more is becoming a dependent variable, towards this world of virtual product development [Anderl, 2006] and product planning where at the moment 'things are happening'.

The third specifically new feature of the IC-technologies is their effect on space and time. By way of informatization, information and communication networks become possible which are able to operate globally and in real time. This became visible for the first time at the end of the 70ies by the financial and capital markets working worldwide 'on the spot'; and if some years ago the then VW boss Piech, while referring to Charles V.'s famous sentence said that for his trust the sun went never down, this makes clear how important just-in-time production is also for this producing company. Globalized socio-technological systems – this way the tendency may be described in summary – have been created which generate, communicate, and process information, and they do it in 'real time'. It is not only that in principle they make worldwide access to any content possible, they are also the technological basis of the IC-technologies becoming reflexive, as mentioned for the second point. If in the 80ies and the early 90ies of the 20th century the spread of network technologies was still limited by proprietary formats, by the client-server principle, as well as by the command line-form of the Internet, the standardized graphic access (in the World Wide Web) brought the breakthrough of mass and universalized use of Internet technologies. Currently, by service-based system architectures a qualitatively new step is indicated where that might become true what was some years ago predicted by Tim Berners-Lee, the inventor of the web-standard: that the net itself will become the computer, today's (workplace-) computer only being the front-end [Schmiede et al., 2006, ch. 3.6; Silberberger, 2003].

These three new specific features of the digital IC-technologies – the creation of an in principle unlimited virtual world of information by help of the universal machine, the computer; the IC-technologies becoming reflexive within this space of the autonomization of the machine system; the spread of globalized real-time information and communication networks with increasing functionalities – are what makes the structural changes of economy and society, of markets and organizations, as sketched in the first paragraph, possible. This internal coherence can be made even clearer by reminding to the fact that the just mentioned steps of development were preceded by the age of mainframe technologies with their proprietary and closed networks; for large-scale one-purpose applications like e. g. early stock exchange-information systems they were sufficient for some time. Thus, the argument is that the steps of globalization and steps of the development of IC-technologies can be closely paralleled and that this way their mutual dependence can be made visible.[7]

Castells in his analysis of 'informational capitalism' not only emphasized the role of network-shaped information technologies but also the spread of network-based forms of organization and cooperation, which again were a mighty impulse for the development, and spread of the appropriate technologies. Indeed, in the course of the last quarter of a century various kinds of networks, most of all in the field of business, have developed, which shall here be shortly summarized by an overview. Most clearly visible are *inter-organizational* networks. They are known as information-processing combines from the world of financial services, where usually they come along with the development of 'flexible bureaucracies'.[8] For some time, these networks have been influential also in the form of production combines, as they have been spreading among car industries in the context of 'lean production'; meanwhile, they operate on a global level and have differentiated to be continent-wide material production networks which to a great extent cooperate by way of information technology. Similar structures can be found for electronics production in various fields.[9] Common guideline for these kinds of networks is the 're-organization of value chains', i. e. the rationalizing re-adjustment of the complete value chain by way of specialising and adjusting their material and digital links.[10] *Intra-organizational* networks closely follow the tendencies of re-organization as already mentioned under the headword of 'lean production': the spread of groupwork, teamwork, and projectwork; the levelling of organization by way of flattening hierarchies, something, however, which often comes along with eroding the middle ranks; organizational de-centralization which creates units to be as clearly identifiable, but also controllable, as possible; and the creation of graded forms of self-responsibility going towards the 'company within the company' and which find expression e. g. by profit centres, competitive relations between parts of the same company and other companies, are important forms of this network level. In the course of intensified economic control, the partition walls and structures have rather been influenced financially than organizationally.

As already mentioned, both types – inter- and intra-organizational networks – do not only serve for adjusting to more flexible and globalized market demands. At the same time they are an important way of dealing with the increased insecurities and uncertainties which are connected to these, of at least transforming them into calculable risks. Both in the material and in the immaterial sense they serve for mobilizing resources as well as for securing their availability and their access. That what at first was propagated as 'business process re-engineering' at the beginning of the 90ies has after the middle of the 90ies most of all concentrated on mobilizing the stocks of experience and knowledge within organizations and networks. Under the flag of 'knowledge management' a whole lot of approaches have been created to support the exchange of knowledge of all kinds by way of intensifying network relations.[11] This, too, aims at orientating these professional activities towards the value chain; following the older concept of 'human capital' it is now about mobilising and exploiting the 'intellectual' capital of the company [Edvinsson and Malone, 1997]. However, the practical experience with this approach is rather sobering. It is not only that the technological basis of electronically supporting these processes is not at all fully matured; additionally, in the course of many experiments it soon turned out that networks are highly complex social structures and that dealing with knowledge is strongly interwoven with them. Knowledge processes are closely connected to motivation, interest, and power structures. Every employee is conscious – even if he does not know the slogan which is ascribed to Francis Bacon – of the fact that knowledge is power; whether one is ready to give up on this instrument of power, is – apart from hierarchically exerted pressure – dependent on contradictious processes like trust, acceptance, and gratifications, i. e. on the shape of the networks and their embeddedness in that what – often euphemistically – is called corporate culture.

These experiences and insights draw the attention to a third form of networks which come from practical work and which take the inter-personal dimension more strongly into account, and which I thus like to call *micro-structural* networks. Their discussion – most of all in US literature and research – also comes from the context of knowledge processes, i. e. from learning and acquiring knowledge in and by way of practice; accordingly, they are mostly called 'communities of practice' but sometimes also communities of collaboration or communication.[12] Here it is mostly about observing and analysing the transfer of experience and knowledge and – the more recently the more often – also the appropriate use of IC-technologies for real cooperation and communication. The background of this increased and still increasing attention is definitely to be seen in the fact that with the spread of network-shaped cooperation structures, cooperation and communication – also beyond the immediate work context – has become economically, organizationally, and also technologically more important. Furthermore, for the practice of cooperation the use of digital technologies plays a crucial infra-structural role. The communities of practice are defined by a common domain, by being member of a social community, and by being tied together by a common practical context of work.[13] Until now, however, only a limited number of investigations of work processes has been presented; many investigations refer to local communities. But they can be supplemented by studies from a workfield which has up to now been rather information technologically influenced and has been supported by only a few psychologists, i. e. the research on 'Computer Supported Cooperative Work' (CSCW), as well as by a few other investigations.[14] Altogether, these connections of practical cooperation, kinds of networks, use of IC-technologies, knowledge transfer, and work are a little researched field, i. e. there is a distinctive research deficit. If one wants to develop an empirically rich concept of informatized work, one will have to accept the laborious investigation of this sub-levels of work and cooperation.

4   Flexibilization of Work and Forms of Digital Divide

What becomes most clearly visible with the structural change of work is not the concrete operational *working conditions* which have already been mentioned in the context of the dimension of work organization but much more the changes of the *conditions of employment* which become manifested by the ways of deployment of work and in the labour markets but which have also a subjective biographical dimension. This structural change is commonly described by the rather vague expression of 'flexibilization' of work, and already for about 20 years there has been wide agreement among German industrial sociology and labour market research on the fact that an erosion of the 'normal' or 'regular employment condition' (i. e. regulated, fulltime, qualification-adequate, and long-term work which traditionally was most of all typical for men's labour) is to be observed. Both tendencies are expressed by different dimensions of labour: *working times* have become clearly more variable during the last decades. This does not only address the successive extension of part-time work to meanwhile almost one fifth of all gainfully employed as coming along with increasing employment of women; working time is varied according to order situation, season, or time of day, and in the biographical dimension continuity decreases while particularly at the beginning and the end of working life work is increasingly unstable. The average *duration of employment* at one company decreases. Although the employment situation in Germany is still miles away from the hire-and-fire practices in the Anglo-Saxon world, nevertheless in the environment of mass unemployment *dismissals, redundancies,* and *transfers to a different position* have become much easier and thus happen much more often. Meanwhile, *fixed-term* employment is not the exception but the rule for the first years of gainful employment. The continuous extension of *temporary work* and *subcontracted employment* also serves for shifting the risk beyond the walls of the company. Finally, the frequent change of the *professional status* of gainfully employed people counts among this, who partly voluntarily but to a great extent also are forced to change between dependent employment, self-employment, and the manifold forms of partial or falsely designated self-employment between these two poles.[15]

The decreasing biographical continuity of gainful employment is not without consequences for the working people's *way of life*, for the *way they see themselves*, and for their *self-confidence*. Inevitably, long-term biographical plans are replaced by short-term or at the most mid-term perspectives. The employee is at the mercy of market powers he/she is not able to control, he/she becomes a haunted person – an effect which Richard Sennett by way of a number of case studies describes most impressively as a 'drift' but which he also makes clear to be a 'corrosion of character', as the original title of his book calls it, due to their potentially personality-affecting consequences [Sennett, 2000]. The social pathology of flexibilized and informatized work is still an unwritten chapter of labour research, something which is surely connected to the fact that its manifestations are made a taboo subject: the estimations according to which about one third of all employees in Germany are the victims of manifest mobbing, mostly by superiors, or those saying that work-related depressions have meanwhile reached the size of some million cases, are far from being popular. Nevertheless they are part of the overall picture of the structural change of work in the age of informatization.[16]

Flexibilization of work has also lastingly changed the *structures of the labour market*. Not only the continuity of employment has drastically decreased, at the same time also the internal labour markets, which were typical for many industries and for great parts of the 20th century and which offered a high degree of employment security and often even well-ordered career conditions for the permanent staff, have eroded to a large extent. Instead, fluctuating forms of employment – named by the appropriate term of 'contingent work force' in the US – are gaining increased significance. As the already quoted David Knoke has it, employment conditions which were to a large extent law-established and organized by collective contracts have been replaced by a 'new employment contract' which are characterized by the increased significance of external labour markets or external employees for usually only mid-term recruiting, but most of all by 'high-performance workplace practices' inside the company. Among the latter there count an intensified economy of time by way of just-in-time structures, inclusion into groupwork, teamwork, and project work, performance-orientated short-term skills training, changing the workplace between inside and outside, the omni-present information technologies, total quality management, and performance-dependent ways of payment.

These changes of employment and of labour markets come along – at least for the time being – with a clear *shift of power* from waged work towards capital. The flexibilization of employment conditions, which as a matter of fact comes along with increased exchangeability of workers (increase of contingent work force), weakens the individual's position towards the company; furthermore, he/she becomes more susceptible to reprisals of open or hidden nature. The limits of reasonableness at the workplace are extended. Thus, for many years we have been observing a continuous decrease of the readiness to be organised in trade unions.[17] For the time being, the trade unions have not succeeded with offering a perspective of representation and organization which is considered attractive by the employees of modern industrial branches and particularly of the IT branches. Instead, particularly in the IT-sector almost 'trade union-free zones' come into existence. To further trace back these changes it is reasonable to go back once again to the already partly discussed changes of working conditions.

Particularly in the informatized, high-technology fields of societal work the questions of gain, of security, of adjusting and further developing one's own *qualification* has more and more become the focus of the workers' interests. It has clearly gained a dominating position towards the traditional goals of higher wages and shorter worktime. Why? Because the possibility and the perspectives of employment (the much quoted 'employability'), on which all the other factors are dependent, are closely connected to qualification and its appropriateness to the permanently newly arising tasks. With the rapid change of technologies in the course of increasing informatization the half-life of the decline of the respectively valid knowledge and experience has dramatically decreased. However, for the time being no social pattern of '*life-long learning*' as it is demanded by many has developed.

Despite the everywhere observed informatization of work, experience-based knowledge coming along with work and the use of technologies still plays a crucial role. Informatization and need for subjectivity are not alternatives but complementary processes. This is true both for the restricted field of professional knowledge and for the wider field of work, organization, and social experience. This combination of increased, continually changing specialized knowledge on the one hand and process- and dimension-related experience on the other hand are subsumed under the concept of *competencies*. The already mentioned crucial significance of qualification together with acquiring and securing broad competencies becomes clear by Chris Benner's results when investigating information work in Silicon Valley: particularly in the field of 'high-tech qualifications', networks ('occupational communities') play an important role for the exchange of knowledge. They have resulted in the creation of guild-like or profession-orientated employees' organizations (called 'guilds' or 'new occupation-based associations' by Benner). In some cases also trade unions have opened up towards these specific interests of 'information workers' and have thus achieved organizational success in this otherwise completely union-free field ('next generation unionism').[18]

Altogether, when looking at the changes of work in informatized capitalism we come to the conclusion that the forms of *social inequality* connected to it have clearly increased, a development which is often called 'digital divide' or more precisely 'social digital divide'. At least for the USA, *tendencies of splitting* in the employment structure have been named which are closely connected to informatization: at the upper end of the qualification hierarchy there appeared the 'symbol analysts' (Reich) or 'knowledge workers' (Burton-Jones) or the information workers of the so called new economy.[19] At the lower end, an obvious class of to a great extent degraded mass workers, most of all in the services sector (retail trade; personnel for cleaning, housework, and security), has developed which so to speak must provide for the material working conditions of the information workers. Even if by the crisis of the 'new economy' in 2001-2004 a significant part of the information employees were taken back from temporarily dominating special conditions regarding their chances of career and income to the normality of capitalist labour markets, both groups are drifting apart; both are growing; on the other hand, there seem to be tendencies of erosion for the middle-class between them. Manuel Castells, however, points out to the fact that these tendencies of social polarization and splitting have not primarily originated in their qualifications drifting away from each other but most of all are observed for employment conditions. We thus observe an overlap of several tendencies of development: on the hand, the general, average level of education and qualification is rising. At the same time, however, the fringes of the qualification spectre seem to drift apart, which results in a suction for medium qualifications. But these polarization tendencies are thirdly much more distinctive for employment conditions and job chances. Finally, they are fourthly eclipsed by a clear spread of income levels.

5   Knowledge and Information

The already mentioned contradictory character of the informatization processes is closely connected to the tension between knowledge and information which is thus worth discussing in more detail, as there can be found decisive conditions for the constraints, but also for the leeways the working subjects are confronted with. *Information* is only a raw material for work, knowledge and organizational processes: abstracted, shaped, and thus formalized content. Information must not only, like the data of technical communications models, be technically understood by transmitter and receiver but the contents transported by them must also be syntactically understandable. Nevertheless, the information stays to be free from the context: a newspaper report may be completely understandable concerning its words and their meaning for me as a reader, but due to lacking context its meaning may be completely incomprehensible at the same time. To have it more generally: information is always positively determined and must always be so, as only clearly defined objects and relations – also if they are only be clearly defined statistically – can be technically modelled. This, however, makes it at the same time restricted in principle, for positive determination can only be reached by disregarding variety, i. e. by abstraction. Thus, information always includes only designed and formalized excerpts of reality, i. e. those cleared of disturbing conditions and complexities.[20]

Knowledge, on the other hand, in principle stays tied to the knowing subject, for it is always context-related, dependent on interpretation and understanding. It is – as Michael Polanyi has it – always 'personal knowledge'. There are no stocks of knowledge which are not communicated by the thinking subject's head; without being worked on by it they stay dead material. Dealing with those stocks of information and knowledge as being outside the individual, i. e. changing information into knowledge and connecting knowledge to practice, stays to be an intellectual performance which cannot be taken away from the individual subject. As all previous experience shows, it can only to a very limited extent be replaced by intelligent technological systems, i. e. artificial intelligence. Like in the case of other technologies this conversion of information into knowledge may be supported by means of production (and here there is for the present and in the foreseeable future a significant shaping potential for the sciences as well as for business and society) but it can never or only partly be substituted. Thus, knowledge is 'information critique' (Gamm) in a certain sense. Furthermore, it is dialectically related to not-knowing: due to the increasing complexity of society and its sub-systems (in the system-theoretical diction) or rather due to the insecurity of all social and individual living conditions, growing together with globalization and the thorough-going capitalization of economy and society (from the critical-theoretical point of view), not-knowing is increasing despite all efforts of increasing knowledge. Knowledge – to pointedly follow Willke – increasingly becomes knowing about ways of how to deal with not-knowing; knowledge and not-knowing, as his diagnosis of today's 'knowledge crisis' says, are complementary manifestations of the same social development.

Thus, one cannot simply, as done for naïve concepts of knowledge management, transform implicit knowledge to a great extent into explicit knowledge but must provide space for processes which do make it possible for tacit knowledge to come into effect. How is that to be understood? Knowledge is defined only by negation: I am able to know what I do not know. In contrast, a positive definition of that what is known is only apparently possible, as it becomes again and again clear for everyone confronted with the comparably simple task of marking at school or university. For, first, knowledge includes experience of all kind –memories of the body, emotional experience, experience of relationships, estimating people, experience of practically dealing with objects and organizations etc. Secondly, knowledge, as the linguistic cognation shows[21], is tied to certainty, i. e. to subjective interpretations and convictions. Thus, in this context it becomes, thirdly, visible that knowledge – as it is always about the question for truth – cannot be separated from reason; reason, as we know after Kant and Hegel, presupposes a social individual, i. e. the constantly socially interacting subject. This makes, fourthly, clear that knowledge is closely connected to processes of the appreciation of knowledge contents themselves, but also of the person (as the English term 'acknowledgement' signifies), i. e. to genuinely social processes. Finally, knowledge is in an even more comprehensive way socially and politically embedded: the slogan 'Knowledge is Power', ascribed to Francis Bacon, is again and again confirmed by everyday knowledge processes. Thus, knowledge is – summarized – not a positively stateable matter of fact but a constant process, infinite effort, fight against not-knowing, fundamentally subjective but always also objectively communicated probation in a fundamentally undetermined world.

Beyond this, new contents and kinds of knowledge have developed which have been made possible at all only by the informatization of knowledge: in the *quantitative dimension,* by informatization facts, relations, and structures become depictable and calculable which before could not be dealt with at all due to the amounts of information. The terabytes of information which are produced daily by the great international geologic and geographic projects; the modelling and calculation of the characteristics of materials and free forms by help of systems of infinite equations in the field of mechanics; the modelling and visualizing of energetic processes in the fields of thermodynamics or construction physics; recognizing patterns and the numerical comparison of genetic sequences in the field of bio-genetics; modelling and increasingly small-scale calculation of weather development by help of a variety of parameters in the field of meteorology; but also the extensive statistical calculation of cluster structures in the sociological analysis of social structures which has become a new basis for the formation of concepts and terms – all these are examples which make clear the enormous potential of informatized procedures. They lead to the procedures and techniques of *simulation*, used from technological development and design as far as to risk calculation, from the analysis of chemical compounds in respect of their characteristics as far as to traffic planning, from water management in settlements as far as to critical decisions of companies. It must be asked how far these kinds of quantitative insight and decisions based on this, i. e. the manifestations of 'informatized knowledge' – for which Daniel Bell coined the term of 'intellectual technology' more than 30 years ago – have today become the dominating kind of thinking and knowledge among the sciences.[22]

Inevitably, *standardization processes and the creation of norms* go along with informatization at the same time, which mostly also include the pushing through of the English or American language as a standard. On the one hand, standards make the general access to resources possible, but on the other hand regarding content matter they mean a restriction of variety. Maybe the first aspect becomes most visible with the massive processes of de-facto standardization of technological objects in the field of construction, which makes the technological integration of development networks possible at all; the effects of the second aspect become visible by the standardization of contents of naturally complex facts like in the case of diseases by the ICD 10 (International Classification of Diseases), which meanwhile has lead to a worldwide accepted and practically (e. g. in the form of acceptance by health insurances) highly momentous canon of accepted diseases or syndromes (with the effect that non-conventional symptoms are excluded by definition or at least can only indirectly be described and defined). The effect of informatization as re-structuring the world by standardization cannot at all be over-estimated.

6   Subject and Leeways for Shaping Work, Organization and Technology

Here, today's information and communication technologies, which to a great extent aim at mobilizing, making accessible, and keeping knowledge stocks, become visible as part and arena of a new kind of the dialectic of individual and society. The *increased role of knowledge* in society in general and for production and administrative processes in particular – this should be made clear – comes along with the *more important role of the subject* for these processes. At the same time, however, this increased importance of subjectivity in the social reproduction process is accompanied by an intensification of the *fundamental contradictoriness* in which the subject finds itself in modern society: the extended demands on subjectivity are contrasted by the massive tendencies of formalization and objectification of the contexts in the spheres of technology, organization, and economy. The individual must continuously deal with the relationship of freedom and force in his/her concrete life situation. Again and again one's own reflection is limited by social norms which shape our interpretations and thoughts. Subjective creativity is confronted with the previous social and technical imprint of the offer and the structuring of information which contradict and limit the desire for knowledge. The freedom of market – in the double sense of freedom in the market and of being free from the market – is constantly thwarted by the universal dependence on the market. Now, by this dichotomy the conditions of the origin of the individual at the beginning of the bourgeois age is named. Are we thus at the beginning of a renewed rise of the chances for the realization of individuality?

The *new immediacy of the economy*, as addressed in the description of economic and organizational changes by which each individual is confronted particularly in the context of informatized work seems to indicate a comparable socio-structural constellation of the freedom of market and market-dependence; however, the detailed description of this changed status as a 'labour power-entrepreneur' [Voß and Pongratz, 1998, 131-158] makes clear also the limitation of this analogy. Today's freedom of market is essentially restricted to giving shape to one's own position as an employee. Subjectivity is demanded and at the same time restricted. However, it can hardly be doubted that these changes of the subject's status in the informatized society – the erosion of community, the tendencies of disintegration of society, and the tendencies of dissolving solidarity – reach far into personality. Subjectivity itself changes. Just like Don Quichotte at the threshold of modern society fought in vain against the bats of the new windmills, it seems, as Richard Sennet describes it very illustratively, that who trades his own labour power most successfully in a business-like manner rather pushes forward than impedes the disintegration of community and the concrete forms of socialization.

On the other hand, with today's changes of organization and work subjectivity is just demanded. Its mobilization and practice is so to speak a condition of productivity, i. e. economic and social necessity. For dealing with digital information and with informatized knowledge, which is communicated in a highly technological way, needs a broad specialist and social background of experience and embedding into social, practice-orientated networks which meanwhile have become name-giving for modern society. According to the here suggested interpretation, the informatization of work and the parallel increasing significance of knowledge work play a key role: knowledge processes are essentially not one-dimensional but contradictory; they contain a potential of contradiction and conflict, the more as in reality they often come along with different interests. They will not be able to invalidate the tendency towards abstract socialization. But they offer a starting point for preventing individuals from becoming pure function bearers of the technologically and organizationally mediated economy and that what is possible within it.

The support and at the same time the exploitation of the employee's subjectivity by modern management concepts, however, indicate a danger by which formation, maintenance, and further development of individuality are threatened due to the close determination of the purposes of subjective efforts. The pushing through of the not peripheral but subordinated, adapted, integrated individual, for which in the face of the superior forces and rationalities of the system there is only mimetic adaptation, cannot be ruled out. However, we must assume that such a development, as it is accompanied by severe experiences of suffering due to the loss of one's own identity, could not at all happen without contradictions. Particularly under the aspect of further functionality and of extending the information and communication technology the *fight for the subject* has already started today. For their operation the current information and communication technologies demand the more the active subject the more they serve for dealing with knowledge. Thus, far-reaching questions of our society's future will be decided by the direction which the development of information, knowledge, and society will take and by the question of how to handle the information and communication technologies on which they are based.

Under these conditions, what can be meant by *leeways for shaping* in the fields of technology, organization, and work? To a great extent, the organization of today's information and communication technologies is still technology-focused. Computer specialists, system developers, and programmers in their great majority understand themselves as technology-designing engineers or handicraft enthusiasts whose guideline – according to the classical understanding of the engineer – is the elegant realization and optimization of given technological goals or functionalities. Awareness of the fact that technological design is at the same time a formation of social matters – pointedly formulated: that the development of information systems is applied sociology – is either non-existent at all, or this connection is considered a problem and task outside the field of development. This orientation is the subject of immanent, technologically and economically arguing criticism as well as a critique formulated from the outside, referring to organization and work.

The immanent critique states that by restricting its horizon in this way systems' development sets up artificial but nevertheless hardly surmountable hurdles for its own work. The assumptions as usual for development projects, that clients knew exactly what they wanted and that they and the users were the same group, are both not in accordance to reality and are based on neglecting the fundamental social facts of organizations. Accordingly, often there result information systems which show unnecessary complexity and on the other hand lack important functionalities, which furthermore do not meet expectations and are designed in a not very user-friendly way. The strongest confirmation of this criticism is in the still extremely poor success record of software projects themselves: the estimations – according to which about half of the projects fail without any result, on the other hand about one tenth reaches their goals with the available resources of time and money, and the rest is finished with significant additional expenditure and/or reduced functionality – have hardly changed during the past 20 years.[23] In other fields – just think of e. g. a similar project record in flight technology or in the generation of energy – such results would simply be considered disastrous and would soon be deprived of their legitimacy or even their existence. The alternative of an *anthropocentric development of technology* can only be imagined on the basis of an extended, interdisciplinary approach in regard of content matters and the persons involved.

The external critique holds that the thus created information systems follow logics alien to the organizations and to work and thus do not appropriately support them. The again and again observed needs of adjusting organizational processes and work subjects and routine to the demands of information technology is the empirical background of this criticism. This is sure to become clear by the almost proverbially permanent complaints by the great majority of users and affected persons about the jungle-like enigmatic nature of SAP/R3 and the thus not accessible or actually not existent functionalities. The structuring imprint of the organizational realities by IT-technology becomes tangible here. These thoughts imply as a strong support for the arguments in favour of *open and modular system architectures*. In their nucleus they state that only by decentralized system structures also decentralized organization and work forms can be appropriately depicted and supported [Schmiede, 2005]. The alternative to the above mentioned danger of mimetic adaptation of individuals to formalized social processes and pressure is the mimetic adaptation or 'cuddling up' of a small-scale IT-technology, which nevertheless stays to be able to interact by a reasonable modularization, standardized interfaces, and prudent semantic relationships, to the actual working processes and organizational units. Here there is a wide and significant field for further technological development. In my opinion, the increasing role of knowledge processes will exert increasing pressure towards this direction, as knowledge work is usually tied to individual activities and small units.

However, the necessity of facing the demands of interdisciplinary and anthropocentric technology design is also true for the opposite direction. Today, criticism of existent IC-techniques or -technologies is mostly criticism of the effects of technology. Even if in many cases correct in its statements, in principle it is defensive and mostly ineffective because it comes too late. In this sense, struggles against certain information technologies are in most cases nothing but Don Quichotte-like behaviour, for they are confronted by faits accomplis. Potentially effective struggles, fights, and decisions on directions happen in the fields before: by designing the basic structure and the architecture of the information systems. The above used, pointed formulation that the development of information systems was applied sociology is also true for the inversion of arguments: a significant application of sociology is in the development of information systems. Here, social reality is shaped and structured. This is a suggestion which is unusual for humanities and social science scholars and surely is considered strange by most of them. But if one makes clear to oneself that this distinguished reserve is a mirror-image equivalence of the sketched engineer's rationality, i. e. the humanities and sociology variant of shifting a problem away by help of division of labour, one's own obligation to deliver becomes clearer. *Openly facing and getting involved involvement into technology design* will definitely be connected with problems of understanding, frustration, communication difficulties, extended learning processes, and efforts, and it will not produce short-term success; on the long run, however, it promises to approach goals which otherwise would not even come into view.

To have it more generally: where social contradictions become apparent, there usually also leeways for action and shaping reality are created. The radical changes of society coming along with the informatization of work are again and again followed by spaces of 'undeterminedness'. Despite structural affinities there is no automatism, no inevitable relationship of causes between the different social fields; here there are leeways for shaping the future. The condition for influencing, however, is an attitude (and a culture) of facing realities – both in the theoretical-scientific and in the practically organizing sense. To use the really existing uncertainties as a potential, to draw a potential for one's own certainties in the sense of self-determination is only possible under today's conditions by including organizations and information technologies. It is inevitable to be confronted with powerful competitors or opponents but surprising coalitions are also possible. The social struggles for the access to worldwide digital information incl. medial contents, for those standards as characterizing the future, opening up or closing off chances, for the privatization of software by way of granting patents, for the alternative of open source development, as well as for the future of technological network structures are only some of the fields where currently more or less heavy power struggles are happening. Who wants to shape future technological and social reality will not be able to avoid interfering with them.

References

Anderl, Reiner, 2006: Virtuelle Produktentwicklung in der Automobilindustrie, in: Baukrowitz, Andrea, et al., eds., 2006: *Informatisierung der Arbeit: Perspektiven zur Gestaltung eines gesellschaftlichen Umbruchprozesses*, Berlin: edition sigma (forthcoming)

Baukrowitz, Andrea, 1996: Neue Produktionsmethoden mit alten EDV-Konzepten? Zu den Eigenschaften moderner Informations- und Kommunikationssysteme jenseits des Automatisierungsparadigmas, in: Schmiede, Rudi, ed., 1996: *Virtuelle Arbeitswelten*, Berlin (edition sigma), pp. 49-77

Baukrowitz, Andrea, et al., eds., 2006: *Informatisierung der Arbeit: Perspektiven zur Gestaltung eines gesellschaftlichen Umbruchprozesses*, Berlin: edition sigma (forthcoming)

Benner, Chris, 2002: Work in the New Economy. Flexible Labor Markets in Silicon Valley, Malden/Mass.,

Benner, Chris, 2003: 'Computers in the Wild': Guilds and Next-Generation Unionism in the Information Revolution", in: Aad Blok/Greg Downey, eds.: Uncovering Labour in Information Revolutions, 1750-2000. *International Review of Social History* IRSH 48 (2003), Supplement, pp. 181-204

Bielefeld, Ulrich, 2003: *Nation und Gesellschaft*, Hamburg

Boes, Andreas; Baukrowitz, Andrea, 2002: *Arbeitsbeziehungen in der IT-Industrie - Erosion oder Innovation der Mitbestimmung?*, Berlin

Boltanski, Luc/Chiapello, Ève, 2003: *Der neue Geist des Kapitalismus*, Konstanz

Bradner, E./Gloria Mark, 2002: Why Distance Matters. Effects on Cooperation, Persuasion and Deception, in: *Proceedings of the ACM Conference on CSCW (CSCW '02)*, New Orleans, November 16-20, New York, pp. 226-235

Bratton, John, 1992: *Japanization at Work*, London

Burton-Jones, Alan, 1999: *Knowledge Capitalism. Business, Work, and Learning in the New Economy*, Oxford

Castells, Manuel, 2001a: *The Internet Galaxy. Reflections on the Internet, Business and Society, New York*

Castells, Manuel, 2001b: *Der Aufstieg der Netzwerkgesellschaft. Das Informationszeitalter*, Teil 1, Opladen (Engl. Orig. 1996)

Collard, Ron, 1993: *Total Quality. Success Through People*, 2nd ed. London

Degele, Nina, 2000: *Informiertes Wissen. Eine Wissenssoziologie der computerisierten Gesellschaft*, Frankfurt a.m./New York

Dose, Carsten, 2003: 'Flexible Bürokratie. Rationalisierungsprozesse im Privatkundenbereich von Finanzdienstleistern', Diss. TU Darmstadt

Dostal, Werner, 2006: IT-Beschäftigung als Frühindikator neuer Arbeitsformen?, in Baukrowitz, Andrea, et al., eds., 2006: *Informatisierung der Arbeit: Perspektiven zur Gestaltung eines gesellschaftlichen Umbruchprozesses*, Berlin: edition sigma (forthcoming)

Edvinsson, Leif/Malone, Michael S., 1997: *Intellectual Capital. Realizing Your Company's True Value by Finding its Hidden Brainpower*, New York

Ehrenberg, Alain, 2004: *Das erschöpfte Selbst. Depression und Gesellschaft in der Gegenwart, Frankfurt*

Fairchild, Alea M., 2004: *Technological Aspects of Virtual Organizations*. Boston/Dordrecht/London

Faust, Michael/Voskamp, Ulrich/Wittke, Volker, 2004: European Industrial Restructuring in a Global Economy: Fragmentation and Relocation of Value Chains. Paper presented at the International Workshop: European Industrial Restructuring in a Global Economy: Fragmentation and Relocation of Value Chains., Göttingen, March.

Gamm, Gerhard, 2000: Wissen und Information, in: Gamm, ed.: *Nicht nichts. Studien zu einer Semantik des Unbestimmten*, Frankfurt am Main, pp. 192 – 204

Goll, Michaela, 2002: *Arbeiten Im Netz. Kommunikationsstrukturen, Arbeitsabläufe, Wissensmanagement*. Wiesbaden

Haase, Anabel Quan, and Cothrel, Joseph, 2003: Uses of Information Sources in an Internet-Era Firm: Online and Offline, in: Huysman, et al.: *Communities and Technologies*, pp. 143-163

Haug, Wolfgang Fritz, 2003: *High-Tech-Kapitalismus. Analysen zur Produktionsweise, Arbeit, Sexualität, Krieg und Hegemonie*, Hamburg

Heintz, Bettina, 1993: *Die Herrschaft der Regel. Zur Grundlagengeschichte des Computers, Frankfurt/New York*

Holling, Eggert/Kempin, Peter, 1989: *Identität, Geist und Maschine. Auf dem Weg zur technologischen Zivilisation*, Reinbek bei Hamburg, pp. 139 sqq.

Hooff, Bart van der/Elving, Wim/Meeuwsen, Jan Michiel/Dumoulin, Claudette, 2003: *Knowledge Sharing in Knowledge Communities*, in: Huysman, et al.: Communities and Technologies, pp. 119-143

Huysman, Marleen/Wenger, Etienne/Wulf, Volker, eds., 2003: *Communities and Technologies*, Amsterdam/ Dordrecht/Boston/London,

Jackson, Tim, 1993: *Turning Japanese. The Fight for Industrial Control of the New Europe*, London

Knoke, David, 2001: *Changing Organizations. Business Networks in the New Political Economy*, Boulder/Co.

Köhler, Holm-Detlev, 1999: Auf dem Weg zum Netzwerkunternehmen? Anmerkungen zu einem problematischen Konzept am Beispiel der deutschen Automobilkonzerne, in: *Industrielle Beziehungen*, vol. 6 (1999), number 1, pp. 36-51

Klug, Tina, 2006: Flexibilisierung von Arbeit und Beschäftigung: Faktoren sozialer Ungleichheit? Chris Benners Analysen aus Silicon Valley, in Baukrowitz, Andrea, et al., eds., 2006: *Informatisierung der Arbeit: Perspektiven zur Gestaltung eines gesellschaftlichen Umbruchprozesses*, Berlin: edition sigma (forthcoming)

Krämer, Sybille, 1988: *Symbolische Maschinen. Die Idee der Formalisierung in geschichtlichem Abriß*. Darmstadt

Krämer, Sybille, 1989: Geistes-Technologie. Über syntaktische Maschinen und typographische Schriften, In: Werner Rammert/ Gotthard Bechmann, eds. : *Technik und Gesellschaft, Jahrbuch 5*, Frankfurt am Main/New York, pp. 38-52

Lave, Jean/Wenger, Etienne, 1991: *Situated Learning. Legitimate Peripheral Participation*, Cambridge/UK

Lüthje, Boy/Schumm, Wilhelm/Sproll, Martina, 2002: *Contract Manufacturing. Transnationale Produktion und Industriearbeit in der IT-Branche*, Frankfurt am Main/New York

Mark, Gloria, 2002: Conventions and Commitments in Distributed Groups, in: *Computer Supported Cooperative Work. The Journal of Collaborative Computing*, vol. 11, no. 3-4, pp. 349-387

Mark, Gloria/Abrams, Steve/Nassif, Nayla, 2003: Group-to-Group Distance Collaboration. Examining the 'Space Between', in: *Proceedings of the 8th European Conference of Computer-supported Cooperative Work (ECSCW '03)*, 14-18. September 2003, Helsinki, pp. 99-118

Mills, C. Wright, 1955: *Menschen im Büro. Ein Beitrag zur Soziologie der Angestellten*, Köln-Deutz (amerik. Orig. White Collar 1951)

Mishel, Lawrence/Bernstein, Jared/Boushey, Heather, 2003: *The State of Working America 2002/2003*, Ithaca/NY

Nonaka, Ikujiro/Takeuchi, Hirotaka, 1997: *Die Organisation des Wissens*, Frankfurt a.M., New York

Nora, Simon/Minc, Alain, 1979: *Die Informatisierung der Gesellschaft*, edited by Kalbhen, Uwe (Veröffentlichungen der Gesellschaft für Mathematik und Datenverarbeitung), Frankfurt am Main/New York (Franz. Orginal 1978)

Osterlund, Carsten/Carlile, Paul, 2003: How Practice Matters: A Relational View of Knowledge Sharing, in: Huysman, et al.: *Communities and Technologies*, pp. 1-23

Pirker, Theo, 1962: *Büro und Maschine*, Basel

Pirker, Theo, 1963: *Bürotechnik*, Stuttgart

Polanyi, Michael, 1958: *Personal Knowledge. Towards a post-critical philosophy*, London

Probst, G. et al., 1999: *Wissen managen. Wie Unternehmen ihre wertvolle Ressource optimal nutzen*, Wiesbaden

Reich, Robert B, 1994: *Die neue Weltwirtschaft. Das Ende der nationalen Ökonomie*, Frankfurt am Main (Engl. Orig. 1992)

Ruuska, Inkeri/Vartiainen, Matti, 2003: Communities and Other Social Structures for Knowledge Sharing - a Case Study in an Internet Consultancy Company, in: Huysman, et al.: *Communities and Technologies*, pp. 163-85

Schiller, Dan, 2000: *Digital Capitalism. Networking the Global Market System*, Cambridge, Mass./London

Schmiede, Rudi, 1979: Das Ende des westdeutschen Wirtschaftswunders 1966-1977, in: Die Linke im Rechtsstaat, Bd. 2: *Bedingungen sozialistischer Politik 1965 bis heute*, Berlin/West, pp. 34-78

Schmiede, Rudi, 1989: Reelle Subsumtion als gesellschaftstheoretische Kategorie, in: Wilhelm Schumm, ed.: *Zur Entwicklungsdynamik des modernen Kapitalismus. Beiträge zur Gesellschaftstheorie, Industriesoziologie und Gewerkschaftsforschung*. Symposium für Gerhard Brandt, Frankfurt/Main, New York (Campus), pp. 21-38

Schmiede, Rudi, 1996: Informatisierung, Formalisierung und kapitalistische Produktionsweise - Entstehung der Informationstechnik und Wandel der gesellschaftlichen Arbeit, in: Rudi Schmiede, ed.: *Virtuelle Arbeitswelten. Arbeit, Produktion und Subjekt in der 'Informationsgesellschaft'*, Berlin (edition sigma), pp. 15-47

Ibid., pp. 107-128

Schmiede, Rudi, 2000: Virtuelle Arbeitswelten, flexible Arbeit und Arbeitsmärkte, in: Silvia Krömmelbein/Alfons Schmid, eds.: *Globalisierung, Vernetzung und Erwerbsarbeit. Theoretische Zugänge und empirische Entwicklungen*, Wiesbaden, pp. 9-21

Schmiede, Rudi, 2003: Informationstechnik im gegenwärtigen Kapitalismus, in: Gernot Böhme/Alexandra Manzei, eds.: *Kritische Theorie der Technik und der Natur*, München, pp. 173-183

Schmiede, Rudi, 2005: Scientific Work and the Usage of Digital Scientific Information – Some Notes on Structures, Discrepancies, Tendencies, and Strategies, in: Matthias Hemmje/Claudia Niederee/Thomas Risse, eds.: *From Integrated Publication and Information Systems to Virtual Information and Knowledge Environments*. Essays Dedicated to Erich J. Neuhold on the Occasion of His 65th Birthday, Berlin/Heidelberg/New York: Springer Lecture Notes in Computer Science 3379, pp. 107-116

Schmiede, Rudi et al., 2006: Virtuelle Organisation und verteilte Anwendungen – Web Services-basierte Netzwerke als neue Stufe der IT-Technologie, in Baukrowitz, Andrea, et al., eds., 2006: *Informatisierung der Arbeit: Perspektiven zur Gestaltung eines gesellschaftlichen Umbruchprozesses*, Berlin: edition sigma (forthcoming)

Sennett, Richard, 2000: *Der flexible Mensch. Die Kultur des neuen Kapitalismus*, München (Engl. Orig. The Corrosion of Character, 1998)

Silberberger, Holger, 2003: *Collaborative Business und Web Services*, Berlin

Spinner, Helmut, 1998: *Die Architektur der Informationsgesellschaft. Entwurf eines wissensorientierten Gesamtkonzepts*, Bodenheim

Sydow, Jörg/Guido Möllering, 2003: *Kompetenzentwicklung in Netzwerken*, Wiesbaden

The Information Society (http://www.indiana.edu/~tisj/)

Voß, Günter G. /Hans J. Pongratz, 1998: Der Arbeitskraftunternehmer. Eine neue Grundform der Ware Arbeitskraft?, in: *Kölner Zeitschrift für Soziologie und Sozialpsychologie*, vol. 50, number 1, pp. 131 – 158

Warnke, Philine, 2002: Computersimulation und Intervention. Eine Methode der Technikentwicklung als Vermittlungsinstrument soziotechnischer Umordnungen, Diss. FB Gesellschafts- und Geschichtswissenschaften an der TU Darmstadt (http://elib.tu-darmstadt.de/diss/000277/)

Welsch, Johann, 2006: Flexibilisierung und digital divide – Ein verhängnisvoller Kreislauf in: Baukrowitz, Andrea, et al., eds., 2006: *Informatisierung der Arbeit: Perspektiven zur Gestaltung eines gesellschaftlichen Umbruchprozesses*, Berlin: edition sigma (forthcoming)

Weltz, Friedrich/Ortmann, Rolf G., 1992: *Das Softwareprojekt. Projektmanagement in der Praxis*, Frankfurt am Main/New York

Wenger, Etienne, 1998: *Communities of Practice. Learning, Meaning, and Identity*, Cambridge/UK

Wenger, Etienne, 2000: Communities of Practice. The Key to Knowledge Strategy, in: E.L. Lesser/M.A. Fontaine/J.A. Slusher, eds.: *Knowledge and Communities. Resources for the Knowledge-based Economy*, Woburn/MA, pp. 3-20

Wenger, Etienne/Richard McDermott/William M. Snyder, eds., 2002: *Cultivating Communites of Practice*, Boston/MA

Wickens, Peter, 1988: *The Road to Nissan. Flexibility, Quality, Teamwork*, London

Willke, Helmut, 2001: *Systemisches Wissensmanagement*, Stuttgart

Willke, Helmut, 2002: Die Krisis des Wissens, in: Willke, Helmut, ed.: *Dystopia. Studien zur Krisis des Wissens in der modernen Gesellschaft*, Frankfurt am Main, pp. 10 - 47

Windeler, Arnold, 2002: *Unternehmungsnetzwerke*. Wiesbaden

Windeler, Arnold, 2004: Organisation der TV-Produktion in Projektnetzwerken. Zur Bedeutung von Produkt- und Industriespezifika, in: Jörg Sydow/Arnold Windeler, eds.: *Organisation der Content-Produktion*, Wiesbaden, pp. 55-76

---

[1]   The term 'informatization' is not very common in the German language, it is more common in the American language; its linguistic advantage is that it names the process nature of the penetration of all social dimensions by new contents, forms, and techniques

of information. It became popular at first by the French government report, published in 1978, on *L'Informatisation de la Société* by Simon Nora and Alain Minc (in German under the title of [Nora and Minc, 1979]), but in those days it meant primarily the spread of information and communication technologies and their fusion to 'Telematics'; further below I will discuss its further theoretical dimensions.

2   This paper presented the theoretical frame for a conference on 'The Informatization of Work – Society in Fundamental Change', held at Darmstadt, Germany, in January 2005.

3   Castells presented the broadest analysis of the new mode of production and the new form of society, but he is not at all the only sociologist to see a close connection of economic, technological, social, and political changes; see [Reich, 1994]; [Sennett, 2000]; [Burton-Jones, 1999]; [Schiller, 2000]; [Haug, 2003]; [Boltanski and Chiapello, 2003]. See also Castells's empirical network analysis: [Castells, 2001a].

4   At several occasions I have called this tendency the 'new immediacy of economy': both markets and organizations are changed in such a way that economic and political interests of rule and control come into effect for the individual or the group or the organization in the most possible direct way; this institutional change of markets and organizations, however, cannot be called the same as the rule of 'true' (model) economy. See [Schmiede, 2000 (pp. 9-21)], and [Schmiede, 2003 (pp. 173-183)].

5   On lean production in Europe see e. g. [Wickens, 1988]; [Bratton, 1992]; [Jackson, 1993]; [Collard, 1993]

6   In [Schmiede, 1996 (pp. 15-47)], I explained this in more detail; see also the references there. In the field of industrial sociology this development has not been paid much attention to. Exceptions in Germany are: [Pirker, 1962]; and [Pirker, 1963]; in the United States: [Mills, 1955, there part. chapt. 9 (pp. 262-293)]

7   [Baukrowitz, 1996 (pp. 49-77)], showed this in detail for the technological development until the mid-90ies.

8   This term comes from the investigation by [Dose, 2003]

9   See [Lüthje, Schumm and Sproll, 2002]; [Faust, Voskamp and Wittke, 2004]; see on car industries [Köhler, 1999 (pp. 36-51)]

10 See on this [Knoke, 2001], and as an overview [Fairchild, 2004]; for Germany: [Windeler, 2002];[Windeler, 2004 (pp. 55-76)]

11 See on the concept [Probst et al., 1999]; [Willke, 2001]; on the theoretical basics see [Polanyi, 1958]; on the popularized version: [Nonaka and Takeuchi, 1997]

12 This concept was at first developed and propagated by Etienne Wenger. See [Lave and Wenger, 1991]; [Wenger, 1998]; [Wenger, 2000 (pp. 3-20)]; [Wenger, McDermott and Snyder, 2002]; an overview at the state of research is offered by the conference volume [Huysman, Wenger and Wulf, 2003], and by the issue 2/2005 of the journal *The Information Society*

13 See in more detail [Wenger et al., 2002], Chapter 2: 'Communities of Practice and Their Structural Elements'

14 [Haase and Cothrel, 2003 (pp. 143-163)]; [Hooff, et al., 2003 (pp. 119-143)]; [Osterlund and Carlile, 2003 (pp. 1-23)]; [Ruuska and Vartiainen, 2003 (pp. 163-185)]; see for Germany: [Goll, 2002]; [Sydow and Möllering, 2003]; see on the CSCW-context e. g.: [Bradner and Mark, 2002 (pp. 226-235)]; [Mark, 2002]; [Mark, Abrams and Nassif, 2003 (pp. 99-118)]

15 Here, I introduce these tendencies only as a summary; for a more detailed overview see [Dostal et al., 2006 (chapter 3.4)]. An older, summarizing overview is found in [Schmiede, 1996 (pp. 107-128)]; a good overview at the development in the USA is found in [Knoke, 2001 (pp. 164-203)]

16 A recently completed study by the Institut für Arbeit und Technik (Institute for Work and Technology) in Gelsenkirchen, Germany, estimates the share of chronically exhausted members of staff of IT-projects to be one third; quoted from: *Computer-Zeitung*, No. 18, May 2, 2004. According to estimations by the Bundesanstalt für Arbeitsschutz und

Arbeitsmedizin (Federal Institute for Health and Safety Protection at the Workplace and Industrial Medicine), EU-wide 28% of all employees complain about stress-related problems; according to estimations, stress at the workplace causes up to 60% of all sick days, i. e. yearly costs of several hundred billions – this is also a way of externalizing costs! Regarding retirement due to reduced ability to work, psychological illnesses caused by the 'basic noise of fear' of failure and unemployment have meanwhile become the most important single complex of causes; in 2002 their share was 28% (tendency rising); quoted from the German newspaper *Darmstädter Echo*, September 30, 2004. Finally, see more generally [Ehrenberg, 2004]

[17] Even if in the face of an increasingly difficult situation crossing a certain threshold we can observe increased readiness for inner-company representation of interests (see [Boes and Baukrowitz, 2002]), for the time being this has not led to a positive trade union commitment of employees.

[18] See [Benner, 2002], as well as [Benner, 2003 (pp. 181-204)]; see on these studies the essay by [Klug, 2006].

[19] See on digital divide [Welsch, 2006]; on information workers see [Dostal, 2006]. On the empirical analysis of the development in the US: [Mishel, Bernstein and Boushey, 2003]; on the following also [Castells, 2001b, Chapter 4]

[20] See on this in more detail: [Schmiede, 2000] as well as further: [Gamm, 2000 (pp. 192-204)] and [Willke, 2002 (pp. 10-47)] as well as [Polanyi, 1958]

[21] In German language, knowledge ('Wissen') is closely related to certainty ('Gewissheit').

[22] See [Warnke, 2002]. By the way, this question can also be extended to traditional *fields of qualitative analysis*: by way of computer-based possibilities of retrieval and analysis the work with texts – traditionally in the focus of humanities from theology to philosophy and linguistic sciences as well as history and condensed in the hermeneutic procedures – is provided with a new basis (the development of computer philology shows this clearly). If in the past a theologist or a literary specialist could be reasonably occupied with the comparison and analysis of texts, this traditional scientific activity tends to becoming obsolete in favour of new – though hardly developed – complex procedures of comparing contents. The comparatively low degree of informatization in the humanities and the social sciences indicates openness towards experience and variety as well as analytical weakness and a backlog of procedures at the same time. [Degele, 2000] made this philosophically and sociologically highly significant fact of the change of knowledge by way of being informatized a matter of discussion, but did not solve it theoretically.

[23] [Weltz and Ortmann, 1992] investigated these connections as early as 15 years ago in a very concise study; despite all further development of computing science the problems as described by the investigation are still existent.

Designing the Accountability of Enterprise Architectures

Gian Marco Campagnolo and Gianni Jacucci
University of Trento, Sociology and Social Research, Italy
gianmarco.campagnolo@soc.unitn.it, gianni.jacucci@soc.unitn.it,
http://www.soc.unitn.it/dsrs

Abstract: Designing enterprise architectures for accountability is to reason about options. Instead of taking enterprise architectures as products, the paper seeks to comprehend how they are produced. Considering enterprise architecture as an entangled category of sociological, political and democratic challenges provide an opportunity to determine the political *topos* of enterprise architectures.

Keywords: Design for Accountability, Enterprise Architecture, Actor Network Theory, Circulating System of Scientific Objects, Located Accountabilities.

1   Introduction

In information engineering, a model is a guide for writing the code of applications. It is used as a protocol for the exchange of specifics among engineers. For enterprise architects, instead, a model gives guidance in visualizing the overall organizational activity [Zachman 1987]. Previously, different models coexisted in enterprises, and each model had its application. A model for the development of a software application would be devised using MS Visio, for example. A model for product development would be developed using CAD. A blueprint would be the model of the organization. And a model of business processes would be constructed using a business process modelling (BPM) application. Today, enterprise architects envisage the use of a single information platform (the 'enterprise architecture') to model all organizational activities: product, processes, human resources and information systems. This phenomenon can be interpreted as the radical modernization, or 'reflexive modernization' [Beck 1994], of enterprise systems (where 'enterprise systems' means the overall family of enterprise modelling tools). The radical modernization of enterprise systems represented by enterprise architectures (EA) has two distinctive features:

Please use the following format when citing this chapter:

Campagnolo, G. M., Jacucci, G., 2006, in IFIP International Federation for Information Processing, Volume 223, Social Informatics: An Information Society for All? In Remembrance of Rob Kling, eds. Berleur, J., Numinen, M. I., Impagliazzo, J., (Boston: Springer), pp. 355–366.

1. EA are turning from applications on single functions - like expert systems or business process automation - into systems to control overall organizational action;
2. EA is not about introducing a new technology into organizations where there is none; it is about introducing a new technology on top of existing ones.

These features make 'enterprise architecture' a category that must be reconfigured both in political terms and from the point of view of sociological analysis. Moreover, the radical or reflexive modernization of the domain of enterprise systems [Beck 1994] informs public debate on reform of the control systems of democratic institutions.

In this paper we will use the term 'enterprise architecture' to denote the modelling platform (the enterprise architecture modelling tool) as well as the enterprise model produced from it. The question that we shall seek to answer is this: what would a design for the accountability of enterprise architectures look like?

The paper is structured as follows. First we describe enterprise architecture as an entangled category of sociological, political and democratic challenges. We then review the current literature on accountability in the information system field. The limitations of the current literature are presented. Thereafter, we develop our own proposal of design for accountability based on actor-network theory. The empirical part of the paper is devoted to the case of an enterprise architecture modelling platform observed in a Scandinavian software company. The role of enterprise architectures (EA) in the context of US regulations on financial reporting is presented. In particular, we present how EA facilitate fulfilment of templates required by the Office of Management and Budget for allowing investments of public money on IT. We will underline how the dimension of financial reporting is related to the work of modellers and how the work of modellers is related to the scientific acceptance of a modelling approach. We will also present the relation between the scientific acceptance and the way modeller gather user requirement. Drawing on interviews and ethnographies of modellers gathering requirements, we witness a series of attempts to foster connections through which to gain access to the organization to be modelled and then immediately afterwards, to cut them, nullify them, obliterate them. Our interest for accountability raises from this observed trend. The data will be structured and analyzed according to the theoretical framework proposed. Discussion and final remarks conclude the paper.

2   Enterprise Architecture as an Entangled Category of Sociological, Political and Democratic Challenges

2.1   The Superseding of the Political System

In the case of EA, the material to be modernized is not material provided by a political representation. What is to be replaced by the introduction of computer-based technology is not labour and its union representatives. The modernization concerns a previous modernization process that has already dealt with the problem of reference. In industrial society, the problem of reference was a problem of accuracy and precision. In today's risk society, the problem of reference is one of trust, election, obedience. In industrial society the formula was 'technology replaces labour': an object took the place of subjective performance. In the risk society, technology supersedes technology: objectivity applies to itself [Beck 1994].

2.2   The Elusion of the Sociological Analysis

It is not only the political system that has been superseded. The sociological analysis is also eluded. The category of 'accountability' in its sociological version cannot be used to make enterprise architectures 'visible and reportable'. Accountability is a category of ethnomethodology conceived by Alfred Schutz [Schutz 1953/1971], developed by Garfinkel [Garfinkel 1967], Sacks [Sacks 1966-7,1992] and Cicourel [Cicourel 1974] and applied in organizational studies by Bittner [Bittner 1965], Silverman and Jones [Silverman and Jones 1976] and Boden [Boden 1994]. This tradition postulates that accountability is the main bond of human interaction. Accountability is considered to be a 'members concern'. It doesn't seem to be explained in what are the relations between different accounting rules, which suggests an implicit naturalism [Lynch and Bogen 1994]. We still consider accountability to be a bond, but we extend the notion to non-human interactions as well. What is specific to accountability in technology production is its 'dismemberment' [Beck 2005] from the social setting taken as a gathering of humans with some kind of shared membership. What we have in mind in developing the concept of accountability is not a social community but a still-to-be-organized number of human and non-human actors jointly implicated by an issue [Marres 2005].

2.3   The Debate on Reform of the Control Systems of Democratic Institutions as an Integral Part of EA Analysis

The debate on reform of the control systems of Western democratic institutions is an integral part of enterprise architecture analysis. The regulations of the US Congress contain provisions on a 'sound and integrated information architecture technology' [CCA 1996] and 'graphical representations' [SOA 2002] that governmental agencies and corporations have to provide on the investment of public money and the reliability of their disclosures.

This represents a shift from the idea of the 'state manager' – with the capabilities and the instruments to intervene directly in the market – to the idea of a 'regulatory state' [La Spina and Majone 2000] which delegates regulation of the markets for both private and public goods to private actors. The state oversees this shift via specific regulatory authorities, which supervise the action of private actors, considered valuable for a community by implementing regulations.

Because these regulations establish internal control procedures in the form of monitoring techniques, they help create what in anthropology has been termed an 'audit culture' [Strathern 2002].

Technology plays a key role. Michael Power, a leading scholar of audit studies, states that a distinctive feature of an audit culture is the switch to system accountability [Power 1994]. Technology is said to ensure a more 'neutral' system of control. Enterprise architecture has been advocated as one such control system by the 'Information Technology Reform Act' [CCA 1996] of the US Congress and by the more recent 'Sarbanes Oxley Act' of 2002 [SOA 2002].

Studying enterprise architecture as an entangled category of sociological political and democratic challenges provides an opportunity to determine the locus of the conditions of possibility within which we want to live, this being the political *topos* of enterprise architectures. Designing enterprise architectures for accountability is to reason about options [Mol 1999:80]. Instead of taking enterprise architecture as a product, we want to comprehend how it is produced.

3   Design for Accountability

Accountability is on the list of desiderata of system developers [Leven 1995, Paulk et al. 1993]. However, the expression 'design for accountability' is a more recent coinage by Sara Eriksen [Eriksen 2002]. In her paper, citing the ethnomethodological definition of accountability – 'visibly-rational-and-reportable-for-all-practical-purposes' [Garfinkel 1967:vii] – Eriksén remarks that design methodologies lack an understanding of accountability 'from a user perspective'.

The scholars that Eriksen considers in regard to the concept of 'design for accountability' are Paul Dourish [Dourish 1993, 2001], Harold Garfinkel [Garfinkel 1967] and Lucy Suchman [Suchman 1994,2000]. Although Eriksén acknowledges that all these authors have influenced her work, the most influential of them is certainly Lucy Suchman.

Suchman can be indeed considered a pioneer in the study of accountability in design practices. In 1993 she published 'Technologies of Accountability' [Suchman 1993] on the work of air traffic controllers, in 1994 'Working Relations in Technology Production and Use' [Suchman 1994], and drawing on the former paper, in 2000 she issued a work in progress entitled 'Located Accountabilities in Technology Production' [Suchman 2000]. Suchman distinguishes three design practices on a scale of increasing accountability:

1. 'design from nowhere', where the designer is only concerned with system accountability, that is, how the system feeds back on the function assigned to it by the developer;
2. 'detached intimacy', which is when the circuit of accountability is limited to the community to which the engineer belongs; and
3. 'located accountability', when the designer makes him/herself politically accountable for his actions to a public wider than the community of system engineers.

The notable aspect of the notion of 'located accountability' is that it goes beyond Garfinkel's idea of accountability as a member concern. Suchman instead adopts a deliberately political stance. As also noted by Eriksén [Eriksen 2002], the concept of 'located accountability' implies reflexivity and awareness of our personal participation in various communities and of the possible benefits to be derived from 'boundary-crossing networking' [Eriksen 2002:182]. Each of us must be accountable for our actions in a wider and 'commonal' sense [Eriksen 2002:182]. The design and use of technologies are collective attainments for which each of us is, in some way, responsible.

The notion of 'located accountability' gives a broader and civic meaning to designer responsibilities. The question to bear in mind in technology production is, Suchman writes, 'Who is doing what to whom?' [Suchman 2000:5]. We would point out that, although we too adopt Suchman's stance, we do not maintain that designers inscribe their will in objects and that objects serve them. We instead distinguish between a 'substantive' view of design and a 'propositional' one. Developing a propositional view of design means seeing 'design' not as a noun but as a verb. <requirement>, <design> and <user> are not separate terms in a list, but instead form a proposition. On the substantive view of design, the political *topos* – where a decision is made – is always deferred to an elsewhere. 'Design' is determined by 'requirement', and 'requirement' is motivated by 'design', so that the decision defers to a matter of fact, making impossible to track the trajectory of accountability. On a propositional view of design, a chain of inscription between human and non-human actors takes the place of the dichotomy between matters of fact and designer decisions.

4   Actor-Network Theory

The notion of 'located accountabilities' has a drawback. It gives no indication as to the 'broad sense' in which the designer must take responsibility for his/her actions. Even when referring to Suchman's writings on accountability in design practices [Suchman 1993,1994], it is not easy to garner clarification of the 'wider and 'commonal' sense' in which the designer must take responsibility for his/her actions. A similar criticism of this aspect to the concept of 'located accountabilities' is made by Neyland and Woolgar [Neyland and Woolgar 2002], when they write:

> across the wide range of ethnomethodological studies of accountability, the analytic status of the 'public', that is, the nature and identity of those for whom practical actions are 'publicly observable' varies considerably. The nature of the 'public observation' also varies. [Neyland and Woolgar 2002:263]

In order to determine the 'nature and identity' and the 'ontological status' of the 'public observation' that makes an action accountable in the ethnomethodological version of accountability, we may resort to actor-network theory. Actor-network theory has never been codified into a full fledged theory; it is better described as an interpretative approach and a literary genre. Its two sources of theoretical inspiration are actant theory [Greimas and Courtes 1982] and the notion of translation [Callon 1975]. We make use here of actant theory, a version of structuralist analysis introduced by the French semiologist Algirdas Greimas [Greimas and Cortes 1982], who propounded the notion of 'narrative program': a change of state produced by any subject affecting any other subject. Greimas speaks of grammatical subjects, which may or may not reveal themselves as persons. He accordingly replaces the term 'character' with the term 'actant', "that which accomplishes or undergoes an act" [Greimas and Cortes 1982], because it applies not only to human beings but also to animals, objects and concepts. Narrative programs are chained together in a logical sequence to form a narrative trajectory. The circulating system of scientific facts [Latour 1999:70] used to structure field data is an adaptation of Greimas's narrative trajectory to description of the making of technological objects. In our proposed design for accountability, the circulating system of scientific and technological facts assigns analytical status to the public observation that makes designer actions accountable, thus filling the analytical gap in the ethnomethodological version of accountability. The use of actor-network theory [Callon and Latour 1981] in a proposed design for enterprise system accountability focuses attention on the carefully arranged sequence of steps and movements that involve actors (models and enterprises, referents and modellers) in negotiations and associations.

Moreover, actor-network theory provides a topology for accountability design that allows us to do away with the 'requirement', 'design' and 'user' triad. We can thus study the multiplicity of enterprise architecture accounts and how this multiplicity produces the modelling platform in relation. Multiplicity is different from plurality. In plurality there are mutually exclusive, discrete perspectives existing side by side in a transparent space, while at the centre the object of attention is singular, intangible, untouched. In multiplicity, reality is performed and enacted rather than observed. Instead of being seen by diverse watching eyes while remaining untouched in the centre, reality is manipulated by various tools used by diverse practices [Mol 1999:77].

5   Empirical Study

5.1   Data Source

We report a field study carried out at the production site of an enterprise architecture tool – which we call 'EPISTEME'. EPISTEME is delivered by a software company headquartered in Scandinavia. We gained access to the software company as a result of longstanding collaboration between the Information Engineering Laboratory of the University of Trento and the software company producing EPISTEME. Preparation for the fieldwork started in January 2004 with preliminary interviews, and the fieldwork itself was conducted at the EPISTEME production site from September to December 2004 using ethnographic methods. The data were obtained by means of regular weekly interviews with the managers of the company's Product Business Unit and Research & Development Business Unit (BU), and with developers working in its R&D BU. In progress at the same time as the field study was an EU research project – let us call it MINERVA. We were able to discuss the MINERVA requirements, at their various stages of modelling, with the developers working on them. Further data were collected from the minutes of meetings held by the modellers with one industrial project partner and from the MINERVA deliverable documents. Other sources of data were the scientific papers published by the manager of the Research & Development Business Unit (BU). The company has a branch in North America, and data on EPISTEME's American market were gathered from mail exchanges between the North American branch manager and the Product Business Unit manager at the headquarters in Scandinavia. Finally, marketing materials were analyzed and compared with the on-line marketing materials of competitor companies in North America.

5.2   Data Structure

The data are structured according to the scheme known as the 'circulatory system of scientific facts' [Latour 1999:98]. Obtaining requirements from users (mobilization) is the first of a number of loops that must be measured in order to calculate a model's accountability. Together with 'mobilization', the model is then translated into scientific text to convince the enterprise architects' audience of its autonomy from competing approaches (autonomization). Third, the model is sold on the market. (alliances). Finally, Enterprise Architectures reaches the public controversy of financial reporting (public).

5.3   Data Presentation

The role of EPISTEME in the context of US regulations on financial reporting has been investigated. We quote an excerpt from an article by BW, the manager of the company's North American branch. 'Clinger Cohen Fulfilled? Agency Officials are Taking Enterprise Architecture and Capital Planning Seriously'. In this article BW relates success in compliance with the regulations to success in selling EPISTEME to governmental public agencies. He writes:

Cohen might be gratified by the sophistication of agencies' compliance with the act..1

This sentence comes exactly one year after Government Accountability Office reports 1% of governmental agencies applying Enterprise Architectures following the criteria of the OMB provision of 20022. He adds:

For more than a year some agencies [...] have been developing prototype models for a single line of business that could be duplicated department wide.

The gratification derives from the fact that if the EPISTEME application is applied to one single line of business, it will be 'duplicated' (without variations) to the scale of the entire organization. Since it is used by 1% of agencies, it will be soon used by the remaining 99%. In addition, the article furnishes an example of the 'sophistication' with which agencies use enterprise architectures. The example is 'the marriage' with 'capital planning' and 'investment control':

An example is the marriage of the capital planning and investment control process – the financial rationale behind funding requests – with the enterprise architecture model that officials must incorporate into agency business cases contained in the OMB Exhibit 300s.

OMB Exhibit 300 is the format for IT investment proposals that agencies submit to OMB in order to obtain a 'Delegation of Procurement Authority' (DPA). A DPA is approval for IT investment issued by OMB. EPISTEME is presented as a product able to speed up and facilitate fulfilment of the Exhibit 300 by generating them dynamically.

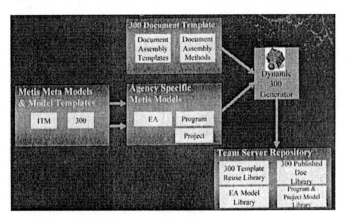

Fig. 1. The dynamic 300 generator

Here EPISTEME performs the highly specific role of dynamically generating the format to obtain funding. The general name for this function is 'Capital Asset Planning', which is the key factor in the marriage between enterprise architecture and financial reporting.

In fig.1 a very simple diagram depicts what EPISTEME does. A number of square shapes, represent causes and consequences in a line. Our analysis did not stop to this frame. Our ethnography has been driven by the following question: what do we find if we expand the diagram a bit more? Where an imaginary arrow pointing to the box 'EPISTEME Meta Model & Model Templates' departs from? The answer can be found drawing on other sources of data analyzed. Namely we had: scientific papers published by the R&D department of the Company and by observation of meeting modellers had with users in the MINERVA project. We will be fast stepping through these other sources of data, for our aim is to make our point on accountability. The element framed out from the dynamic Exhibit 300 generator is the work of modellers developing EPISTEME. To understand modellers' work we have to go back to the 'scientific foundations' of the modelling approach used to build EPISTEME. The scientific foundations of the modelling approach, to its turn, involve the discourse on the empirical base, that is, the way in which the requirements are collected. The empirical base is populated by 'referents' and by their knowledge about the organization. The knowledge of the organization's referent providing the empirical base is defined by a modeller in the following way:

> I enter a company and I have a contact with a referent that gives me the data. The referent has a *limited knowledge* that is *unstructured*. It is *tacit*.[3]

6   Data Analysis

The modeller first credits the data gathering process with the presence of a referent ('I have a contact with a referent that gives me the data'). Then s/he quickly discredits it, ascribing to that referent 'limited', 'tacit' and 'unstructured' knowledge of his/her daily work practice. On following the itinerary of the 'data' step by step from the data collection site to that of their elaboration in EPISTEME, we witnessed a series of attempts to foster connections through which to gain access to the organization to be modelled and then immediately afterwards, to cut them, nullify them, obliterate them. First memory of the passages accomplished is impaired. Later there is a quest for the model appearing on the computer screen to be an accurate representation of the organization where the data come from.

This reconstruction prompted us to enquire as to the reason why this question about accuracy is asked. According to our empirical findings, the reason was to obtain a perfectly defined product from EPISTEME. It is only by defining the referent's know-how as unstructured knowledge that the call for a different kind of knowledge can be sustained. Only by opposing two different kinds of knowledge can structured knowledge be preferred instead of unstructured know-how. And finally, only by leaving out of the scene the dependency of one form of knowledge (straight and scientific) on the other (clever and crooked) that a perfectly defined product can be obtained.

We can extend this argument to analysis of the role of EPISTEME in the context of US regulations on financial reporting. Analysis of SOA provisions shows the know-how of independent auditors as inadequate because of a conflict of interests. Enactment of this inadequacy produces an image of enterprise architecture as know-how free from conflicts of interest. As a consequence a last relation is made: that of the public with the private. The felicity condition of the financial reporting triangle [Cullinan 2004], where the resolution of urgent financial controversies in real time is secured by the presence of a heterogeneous and odd system of actors (independent auditor, CEO, internal audit committee), is represented by enterprise architecture software firms as places where the intervention of a 'built-in system' with no need for consultation is beneficial and resolutive. It is now that the technical problem becomes totally political. It is not a system clash but an interest clash that the technology must prevent. What is now required by a piece of technology is accountability, election and obedience. No longer accuracy.

7   Discussion

The foregoing description of EPISTEME using the circulatory system of scientific facts [Latour 1999:98] has shown that the interests that lie behind technology are significant and diverse. For this reason, requiring all these interests to fit together without any clash is problematic. To make EPISTEME a system that prevents interest clashes, without any additional warranty, is to erase what makes EPISTEME a secure system: the visibility of its interest clashes. If EPISTEME is maintained as something neutral that supplies decisive knowledge, something is created that is precisely what is to be avoided: a thousand times bigger interest clash between technology and politics. Because financial reporting is subject to regulations, it can be shaped as a 'public' discourse. According to Dewey [Dewey 1927], 'public' is a place deprived of the option of decisive knowledge. In the 'public' dimension, decision making have to be made in 'real-time' under the constraints of 'number, priority and urgency' [Latour 1999:263]. There is no alternative or substitutive decision-making procedure under these conditions. Why, then, is EPISTEME deemed to be a more neutral system of control? What EPISTEME can do in this frame is constantly to enrol new elements, increase the list of entities that must be taken into account.

Continuous backward references instead turn EPISTEME into a structured scientific method, so that it becomes insecure and decision making by the financial reporting system becomes impossible.

For this to be avoided, it is necessary to make apparent all the connections among the loops in the EPISTEME circulatory system.

8   Conclusion

Finally: what would a design for the accountability of enterprise systems look like? We outline some features. First, enterprise models should be represented as different from independent objects, perhaps as *assemblies*. The visual metaphor must be replaced by an *industrial metaphor* taking account of each intermediary in the circulatory system of technological facts. Moreover, the work of modellers, and the role played by the referents of the organizations that give them the data, together with their *bodies* and their *voices*, must be better represented, all the way down to the model's production line. Finally, new strategies and new media for the *distribution of responsibilities* in engineering must be identified and developed. These various aspects warrant further investigation.

References

[1]   Beck, U. & Giddens, A. & Lash S. (1994) *Reflexive Modernization. Politics, Tradition and Aesthetics in the Modern Social Order*. Cambridge : Polity Press.

[2]   Beck U. (2005), Neither Order Nor Peace, *Common Knowledge* 11:1, Duke University Press.

[3]   Bittner, E. (1965), The Concept of Organization, *Social Research* 31:240-55.

[4]   Boden D (1994), *The Business of Talk. Organization in Action*, Polity Press, Cambridge.

[5]   Callon Michel and Latour Bruno, (1981), Unscrewing the big Leviathan: how actors macro-structure reality and how sociologists help them to do so, in Knorr-Cetina K. and Cicourel A.V. eds, *Advances in Social Theory and Methodology*, Routledge & Kegan Paul, Boston.

[6]   Callon Michel (1975), L'opération de traduction, Roqueplo M. (eds.), *Incidence des rapports sociaux sur le développement scientifique et technique*, 1-28, CNRS, Paris.

[7]   *Clinger-Cohen Act of 1996, Public Law*, 104-106, 110 Stat. 684 (1996), 40 U.S.C. 11315.

[8]   Cicourel A.V. (1974), *Cognitive Sociology. Language and Meaning in Social Interaction*, Free Press, New York.

[9]   Cullinan C. (2004), Enron as a a symptom of audit process breakdown: can the Sarbanes-Oxley Act cure the disease?, *Critical Perspectives on Accounting* **15**: 853-864.

[10] Dewey J. (1927), *The Public and its Problems*. Holt, New York.

[11] Dourish P. (2001), *Where the Action Is? A new foundation for embodied interaction*, Cambridge, MIT Press.

[12] Dourish P. (1993), *Technomethodology: Paradoxes and Possibilities*, Proceedings of an ACM Conference on HCI 96, Vancouver, Canada, April 13-18.

[13] Eriksen S. (2002), Designing for Accountability, in *Proceedings of the Second Nordic Conference on Human-Computer Interaction*, October 19-23, Aarhus, Denmark.

[14] Garfinkel, H. (1967), *Studies in Ethnometodology*, Prentice-Hall, Englewood Cliffs, NJ.

[15] Greimas Algirdas Julien, Courtés Joseph (1982), *Semiotics and language. An analytical dictionary*, Indiana University Press, Blumington, IN.

[16] Latour Bruno, (1999), *Pandora's Hope: Essays on the Reality of Science Studies*. Harvard University Press, Cambridge.

[17] La Spina A., Majone G. (2000), *Lo Stato Regolatore*, Il Mulino, Bologna.

[18] Levén P. (1995), 'From use to action. Concerning quality in a market-oriented information system', Licentiate Thesis. Dept. of Informatics.

[19] Lynch M. and Bogen D (1994), Harvey Sacks primitive natural science. *Theory, Culture & Society*, **11**: 65-104.

[20] Marrres N. (2005), Issues Spark a Public into Being, A Key but Often Forgotten Point of the Lippman-Dewey Debate, in Latour B. and Wiebel P. (eds), *Making Things Public. Atmospheres of Democracy*, Engelhardt & Bauer, Karlsrhue.

[21] Mol Annemarie (1999), Ontological Politics. A word and some questions, in J.Law and J.Hasseard eds. *Actor Network and After*, The Editorial Board of Sociological Review, Oxford: Blackwell Publishers.

[22] Neyland D. and Woolgar S. (2002), Accountability in action?: The case of a database purchasing decision, *British Journal of Sociology* **53**:259-274.

[23] Paulk M., Curtis B., Chrissis M.B., Weber C., Capability Maturity Model, *IEEE Software*, July 1993: 18-27.

[24] Power Michael, (1994), *The Audit Explosion*, Demos, London.

[25] Sacks H. (1966-7,1992), *Lectures on Conversations* (vol.1 2). Blackwell, Oxford.

[26] Sarbanes-Oxley Act of 2002, *Public Law* 107-204, 107th Cong., 22nd sess. (30 July 2002).

[27] Schutz A. (1953), Common-Sense and Scientific Interpretation of Human Action, *Philosophy and Phenomenological Research*, **14**:1-38.

[28] Silverman, D. and Jones J. (1976), *Organizational Work*, Collier MacMillian, London.

[29] Strathern Marilyn (2002), *Audit cultures: anthropological studies in accountability, ethics and academy*, Routledge, London.

[30] Suchman Lucy, (2000), 'Located Accountabilities in Technology Production.' Sawyer Seminar on Heterarchies, Santa Fe Institute, October.

[31] Suchman Lucy (1994), Working Relations in Technology Production and Use, *CSCW* 2: 21-39, Nedherlands, Kluwer Academic Publisher.

[32] Suchman, L. (1993) Technologies of Accountability: of lizards and aeroplanes, in G. Button *Technology in Working Order: Studies of work, interaction and technology*, London: Routledge.

[33] Thomas, N. (1991), *Entangled Objects. Exchange, material culture and colonialism in the Pacific*. Cambridge, Mass: Harvard University Press.

[34] Zachman, J.A. 'A Framework for Information Systems Architecture,' *IBM Systems Journal*, vol. 26, no. 3 (1987).

---

1   BW (2004), Clinger-Cohen Fulfilled?, http://www.fcw.com/fcw/articles/2004/1115/oped-wright-11-15-04.asp
2   Davis T., Turner J. (2003), Enterprise Architecture, GAO 04-40.
3   Excerpt from interview with TT of 10-01-2004, Rovereto.

Creating a Framework to Recognize Context-Originated Factors in IS in Organizations

Tuija Tiihonen, Mikko Korpela, and Anja Mursu
University of Kuopio, HIS R & D Unit, Finland
tuija.tiihonen@uku.fi, mikko.korpela@uku.fi
University of Kuopio, Department of Computer Science, Finland
anja.mursu@uku.fi

Abstract. Information system (IS) is a complicated structure of social and technical systems. They are part of every organization in western and developing countries. Uncertainty has always been a part of software and information system development, and working globally increases the uncertainty. To know some basic factors of the IS context, the interconnectedness of human and technological informatics in everyday work could be a way to decrease this uncertainty. In this paper, we present the theoretical basis of three context models to construct a framework to be used as one method when evaluating different IS contexts in IS use and development.

Keywords: information system, context, information system development, information system use, organization

1 Introduction

In the age of globalization, the world is becoming more and more interconnected, and information and communication technology (ICT) is becoming more important for everyone [Heeks 2002, Moyi 2003, Walsham et al. 2006, WITFOR 2005]. All organizations utilize information systems (IS), which increasingly use ICT. Good application or design of an information system is not obvious when it is based on technical requirements only, without understanding how people work and what their environment and context is [Kling 1999]. Even if ICT and IS development include universal codes and rules, the transfer of information systems is not an automatic success. Uncertainty has always been a part of software and information system developing projects; the mismatch of cultures and contexts can cause problems

Please use the following format when citing this chapter:

Tiihonen, T., Korpela, M., Mursu, A., 2006, in IFIP International Federation for Information Processing, Volume 223, Social Informatics: An Information Society for All? In Remembrance of Rob Kling, eds. Berleur, J., Numinen, M. I., Impagliazzo, J., (Boston: Springer), pp. 367–379.

especially when working globally [Lai et al. 2003, Molla et al. 2005]. Knowing the basic factors of the IS context could be a way to decrease this uncertainty. To find these factors the information systems should be approached not only as a technical but also as a social system, [Walsham et al. 1990], which is also the principle of Social Informatics (SI) research [Kling 1999].

This research is part of the INDEHELA -programme. INDEHELA [Korpela et al. 2006] (*Informatics Development for Health in Africa*) has, in its previous phases, produced knowledge about information systems development practices mainly in Nigeria [Mursu 2002, Soriyan 2004]. In IS development there is need for context-oriented implementation, yet there is not much analytical research conducted on the social context [Avgerou et al. 2004]. The existing IS context studies are not particularly focused on producing theories, frameworks, or methods to observe the working environment, but more on the technical and economical aspects of developing IS. The object of the present phase of the INDEHELA is to focus on this deficiency. The aim is to develop a framework as a method to evaluate different IS contexts in IS use and development. The partners of the INDEHELA in this phase are in Finland, Nigeria, Mozambique, and South Africa.

The main research question is: *How to recognize contextual factors that affect IS development and use?* How would we find these factors? What are these factors like? How can the factors be used in the evaluation of IS use and development? The objective of this research is to create a framework to help observe the context and to find answers to the former questions.

In this paper, we present the theoretical basis to create this framework. Section 2 presents the theoretical background and it includes three models of context: the scopes of context, the categories of contextual factors, and the analysis levels of contexts. Section 3 concerns the methodology we use. Section 4 is a first attempt to use the ideas of the context models as a framework to elicit different contextual factors.

2 Theoretical background

The concept of context is huge and very difficult to define or explain. In this section, we define these sub concepts of context: the scopes of contexts, the categories within contexts, and the levels of contexts.

2.1 Scopes of Context

Context surrounds and affects every item, idea, or action. The context may create or increase, as well as hinder, limit, or decrease those phenomena. Context is an essential concept in different fields of science. On the most concrete level, for example, the context applies in archaeology. Any artefact found by an archaeologist is tightly connected to the context it is found in. The context may help define the purpose of an object, or an object can lighten the surrounding context and culture.

Anthropology is a science that studies humankind. In anthropology, context is a little more abstract concept than in archaeology, but very essential as well. In the context definition of Tapaninen (2005), there are three levels of contexts: cultural context, historical context, and immediate context. Since this research considers the information system in organization mostly as a social system, a system that exists only when humans are acting in it, the idea of context used here is the anthropologist definition.

To the three anthropological levels of contexts, we have added *nature*, which is the largest concept. Nature is everything that exists without humans such as vegetation, fauna, the ground, and weather. Nature is the basis that has to exist before any kind of culture can appear, and where there is human made culture there is *cultural context*. Cultural context is all that human actions and ideas have created. Cultural context includes all habits, ideas, norms, values, or beliefs. Because of cultural context is the *historical context*, which is all of the historical events that have marked its cultural context. The innermost 'top' context is the *immediate context*, which includes all of the other contexts in it: the entire environment, its action and interaction, the actors and roles, in the situation where it exists. On this basic idea of different contexts, we have created the bowl model of scopes of context (Fig. 1).

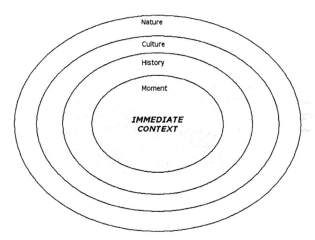

Figure 1. The bowl model of scopes of contexts

As illustrated in Figure 1, the context is like a bowl of water: nothing can be separated to belong to only one part of the context. We can take, for example, skills of an individual in an organization: the cultural context may define what kind of education is respected. The historical context may affect how this kind of education in this culture is possible to arrange. In addition, the history of every individual, her/his experiences of life, in the surrounding nature and culture, history and the moment are relevant. Accordingly, the education and experience, which lead to the skills of an individual, is a wholeness of culture, history, and the moment. The lines between these different contexts are lines drawn on the water. Different layers of contexts are present in the everyday working environment of any information system.

2.2   Categories of Contextual Factors

Within context, many environmental factors affect the information system. In this research, we have separated five main categories: *socio-political environment, infrastructure, organizational culture, economy, and human resources*. (See Figure 2.) The selection of these categories is based on the findings in literature [Ciborra 2004, Lai et al. 2003, Molla et al. 2005, Mosse 2005, Soriyan 2004], and on our own work and research experiences in information systems. In this phase, the categories are quite tentative; the categorization will elaborate along the research process.

The socio-political environment includes political and military safety and stability, as well as hierarchical constructions and social security of the citizens of the country [McGrew 2002]. In addition, beliefs, values, norms, and habits are parts of socio-political environment. Socio-political environment sets the potentiality to all the other categories.

The definition of infrastructure we use in this research is all manmade possibilities, which include roads, buildings, power supplies, communication systems, water systems, et cetera. We may call this kind of infrastructure a 'technical infrastructure', although in some definitions the technical infrastructure includes only the machinery used inside an organization. There are wider definitions to infrastructure as well, which include education and banking [Okunoye 2006] or qualifiers like human resource infrastructure and economic infrastructure [Williamson et al. 2004].

Organizational culture is a specific manmade ecosystem that can only appear inside the surrounding culture, but within an organization's own rules and habits. Organizational culture defines the ways of communication, hierarchy, and all of the habits of work inside the organization. It includes the shared values, beliefs, norms, and expectations within the system [Okunoye 2003]. Organizational culture is the personality of the organization [McNamara 2005]. It is a daughter of culture, or cultural context; it varies between countries, but also between organizations within a country.

In information systems, as well as in many other manmade systems, almost everything depends on economy. It is not only the question of 'how much money do we have', but also 'how do we use this money we have', concerning the economic skills and decisions [McGrew 2002, Wilson et al. 2002].

The last category is something that needs all other categories, but it is also needed to realize all others: human recourses. Again, we have the fact that an information system is a human system; thus, it cannot exist without human resources [Ciborra 2004, Wilson et al. 2002]. Human resources include all the knowledge and skills that are to be used in the organization, and how these resources are used. The human resources are tied tightly with economy, socio-political environment, and organizational culture.

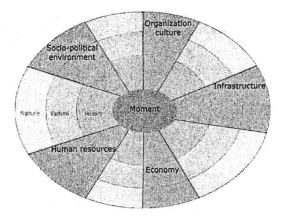

Figure 2. Categories of contextual factors

All five categories relate to each other and they are present in every information system. These categories appear as sector slices in the bowl model as presented in Figure 2. The empty space between the slices implies other parts of society that are not significant in light of this research.

2.3 Levels of context

When examining information systems there are many different social and technical levels with relation to the viewpoint the system is studied. Yet not all the levels exist in every context. For example, the working cultures of Africa can be radically different from those in Western countries [Walsham 2000]. However, in the IS study it is significant to have models to approach the use of information systems and IS development, regardless of the culture we are working on [Walsham et al. 2006].

Two times four levels of analysis model was created by Korpela et al. (2001) to define on which level of surrounding social ecosystem the information system is situated, despite the culture or context, on a globally comparable way. Figure 3 is modified from the original figure to be more illustrative.

The different rows of the model represent the level in the human society, and the columns are for units to be analyzed, and the relations between these units. The lowest level is individual and on this level, the unit is a person. These persons can form different kinds of groups like women, men, doctors, clerks, and so on. Second, group or activity level is for groups, operational units that together create 'product'. On the second level we can define groups like operating groups and first aid groups, which can interact with each other. The third level in this model is the organizational level. It signifies mainly organizations or units of organizations that work locally (e.g. district hospital), and the cooperation between organizations. The highest level in the original model was the societal level, which represents country. Yet globalization brings international connections between countries, and to this version, we have added the global level, which is the top level of information systems. On the societal and global levels stay the big and multinational organizations, e.g. at the societal level is the governmental health care system and at the global level international health programmes.

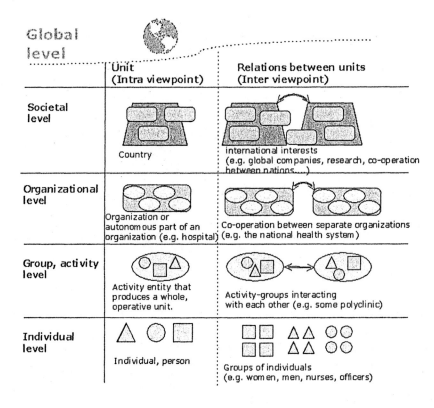

Figure 3. Levels of analysis. Modified from Korpela et al. (2001).

All of the higher levels are present and affect the lower levels. Depending on the analysis level, the bowl model has different status. In the societal and organizational levels, the impact of cultural and historical context is very strong. Therefore, we should view the factors of this level in the light of the culture and history of the surrounding human ecosystem. The immediate context then appears on the lower, group, and individual levels.

In this study, the focus is to study information system in organizations. On an organizational level, we look at organizational information systems affected by the culture, history, and the society as a whole, but the functionality of the organization realizes on the group level and individual level and is a construction of immediate contexts.

3   Methodology

Our objective is to create a framework to recognize context-originated factors. We have started this based on the theoretical models presented in the previous chapter. In this section, we describe how we have applied the models, the research approach, and the research data.

3.1   Research Approach

This research began from literature, articles, reports, and other secondary data. This data has been the basis for the three models of context in the theoretical background. The assumptions for building the interview material are based on the secondary data. Yet all the existing literal material is in practice for some other reason than describing context, so it can only help to make some guidelines, not work as a research material itself. The research is iterative: the first frame to the research was created with secondary data, and first part of primary data was collected by using this frame. This primary data will be analysed by applying the first frame, and the analysis will produce a new iteration to create the final framework.

The research is qualitative and interpretive. Contextual factors in the use of information systems are very little researched outside of risk management. This research aims to find contextual factors, not classify them. We are not looking for good or bad factors, nor are we going to find any causes and effects. This is a research of context, but not a contextual analysis, for the objective is not to understand the immediate context but detect the context and to define it as neutrally as possible. In this research, the objective is to apply the frame under development in as many different information systems as possible.

3.2   Primary Data and Fieldwork Methods

The intention is to get material as widely as possible, so the deep case studies, action research, or any other deep interpretive methods are not part of this study. Furthermore, there is no resource to stay longer in Africa or travel there often, so the methods to collect primary data in this research are mainly by interview and conversation. We obtained primary data from Finland, South Africa, and Mozambique.

First, we had to decide what kind of factors we were looking for. To research information system context is quite a large area, and there are neither certain questions nor right answers. Again, the information system is a human system, and the reality for every individual is different. To build an interview we used the five categories (infrastructure, economy, socio-political environment, human resources, and organization culture) and created questions that would be situated in a certain category.

We structured the interview on certain question groups: *1) Basic Questions* (name, age, and so on), *2) Work* (working title, role in the organization, and so on), *3) Technology* (availability of technology), *4) Motivation, 5) Environment and Infrastructure, 6) Hierarchy,* and *7) Human Relations in Working Environment.* The structure of the questions was quite strict, including a detailed question series for all of these groups. Some questions included word lists, which we illustrated during the interviews, and we asked some questions about these words. Most important was the list of items that might threat the functioning of the information system. These items were collected from different reports and articles, mostly about information system risk management.

The strict questions worked quite well in Finland. However, during the first interview in South Africa, we realised the difference between cultures: These people talk! One does not have to ask every detail separately, only themes. According to our experience, all of the people in the world like to talk about their work, but the way they do it depends on their culture. Therefore, after the first interview in Africa we combined the strict questions to wider, more thematic questions.

Soon we found that the questions were not important at all. Instead, the value of the word lists proved to be the most important part of the interview. Instead of questions, which always include some kind of supposition, the neutral list of words gave the people interviewed a wider area to tell what she/he really thought. The viewpoint, values, and the meaning of word came from her/his reality. We still have some questions, but the basics of the interviews are the wordlists. An interviewed person is able to talk freely and the interviewer(s) could make defining questions as needed. This method seems to work really well in this kind of research, where there are no straight answers, not even straight questions.

3.3 Secondary Data

Secondary data from INDEHELA and Health Information Systems Programme (HISP) partners will be used to complete the primary data. HISP is a health information system program at the University of Oslo. It started as a local pilot project in South Africa in 1994; nowadays it has broadened to several other developing countries in Africa and Asia [HISP 2006].

This research was conducted mostly in Finland; thus, the collection of the material is and will be done in Africa. Since the resources for us to stay doing field research are quite limited, and we have partners staying in Africa (and also other parts of the world) in INDEHELA and HISP programmes, the co-operation in research gives us quite a large amount of secondary data we use in this research. Co-operation is crucial, firstly to cover a wider area than one could do alone; secondly, a cross-cultural research team is quite essential when trying to create a framework that would work in different cultures. In addition, the local contacts are most important when arranging interviews to other countries.

4   Testing the framework: Situation analysis of HMIS, South Africa

At this moment, we have created a theoretical basis frame of the three context models. To improve this towards a working framework it requires testing with different kinds of research materials (e.g. case reports and interview material) of different information systems to find the weaknesses and the strengths of the frame. This section presents the first applying of the context models as a framework.

The material studied here is from HISP partners: the report of situation analysis of HMIS by Louisa Williamson and Vincent Shaw [Williamson et al. 2004]. It is a report of the status of the District Health Information System (DHIS) and hospital and Primary Health Care (PHC) services in the North West Province in South Africa. The report itself is an analysis of information systems with key objectives, components of functioning IS, mainly on the data flow inside the health organization. The material of this report was collected through a survey of selected facilities, and with interviews with key personnel. Since the purpose of this report is mainly to develop the dataflow, it will not include all of the information we need to use this framework in full. The test output is also biased, since data in this report emphasis is to find possible faults in the context; the existing positive factors are reported less than negative factors. The country (societal level) context is not described in this report; hence, this report applies to people familiar with it.

The reported units are on the *organizational level*: district or sub-district hospitals and one provincial office. Although the analysis report concentrates on the functioning of the information system, its dataflow through the group, or even individual level (primary health care can be a health station with only one nurse) to the top, societal level, so that the level of the contexts depends on the analyzed item. In this paper, we have taken the liberty to combine the different source units; although the data of the report was collected in separated units, it was studied as data from one organization.

The *socio-political environment* in South Africa has gone through a major change during the last ten years, which also includes the health care system. The importance of health management is approved, and nowadays it is beginning to be realized. Since the nature, culture, or historical scopes of context are not part of the report, we feel it worthwhile to add a little about the *cultural and historical contexts* of South Africa from our own point of view. We have seen when visiting South Africa how strongly the cultural and historical contexts are present and how society has and is going through major changes. Yet this does not affect the *immediate context* in information systems as much as could be presumed. Instead, the people are willing to build a new working society together; there cannot be seen fear of the new. In the report studied, we can see this through the enthusiasm to work in new systems and desire for training. However, some doubts about the usefulness of training are also mentioned.

The factors of *organizational culture* and closely related *human resources* are often noticed in this report. Major changes have occurred in the organizational structure, and senior management has been changed. The conventions inside the organization are not clear or are often quite vague. The lack of continuity in management has affected negatively upon the ensured stability of cohesive policy and capacity development. The organizations lack job descriptions, as well as data flow, communication, and feedback policy. Lack of determination of the information needed causes an overload of information. Furthermore, there is a wide range of data collection tools.

The enthusiasm of the staff is mentioned. However, there is a lack of knowledge, skills, and experience, which complicates working. There is also a lack of 'buy in': the people cannot see the point of the data collection, the data can be too difficult, the tools are inappropriate, and the employees are too busy to do this 'extra' work. They feel that they do not get enough support from management. Heavy workload is also reported. The turnover is remarkable and rapid through the organization, both at the organizational management level and at the group level employees.

Economy or *infrastructure* is not the focus of this report; accordingly, many factors of these categories do not appear. The importance of financial resources is clearly present in many factors: lack of human resources as the ongoing need of training and deficient staff; lack of adequate computers and tools; and heavy workload. Infrastructure is mentioned in that the staff members have general access ICT equipment, but there are problems in connectivity, as well as a lack of willingness to use them. In addition, the lack of office space is mentioned, but with no further explication.

5   Discussion

The most positive aspect about testing the context models was to realize how some factors, which were already familiar before, were found again from a different view. This kind of finding supports one of the objectives of the framework: how to find the 'obvious things' in the information system of the working environment. The framework is not at its best when used on a single case, but still is useful to give different viewpoints. It helps to gather items (or factors) with similar categories or scopes, but it would be most useful when comparing different information systems.

As mentioned earlier, the report studied here is an analysis mainly on the data flow inside the health organization. If the three models of contexts would have been on the base when this report material was collected and analyzed it might had given a richer picture of the system environment. For example, separating the level of context would have located the data more clearly; also, some description of the historical and cultural context would have been illustrative, not only to the view of foreign researcher, but also for the local researchers to 'take a step back' in order to get a wider viewpoint. The specified data from economical and infrastructural categories in the report is also quite limited. Even if these items were not essential to the report, they still may have affected the contextual factors in the information system.

The categories of contexts will need some redefinition. Some factors did not exactly fit in any category of the bowl model, e.g. the data collection tools (registers, books, forms). Generally, we can see them as a part of the organizational culture, when the tools are defined by management or in practice approved. However, what if there is no real organizational culture yet? Could the choosing of the tools be a reflection of socio-political environment, or is it only an economical necessity? Testing the context framework surfaced many questions similar to these. There may be a need for some different categories, and the existing ones should be defined more exactly, if possible.

6   Conclusion

The object of this study was to construct a theoretical basis to a framework for IS contexts study. Now we have three basic models (scopes of contexts, categories of contextual factors, and levels of contexts), which we can use as a frame to study different IS context material. We have collected primary data such as interviews in South Africa and Mozambique during November 2005. Further interviews will take place in Finland, as well as in rural areas regarding health information systems and in urban areas regarding non-health information systems. Cooperation with partners will also bring some secondary data to study. The research will get clearer points as to where to approach when this material is studied within the frame. The categories on the contexts will get some kind of priority, and the structure of the categories may change. The iteration is going on.

In the first test, the frame showed some positive aspects as well as some imperfections. In any case, it appears to be quite useful, at least worth further development. The frame of models of contexts is free to use for anyone interested, and as we need as many cases studied as possible, we would be very interested in the results that using this frame may produce.

References:

1.   [Avgerou et al. 2004] Avgerou, C, and Madon, S, Framing IS Studies: Understanding the Social Context of IS Innovation. In: Avgerou, Ciborra, Lang (eds.) *The Social Study of Information and Communication Technology,* (Oxford University Press 2004) pp. 162-184

2.   [Ciborra 2004] Ciborra, C, Encountering Information Systems as a Phenomenon. In: Avgerou, Ciborra, Lang (eds.) *The Social Study of Information and Communication Technology,* (Oxford University Press 2004) pp. 17-37

3.   [Heeks 2002] Heeks, R, Failure, Success, and Improvisation of Information Systems Project in Developing Countries, *Development Informatics,* WP series, Paper No. 11, (Institute of Development Policy and Management, Manchester 2002) http://unpan1.un.org/intradoc/groups/public/documents/NISPAcee/UNPAN015601.pdf (March 16, 2006)

4.   [HISP 2006] The homepage of HISP (Health Information Systems Programme), University of Oslo, http://www.hisp.org (January 1, 2006)

5.   [Kling 1999] Kling, R, What is Social Informatics and Why Does it Matter? *D-Lib Magazine,* Vol. 5 No. 1, January 1999
http://www.dlib.org/dlib/january99/kling/01kling.html (February 23, 2006)

6.   [Korpela et al. 2001] Korpela, M, Mursu, A, and Soriyan, H. A, Two Times Four Integrative Levels of Analysis: A Framework. In: Russo NL, Fitzgerald B, DeGross JI, (eds.) *Realigning Research and Practice in Information Systems Development. The Social and Organizational Perspective. IFIP TC8/WG8.2 Working Conference,* Boise, Idaho, USA, July 27-29, (Boston: Kluwer Academic, 2001) p. 367-377.

7.   [Korpela et al. 2006] Korpela, M, Mursu, A, Soriyan H. A, de la Harpe, R, and Macome, E, Information Systems Practice for Development in Africa: Results from INDEHELA. In: Howcroft, D, and De Gross J. I (eds.) *Social Inclusion: Social &*

Organizational Implications for Information Systems, Trauth, E, (Kluwer Academic, Boston, MA 2006) (forthcoming)

8. [Lai et al. 2003] Lai, S-Y, Heeks, R, and Nicholson, B, Uncertainty and Coordination in Global Software Projects: A UK/India - Centred Case Study, *Development Informatics,* WP series, Paper No. 17. (Institute of Development Policy and Management, University of Manchester 2003) http://www.sed.manchester.ac.uk/idpm/publications/wp/di/di_wp17.pdf (March 13, 2006)

9. [McGrew 2002] McGrew, A, Sustainable Globalization? The Global Politics of Development and Exclusion in the New World Order. In: Allen and Thomas (eds.) *Poverty and Development into the 21st Century,* (Oxford University Press 2002) pp. 345-364

10. [McNamara 2005] McNamara, C, Organizational Culture. *Free Management Library,* http://www.managementhelp.org_thry/culture/culture.htm (December 21, 2005)

11. [Molla et al. 2005] Molla, A, and Loukis, I, Success and Failure of ERP Technology Transfer: A Framework for Analysing Congruence of Host and System Cultures, *Development Informatics,* WP series, Paper No. 24, (Institute of Development Policy and Management, Manchester 2005) http://www.sed.manchester.ac.uk/idpm/publications/wp/di/di_wp24.pdf (March 16, 2006)

12. [Mosse 2005] Mosse, E, *Understanding the Introduction of Computer-based Health Information Systems in Developing Countries: Counter Networks, Communication Practices and Social Identity, A Case Study from Mozambique,* Doctoral Thesis (University of Oslo 2005)

13. [Moyi 2003] Moyi, E. D, Networks, Information and Small Enterprises: New Technologies and the Ambiguity of Empowerment, *Information Technology for Development,* vol. 10 No 4 (IOS Press 2003) pp. 221-232

14. [Mursu 2002] Mursu, A, *Information Systems Development in Developing Countries - Risk Management and Sustainability Analysis in Nigerian Software Companies,* Doctoral Thesis (University of Jyväskylä 2002)

15. [Okunoye 2003] Okunoye, A, Context-Aware Framework of Knowledge Management: Cultural and Infrastructural Considerations. In: Korpela M, Montealegre R, Poulymenakou A, (eds.) *Organizational Information Systems in the Context of Globalization. IFIP TC8 & TC9 / WG8.2 & WG9.4 Working Conference on Information Systems Perspectives and Challenges in the Context of Globalization. In Progress Research Papers [CD-ROM],* Athens, Greece, June 15-17, (IFIP 2003), pp 59-71

16. [Soriyan 2004] Soriyan, H. A, *A Conceptual Framework for Information System Development Methodology for Educational and Industrial Sectors in Nigeria,* Doctoral Thesis (Obafemi Awolowo University 2004)

17. [Tapaninen 2005] Tapaninen, A-M, *Sosiaaliantropologian perusteet* http://www.avoin.helsinki.fi/Kurssit/sosAntr/materiali/ (May 4, 2005), (Course material, in Finnish)

18. [Walsham 2000] Walsham, G, Globalization and IT: Agenda for Research. In Baskerville, R., Stage, J. and DeGross, J. (eds.) *Organization and social perspectives on information technology: IFIP International Working Conference on the Social and Organizational Perspective on Research and Practice in Information Technology (TC8*

WG8.2), 9-11 June, Aalborg, Denmark. (Boston: Kluwer Academic Publishers 2000), pp.195-210

19.   [Walsham et al. 1990] Walsham, G, Symons, V, and Waema, T (1990) Information System as Social Systems: Implications for Developing Countries. In: Bhatnagar and Bjorn-Andersen (eds.) *Information Technology in Developing Countries,* (Elsevier Science Publishers, Amsterdam 1990) pp 51-61

20.   [Walsham et al. 2006] Walsham G, and Sahay, S, Research on Information Systems in Developing Countries: Current Landscape and Future Prospects, *Information Technology for Development,* Vol. 12 No 1 (Wiley Publishers 2006) pp 7-24

21.   [Williamson et al. 2004] Williamson, L, and Shaw, V, Situation Analysis of HMIS in North West Province, Health Information Systems Programme South Africa, report 2004 (Unpublished)

22.   [Wilson et al. 2002] Wilson, G, Heeks, R, Technology, Poverty, and Development. In: Allen and Thomas (eds.) *Poverty and Development into the 21st Century,* (Oxford University Press 2002) pp. 403-424

23.   [WITFOR 2005] IFIP Wold Information Technology Forum, Gaborone Declaration 2005, http://www.witfor.org (December 2, 2005)

Methods and Concepts

Social Informatics – From Theory to Actions for the Good ICT Society

Gunilla Bradley
IT University, Royal Institute of Technology, Sweden
Bradley@imit.kth.se, http://web.it.kth.se/~bradley/gunilla/

Abstract: This paper presents ongoing social changes related to the use of ICT. They are analyzed under the headings: workforce, organizational design and structure, psychosocial communication, and work content. A theoretical model entitled 'The Convergence theory on ICT and Psychosocial Life Environment' is described, which reflects main ongoing processes in the Network society encompassing various spheres of life, environments, and human roles. A special section analyzes the ongoing changes in the home and home environment. Social Informatics is discussed related to the model and special attention is devoted to the individual level and humans. Concluding remarks deal with visions and actions. Figures with circles and converging circles are used to illustrate and summarize.

Keywords: ICT society, theory, work life, network organization, psychosocial

1 Introduction

The area Information and Communication Technology (ICT) and its interaction with social changes on organizational, individual and societal levels has in the 2000'th become of growing attention, due to the depth and wide use of ICT. The focus in the ICT related disciplines has so far been too much on the 'technology push' in contrast to focus on human needs and requirements at the development, introduction and use of ICT. New universities, sometimes entitled IT universities, are appearing in many European countries trying to bring together disciplines from the traditional university and disciplines from the technical university in order to facilitate a necessary rethinking and reorientation of R&D. This sometimes results in new centres directly named 'Humans in the ICT-society' focusing on the human, organizational, and societal aspects of ICT use. Empirical experiences show that it is important to keep a balance between pure technical research and development in software and hardware

Please use the following format when citing this chapter:

Bradley, G., 2006, in IFIP International Federation for Information Processing, Volume 223, Social Informatics: An Information Society for All? In Remembrance of Rob Kling, eds. Berleur, J., Numinen, M. I., Impagliazzo, J., (Boston: Springer), pp. 383–394.

technologies, new fields such as nanotechnology and on the other hand the behavioural and social science disciplines such as psychology, sociology, cultural anthropology, urban/rural planning, and ethnography.

2   Ongoing Social Changes in the 'Net Era'

Changes related to the use of ICT are occurring in workforce structure, the structure and design of organization, communications patterns, work content/work tasks, management, and the relation between work, private and public life. The results below are primarily derived from our research over the years in developed countries.

2.1   Workforce Structure

We get more and more organic organizational structures, with a focus on flexible work processes, including dynamic networks for capital and human resources, often summarized under the concept of network organizations. Economic systems are being created where the present boundaries are increasingly becoming eroded.

Core Workforce in the Flexible Company is decreasing

Figure 1. Core Work Force and Peripheral Work Force (Bradley 2001, 2006)

So-called flexible companies are becoming frequent in the present Net Era. At the centre of Figure 1, a core workforce exists that consists of permanent full-time employees. They enjoy a wide range of employment rights and benefits. In the flexible company, the *core workforce* is decreasing. However, the other part, the *peripheral workforce*, is growing (see the outer circle sectors in Figure 1). It consists of part-time staff, self-employed consultants, sub-contracted and outsourced workers, and temporary and agency employees. Some of the knowledge workers are key resources, while others can easily be replaced. This is not due to competency, rather due to the applied rules for hiring persons. They might have very strong positions in the company through the network organizational structure, and based on their expertise or social contacts. This phenomenon is invisible. Power is invisible in these new forms of organizations: power has no outward manifestation and is not reflected to the same extent as before in properties belongings associated with leadership.

2.2 Organisational Design and Structure

Traditional organisational structures have a 'military' form with boxes and one directed arrows in tree-like shapes showing attributes such as chain of command and responsibility. Such bureaucracy was originally meant to support and protect individual rights; however, it developed to function in the opposite direction. These organisations still exist, but they are complemented by and sometimes replaced by networks. Network organisational structures are like crocheted tablecloths or bed covers, easily handled by women through history. The loops in the fabric or organizational units (computers) are connected through the same yarn (network, tele-technology). The future structure of the world - social systems, organizations, official authorities, NGOs have this basic form, even if the pattern might differ. The networks interact more and more *wirelessly*. In these networks, *power* can both be centralised and decentralised and the process of building up power is invisible, it takes place in cyberspace. Industrialization and industrial technology during the mainframe period of the computerization era were fading away as well as the *hierarchical structures* of companies. We concluded in early studies of the use of knowledge-based systems (KBS) or use of applied AI that the *distribution of power* became possible in quite a deep sense (Bradley and Holm 1991). Competence was being transferred to the periphery, out to the lower levels of the organisations and even to people's homes. We can also explain the present trend towards the flattening of hierarchies because the hierarchical regulation and control are built into information and communication systems.

Characteristics of the network organizations are as follows: Direct communication between the various levels of the organization is more and more applied. Barriers between organizational units that deal with on one hand development of ideas and on the other hand execution of those ideas are disappearing. Power is relocated in the organization, also internationally - headquarters as well as production units are moved. The permanent changes of the organisational structure and the professional roles are partly due to and result in an increased openness and awareness of the surrounding world. New professional cultures are being developed and they are often complemented by being part of virtual cultures. The latter are entitled virtual communities and web based communities (WBC), new forms of collaboration. More and more individuals function as self-governing company units, with new challenges.

2.3   Psychosocial Communication

In network based organizational structures *psychosocial communication* has come in focus. The communication circle in Figure 2 illustrates how ICT direct and indirect affect qualitative and quantitative aspects of communication between people. As an example, leadership (the sector lower right in the circle) is directly affected by the use of ICT and in addition the changing role of leaders as becoming more of coaches, is affecting communication pattern (in the middle of the circle).

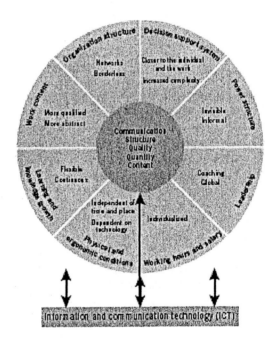

Figure 2.   The Communication Circle and Psychosocial communication in the Net Era
(Bradley 1977, 2006)

When people are working more and more from their computers, greater demands appear on the social and emotional components of communication (Bradley et al. 1993). This is valid still more in the Net Era when people are "working together when being apart" (Jansson 2005) as well as being together when being apart. Working in distributed environments internationally is a common work pattern.

An environment were people trust each other, have a feeling that they belong together and are part of a group, are aware of each other's competences, and where the communication is open and frequent, will have a much higher chance of being sustainable. To be able to achieve such communication cultures, one should consider different areas in the communication circle. In addition, one should include action strategies on how to handle distance, design in psychosocial work, and examples of activities that concern different sectors in the communication's circle. The objective work environment includes organizational structure, power structure, how important the project is considered, leadership and time management, reward system that supports the building of an environment that is motivating and comfortable to work in, team composition, the organizational design of a project, the content of the work tasks, and the communication patterns. In addition, it includes the physical environment, distance per se, and the subjective work environment (Jansson and Bradley 2004, Jansson 2005).

2.4   Work Content

Accelerated changes at work and in the content of work tasks are occurring in the 'net era'. We have achieved more *flexible work processes* regarding both in the professional role and in leadership. All human roles (the professional role, the learning role, and the role of citizen) are becoming more and more *integrated*. Changes that dominated for many years in industry as well as in office (e.g. repetitive jobs, physically strenuous jobs including routine work) are disappearing and a total upgrading of qualifications occurs. Consequently, the organizations have flattened out, even if we still can see organizations that keep levels that are not required by company goals. The worldwide sale and application of the *same type of software programs* continues and hence people carry out the work tasks in a more and more similar way. This facilitates the mobility in the labour market.

Our studies of young IT people in the city centre of Stockholm show that they have *strong social networks* that were an important part of their work situation. Workmates and friends were often the same people and *trust* had an important role. Work tasks should have a *meaning* to their life. Most people were deeply involved in their work and found their work tasks *fun, stimulating, interesting, and independent*. *Flexibility* concerning time and space was a key aspect in their work situation. Due to much of responsibility in both work and private lives, they felt a great freedom. They took care of themselves in professional *development* and learning became a part of their daily work (Danielsson 2002).

3   The Convergence Theory on ICT and the Psychosocial Life Environment – and some Future Trends

3.1   Convergence Theory

The convergence model on 'ICT and the Psychosocial Life Environment' is a graphical illustration of ongoing changes in the 'net society', which will appear in detail in my forthcoming book (Bradley 2006). Some comments to the model in Figure 3 will follow and the description is structured with reference to concepts in the outer circle in the figure.

The current network period very much follows the convergence and integration of three main technologies: computer technology, teletechnology, and media technology. The convergence process (Figure 3) is enforced all the time by smaller, cheaper, and more powerful components. More and more, people are using ICT in almost every activity and we find it embedded in more and more things (ubiquitous computing). The converging circles reflect graphically the ongoing process.

Both convergence and interactions are important features in the model. Convergence here means a move towards a common content. Interaction means that technology interacts with the social world with values and believes. There is also an ongoing interaction between the 'clusters of circles'.

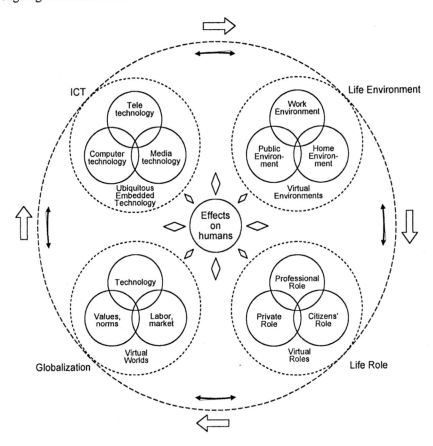

Figure 3.   Convergence Model on ICT and Psychosocial Life Environment
(Bradley 2005, 2006)

Globalization (lower left in the circle in Figure 3): We see that a convergence is occurring between technology, economy, values and norms, and labour market and is entitled *Globalization*. The geographical span is changing. At present, our work life is mainly based on national and international trade that will become more global. Electronic commerce and electronic market places are creating a strong change factor behind the structure of work life. The geographical space in the future is both global and beyond – including applications of virtual reality (VR).

- *ICT* (upper left): A convergence of computer technology, telecommunication technology and media technology is occurring and it is becoming what we define as ICT. Knowledge companies and knowledge workers are increasing. In these organisations, *knowledge* is managed in new ways. In the early 2000s, multiple communication channels exist such as word of mouth, writing, and audio visual, electronic. In the future, we should expect to apply meta-channels (e.g. meta-media of virtual reality (VR)) and controlled reality environments (environments that we manipulate and manage in VR).

- *Life Environment* (upper right): Work environment, home environment, and public environment are converging to a 'life environment' where the work and public environments move into our homes. We should see a new *emphasis* on certain dimensions in the current psychosocial environment as well as new *dimensions* in the psychosocial environment. We have to be open for unforeseen implications.

- *Life Role* (lower right): The professional role, the private role, and citizen's role converge to become a 'life role'. Role and role formation are central concepts in social psychology and they represent a level between structures and the individual. A 'role' appears where psychology and sociology meet and social psychology emphasizes the interaction between the levels. In democracies, the individual *can* influence and form his/her role/roles that are not solely a victim for structures;

- *Effects on Humans* (in the middle): In Figure 3, we represent the 'effects on humans' by the circle in the middle with two ways arrows around as a flower, which illustrate interactions. ICT, the life environment with its three sub-environments, the life role with its three sub-roles, and globalisation with its three components of values, technology and labour market all affect the individual. However, the individual can also influence the technology, the environment, and her/his own roles and phenomena on the organisational and societal level and the new virtual reality. Complexity characterizes the society and is mirrored by the fact that effects on the *individual* become more *multi-faceted and complex*. The way humans handle his/her situation can roughly be categorised as *active or passive reactions*.

- *Virtual Reality* (VR): We illustrate virtual reality by four circles marked with dotted lines, surrounding the four clusters of converging circles. These circles reflect our participation in cyberspace on various levels.
  - To the lower left part in Figure 3 we could talk about *Virtual Worlds* on the global level.
  - Within the concept of ICT the step taken by applied *Embedded and Ubiquitous technology* make the technology more hidden for the individual and in the society as a whole.
  - *Virtual Environments* in the upper right part of Figure 3 is already a common concept.
  - *Virtual Human Roles, in* the lower right part, is in a more extreme form another person/personality that people take on e g avatars.

- The thin double-directed arrows represent interaction, the broader one-directed arrows represent the main direction for the movement, and the process described in the circle model. Transferred to *actions* we can in our professional role, private role and citizen's role influence our life environment on various levels of analyses (see further Section 4).

• *Home of the Future*: Close connected to the convergence model is home and home environment. During the last few years we have studied changes in society and human behavioural patterns at the use of ICT in homes and home environments in USA, South East Asia (Singapore, Malaysia) and Japan (Bradley, Linda et al 2000, Bradley, L. and Bradley, G. 2001, Bradley L. 2005, Danielsson 2002). A general trend is that in the home many human roles are converging to *one life role* and the home is moving towards encompassing also a *virtual space* as well as *physical space*. Driving forces are converging and embedded technologies are appearing. We could regard the home as an extended family centre, a care centre, a multimedia centre, a centre for democratic dialogue, a market place, a learning centre, or an entertainment centre. We could summarize all of these as a *communication sphere*.

3.2 Convergence and Allocation Issues

Despite the observable tendencies of convergence in the ICT society, there are also *counter-movements*. We can observe that regions, nations, and subgroups in the world work towards separation, self-government, autonomy, and sometimes isolation. Related to this phenomenon is the allocation issue in a broad sense.

Throughout computerization, it has been possible to make huge profit and the question of allocating the profit should have been a key issue at an early stage. However, even if we could foresee the global economy, it was not until recently that the allocation issue has come in focus for actions both at the national and global level. The allocation issue has very much to do with allocating:
• work and leisure time
• citizens' services (paid/unpaid)
• production and reproduction
• cities and rural areas
• profit between sectors within a country (profit between industrialised countries, profit between industrialised countries and industrially developing countries.

In the Western countries, we have achieved a subdivision with one group that is overworked and another that is shut out from the workforce. It is not a necessary development and there are many alternatives. In later years, they used ICT to support the 'weak' in society and the people with various kinds of handicaps: linguistic, physical and intellectual. The 'digital divide' is a descriptive and analytical term whereas the 'allocation issue' and allocation of resources are terms that are more political. There is a call for actions incorporating social and humane costs and the gains of globalization, in a short and long-term perspective. The potential of balancing deep divides in resources is inherent in ICT, but plans are needed.

3.3 Individual reactions

The individual level needs more attention with respect to interaction between ICT – Society – Individual. There are both positive and negative impacts on the Individual. In the present flexible network of organisations, too much of responsibility is placed on the individual who loses permanent employment. The peripheral work force (see Figure 1) has to manage his/her competence development and market himself/herself. These new knowledge workers are as individuals exposed to a competitive world market.

We might view this pattern as freedom from paid work in a traditional sense, freedom to choose your life. However, some questions have to be raised. Should our schools prepare for educating so-called 'free agents' or prepare for acting proactively? We all need a basic security as employees and citizens, but there is a need for balance between a strong society and strong individuals. Most people are not 'strong' throughout the life and we need to think in terms of *sustainability* regarding physical and social environments and thus sustainable human beings.

Regarding the 'Effects on Humans' in Figure 3, we can conclude that the use of ICT has changed human qualities so far. They include identity and self-perception, social competence, creativity, integrity, trust, and dependency. We could either strengthen or weaken each of these qualities.

In stress-theoretical terms, we often talk about the importance of balance. ICT is contributing to a balance or an imbalance between emotional - rational components of life, female - male aspects, and involvement - alienation.

Research shows that an *accelerated tempo* is occurring in the industrialized world. There are reasons to talk about 'ICT stress' or 'Internet stress'. Certain ICT stress is related to the fact that we have an increased *dependency* on computers and networks and an increased expectancy that these technologies are functioning well. Stress phenomena in the Internet world are *information overload, contact overload,* demands for *availability,* lack of *organizational filters,* and difficulty of separating 'noise' from essentials, changing level of expectations and an altered *perception* of time and space in general.

[Tasks and environments that expose people to one of the two poles of over stimulation and under stimulation should be avoided in our society. The reason is due to the risk of stress (the individual level), the risk of a fragmented labour force (group/organization levels), the risk for a digital divide in nation states, and the risk of marginalization and exclusion from the mainstream of society (individual, group and societal levels] (Bradley 1989).

3.4 Social Informatics and the Convergence Theory

In the web page for the TC 9 world conference on Social Informatics it is pointed out that terms such as 'human choice and computers', 'computers and society', and 'social informatics' refer to a similar concern. The key question is formulated as follows: 'How is the human being and its societal environment kept in the centre?' and in particular, 'How to build up an 'Information Society for All' (UNESCO, 2002; eEurope, 2002) when developing our more and more complex ICT systems?" For example, we refer to a definition by Rob Kling as: "Social Informatics is the interdisciplinary study of the design, uses and consequences of information technologies that takes into account their interaction with institutional and cultural contexts" (Kling, 1999).

Earlier sections in this paper, both the empirical and theoretical one, confirm and underscore this basic perspective and the need to focus on *actions*.

4   Concluding Remarks – From Theory to Actions

In 1986, I visited Rob Kling at UC Irvine and lectured on 'Psychosocial Work Environment and Computers', which was the title of my book that appeared the same year (Bradley 1986). We very much shared the same perspective in our research but we used different terms depending on our backgrounds. At that time, I looked at myself as a behavioural scientist, educated as a psychologist and working at a department of sociology, doing cross-disciplinary research together with computer and system scientists, economists, and sociologists.

One way to summarize the discussion on the ICT, society and the individual are to address *psychosocial processes*. These could be formulated as policy statements and with positive formulations of goals to be reached. ICT should contribute to goals such as:

- Information access for all
- Wellbeing and quality of life for all
- Enrichment in the social contact between people
- Integration and respect for diversity
- Greater autonomy for the individual
- Prevention of various kinds of overload and stress
- Deepening of true human qualities
- Deepening and broadening of democracy
- E-cooperation and peace
- Sustainability in a broad sense (the environment, economy, and human side)

Internationally, the first official statements of goals for the ICT society were formulated at the World IT Forum (WITFOR 2003). The so called Vilnius Declaration brought forward goals which had a great implication for the involvement of the developing countries e. g. *bridging* the digital divide between rich and poor in the world; urban and rural societies; men and women; different generations. Another main concern was *reducing* poverty using education and information and communications technology (ICT).

Many concepts in the list above are overlapping and possible to analyze from various angles. By now we need to move to action-oriented and value-oriented research to support and influence actions strategies. TC 9 World Conference is highlighting a field of research, practice, and education with accelerated speed of change and complexity as well as urgency. There is a need for a much stronger support internationally for cross-disciplinary, cross-cultural, and action-oriented research on the topic 'ICT for Deepening of Humane and Societal Qualities'. Social informatics has to be a mandatory part in education and training in ICT-related disciplines.

Official bodies on the international and national level such as WSIS (World Summit on the Information Society) and national ICT programs are actors as we move to an ICT society on a global scale. ICT applications as Internet, web, and blogs should be used for dialogue between cultures, increase mutual understanding, and enrich us all. How can human rights be more deeply understood, exemplified, and applied in the ICT society? In 2006, the United Nations is reviewing human rights; can IFIP and Social Informatics contribute?

Sustainability as Convergence

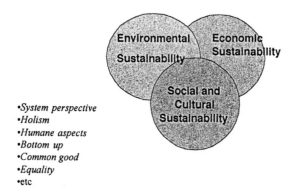

•*System perspective*
•*Holism*
•*Humane aspects*
•*Bottom up*
•*Common good*
•*Equality*
•etc

Figure 4. Sustainability and the use of ICT are close connected

Social informatics can be defined in various ways, but visions are shared about wellbeing, democracy, and quality of life for all as well as social, economical and ecological sustainability as illustrated in the convergence circles of Figure 4. We can all be 'actors' in this process, researchers, IT professionals, NGOs, and the individual.

References

Bradley, G. (1977). *Datateknik, Arbetsliv och Kommunikation.* (*Computer Technology, Work Life, and Communication).* The Swedish delegation for long-term research. FRN. Stockholm: Liber (in Swedish).

Bradley, G. (1979). Computerization and some Psychosocial Factors in the Work Environment. *Proceedings of the conference Reducing Occupational Stress,* New York, 1977. U.S. Department of Health, Education, and Welfare, NIOSH Publication No. 78-140, pp. 30–40.

Bradley, G. (1986 & 1989). *Computers and the Psychosocial Work Environment.* London/Philadelphia: Taylor & Francis. (Published in Swedish, 1986.)

Bradley, G. (ed.) (2001). *Humans on the Net. Information and Communication Technology (ICT) Work Organization and Human Beings.* Stockholm: Prevent.

Bradley, G. (2005). The Convergence Theory on Information and Communication Technology (ICT) and the Psychosocial Life Environment – The Connected Home. In Salvendy, G. (ed.). *Proceedings of the HCI International 2005 conference,* 22–27 July 2005, Las Vegas, USA. (CD). Mahwah, NJ: Lawrence Erlbaum Associates.

Bradley, G. (2006). *Social and Community Informatics - Humans on the Net.* London: Routledge

Bradley, G. and Holm, P. (1991). *Knowledge based systems – Organizational and Psychosocial Aspects – Early experiences from a Swedish commercial bank.* Research report. Stockholm: Stockholm University, Department of International Education.

Bradley, G., Holm, P., Steere, M. and Strömqvist, G. (1993). Psychosocial Communication and Computerization. *Computers in Human Behaviour,* 9:157–69.

Bradley, Linda (2005). Home of the Future Japan – Information and Communication Technology (ICT) and Changes in Society and Human Patterns of Behaviour in the Network Era. KTH Research report ISBN 91-7178-052-1. Stockholm: Royal Institute of Technology (KTH).

Bradley, Linda, Andersson, N. and Bradley, G. (2000). Home of the Future – Information and Communication Technology (ICT) – changes in society and human behaviour patterns in the net era. FSCN Report R00–1. Mid-Sweden University. (in Swedish).

Bradley, L. and Bradley, G. (2001). The Home as a Virtual and Physical Space – Experiences from USA and South-East Asia. In Smith, M. and Salvendy, G. (eds). *Systems, Social and Internationalization Design Aspects of Human-Computer Interaction.* Mahwah, NJ: Lawrence Erlbaum Associates, pp. 81–5.

Danielsson, U. (2002). Unga IT människor i storstad – En studie inom projektet 'Home of the Future'. (Young IT people in Stockholm – A study within the project 'Home of the Future'.) FSCN report R-02-34. Mid Sweden University. (in Swedish).

Jansson, E. (2005). Working Together when Being Apart. An analysis of distributed Collaborative Work through ICT from Psychosocial and Organizational Perspective. Doctoral dissertation at Department of Computer and System Sciences, IT University, Royal Institute of Technology, Stockholm.

Jansson, E. and Bradley, G. (2004). Sustainability in Collaborative Network Structures – with focus on the Psychosocial Work Environment in Distributed Teams. *Proceedings of the CIRN conference on Sustainability and Community Technology: What does this Mean for Community Informatics,* Vol 1 p 271-283. Prato, Italy, 29 September–1 October, 2004.

Kling R. (1999). What is Social Informatics and Why Does it Matter ? *D-Lib Magazine*

On Similarities and Differences between Social Informatics and Information Systems

Pertti Järvinen
Department of Computer Sciences, University of Tampere, Finland
pj@cs.uta.fi

Abstract. Rob Kling strongly advocated the term Social Informatics. He demonstrated that equipment, equipment vendors, technical specialists, upper-level managers, ICT policies, internal funding, and external grant funding with the people who will use information systems in the course of other work are not simply a static list but are interrelated within a matrix of social and technical dependencies. In Information Systems there has recently been heated debate about the core content of the discipline. In this paper we study whether Social Informatics and Information Systems are similar or not. According to the broad view on Information Systems, they appear quite similar. The few differences we identified are in research approaches, when most Social Informatics researchers use intensive case studies while most Information Systems researchers surveys. Such minor differences do not support the view that these two sciences should have different names. The researchers in both sciences seem to believe that people's behavior can be predicted, but we demonstrate that this is not true. Hence we propose that theories with people as a component must be adjusted accordingly in both sciences.

Keywords: social informatics, information systems, dynamic systems, conception of human being, prediction

1 Introduction

Social Informatics (SI) as "the interdisciplinary study of the design, uses and consequences of information technologies that takes into account their interaction with institutional and cultural context" [Kling 1999]. The label 'social informatics' emerged from discussions in 1996 within the community of researchers who conduct the kind of research discussed in Kling [1999]. Several social informatics researchers (Phil Agre, Jacques Berleur, Brenda Dervin, Andrew Dillon, Rob Kling, Mark Poster, Karen Ruhleder, Ben Shneiderman, Leigh Star and Barry Wellman)

Please use the following format when citing this chapter:

Järvinen, P., 2006, in IFIP International Federation for Information Processing, Volume 223, Social Informatics: An Information Society for All? In Remembrance of Rob Kling, eds. Berleur, J., Numinen, M. I., Impagliazzo, J., (Boston: Springer), pp. 395–406.

participated in a workshop at UCLA on social aspects of digital libraries in 1996. The topic was then about 25 years old.

The history of the discipline called Information Systems (IS) is longer. In the journal *Management Science* the first IS research articles concerning early visions of decision support systems were published in 1956 [Banker and Kauffman 2004]. The proposal for its curriculum was prepared [McKenney and Tonge 1971, Teichroew 1971] and presented by Ashenhurst [1972]. One reason why consideration of IS is now important is based on the lively discussion on its nature recently initiated by Benbasat and Zmud [2003]. A definition of information systems suitable for our purposes is: the effective design, delivery, use and impact of information technology in organizations and society [Gregor 2002].

In both SI and IS there is debate on the boundaries of the discipline, which topics are to be included and excluded. As a preliminary comment, it seems to me that the domains of SI and IS much overlap. Hence it is interesting to identify their similarities and differences.

Neither SI nor IS, in to my opinion, has an adequate conception of people; there is still room for innovations and improvements. In this sense we try to bring Aulin's [1989] self-steering system as a potential model of the human being into the discussion.

In this paper we start with an analysis of some fundamental characteristics of SI. We then briefly review the recent discussion of the nature of IS. Thereafter, we compare SI and IS. Finally, we propose some improvements to both.

2   Social Informatics (SI)

In a section of the Rob Kling Center of Social Informatics (SI) portal [2005] it is claimed that "SI studies aim to ensure that technical research agendas and system designs are relevant to people's lives. The key word is relevance, ensuring that technical work is socially-driven rather than technology-driven. Relevance has two dimensions: process and substance. Design and implementation processes need to be relevant to the actual social dynamics of a given site of social practice, and the substance of design and implementation (the actual designs, the actual systems) need to be relevant to the lives of the people they affect. SI sets agendas for all the technical work in two ways: 1) more superficially, by drawing attention to functionalities that people value, thus setting priorities for design and implementation; and 2) more fundamentally, by articulating those analytical categories that have been found useful in describing social reality, and that which therefore should also define technical work in/for that reality as well. Unfortunately, many technical professionals have viewed social concerns as peripheral. One key role of SI is to stand things back on their feet, so that social concerns are central and define the ground that technical work stands on [Phil Agre, 1996]."

Kling [1999] describes how the professional systems designer oriented to social informatics could design a new system. "A systems designer with a socio-technical orientation does not simply consider these elements while working in a 'design studio' far away from the people who will use a specific system. Effectively designing socio-technical systems also requires upon a set of 'discovery processes' to help the designers understand which features and tradeoffs will most appeal to the people who are most likely to use the system. There are a number of discovery processes for learning about the preferences of the men and women who are likely to use these systems. These discovery processes include workplace ethnography, focus group, user participation in design teams, and participatory design strategies. These approaches differ in many significant ways, such as the contextual richness of the understandings that they reveal and the extent to which they give the people who will use systems influence and power in their design. These issues are the subject of a lively body of research that overlaps social informatics."

Kling [2000] writes that "as we develop more elaborate ICTs and try to use them in almost every sphere of social life, we face fresh theoretical challenges for social informatics. Its possibilities and value are illustrated by some of key ideas: 1) the social shaping of ICTs, 2) the conceptions of highly intertwined socio-technical networks, 3) roles of social incentives in energizing new electronic media, and 4) the conceptualization of ICT infrastructure as socio-technical practices and resources."

First, to set the groundwork for socio-technical networks, Kling [2000] starts with a more general concept, that ICT, in practice, *is socially shaped*. In the standard (non-social informatics) accounts of ICT and social change, it is common to hear information technologies characterized as tools, and questions are asked about their social impacts. To take a wider perspective, the combination of equipment, people, governance structures, and ICT policies is called "the local computing package" [Kling 2000].

Secondly, the local computing package is also an example of a socio-technical network. A *socio-technical network* brings together equipment, equipment vendors, technical specialists, upper-level managers, ICT policies, internal funding, and external grant funding with the people who will use information systems in the course of other work (such as policing, accounting, taxing, or planning) [Kling 2000]. These elements are not simply a static list but are interrelated within a matrix of social and technical dependencies.

Thirdly, one key idea of social informatics research is that the social context of information technology development and use plays a significant role in influencing the ways in which people use information and technologies, and thus affects the consequences of the technology for work, organizations, and other social relationships. Social context can be characterized by particular *incentive* systems for using, organizing and sharing information in different work groups and work roles [Kling 2000].

Finally, workable computer applications are usually supported by a strong socio-technical *infrastructure* [Kling 2000]. The surface features of computer systems are the most visible and are the primary subject of debates and systems analyses. But they are only one part of computerization projects. Many key parts of information systems are neither immediately visible nor interesting in their novelty. They include technical infrastructure such as reliable electricity. They also involve a range of skilled support – from people to documents system features and training people to use them, to rapid-response consultants who can diagnose and repair system failures.

3   Information Systems (IS)

In his historical review Davis [2000] stated that "the academic field of information systems has developed because organizations use a specialized body of knowledge about information and communication systems. Teaching and research support these organization needs. The field may be defined in terms of observed information systems in organizations and also in terms of the function or field of activity for system planning, development, management, and evaluation. Since the systems deal with capture, repositories, processing, and communication of data, information and knowledge, these are also defined. – Conceptual foundations for the field are set of concepts and propositions that explain why structures are designed the way they are, tasks are scheduled and accomplished in the way they are, and activities are performed the way they are."

Benbasat and Zmud [2003] were concerned that the IS research community is making the discipline's core identity ambiguous by, all too frequently, under-investigating phenomena intimately associated with IT-based systems and over-investigating phenomena distantly associated with IT-based systems. They discussed why establishing an identity for the IS field is important. They conceptualize the IT artifact (see Figure 1) as the application of IT to enable or support some task(s) embedded within a structure(s) that itself is embedded within a context(s).

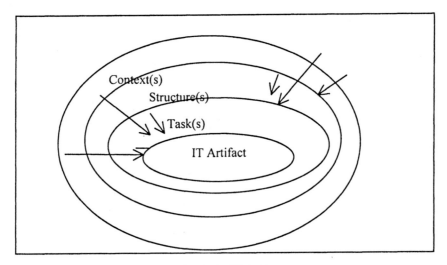

Fig. 1. The IT Artifact

They then described what such an identity might look like by proposing a core set of properties, i.e., concepts and phenomena, that define the IS field.

Benbasat and Zmud's view (Figure 2) of the phenomena studied by IS scholars and hence the set of core properties of the IS discipline includes:

- The managerial, methodological, and technological *capabilities* as well as the managerial, methodological, and operational *practices* involved in planning, designing, constructing, and implementing IT artifacts.

- Human behaviors reflected within, and induced through both the (1) planning, constructing, and implementing, and (2) direct and indirect usage of these artifacts.
- The managerial, methodological, and operational practices for directing and facilitating IT artifact *usage* and evolution.

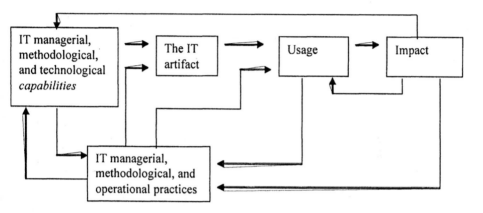

Fig. 2. IT artifact and its immediate nomological net

- As a consequence of use, the *impacts* (direct and indirect, intended and unintended) of these artifacts on the humans who directly (and indirectly) interact with them, the structures and contexts within which they are embedded, and associated collectives (groups, work units, organizations).

Next, Benbasat and Zmud [2003] discussed research by IS scholars that either fails to address this core set of properties (labelled error of exclusion) or that addresses concepts/ phenomena falling outside this core set (labelled error of inclusion). They concluded by making three suggestions for redirecting IS scholarship toward the concepts and phenomena that they argued define the core of the IS discipline:

- "Does a study investigate the relationships that fall within the IS *nomological net* – that is, investigate relationships involving one or more of the constructs included in Figure 2?
- How many *degrees of separation* are there between the IS constructs and the key consequent construct(s) in a study's research model – that is, how far *outside* the boundaries of the nomological net shown in Figure 2 are the primary constructs being investigated? (Here, by primary constructs we refer to those constructs associated with a study's principal scholarly contribution.)
- What is the *nomological density* of the IS constructs in a study's research model – that is, do relationships involving only IS constructs represent a majority of the relationships in a research model? To measure nomological density, count the number of two-way relationships among the constructs in the research model that fall within the nomological net (i.e., those relationships that exist between

constructs in Figure 2), then divide this total by the total number of two-way relationships in the research model."

Agarwal and Lucas [2005] wrote that "since the publication of Benbasat and Zmud's [2003] article, the response from the IS community has been heartening. Many scholars have elected to engage in this debate and offer their perspectives on the field. As might be expected, these commentaries and perspectives offer divergent views on a variety of issues raised by Benbasat and Zmud, such as the existence of a crisis, the need for a defined core for the IS field, and recommendations for the nature of this core." Agarwal and Lucas summarize the key assertions made in the 18 articles.

Agarwal and Lucas [2005] presented an alternative view of the Information Systems identity crisis recently described by Benbasat and Zmud. Agarwal and Lucas agreed with many of their observations, but Agarwal and Lucas were concerned with their prescription for IS research. Agarwal and Lucas criticized their discussion of errors of inclusion and exclusion in IS research and highlighted the potential misinterpretations that are possible from a literal reading of their comments. Agarwal and Lucas' conclusion is that following Benbasat and Zmud's nomological net will result in a micro focus for IS research. The results of such a focus are potentially dangerous for the field. Agarwal and Lucas "classify research that has a narrow focus as *micro* while they consider research on the transformational aspects of IT as more *macro* in focus. Agarwal and Lucas' distinction between micro and macro research parallels that drawn in the organizational sciences where micro research is generally viewed as being at the individual or group level of analysis, while macro research focuses on organizations, environments, and strategy. Agarwal and Lucas include work related solely to the IT artifact in the former category. To the extent that macro research seeks to understand how technology is changing organizations, environments, and strategy, they label such research as *transformational* (my emphasis) in nature."

Agarwal and Lucas present an alternative set of heuristics that can be used to assess what lies within the domain of IS scholarship. They offer the following three questions to help determine if research is relevant to the IS field: (1) "Is there a non-trivial aspect of underlying theory that draws upon the unique nature of the IT artifact? (2) Would the phenomenon have been approached differently were the IT artifact not involved? (3) Does the research illuminate scholarly and practitioner understanding related to the construction, management, and effects of the IT artifact?" Agarwal and Lucas argue that the IS community has a powerful story to tell about the transformational impact of information technology. They believe that a significant portion of our research should be macro studies of the impact of IT. It is important for academic colleagues, deans, and managers to understand the transformational power of the technology. As IS researchers with a profound knowledge of the underlying artifact, we are best positioned to undertake such research.

4   Comparison of SI and IS

To start our comparison we would first like to refer to differences between standard tool models and socio-technical models identified by Kling and Lamb [1999].

To our mind, Benbasat and Zmud [2003] had some kind of tool model in mind, but Agarwal and Lucas [2005] and their ideas are closer to socio-technical models. They mentioned that "Figure 1 in Benbasat Zmud presents the IT artifact as embedded within a structure and context, with arrows running from contexts to structure to tasks to the IT artifact. Agarwal and Lucas' view inserts a set of arrows running in the opposite direction as well; the IT artifact has had a dramatic impact on tasks, structures, and the context of organizations and industries." – Roberta Lamb [2005] noted that IS researchers often perform their studies with 'management' in mind but SI researchers expect a wider audience for their studies.

Table 1. Conceptions of ICT in organizations/society

Standard (tool) models	Socio-technical models
ICT is a tool	ICT is a socio-technical network
A business model is sufficient	An ecological view is also needed
One-shot ICT implementations are made	ICT implementations are an ongoing social process
Technological effects are direct and immediate	Technological effects are indirect and involve different time scales
Politics are bad or irrelevant	Politics are central and even enabling
Incentives to change are unproblematic	Incentives may require restructuring (and
Relationships are easily reformed	may be in conflict)
Social effects of ICT are big but isolated and benign	Relationships are complex, negotiated, multivalent (including trust)
Contexts are simple (a few key terms or demographics)	Potentially enormous social repercussions of ICT (not just quality of work life, but overall
Knowledge and expertise are easily made explicit	quality of life)
ICT infrastructures are fully supportive	Contexts are complex (matrices of businesses, services, people, technology history, location, etc.)
	Knowledge and expertise are inherently tacit/implicit
	Additional skill and work are needed to make ICT work

Agarwal and Lucas extended Benbasat and Zmud's definitions of 'impact' and 'IT artifact'. The nomological net in Benbasat and Zmud's Figure 2 includes a variable called 'impact', which is defined to be the (direct or indirect, intended or unintended) impact of these artifacts on humans who directly (and indirectly) interact with them, structures and contexts within which they are embedded, and associated collectives (groups, work units, organizations) (p. 186). It is possible that Benbasat and Zmud agree with Agarwall and Lucas' call for macro research, given the inclusion of the impact variable in their nomological net. However, their paper does not suggest a need for macro-oriented research, nor does it discuss the transformational nature of information technology. In particular, the impact (or a new set of variables) should include the transformation of industries, firms, and individual tasks as well as new bases for competition and new business models. Agarwal and Zmud recommend expanding the definition of the IT artifact from "enabling or supporting some tasks" to specify IT as the integration of the processing logic found in computers with the massive stores of databases and the connectivity of communications networks. The IT artifact includes IT infrastructure, innovations with technology, and especially the Internet.

Kling [1999] describes the use of socio-technical systems as follows: "As socio-technical systems, we can pay special attention to:
- people in various roles and relationships with each other and with other system elements;
- support resources (training/support/help); and
- information structures (content and content providers, rules/norms/regulations, such as those that authorize people to use systems and information in specific ways, access controls).

He asks about the importance of their content for various constituencies, who is authorized to change content and how that matters, etc." He adds
- "The networks' content for various constituencies, who is authorized to change content, and how that matters." [Kling 2000].

In the list above there are many such elements that connect technological artifacts to their social world. To our mind, the relationships between technological artifacts and social world in Social Informatics as described by Kling are much richer than in Information Systems as described by Benbasat and Zmud, and by Agarwal and Lucas, too.

5   Some Ideas to Supplement Both SI and IS

So far the human being has only been implicitly considered, and writers in both Social Informatics and in Information Systems supported the macro view. We shall below analyze some characteristics of the human being. Our motivation in so doing is based on two disparate views. First, Hevner et al. [2004, p. 82] indirectly define IT artifact: "We include not only instantiations in our definition of the IT artifact but also the constructs, models, and methods applied in the development and use of information systems. We do not include people or elements of organizations in our definition nor do we explicitly include the process by which such artifacts evolve over time." In addition, Alter [2003] criticizes Benbasat and Zmud's idea to take the IT artifact as core concept of information systems, its main role in their nomological net (Figure 2). He starts by examining the meaning of 'IT artifact' and concluding that this term is too unclear to serve as a basic concept for delineating the field. "The concept of work system is useful in trying to interpret Benbasat and Zmud's definition of IT artifact. A *work system* can be defined as a system in which *human*

participants and/or machines perform *work* using *information, technology,* and other
resources to produce *products and/or services* for internal or external *customers.* A
rudimentary understanding of a work system requires a basic description of those six
underlined elements in the definition plus some understanding of three additional
elements: the relevant environment, infrastructure, and strategies." To this end we
pose the question: Why do Hevner et al. not want to include people into their
definition? Is there something problematic about people for building information
systems?

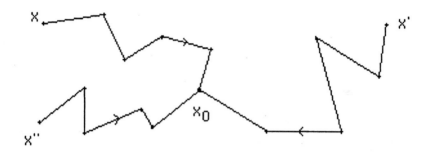

Fig. 3. A nilpotent dynamic system

We consider information systems as dynamic systems and we use Aulin's [1989]
classification of those systems. Aulin [1989] states that the initial state x_0 is called
the *rest state* and the *nilpotent* dynamic system (Figure 3) has the property that it
comes back to its initial state after a finite number (s) of units of time. A dynamic
system with a *full causal recursion* does not have any rest state to be reached in a
finite number of steps (in a finite time). The causal systems can be classified to two
categories: nilpotent systems and systems with a full causal recursion.

.Causal systems
|
|--- nilpotent systems
|
|--- systems with a full causal recursion

The causal systems with full causal recursion can be divided into four classes
depending on whether the system will *disintegrate* after a certain disturbance and its
trajectory disassociate from the path of its old goal function, or whether the system is
steerable from outside and its path goes in the constant distance of the path of its old
goal function or comes closer to the path of its old goal function in time. The latter
can be either finite (*self-regulating systems*) or infinite (*self-steering systems*).

Causal systems
|
|--- nilpotent systems
|
|--- systems with a full causal recursion
  |
  |--- self-steering systems
  |
  |--- self-regulating systems
  |
  |--- systems steerable from outside
  |
  |--- disintegrating systems

If the uniqueness of the states of mind, along with the goal-oriented nature of thought processes, is typical of human consciousness, the only thinkable causal representation of what takes place in the human mind in an alert state is the self-steering process. According to Aulin [1989, 173] it is, however, necessary to limit the interpretation so that what is *self-steering* in the human mind is the *total intellectual process*. Not all the partial processes need be self-steering.

Real-world examples of *self-regulating* systems are: a room equipped with a good *thermostat* (self-regulating equilibrium systems); some *living organisms* like a heart (periodically pulsating self-regulating systems); etc. A flying ball (the resistance of the air is negligible), a frictionless oscillator and a *robot* are examples of systems *steerable from outside*. A *radioactive atom* and a dead organism are *disintegrating systems*.

Aulin's classification gives us a partial explanation for the exclusion of people made by Hevner et al. All the components (e.g. hardware, software and data as nilpotent systems) of the IT artifact are then behaving regularly, because people as self-steering sub systems whose behavior cannot be predicted do not belong to the IT artifact.

But what does the combination of hardware, software and data as nilpotent sub systems, and people as self-steering sub systems mean for the practice (design, use and management) of information systems?

Design: use the participative development method, allow people to design their jobs themselves; base the distribution of tasks between people and computer on the novice user, develop flexibilities for the computerized sub system for the expert user.

Realization: Because people learn some tasks, allow them to move their routine tasks to the flexible computerized sub system, i.e. allow them to change the distribution of tasks between people and computer.

Management: Apply process innovations, i.e. integrate consecutive tasks into one job; reduce unnecessary hierarchies (The Law of Requisite Hierarchy in [Aulin 1989]).

What does the combination nilpotent and self-steering sub systems mean for the *science* (research) of information systems?

People: Repetitive research settings are not allowed, because a human being is always moving into a new state. Gather data by asking human subjects; confirm raw data by triangulation, apply Klein and Myers's [1999] principles.

IT artifacts: Apply Orlikowski and Iacono's [2001] five premises. Follow the seven guidelines of Hevner et al.'s [2004].

6 Discussion

Researchers in Social Informatics do not want to use research models typical for the controlled experiment where one independent variable is manipulated and its influence on the dependent variable is studied when all the other variables are kept constant or carefully controlled. The testing of a certain theory or theoretical framework in wide surveys is not typical for social informatics researchers who "study specific ICTs in specific settings to develop concepts and theories that apply to many kinds of ICTs in many kinds of settings" [Kling 2000]. Information systems researchers, too, seek knowledge applicable to many contexts, but, to my mind, their research models are narrower than the models of social informatics researchers, because surveys play a central role in IS studies [Orlikowski and Baroudi 1991]. Social informatics researchers prefer more realistic research models of the matrix of social and technical dependencies.

According to Gregor and Jones [2004] Information Systems (IS) as a discipline is concerned with action - the design, construction and use of software and systems involving people, technology, organizations and societies. In acting in building information systems it is preferable not to approach every new development problem afresh. We would like some guiding knowledge that can be transferred from one situation, in which action is taken, to another. Generalized knowledge of this type can be referred to as design theory. In Information Systems people are considered to behave in a similar way to technology, i.e. regularly. The purpose of Social Informatics is "to understand how people's behavior can help scientists develop empirically-grounded concepts that help scientist to predict (or at least understand) variations in the ways that people and groups use information technologies" [Kling 1999]. But we demonstrate here that because of free will, people do not always behave regularly or predictably, and hence both Social Informatics and Information Systems must be improved by new, more realistic models of the human being.

References:

R. Agarwal and H. C. Lucas Jr, The Information Systems Identity Crisis: Focusing on High-Visibility and High-Impact Research, *MIS Quarterly* 29(3), 381-398, 2005.
P. Agre, Toward a Critical Technical Practice: Lessons Learned in Trying to Reform AI, in: *Bridging the great divide: Social science technical networks, and cooperative work*, edited by Bowker, Gasser, Star and Turner, Erlbaum 1996)

S. Alter, Sidestepping the IT Artifact, Scrapping the IS Silo, and Laying Claim to 'Systems in Organizations', *Communications of the Association for Information Systems* 12(30), 54 p [2003.

R.L. Ashenhurst, A Report of the ACM Curriculum Committee on Computer Education for Management, *Communications of the ACM* 15(5), 363-398 [1972.

A. Aulin, *Foundations of Mathematical System Dynamics: The Fundamental Theory of Causal Recursion and its Application to Social Science and Economics*, Pergamon Press, Oxford, 1989.

R.D. Banker and R.J. Kauffman, The Evolution of Research on Information Systems: A Fiftieth-year Survey of the Literature in *Management Science, Management Science* 50(3), 281-298, 2004.

I. Benbasat and R.W. Zmud, The Identity Crisis within the IS Discipline: Defining and Communicating the Discipline's Core Properties, *MIS Quarterly* 27(2), 183-194, 2003.

G. B. Davis, Information Systems Conceptual Foundations: Looking Backward and Forward, in: *Organizational and Social Perspectives on Information Technology*, edited by R. Baskerville, J. Stage and J. DeGross, Kluwer, Boston. 2000, pp. 61-82.

S. Gregor, Design Theory in Information Systems, *Australian Journal of Information Systems*, Special Issue, 14-22, 2002.

S. Gregor and D. Jones, The Formulation of Design Theories for Information Systems, in: *Constructing the infrastructure for the knowledge economy: Methods and tools, theory and practice*, edited by Linger, Fisher, Wojtkowski, Zupancic, Vigo and Arold, Kluwer Academic, New York, 2004, pp. 83-93.

A.R. Hevner, S.T. March, J. Park and S. Ram, Design Science in Information Systems Research, *MIS Quarterly* 28(1), 75-105, 2004.

H.K. Klein and M.D. Myers, A Set of Principles for Conducting and Evaluating Interpretive Field Studies in Information Systems, *MIS Quarterly* 23(1), 67-94, 1999.

R. Kling, What is Social Informatics and Why Does it Matter?, *D-Lib Magazine* 5(1), 1-22, 1999.

R. Kling, Learning about Information Technologies and Social Change: The Contribution of Social Informatics, *The Information Society* 16(3), 217-232, 2000.

Rob Kling Center of Social Informatics portal, History of the Term, (http://rkcsi.indiana.edu/article.php/about-social-informatics/35 , November 7, 2005)

R. Kling and R. Lamb, IT and Organizational Change in Digital Economies: A Socio-technical Approach, in: *Understanding the Digital Economy – Data, Tools and Research*, edited by Kahin and E. Brynjolfsson, MIT Press, Cambridge MA, 1999; http://mitpress.mit.edu/ude.html

R. Lamb [2005], A Private Communication, December 1, 2005 at Turku, Finland.

J.L. McKenney and F.M. Tonge, The State of Computer Oriented Curricula in Business Schools 1970, *Communications of the ACM* 14(7), 443-448, 1971.

W.J. Orlikowski and J.J. Baroudi, Studying Information Technology in Organizations: Research Approaches and Assumptions, *Information Systems Research* 2(1), 1-28, 1991.

W.J. Orlikowski and C.S. Iacono, Research Commentary: Desperately Seeking the 'IT' in IT Research – A Call to Theorizing the IT Artifact, *Information Systems Research* 12(2), 121-134, 2001.

D. Teichroew, Education Related to the Use of Computers in Organizations, *Communications of the ACM* 14(9), 573-588, 1971.

Work Informatics – An Operationalisation of Social Informatics

Markku I. Nurminen

University of Turku, Department for Information Technolgy and TUCS
Turku, Finland, markku.nurminen@utu.fi

Abstract. A new approach to informatics and Social Informatics is introduced called Work Informatics. It is compared with Social Informatics, and it turns out that there is a high resemblance between their scopes and objectives. Work Informatics is more operational and therefore, we can use it more easily for practical purposes. Social, technical, and socio-technical aspects of both are analysed. The focus, unit of analysis and contents of Work Informatics are briefly outlined.

Keywords: Social Informatics, Work Informatics, Socio-Technical Design, Participative Design, Unit of Analysis

1   Introduction

Social Informatics has been characterised [1] in the following way:

"Social Informatics refers to the interdisciplinary study of the design, uses and consequences of ICTs that takes into account their interaction with institutional and cultural contexts."

It is clear that the purpose is to emphasise the social aspects of information and communication technology (ICT). In this definition, we do not view that intention only in the name of Social Informatics, but also in the expressions of *interdisciplinary contexts* and *institutional and cultural contexts.* The definition is probably intentionally open, as it does not tell in full detail what should be the object of study or what characteristics one should study. The expectation of type of results from such studies is also open and how and for whom these results might be useful.

One conclusion of the general nature of Social Informatics is that each application of it has to begin by articulating many things to make the study specific enough. In this paper, I shall analyse one possible application area that I have called *work informatics.* Work Informatics is the name of a new master's programme at the

---

Please use the following format when citing this chapter:

Nurminen, M. I., 2006, in IFIP International Federation for Information Processing, Volume 223, Social Informatics: An Information Society for All? In Remembrance of Rob Kling, eds. Berleur, J., Numinen, M. I., Impagliazzo, J., (Boston: Springer), pp. 407–416.

University of Turku, but it is also a research area within information systems research and probably also within Social Informatics.

Intuitively it seems reasonable to look for similarities rather than dissimilarities between Work Informatics and Social Informatics. Both of them have an important mission that aims at broadening and enriching the technically biased understanding and self-understanding of IT and IT artefacts. In this paper, we identify more approaches that share this objective and outline a concretisation towards its fulfilment based on informatics work.

2   Social or/and Technical

The emphasis on social aspects in Social Informatics raises two questions to the surface. (1) Does Social Informatics expand the area of Informatics by bringing some new research questions to the agenda? (2) What parts of informatics do not belong to Social Informatics? It is clear that the second question is more central for our interest in Work Informatics.

If we consider Social Informatics people sitting on one side of a border, who are sitting on the other side of it? Are they unsocial, non-social, or asocial? I am afraid that these labels are tautological and they do not add very much to the understanding of the substance of the difference. It is probably more fruitful and truthful to realise that *we* are sitting on the other side, as deviants from the mainstream. Moreover, it is not so difficult to find the name of the mainstream to be information technology. The identity of information technology people arose from the concept of technology and the technical. Information technology simply cannot escape its technical connotation. The message from Social Informatics is that this interpretation may not be the complete truth and perhaps not even its most important dimension.

The reference to the technical aspects of informatics brings a new challenge to the discourse reflected in the recent debate about the IS Core that divides the discipline in two main camps [2,3,4]. They have identified the two camps as the 'IT Artefacts' and 'IS in Organisations'. Without a deeper analysis, it seems natural that the latter one is a better candidate for an ally to Social Informatics, if it turns out that this kind of choice is necessary. Perhaps we can even use the label 'IS in Organisations' as a synonym to Social Informatics. Of course, Work Informatics would even be on the same side of this borderline.

It is possible to view this confrontation between the two fractions of IS Research (IT Artefact and IS in Organisations) one possible expression of another confrontation: ICT is fundamentally social or technical. This issue has been with us quite a long time. *Information systems are technical systems that have also social consequences* is a slogan expressed by the advocates of the technical orientation whereas the socially oriented people would favour a slogan *Information systems are social systems, part of which are technically implemented.* In addition, many groups obviously want to avoid making this choice as if they would like both to eat the cake and to have it.

It is beyond the scope of this paper to find an ultimate solution to the question whether information technology is technically or socially determined. It is, however, still interesting to examine the role taken by IT on issues relevant to Social Informatics and Work Informatics.

The power of the computer to support human work and enhance organisational activities is based on the computer's ability to execute stored programs without frequent intervention of a human operator. This property seems to give support to the technical orientation. It also has the risk that the IT artefact is conceived as an actor that nobody needs to control and therefore can function more or less on its own. The other, more socially oriented option comes from the tool metaphor. Even if the execution of programs seems to happen independently of the human operator, a user makes use of the artefact as a tool that is ultimately responsible for the outcome, whether performed partly or entirely by means of computers. This is an interpretation that Work Informatics (and in my opinion Social Informatics) must do.

The actor issue is of crucial importance. This importance is underscored by the fact that the issue is not too often addressed. Most textbooks on information systems research and design silently accept the state of affairs that the computers perform certain tasks because they are better, faster, and more accurate or have other benefits when compared to human performance. There is an implicit division of labour between human and computerised tasks. It remains implicit, because we discuss the collaboration between people and computers quite seldom from the actor perspective. This is natural because it is extremely difficult. One must present a theory about the particular characteristics of the machine actor and, if the information system is supposed to perform some functions, what kind of actor it is? If something goes wrong, who takes the responsibility?

The problem does not boil down to the dichotomy between objective and subjective. A bullet does have an objective effect upon human flesh [5]. However, shooting people is socially and subjectively unacceptable rather than technically determined.

3   Socio-Technical Approaches

Our discussion above can be summarised in two issues. One issue is, how we conceive the relationship between technical and social phenomena? Many questions arise. Are they different or distinct? Do their domains consist of or contain same elements or are their units entirely different? Are they overlapping to some extent or is one of them perhaps a subset of the other? These questions are valid for any area that deals with technical and social phenomena, for example traffic, energy production, or home electronics.

In addition, another set of questions exists that are specific for IT. The actor problem discussed above is a good example of this. One may find another question, for example, in the complicated and integrated structures characteristic for many information systems. Are these structures social or technical? Do they coordinate social or technical activities?

The socio-technical school offers one consistent suggestion to both question groups. Emery and Trist [6] distinguish between two more or less separate systems: the technical system and social system. The innovation made by the Tavistock

School at that time was that these two systems are fundamentally different and therefore, one should design them according to their different principles. We should remember that we still in the 40's the ideal for the design of work organisation and other social systems was based on an analogy with technical systems. In this context, the socio-technical initiative was revolutionary.

The socio-technical principles soon received applications in information technology as well. Enid Mumford developed and introduced the successful development method ETHICS [7]. She supplemented the Tavistock approaches with her own theory of factors of job satisfaction. The design should aim at a good fit between the employer requirements and employee needs. The social and technical systems are designed separately and finally, they chose an optimal joint design of the alternatives given by both tracks.

We could interpret Social Informatics in terms of socio-technical approaches. This is a suggestion, for example, presented by the frequent use of the term socio-technical in the communities close to Social Informatics [8]. For some reason, the two socio-technical groups do not seem to belong fully to the same tradition. It is not, for example, easy to say whether Social Informatics people regard the technical and social systems as separate in the same way as the older socio-technical tradition. The phrases used in the definition of Social Informatics unfortunately indicate such separation. *The consequence of ICT* already gives a hint to that direction. The *interaction* of ICTs with institutional and cultural contexts is a stronger indication, because interaction does have identifiable parties.

I would personally hope that this Social Informatics does not subscribe to the separate and consequently non-social character of ICTs. The doubts I expressed above are probably a sign of widespread (but not therefore harmless) inaccurate words and idioms that give unintended connotations when read accurately. This is my hope, because the separate technical systems are likely to grow to autonomous systems. If this happens, reified technical arguments (that we need not or can not discuss) will confront us because they are not socially determined. In other words, no people exist behind these arguments and they do not necessarily serve human interest.

In Work Informatics, we can resist such reification; we should just remember the aphorism by Irmeli Sinkkonen [9]: *The work of the users is not to use the system.* Les Gasser [10] has also given a similar statement by:

"Use of computers is any employment of computer-based information or analyses in the performance of other tasks. Thus, computer use presumes existence of other work..."

Work is a primarily social phenomenon. We cannot do work so that you first do some work, then interrupt it and do some technical tricks with the system, and then return to work. The system must be an embedded one that performs as an inherent part of work; we must not conceive it as a separate effort. Therefore, Work Informatics should reject the conceptual separation of the social and technical systems.

4   Discovery of Context and Participation

One possible way to give more emphasis to the social aspects of informatics is to pay greater attention to the contexts. This is exactly what Rob Kling has done in his definition by his reference to institutional and cultural contexts. His interest in context can be seen in the context of the widely spread interest in context during the last fifteen years. *Computers in Context* was the name of at least one conference [11] and monograph [12] in 1990s. Context has, in my interpretation, been an expression of the desire to escape from the narrow definition of IS area with dominantly technical label. There are so many aspects to consider such as work and its organisation, communities of practice, and motivation and skill.

Unfortunately, context is a poor concept since its analytical power is so minimal. Context somehow stands for anything that is not in the focus; yet it relates to the focused object. In informatics, for example, the discourse surrounding a context reveals the fact that the focus still was in the design and implementation of information systems, conceived as dominantly technical constructs. Now many scholars required that the focus should shift from ICT to the context. This is, however, impossible because when a new focus is taken into focus, the earlier focus becomes part of the new context. However, the new focus in the earlier context does not mean that everything is lost. Rather, it may open new ways of thinking about the relationship between ICT and work activities that follow the wisdom of the aphorism by Irmeli Sinkkonen, namely, that the work of the users is not to use the system.

This statement is insightful because it calls for a formulation of the work in terms that do not rely on information systems. The essential things reside outside the ICT artefacts. This reallocation of focus has an interesting parallel with the changes in the organisation of information systems development (ISD). Increasingly, outsourced companies have replaced in-house development. If we move ICT from the focus to the periphery, the same will largely happen to ISD. This has far-reaching consequences to participative design that has been one of the flagships of Social Informatics.

Participation has been justified by at least three groups of argument, namely 1) human right, 2) acceptance, and 3) quality of the future system. Happily, both Social Informatics and Work Informatics share the first argument, even if both have to articulate what is the object and process of participation. The acceptance of the users is likely to be higher if they have the opportunity for participation. However, this argument may have a flavour of manipulation, unless the genuine improvement of the future use or work situation forms its foundation. Hence, the third argument is the core of all participation.

The discourse on the quality of information systems is, again, dependent upon the choice; that is, that which we decide to place in the concept of information system. Shall we regard it as an IT artefact? On the other hand, shall we want to include the organisational context as well? This question is not only an academic or intellectual exercise, but it has an important practical significance. This is because the production and delivery of information systems more and more seldom takes place as an in-house development. Therefore, the design and production of the ICT artefacts is often finished when a customer organisation considers a purchase. Thus the decisions on the structure and functioning of the software have already been made and beyond the potential participation of these particular users. One decision remains: the choice between alternative software products.

However, if we decide to consider the organisational context as a domain of participation, there is much to do in terms of designing work roles and responsibility areas and assigning them among employees. We need to decide user education and training, coordination practices, and many other aspects. One can even argue that organisational implementation is impossible without participation. This is because during an implementation, users must produce an interpretation of their own – no one else can do it for them. This kind of appropriation is an active form of participation performed both individually and collectively.

To sum up, participation in the design does not guarantee a successful implementation or appropriation. Work Informatics emphasises naturally the organisational implementation and appropriation; it is possible to accomplish good work and use situations even for a system designed without direct user participation, whereas it is not possible without participation in organisational implementation. I am convinced that Social Informatics shares these concerns of Work Informatics.

5   Unit of Analysis

After a shift of focus (ICT) to the earlier (organisational) context, the new focus is on the side of working (or organisational activity) instead of information systems. One fruitful trick of assessing the benefit of such redefinition is to identify the 'Unit(s) of Analysis' (UoA) within the new research focus. We often view units of analysis as an answer to the question: Facts about what? In other words, what are we talking about? It is difficult to overestimate the importance of the UoA discussion because very many misunderstandings are because people are not talking about the same thing. Furthermore, people use the term 'Unit of Investigation' for the same thing [13].

I have earlier [14] suggested that one feasible candidate to the primary UoA could be a work role. Here, we use the concept of work role to signify a meaningful collection of work tasks and processes connected to the rights, responsibilities, and resources needed for successful performance of work tasks. In organisation of work, the work role is a flexible building block that has a many-to-many relationship with the employees. What is important in the discussion of Work Informatics is the place of the ICT artefacts. The work role as the UoA embeds these artefacts in the work roles and the processes included in them.

This choice is of crucial importance. The work role as a central structural unit transcends the distinction between technical and social, because it embraces both of them. There is no separate social or technical system as both aspects integrate with each other within each work role. Integration takes place between work roles, not between their technical or social components. Of course, the work roles are not isolated islands; they have many connections to other work roles by means of communication and shared databases. In addition, the work role aims at being scalable to fit if small and large units of work. If we decide to regard the work role as a more social than technical construct, we have given the social sphere the superior role subordinated to the technical one.

Here we cannot be completely sure about Social Informatics. To what extent do different scholars agree with Work Informatics about the dominance of social over technical? The name Social Informatics creates, however, expectations to this direction. The work role framework for the use of information technology is not alone in the manifestly social approaches to IS use and research. Steve Alter introduces one significant framework; he uses the term 'work system' as the name and basic construct. Just like with work roles, it is not meaningful to talk about Information System Development as an isolated enterprise, because the real issue is in the development of the work system and information systems as a part of it.

While it was quite straightforward to construct a natural Unit of Analysis for Work Informatics, it is not quite easy to do the same for Social Informatics. What could be the most obvious Unit of Analysis for Social Informatics? This question and the difficulty in finding an answer to it indicate that Social Informatics, indeed, is more a perspective to research than a well-defined set of problems. In this respect, Work Informatics offers a sub-discipline that is more operational. We now give some examples of its possible application.

6   Work Informatics in Action

We outlined above the meaning of Work Informatics as a discipline or sub-discipline within informatics primarily anchored to the work concept and only secondarily in informatics, as far as it is understood as IT artefacts. The technical perspective does not have an autonomous existence; rather, we always regard it in the context of the social perspective of work. This became clear in the discussion about the 'unit of analysis' above. We determined that the primary UoA was to be a work role that undoubtedly belongs to the social rather than to the technical side of this dichotomy. IT artefacts were not regarded as independent units of analysis; rather, they were seen as characteristics of the work roles.

This shift of perspective from the IT artefact to the organisational context reduces the autonomy of the technical system that cannot have any objectives of its own. It is, indeed, fine if we can do tasks effectively and reliably. However, people also determine these objectives, not by a nameless and faceless technology.

The new emphasis around work and its organisations does not imply that Work Informatics allocates itself in a small corner of 'information systems research', or even partly outside of it. Work Informatics actually more or less coincides with the ISR domain. This coincidence is not, however, a coincidence. What is different is the perspective: not from the IT artefact to the context, but from the work context to the artefacts. The difference in perspectives leads to different problem formulations. Most of the IS research really aims at creating some benefit. Furthermore, the greatest benefits are waiting in work organisations that hope to collect the fruits of the ICT artefacts.

Once this kind of theoretical conceptualisation occurred, it opened a question of demonstrating the legitimate status as a discipline. In information technology, one important characteristic for a new theoretical approach is its fruitfulness. During the last fifteen years, our research group has performed a series of case studies that have taken the form of evaluation of the success of deployment of information systems in the collaborating work organisations. The experiences of these projects will now be replicated to parts of the master's programme in Work Informatics. The common part in all successful approaches has been that the current state is analysed in terms of non-technical abstraction: the work activities and their objectives are described in terms that are independent of the current ICT solution. This is because otherwise it is not possible to give an evaluation of the current solution, how well one achieved the work-related objectives. The abstraction often also gives good hints for discovering alternative solutions for the work and its organisation as well as for the development of skills and knowledge, not to forget improvements in the ICT artefacts.

The experiences are promising. We have given suggestions for moderate to significant changes that are most often to the satisfaction of the customers. Often the suggestions have been conflicting. This is not strange; it rather confirms many findings of Social Informatics. Here the reasons and mechanisms of impact have been expressed more analytically. There is a good reason to believe, that Work Informatics as a sub-discipline of ISR can contribute to a paradigm shift that has a positive effect in both work and business.

7   Structuring Work Informatics

Work Informatics is also the name of a recently established Master's Programme in the University of Turku in Finland. The Department of Information Technology hosts the programme that is the major educational effort of its information systems group. The contents of the programme are structured through the concept of work rather than one or other attribute of the IT artefact. The work is conceptualised according to three modalities: individual work, collective work, and services. One of the modalities is usually dominant in a particular work situation, even if the other two often are also present at least implicitly.

This kind of general study of work becomes Work Informatics when we find out that ICT takes different roles in different modalities. The modalities also provide a map over the field of information systems research. Various approaches, such as for example BPR, CSCW, or CRM get their natural favourite modalities. Similar connections emerge also to other theoretical frameworks often borrowed from reference disciplines. For example, communities of practice, activity theory, actor-network theory, articulation work, and situated action find their place on the map.

Two more aspects further strengthen the informatics connection of Work Informatics: knowledge and change. Knowledge has already turned out to be a crucial aspect for the use of ICT. Knowledge is embedded in the artefacts themselves and their skilful use is possible only by employees with sufficient knowledge. Nevertheless, probably the most important knowledge is related in the activities and processes of the work organisation. Moreover, of course, not all these dimensions of knowledge are independent on each other. We must absolutely address this theme (as addressed in ISR before).

Change is change of work and its organisation, with their tools and infrastructures. This is the emphasis that traditional IS Research had already in 1960s and 1970s. The problem is how to make analysis and design of systems to get them implemented in organisations – all activities were strongly change-driven. It is important to remember this change aspect so deeply rooted in all technology, but the new emphasis in Work Informatics makes the object of change broader and the process of change to be more dominated by technology-pull than –push.

8   Discussion

In this paper, I have introduced the concept Work Informatics and given it a characterisation by comparing it with Social Informatics. It comes as no great surprise that these two approaches have much in common: work is essentially social. Both approaches are concerned with the often-technical emphasis in the development and application of information technology. This concern gives them a perspective from which we can reformulate old research problems and invent new ones.

The discussion above has come to a suggestion that Work Informatics is more specific and thus, also more operational than Social Informatics. For people working in Work Informatics it is straightforward to find different work organisations, identify units of analysis, collect qualitative and sometimes quantitative data, interpret them, and advance towards new concepts and theories. Social Informatics, on the other hand, has its power in its abstract and general nature. Hence, we can find fruitful research problems in various different areas.

Work Informatics has an important contribution to give informatics in general and to Social Informatics in particular. This is because the vast majority of the benefits that ICT is expected to create to our societies is likely to emerge from work organisations. For example, these organisations make most decisions on purchasing and implementing ICT. This means that the industry should be interested in hiring people who have a special competence in Work Informatics. This justifies the introduction of the new master's programmes in Work Informatics.

References

1. R. Kling, What is Social Informatics? (2001);
   http://www.slis.indiana.edu/SI/concepts.html.
2. W. Orlikowski and S. Iacono, Desperately Seekint the IT in IT Research, *Information Systems Research* 2(1), 400-408 (2001).
3. I. Benbasat and R. Zmud, The Identity Crisis within the IS Discipline: Defining and Communicating the Discipline's Core Properties, *MIS Quarterly* 27(2), 183-194 (2003).
4. K. Lyytinen and J.L. King, Nothing at the Center? Academic Legitimacy in the Information Systems Field, *Journal of the Association for Information Systems* 5(6), 220-246 (2004).
5. K. Grint and S. Woolgar, *The Machine at Work; Technology, Work and Organization*, Polity Press, 1997.

6. F.E. Emery and E.L. Trist, Socio Technical Systems, in: *Management Science, Models and Techniques*, edited by C.W, Churchman and M. Verhulst, Pergamon, 1961, pp. 83-97.

7. E. Mumford and M. Weir, *Computer Systems in Work Design: The ETHICS Approach*, Wiley, New York, 1979.

8. W. Scacchi, Socio-Technical Design, in: *Berkshire Encyclopedia of Human-Computer Interaction*, edited by W.S. Bainbridge, Berkshire Publishing Group, 2004.

9. I. Sinkkonen, private communication (1996).

10. L. Gasser, The Integration of Computing and Routine Work, *ACM Transactions on Office Information* 4(3), 205-225 (1986).

11. M. Kyng and L. Mathiassen (editors), *Computers in Context: Joining Forces in Design*, Third Decennial Conference, Aarhus, Denmark, August 1995.

12. B. Dahlbom and L. Mathiassen, *Computers in Context: The Philosophy and Practice of Systems Design*, NCC Blackwell, 1993.

13. T. Nordström, *Information Systems Stewardship; Advancing utilisation of information technology in organisations*, Print & Media, Umeå, 2003.

14. M. I. Nurminen, *Unit of Analysis*, Keynote presentation at the IRIS'27 Conference, Falkenberg, Sweden , 2004.

Philosophical Inquiry into Social Informatics – Methods and Uses of Language

Rocío Riueda Ortiz, Henrik Herlau, and Leif Bloch Rasmussen
Central University, Bogotá, Colombia, rruedaortiz@yahoo.com
Copenhagen Business School, Denmark, lbr.inf@cbs.dk, herlau@cbs.dk

Abstract. This paper inquires into the possibility of the development of ICT at the Bottom of the Pyramid. Its focus is on philosophically founded methods and languages applicable on a universal and exemplary basis. The methods are taken to be based on abduction and sweeping-in-processes and the languages are taken to be based on categorical imperatives of Kant and the discourse ethics of Habermas/Apel. These 'taken to be's' are contrasted with Jacques Derrida's 'Deconstruction'. Paul Feyerabend's 'Against Method' as well as complexity theory. The explicated monological/dialogical and formal / procedural methods and languages together with its counterparts are used to start a sweeping-in-process on 'Social Informatics'.

Keywords: deconstruction, inquiry, method, language, philosophy, social informatics, sweeping-in-process

1 Introduction – Questions Asked

During 2003-2005 a lot of work has been carried out on ICT in a globalized world. At the Global Level: WSIS in Geneva and Tunis, UN ICT Task Force and ILO's Fair Globalization. At the European Level: Lisbon Strategy, Agenda for Key Technologies, i2010, Preparation of CIP and 7-the Framework Programme and Strategic Partnerships with other countries. The call for papers for HCC7 on Social Informatics can be seen as part of that work.

This paper will try to inquire into the philosophical foundation of Social Informatics and beyond. The questions asked in Social Informatics and HCC's may be taken to be based in a Western quest for Enlightenment. We therefore start with two of the most prominent formulators of that quest, Immanuel Kant in 1784 and Foucault in 1984. In *What is Enlightenment?*, Kant said: "Enlightenment is man's

Please use the following format when citing this chapter:

Ortiz, R. R., Herlau, H., Rasmussen, L. B., 2006, in IFIP International Federation for Information Processing, Volume 223, Social Informatics: An Information Society for All? In Remembrance of Rob Kling, eds. Berleur, J., Numinen, M. I., Impagliazzo, J., (Boston: Springer), pp. 417–430.

release from his self-incurred tutelage. Tutelage is man's inability to make use of his understanding without direction from another. Self-incurred is this tutelage when its cause lies not in lack of reason but in lack of resolution and courage to use it without direction from another. *Sapere Aude!* 'Have courage to use your own reason!' – that is the motto of enlightenment."

Foucault responded 200 years later, that Enlightenment could be taken to be [11]: the art of not being governed quite so much by

• Dogma from the (Christian) scriptures
• Authorities
• Language and text from sciences (humanities, social and natural)

... in such a way that [11, p. 132] "The critical ontology of ourselves has to be considered not, certainly, as a theory, a doctrine, nor even as a permanent body that is accumulating; it has to be conceived as an attitude, an ethos, a philosophical life in which critique of what we are is at one and the same time the historical analysis of the limits that are imposed on us and an experiment with the possibility of going beyond them."

Thus we take the quest for Enlightenment to be an ongoing courageous process based on an endless search for better methods and uses of languages. That search also means for us the study of the conditions of possibility, in terms of Foucault, that each epistemology with its language and methods bring us a particular set of tools to create a kind of reality, a kind of world.

2   On Method

As a way of starting on the methods and uses language we take as a point of departure the fundamental foundations of pragmatism and studies in empirical idealism on scientific methods as expressed in the writings of Edgar A. Singer and C. West Churchman. They both tell us, that when we reach a conclusion after having exposed our ideas to the most severe test we can imagine, then we have done the best that inquiry can possibly accomplish.

"The *only* trouble with this telling, they say, is *all* the trouble in the world: How do we know we have exposed our ideas to the severest test? If we have bound ourselves by our thinking into one corner of reality, then we shall never expose ourselves to the really severe test. Instead, we shall wander aimlessly about in our own narrow muddle, thinking we are progressing, but getting nowhere at all. The possibility that we have become prisoners of our own concepts is a topic that demands a separate study in the next part."

In his search for methods Churchman uses the work of E.A.Singer (especially *'Experience and Reflection'* [26] and *'Mind as Behavior'* [25] to develop a methodology using induction, deduction, abduction and beyond in a process called the 'sweeping-in-process'. Churchman tells that there are four possible situations in this process, based on [6, p. 191]:

1. the object remains the same over the period of time in which the methods are used, as does the methods
2. the object fluctuates in while the methods does not
3. the object remains the same while the methods fluctuate
4. both fluctuate.

"Our question of how the system should behave in each of the four conditions is thus Hegelian in kind: how can the over-observer be created?"

When we decide that a hypothesis on 'reality' is not consistent with a set of readings from our methods then we can choose among three strategies, [6, p.194]:

1. revise the hypothesis by adding new variables, or changing the functional form of the hypothesis;
2. revise the methods used in obtaining the hypothesis (including discarding one or more of them as being incorrectly used); or
3. tolerate the inconsistency until more evidence is available.

We may begin to sense the sweeping-in process of the Singerian Inquiring System as endless. One might for example take the third possibility: the object may be taken to be constant while the methods may be taken to fluctuate. Then the question will be: Can we have any certainty in that our catalogue of sciences and their measuring 'rods' should start with logic? And then we may 'conclude' in the words of Churchman [6, p. 196]: "At this point, those who hold precision and certainty as high values of inquiring system may feel that the whole foundation has slipped. Once the measuring system engages in the game of adjusting imagery, and hence data, to 'save' its view of the world, all fundamental control seems to be lost: there is no ultimate court of appeals. One has only to recall the very flexible and subtle strategies open to Ptolemaic geocentric theory to see how far this game can be extended.

But such a reaction arises out of the kind of parsimony that no longer is suitable as a criterion for the design of inquiring systems. The parsimony is based on the erroneous theory that authority or authorization is essential for design. The word 'authority' derives from the concept of leadership, a component of the system to which one can turn when in doubt. It is similar to the concept of control, which implies that a component can observe and correct the behavior of the system. But Singerian inquiring systems have no such component. Put otherwise, authority and control are pervasive throughout the system and have no location; the system is controlled, but no component is the controller. The idea has already been mentioned several times under the labels 'tactics' and 'strategies'; a tactical decision assumes an authority while a strategic decision does not. Thus a Singerian inquiring system must encompass the whole breath of inquiry in its attempt to authorize and control its procedures."

Our methodology thus begins with data or theory, collects data or theories, interpret them, find new opportunities for data and/or theories in other fields than originally aimed at, reaches out for 'conclusions' for action/experiments, stops, wonders, rests ... and: starts the journey again. During the process abduction plays a crucial role, as it makes it possible once in while to switch from a culture of logic to a culture of imagination. Abduction is part of the sweeping-in process in that it is not a systematic and logic method; rather it introduces intelligent guesswork and imagination. In that way abduction is using experiences, reflections and experimental actions in the sweeping-in process as the building blocks for qualitative shifts in methods and use of languages in search of a theory.

This demands the spirit of the artistic and heroic mood in our search for more complex methods.

Instead of assuming that there is a specific external reality upon which we can ground our efforts to know the world, Foucault, Derrida, Deleuze, mobilize metaphors such as flux to index the sense that whatever there is in the world can not be properly or finally caught in the webs of inquiry found in science. They talk of discourse to point to the methodological efforts to make and know limited moments in the fluxes that make up reality [18, p. 2-10]. For these post-structuralist thinkers making anything present implies that other but related things are simultaneously being made absent, pushed away from view; that presence is impossible without absence. Thus representations go along with something out there to represent and a lot more besides. Then, method, on the one hand, is not a more or less successful set of procedures for reporting on a given reality. Rather it is performative. It helps to produce realities. Nevertheless, there is a hinterland of realities, of manifest absences and otherness, resonance and patterns of one kind and other, already being enacted and it cannot ignore these.

Methods are not, and could never be, innocent, neutral or purely technical. In fact, method produces not only truths and non-truths, realities and non-realities, presences and absences, but also arrangements with political implications. In this framework, the complexity paradigm, which for us go further post-structuralism and Derridian strategy of knowing, subvert 'the method' by helping to remake methods –in plural- that imagine and participate in politics and other forms of knowing in novel and creative ways by escaping the postulate of singularity and responding creatively to a world that is taken to be composed of an excess of generative forces and relations. Other recent works inspired in STSS (science, technology and society studies) emphasized that scientific and technological knowledge does not evolve in a vacuum. Rather they participate in the social world, being shaped by it and simultaneously shaping it. For Latour, Wooglar, Callon and Law (STS researches), reality is not out there beyond ourselves, independent of our actions or perceptions, neither reality presents itself to us in definitive forms of relations. For them, it is not possible to separate (1) the making of particular realities; (2) the making of particular statements about those realities and (3) the creation of instrumental, technical and human configurations and practices because they are all produced together. So, reality is not independent of the methods that produce reports of reality.

That means that we need to unmake/deconstruct many of our methodological habits including the desire of certainty, security and universalism and the expectation for stable conclusions and universalism. Laws [18] says that method is not simply about the kinds of realities that we want to recognize or the kind of worlds we might hope to make. It is also and most fundamentally, about a way of being. It is about what kinds of social science we want to practise. And then, and as a part of this, it is about the kind of people that we want to be, about how we should live. So, method goes with ways of working, ways of being: happy, creative, generous, reflecting and cooperating.

Of course, new method also means that we need to create other-s language-s. One interesting possibility for us is provided for narratives, as a valid way of knowing. Narratives are the mediator that makes actions and their unity compatible. It is not merely a passive intermediary linking two distinct and pre-existing levels of reality (individual action with the story). Narrative mediation is situated in-between; it reveals both realities, individual and collective; and it does so by organizing the unexpected overflowing that, by renewing the action, reveals the existence of a story-already-there, which might have been concluded but which the actor opens and sets off again in an unexpected directions.

3   On Use of Language

The use of the method of 'sweeping-in process' can also be used in a search for uses of language for the Quest for Enlightenment and the search for answers to our questions on Social Informatics.

Again Kant is taken as a point of departure. According to a recent inquiry Bordum [2] shows, that at least four formulations of Kant's Categorial Imperative can be identified:

(1)   The categorical imperative formulated as a principle of universalization
I should never act except in such a way that I can also will that maxim should become a universal law. [16: 14, 402]

Act only according to that maxim whereby you can at the same time will that it should become a universal law. [16: 30, 421]

Act according to that maxim which can at the same time make itself a universal law. [16: 42, 437]

(2)   The categorical imperative formulated as a practical principle
Now I say that man, and in general every rational being, exists as an end in himself and not merely as a means to be arbitrarily used by this or that will. He must in all actions, whether directed to himself or to other rational beings, always be regarded at the same time as an end. [14: 35, 428]

Act in such a way that you treat humanity, whether in your own person or in the person of another, always at the same time as an end and never simply as a means. [14: 36, 429]

(3)   The categorical imperative formulated in relation to the kingdom of ends
Therefore, every rational being must so act as if he were through his maxim always a legislating member in the universal kingdom of ends. [14: 43, 438]

Act in accordance with the maxims of a member legislating universal laws for a merely possible kingdom of ends. [14: 43, 439]

(4)   The categorical imperative formulated as the absolute good will's self-legislation in analogy to the laws of nature
Act as if the maxim of your action were to become through your will a universal law of nature. ([14: 30, 421]

Act according to maxims, which can at the same time have for their object themselves as universal laws of nature. [14: 42, 437]

And Bordum concludes [2, p. 854-5]: "When I state that the formulations of the categorical imperative are different, it is due to the fact that each of them is specially formulated with different referents. They are respectively formulated in relation to: (1) the rational self-legislating person himself or herself and to self-legislation as such, (2) other rational self-legislating persons both themselves and others, (3) an objective law that can unite all persons' rational self-legislation, (4) self-legislation in analogy with the laws of nature."

Habermas has questioned the monological and formal approach used by Kant, yet they acknowledge the importance of these four formulations as basic for further developments of languages for statements of truths. As Bordum writes, [2, p. 868]:

"Habermas has two main objections to Kant's approach. The first is that it is monological and the second is that it is formal. Habermas's main improvements to Kant's theory are to give it a new dialogical (intersubjective) and procedural foundation."

The requirements for dialogical action may be found in four universal validity claims for a power-free communication (Jürgen Habermas: *On the Pragmatics of Communication,* [12, p. 22-23]):

a. uttering something *intelligibly,*
b. giving (the hearer) *something* to understand,
c. making *herself* thereby understandable, and
d. coming to an understanding with *another person.*

Agreement thus is based on recognition of the four corresponding validity claims: comprehensibility, truth, truthfulness, and rightness.

If these validity claims are not met, then any dialogue for mutual understanding breaks down. Bordum then states the following principles for discourse in a supplement to Kant's [2, p. 867-870]:

*   *the principle of discourse*: 'Just those action norms are valid to which all possibly affected persons could agree as participants in rational discourse'
*   *the principle of universalization*: 'For a norm to be valid, the consequences and side effects that its general observance can be expected to have for the satisfaction of the particular interests of each person affected must be such that all affected can accept them freely'

Karl-Otto Apel has inquired into Habermas' position in order to find out whether Habermas can be said to have the final word. Obviously – as might be expected – the answer is no, yet he convincingly shows that this 'no' must be taken to be just a pause in the dialogue; a sort of safe and comforting resting place before the journey continues.

In an article on Habermas' theory of communicative use of language Karl-Otto Apel [1]: tries to think with Habermas against Habermas. The idea of Apel is that it is not possible to prove by empirical means these intuitive theses of validity claims in an ethical discourse. This is not possible as the empirical proof in itself presupposes similar validity claims.

In order to avoid such difficulties that Habermas experiences in trying to do empirical justice to his validity claims Apel suggests another strategy for the ultimate justification (German: *Letztbegründung*) of the validity claims (constituting norms of the ethical discourse). He suggests a strict reflection that incorporates the necessary presuppositions for any claim of truth.

Apel (in accordance with Habermas) makes the following distinctions on use of language:

*   Openly Strategic Use of Language, as an alternative to
*   Closed Strategic Use of Language, which is one kind of
*   Instrumental Use of Language which are contrasted with
*   Use of Language for Mutual Understanding

In the theory on communicative action Habermas proofs convincingly that the Closed Strategic Use of Language and Instrumental Use of Language works against use of languages for mutual understanding. But Apel asks if this proof also holds for Open Strategic Use of Language? Apel is of the opinion, that it is not possible to make such a proof [1, p. 275]: "The reason for this is that, in the case of OSUL, it is impossible to in principle to decide which use of language – the *strategically rational* or the *consensually communicatively rational* – is more fundamental, without appealing to controversial *philosophical* presuppositions concerning the rational norms of language. Indeed, it is impossible to decide whether there is a *fundamental* use of language at all.

This means that the question cannot be decided on the basis of a formal pragmatics, which ultimately aims to demonstrate the presuppositions of language use in an *empirical-descriptive* manner. However, my thesis is that the question can be decided on the basis of a *universal pragmatics* which understands itself as a *transcendental pragmatics* of language. Such a transcendental pragmatics does not back away from the problem of an *ultimate reflexive justification of rationality* – so it is also able to address the problem of the relations of dependence between different types of rationality."

It is here that we find a recognition of the *priority* of the consensual-communicative rationality of argumentative discourse. And this may be taken by some to be a resting place, as we might formulate some important statements on Social Informatics.

4   Sweeping-in-Process on Social Informatics

We take Social informatics to refer to the interdisciplinary study of the design, uses and consequences of ICTs that takes into account their interaction with institutional and cultural contexts. Key ideas of Social Informatics [17]:
1.   The context of ICT use directly affects their meanings and roles.
2.   ICTs are not value neutral: their use creates winners and losers.
3.   ICT use leads to multiple, and often paradoxical, effects.
4.   ICT use has moral and ethical aspects and these have social consequences
5.   ICTs are configurable; they are actually collections of distinct components.
6.   ICTs follow trajectories and these trajectories often favor the status quo.
7.   ICTs co-evolve during design/development/use (before and after implementation)
These few statements can be taken into the endless sweeping-in process on knowing Social Informatics. As a suggestion we start by taking a few examples as a starting point:
From Kant:
1.   Social Informatics should never act except in such a way that Social Informatics can also will its maxims should become a universal law
2.   Act in Social Informatics in such a way that you treat humanity, whether in your own person or in the person of another, always at the same time as an end and never simply as a means
3.   Act in Social Informatics in accordance with the maxims of a member legislating universal laws for a merely possible kingdom of ends
4.   Act in Social Informatics as if the maxims of your action were to become through your will a universal law of nature
From Habermas:
1.   Just those action norms in Social Informatics are valid to which all possibly affected persons could agree as participants in rational discourse

2. For a norm in Social Informatics to be valid, the consequences and side effects that its general observance can be expected to have for the satisfaction of the particular interests of each person affected must be such that all affected can accept them freely

From Apel

1. Use of language for mutual understanding is the only language applicable for Social Informatics

A dialogue on these few principle/maxims is what we are arguing for in the design and possibly needed re-construction of the methods and use of languages in Social Informatics. From there we may embark on a journey in order to de-construct Social Informatics. We may even go against methods and look for the art of *not being governed quite so much* by

*   Dogma from the (Christian) scriptures
*   Authorities
*   Language and text from sciences (humanities, sociology, natural)

As said by Bertrand Russell on philosophy: "The goal of philosophy is to begin with something so obvious that it is nearly not worth mentioning and end with something so absurd that nobody will believe it."

5   Twist of the Knife

So, our journey on the quest for Enlightenment starts again; guided by Jacques Derrida [7, 8], Paul Feyerabend [10] and Eric Jantsch [15].

In the tradition, language is considered something neutral, transparent and essential that represents reality. That means that there is a natural relation between the field of worlds and the field of things. Actions, subjects and experiences are simply reflected by words. Sounds emitted by voice are the symbols of the soul, and the written words, symbols of the words emitted by voice. So, reality is understood as exterior of language, belong to a fixed order that language simply express.

Nevertheless, with the linguistic turn, language is criticized –as many other issues- and it is pointed out the role of the categorizations and divisions established for language and discourse, which defined reality. So the role of the language is important because the big changes that happen in the social interaction where new languages and 'games of languages' appear. For the philosophy of difference –and deconstruction- there is not any discourse which can be considered the 'center', synthesis or neutral point for a supposed unity or universality

Deconstruction consists in un-made, without destruction, a system of thoughts which is revealed as unique and/or, hegemonic and/or, dominant. Deconstruction implies put in question and under suspicious the authority of one term (male, black, poverty, richness) and the naturalization the other terms as subaltern, minority and otherness. So, deconstruction produces 'other', 'the other invisible, absent, silent'.

The first step in de-construction is to locate the historic (etymological) roots of the concepts involved in the theme under inquiry. This leads to the identification of pairs of opposites that might illuminate the theme in new and most often radically different perspectives. The next step then is to bring these pairs of opposites into broad daylight and dig deeper into their interrelationships. The third step is to show that these pairs of opposites are hierarchically related. As part of this third step he can show that any concept is bound to its historical context and will imply certain ways of dialogue and acting that excludes other potential ways of communicating and acting, experiencing and reflection. The fourth step is to bring disorder on these pairs of opposites and showing that communications and actions taken based on these hierarchical ordered pairs of opposites will lead to paradoxes and questions on how communications and actions might have been different – and could be different.

Then, for Derrida deconstruction produces 'otherness', 'other' which implies dialogue with that/those other/s, respect for their singularity. It is just to be fair with other, as a same way to be fair with ourselves. Deconstruction is not only a process of dissociation, disarticulation, or destruction; it is as Derrida says, a condition for 'construction', for invention, that means as a condition for an affirmation. In this comprehension of the deconstruction as commotion and reconstruction, deconstruction is not only an analytic strategy but an impulse that pushed us to other interpretation of experience, to other experience of the other far of the idea of a centered subjectivity which is ordered by one reason or logic of thought. In our critic to Kant and Habermas, we can say that their ideas are stated in the reason and its 'light' which of course, illuminate just some kinds of reality leaving in the darkness others. For instance, the principle of 'universalization' needs to be confronted with the concepts of situated/local and contextualized knowledge. But also we need deconstruct who defines the 'ends' of the humanity. Moreover, the principles centered in human being, need their others: environment, animals, machines. We do know that consensus and hegemonic discourses about reality are always connected with power (in science, culture, and politics). Our challenge is that dialogue for mutual understanding guarantees other kind of discourses, even some of them which are not considered rational (in the universal idea of Kant or rationality).

The de-construction of ICT-concepts and design-methods would thus be needed before we embark on the task of ICT from BOP, SI and ICT for Fair Globalization, even the terms themselves in the first place. Such deconstruction is an endless process which is followed by reconstruction and invention process as we pointed out before. That is why we cannot feel comfortable with concepts on ICT and Social Informatics. We always need an attitude of alert against the idea of a closed or unitarian truth about them. But we need a permanent dialogue 'with others' as well which allow us to reach that process of invention and reconstruction, even if we do not have consensus, even there is not total agreement, there will appear partial consensus, partial truths, that permit the movement.

Feyerabend wrote his book 'Against Method' as a reaction to all methodologies proposed by science, but especially the methods put forward by logical positivism, Karl Popper and Imre Lakatos. His trouble with these 'scientific methods' relates to the fact that any break through in science, especially in modern physics, come about by breaking away from any scientific methodology put forward at the time. It is his aim to show that it is not possible to find any universal methodology. Science and scientific method is for Feyerabend an ideology and just one form of knowing of the world. The scientific methods exist with their rituals without having any 'true knowledge' or even any better description of the world. This means that scientific methods cannot claim to be better or to be prioritized than any other form of methodology or knowledge. Therefore 'anything goes', any methods has its advantages and its backdrops.

Feyerabend then postulates that there is a close relationship between science and myth [10, p. 284]: "The two areas are very close. The massive dogmatism that I have described is not just a fact, but it also has an important function. Science would be impossible at all without it. 'Primitive' thinkers showed a better understanding of the nature of knowing than their 'enlightened' philosophical rivals. Thus it is necessary once again to inquire into our attitude towards myth, religion, magic, witchcraft and all the attitudes that rationalists should like to see eradicating from the surface of the earth (without even having looked upon them – a typical taboo-reaction.)"

6   New Guiding Images

Our sweeping-in-process thus far is trying to choose all the methods and languages put forward by Eric Jantsch [14], that shows a way out by combing different inquiring approaches with spaces in which we inquire. Jantsch starts by defining three inquiring approaches [14, p.84ff]:

- The *rational approach* assumes separation between the observer and the observed, and focuses on an impersonal 'it' which is supposed to be assessed objectively and without involvement by an outside observer; the basic organizing principle here is *logic*, the results are expressed in *quantitative* or *structural* terms, and the dynamic aspects are perceived as *change*
- The *mythological approach* establishes a feedback link between the observer and the observed, and focuses on the relationship between a personal 'I' and a personal 'Thou.' Its basic organizing principle is *feeling*, the results are obtained in *qualitative* terms, and the dynamic aspects are perceived as *process*, or order of change.
- The *evolutionary* approach establishes union between the observer and the observed and focuses on the 'we', on the identity of the forces acting in the observer and the observed world; the organizing principle is *'tuning-in'* by virtue of this identity, and the results are expressed in terms of *sharing* in a universal order of process (namely, *evolution*).

All three approaches are part of our world and are taken to elucidate different aspects of it. They constitute but partial aspects of a multifaceted subject/object relationship as it is evoked most suggestively in a thirteenth century Japanese parable: "Two monks were arguing about a flag. One said: 'The flag is moving.' The other said: 'The wind is moving.' The sixth patriarch happened to be passing by. He told them: 'Not the wind, not the flag; mind is moving.' Wind, flag, mind move. The same understanding. When the mouth opens, all are wrong."

Jantsch defines three spaces in which we might be taken to inquire [14, p. 50-1]:

- *physical space* where man lives like other creatures
- *social space* which is created through differentiation, through the design of social roles and systems of such roles as they come into being with all kinds of social invention and innovation... Labor and task-sharing, crafts and industries, trade and accumulation of wealth, government and education, physical and conceptual mobility, collective health and organized fighting – they are all social inventions with their corresponding patterns and systems of roles
- *spiritual space* that holds man's relations with the numinous; his quest for purpose, direction, and meaning; his cultural inventions from values to religions, from the arts to philosophy and science.

	GROUNDING *(Physical Space)*	SOCIALIZATION (Social Space)	*INDIVIDUATION* *(Spiritual Space)*
EVOLUTIONARY LEVEL	Tao of the " Earth Vitalism	Tao of Man Humanity Legitimacy *Li*, ethics of whole systems	Tao of Heaven Shunyata God Within Man-becoming- in-universe- becoming Self-realization Alchemy
MYTHOLOGICAL LEVEL	Gestalt Animism Magic	Polytheistic religions Morality Individual ethics	Monotheistic religion Virtue
RATIONAL LEVEL	Regularities Natural Laws Physical technology	Behavioral laws Ceremony Social technology	Humanistic psychology Ritual Human technology

Fig. 1. Images of Man Forming through the Processes of Re-ligio in the Three Aspects of Man's Total Space (adapted from [15, p.233].

Combining these inquiring approaches with spaces of inquiry we may suggest the following ways of knowledge creation and knowledge sharing for the inquiry into ICT and Social Informatics.

In order to act collectively it is our understanding that we need new guiding images. In *The Image of the Futures*, the Dutch sociologist Fred Polak [23], noted that when the dominant images of a culture are anticipatory, they 'lead' social development and provide direction for social change through a 'magnetic pull' toward the future. Markley [20, p. 214] explains:

"By their attractiveness and legitimacy they reinforce each movement that takes the society toward them, and thus they influence the social decisions that will bring them to realization. As a culture moves toward the achievement of goals inherent in its dominant images, the congruence increases between the images and the development of the culture itself – the implications of the images are explored, progress is made, and needs are more fully satisfied. [Illustrated in Fig. 2]

If the progress of the human system outstrips that of its traditional images, however, its policies and behavior (which are based on the old dominant images) becomes increasingly faulty – even counterproductive – precipitating a period of frustration, cultural disruption, or social crisis. The stage is then set for basic changes in the underlying images and the organization of the system. Various indicators suggest that our culture may now be nearing, if not at, such a stage."

It is thus our hypothesis that we need a new guiding image based on mythological and evolutionary approaches to social and spiritual space. This hypothesis tries to go ahead of Kant, Habermas and Derrida approach. At least that can be taken to be true for the Western World, yet one might wonder whether the dialogue might not better take the form of a dialogue between the Western World's methods and use of languages taken from rational approaches to physical (and partly social) space and an Eastern or Southern World's mythological and evolutionary methods and uses of language in social and spiritual spaces.

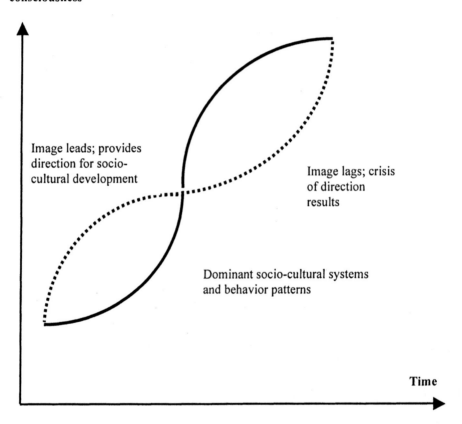

These mythological and evolutionary methods, need to surpass the debate of the simplification of the complexity of the social world. Following John Law [18, p. 152-3], some of the more obvious possibilities and challenges are:

- Process: In Euro-American method the bias is against process and in favour of product. If we look at any grant application form, the rules of method are imagined as a means to an end for knowing better or intervening. The practicalities of knowing are bracketed and treated as technique. So we should start of attending the mediations of method rather than being concentred in the final product. Means/ends divisions cut the cake in a particular way. Parts of process, enactment, can be pushed into a means/ends scheme, but others cannot.

That means that we need to treat with the uncertainties and 'undecidables' of process as well as with means and ends.

- Symmetry: Instead of considering just one approach as good or bad (and the fixed ways and rules that they have to discovering realities), we should consider all practices of knowing as appropriate methods. We need to understand the different methods, so they have to be treated symmetrically, to explore them without, in the first instance, judging their adequacy in terms of our prior assumptions about what is methodologically right and what do not.

- Multiplicity: If we focus on practise then we are led to multiplicity since there are as many practises as many realities. Truth is no longer the only arbiter and reality is no longer destiny. There are choices to be made between the desirability of different realities. The world could always be otherwise. We need ways of knowing about and enacting fractionality or partial connection.

- Reflexivity: We need to ask whether we are able and willing to recognise that our methods also craft realities. It is necessary to be alert and aware that one method enacts divisions between different forms of absence: absence made manifest, and absence as Othering. So, boundaries made and remade, the point of view of the researcher/observer and his/her unavoidable complicity in reality-making, and the situated context of knowing are central concern.

- Imaginaries: John Law suggests use allegory as a way of knowing the multiple and ambivalent, avoiding discourses about coherence or consistency. But this is just a beginning. Maybe the mythological and evolutionary level that we suggested in the fig. 1, can offer other metaphors and experiences of knowing that open our frameworks in order to create new possibilities of dialogue and understandings –even without oral or written language-. Flux, multiplicities, fractionalities, resonance, process of weaving, spirals, vortices, dances, passions, interferences, there are some of the metaphors for imaging creative methods and languages.

- Materialities: If we accept that possibility of imaginaries, then we should move beyond academic texts to texts in other modalities, and not just texts and figures, but bodies, devices, theatre, apprehensions, buildings, art, music, food. There is need for a whole range of materially innovative methods.

- Indefiniteness: Instead of expect definite results out methods, should, sometimes, perhaps often, manifest realities that are indefinite, and that as apart of this, allegory, non-coherence, and the indefinite are not necessarily signs of methodological failure.

If we agree there is not universal method, we have to think well about the modes of relating between sites and specificities. These are not split off from one another by 'external acts'. Science, politics and aesthetics, these do not inhabit different domains. Instead they interweave. Their relations intersect and resonate together in unexpected ways.

References

1. Apel, Karl-Otto (1999), Openly strategic uses of language: a transcendental-pragmatic perspective - a second attempt to think Habermas against Habermas, in Dews, Peter (ed.) (1999): *Habermas – a Critical reader*, Blackwell

2. Boisot, Max (1995), *Information Space*, Routledge, London
3. Boisot, Max (1998), *Knowledge Assets*, Oxford University Press, New York
4. Bordum, Anders (2005), Immanul Kant, Jürgen Habermas and the categorical imperative, *Philosophy & Social Criticism*, Vol. 31, no. 7, Nov., Sage Publ.
5. Borradori, Giovanna (2003), *Philosophy in a time of terror – Dialogues with Jürgen Habermas and Jacques Derrida*, University of Chicago Press
6. Callon, Michael (2002) Writing and (Re)writing devices as tools for managing complexity. In: Law, John; Mol Anne Marie (ed). *Complexities. Social studies of knowledge practices.* Duke University Press. Pp. 191-217.
7. Churchman, C.W. (1968), *Challenge to Reason*, McGraw Hill
8. Churchman.C.W. (1971), *Design of Inquiring Systems*, Basic Books
9. Derrida, Jacques (1986), *De la gramatología.* México: Ed. Siglo XXI, 4ª. Ed.
10. Derrida, Jacques (1998), *Espectros de Marx. El estado de la deuda, el trabajo del duelo y la nueva internacional.* Madrid: Ed. Trotta. Original source: *Specters of Marx, the state of the debt, the Work of Mourning, & the New International,* translated by Peggy Kamuf, Routledge 1994
11. Dews, Peter (ed.) (1999): *Habermas – a Critical reader*, Blackwell
12. Feyerabend, Paul (1975), *Against Method*, NLB, London
13. Foucault, Michel (1997), *The Politics of Truth* (ed. Sylvère Lotringer), Semiotext(e)
14. Habermas, Jürgen (2000), *On the Pragmatics of Communication*, (ed. Maeve Cooke), MIT Press
15. Hardt Michael; Negri Antoni (2003), *Imperio*, Buenos Aires: Paidós.
16. Jantsch, Eric (1975), *Design For Evolution*, Brazille
17. Jantsch, Eric (1976) Evolving Images of Man: Dynamic Guidance for the Mankind Process, in E. Jantsch C.H.Waddington: *Evolution and Consciousness – Human systems in Transition*, Addison-Wesley, 1976
18. Kant, Immanuel (1994), *Ethical Philosophy: Grounding for the Metaphysics of Morals*, Hackett
19. Kling, Rob et.al. (2000), *Learning from Social Informatics: Information and Communication Technologies in Human Context* (v 4.6, Aug. 2000), Center for Social Informatics, Indiana University
20. Law, John (2004). *After method. Mess in social science research.* Routledge, London Press.
21. Law, John; Mol Anne Marie (ed) (2002). *Complexities. Social studies of knowledge practices.* Duke University Press.
22. Markley, O.W. (1976) Consciousness in Transformation, in E. Jantsch C.H.Waddington: *Evolution and Consciousness – Human systems in Transition,* Addison-Wesley, 1976
23. Negri, Antonio (2003), *Time for revolution*, Continuum, London
24. Prahalad, C.K. (2005), *The Fortune from the Bottom of the Pyramid*, Wharton School Publishing, Wupper Saddle River, NJ
25. Polak, Fred (1973) *The Image of the Future*, (E. Boulding transl., Abridged English ed., San Francisco, Jossey-Bass
26. Rasmussen L; Herlau, H; Rueda, R. (2004), ICT from the Bottom of the Pyramid, in: *The Information Society: Emerging Landscapes*, Zielinski, Chris, Duquenoy, Penny; Kimppa, Kai (Eds.), IFIP International Conference on Landscapes of ICT and Social Accountability, Turku, Finland, June 27-29, 2005, 354 p., ISBN: 0-387-30527-0IFIP, Springer Verlag, 2006
27. Singer, E.A. (1924), *Mind as Behavior*, R.G.Adams & Co.
28. Singer, E.A. (1959), *Experience and Reflection*, University of Pennsylvania Press (C.W.Churchman ed.)

Strategies for the Effective Integration of ICT into Social Organization – Organization of Information Processing and the Necessity of Social Informatics

Klaus Fuchs-Kittowski
University of Applied Sciences Berlin, (Germany)
fuchs-kittowski@t-online.de

Abstract. This paper discusses strategies and concepts of information and communication-support for knowledge-intensive work processes. The necessity of social informatics or organizational informatics according to Rob Kling results from the complementarity of formal (syntactic), product oriented and informal (semantic), process oriented, technical, and social view in informatics. The understanding of man/computer communication as a problem of linking syntactic and semantic information processing, led to the idea of information centers. The importance of social (organizational) informatics is illustrated in connection with the development of modern information and communication technology; new forms of communication to support international collective research; computer supported knowledge work, as a problem of linking syntactic and semantic information processing. The automated information processing, software use, must be organized, before and during knowledge-intensive work processes take place.

Keywords: organization of information processing, social oriented informatics, knowledge-intensive work processes, complementarity, syntactic and semantic information processing, computer networks, information centers.

Please use the following format when citing this chapter:

Fuchs-Kittowski, K., 2006, in IFIP International Federation for Information Processing, Volume 223, Social Informatics: An Information Society for All? In Remembrance of Rob Kling, eds. Berleur, J., Numinen, M. I., Impagliazzo, J., (Boston: Springer), pp. 431–444.

432 Klaus Fuchs-Kittowski

1 The Complementarity of technical and social views in Informatics and the Necessity of a social oriented Informatics

The decisive basic problem that we have to face when directing our attention to the subject 'Human Choice and Computers' and therefore to social and methodological problems of information processing is the relation between computer and Man, automation and its social environment, between the mechanism and living reality. Informatics especially develops due to the necessity of bridging the gap between the technological automation, working in purely syntactic terms (as information transformer) and the creative, active human being (as a social being), enabled to perform information and knowledge generation and to carry out semantic information processing. Because of these decisive differences, the software use has to be organized and the formal operations have to be integrated into the complex work process of Man.

With today's conference, we want to remember and honor Rob Kling. The author immediately remembers the first encounter with him. Rob Kling was the representative of the USA in the working group 'computers and work' of IFIP TC9. Even if he seldom took part in the meetings, we repeatedly met and talked with each other. I visited him at the University of California Ervine. This visit at his home is for various reasons unforgettably to me. I asked him, what the core of the master course on 'computer science and society', introduced by him at the university, was. He answered: "The core of the education in this field is of course organization theories. I don't need to tell you, because you were one of the first, demanding the inclusion of organization theories in information systems design." But our IFIP/TC9 Working group 1 conference in Berlin on 'Information system, Work and Organization design', had not taken place yet [1]. With this remark, he could have hardly referred to our national conferences on 'organization of the information processing' at Humboldt University. However, he could very well have referred to the IFIP/IFAC Conference on 'Socio-technical Aspects of Computerized Automation' (SOTAC) in Budapest, 1979 [2], on discussions in the TC9 (unpublished contributions). He referred to the idea of 'information centers' as an organizational form for the realization of indirect man computer communication, as we had discussed on an IIASA workshop on Data Communications". [3] Like me, he saw this as a proof for the necessity to develop orgware[1] [4] next to hard- and software. One must develop a new discipline in or with computer science, an organization computer science. Further we discussed the necessity of a social oriented computer science because of the complementarity of formal (syntactic), product-orientated and informal (semantic), process-oriented, technical and social views in informatics. The computer scientist must primarily recognize that this complementarity goes right through the center of the discipline computer science itself. Software must be formally correct and at the same time as a tool adequate for the work process. This complementarity of correctness and task adequacy was the inside, which made the paradigm change in software engineering necessary and led to a social orientation of informatics.

During our 'IV colloquium for the organization of the information processing' Christiane Floyd for the first time spoke about the necessity of a paradigm change in the computer science or software technology. She writes: *"My topic was: ,essential features of a paradigm change in software technology' a precursor to my English paper to which I dared me at that time for the first time"* [5].

The emphasis on qualification and users' participation as a source of democratic participation at work and at the processes of change taking place was only one aspect of the problem. The other one was the attention of the abilities and skills as well as the participation in the system design and software development process as a creative process of learning and communication. They then worked this out especially in the STEP-methodology of Christiane Floyd and her coworkers [6], [7], [8].

With reference to the work of Rob Kling, organization informatics developed further in the department of Informatics of the University of Hamburg by Arno Rolf [9] and his coworkers. The development of software and design of complex information systems must occur in a structural coupling with a social organization to integrate complex information systems into the social context. Based on it, Bernd Pape [10] points out that we must organize software use and information processing. In this contribution, we especially want to show that we must organize software also during its use, particularly at problem solution processes, as it is characteristic for knowledge intensive work processes and scientific work. Information centers (or other organizational forms) could be helpful by this necessary organization of software use.

The support of knowledge-intensive work processes and of knowledge management in knowledge-intensive organizations by modern information and communication technologies has become an important topic in informatics. The vision is as follows: ICT-support of cooperation, of knowledge provision, and generation helps to develop creative-learning organizations. If one also takes the local and global social structures of the human society into account, it could be the basis for an information and communication society for all, or even, the basis for the development of the Noosphere in the sense of Teilhard de Chardin and Vladimir I. Vernadsky [11], [12].

2   New Forms of Communication to Support knowledge Work and International Collective Research

2.1   Basic Concepts and the Development of Modern Information and Communication Technology

The development of a social oriented informatics has proven necessary to integrate computer application systems into the social context and to adapt the computer application systems to the needs of users, though not vice versa. Above all, it is necessary to ensure that we design information systems not according to technical principles alone, but also according to social concepts, values, and objectives.

The question of the relation between the computer and society, and between computer and human choice leads to the discussion of the following issues.

1. Different positions in world outlook regarding the position of Man to his tool
2. Different basic lines resulting from this for the automation of intellectual activities
3. Different directions for the use of computers in various spheres of social life.

As to the position of Man to his tool, the following basic concepts may be distinguished.

1. The concept of the direct and indirect identification of Man and the computer, the position of the most classical, strong AI-researcher (technicism)
2. The concept of a mystic exaggeration of Man's abilities, which is often related to an unjustified criticism of technology (technology pessimism)
3. The concept of a purposeful an effective Man-machine combination, uniting the advantages of human and machine-performed information processing to form an efficient overall system and giving full consideration to the creative abilities of Man.

Obviously, the fist two concepts represent extreme viewpoints resulting from a unilateral visualization of the interaction between Man and computer. We can only overcome this by a dialectical approach to this relationship.

The application of modern information and communication technologies faces us with a multitude of new problems. They not only concern technical and technological problems, but above all, the position of human beings in such complicated technical and technological systems and in the organization, which includes these systems. In this context, explicitly and implicitly extremely varying fundamental attitudes exist that differ in providing a response to this question. That is, we must determine whether we can understand the human being as a disturbing factor, as a relatively imperfect being as compared with automation (so as can be more or less completely replace Man by automation), or whether Man is really seen as the genuine master of these modern technologies. Dependent upon the manner in which we answer this question, we powerfully influence the basic strategies for the utilization of modern information and communication technologies, and research and training programs in informatics. The answer to this question also influences the development of local and global digital networks.

In the late 1960s, U.S. scientists created the so-called ARPA-Net that connected military computers and computers of universities with one another. In the early 1980s, the research institutions used the network to an ever-increasing extent. The U.S. government transferred the network's operation to the National Science Foundation. This also allowed other countries to connect with this network gradually. This became possible, because the ARPA-NET is fundamentally connected to and born of computer science rather than of the military, as Licklider stated in his ARPANET Completion Report [13, p. 96].

At that time, the author took part in further elaborating and developing this approach on intellectual lines, by active participation at the IIASA conference on data communications and further workshops. The title of our paper was 'Man machine communication' – a problem of linking semantic and syntactic information processing [3].

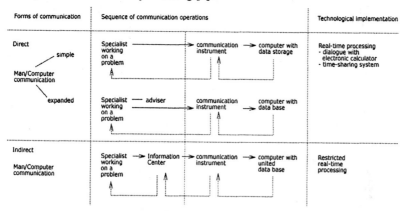

Figure 1: The Need for an Information Center – Different Forms of Man/Computer communication: direct (online) dialog and indirect dialog (via an Information Center) [3]

These ideas were very well received at this conference, but not at home. We always wondered why? Now we know at least part of the answer!

2.2 Information centers / Thinking center

In our book *Informatics and Automation* [7], our thesis, that problem solution processes are not steadily automated, plays a large role. Therefore, different dialogue forms (direct dialog and indirect dialog via an information center) can or must support a combination of man and computer because man/computer communication is a meaningful combination of syntactic (machine) and semantic (human) information processing.

Semantic information processing is the combination of meanings of information to form new meanings. It is typical of man's intellectual information processing that it is concentrated upon the contents. Man carries out the structural processes, which are underlying the meaning of words and sentences, unconsciously.

Syntactic information processing is a transformation of the structure of information carriers. Because of specific rules between information carriers and their meanings, we ascribe new meanings to them. The mediation of structural transformations processes the contents of semantic statements.

A reviewer of our book wrote that our strategy of the information center clearly shows how strongly the authors underestimate the forthcoming performances of the artificial intelligence (AI) research. To our satisfaction, we experienced exactly the opposite reaction at the IIASA conference, one of the first public meetings for the development the ARPA-Net. Davis, the developer of the packet switching, jumped up and cried out, *"You are right! If the technical net stands once, then the net of the information centers will be the real net."*

This different reception of our concept was based on the fact (as we know today) that the net development under J.C.R. Licklider [14] supported the consideration of man and machine having things in common and significant differences. Therefore, we need a sensible man-computer interaction (symbiosis). As a prerequisite for this man-computer symbiosis, Licklider also saw (of course we did not know this at that time) the so-called 'Thinking center' [14]. The leading vision for research on the development of modern digital nets was a technical net by which the people could cooperate internationally. The basic scientific visions developed this for a new way of computer use.

These visions lead once to the understanding of the computer as a medium and on the other hand, to the thought of a combination of the special abilities of the computer with the special abilities of man; J.C.R. Licklider expressed as by his concept of 'Man Computer Symbiosis'.

J.C.R. Licklider wrote *"It seems reasonable to envision, for a time 10 or 15 years hence, a 'thinking center' that will incorporate the functions of present-day libraries together with anticipated advances in information storage and retrieval and the symbiotic functions suggested earlier in this paper. The picture readily enlarges itself into a network of such centers."* [14].

We wrote, *"By appropriate organizational measures, it is therefore possible to obtain dynamic forms of linking human and machine-operated information processing without having to develop completely new foundations in programming technology. In this respect, the setting up of an information center, by which a special form of man/computer communication is carried out, plays an important role."* [3].

With this statement, we were suddenly, without realizing all its consequences, in the middle of an international struggle for a paradigm change: from an understanding of the computer as a competitor for Man to an understanding of the Computer as an effective part of a Man-Computer-Combination. However, it was not easy to overcome the first position and to introduce the concept of a purposeful and effective Man-Computer-Combination. Therefore, even J.C.R. Licklider had to fight for his idea of a

'Man Computer Symbiosis', put forward in connection with the development of new forms of communication to support international collective research. H. Dreyfus wrote in his book, *What Computers Can't do. The Limits of Artificial Intelligence* that at MIT, J.C.R. Licklider wanted to defend him with the words "an interplay of man and machine is presumably most successful". A paper from a scientist at the time working at MIT protested vehemently against it [15, p. 379].

2.3. Computer aided Knowledge-intensive work processes – a problem of linking semantic and syntactic information processing

We proceed from the assumption that the scope for setting up new organizational structures has increased decisively with the recent development in modern information and communication technologies, especially with the global electronic network–the Internet. Due to their ability to overcome the restrictions of time and space, network systems promise to enable new types of work, a new culture of knowledge work and scientific work.

With Figure 2, we especially want to stress the point that knowledge as a process and product of a social process is embedded in distributed social activities and that knowledge is generation in cooperation in a work community.

The proposed fundamental difference between syntactic and semantic information processing, the difference between store and memory, the difference between information processing and information generation of forming meanings, is also fundamental here.

Nevertheless, a knowledge-gap characterizes knowledge-intensive work process and even more a scientific work process. It is a problem-solving process. Due to the knowledge-gap, a problem solving process cannot continuously be formalized and thus not generally be automated. In the case of creative aspects of knowledge intensive work processes and scientific work – in the case of cooperative knowledge production the communication-oriented (personal-oriented and social-oriented) approach has therefore to be dominant. Integration with the information-oriented approach (with the formalization and codification strategy) seems to be sensible because the knowledge intensive work process and the scientific work process need both, the provision and the generation of knowledge. The knowledge-intensive and scientific work processes are different mixtures of creative work, routine work and of non-schematic and schematic tasks, which can be formalized. [16], [17, pp 195-210].

If the aim is to increase the cooperation of Man, then from this viewpoint also some various directions complementing each other necessarily are to be discussed in the use of the computer.
1. We can use computers primarily to support the functions of major systems.

438   Klaus Fuchs-Kittowski

2. We can use computers in support of the functions of the individual human being as the only productive force.

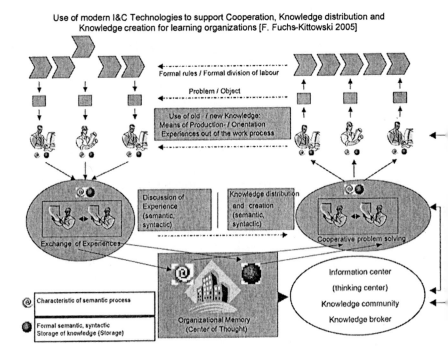

Figure 2: *Provision and Generation of Knowledge intensive work processes*

The first direction led above all to support managerial and administrative functions and to the immediate process control. In addition, as A. Rolf points out, we can only see certain strategies of knowledge management as a modern version of this direction [18].

The second direction led to computer support in current individual work processes. As the result of the development of interactive systems and, owing to the communication systems, the information processing function of the individual human being, individually or in groups, more and more is assisted in the immediate work operations. Therefore, we could bring information and communication technology closer to the work place. This became the basis for a computer support of knowledge intensive work processes.

We find both directions in the different strategies of the modern knowledge management. In the book *Interaktionsorientiertes Wissens Management* [16] (Interaction-oriented Knowledge Management) the authors show the necessity of their integration.

We might suppose that this direction of 'interaction oriented knowledge management' will lead to an essential reinforcement of social organization because of widening the range of abilities proper to the human beings working in knowledge intensive work processes.

The knowledge-intensive work processes requires new cooperative, self-organizing forms for work, organization and learning that support creativity and can be supported by information and communication systems (in particular Tele-cooperation systems).

2.4 An information center can be useful to organize Software use

For knowledge workers, people working on problems, we must aim at designing possibilities for ICT applications allowing a very simple transition to a machine-readable formulation of a task. Knowledge workers often require very detailed special knowledge in the field of computer technology and of modeling processes. Above all, non-schematic tasks occur. Nevertheless, the necessity of immediate action and decision is not typical of the creative problem solving process in knowledge work or scientific work. Therefore, it is not necessary to build only direct man/computer systems with real time processing. To give aid to the process of working on problems and solving them, especially for management staff of higher levels, and other knowledge workers indirect man/computer communication is by far a more advantageous solution. In indirect communication, a special process of work is switched between the syntactic and the semantic information-processing operations.

This process of work comprises the fact process to be modeled until the formulation of a machine-intelligible data processing task, including cooperation of the user with the modeler (problem analyst) on the semantic level. Therefore, a special organizational component of man/computer communication that is often called an information center (a thinking center) or a knowledge broker carries out the function of mediating.

It is necessary, as F. Fuchs-Kittowski and P. Stahn showed [17], to differentiate between different approaches and strategies of knowledge management: information-oriented approach (with the formalization and codification strategy) and the communication-oriented approach (with the personification and socialization strategy). It also becomes necessary to differentiate between levels of the enterprise organization: a) the individual, b) the group, c) the whole organization, which have to be integrated for an effective knowledge management [16, 17]. On the different levels of organization (and strategies), we will have a different use of an 'information center' (or 'thinking center'). First, (see Figure 2, organizational memory) we have the orientation towards syntactic storage of knowledge and its retrieval. Here, we will still need the information center (or knowledge broker). On the next level (see Figure 2, cooperative problem solving), an information center in the proposed sense, will not always be necessary. Not that the reductive concept of the direct and indirect identification of Man and computer has succeeded! The opposite is true, because the concept of a purposeful an effective Man-computer combination, considering fully the creative abilities of Man, has succeeded, with a strong social orientation. The understanding of knowledge as a social product, the insight, that knowledge generation takes place in social groups, has led to the communication-oriented approach. In these communities of practice, in the process of cooperative problem solving, the function of the 'special organizational form: information center' linking semantic and syntactic information processing can, when needed, also be delegated to specialists in the group. The cooperative problem solving takes place in a group of experts. They might be engaged in this task in such a manner, that not all have to use the information and communication technology themselves, but they now need the knowledge broker: a) to keep updated the knowledge base, b) to organize the experts and c) to gather the results of the individual problem solving processes.

If we look at the information-oriented approach, we see the support of always repeating schematic tasks as typical for the formalizing strategy. Characteristic for the codification's strategy is the support of routine activity. Not formalized routine activities have also creative aspects, because known methods are used in different context. Here an information center in the original proposed sense could be useful, because it becomes necessary to link semantic and syntactic information processing.

If we look at the communication-oriented approach, we see that also the personification strategy deals with the support of routine activities. I n addition, we can introduce an information center, a knowledge broker, linking the syntactic and semantic information processing. Only with the socialization strategy, dealing with the support of creative activities in communities, the main task is the organization of the communication between human beings. This means we can but must not link semantic information processing with the syntactic information processing. The computerized (syntactic) communication system supports the organization of the semantic communication between the experts.

We understand the knowledge intensive work process as a problem solution process. Because of a knowledge gap, we cannot address the problem solution simply by a task solution. Due to the knowledge gap, a problem solution is not a general formalization. We must provide knowledge for the solution of the problem or we must create equipment and conditions to generate the missing knowledge. Here the IKT support needs the organization of software use, it becomes specifically important to select ore construct the prerequisite for the problem solution. The problem aims determine the prerequisites for the problem-solution.

Thus, Frank Fuchs-Kittowski and Peter Stahn [17] differentiate between schematic and non-schematic tasks, between routine and non-routine activities. This leads to a differentiation between an automation of information processing: a) on the basis already existing, b) as a general potential existing and c) yet without existing prerequisites:

a) Prerequisites already exist and remain constant; we can support always-repeating tasks based on standards.

b) Prerequisites selection, we select the prerequisites for the problem solution from already existing information and operation funds. Therefore, we select or generate them from general prerequisites already created. The prerequisites, required as an information and operation fund, can, however, either already exist or are not yet available.

c) Prerequisite construction, the creation of information and operations funds for the problem solution becomes necessary. In knowledge intensive work process, as problem solving, the aim usually develops and therefore the prerequisites must be created. For a prerequisite construction, the information and operations required for the processes of information processing have to be conceived first, only gradually enlarging the necessary information and operation funds. We have no routine problems here. No knowledge is ready for their solution yet. The prerequisites to make use of the IKT, according to the solution of routine problems, must be created first. This prerequisite construction can, however, be supported by the system of the communication effectively. We can use different forms of organization for the prerequisite construction (see Figure 2, information center, knowledge broker, knowledge community).

3   Informatics as a socially oriented science

Automation as an essential element of scientific and technological advance of our time is in no way a purely technological problem to be solved only by knowing and mastering the technological application conditions. This worldwide insight has led to the development of a specific scientific discipline, informatics – and social oriented informatics.

In our article 'Future Expectations to the Designer of modern Information Technologies' [19], we state "If one takes into account, as Rob Kling [20] has worked out in the context of the Curricular debate in the USA, that the predominant part of the computer science graduates gets working for the development and the use of the IKT in social organizations, in the education one must take into account these IKT application areas and their problems correspondingly. An orientation towards the problems of an 'organizational computing', [20] an 'Organisationsinformatik' wasn't, at least in the context of computer science, carried out till now" [19].

One overlooks there that this change of the guidelines (paradigm change) is forced from the technological development, the economic requirements, and the social development. An economically effective and socially justified application of modern information and communication technology requires a social orientation, which is carried at least by the insight that information system design at the same time has to be work and organization design. It definitely would be important, as R. Kling stated, to determine once, which economic damage is caused, how expensive the failure is for the society, not to include social – and also information science cognition's in the information system development.

Informatics has especially the task of elaborating some principles for understanding and methods for describing the interrelations between man and the automation, as well as between man and his working environment [21], and of working out viewpoints for judging and forms of computer application, as well as recommendations and criteria for a humanistic system design [22]. Above all it is necessary to ensure that the design of automata-supported information systems in economics, education, the legal system and the health service are not only derived from technological principles but performed according to social ideas of values and goals [23], [24], [25].

To develop an information society for all is a very important technical and social goal. Seen together with the concept of sustainable development this would be a substantial social innovation [26], [27]

Nevertheless, it is not a very deep concept that concerns real social development. We rather think that a further task actually lies before us. The one that must be carried out is really to integrate the potentials of information – and communication technologies in the process of shaping social and individual development, on the basis of a modern scientifically proven social concept and humanistic social visions, as the Noosphere Vision of Pierre Teilhard de Chardin and Vladimir I. Vernadsky [28].

We should do this task in such a way that man is and remains the stating point and aim of the shaping of systems of social organization.

Acknowledgement

The author thanks Frank Fuchs-Kittowski for many helpful discussions on this topic.

References

1. P. van den Besselaar, A. Clement, and P. Järvinen, *Information system, Work and Organization design*, North Holland, Amsterdam, 1991
2. K. Fuchs-Kittowski, U. Schuster, and B. Wenzlaff, Organizational, Technological and Social Problems of Computerization, *Computer in Industry* (2), 275-285 (1981).
3. K. Fuchs-Kittowski, K. Lemgo, U. Schuster, and B. Wenzlaff, Man / Computer Communication – A Problem of Linking Semantic and Syntactic Information Processing, Workshop on Data Communications (International Institute for Applied Systems Analysis, Laxenburg, 1975), pp. 169-188.
4. Le Programme FAST II (1984-1987) Perspective et évaluation de la science et de la technologie, Synthèse des Résultats, First Draft
5. C. Floyd, Laudatio, in: *Stufen zur Informationsgesellschaft* – Festschrift zum 65. Geburtstag von Klaus Fuchs-Kittowski, edited by C. Floyd, C. Fuchs, and W. Hofkichner, (Peter Lang Verlag, Frankfurt/Main, 2002).

6. C. Floyd, Software-Engineering – und dann?, *Informatik Sprektrum* **17**(1), pp. 29-37 (1994).
7. K. Fuchs-Kittowski, H. Kaiser, R. Tschirschwitz, and B. Wenzlaff, *Informatik und Automatisierung – Theorie und Praxis der Struktur und Organisation der Informationsverarbeitung*, Akademie Verlag, Berlin , 1976.
8. K. Fuchs-Kittowski, Informatik und Computer – Organisationstheorie als ein konzeptioneller, theoretisch-methodologischer Bezugsrahmen für die effektive Integration der modernen Informationstechnologien in soziale Organisation, in: *IV. Wissenschaftliche Kolloquium zur Organisation der Informationsverarbeitung,*, Humboldt Universität, Berlin, 1983.
9. A. Rolf, *Grundlagen der Organisations- und Wirtschaftsinformatik*, Springer Verlag, Berlin et al., 1998.
10. B. Pape, *Organisation der Softwarenutzung – Theorienbildung und Fallstudien zu Softwareeinführung und Softwarebetreuung*, Logos Verlag, Berlin, 2005.
11. T. de Chardin, *Der Mensch im Kosmos*, Union Verlag, Berlin, 1959; (C.H. Beck, München, 1959).
12. V. Vernadsky, The biosphere and the noosphere, *American Scientist* **33** (1), 1-12 (1945).
13. M. Hauben, and R. Hauben, *Netizens – On the History and the Impact of Usenet and the Internet*, IEEE Computer Society Press, Los Alamitos, 1997.
14. J.C.R. Licklider, Man-Computer Symbiosis, *IRE Transactions on Human Factors in Electronics*, (1) 4-111 (1960); J.C.R. Licklider, Man-Computer Symbiosis, 1990, http://memex.org/licklider.pdf (March 31, 2006).
15. H. Dreyfus, *Die Grenzen künstlicher Intelligenz – Was Computer nicht können*, (Athenäum, Königstein, 1985) (What Computers can't do – The limits of Artificial Intelligence, New York)
16. F. Fuchs-Kittowski, and W. Prinz, *Interaktionsorientiertes Wissensmanagement* (Peter Lang Verlag, Frankfurt/M., 2005).
17. F. Fuchs-Kittowski, and P. Stahn, Kooperative Wissensarbeit in wissensintensiven Dienstleistungen – IT-Unterstützung mit der WiKo-Anwendung aus Anwendersicht, in: *Entwicklung innovativer Dienstleistungen – Wissen, Kreativität*, Lernen, edited by T. Schlegel, and D. Spath, Dieter Fraunhofer IRB Verlag, Stuttgart, 2005, pp. 195-210.
18. A. Rolf, *Informatiksysteme in Organisationen und globalen Gesellschaften*, IMG 4-Skript, WS 2004/05, 2004, Fachbereich Informatik, Universität Hamburg
19. K. Fuchs-Kittowski, and H. Juncker, Zukünftige Erwartungen an den Gestalter moderner Informationstechnologien, in: *InfoTech – 5* (4) 42-50 (1993).
20. R. Kling, Organizational Analysis in Computer Science, *The Information Society* **9** (2) (1993).
21. K. Fuchs-Kittowski, and F. Fuchs-Kittowski, Quality of working life – knowledge-intensive work processes and creative learning organizations – Information processing paradigm versus self-organization theory, in: *Human Choice and Computers – Issues of Choice and Quality of Life in the Information Society*, edited by K. Brunnstein, and J. Berleur, Kluwer Academic Publishers, Boston, 2002, pp. 265-274.
22. M. Nurminen, *People or Computers – Three Ways of Looking at Information Systems*, Chartwell-Bratt, Lund, 1988.
23. J. Berleur et al., Risks and Vulnerability in an Information and Artificial Society, *Proceedings of the IFIP 12th World Computer Congress*, Madrid, Spain, Volume II, 1992, pp. 309-310.
24. K. Brunnstein, Perspectives of the Vulnerability of IT-based Society,:in *Proceedings of IFIP 12th World Computer Congress*, Madrid, Spain, Volume II, 1992, pp. 588-592.

25. K. Fuchs-Kittowski, H.A. Rosenthal, and A. Rosenthal, Die Entschlüsselung des Humangenoms – ambivalente Auswirkungen auf Gesellschaft und Wissenschaft. EWE – *Erwägen, Wissen, Ethik* **16** (2) (2005) pp. 149 – 162 u. 219- 234

26. A. Rolf, and A. Moeller, Sustainable Development – Gestaltungsaufgabe der Informatik. *Informatikspektrum* **19** (4) 206-213 (1996).

27. K. Fuchs-Kittowski, J.L. Heinrich and A. Rolf, Information entsteht in Organisationen – in kreativ lernenden Unternehmen – wissenschaftstheoretische und methodologische Konsequenzen für die Wirtschaftsinformatik, in: *Wirtschaftsinformatik und Wissenschaftstheorie*, edited by Becker,, König, Schütte, Wend, Zelewski (Gabler Verlag, Wiesbaden, 1999).

28. K. Fuchs-Kittowski, and P. Krüger, The Noosphere Vision of Pierre Teilhard de Chardin and Vladimir I. Vernadsky in the Perspective of Information and of World-Wide Communication, in: *The Quest for a Unified Theory of Information, World Futures General Evolution Studies* Vol. 13, edited by W. Hofkirchner, Gordon and Breach Publishers, Amsterdam, 1999.

---

[1]   G. Dobrow and I had introduce the term orgware in the International Institute of Applied Systems Analysis (IIASA). From there the term orgware was taken and advocated in the FAST-Report (FAST : Forecasting and Assessment in Science and Technologie [4]).

A User Centred Access Model

Olof Nilsson
Mid Sweden University, CITIZYS Research Group, Dept of Information
Systems & Media, Sweden
olle.nilsson@miun.se

Abstract. This paper presents a model to assist in the ability to judge access by private persons to the Internet in general, and to Public Information Systems (PIS) particularly. It has its starting point in the Swedish Government's endeavour to turn Sweden into the first 'information society for all'. When the available statistics concerning the access to a PC and the Internet in Swedish homes are studied it is easy to think that this vision may soon be realised. Of course, access to the technical equipment is a fundamental condition in order to be able to use the Public Information Systems, but unfortunately, is not the only one. Several studies have shown that it is not possible to equate possession and use. A number of access models or frameworks designed to judge whether or not a person has access to the ICTs do exist. However, it is my opinion that there is a deficiency in these models; they do not start out from the individual user's prerequisites, but rather judge the external conditions available for possible access. Assisted by four empirical studies, interviews and questionnaires, a number of access barriers experienced by the users have been identified. The studies show that in addition to the technological hindrances, a series of more elusive ones also exist originating from prevailing norms and values in the environment the user lives in. The barriers are categorised into five groups: to have, to be able, to will, to may and to dare. Together these notions form the User Centred Access Model, UCAM, which is suggested for use in charting and communicating the necessary considerations that must be taken into account in the development of Public Information Systems aimed for e-governmental issues.

Keywords: User centred access, access barriers, digital divide, information society

1 Introduction

A prayer for the information society:
  "Dear God:

Please use the following format when citing this chapter:

Nilsson, O., 2006, in IFIP International Federation for Information Processing, Volume 223, Social Informatics: An Information Society for All? In Remembrance of Rob Kling, eds. Berleur, J., Numinen, M. I., Impagliazzo, J., (Boston: Springer), pp. 445–455.

Please remove the have *nots*, the can *nots*, and the do *nots* that invade my mind.
Please erase the will *nots*, may *nots*, might *nots* that invade my heart.
Please release me from the could *nots*, would *nots* and should *nots* that invade my life." [1]

A number of studies reveal that possession a PC and an Internet connection in your home do not automatically imply that all the members of the household are users [e.g. 2, 3, 4, 5, 6]. Despite this fact, we could find all these individuals in the official statistics as households or citizens with access to an Internet connected PC in their home. This indicates two of the main ideas associated with this paper. The first is that possession, access, and use are notions that we cannot treat as being equal. The second is that circumstances other than the technical ones must come into consideration to be able to judge the options available for citizens to have access to the Internet and the ability to use Public Information Systems, PIS.

A great body of research has pointed out the inequalities in access to IT. I venture to say that it is now possible to have an overall picture of these inequalities. Generally speaking, more men than women have access to the Internet, more young people than elderly, more highly educated than less educated, more employees than unemployed, more rich than poor, and so on [e.g. 6, 7]. It is tempting to draw the conclusion that the inequalities in access to IT do mirror previously existing societal disparities [8]. In order to change these conditions, if indeed it is the ambition to one day achieve the 'information society for all', it is necessary for us to seek understanding for the reasons behind why it appears as it does, i.e. why the user is a user and why the non-user is a non-user. By investigating and understanding these mechanisms or hindrances to access, we are better equipped with the necessary tools to complete or bridge the digital gap.

2   The Access Concept

The purpose of this paper is to identify and analyse barriers that affect the individual user's experiences concerning access, and the use of the Internet for personal use. To be able to utilise the technology, access is essential. In this paper, we use the access concept in a somewhat broad perspective, covering all the aspects that we should take into consideration. In addition to the technical, physical and knowledge factors, economic, social, cultural, and mental aspects will be included.

We could either assume that those in households with an Internet-connected computer have access to the Internet. We could also assume that we also must add the possibilities for the household members to use the equipment and to talk about access. Beyond possession and possibility, we also must include the actual use for the given access to obtain the correct picture. Kling et al [9] emphasise that one PC is not equal to another PC, or "ICTs are configurable – they are actually collections of distinct components". This quote implies, that if we are satisfied with the answer if a person has a PC at home or not, we cannot say anything about the purpose of this specific equipment.

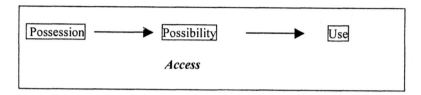

Figure 1: The widened access concept [14]

Clement & Shade [11] suggest three questions whose answers could assist in the formulation of a feasible description of the access concept, adapted to the actual situation:
1. Access to what? What is it that the individual should have the possibility to use, and how should this possibility be provided?
2. Access for whom? Should this possibility be provided to everyone or merely for specific individuals or groups?
3. Access for what purpose? For what purpose is this possibility provided?

As a starting point for a detailed formulation of a description of access that serves this paper's purpose, use is made of the answers to the above questions. The answer to the 'to what' question, will be access to Internet-based public information and services. Provision should be in a way that does not limit the individual's possibility of using the access. This implies that a computer with an Internet connection at home is a prerequisite for the possibility to use the Internet as a daily tool [15]. The second question, regarding whom, could only have one answer, namely all citizens. In Sweden and in a number other countries (e.g. the UK, Canada, and Australia to mention but a few) this requirement is stated in governmental bills or in other official documents [16]. We could view the purpose of providing the access as two-fold; one is to make it possible for the citizen to take part in their rights and to fulfil their duties in a desired way, and the other to make the public administration less expensive and more effective [17].

Having come this far, consideration must be given as to whom should make the judgement regarding whether or not a person has access. Is it the individual himself or herself who makes a subjective interpretation, or should the judgement be made by anyone else based on a more objective basis? Two different perspectives can be separated out, a 'from-outside' view and a 'from-inside' view.

From outside	From inside
External actors perspective	Individuals perspective
What are offered?	What are offered?
To who is it offered?	Am I able/allowed to use it?
What are the benefits for us?	What are the benefits for me?
More objective	Personal, subjective

Figure 2: Two different perspectives to study access [14]

It is the opinion of the author that the main part of current research and official reports and statistics is based primarily on the former perspective [e.g. 6, 7]. These reports and statistics have provided a substantial body of knowledge about what technology, education, and information offers or provides the individual. It can be stated that it determines the external actors' (i.e. the Internet Service Providers, the companies, the organisations, and the authorities) activities and efforts, and the results in the form of the number of PCs and Internet connections in a country. It also provides demographic information about the users and non-users, and to the extent in which they use it. This knowledge is of course necessary. However, to handle the question regarding how and why the individual uses or does not use the provided technology and its applications, requires a 'from-inside' perspective.

The most commonly used pair of notions to describe the differences in access is that of the 'haves' and 'have-nots' [e.g. 18, 19], which gives information about who has the technology at home and who has not. The shortcoming of this dichotomy is that it merely describes the possible access to IT, which is only one part of the problem. We could also find those who do not can, want, may, or dare use the technology among the non-users. This provides four additional dichotomies namely 'want to' and the 'not want to' or the 'be able to' and the 'not be able to', of the 'be allowed to' and the 'not be allowed to', or finally the 'dare to' and the 'not dare to' people. To be aware of these latter dichotomies is important and has an underpinning by reports that show that possession is not the same as actual use [e.g. 2, 6].

2.1 Driving Forces or Barriers

If our goal is to bring about or facilitate a change, it is more fruitful to look forward than backward [20]. The question to answer will then be: What are the hindrances for us to do what we want to do, or why do we act in a way we do not want to? The focus will be to identify and to study the factors and the barriers that the individual experiences as standing in the way of the everyday use of the Internet.

Driving forces	Barriers
Causal	Intentional
Looking backwards	Looking forward
What made us acting?	What hampers the acting?
Tells what has happened	Tells what has to be changed

Figure 3: Characteristics for driving forces and barriers [21]

We should not look upon the driving forces and the barriers as dichotomies. The lack of a driving force does not imply a barrier, and similarly, the absence of a barrier does not automatically denote a driving force. For example, a common driving force for Swedes to obtain an Internet connected PC at home is school age children [7], but we should not view being without children as a barrier, only as the absence of a driving force. Israel [20] suggests that we should study hindrances or barriers at five levels. (a) Hindrance concerning our biological equipment and the structure of the physical world should be a mission of technology that often provides a bridge for these obstacles. (b) Existing economic, social, political, and cultural processes in society limits our actions if we are willing to follow the rules and accept sanctions for breaking them. (c) Organisational structures such as the family, school, workplace, and organisations where we live and work have obstacles at two levels: (i) the existing social division of labour and the power and authority conditions in these structures' daily function, and (ii) norms and rules in relation to their activities and goals as well as their resources has a limiting function. (d) Interpersonal relations and interaction could bring about two types of hindrances: (i) formal rules and dictated roles that limit actions and (ii) the communication process. (e) Hindrance may originate from the individual's own mind because of fear, uncertainty, or a lack of confidence in his or her own ability.

When we adopt Israel's suggested barriers for this study, we obtain the following categories: 1) Technical barriers; 2) Physical barriers; 3) Economical barriers; 4) Cultural and social barriers; and 5) Mental barriers. In this context, these five categories will generate a necessary sixth one, namely knowledge and skill barriers, used in the following empirical studies to discuss and propose an access model.

We studied and applied four current access models (Aspden and Katz [10], Clement and Shade [11], Poland [12], and Van Dijk and Hacker [13]) to these six categories of barriers, which gave the following result.

Barrier	Aspden & Katz	Clement & Shade	Poland	van Dijk & Hacker
Technological		X	X	X
Physical			X	
Economical	X			X
Knowledge and skills		X		X
Social and cultural	X	X	X	X
Mental	X		X	X

Figure 4: Access models applied to the access barriers [14]

As one can see, none of the above mentioned access models cover all of the suggested aspects. Thus, it is necessary to take the process one-step further in the attempt to design a user centred access model, UCAM. We can view the aspects as circumstances that affect the individual's conception of IT, and the extent to which he or she will, can, allowed, and dares to use IT. We have named the barriers in the UCAM with commonplace notions such as have, want, may, able, and dare to make them easier to communicate to people who are outside academia.

Barriers	Description
Have	Technical, physical possibility to use
Want	Will to use
May	Allowed to use
Able	Knowledge to use, economical prerequisites
Dare	Familiar to use

Figure 5: The user centred access model, UCAM [14]

3   Identifying the experienced access barriers

We made this study as a critical analysis [23] applied on the results from four empirical studies, made in the period October 2001 to May 2005. From these studies developed a number of access barriers identified and categorised in the UCAM as technological, physical, economic, knowledge and skills, and social-cultural-psychological barriers.

We made the first empirical study in the municipality of Härnösand during October and November 2001 [3]. The tool used in the survey was a questionnaire distributed to 500 persons, born 1985 or earlier, of which 400 completed the form. The form contained of 53 questions, of which 52 had fixed answering alternatives. We invited informants to leave comments to any the questions if they felt limited by the fixed alternatives.

The second study was an interview study made among parents of pupils at two schools in two different town districts in Gothenburg, which had taken place at the end of February 2002 [23]. We made the data collection by semi-structured interviews. The two head teachers, ten teachers, one school assistant, one administrator, and two from school healthcare were interviewed individually. In addition, we interviewed 20 parents with children in the 13 to 15 year age category by telephone, and 22 pupils in groups at the schools.

We carried out the third study in April and May of 2003 [14]. The study included 290 parents from 182 families in Härnösand and Gothenburg with children in the 7 to 12 year age category who answered a questionnaire concerning their use of Internet at home.

The last study was an interview study among parents to children in compulsory schools and teachers at the schools in the municipality of Sundsvall [4, 5]. We conducted the parental interviews as focus group interviews [24]. This included 5 interviews with five to six parents in each focus group, and 9 individual interviews with the teachers.

The identified access barriers has been categorised in the five groups or categories. A summary of these hindrances was categorised and applied to the User Centred Access Model in the table below. These categories are not independent of, or isolated from each other; they are rather interdependent. That fact generates a factor that could occur in more than one category, which could affect one or more other factors.

Barrier	Experienced hindrances
Have	• Lack of PC; • Lack of Internet connection due to infrastructural circumstances; • Lack of Internet connection due to considerations for the own children; • Registration problems; • Economic constraints;
Want	• Slow transmission due to bandwidth; • Unattractive service; • Unwanted pop-ups and spam; • Attitude to the service provider;

May	• Unreliable information; • Lack of use worthiness; • Lack of interest in the technology; • Lack of time; • Gets all necessary information the 'traditional way'; • Threat against the personal contact; • Limitations in use opportunity due to the division of the domestic work; • Limitations in use opportunity due to the number of family members; • Limitations in use opportunity due to the placing of the equipment; • Economic constraints;
Able	• Lack of skills and knowledge; • Information incapability; • Economic constraints; • Lack of time; • Registration problems; • Problems with the size of fonts; • Problems with the language; • Problems with the combination of colours;
Dare	• Risk for the children to get in contact with inappropriate persons or material; • Risk for the children's health; • Risk for the children's social life; • Replacement of personal contacts; • Risk becoming addicted to the use; • Risk for virus, modem napping and unauthorised trespassing; • Risk for fraud; • Risk for the personal integrity

Figure 6: The identified access barriers applied to the UCAM [14]

4   Discussion and Conclusion

The first conclusion drawn from the study is that it was possible to use the User Centred Access Model to categorise the identified barriers. We could place all the hindrances experienced by the respondents in the empirical studies in a feasible category. The use of the UCAM also offers the possibility to present the access barriers in a structured way that is easy to understand and communicate with the experts and with the uninitiated.

Later, I will state the identified access barriers, which we can divide into two rough categories or groups according to their origin or causing factors. These two groups are:

• Access barriers whose origins are in, or are caused by the infrastructure, the design of the applications and the equipment, the use and political and economic circumstances.

- Access barriers that have their origin in, or are caused by prevailing values and norms in society or in the user's environment or own mind.

Constraints (such as the possibilities to obtain a broadband connection, slow modem transmission, old equipment and software, hyperlinks that do not work, virus attacks, and design problems to mention but a few) appear in the first category. We can state that this category of access barriers is not the major problem in the endeavour towards the 'information society for all'. Of course, we cannot ignore them, as we must also accommodate them while obstructing the possibilities to use technology. I base this statement on my firm conviction that today the knowledge and skills are available to remove these access barriers; it is merely a question of money, politics, and will.

The other challenge occurs when the goal is an equal possibility to access and to remove the barriers that exist in an individual's own mind formed by the structures and norms in the social and cultural environment in which we live. Lindblad-Gidlund [25], Bijker and Pinch [26], and Popper [27] showed the shaping and the presence of these individual concepts of technological artefacts as well as the individual's relation to them. These barriers, experienced by the individual, are more difficult to handle when they created from their own feelings, interpretations, and concepts. This does not only concern gender issues, education or income, but also how we regard the way in which we should live our lives, or our form of life, life cycle, and life style as suggested by Selg [2].

In the Swedish Government's bill 1999/2000:86 [16], there are three prioritised areas: the confidence in IT, the competence to use IT, and the accessibility to the services in an information society. The bill also points out where the efforts should lie in order to create the 'information society for all'. When we view the identified hindrances experienced by Swedish citizens in this study, one realises that a great deal of work remains before we cam move the focus from these three prioritised areas. However, we could place all of the identified barriers into the three areas. The study shows that an obvious lack of confidence exists in both the technology and its use among the respondents. I dare to state that this is the most crucial 'piece in the puzzle' that requires full attention and effort. We must view confidence as a subjective factor that is dependent on the individual observer; confidence is also a dynamic factor that could change very quickly. Our ideas concerning the technology are formed, affected, and changed by not only by our own experiences, but also by the environment in which we live. Newspapers, radio and television, strongly influence our trust or distrust in IT. Headlines such as "Giant bluff against Nordea – false website panic closed net services" (Aftonbladet, 2005-10-04) will not contribute to making those who feel dubious any more friendly to their own use of technology. Nevertheless, in the same way as media scares the users or the potential users, it also encourages or stimulates them to use technology with lyrical descriptions and stories about different equipment or applications fantastic qualities. For example, in DN (2005-10-19) you could read that the "iPod is the first technical apparatus that makes it possible to carry with you a part of your cultural heritage. An extra memory to your brain that could be filled with that, that have stamped and formed your identity".

Beside the mistrust in the technological artefacts, the applications, and the eventual unwanted consequences, there is also an expressed lack of confidence in one's own capability or skill in handling the machine and using the applications. A third experienced area of confidence problems is the reliability of the information and sources associated with the Internet. This result corresponds to the results in the report from the World Internet Institute [28] that shows that 58,7% of the Swedes trust at least half of the information at the Internet. A common feeling of uncertainty and anxiety was expressed particularly among the female respondents, when it came to risk associated with the use of the Internet. These feelings did not relate to their own use, but to the children's use. Almost 80% of the Internet users also experienced concerns that the authorities and the employers obtain the possibility for increasing control and supervision [28]. The same study shows that 86,9% of Swedes are worried or greatly worried about being attacked by a data virus.

A common opinion among the users was that they did not feel that they had sufficient knowledge or skills to feel comfortable in front of the computer. As long as everything worked as it was supposed to work, and everything on the screen looked as it usually looked, there were not many problems. Unfortunately, this idealistic situation is not very common. For many it is sufficient to encounter an unexpected pop-up window or a change in the appearance of the desktop, to feel insecure as to how to act. Many of the confidence problems originate from a lack of knowledge and skills and they will probably decrease as competence levels increase. However, some of them (e.g. the worry to be attacked by a virus is 79%) consider themselves very experienced users [28].

Often public access points such as libraries, workplaces, or schools are used as an argument for everyone's possibility to use IT. If you, for one reason or another, do not have the necessary equipment at home, one would expect you to use IT in some other place. The participants in my studies put forward a number of reasons why they did not see these external access points as a realistic alternative for their private use of the Internet and Public Information Systems. The lack of privacy at a public access point limits the services you feel comfortable in using. Additionally, you must also face restrictions to the hours of service, thus reducing the advantages of the 24/7 promoters. At many workplaces, the private use of the Internet is strictly limited either by the employer or by the employees' own conscience. These arguments support Grönlund [15] who states that access to the equipment at home is a requirement to become a daily user.

The occurrence or experience of a specific access barrier is not a static condition; the changes over time and the differences in use between men and women are decreasing [7]. The elderly have always been noted as being a group who have been unfairly treated in this context, but according to a new report from the European Union named *eInclusion revisited: the local dimension of the Information Society* [29], "the elderly are crossing the digital divide". This is perhaps not so surprising, as the group referred to as 'elderly' is defined as those who are 55 or older and a huge difference exists between a 55-year-old today and one of ten years ago with reference to the options and availabilities offered by the information technology.

I will also draw the conclusion that Israel's suggestion [20] concerning changes of an unwanted situation; it is more fruitful to concentrate on the barriers than the driving forces; the results of this work support this concept. We realize that a number of the access barriers identified here are not possible to overcome simply by means of increased driving forces. The worry many parents feel for their children and the

454   Olof Nilsson

lack of design expressed by some users will not decrease by means of a driving force. A driving force could on the other hand, stimulate other barriers such as the lack of reasons for IT use.

References

[1]   [http://beliefnet.com/story/95/story_9522_1.html]
[2]   H. Selg, *Vem använder Internet och till vad? Spridning av Internet bland befolkningen,* IT-kommissionens rapport 1/2002, SOU 2002:24, Stockholm, Sweden, (2002)
[3]   O. Nilsson, *The use of, and access to PC, Internet and a local government's web site - A study of a strategic chosen group of residents in Härnösand* – in Proceedings of Promote IT Conference 2002, Skövde, Sweden (2002)
[4]   O. Nilsson, *Vardagskommunikation skola-hem, delrapport 2,* Sundsvalls Kommun rapport 2005:4, Sundsvall, Sweden (2005)
[5]   O. Nilsson, Sefyrin, J. *Vardagskommunikation skola-hem, delrapport 1,* Sundsvalls Kommun rapport 2005:2, Sundsvall, Sweden, (2005)
[6]   O. Findahl, *Svenskarna och Internet 2003,* World Internet Institute, Gävle, Sweden, (2004)
[7]   SCB, *Use of computers and the Internet by private persons in 2004,* SCB, Stockholm, (2004), [http://www.scb.se/statistik/_publikationer/IT0102_2004A01_BR_TKFT0404.pdf]
[8]   B. Barber, Open lecture at Örebro University 2001-03-30, unpublished
[9]   R. Kling, H. Crawford, H. Rosenbaum, S. Sawyer, S. Weisband, *Learning from Social Informatics: Information and Communication Technologies in Human Context,* Center for Social Informatics, Indiana University, USA retrieved from [www.slis.indiana.edu/CSI/2003-12-10 (2000)
[10] P. Aspden, J. Katz, *Social and Public Policy Internet Research: Goals and Achievements,* Dr Aspen's talk at the University of Michigan School of Information February 2, 1998 retriewed from [www.communitytechnology.org/aspden/aspden_talk.html 2003-12-02
[11] A. Clement, L.R. Shade, *The Access Rainbow: Conceptualizing Universal Access to the Information/Communication Infrastructure*, in Gurstein, M, (ed) *Community Informatics: Enabling Communities with Information and Communications Technologies,* Idea Group Publishing, London, UK, (2000)
[12] P. Poland, *Online Consultation in GOL Countries: Initiatives to Foster E-democracy,* Government Online International Network, (2001) http://governments-online.org/articles/18.shtml]
[13] J. Van Dijk, K. Hacker, *The Digital Divide as a Complex and Dynamic Phenomenon,* The Information Society, 19:315-326, 2003
[14] O. Nilsson, *Access Barriers – from a user's point of view,* Doctoral thesis, Department of Information technology and Media, Mid Sweden University, Sweden, (2005)
[15] Å. Grönlund,. *En introduktion till Electronic Government,* in Grönlund, Å. & Ranerup, A.(red) *Elektronisk förvaltning, elektronisk demokrati – Visioner, verklighet, vidareutveckling,* Studentlitteratur, Lund, Sweden (2001).
[16] Government bill 1999/2000:86, *Ett informationssamhälle för alla,* Riksdagens tryckeri, Stockholm, (2000)
[17] The Ministry of Industry, Employment and Communications, *An Information Society for All – a publication about the Swedish IT-policy,* Government Offices of Sweden, (2004)

[18] E. Boyd, *Introduction to the Special Series on the Digital Divide*, in Informing Science, vol. 5, No 3, 2002, p. 113-114, (2002)

[19] Carveth, Kretchmer *Policy Options to Combat the Digital Divide in Western Europe*, in Informing Science, vol. 5, No 3, 2002, p. 115-123 (2002)

[20] J. Israel, *Har vi behov?* I Aronsson & Berglind (ed) *Handling och Handlingsutrymme*, p.51-68, Studentlitteratur, Lund, Sweden (1990)

[21] J. Israel, *Handling och samspel. Ett socialpsykologiskt perspektiv*, Studentlitteratur, Lund, Sweden (1999)

[22] L. Kvasny, E.M. Trauth, *The Digital Divide At Work and Home: The Discourse About Power and Underrepresented Groups in the Information Society*, in Wynn, E. Myers, M.D. and Whitley, E.A. Global and Organizational Discourse about Information Technology, pp. 273-291, Kluwer Academic Publishers, Boston, USA (2002)

[23] O. Nilsson, *Confidence or Control*, in Proceedings of ITiRA 2002 Conference, Rockhampton, Australia (2002)

[24] E. F. Fern, *Advanced Focus Group Research*, Sage Publications Inc, Thousand Oaks, USA (2001)

[25] K. Lindblad-Gidlund, *Techno Therapy, a relation with technology*, Doctoral thesis, Department of Informatics, Umeå University, Sweden (2005)

[26] W. Bijker, T. Pinch, *The Social Construction of Facts and Artefacts: Or How the Sociology of Science and the Sociology of Technology Might Benefit Each Other*, Social Studies of Science, no. 14, (1984)

[27] K. R. Popper, *The Worlds 1, 2 and 3*, in Popper, K. R. & Eccles J. C. *The Self and ITs Brain*, Springer, Berlin, Germany (1977)

[28] World Internet Institute, *Virus, spam och tillit*, Faktablad nr.1 2005-11-01, retrieved 2005-09-15 at [http://www.wii.se]

[29] EU, *eInclusion revisited: the local dimension of the Information Society* (2005) [http://europa.eu.int/comm/employment_social/news/2005/feb/eincllocal_en.pdf]

Cross-Cutting Issues

Computers and Internet Related Beliefs among Estonian Computer Users and Non-Users

Pille Pruulmann-Vengerfeldt
University of Tartu, Department of Journalism and communications
pille.vengerfeldt@ut.ee, http://www.jrn.ut.ee/

Abstract. This paper aims to look at the computer and Internet related beliefs among Estonian computer users and non-users. It uses data from two nationally representative surveys to analyze seven Internet and computer related beliefs. The paper also discusses how understanding the opinions of computer users and non-users should influence the policies of the information society. As a conclusion, policy suggestions on visibility of the technologies, digital literacy, and data monitoring needs are made.

Keywords: technology related beliefs, computer users and non-users, information society policy, adaptive theory.

1 Introduction

As new technologies emerge and constantly outdate each other, it is difficult to imagine that only less than fifteen years ago, there was no Internet connection in Estonia and that computers were highly specialized tools kept in labs. No one thought that usage and distribution of these technologies might become an important part of the notion of information society. Yet, nowadays, it is hard to imagine anyone living in Estonia who has not heard about these technologies. The Estonian case in interesting because of the simultaneous co-occurrence of several 'revolutions', alongside with the 'singing revolution' contributing to the political collapse of the Soviet Union, Estonia witnessed a rapid turn towards capitalism and market economy. At the same time, international 'technology revolution' also reached Estonia and flooded society with options and possibilities that were very positively received.

The aim of this paper is to look at the context of Estonian information and technology developments from the perspective of social informatics. Social

Please use the following format when citing this chapter:

Pruulmann-Vengerfeldt, P., 2006, in IFIP International Federation for Information Processing, Volume 223, Social Informatics: An Information Society for All? In Remembrance of Rob Kling, eds. Berleur, J., Numinen, M. I., Impagliazzo, J., (Boston: Springer), pp. 459–468.

informatics has several different aspects – micro level of design and uses and macro level of institutions and societies. It also has many disciplinary backgrounds and as Rob Kling [1] puts it: "It is a field that is defined by its topic rather than family of methods". Diversity of the disciplines and ever-expanding research objects makes social informatics somewhat difficult to comprehend; yet we need to learn many valuable lessons.

The aim of this paper is to look at the computers and Internet related beliefs of the Estonian people and draw some policy conclusions from this material.

2   Theoretical Context and Focus of the Study

One of the major problems with technology research is that it either is overpowered by political assumptions or hopes nicely referred as punditry [1] or that they are very empirical and lack theorization. Social informatics has been building the body of research over twenty-five years and has connected the ideas of empirical and theoretical research.

Derek Layder [2] is one of those who seek an answer on how to connect theoretical and empirical work. In his opinion, social theory often lacks the connection between well-grounded empirical research and more theoretical approaches. He proposes a notion of adaptive theory.

"The word 'adaptive' is meant to convey that the theory both adapts to, or is shaped by, incoming evidence while the data itself is simultaneously filtered through, and is thus adapted by, the prior theoretical materials (frameworks, concepts, ideas) that are relevant to their analysis"[3].

This paper tries to follow the ideas of the adaptive theory by first providing a conceptual framework for the data, by using the notions of social informatics and information environment. In the second half of the paper I will analyze the data with the help of the questions that social informatics asks and provide some policy suggestions. We can consider social informatics to be a very good example of what Layder considers as adaptive theory, as it is constantly revising itself in the face of the empirical material provided.

Social informatics has used the methods of the adaptive theory to help empirical material to understand better and often to overthrow some of the everyday beliefs that have received the status of theories, like for instance the direct effect theories [4]. One of the key aspects of the social informatics is to find and to stress the importance of the socio-technical character of the information technologies. The present study will investigate one aspect of the socio-technical network, namely people and their beliefs. We will look at the everyday understanding of the state of the information society in Estonia and the way it has changed in the years of 2002-2005.

Beliefs and attitudes are expressions of the human emotional disposition, subjective preferences and goals [5]. Beliefs are communicated through interpersonal communication or media; they can be acquired also though individual contemplation. Beliefs and attitudes do not guarantee behavior in desired direction, but rather reflect the overall disposition towards the topic. Therefore, we cannot conclude that positive beliefs will result in positive behavior. Investigation of computer and technology related beliefs shows a more general public opinion and helps to understand the cultural context of the technology adoption.

Focus on the Information Environment

Estonia is one of the fastest developing countries in Europe in the late 1990s. Its speedy developments in the field of electronic governance and Internet in schools has influenced Estonian people. The general understandings of the technological developments have been supportive and that understanding has spread to individual use of the new technologies. Although the Internet adoption rates are not as good as in neighboring countries such as Finland and Sweden, they are significantly higher than in other Baltic states [6]. That advantage has also supported Estonian's self-image as active and technology-savvy country.

There have been many discussions as to what contributes to such rapid developments. Estonian society has been welcoming different initiatives with open arms. Hence, the aim of this article is to look at one of the possible reasons as to why ICTs have been so popular in Estonia. There are number of different explanations as to what contributes to the social environment that is so encouraging for the take-up of new information technologies.

Social informatics helps us in asking the question about the cultural context of specific adoption process. Leah Lievrouw [7] in her article about knowledge dissemination in society defines *information environments* as social settings or milieu in which these resources, relations and technologies undergo a structuration-type process of change called *informing*. In her schematic model, she divides the environment into "an *institutional aspect* and a *personal/relational aspect*, which are closely related and interact" [8]. Looking at those different aspects of information environment enables us to locate a variety of factors that influence ICTs dissemination in culture-specific contexts. Government, businesses, and media provide the institutional aspect; individual beliefs, values and understandings as well as social networks like family, kin, and workmates constitute the personal/relational aspect. They are strongly influenced by one another and therefore very complex to research. From these different factors, this article focuses on the technology related opinions among Estonian computer users and non-users. Their beliefs provide one measurable aspect of the social and cultural context in which the adoption of new technologies takes place. It is important to understand that the technology adoption is not a once-off experience, but rather a repetitive cycle where each new application of the same, already adopted technology, needs to be re-adopted continuously. Beliefs and understandings form an important background for such a process.

I am going to compare the different opinions and attitudes among computer users and non-users. I think this is an important step in understanding the notion of human choice in computer and Internet adoption as our opinions and beliefs strongly govern the way we behave. This paper is part of a larger study that uses longitudinal data to investigate Estonian people at the wake of the 21st century. Data gathered within this project is versatile and covers many areas of people's everyday life, media use, values, beliefs, relation to money, politics, culture, and to other people [9]. This paper only manages to introduce very few of the issues covered – namely Internet and computers related beliefs, but I think they are very important ones to be considered when talking about the social and cultural context of the particular adoption.

3   Method

I will look at data from two representative longitudinal surveys conducted in Estonia – in late 2002 and early 2003 and late 2005. The survey was conducted in Estonia, with the representative sample of 1470 people in 2003 and 1475 in 2005. We collected data with a written questionnaire complemented by an oral interview. Interviewers left the respondents the survey booklet containing about 700 questions. In addition to that, interviewers agreed time to meet with the respondents, collect the questionnaire and ask additional 80 questions from those who qualified for the oral interview. The survey was conducted in 150 survey points across Estonia with the 'youngest male method' where interviewers asked to speak with the youngest male member of the household and if he was not present, the youngest female was asked to participate. The survey was conducted within the age group of 15-74 and 500 of the respondents were Russian speakers (for more detailed information about the study see Kalmus, Lauristin, Pruulmann-Vengerfeldt [9]).

For the present paper, the following question asked from the respondents is most relevant: With computers and Internet becoming a part of everyday life, there are many opinions about them. Hereby we provide you a list of some of those opinions that have been circulating about computers and Internet. To which extent do you agree with them? The following options were given: 'agree completely', 'agree to a certain extent', 'disagree to a certain extent', 'disagree completely', and 'I don't know, don't have an opinion' were given. In 2003, there were fourteen and in 2005, there were twenty statements in the survey. For the present analysis, I have divided the answers into three subsets: complete and partial agreements, complete and partial disagreements, and no opinion. I have selected seven variables that are comparable between the years and that I consider more related to the computer and Internet adoption rates.

I will compare the answers of users and non-users of the computers as well as compare different years. For the purpose of this study, I define computer users as those who answered 'Yes' to the following question: 'Do you use a computer?' We asked the question with no specific definition of the use and without a timeframe, which leaves the definition of the use up to the respondent.

Statements that are under investigation cover both computer and Internet use, but the variable we compare them against is only computer use. This is because the number of people who use computers, but do not use the Internet is relatively small in our sample. In 2003, 48% of the respondents were computer users and 90% of them were Internet users. In 2005, the level of computer usage has risen to 68,5% of respondents, and the level of Internet usage has risen to 94% of the computer users. As the computer-use variable was used as the gatekeeper variable to the Internet use question, then there is no information about those people who would say that they are Internet users without actually defining themselves as computer users. We have assumed that the number of those people is very marginal.

4   Internet Related Beliefs and Opinions in Empirical Material

In Table 1, we have gathered information about seven statements that we asked the computer users and non-users to rate.

Table 1: Internet and computer related opinions of the computer users and non-users in Estonia, in 2003 and 2005

Statement	Year	Computer use/non-use	Agreement with the statement	Disagreement with the statement	Uncertain, don't know
Frequent use of computers and the Internet is not good for your health	2003	User	53%	37%	10%
		Non-user	59%	12%	29%
	2005	User	56%	37%	6%
		Non-user	58%	8%	27%
The Internet makes people to waste work and study time	2003	User	35%	60%	5%
		Non-user	31%	38%	30%
	2005	User	38%	56%	5%
		Non-user	39%	33%	21%
The Internet enables citizens to influence politics more	2003	User	25%	55%	20%
		Non-user	14%	40%	46%
	2005	User	17%	64%	17%
		Non-user	13%	41%	40%
The Internet alienates people from each other	2003	User	36%	54%	10%
		Non-user	41%	23%	36%
	2005	User	46%	45%	8%
		Non-user	42%	23%	28%
Using computers and the Internet scares me	2003	User	5%	89%	6%
		Non-user	17%	49%	34%
	2005	User	9%	83%	7%
		Non-user	19%	37%	35%
All children must have the possibility to use computers and the Internet as early as possible	2003	User	71%	24%	5%
		Non-user	64%	23%	14%
	2005	User	46%	45%	8%
		Non-user	37%	36%	20%
All people who don't have access to the Internet are disadvantaged in all aspects of life	2003	User	54%	39%	8%
		Non-user	50%	28%	22%
	2005	User	53%	38%	8%
		Non-user	35%	37%	20%

The most significant difference between the users and non-users are that besides being more positive and optimistic about the Internet and computers, in general,

464   Pille Pruulmann-Vengerfeldt

computer users are more opinionated. The number of computer non-users, who do not have an opinion about the statements, is remarkably larger than the proportion of computer users who are unsure about the given statement.

These statements demonstrate the positive attitudes prevailing among the Estonian public. I will now discuss each of those statements separately.

Connection between Internet or computer use with health issues is very common in everyday discourses in Estonia. People are mostly worried about their eyesight, but sedentary lifestyle of computer users is also an issue. Very common is the understanding that children who are using computers are not interested in participating in sports. Also in our sample, more than half of the people agree with the idea that frequent computer use may not be good for your health. The opinions about this statement show that more computer users have became to agree with that statement.

Wasting time with computers has been one of the negative attitudes among general optimism. We expected a rise in productivity, although social informatics studies elsewhere are not supporting this optimism [1]. Similarly in Estonia, people, who originally placed much hope on computers diminishing the workload and increasing productivity, found that people could do so many things with computers and the Internet. People tend to start dividing their attentions and not concentrating on the issues of work alone. Results from the survey show that more than half of the computer users disagree with the idea that computers make you waste the time. The number of non-users who disagree with the statement has decreased over the years. The concept that new technologies are adopted in the context of the existing lifestyle is not new. Non-users who feel that meaningful activities fill their lives, they fear that using computers may make them waste the time they have now for other things like reading and spending time with the family. However, the levels of being uncertain about this issue have decreased quite significantly among the non-users, indicating that people who have remained non-users are more sure in their opinion whether ICTs are waste of time or not.

The next statement is strongly connected with the optimistic hopes that people have had towards the technology. Estonia's e-government is a very successful project that received much attention. For instance, Network Readiness Index has rated Estonia to the 5th place in e-governance index in 2001 and to the 8th place in e-governance index in 2002 [10]. Estonia has also a digital democracy project called Today I Decide (TOM in Estonian) that received much media attention at the time of its creation in June 2001. It is possible to see disappointment of the computer users in this system – the number of computer users who believe that Internet enables citizens to influence politics has dropped and the number of those who disagree with the statement has risen.

Discussion that has received a lot of attention from social scientists is the issue of alienation and social capital of the Internet users [11, 12]. Different reactions have made this issue to be on the top of the Internet related agenda for quite some time. The data reveals that in 2003 more than half of the people who used computers did not believe that computers cause alienation, but in 2005, the percent has dropped below half. At this point, it is difficult to say what causes this: changed opinions, changed experiences, or enlarged user-body are probably all part of the explanation.

A number of people are hesitant to adopt new technologies because they are scared of them. People might be afraid of the consequences of technology adoption or fear that they look stupid or that they might break something. In our sample, it is interesting to see that the number of people who are afraid of using ICTs has risen among the computer users and declined among the non-users. It may be that the pressures in the society to apply new technologies are so remarkable that people are adopting them in spite of their fears and use of the technology has not made them overcome their fears

In recent years the debate of computer addiction and children has became livelier in Estonia. The result is that 73% of the population thinks that children's computer addiction has become a serious problem. The replies to the question of whether children must have early contact with the computers also reflect this. The percentages of people who agree with this statement have declined among the computer users and the non-users.

In spite of the pessimistic and cautious beliefs, more than half of the computer users believe that people who don't have access to the Internet are disadvantaged in their life. The number of non-users who believe the same thing has decreased and partially probably because they are computer users now.

With the negative statements, the health related statement is the only one where more than half of the people agree with it, be they computer users or not. All other negative statements have less than half of the population supporting them. On the other hand, the positive statements receive also less than half of the population's support. It shows there is overwhelming agreement does not exist with either positive or negative attitudes. However, in general, computer users are more inclined to have positive beliefs towards the information and communication technologies, whereas non-users have more people among them who are uncertain.

5 Implications for the Information Policy of Estonia

Most of the statements under investigation here are common day-to-day statements that circulate between people, in public and private texts. It seems that although people sometimes consider Estonia very optimistic and positive in attitudes towards the Internet and computers [13, 14], the data indicates that the optimism is not so overwhelming. There are several policy lessons we can learn from these findings.

Without wanting to go too deeply into policy analysis, I would still like to draw a few conclusions from the current study that the Estonian information society policy could find useful. Estonia is currently in the process of formulating new principles in the information society policy for the years 2007-2010. This is the first policy document where active involvement of the researchers has been encouraged and enabled. Previous policies have been technology and economic centred [15, 16] whereas there is a strong possibility that the policy document under construction will also consider human and social aspects of the new technologies.

Firstly, we consider a lesson that is strongly connected to Roger's [17] theories about diffusion of innovations. It is clear that information about the innovation is very important. The fact that approximately one fifth of the non-users doesn't have an opinion about the statements that were provided shows that there is still not enough information, not enough possibilities to observe other people using information and communication technologies. If information policy-makers are interested in influencing the human choice towards adopting new technologies and government-provided services in new media environment, they must foster a well-balanced and open information environment.

Today, the ICTs related information provided by the government is hectic and inconsistent. It is also not focusing on the day-to-day usage by the individuals, thus not providing the necessary observation moment for the non-users. There are different possibilities for local or state government to promote their own services in a way where use of those services can be observed publicly and therefore people would be more inclined to try themselves. However, the indifference towards a technology might mean that people generally ignore the public messages about technology related activities and might therefore be more difficult to reach. For them, the educational aspects of the information environment may be available through the personal aspects of their information environment where friends and relatives can become proxies for mediating the ICTs related information provided by different institutions.

Second, a policy lesson that can be learned is that the issue of young children's use of computers and Internet is something that needs even wider public discussion and probably some political decisions. Children seem at risk from computers and Internet and often parents even do not know how to help them. Information society policy should acknowledge the concern and find ways to support parents in their attempts to regulate children's exposure to new information and communication technologies. Thus, information society for all needs clear political activities to provide digital literacy not only in a way to be able to use technologies, but also to interpret the content accessed by those technologies in a safe way. The role of the policy makers is to make sure that digital literacy skills are included in the school programmes and that they are meaningful and helpful for all different levels of user competences and abilities.

Another idea that can be taken to policies outside Estonia is that monitoring these kinds of opinions and understandings through surveys can help to see how they are changing, what is on agenda and what concerns people have in relation to the technology. The set-up of the current study was the following – for the first questionnaire we devised our questions based on an international survey (World Internet Project [18]) and modified them to suit our survey In 2005, however, we took the same questions, removed some that had vague wording and added new ones that we had derived from media analysis. Media, especially traditional media that is most popular for that particular cultural context, is an important source for information in today's 'mediatised' world and sometimes it seems that computer and Internet studies do not pay enough attention to the content of 'old' media. At least in Estonia, where for instance newspaper readership is relatively high, the press is a very important shaper of the public opinion.

6   Conclusion

Researching the Internet and computer related beliefs and opinions, gives an important insight into human choice and ICTs. It shows some underlying principles that people use in their decision making whether to adopt new technologies or not. The more complex the technology under investigation, the more important the issue of knowledge about the innovation becomes. In order to understand the human choice in the question of information technology adoptions, understanding attitudes towards the common beliefs related to that technology is a first step. The complexity of the information environment exposed to modern people is too large to address in only one paper. This study is only part of a larger project that investigates the different aspects of the institutional and personal information environment.

There are several policy lessons that we can learn from the study, mostly showing the key aspects of the concern by the public, but also helping to understand the factors underlying the decisions people make in relation to the information technologies. Today, data about the beliefs in the different countries is relatively difficult to access and probably not available at all in many cases. However, knowing the stronger currents in public opinion related to information and communication technologies would make the information society more accessible and understandable for all. Having material for international comparison would give better understanding of the different factors in shaping the social and cultural context of the particular technologies adoption.

Social informatics is a good example of adaptive theory that helps us to understand that empirical research, theoretical generalizations, and policy lessons are all strongly interconnected; we cannot and should not consider them in isolation.

References

1.   R. Kling, What is social informatics and why does it matter? *D-lib Magazine* **5**(1) (1999), http://www.dlib.org/dlib/january99/kling/01kling.html (Last accessed 30/03/2006)
2.   D. Layder, *Sociological Practice: linking theory and social research*, (Sage, London, Thousand Oaks, New Delhi, 1998)
3.   Ibid., pp.5.
4.   R. Kling, H. Crawford, H. Rosenbaum, S. Sawyer and S. Weisband, *Learning from Social Informatics: information and communication technologies in human contexts*, (Centre for Social Informatics, Indiana University, 2000), http://rkcsi.indiana.edu/media/SI_report.pdf (Last accessed 30/03/2006)
5.   M. Lauristin and P. Vihalemm, *Massikommunikatsiooni teooria: õppevahend _urnalistika üliõpilastele*, Tartu Riiklik Ülikool, Tartu, 1977.
6.   M. Bogdanowicz, J. Burgelman, C. Centeno, E. Gourova and G. Carat, Factors of regional/national success in information society developments: Information society strategies for candidate countries, *First Monday* **8**(10) (2003), http://www.firstmonday.org/issues/issue8_10/ (Last accessed 30/03/2006)
7.   L. Lievrouw, New media and the 'pluralization of life-worlds': a role for information in social differentiation, *New Media and Society* **3**(1), 7-28 (2001) pp.12
8.   Ibid., pp.13

9.   V. Kalmus, M. Lauristin, P. Pruulmann-Vengerfeldt, *Eesti elavik 21. sajandi algul : ülevaade uurimuse Mina. Maailm. Meedia tulemustest,* Univeristy of Tartu Press, Tartu, 2004.
10. P. Vengerfeldt, and P. Runnel, Uus meedia Eestis in: *Meedia süsteem ja meediakasutus Eestis 1965-2004,* edited by P. Vihalemm, University of Tartu Press, Tartu, 2004, pp. 233-256.
11. A. Quan-Haase, B. Wellman, J. C. Witte and K. N. Hampton, Capitalizing on the Net: social contact, civic engagement and sense of community, in: *The Internet in Everyday life,* edited by B. Wellman and C. Haythornthwaite, Blackwell Publishing, Malden, 2002 pp. 291-324.
12. J. Boase, J. B. Horrigan, B. Wellman and L. Rainie, The Strength of Internet Ties The Internet and email aid users in maintaining their social networks and provide pathways to help when people face big decisions (Pew Internet and American Life Project, Washington, 2006), http://www.pewinternet.org/pdfs/PIP_internet_ties.pdf (Last accessed 30/03/2006).
13. Accenture, Markel foundation and UNDP, *Creating a development dynamic: Final report of the Digital Opportunity Initiative* (2001) http://www.opt-init.org/framework/pages/contents.html (Last accessed 30/03/2006).
14. Lander, M, Hot technology for chilly streets in Estonia, *New York Times* (13/12/2005).
15. Information policy principles for 2002-2003, http://www.riso.ee/en/information-policy/policy-document (Last accessed 30/03/2006).
16. Information policy for 2004-2006, http://www.riso.ee/en/files/Policy.pdf (Last accessed 30/03/2006).
17. E. Rogers, *Diffusion of innovations,* Free Press, New York, 1995
18. The World Internet Project, http://www.worldinternetporject.net, (Last accessed 30//03/2006).

Understanding Socio-Technical Change: Towards a Multidisciplinary Approach

Edouard J. Simon, Monique Janneck, and Dorina Gumm
University of Hamburg, Department of Informatics, Germany
{simon, monique.janneck, gumm}@informatik.uni-hamburg.de

Abstract. Designing information technology involves the responsibility to be aware of the possible consequences that arise from its use. This can hardly be achieved from a single discipline's viewpoint. The paper describes an approach that is currently being developed to support a multidisciplinary perspective on the reciprocity between society and computers. It is a work in progress that is being developed by a network of scholars located mainly at the University of Hamburg, Department of Informatics.

Keywords: Ethics, Socio-Technical Change, Multidisciplinarity, Innovation, Reciprocity

1   Innovation as an Ethical Challenge

Social Informatics deals with the interrelation between human action and computers [1] – a reciprocity that influences not only our view on labour and economic development but also the very way we communicate and cooperate. Information technology (IT) is increasingly setting the pace and direction of what is supposed to be innovation. This is true at a global level where politicians are forced to rethink their notion of national interest and to cooperate internationally. It is also true at a national and local level, where IT helps in developing new markets, destroys whole lines of industry, and allows for undreamed of productivity increase resulting in unheard of unemployment. Finally, it is true at a personal level, shaping new social behaviour and deepening a new, digital divide.

But speaking only of technology changing our world would be a technological determinism that has been discarded quite some time ago [1]. Technology provides us with the means to do different things, or things differently, than we could do without it. It is up to us to decide what we want to do and which instruments we need. The ethical challenge intrinsically tied to social change is part of the

Please use the following format when citing this chapter:

Simon, E. J., Janneck, M., Gumm, D., 2006, in IFIP International Federation for Information Processing, Volume 223, Social Informatics: An Information Society for All? In Remembrance of Rob Kling, eds. Berleur, J., Numinen, M. I., Impagliazzo, J., (Boston: Springer), pp. 469–479.

innovation process. Nevertheless, innovation is often treated as an appendix to technological research and development. Some consider innovation to be unpredictable, stating that no one could tell what benefit might arise from new technologies. Some assume that embedding technological artefacts in society is a different task than inventing them, involving different actors. Thus IT researchers and developers would not need to bother about the social consequences [2]. Some even regard technological change as a market-driven process which is (and should be) beyond social or political intervention.

To hold these views means to actually negate the very possibility of innovation in terms of social progress. The meaning of innovation is separated from the process of research and development and delegated to specialised professionals, like politicians or even left to the market. Without an understanding of how research and development affects, or at least might impact, society there can be no progress. Understanding is the first step in any approach to change the world for better – at least it should be.

2   The Need for a Multidisciplinary Approach

The widespread use of IT is a complex phenomenon, promoting economical, political, social, and behavioural change at all levels of human action. It is thus a phenomenon that can only be understood from a multidisciplinary point of view. Such a multidisciplinary approach brings in questions that deal with the self-conception of academic research. The questions are posed from the different viewpoints of the involved disciplines, such as: What exactly are we looking at? What do we want to find out? What will all the research eventually be good for? In other words, at least two fundamental issues have to be addressed in a multidisciplinary approach:

- *Make clear what our subject is.* What looks like a technological artefact to one researcher will appear like a set of behavioural constraints to another. A third will neither perceive how it works nor how it affects behaviour, but will recognise the social and economic interaction that leads to the creation of it. What one studies as a black box will be obviously transparent to another, and vice versa. The subject of a profession is constructed according to its particular self-conception which is not necessarily (and most often actually not) compatible among professions. A multidisciplinary approach can help to build bridges: by providing conceptual links that mediate between different perceptions of similar phenomenons; and by developing a conceptual framework that acts as a map that can help to locate different academic approaches within an integrative heuristic approach.
- *Make clear what our cognitive interest is.* Computer Sciences and related disciplines aim at changing – that is, somehow improving – working and living conditions. For many other disciplines – like social science or psychology – this involves a shift, from mere contemplation about how things are related, towards a more constructive and targeted reasoning. Since, there is little a profession can do on its own to find out about what actually is an improvement from a society's

point of view, only a few professionals are aware of the consequences that arise from their efforts to change the world. This is where a multidisciplinary approach becomes necessary. Knowledge about the interplay of social action and information technology is not only favourable to, but a necessity for, independent academic research. Without it we are not able to know whether we aim in the right direction and thus know nothing about innovation. The improvement of living conditions is not only a highly contingent process, but also, for many reasons, there can be no impartial definition of what is an improvement. Therefore, a multidisciplinary approach should allow for normative issues, statements about the quality of technological improvements in terms of social progress.

3 *Mikropolis* – a Multidisciplinary Approach to Understand Socio-Technical Change

Mikropolis – derived from *Mikro*elektronik (german for microelectronics) and *polis* – is the name of a multidisciplinary research initiative and approach. Mikropolis aims at describing, analysing, and understanding the interplay between information technology development and social and political action [3].

The Mikropolis approach is not designed to replace or even complement existing theoretical examinations of socio-technical systems. We use the metaphor of a *travel guide* to describe its scope [4]: It provides a map that allows for orientation within the landscape of theories about technological innovation. In some cases, the conceptual attribution is quite obvious while sometimes there is a need for further investigation before a theory can be mapped to our framework.

In the following paragraphs, we first describe the Mikropolis Initiative, a group of researchers from different disciplines. Then we present the basic elements of the Mikropolis approach itself.

3.1 The Mikropolis Initiative: Bringing the Disciplines Together

The Mikropolis initiative consists of an interdisciplinary group of researchers working mainly at the Department of Informatics at the University of Hamburg, complemented by researchers from other universities and also practitioners (e.g. consultants). The disciplines represented in our group include Informatics, Information Systems, Political Science, Psychology, Social Science and Environmental Informatics.

Concerned with various topics in the fields of Information Systems, Human Computer Interaction, Computer Supported Cooperative Work (CSCW) and Learning (CSCL) and Virtual Organisations, we share a common understanding that designers and developers of software and information technology need to take into account the social and organisational conditions as well as the consequences of technology use.

We work on the Mikropolis approach because it serves as a tool to explain phenomena we observe in our respective application domains or even as a guide for socio-technical design decisions. In our various research areas and projects we take different perspectives on the Mikropolis approach:

*   *Theoretical perspective*: We aim for strengthening the Mikropolis approach theoretically, relating it to existing theoretical frameworks and models of socio-technical interdependencies, as well as organisational theories and models of human behavior.
*   *Empirical perspective*: We seek to ground the Mikropolis approach in our empirical work, e.g. case studies of virtual organisations, using it as an analytical instrument and testing its explanatory and predictive power.
*   *Consulting perspective*: We are interested in using the Mikropolis approach as a guide to advise organisations with respect to IT development and use.

3.2   The Mikropolis Approach: Constructing a Multidisciplinary Conceptual Framework

The Mikropolis approach has its origins in higher education. It has been developed since the late 90s at the Department of Informatics at the University of Hamburg and has been modified and enhanced by students and researchers. From a theoretical perspective we use our approach for educational purposes. As a didactical framework it is being used by several scholars and has recently been published by the German Federal Agency for Civic Education [5, 6]. With regard to the empirical and consulting perspective it is already in use by an IT-consultant who is part of the Mikropolis network.

We adopt a multidisciplinary perspective by integrating concepts from different professions into a conceptual framework. This framework may be characterized as a template consisting of specific cognitive patterns that are familiar across disciplines.

The Mikropolis approach takes a close look at the actors and their interests and motives. There is a distinction between the micro- and macro-level of analysis, which corresponds to social, political, or economic contexts of interaction. In addition to this structural view there is a longitudinal perspective allowing for the analysis of temporal aspects. Last but not least, there are basic assumptions about the interrelation between human action and information technology – in other words, the analysis of reciprocity can be considered as the core issue of our approach.

The Mikropolis approach must not be understood as a theory. Rather it serves as a heuristic approach to analyse the interplay between social action and information technology from different disciplinary perspectives and to act as a translator. For in-depth explanations of the phenomena studied, it is necessary to 're-embed' the multidisciplinary discourse into a discipline's theoretical framework.

3.2.1 Reciprocity as an analytical perspective
Reciprocity operates as the basic analytical perspective in our approach. In terms of *individual* IT use and development, reciprocity means on one hand the interrelating process of formalising human action and 'translating' it into computer executable routines and re-embedding those routines into the social context on the other hand. Since this process involves a generalising description of context-specific action,

which is then somehow transferred back into a context, we call it the reciprocity of *de*contextualisation and *re*contextualisation.

On an *organisational* level we make a distinction between those organisations using and those developing IT. It should be emphasised that this distinction is an analytical one, since many organisations using information technology develop or at least customise the products they use in-house, and those developing are themselves users of IT. Therefore we accent the complex system of different actors that are involved in advancing information technology, involving, for example globally operating software vendors, publicly funded research institutions, or IT-related R&D-sections of a larger organisation.

The relation between these actors can be characterized as a sectoral system of innovation [7]. The interaction between organisations using IT and the IT-related sectoral innovation system is used for the analysis of the interplay between development and use of IT, which can be characterized as either demand-driven or technology-driven.

3.2.2 The structural perspective

We make an analytical distinction between the micro-context and the macro-context of socio-technical systems. This allows for a view on organisational aspects of computerisation and the societal influences on these, as well as the impact of IT-related organisational change on economy, society, culture, and politics.

The micro perspective focuses on the interplay between IT and its embedding into organisational contexts. IT is used and developed, in specific contexts of interaction, where people work together and communicate, consisting of a specific set of rules, tradition, and history that it emerged from.

The macro perspective focuses on the socio-political context in which the organisations are themselves embedded, consisting of social and political norms as well as cultural habits and values and economic pressures in a globalised world.

3.2.3 The temporal perspective

The longitudinal analysis of socio-technical contexts provides a deeper insight into patterns of the development and adoption of technologies. The history of such a context can be described as a chronology of decisions for certain technological options, leaving others behind. The development of socio-technical systems can thus be seen as a reduction of contingency in IT-usage based on the status quo, which, in turn, stimulates the future development of IT.

Successful technological innovations form a historically determined path of technology development and the associated organisational development. Tracing this path of technology use shows that 'history matters' [8]. Decisions of technology use (or non-use) set the course for the future, subsequently enabling further development or preventing possible alternative practices. Decisions to take one way or another are not merely a matter of rational choice, but also of cultural beliefs and emotions (e.g., technology friends and foes) as well as of power, defining winners and losers. Thus, technology becomes a matter of scientific and ethical discourse.

Analysing the technology use path is important to assess what ways future design decisions might pave. Of course, future developments cannot be predicted using the

Mikropolis approach, but knowing crucial switches of the past helps to appraise future paths of development.

3.2.4 Actors

Looking at socio-technical systems makes it inevitable to take an analytical view on actors. Their specific interests, tasks, and activities and the technology used to support them are at the center of the socio-technical system.

The Mikropolis approach integrates different concepts of actors focusing different roles, like computer users [9] or participants of market transactions ('homo oeconomicus'). Such concepts highlight aspects of intential behaviour that are important from their point of view, but fail to provide realistic assumptions adequately reflecting the complexity of human interaction. Therefore, we rely on a concept of actors that does not presume any role or context but instead provides categories that inform us about the specific abilities, perceptions, and preferences, which, analytically speaking, form an actor's identity [10].

Within the Mikropolis approach, we look at micropolitical processes – i.e. actors' strategies to gain influence and power within their institutional and hierarchical framework [11] – to explain and interpret the actions of individuals and groups. Another important tool is the analysis of motives, missions, and ideals.

Furthermore, social psychological concepts, findings concerning group behavior, and intergroup relations might inform the Mikropolis approach. This is a prospect for our future work.

4   The Mikropolis Approach as a Framework for the Design of Virtual Organisations – A Case Study

Our approach has proven to be useful for examining the inter-relation between human action and IT design in a research project on the socio-technical design of virtual organisations. In this section, we will present the case study of a *virtual network of freelancers* to exemplify how we use the Mikropolis approach as a heuristic model that can inform us about social issues that affect the use of IT. On the other hand, we use this case study to reveal weaknesses of our approach and advance it.

We developed and customised a groupware system for a network of freelancers in a participatory design process [12, 13, 16] within the scope of a research project focusing on the sustainable development of virtual networks of freelancers, as a new and rapidly spreading form of virtual organisations.

The network was founded in 1997 by freelance IT and management consulting professionals to exchange experiences, knowledge, and work results. It offers its members vocational training and the opportunity to get involved in several occupational working groups or to meet potential clients via the network's contacts. Today about 15 members belong to the community. It is completely self-organised by its members without formal hierarchies or roles, thus relying on its members' involvement and commitment. Financial resources are scarce.

In the past, several project management systems were tested within the network before we got involved as a research group. However, with each of them, the usage turned out to be unsatisfactorly low. The network members blamed this on the respective software, which they regarded as unsuitable for their tasks.

We therefore decided to implement another groupware system, which was to be continually adapted due to the networks' needs, involving as many of the network members as possible in the process. A systematic evaluation was carried out to investigate the network's requirements for software support. Semi-structured interviews were chosen as an appropriate method to grasp the subjective views of the community members. Additionally, this approach allows for addressing specific topics and comparing between interviews [14]. We conducted three group interviews with a total of twelve community members.

The interviews were audio-taped, with the interviewee's permission and transcribed verbatim, resulting in over 200 pages of interview-transcripts. Data analysis was carried out following the three steps of paraphrasing, generalisation, and reduction suggested by Mayring [15]. In the first step, the respective units of analysis (usually singular phrases) are paraphrased to reach a uniform level of speech. In the next step, the paraphrased expressions are generalised on a higher level of abstraction to enhance comparability (generalisation). Thirdly, synonymous or correspondent expressions are omitted or combined (reduction).

Furthermore, we observed the network's system usage while working with two core members acting as representatives to discuss their usage experiences, analyse usage problems, and plan further developments for about 18 months. We conducted regular workshops every two or three months with these network representatives, applying scenario techniques, and using mock-ups for elaborating design ideas [16].

Even though the network members stressed the general necessity of communicating online and agreed that the platform was suitable for their needs, the intensity of use still turned out to be very low after approximately a year and a half, frustrating the small number of active users. Since we suspected social and organisational reasons for this, we used the Mikropolis approach to analyse the network situation. A detailed account of this analysis is given by Finck et al. [17].

The following analytical tools supplied by the Mikropolis approach turned out to be helpful: At the micro level we looked at the changes the freelancers had to face with regard to their work organisation when they started to collaborate within their network and identified conflicts that might have interfered with their usage. This addressed issues like different experiences with individual desktop applications that were no longer applicable to a shared web-based workspace, or preferences for different ways of organising work that had to be negotiated within the network.

Tracing the path of technology use showed that decisions regarding IT support had seldom been discussed with a substantial number of network members, but rather been made by individual members who were especially competent and interested in IT use. This led to confusion and insecurity within other members regarding the continuity of IT use, reducing their motivation to use the system. Analysing the actors' interests, actions, and motives showed a clear area of conflict between the ideal of equal, non-hierarchical cooperation that was propagated within the network and its actual practices. We found that decision-making processes were clearly dominated by certain core members, showing hierarchical structures.

Furthermore, we observed tension concerning the network's main purposes and goals. These purposes varied from mainly social exchange and support to economic interests, such as improved possibilities for aquisition and a stronger market position. An economic orientation, however, raises issues of competition between individual network members, presumably hindering both social exchange and true cooperation. The implicit competition within the network is heightened by the rough economic situation on the macro level that the freelancers are currently facing.

We concluded that these discrepancies between the network's goals, ideals, and motives on the one hand and their daily practices on the other hand accounted for the low intensity of use that we observed on the network platform.

In this vague collaborative setting, concrete occasions and incentives for use are rare. Furthermore, due to the economic pressures the freelancers are facing, it is rather advisable for them to be careful when investing scarce resources such as time and ideas into the network. This especially applies to providing (economically relevant) content to the shared groupware system. This analysis has several consequences for future socio-technical development: Regarding software support, we need to check whether functionalities supporting equal and intense cooperation are truly suitable for the network's needs. Regarding organisational development, we consider it necessary to explicate, clarify, and, if necessary, change current visions, expectations, and goals within the network.

5   IT-Usage in the Medical Care System: A View on Strategies

In a study on IT usage for medical care from a Mikropolis perspective [18], strategies concerning the promotion of IT related innovations were examined. The study was carried out by a member of the Mikropolis network and was based on empirical findings collected during his work as an IT-consultant.

The examination of strategies concerning IT-support of organisational procedures led to the interesting finding that there is a difference between individual strategies of the various actors involved and an overall strategy, usually set by the management. Moreover, the findings suggested that the latter is usually merely wishful thinking, since the complex interaction of different strategic orientations will most likely render the outcome unpredictable. This is true, at least when the perceptions, preferences, and resources of all stakeholders within the organisation are not taken into account. It might even be necessary to look at external actors, as long as these have relevant preferences and are able to raise a sufficient amount of resources to interfere in the process. This conclusion was based on the results of four different IT-related projects: acquisition of a specialised documentation system, external quality assurance in a surgical ward, introduction of a general surgery planning system, and security orientation of the IT department.

All four projects were analysed, with regard to the distribution of power among the stakeholders, the strategy legitimated by the management, and a collective strategy resulting from an (implicit or explicit) consensus between the actors involved. In two projects a collective strategy could not be achieved, since the preferences of some of the fractions involved directly opposed the legitimated strategy. In these cases the outcome reflected the distribution of power among the fractions. In the other projects, a consensus was achieved either through a change of preferences or by finding a solution that met the needs of all stakeholders.

In our analysis we could identify three resources of power that had an impact on the degree in which actors influenced the results: Institutions, knowledge, and involvement in realisation. Following [10] we use the term 'institutions' for all kinds of more or less stable settings that the actors agree on, like, for example organisational structures, contracts, or cultural habits. There is no doubt that the management of a hospital has most of the institutional power, being able to control almost all contracts and thus being in control of all of the material resources. The second source of power turned out to be knowledge. Mainly the IT department, but also the health professionals could in some cases enforce their position, simply because no one else was able to argue it. In fact, technical knowledge turned out to be one of the most important resources in terms of influence on the result. Nearly equally important was to be actively involved in realising the socio-technical infrastructures, whether socially - as users who could either use or boycott the system - or technically where the IT department was in the position to push or to slow down the development.

As already mentioned, the actors staking their claims were mainly the management, the IT department, and the medical staff. Especially the head physicians played an important role in promoting new technical features, while the IT department usually had the last word on what happened and how it happened. In one project, external software developers developed an interface between two software systems, one of which was preferred by a medical department while the other was pushed by the IT department. It showed that the preferences of the interface developers - namely to get further jobs - had a significant impact on the outcome of the project, even though they were not directly involved in it. Because maintaining the interface turned out to be quite costly and time consuming both departments involved soon agreed on switching to one of the systems.

This case study showed that the analytical concept of actors, as used in the Mikropolis approach, turned out to be useful to explain social phenomena, which would not be visible when only taking into account the measures taken to watch over the implementation of previously agreed-on specifications. It seems to allow, at least partially, for a prediction of the outcome of IT-projects involving complex actor constellations. It has shown the importance of looking at micro-political processes. But there is still work to be done to refine the analytical toolset and take a closer look at strategic processes.

6   Conclusions

In this paper, we introduced the Mikropolis approach as a framework for understanding and shaping socio-technical change in a multidisciplinary setting. We addressed different applications and perspectives of the Mikropolis approach: theoretical, didactical, empirical and consulting. Furthermore, by means of two case studies we presented one possibility to use the Mikropolis approach, for analysing specific settings in which socio-technical problems and questions arise. The Mikropolis approach is work in progress. It needs to be refined and strengthened theoretically, and we need more empirical evaluations to test its usefulness. In order to do so, we plan to take a closer look at the German health care system, where socio-technical innovation is a fundamental issue to civil society, reflecting the need for the advancement of high-tech products and procedures, thereby taking into account the requirements of highly complex organizations and infrastructures as well as institutional entwinements between a multiplicity of different public and private actors. Moreover, ethical and moral issues affect trends and decisions. For many of the activities going on in this sector, IT has become a crucial factor and more often than not a precondition for future development. Analysing those activities, from a Mikropolis perspective, is our prospect for future work.

We are going to expand the Mikropolis initiative to include other researchers and practitioners interested in reflective socio-technical development and design and will gladly get into contact with anyone interested in the field.

References

1. Rob Kling. What is social informatics and why does it matter? *D-Lib Magazine*, 5(1):1–25 (1999).
2. Edsger W. Dijkstra. On the cruelty of really teaching computing science. *Comm. of the ACM*, 32(12):1398–1404 and 1414, (1989).
3. Krause, D., Rolf, A., Christ, M., Simon, E. (in preparation): Wissen, wie alles zusammenhängt – Das Mikropolis-Modell als Orientierungswerkzeug für die Gestaltung von Informationstechnik in Organisationen und Gesellschaft. Published in: *Informatik-Spektrum* (2006).
4. Arno Rolf. Reiseführer für Informatik und Gesellschaft. *fifF-Jahrbuch*, (2005).
5. Arno Rolf. Von der Theoriearbeit zur Gestaltung. In *Wissensgesellschaft. Neue Medien und ihre Konsequenzen*. Bundeszentrale für politische Bildung, Bonn (2004).
6. Arno Rolf, Informationstechnologien in Organisationen und Gesellschaft, In: *Medienpädagogik: 'Wissensgesellschaft'* (2005).
7. Franco Malerba, editor, *Sectoral Systems of Innovation. Concepts, Issues and Analyses of Six Major Sectors in Europe*. Cambridge University Press, 2004.
8. Georg Schreyögg and Jörg Sydow, editors. Strategische Prozesse und Pfade. *Managementforschung 13*. Wiesbaden: Gabler, (2003).
9. Rob Kling and Roberta Lamb. Reconceptualizing users as social actors. In: *information systems research. MIS Quarterly*, 27(2):197–235, June 2003.
10. F. W. Scharpf, *Games Real Actors Play: Actor-Centered Institutionalism in Policy Research*, Boulder, 1997.
11. O. Neuberger, *Mikropolitik: Der alltägliche Aufbau und Einsatz von Macht in Organisationen*. Enke, Stuttgart, 1995.
12. Finck, M., Janneck, M. Hospitality in Hosting Web-Based Communities: Two Case Studies. In: Kommers, P., Isaias, P. (eds), *Web Based Communities 2005: Proceedings of the IADIS International Conference Web Based Communities 2005* (2005), pp. 327-330.
13. Janneck, M., Finck, M., Appropriation and Mediation of Technology Use in Stable Self-Organised Online Communities. In: Kommers, P., Isaias, P., Goikoetxea, A. (eds): *Web*

Based Communities 2006: Proceedings of the IADIS International Conference Web Based Communities 2006, (2006) pp. 149-156.

14. Kvale, S, InterViews: An introduction to qualitative research interviewing. Sage, Thousand Oaks, CA, 1996.

15. Mayring, P., Qualitative Inhaltsanalyse: Grundlagen und Techniken, 8. edn. Weinheim: Beltz, 2003.

16. Janneck, M., Finck, M., Obendorf, H., Participatory Design: An Issue for Web-Based Community Development?! In: Kommers, P., Isaias, P., Goikoetxea, A. (eds): Web Based Communities 2006: Proceedings of the IADIS International Conference Web Based Communities 2006, (2006) pp. 274-277.

17. Finck, M., Janneck, M., Rolf, A., Techniknutzung zwischen Kooperation und Konkurrenz -- eine Analyse von Nutzungsproblemen. In: Lehner, F., Noehsekabel, H., Kleinschmidt, P. (Hrsg.): Multikonferenz Wirtschaftsinformatik 2006, (2006) pp. 636-376

18. Drews, P., IT-Strategie im Krankenhaus: Akteure, Prozesse und Inhalte. Diploma Thesis, Institute for Information Systems, University of Hamburg, 2004 (unpublished).

PART 3 – FAIR GLOBALIZATION

Priorities of Fair Globalization

Leif Bloch Rasmussen, Viktoria Skarler
Institute of Informatics, Business Copenhagen School
lbr.inf@cbs.dk, www.cbs.dk/staff/leif_bloch_rasmussen

The report, *A Fair Globalization: Creating opportunities for all*, by the World Commission on the Social Dimension of Globalization (ILO), seek a process of globalization with a strong social dimension based on universally shared values, respect for human rights and individual dignity. A world that is fair, inclusive, democratically governed and gives opportunities and tangible benefits for all countries and people in the world. To this end the report calls for:

- *A focus on people.* The cornerstone of a fairer globalization lies in meeting the demands of all people for: respect for their rights, cultural identity and autonomy; decent work: and the empowerment of the local communities they live in. Gender equality is essential.
- *A democratic and effective State.* The State must have the capability to manage integration into the global economy, and provide social and economic opportunity and security.
- *Sustainable development.* The quest for a fair globalization must be undertaken by the interdependent and environmental protection at the local, national, regional and global levels.
- *Productive and equitable markets.* This requires sound institutions to promote opportunity and enterprise in well-functioning market economy.
- *Fair rules.* The rules of the global economy must offer equitable opportunity and access for all countries and recognise the diversity in national capacities and developmental needs.
- *Globalization with solidarity.* There is a shared responsibility to assist countries and people excluded from or disadvantaged by globalization. Globalization must help to overcome inequality both within and between countries and contribute to the elimination of poverty.
- *Greater accountability to people.* Public and private actors at all levels with power to influence the outcomes of globalization must be democratically accountable for the policies they pursue and the actions they take. They should deliver on their commitments and use their power with respect for others.

Please use the following format when citing this chapter:

Rasmussen, L. B., Skarler, V., 2006, in IFIP International Federation for Information Processing, Volume 223, Social Informatics: An Information Society for All? In Remembrance of Rob Kling, eds. Berleur, J., Numinen, M. I., Impagliazzo, J., (Boston: Springer), pp. 483–486.

- *Deeper partnerships.* A number of actors are engaged in the realisation of global social and economic aims – international organisations, governments and parliaments, business, labour, civil society and many others. Dialogue and partnership among them is an essential democratic instrument to create a better world.
- *An effective United Nations.* A stronger and more efficient multilateral system is the key instrument to create a democratic, legitimate and coherent framework for globalization (according to the report).[1]

Globalization is a complex phenomenon that has had a long reaching effect. And the term 'globalization' has acquired many emotive connotations and become a frequently contested issue in current political discourses. At one extreme, globalization is seen as an irresistible and good force delivering economic prosperity to people around the world, and at the other, it is blamed as a source of all contemporary ills.

Although, it is widely accepted that the key characteristics of globalization have been the liberalisation of international trade, the expansion of Foreign Direct Investments (FDI), and the emergence of massive cross-border financial flows. This has resulted in increasing competition on the global markets. It is also widely acknowledged that this has come about through combined effect of two underpinning factors namely; policy decisions to reduce national barriers to international economic transactions and the impact of new technology, especially in information and communication technology. These developments created the enabling conditions for the beginning of globalization.[2]

Globalization has set in motion a process of far-reaching change that is affecting everyone. New technology, supported by more open policies, has created a world more interconnected than ever before. This distance not only growing interdependence in economic relations regarding; trade, investments, finance and the organisation of production globally, but also social and political interactions among organisations and individuals around the world.

The effects of the new technology have also given a distinctive character to the current process of globalization, compared to similar episodes in the past. The natural barriers of time and space have been vastly reduced. The cost of moving information, people and goods and capital across the world has fallen dramatically, while global communication is cheap and instantaneous, and continuing ever more so. This has vastly expanded the feasibility of economic transactions across the globe, and markets can now be global in scope and encompass an expanding range of goods and services. Another distinctive subject of the current process of globalization relates to what is absent, and unlike earlier times of globalization that were characterised by massive cross-border movements of people, the current process largely excludes this.

Hopefully we all seek a globalization with social dimension, which sustains human values and enhances the well being of people, in terms of their freedom, prosperity and security. Globalization is seen through the eyes of women and men in terms of the opportunity it provides for decent work, for meeting their essential needs for food, water, health, education and shelter, and for a liveable environment. Without such a social dimension, many will continue to view globalization as a new version of earlier forms of domination and exploitation. The fundamentals of this social dimension include:

- A process of globalization based on universally shared values, which require all actors, including States, international organisations, business, labour, civil society and the media, to assume their individual responsibilities. It demands respect for obligations and duties under international law. It also requires economic development to be based on respect on human rights.
- An international commitment to ensure the basic material and other requirements of human dignity for all, enshrined in the Universal Declaration of Human Rights. The eradication of poverty and the attainment of the Millennium Development Goals (MDGs) should be seen as the first steps towards a socio-economic 'floor' for the global economy.[3]
- A sustainable path of development, which provides opportunities for all, expands sustainable livelihoods and employment, promotes gender equality, and reduces disparities between countries and people. It calls for greater coherence between economic, social and environmental policies.
- A more democratic governance of globalization, which permits for greater voice and participation, and ensures accountability, while fully respecting the authority of institutions of representative democracy and the rule of law.[4]

The resources exist to overcome the most urgent problems of poverty, disease and education. Mahatma Gandhi put it very simply:

"There is enough in the world for everybody's need, but there cannot be enough for everybody's greed".[5]

This report set out the broad goals and principles that can guide policy to handle more effectively with the social dimension of globalization, fully recognising that their implementation shall respond to the needs and specific conditions of each country. From this perspective it is clear that national governance have to improved in all countries, however more radically in some than in others, and there is wide international agreements on the fundamentals, which we all must strive for:

- Good political governance based on a democratic political system, respect for human rights, and the rule of law and social equity.
- An effective State that ensures high and stable economic growth, provides public goods and social protection, raises the capabilities of people through universal access to education and other social services, and promotes gender equity.
- A vibrant civil society empowered by freedom of association and expression, that reflects and voices the full diversity of views and interests. Organisations representing public interests, the poor and other disadvantaged groups are also fundamental for ensuring participatory and socially just governance.
- Strong representative organisations of workers and employers are essential for fruitful social dialogue.[6]

The proposals call for a wider and more democratic participation of people and countries in the creations of policies that affect them. They also require those with the capacity and power to decide: governments, parliaments, business, labour, civil society and international organisations, and to assume their common responsibility to promote a free, fair and productive global community.

[1]   World Commission on the Social Dimension of Globalization, February 2004, Report: 'A Fair Globalization: Creating opportunities for all', Synopsis, pp. ix-x. Photocomposed by ILO, Geneva, Switzerland.

[2]   Ibid. pp. 24-25.

[3]   The Millennium Development Goals: In: September 2000, 189 Heads of State and Governments committed their countries – rich and poor – to meet a set of time-bound and measurable goals by 2015: eradicate extreme poverty and hunger, achieve universal primary education, promote gender equality and empower women, reduce child mortality, improve maternal health, combat HIV/AIDS, malaria and other diseases, ensure environmental sustainability, develop a global partnership for development. http://www.un.org/millenniumgoals/

[4]   World Commission on the Social Dimension of Globalization, doc. cit. p. 5. Photocomposed by ILO, Geneva, Switzerland

[5]   Ibid.

[6]   Ibid. p. xii.

Subject Index